WITHDRAWN

Sociology

Exploring the Architecture
of Everyday Life

A companion anthology entitled
SOCIOLOGY: EXPLORING THE ARCHITECTURE OF EVERYDAY LIFE: *Readings*
accompanies this book and is available from
your instructor and college bookstore.

Sociology

Exploring the Architecture of Everyday Life

David M. Newman

Department of Sociology
DePauw University

Pine Forge Press

Thousand Oaks, California • *London* • *New Delhi*

For information address:

Pine Forge Press
A Sage Publications Company
2455 Teller Road
Thousand Oaks, California
91320
E-mail: sales@pfp.sagepub.com

Production Manager: Rebecca Holland
Designer: Lisa S. Mirski
Cover Design: Cheryl Carrington
*Visual essays in chapters 4, 5, 6, 7, 8, 10,
and 14 designed by:* Claire Vaccaro
*Visual essay in chapter 2
designed by:* Cheryl Carrington
Desktop Publisher: Rebecca Evans

Printed in the United States of America

1 2 3 4 5 6 7 8 9 10—99 98 97 96 95

Cover photograph by Helen Levitt. Printed by arrangement with Knox
Burger Associates Ltd. Reprinted from *In the Street*, published by Duke
University Press. © 1987, Helen Levitt.

Library of Congress Cataloging-in-Publication Data

Newman, David M., 1958-
    Sociology : exploring the architecture of everyday life / David M.
Newman.
       p. cm.
    Includes bibliographical references and index.
    ISBN 0-8039-9004-9 (pbk. : alk. paper)
    1. Sociology—Study and teaching—United States. 2. Sociology.
I. Title.
HM47.U6N48   1995
301—dc20
                                                        94-38140
                                                           CIP

About the Author

David Newman (Ph.D., University of Washington) is an Associate Professor of Sociology at DePauw University. In addition to the introductory course, he teaches courses in research methods, family, social psychology, and deviance. He has won teaching awards at both the University of Washington and DePauw University.

About the Publisher

Pine Forge Press is a new educational publisher, dedicated to publishing innovative books and software throughout the social sciences. On this and any other of our publications, we welcome your comments, ideas, and suggestions. Please call or write to:

Pine Forge Press

A Sage Publications Company
2455 Teller Road
Thousand Oaks, CA 91320
(805) 499-4224
E-mail: sales@pfp.sagepub.com

For my Dad

CONTENTS IN BRIEF

DETAILED CONTENTS

PART II CONSTRUCTING SELF AND SOCIETY

Preface

The ink had barely dried on the contract I had signed to write this book when a wave of panic and sheer terror crashed over me. "My God, what have I gotten myself into this time?! I can't write a book," I whispered to myself (making sure my new publisher was out of earshot). "Authors write books. I'm a teacher, not an author." Perplexed and increasingly anxious, I did what anyone would do under these circumstances—I turned to those closest to me for assistance.

I gingerly approached my younger son, who was 3 years old at the time. "Seth," I said, "I just signed a contract to write a book. What should I do?" He responded, "Daddy, I want some apple juice . . . and put it in the choo-choo train cup!" Failure.

I then sought the advice of my older son, who was then 6. "Zach," I said, "I'm going to write a book. What do you think about that?"

"That's great, Dad," he replied inattentively. "Now could you move, I'm trying to watch TV."

I pressed on. "How do you think I should write it?" I asked.

At first he was annoyed as he turned away from the television. But then he became pensive.

He began to speak. I inched closer. "Dad," he said, "people don't like words, they like pictures. Why don't you write a picture book? No, wait! Just make some empty boxes for *me* to draw pictures, because you can't draw. When are you going to start making dinner, anyway?"

It was with this unwavering encouragement solidly embedded in my mind that I set out to write this book.

Depth Versus Breadth

It has always been my belief that instructors do their best when they teach what they enjoy, what excites them, what they know about. The same, I think, should go for textbooks. I didn't want this book to be a massive information smorgasbord that gives you a little taste of every conceivable sociological topic but not enough detail on any of them to satisfy your hunger. Perhaps the most common criticism directed toward textbooks today is that they try to cover too much. So

I have opted for deeper coverage of fewer general topics than you'll find in most introductory textbooks.

This approach has allowed me to write a book that is designed not for memorizing a string of sociological facts and definitions but for provoking thoughtful analysis and evaluation. I believe that part of my role as a teacher and author is to make students think about their lives in new ways. By devoting greater space to a narrower set of important issues and concepts, this book offers you the depth of detail necessary to fully examine what society is, how it works, and, most important, your place in it.

The Sociology of Everyday Life

One of the greatest challenges I face as a teacher of sociology is trying to get my students to see the personal relevance of the course material, to fully appreciate the connection between the individual and society. I teach my students to see that sociology is all around us. It's in our careers, our media, our families, our goals, our interests, our desires, even our minds. Sociology can be found at the neighborhood pub or in the maintenance bay at the local gas station. Sociology can answer questions of global as well as private significance, from why poverty, discrimination, and homelessness continue to grow to why we are attracted to some people and not to others; from why people become criminals to why we enjoy scrambled eggs for breakfast rather than rice.

In order to drive home these ideas, this book uses an "everyday life" approach, employing common personal experiences as a vehicle for understanding the relationship between individuals and society. The guiding theme of the discipline is that our lives are ordered and influenced by powerful social forces that are larger than we are. At the same time, individual action can influence those forces. Hence, the true value of sociology lies in its unique ability to show the reciprocal connection between the most private elements of our lives—our characteristics, experiences, behaviors, and thoughts—and the cultures, groups, organizations, and institutions to which we belong. To put it into more sophisticated language, this book emphasizes the mutual link between the *micro*sociological—what happens to us and what we experience in our day-to-day lives—and the *macro*sociological—the larger structural characteristics of society.

My purpose in introducing sociology to you in such a fashion is to make the familiar unfamiliar—to make you critically examine the commonplace and the ordinary in your own life. Only when you are able to take a step back and examine the taken-for-granted aspects of your personal experiences can you see that there is an inherent, sometimes unrecognized, organization and predictability to them. At the same time, you will see that the structure of society is greater than the sum experiences and psychologies of the individuals who reside in it.

I have included some special innovations that I hope will aid in this endeavor:

Micro-Macro Connections and Research Illustrations

Each chapter has several in-depth features that either focus on a specific piece of sociological research or on some issue that illustrates the connection between micro- and macro- sociology. Through these extended illustrations I show the important links between social institutions and personal experiences as well as provide some insight into the methods sociologists use to gather information and draw conclusions about how our world works.

Visual Essays

The book contains visual essays on such interesting social phenomena as graffiti, funerals, multiracial families, and the varied experiences of immigrants. These essays make use of photographs or other graphic material that help you "see" the sociology embedded in everyday life. Each one is designed to tell a sociological story through the use of vivid and provocative images.

Your Turn Exercises

At the end of each chapter I have included an exercise that will allow you to go outside the classroom and systematically observe certain sociological phenomena. Some of these exercises require you to talk to other people in order to gain insight into their firsthand experiences; others require you to venture into some common social settings—restaurants, businesses, shopping malls—to observe the activities taking place around you; still others ask you to analyze the content of existing material: books, magazines, television shows. I believe that learning is most effective when it occurs actively, not passively. These exercises are designed to give you a sense of what it is like to "do" sociology, to see how the sociological concepts and ideas you've been reading about actually work in the real world.

Companion Reader

Finally, this text comes with a carefully constructed companion reader that includes short articles, chapters, and excerpts written by other authors. These readings are provocative and eye-opening examples of the joys and insights of sociological thinking. They examine common everyday experiences, important social issues, and distinct historical events that vividly illustrate the relationship between the individual and society.

The Architecture of Society

I have chosen to use the image of architecture in the title to convey one of the driving themes of this book: that society is a human construction. Society is not "out there" somewhere waiting to be visited and examined. It exists in the minute details of our day-to-day lives. Whether we follow its rules or break them, enter its roles or shed them, work to change things or keep them as they are, we are adding another nail, plank, or frame to the structure of our society. In short, society—like the buildings around us—couldn't exist were it not for the actions of people.

At the same time, however, this structure that we have created appears to exist independently of us. We don't usually spend much time thinking about the buildings we live, work, and play in as human constructions. We see them for the finished products they are, not the processes that created them. Only when something goes wrong—the pipes leak or the walls crack—do we realize that people made these structures and that people are the ones who must fix them. When buildings outlive their usefulness or become dangerous to their inhabitants, it is people who must renovate them or, if necessary, decide to tear them down.

Likewise, society is so massive and has been around for so long that it *appears* to stand on its own—at a level above and beyond the toiling hands of individual people. But here, too, when things begin to go wrong—widespread discrimination, extreme poverty, lack of affordable health care, escalating crime rates—it's people who must do something about it.

So the fascinating paradox of human life is that we build society, collectively "forget" that we've built it, and live under its enormous and influential structure. But we are not "stuck" with society as it is. Human beings are the architects of their own social reality. Throughout this book I examine the active role individuals play in planning, maintaining, or fixing society.

Writing Style

Finally, I would like to say a bit about the writing style I've used in this book. Before I began to write, I thought back to my own college days and the courses that meant the most to me. I realized that the ones I felt were influential, intellectually challenging, and enjoyable were those taught by interested and caring instructors—people whose personalities and philosophies seeped into every crack and crevice of their courses. They were the people who showed an infectious love of the discipline through their hands-on, active roles in the teaching process.

Well, I thought, if this is what makes good teachers, perhaps it's what makes good textbook authors, too. So I decided early on that I wanted this book to sound like I do when I teach. Textbooks have a reputation for using a cold and distant voice, one clearly different from the one instructors use in their classrooms. This book is, by design, informal, conversational, and personal in style and tone.

Each chapter is peppered with anecdotes and personal observations. Many of the examples you will read are taken from today's news headlines; others are taken from incidents in my own life. All of these illustrations are meant to show you the pervasiveness and applicability of sociology in our everyday experiences in a way that, I hope, rings familiar to you.

It is my conviction that the teaching/learning experience can and should be a personally relevant, thought-provoking, and enjoyable excursion. Reading a textbook doesn't have to be boring or, even worse, the academic equivalent of a trip to the dentist (although I personally have nothing against dentists). I believe that part of my task as an instructor is to provide my students with a challenging but comfortable classroom atmosphere in which to learn. I wanted to do the same in this book.

A Final Thought

Your instructor has chosen this book not because it makes his or her job of teaching your course any easier but because he or she wants you, the student, to see how sociology helps us to understand how the little private experiences of our everyday lives are connected to this thing we call society. I hope you come to appreciate this important message, and I hope you enjoy reading this book as much as I enjoyed writing it.

By the way, if you have a chance, please let me know what you liked or didn't like about the book, either by writing me directly or by sending in the Reader Response sheet at the back of this book.

Thanks,

David M. Newman
Department of Sociology and Anthropology
DePauw University
Greencastle, IN 46135
E-mail: NEWMAN@DEPAUW.EDU

Acknowledgments

$\mathbf{A}$ book project such as this one takes an enormous amount of time to develop. I spent thousands of hours toiling away at the computer, holed up in my isolated third-floor office. Yet as solitary as this project was, it could not have been done alone. Many people provided invaluable assistance to make this book a reality. Without their generous help and support, it wouldn't have been written, and you'd be reading some other sociologist's list of people to thank. So I hope you will allow me some space to show my appreciation to the people who helped make this book a reality.

First I would like to thank the publisher and president of Pine Forge Press, Steve Rutter. He pushed and prodded and cajoled me into exceeding my expectations and overachieving. At times, I resented the fact that he was so ambitious with my time. But the numerous suggestions he offered made this book a better one. For that I am eternally grateful.

Likewise, the staff at Pine Forge—Rebecca Holland, Sherith Pankratz, and Mary Sutton, and freelancer Susan McKie—must be thanked for helping me through the maze of details and difficulties that crop up in a project of this magnitude. In addition, Becky Smith and Dianne Woo provided firm but kind editorial hands in helping me polish the ugly early drafts of the book. I would also like to express my gratitude to Toska Olson and Marie Bricher for compiling an excellent instructor's manual and to Michele Pinkow for aiding in the selection of readings for the companion reader.

I appreciate the many helpful comments offered by the reviewers of this book:

Bernice Pescosolido, *Indiana University, Bloomington*
David Bogen, *University of North Carolina, Charlotte*
Barry Goetz, *University of California, Los Angeles*
Deborah A. Abowitz, *Bucknell University*
Rebecca Adams, *University of North Carolina, Greensboro*
Carol Auster, *Franklin and Marshall College*
Larry Perkins, *Oklahoma State University*
Sally S. Rogers, *Montgomery College*
Mark Winton, *University of Central Florida*

Melissa Latimer, *University of Kentucky*
Marty Wenglinsky, *Quinnipiac College*
Cynthia Woolever, *Midway College*
Susan Hoerbelt, *Hillsborough Community College*
Valerie Gunter, *University of New Orleans*
Tom Kando, *California State University, Sacramento*
Judith Richlin-Klonsky, *University of California, Los Angeles*
John Walsh, *University of Illinois, Chicago*
Robert Robinson, *Indiana University, Bloomington*
Mark Shibley, *Loyola University*
Kandi Stinson, *Xavier University*
Gregory Weiss, *Roanoke College*
Peter Kivisto, *Augustana College*
Rachel Einwohner, *University of Washington*
Toska Olson, *University of Washington*
Doug Currivan, *University of Iowa*

I also want to express my appreciation to the colleagues and friends who offered cherished guidance thoughout the production of this book and who put up with my incessant whining about how hard it all was and my constant barging into their lives as I sought advice on this or that idea. In particular, I'd like to thank Nancy Davis, Rob Robinson, Nafhat Nasr, Tom Hall, James Mannon, Tom Chiarella, Lisa Head, Bizz Steele, and Jodi O'Brien.

I would like to express special gratitude to my students who, throughout the years, have kept me curious and prevented me from taking myself too seriously.

Above all, I want to thank my family, Beth, Zachary, and Seth, for putting up with the frequent late nights, long faces, and lost confidences.

Figure 14.1 from John E. Farley, *American Social Problems: An Institutional Analysis,* 2e, © 1992, p. 344. Reprinted by permission of Prentice Hall, Englewood Cliffs, New Jersey.

Figure 14.2 from *Population: An Introduction to Concepts and Issues* by John R. Weeks (pp. 30, 48), 1994. Belmont, CA: Wadsworth Publishing Co. Copyright 1994 by Wadsworth Publishing Co. Reprinted by permission.

Figure 14.3 from *Readings from Scientific American: Managing Planet Earth* (p. 64), 1990. Copyright © 1990 by Scientific American, Inc. All rights reserved.

To reprint quotes from the following:

From "Proceeding with Caution" by D. M. Gross and S. Scott, 1990, *Time* (16 July). Copyright 1990 Time Inc. Reprinted by permission.

From "Court Rules City May Oust Unwed Couple," 1986, *Seattle Times* (8 November). Copyright 1986 by Seattle Times. Reprinted with permission.

From "A Death Near White House Again Underscores Peril for Homeless" by G. Escobar, 1991, *The Washington Post* (12 December). Copyright 1991 The Washington Post. Reprinted with permission.

From "The New Gradgrinds" by M. Harrington, 1984, *Dissent, 31,* pp. 171-181. Copyright 1984 by *Dissent,* Foundation for Study of Independent Social Ideas. Reprinted by permission.

From "Migrants Create a New World Order With Their Feet" by A. Honebrink, 1993, *Utne Reader* (May/June), pp. 46-49. Copyright 1993 by Lens Publishing Company, Inc. Reprinted with permission.

From Letter to the Editor, 1992, *Greencastle Banner Graphic* (7 March). Copyright 1992 Greencastle Banner Graphic. Reprinted with permission.

From "How Many Is Too Many" by C. C. Mann, 1993, *Atlantic Monthly* (February). Copyright 1993 by the Atlantic Monthly. Reprinted with permission.

From "The Abolition of El Cortito, the Short-Handled Hoe: A Case Study in Social Conflict and State Policy in California Agriculture" by D. L Murray, 1992. © 1982 by the Society of the Study of Social Problems. Reprinted from *Social Problems,* Vol. 30, no. 1, pp. 26-29, by permission.

From "On Being Sane in Insane Places" by D. Rosenhan, 1973, *Science, 179,* p. 253. Copyright 1973 by the American Association for the Advancement of Science. Reprinted by permission.

From "Psychological Warfare" by E. Tims and S. McGonible, 1992, *Indianapolis Star* (5 April). Reprinted by permission of Knight-Ridder Tribune News Service.

From "Give Him a Whistle, He'll Love It" by Elaine Viets, 1992, *St. Louis Dispatch* (29 November). Reprinted with permission of the St. Louis Post-Dispatch, copyright 1992.

Sociology

Exploring the Architecture
of Everyday Life

I

The Individual and Society

*What is the relationship between your private life
and the social world around you? Part I introduces you
to the guiding theme of this book: Our personal, everyday
experiences affect and are affected by the larger society
in which we live. Chapters 1 and 2 discuss the sociological
perspective on human life and how it differs from the
more individualistic approaches of psychology and biology.
You will read about what society consists of and get a
glimpse into sociologists' attempts to understand
the two-way relationship between
the individual and society.*

Private Lives in a Social World

Michael and Carole were college juniors at a large university. They had been dating exclusively for the past 2 years. Both on and off campus they were a loving couple, always reveling in each other's company. By all accounts, the relationship seemed to be going quite well. In fact, Michael was beginning to wonder if it might even become a permanent thing sometime soon, although he wasn't exactly sure what "permanent" meant. Then one day Carole dropped a bomb-shell. She told Michael she thought the relationship was not going anywhere, and perhaps they ought to start seeing other people.

Michael was stunned. "What did I do?" he asked her. "I thought things were going great. Is it something I said? Something I did?"

She said no, he hadn't done anything wrong. She just didn't feel as strongly about him as she once did.

After the breakup Michael became depressed. He turned to his friends for support. "She wasn't any good for you, anyway," they said. "We always thought she was a little unstable. She probably couldn't get serious with anybody. It wasn't *your* fault, it was *hers*."

Fred was a model graduate student. His grades were excellent. He got along well with his professors and even collaborated on a published research paper with one of them. During his last 2 years he taught 2 introductory courses and proved to be a skilled and caring teacher. He completed his dissertation and was granted his PhD. Fred's career script was clear: He would land a job at a top university, where he would establish a national reputation as a top-notch researcher and at the same time become a popular and beloved professor on campus.

But when Fred entered the job market and began applying for faculty positions, he faced a shocking amount of difficulty. No one seemed willing to hire him for a full-time teaching position. The only way he was able to survive was by taking a temporary one-year replacement job. He became frustrated and began to question his own abilities: "Am I good enough? Do I lack the sort of talent they're looking for? Maybe I'm not trying hard enough. What's wrong with me?" His friends and family tried to encourage him, but some of them secretly wondered if Fred wasn't as qualified as they thought he was.

In both these stories the people involved, as well as outside observers, initially try to explain the situation by focusing on *individual* characteristics and attributes. Michael wonders what he did wrong to sour his relationship with Carole; his friends question Carole's psychological stability. Fred blames himself for not being able to land a job; others question his motivation and qualifications. Such reactions are not uncommon. We have a marked tendency to attribute people's achievements and failures to their personal qualities (J. Miller, 1984).

It seems perfectly reasonable, for instance, to conclude that something about Michael or Carole or the combination of the two caused their breakup. We tend to view dating relationships as situations that succeed or fail solely based on the traits or behaviors of the two partners: He does something that bothers her, she does something that bothers him, or they're simply incompatible.

But how would your assessment of the situation change if you found out that Donald—to whom Carole had always been attracted—had just broken up with his longtime girlfriend and was now available? Suddenly things look a little different. We see that Carole's reduced fondness for Michael is based not on some newfound deficiency in his character, but on how favorably or unfavorably he compares to others.

Relationships are not exclusively private entities; they are constantly influenced by outside forces. They take place within a larger network of friends, acquaintances, ex-partners, co-workers, fellow students, and persons as yet unknown who may make desirable or, at the very least, acceptable dating partners. On the one hand, when people believe they have no better alternative they tend to stay with their present partners, even if they are not particularly satisfied. On the other hand, when people think, as Carole did, that better relationships are available, they become less committed to staying in their present ones. According to recent research, the perception of what happens in a relationship (e.g., fairness, compatibility, affection) is less likely to determine when and if it ends than the presence or absence of favorable alternatives (Felmlee, Sprecher, & Bassin, 1990). Couples may endure feelings of dissatisfaction until one partner sees a more attractive situation elsewhere.

Beyond their immediate dating network, Carole and Michael's relationship was certainly influenced by larger social forces. For instance, the very characteristics and features that people consider attractive in the first place are determined by the values of the larger culture in which they live. Fashions and tastes are constantly changing, making particular characteristics, such as hairstyles, body types, and clothing, or particular behaviors, such as smoking and drinking, more or less desirable.

Table 1.1   *Number of Advertisements for Academic Job Openings by Discipline and Year*

Year	English	Foreign Languages	History*	Sociology	Political Science
1982-83	1,354	1,248	268	444	n/a
1988-89	2,146	1,955	849*	844#	1,150#
(% change)	(+58.5)	(+56.7)	(+216.8)	(+90.1)	
1992-93	1,188	1,127	616	840	842
(% change)	(−44.6)	(−42.4)	(−27.4)	(−0.5)	(−26.8)

* from 1990 to 1991
# from 1989 to 1990
Source: Huber, 1994.

In addition, the number of potentially available partners could have indirectly affected Carole's decision. A surplus of college-age men would have increased the likelihood that Carole would eventually come across a suitable alternative to Michael. A shortage of such men, however, might have elevated Michael's relative standing in her eyes. Michael's interpersonal value, and therefore the stability of his relationship with Carole, might well have deteriorated, not because he had changed, but because of forces over which he had little if any control.

And what about Fred, our highly intelligent, well-trained, talented PhD who can't land a permanent job? Is it his fault that he can't seem to find suitable work? The answer might be yes, if we focus only on Fred and his difficulties. In trying to explain a person's failure, most of us initially tend to look at his or her shortcomings. Perhaps some inherent flaw is preventing Fred from being employable: lack of ability, lack of drive, laziness, and so on. Or maybe he doesn't come across as particularly friendly during job interviews.

By focusing exclusively on personal "deficiencies," we overlook the broader societal trends that can affect a person's job prospects. Twenty-five years ago someone with Fred's personality, training, and abilities would have had significantly less trouble landing a job. Faculty positions in higher education were much more abundant then (National Center for Education Statistics, 1989). New PhD's had a wealth of occupational choices. But since that time the nature of the job market has changed and continues to change. During the recession of the early 1990s many university departments—including English, Foreign Languages, History, Sociology, and Political Science—were forced to condense their faculty, thereby reducing the number of openings for new PhD's (see Table 1.1).

So you see, Fred's employability is as much a result of the economic forces operating at the time as any of his personal qualifications. Had he graduated 25 or even 5 years earlier or later, his prospects certainly would have been much brighter. Researchers predict that by the turn of the century, as the large number of professors hired in the 1960s reach retirement age, there will be a shortage of university faculty and a subsequent abundance of openings once again.

The moral of these two stories is that to understand phenomena in our personal lives, it is necessary to move past individual traits and examine broader societal characteristics and trends. External features beyond our immediate awareness and control often exert more influence on the circumstances in our day-to-day lives than our "internal" qualities. We can't begin to explain why relationships work or don't work without addressing the broader interpersonal friendship network and culture in which they are embedded. We can't begin to explain an individual's employability without examining current and past economic trends and the resulting job structure. By the same token, we can't begin to explain the ordinary, everyday thoughts and actions of individuals without examining the social forces that influence them.

Sociology and the Individual

Herein lies the fundamental theme of sociology and the theme that will be present throughout this book: that everyday social life—our thoughts, actions, feelings, decisions, interactions, and so on—is the product of a complex interplay between societal forces and personal characteristics. In order to explain why people are the way they are, we must understand the social, historical, cultural, and organizational environments they inhabit. Neither individuals nor society can be understood without understanding both (C. W. Mills, 1959).

Of course, this is easier said than done. We live in a world dominated by *individualistic* explanations of human behavior that attempt to understand problems and processes by focusing exclusively on the personality, psychology, or even the physical characteristics of each individual. Consequently, most of us take for granted that what we choose to do, say, feel, and think are fiercely private phenomena. Everyday life seems to be a series of unabashedly free choices. After all, *we* choose what to major in. *We* choose what to wear. *We* choose what and when to eat. *We* choose our lifestyles, our mates, and so on.

But how free are these decisions? Think about all the times your actions have been constrained by external circumstances. Have you ever felt that, because of your age or gender or race, certain opportunities were closed to you? Few corporate CEO's are younger than 35, and a 40-year-old ballplayer is considered highly unusual. Some occupations, like bank executive and engineer, are still predominantly male, while others, like nurse and secretary, are almost exclusively female. African Americans are conspicuously absent from the highest management positions in professional sports despite their overrepresentation as players.

Likewise, the doctrines of your religion may limit your behavioral choices. For a devout Catholic, premarital sex or even divorce is unlikely. A strict Muslim would not drink beverages containing alcohol. An Orthodox Jew would never drink milk and eat meat at the same time.

Think about why you find certain hairstyles, clothing, or types of music appealing or unappealing. Large-scale marketing strategies can actually create a demand for particular products or images. Your tastes, and therefore your choices as a consumer, are influenced by decisions made in corporate board-rooms all across the country. Furthermore, what you wear is dictated in part by the organizational setting in which you find yourself. For instance, appropriate attire for a stockbroker is very different from that of a college student.

Broad economic and political trends can also influence your everyday life. You may lose your job as a result of the economic fluctuations brought about by a recession. Or a political decision made at the state or national level might result in the closing of a governmental agency you depend on or reduce the municipal services to which you had grown accustomed. If you are a woman, decisions made by the Supreme Court can increase or limit your options for voluntarily ending a pregnancy or make it easier or more difficult to sue an employer for sexual harassment.

Your private life is sometimes touched by events that occur in distant countries. During the Persian Gulf War, for example, domestic oil consumption was affected by the political and economic fallout of that conflict. A few years ago it may have been difficult for you to purchase the book *The Satanic Verses* by Salman Rushdie because many bookstores in this country refused to carry it. Fundamentalist Muslims in Iran and other countries perceived the content of the book as blasphemous to Islam and vowed to take the life of the author. Fearing violence, some bookstores decided not to carry the novel for some time. So you see, even personal lifestyles may be altered because of events that take place far from one's daily rounds.

The Insights of Sociology

Our lives, private and personal though they may be, are significantly affected by the people, events, and societal features that surround us. There is a structure and pattern to our lives that often is not immediately apparent. By showing how we can be shaped by *social* processes, and how those processes can in turn be affected by individual action, sociology provides unique insight into the taken-for-granted personal events and large-scale cultural processes that make up our everyday existence.

Other disciplines study human life, too. Biologists study how the body works. Neurologists examine what goes on inside the brain. Psychologists study what goes on inside the mind. These disciplines focus almost exclusively on structures and processes that reside *within* the individual. In contrast, sociologists study what goes on *between* people as individuals, groups, or societies. How do social forces affect the way people interact with one another? How do people make sense of their private lives and the social worlds they occupy? How does everyday social interaction create "society"?

Issues like love, poverty, sex, age, and prejudice are better understood within the appropriate societal context. For instance, we may feel that we marry purely for love, when in fact society pressures us to marry within our social class, religion, or race (Berger, 1963). Sociology, unlike other disciplines, forces us to look outside the tight confines of individual personalities to understand the phenomena that shape us. Consider the following situations:

- A young high school girl, fearing she is overweight, begins starving herself systematically in hopes of becoming more attractive.

- A 55-year-old college graduate, unable to find work for the past 3 years, sinks into a depression after losing his family and his home. He now lives on the streets.

- A 36-year-old professor kills herself after learning that her position at the university will be terminated the following year.

- The student body president and valedictorian of the local high school cannot begin or end her day without several shots of whiskey.

What do these people have in common? Your first response might be that they are all suffering or have suffered terrible personal problems—eating disorders, suicidal depression, homelessness, poverty, alcoholism. You may also think that they have some kind of personality defect, genetic flaw, or mental problem that renders them incapable of coping with the demands of contemporary life. Maybe they simply lack the willpower to pick themselves up and move on. In short, your immediate tendency was to focus on the unique, perhaps "abnormal," characteristics of these people to explain their difficulties.

We cannot downplay the importance of *social* worlds. The circumstances described above are all linked to larger phenomena. There is no denying that we live in a society that praises thinness in women, encourages drinking to excess, and values economic success and independence. Some people will suffer under these conditions. This is not to say, though, that *all* people exposed to the same social messages will inevitably fall victim to the same problems. Some people are able to overcome wretched childhoods; others can withstand the tragedy of economic failure and begin anew; and some people are immune to cultural images of beauty. But in order to understand completely the nature of human life or particular social problems, we must acknowledge the broader social context in which these things occur.

The Sociological Imagination

We usually don't see the personal events in our everyday lives as being connected to the larger society. In a country like ours that celebrates individual achievement, we have difficulty looking beyond our immediate situation. When we lose our job, get divorced, or flunk out of school, it's hard to imagine that these experiences are somehow related to massive cultural or historical processes.

The ability to see the impact of these forces on our private lives is what the famous sociologist C. Wright Mills (1959) calls the **sociological imagination.** The sociological imagination enables us to understand the larger historical picture in terms of its meaning in our own lives. Mills argues that no matter how personal we think our experiences are, many of them can be seen as products of macro-level forces. The task of sociology is to help us view our lives as the intersection between personal biographies and societal history.

Take unemployment, for example. Unemployment is a terrible, even traumatic private experience. Feelings of personal failure are inevitable when one loses a job. But if the unemployment rate in an individual's community hovers at 25 or 30%—as it has in many mill and factory towns over the past several decades—then we must see unemployment as a social problem that has its roots in the economic and political structures of society. Being unemployed cannot be viewed as a character flaw or personal failure if a significant number of people in one's community are also unemployed. As long as the economy is arranged so that slumps will inevitably occur, the social problem of unemployment cannot be solved at the personal level (Lekachman, 1991; C. W. Mills, 1959).

The same can be said for divorce. One can experience divorce as an intimate tragedy, but in a society in which approximately one out of every two marriages will someday end in divorce, we must view it within the broader historical changes occurring within the family, the law, religion, and the culture as a whole.

Mills does not mean to imply that the sociological imagination should debilitate us—that is, force us to fatalistically perceive our lives as wholly beyond our control. In fact, the opposite is true. Being conscious of the impact that social forces or world history can have on our personal lives is necessary for any large-scale social change to occur. Without such awareness we fall into the trap of indifference toward both society and one another.

The sociological imagination allows us to recognize that the solutions to many of our most serious social problems lie not in changing the personal situations and characteristics of individual people but in changing the social institutions and roles available to them (C. W. Mills, 1959). Drug addiction, sexual violence, hate crimes, eating disorders, suicide, and so on will not go away simply by treating or punishing the person who is suffering from or engaging in the behavior.

Émile Durkheim
Suicide

Several years ago a tragic event occurred at the university where I teach. On a pleasant night a few weeks into the fall semester, a first-year student shot and killed himself in his dorm room. The incident sent shock waves through this small, close-knit campus. As you would expect in such a situation, the question on everyone's mind was: Why did he do it?

Although no definitive answer was ever obtained, most people simply concluded that his was a "typical" suicide. He must have been despondent, hopeless, unhappy, and unable to cope with the demands of college and the pressures of contemporary social life. In other words, there was something wrong with *him*.

This seems to be an understandable and palatable explanation, but is it sufficient? It is reasonable to assume that this person was frustrated or unhappy. As tragic as this incident was, however, it was not and is not unique. Since the 1950s the suicide rate for people between the ages of 15 and 24 has almost tripled, becoming one of the leading causes of death among young Americans (U.S. Department of Health and Human Services, 1990). People in this age group are significantly more likely to commit suicide than the population as a whole, and teenagers are the only age group for which mortality rates have increased in the recent past (Basch & Kersch, 1986).

Focusing on individual characteristics like depression and frustration doesn't tell us why so many more people in this age group commit suicide, nor does it tell us why there has been such a dramatic increase in youth suicide over the past three or four decades. So, to understand "why he did it," we must look beyond his mental state and examine the social and historical factors that might have affected him.

Clearly, life in American society today is focused on individual achievement more strongly than ever before. Young people are faced with almost constant pressure to "measure up" and define their identities according to standards set by others (Mannon, 1990). Although most can adjust, a growing number of others cannot. The increasing pressure to be beautiful, popular, and successful has taken a particularly heavy toll on young people in this country. Furthermore, as the economy grows more unstable and competition for scarce financial resources becomes more acute, young people are likely to experience unprecedented levels of stress and uncertainty about their own futures. The stakes have gotten higher as the race for the American dream has begun earlier in people's lives.

Within this context we can see that suicide among young people can be linked to certain processes going on in society. Such an explanation occupies a hallowed place in the history of sociology. In fact, one of the classic pieces of sociological research was the first to examine suicide as a sociological rather than psychological issue.

The famous French sociologist Émile Durkheim (1897/1951) argued that suicide is more likely to occur when the social ties that bind people are either too weak or too strong. In college a close friend of his named Victor Hommay committed suicide. Convinced that there was more involved in Hommay's death than psychological factors, Durkheim began to explore the sociological grounds for suicide.

How does one go about determining whether suicide—perhaps the most private act one can commit—is instigated by the structure of society? For about

7 years Durkheim carefully examined the available data on *rates* of suicide among various social groups in Europe—countries, religions, ethnic groups, and so on. He thought that changes in the rate of suicide over time or between communities could not be explained through individualistic disciplines like psychology or biology.

If suicide is purely an act of individual desperation, he reasoned, one would not expect to find any noticeable changes in the rates from year to year or society to society. That is, the distribution of desperate, unstable, unhappy individuals should be roughly equal across time and culture. If, however, certain groups or societies had a significantly higher rate of suicide than others, this would show that something more than individual disposition is at work.

After compiling his figures, Durkheim discovered that suicide rates tended to be higher among widowed, single, and divorced people than among married people; higher in modernized, urbanized communities than in rural ones; and higher among Protestants than among Catholics. Did this mean that unmarried people, Protestants, and city dwellers are more unhappy, depressed, or psychologically dysfunctional than others? Durkheim didn't think so. Instead, he felt that something about the nature of social life among these groups increased the likelihood of suicide.

Durkheim argued that when community ties are weak, people feel disconnected and alone. If one lives in a community that stresses individualism and de-emphasizes ties to the larger group, then one is likely to lack the supportive network that could be used as a buffer against personal difficulties. Durkheim pointed out, for instance, that where the Catholic church emphasizes salvation through community and ties its members to the Church through elaborate doctrine and ritual, Protestantism emphasizes *individual* salvation and responsibility. This individualism, he believed, explained the differences he noticed in suicide rates. Self-reliance and independence may glorify one in God's eyes, but they become liabilities if one is in the throes of personal tragedy and has no supportive community to turn to.

Durkheim felt that life in urban industrialized communities tends to be individualistic and alienating. Contemporary sociologists have voiced this same concern (e.g., Bellah, Madsen, Sullivan, Swidler, & Tipton, 1985; Riesman, 1950). Many people in urban areas today don't know and have no desire to know their neighbors. Strangers are treated with suspicion. In the pursuit of economic survival we have become more willing to relocate, sometimes to areas completely isolated from previous family ties. As we spread out and become more insulated we become more separated from those who could and would offer support in times of need. When the structure of our community *discourages* the formation of ties and bonds to others and to a communal way of life, the likelihood of suicide increases.

Conversely, when the social ties to one's community are *too strong*, suicide also becomes likely. Durkheim suggested that in certain societies individuality is

Figure 1.1 *Proposed Relationship Between Potential Suicide and Density of Religious Integration*

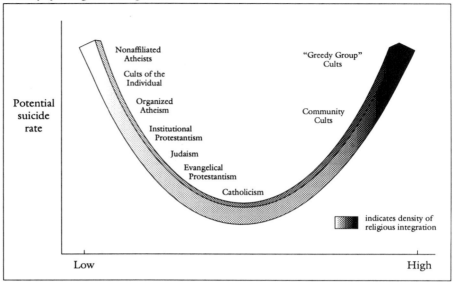

Source: Pescosolido & Georgianna, 1989.

completely overshadowed by one's group membership. Here the individual literally lives for the group. Her or his personality is merely a reflection of the collective identity of the community. Religious cults, for example, require that their members reject their ties to outside people and groups. In such situations obedience to the values and customs of the community can become so powerful that when people feel they can no longer contribute to the group and sustain their value within it, they may take their own lives out of loyalty to group norms (see Figure 1.1). The ancient Japanese suicide ritual, *hara-kiri,* and the mass suicide at Jonestown in 1978 are two examples of people committing suicide not because they were too distant from the group, but because they were too close to it.

In 1989 four young Korean sisters, ranging in age from 6 to 13, attempted to kill themselves by ingesting rat poison. The three older sisters survived; the youngest died. The eldest provided startling sociological insight into this seemingly senseless act. Their family was poor—the father supported everyone on a salary of about $362 a month. She told authorities that the sisters had made a suicide pact to ease their parents' financial burden and leave enough money for the education of their 3-year-old brother. According to Korean culture it is essential that a family be able to send its male children to college. Traditionally, female children are irrelevant and somewhat unimportant.

This situation clearly illustrates the power of the ties to one's cultural values. These young girls attempted to take their lives not because they were depressed or unable to cope, but because they felt obligated to obey the dictates of their culture, which they felt was much more important than their personal well-being.

Just as the suicide pact of these young girls was tied to the social system of which they were a part, so too was the suicide of the young college student at my university. His choices and life circumstances were also a function of his particular society and the values and conditions contained within it. No doubt he had emotional problems, but these problems may have been part and parcel of his social circumstances. Had he lived in a society that didn't place as much pressure on young people or glorify individual achievement, he might not have chosen suicide. That's what the sociological imagination helps us understand.

Conclusion

As we approach the 21st century, understanding one's place within a cultural, historical, and global context is more important than ever. The world is shrinking. Communication technology and global economies connect us to people on the other side of the planet. The growing attention paid to ecological awareness opens our eyes to the environmental degradations that occur in South American rain forests. The events in the former Soviet Union, Yugoslavia, and Czechoslovakia, as well as the unification of Germany, were perhaps the most significant political events of the late 20th century. The consequences of these colossal changes will continue to be felt around the world for many years to come.

When people's lives are changed by such events—as they sink into poverty or ascend to prosperity, stand in bread lines or work at a job previously unavailable, or find their sense of ethnic identity and sense of self-worth altered—we can begin to understand the personal effects of societal and global changes.

The next chapter will provide you with a more detailed introduction to the theme of the book: that individuals simultaneously influence and are influenced by society. In subsequent chapters I will examine the interplay between individuals and the people, groups, organizations, institutions, and culture that collectively make up our society.

CHAPTER HIGHLIGHTS

■ The primary theme of sociology is that our everyday thoughts and actions are the product of a complex interplay between massive social forces and personal characteristics. We can't understand the relationship between individuals and societies without understanding both.

■ The sociological imagination is the ability to see the impact of social forces on our private lives—an awareness that our lives lie at the intersection of personal biographies and societal history.

■ Rather than study what goes on *within* people, sociologists study what goes on *between* people, whether as individuals, groups, organizations, or entire societies. Sociology forces us to look outside the tight confines of our individual personalities to understand the phenomena that shape us.

YOUR TURN

The sociological imagination serves as the driving theme throughout this book. It's not a particularly difficult concept to grasp in the abstract: Things bigger than us affect our everyday lives in ways that are sometimes not immediately apparent; our personal biographies are a function of social history. Yet what does this actually mean? How can you *see* the impact of larger social and historical events on your own life?

One way is to find out what events were going on at the time of your birth. Go to the library and find a newspaper and a popular magazine that were published on the day you were born. What were the major news events that took place that day? What were the dominant social and political concerns in the country at the time? What was the state of the economy? What was considered fashionable in clothing, music, movies, and so forth?

Ask your parents or other adults about their reactions to these events and conditions. How do you think those reactions affected the way you were raised and the values in your family? What have been the lasting effects, if any, of these historical circumstances on the person you are today?

Seeing and Thinking Sociologically

In 1971 Philip Zimbardo, a professor of social psychology at Stanford University, conducted a remarkable experiment in the basement of the campus psychology building. Recent prison uprisings had piqued Zimbardo's interest in what it means psychologically to be a prisoner or a prison guard. Why were prisoners so disposed toward violence? Why were prison guards so brutal? To most of us the answers seem obvious. Prisoners are violent because of the type of people they are: antisocial criminals who have little regard for other people. Guards are brutal because it takes that type of person to be attracted to such an occupation in the first place.

Zimbardo felt there was more to the dynamics of prison life than the personalities of the individuals involved. He wondered whether the structure of the prison situation played a part in turning prisoners and guards into the mean and violent people they were. With the help of several colleagues, he created a mock prison in which he could observe volunteer subjects in the roles of prisoners and guards. Of the 70 or so students who answered his ad for volunteers, Zimbardo chose two dozen mature, emotionally stable, intelligent young men to be part of the study. None had a criminal record. They were, as he put it, the "cream of the crop of this generation" (1971, p. 4).

Some subjects were designated as "prisoners" with a flip of a coin; the rest served as "guards." When it was time for the experiment to begin, the prisoners were unexpectedly picked up at their homes by a city police officer in a squad car, searched, handcuffed, fingerprinted, blindfolded, and taken to the "prison." There they were stripped, given a uniform and number, and placed in a cell with two other inmates. They were told the cell would be their home for the next 2 weeks. When the guards arrived they were informed that they had the authority to make up their own rules for maintaining law, order, and respect in the prison and were free to improvise new ones at any time during their 8-hour shifts on duty. Both prisoners and guards were paid $15 a day for their participation.

Although the experiment was supposed to last for 2 weeks, it had to be stopped after only 6 days. Zimbardo described the situation as follows:

> What we saw was frightening. It was no longer apparent to most of the subjects (or to us) where reality ended and their roles began. The majority had indeed become prisoners or guards, no longer able to clearly differentiate between role playing and self. . . . In less than a week the experience of imprisonment undid (temporarily) a lifetime of learning; human values were suspended, self-concepts were challenged and the ugliest . . . side of human nature surfaced. We were horrified because we saw some guards treat others as if they were despicable animals, taking pleasure in cruelty, while the prisoners became . . . dehumanized robots who thought only of escape, of their own individual survival and of their mounting hatred for the guards. (1971, p. 4)

Some of the prisoners became severely depressed, confused, or hysterical and had to be released after only a few days. On the fourth day of the experiment a Catholic priest, who had once worked as a prison chaplain, talked to the remaining prisoners. He found they were no different from the "first-timers" he had seen in actual prisons. All but three of the prisoners were willing to forfeit all the money they had earned just to get out of the prison. When told they had been "denied parole," however, they returned docilely to their cells. Zimbardo points out that had these individuals been thinking like the college students they were, instead of the prisoners they were playing, they simply would have quit.

Some of the guards became tyrants, arbitrarily using their power and enjoying the control they had over others. Other guards were not as brutal, but they never intervened on behalf of the prisoners and never told the other guards to "ease off."

Zimbardo's reason for calling off the experiment speaks volumes about the nature of society and social life:

> I called off the experiment not because of the horror I saw out there in the prison yard, but because of the horror of realizing that *I* could have easily traded places with the most brutal guard or become the weakest prisoner full of hatred at being so powerless that I could not eat, sleep or go to the toilet without permission of the authorities. (1971, p. 5)

What Zimbardo so poignantly discovered was that individual behavior was largely controlled by social forces and situational contingencies. He took smart, well-balanced people and transformed them overnight into either brutal or cowering animals. In addition, his aborted study illustrated that, given the proper environmental circumstances, individuals can create the very social forces that come to shape their behavior. As the experimenter, Zimbardo merely provided the physical structure of the "prison" and a few general rules. It was the subjects themselves who *created* the reality of their roles and therefore defined the power that the prison structure exerted over them.

Zimbardo's study shows that the relationship between individuals and the social environment in which they live is a reciprocal one. In this chapter I discuss the process by which individuals construct society and how our lives are linked to society. Subsequent chapters examine the specific facets of this process: the social and personal creation of knowledge, culture, social order, social disorder, self, gender, images, intimate relationships, groups, organizations, and institutions.

How Individuals Structure Society

Up to this point I have been using the term *society* rather loosely. Typically, **society** is defined as a population living in the same geographical area who share a culture and a common identity and whose members are subject to the same political authority. Societies may consist of people who share the same ethnic heritage or hundreds of different groups who speak a multitude of languages. Some societies are highly industrialized and complex; others are primarily agrarian and relatively simple in structure. Some societies are self-sufficient and produce most of the goods and services they need; others rely exclusively on trade with foreign countries for survival.

According to the 19th-century French philosopher Auguste Comte, all societies, whatever their form, contain forces for stability, which he called "social statics," and forces for change, which he called "social dynamics." Many sociologists, however, use the term *society* to mean a "static" entity—a natural, permanent, and historical structure. They frequently talk about society "planning" or "controlling" our lives and describe it as a relatively stable set of organizations, institutions, systems, and cultural patterns into which successive generations of people are born and socialized.

As a result, sociology students are often led to believe not only that society is powerfully influential (which it is), but also that it is something which exists "out there," completely separate and distinct from us (which it isn't). It is therefore tempting to view society simply as a "top down" *initiator* of human activity, a massive entity that methodically controls the lives of all individuals within it, like a gigantic puppeteer manipulating his or her marionettes. This characterization is not altogether inaccurate. Society does exert a certain amount of influence on its constituent members. The concept of the sociological imagination discussed in chapter 1 implies that structural forces beyond our direct control affect our personal lives.

But this is only one side of the sociological coin. The sociological imagination also encourages us to see that while every individual lives out his or her life in a particular society with certain identifiable structural features and historical circumstances, each individual also has a role in forming that society and influencing the course of its history. As people process inputs from their social environments, they respond in ways that may modify the effects and even the nature of the environment (House, 1981). As one sociologist wrote:

> No [society], however massive it may appear in the present, existed in this massivity from the dawn of time. Somewhere along the line each one of its salient features was concocted by human beings . . . Since all social systems were created by [people], it follows that [people] can also change them. (Berger, 1963, p. 128)

To fully understand society, we must see it as a human construction. Society is made up of people interacting with one another. It consists of everyday *micro-situations*—what people do, say, feel, and think alone or in small groups. If the nature of society changes, it is because the individuals who enact those changes have altered *their* behavior (Collins, 1981).

The expectations and demands society poses are developed and communicated through interpersonal processes. If people couldn't communicate with one another and understand these expectations, they couldn't live together. In short, society is possible only when there is some agreement as to the cultural rules that govern the minute interchanges of everyday life (see chapter 4).

Communication is what holds society together. Through day-to-day communication individuals construct, reaffirm, experience, and alter the reality of their society. It is the primary means by which we sustain the world of objects in which we live (see chapter 5). This is particularly true of abstract, intangible objects, like society. You can't experience a society directly. You can't "see" a society. You can only see the people who belong to it (Collins, 1981; Collins & Makowsky, 1984).

In turn, society needs our collective recognition in order to exist at all. To experience society, we have to talk about it, and by doing so we reaffirm its reality. Conversation about politics, religion, family, entertainment, love, law, and all the other areas of human activity creates a sense of common membership (Collins, 1981).

Imagine two people sitting on a park bench. They strike up a conversation. Their talk eventually turns to the sour state of the economy—inflation, unemployment, the rising cost of medical care, and so on. Whether or not they agree as to the causes and solutions to these problems, they have collectively acknowledged the reality of these economic phenomena. In dealing with and especially talking about these matters, they give shape and substance to society's ideals and values (Hewitt, 1988). So you see, society is a product of individuals interacting with one another. By responding to other people's utterances and gestures in the manner expected of us and by talking about social abstractions as real things, we contribute our share (Shibutani, 1961). Hence society must also be seen as a "bottom up" phenomenon and might best be regarded as an ongoing process, a *becoming* rather than a *being*. It is a succession of events, a flow of interchanges among people (Shibutani, 1961, p. 174).

When viewed this way we can begin to understand our role in altering society. Whenever we modify the expectations or behaviors associated with a certain social position we occupy, we are simultaneously modifying a part of our society. This is particularly effective for individuals who occupy highly visible and influential positions. It is often argued, for instance, that Franklin D. Roosevelt's turn as president forever changed the nature of the presidency and the role of the federal government in American life (House, 1981).

Not only powerful people can modify society. Sometimes the actions of ordinary individuals mobilize larger groups of people to collectively alter some aspect of social life. On December 1, 1955, Rosa Parks, a black seamstress in Montgomery, Alabama, refused to give up her seat to a white man who had boarded the bus after her. The incident sparked a citywide boycott of the public transit system and galvanized the entire civil rights movement of the 1950s and 1960s. This single act was an individual challenge to the broad societal expectations commonly associated with race at the time and helped set in motion a massive restructuring of American race relations that continues to reverberate through our economic, educational, and political systems today.

Even something so apparently unchangeable as our collective past can be shaped by individuals. We usually think of history as a fixed, unalterable collection of social events that occurred long ago. No one would question that the Civil War took place in the 1860s, or that Thomas Edison invented the light bulb, or that John F. Kennedy was assassinated on November 22, 1963. Only in science fiction can one "go back" and change history.

But even though historical events don't change, there have been frequent attempts to change their meaning and relevance. Individuals and groups engage in the process of making new sense out of old, "undeniable" facts. In the early 1990s a retired bookseller and construction worker in central California named Bradley Smith launched a one-man campaign to convince people that the Nazi Holocaust never occurred. Despite the overwhelming evidence to the contrary and the thousands of firsthand, eyewitness accounts, he argued that the millions of Jews and others who perished in German concentration camps died of typhus and other diseases and not from a concerted German effort to exterminate them. Gas chambers, if they existed at all, were "life saving" chambers meant to prevent disease. Says Smith about his attempt to change history:

> I get up in the morning, I go to the typewriter and write down the simplest things which have the most tremendous implications. I write about how all the historians are wrong, how the scholars and the intellectuals and the universities are all wrong and how I'm right. (quoted in Bishop, 1991)

Not all attempts to revise history have such questionable motivations. Consider the celebration in 1992 of the 500th anniversary of Columbus's discovery of America. Most of us learned as schoolchildren that 1492 represented a triumphant and progressive step forward for Western civilization. However, the increasing sensitivity to the social value of all racial and ethnic groups and the acknowledgment of their past persecution have forced many people to reconsider the historical *meaning* of Columbus's journey. In fact, some historians now consider it one of the most dismal examples of wanton and deadly prejudice.

We live in a world in which our behaviors are largely a product of societal and historical processes. Society is an objective fact that coerces, even creates, us (Berger, 1963). At the same time, we are constantly creating, maintaining, reaffirming, or transforming society. Hence it is part and parcel of the micro-level activities of human beings as they interact with one another (Collins, 1981). We create society, then collectively "forget" we've done so, believe it is independent of us, and live our lives under its influence.

Social Influence: The Impact of Other People on Our Everyday Lives

We live in a world with other people. This is not exactly an earth-shattering statement, but one that is key to understanding the sociology of human behavior. Our everyday lives are a collection of brief encounters, extended conversations, intimate interactions, chance collisions, and superficial contacts with other people. In our early years we have our parents, siblings, uncles, aunts, and grandparents to contend with. Soon we begin to form friendships with others outside our families. Our lives become filled with connections to other people—teachers, bosses, therapists—who are neither family nor friends but who have an enormous impact on us. And, of course, there are the daily encounters we have with total strangers: the clerk at the supermarket, the server at the restaurant, the woman who sat next to you on the bus. Even when we're alone, we feel the effects of other people. Being alone implies the *absence* of social contact, and the only way to understand that is to know what being with *others* is like.

Sociologists tell us that these encounters have a great deal of *social influence* over our lives. Whether we're aware of it or not, other people affect our thoughts, perceptions, and behaviors. We take into account their feelings and concerns before acting. They may be in our immediate presence or hover in our memories. They may be real or imagined, loved or despised. And their effects on us may be deliberate or accidental. Our lives are spent forming or dissolving attachments to other people; we may seek them out one moment, avoid them like the plague the next. As will be discussed in chapters 5 and 6, much of our private identity—what we think of ourselves, the type of people we become, and the images of ourselves we project in public—is derived from our contact with others.

Imagine for a moment what your life would be like if you never had contact with other people (assuming you could survive that long!). Obviously you would be pretty lonely. But beyond that, you'd lack the key experiences that make you a functioning human being. You wouldn't know what love is, or hate or jealousy or compassion or appreciation, for that matter. You wouldn't know if you were wealthy or poor, bright or dumb, witty or boring. You'd also lack some important and basic information. You wouldn't know how much a pound weighed, where England was, or what plants and animals are edible. Furthermore, you'd have no language, and because we use language to think, imagine, and dream, you'd lack these abilities as well.

Contact with people is essential to a person's social development. But there is more to social life than the mere fact that it involves other people. We act and react to things and people in our environment as a result of the *meaning* we attach to them. A squirrel will instinctively run away at the sight of a dog barreling toward it. A human, however, would not have such an automatic reaction. We've learned from past experiences that some animals are approachable while others aren't. So we're able to think, *Is this a friendly or mean dog? Does it want to play with me or tear me limb from limb?* and respond accordingly. In short, we must *interpret* events in our environment before we act. To do this, we often look to others to help us define a particular situation.

Bibb Latané and John Darley
Why Don't People Help?

In the early morning hours of March 13, 1964, a woman named Kitty Genovese was brutally stabbed to death in front of her New York apartment. As we all know, murders are not uncommon in New York City or any other American city for that matter. But what made this case all the more troubling was the fact that about 40 people either heard her scream for help or watched her being stabbed from their apartment windows. No one called the police until about 35 minutes after the attack had begun (Seedman & Hellman, 1975).

When the story appeared in the newspaper the public was outraged. How could people be so insensitive to the suffering of another? Why didn't anyone help her? Some newspaper editors and psychiatrists at the time blamed the behavior on "bystander apathy" or growing "urban alienation." The story became a metaphor for modern city life. Others, however, speculated that the failure of people to get involved might be due more to the social influence that bystanders have on each other than to individual callousness.

To test this theory, two social psychologists, Bibb Latané and John Darley (1970), conducted a series of experiments on helping behavior in emergencies. In the first session the room in which subjects were completing written surveys gradually filled with smoke. In the second experiment subjects heard a loud crashing noise from an adjoining room, followed by a woman's screaming, "Oh my God, my foot . . . I . . . I . . . can't move it. Oh my ankle. I . . . can't get this . . . thing off me" (Latané & Rodin, 1969). In the third study subjects were participating in a discussion over an intercom when one of them suddenly choked, gasped, and called out for help. In each situation, the number of individuals present at the time of the emergency was varied so that some subjects were alone, while others were with several people. The researchers consistently found that as the number of bystanders increased, the likelihood that any one of

Table 2.1

The Diffusion of Responsibility: Percentage of cases in which help was given in emergency situations

Size of Group	Smoke-filled Room	Fallen Woman	Seizure
1 person	75%	70%	85%
3 persons	38%	40%	31%*

*Group consisted of five persons

Source: Latané & Darley, 1970.

them would help decreased. It appeared that people help others more often and more quickly when alone. (see Table 2.1).

There are a number of sociological explanations for this phenomenon, which is often called the *bystander effect*. First, the more bystanders there are, the more likely it is that we will assume someone else will help. If we are by ourselves when an emergency occurs we are 100% responsible for taking action. However, when there are 10 bystanders, each individual has only 10% of the responsibility. The higher the number of bystanders, the less likely each individual is to intervene.

Second, if we are unsure of our own perceptions and interpretations, or if the situation is ambiguous, we look to others for help in defining what is going on. If others appear calm, the individual may decide that whatever is happening doesn't require his or her assistance. Unfortunately, people often try to avoid showing outward signs of worry or concern until they see that other people are alarmed. This sort of caution encourages others not to define the situation as one requiring assistance and therefore inhibits the urge to help. The larger the number of people who don't seem concerned, the stronger the inhibiting influence. Obviously, helping will not be inhibited if others *are* showing visible alarm or if the situation is so unambiguous that one doesn't need to look to the reactions of others, like a car accident, for instance (Clark & Word, 1972).

Kitty Genovese's neighbors weren't necessarily cruel, cold, or apathetic. They simply may have been victims of a tragic case of social influence in which each looked to others for information, waiting for someone else to define the situation and act. Because *everyone* was waiting for someone else to do something, no one did anything.

How Others Influence Our Perceptions

In 1951 social psychologist Solomon Asch devised an experimental situation that examined the extent to which pressure from other people could affect one's visual perceptions (Asch, 1958). Imagine yourself in the following situation: You sign up for a psychology experiment, and on a specified date you and seven others whom you think are also subjects arrive and are seated at a table in a small room. You don't know it at the time, but the others are actually associates of the

Figure 2.1   *Asch's Perceptual Task Cards*

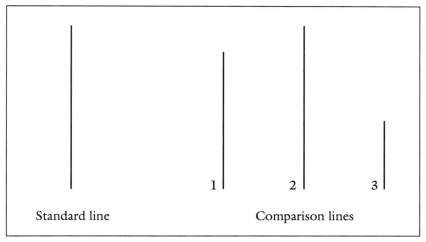

Standard line   Comparison lines

Source: R. Brown, 1986.

experimenter, and their behavior has been carefully scripted. You're the only real subject. The experimenter arrives and tells you that the study in which you are about to participate concerns people's visual judgments.

She places two cards before you. The card on the left contains one vertical line. The card on the right displays three lines of varying length (see Figure 2.1). The experimenter asks all of you, one at a time, to choose which of the three lines on the right card matches the length of the line on the left card. The task is repeated several times with different cards. On some occasions the other "subjects" unanimously choose the wrong line. It is clear to you that they are wrong, but they have *all* given the same answer. What would you do? Would you go along with the majority opinion or "stick to your guns" and trust your own eyes?

In total, about one third of the subjects went along with the clearly erroneous majority. Some of the subjects indicated afterward that they assumed the majority were correct and their own perceptions were wrong. Others knew they were correct but didn't want to be different from the rest of the group. Some even insisted they saw the line lengths as the majority saw them. Asch concluded that it is difficult to maintain that you see something when no one else does. Pressure from other people can make you see almost anything.

How Others Influence Our Actions

Social influence is particularly apparent when it comes to our actions. The presence of other people may motivate us to improve our performance—for example, when the quality of your opponent makes you play the best tennis game of your life. Or, the presence of others may inhibit us—like when you forget your lines in the school play because your family is in the audience.

I'm sure you've been in situations in which other people have tried to persuade you to do things against your will or better judgment. Perhaps a friend convinced you to buy a Ford instead of a Honda. Or perhaps someone persuaded you to steal a candy bar, cheat on your taxes, or disregard the speed limit. On occasion, such social influence can be deadly.

Stanley Milgram
*Ordinary People
and Cruel Acts*

If a being from another planet were to read the history of human civilization, it would probably conclude that we are tremendously cruel, vicious, and evil. From countless wars and crusades to genocides, from backwater lynchings to violent crime and schoolyard bullies, humans have always shown a powerful tendency to turn on their fellow humans.

The curious thing is that people involved in such acts often show a profound capacity to deny responsibility for their actions by pointing to the influence of others: "My friend made me do it," or, "I was only following orders." Can an ordinary, decent person be pressured by another to commit an act of extreme cruelty? Or do evil actions require evil people?

Consider the story of Adolf Eichmann, the mastermind behind the Nazi Holocaust. In 1961 he was found guilty of war crimes and executed in Jerusalem. One would expect someone who had created a meticulous and efficient plan for killing millions of people to look like the devil incarnate or to have a long history of cruelty and violence. Neither was true of Eichmann. Psychiatric evaluations after the war indicated that he was rather ordinary. He loved his parents, wife, and children (Arendt, 1963). He was an avid horticulturist who would spend hours tending to his garden. Eichmann simply claimed that he was doing his job in carrying out the orders of his "boss," Adolf Hitler.

Social psychologist Stanley Milgram (1974) was interested in learning whether ordinary people could be persuaded to commit cruel acts against others. He was familiar with the horrors of Nazi Germany during the 1930s and 1940s in which millions were systematically murdered. After World War II he witnessed the trials of Nazi war criminals like Eichmann and their repeated attempts to deny responsibility for their actions by claiming that they were merely following orders. Milgram wanted to know how far people would go in obeying the commands of an authority figure. He set up an experimental situation in which a subject, upon orders from an authoritative figure, flips a switch, apparently sending a 450-volt shock to an innocent victim.

Subjects were told they would be participating in a study on the effects of punishment on learning. On a specified day each subject arrived at the laboratory with another person who, unbeknownst to the subject, was actually an accomplice of the experimenter. Each subject was informed that he or she would play the role of "teacher," while the other person would be the "learner." The teacher was taken to a separate room that held an ominous-looking machine called a "shock generator." The machine had a series of switches ranging from 30 to 450 volts at 15-volt increments and consecutively labeled "Slight Shock," "Danger: Severe Shock," and, ultimately, "XXX." The learner was seated in another room out of the sight of the teacher and was supposedly strapped to an electrode from the shock generator.

The teacher read a series of word pairs (e.g., *blue-sky, nice-day, wild-duck*) to the learner. After reading the entire list, the teacher then read the first word of a pair (e.g., *blue*) and four alternatives for the second word (e.g., *sky, ink, box, lamp*). The learner had to select the correct alternative. Following directions from the experimenter, who was present in the room, the teacher flipped a switch and shocked the learner whenever he or she gave an incorrect answer. The shocks began at the lowest level, 15 volts, and increased with each subsequent incorrect answer all the way up to the 450-volt maximum.

The learner pretended not to be very bright and made many incorrect responses. As instructed, all of the subjects shocked the learner for each incorrect response. As the experiment proceeded and the shocks became stronger, the learner began to cry out in pain. The cries became more blood-curdling, and the learner's pleas to end the experiment became more intense with each increase in voltage. Most of the teachers, believing they were inflicting serious injury on this other person, became visibly upset and wanted to stop. The experimenter, however, ordered them to continue—and they did. At around 300 volts the learner became silent. Some teachers thought they had actually killed the fellow! The experimenter told them to continue, stating that it was essential to proceed and that he, the experimenter, would be responsible for any harm that might befall the learner. Despite the tortured reactions of the victim, 65% of the subjects complied with the experimenter's demands and proceeded to the maximum, 450 volts.

Milgram repeated the study with a variety of subjects and even conducted it in different countries, including Germany and Australia. In each case about two thirds of the subjects were willing, under orders from the experimenter, to shock to the limit. Milgram showed that one situation, obedience to authority, had the power to cause ordinarily nice people to do terrible things they wouldn't do under other circumstances.

This wasn't a particularly soothing proposition, and Milgram's study generated a tremendous amount of controversy. It's easy to conclude that the brutal acts of inhumanity we read about in our daily newspapers are the products of defective or inherently evil individuals. All society has to do is identify, capture, and separate them from the rest of us. Problem over, case closed. But if Milgram is right, if most of us could become evil given the "right" circumstances, then the only thing that separates us from the monsters is our good fortune and social environment. Just as Philip Zimbardo was horrified to realize that he could easily become a brutal guard in his prison experiment, so too are we horrified at the thought that social conditions could so profoundly influence us to behave in harmful ways.

Societal Influence: The Effect of Social Structure on Our Everyday Lives

Social life is more than just individual people affecting one another's lives. Society also consists of socially recognizable combinations of individuals: relationships, groups, organizations, and so on, as well as the products of human action: roles, institutions, history, and culture. A society is more than just a sum of its human parts; it's also the way those parts are put together, related to each other, and organized (Coulson & Riddell, 1980). Although society is dynamic and may change form from time to time, it persists despite the comings and goings of its members, setting guidelines and influencing our lives. Let's examine some of the important elements that make up a society.

Statuses and Roles

Society is a network of named positions, or **statuses,** occupied by people. "Father" is a status within a network of other statuses—"son," "grandfather," "mother"—that make up a family. "Woman" and "man" are two statuses within a network we call gender. "African American," "Caucasian," "Hispanic," and "Asian" are statuses within a network called race. Professor, uncle, student, shoplifter, brain surgeon, electrician, and alcoholic are other examples.

Statuses are important sociologically because they all come with a set of expectations that include rights, obligations, behaviors, and duties. These expectations are referred to as **roles.** For instance, a professor is expected to teach students, answer questions, be impartial, and dress appropriately. Any out-of-role behavior may be met with shock or suspicion. If your professor consistently showed up for class in a bathing suit, that would certainly violate his or her "scholarly" image and call into question his or her ability to teach. Each person, as a result of her or his own skills, interests, and interactional experiences, defines roles differently. Students enter a class with the general expectation that their professor is going to teach them something. Each professor, however, may have a different method. Some professors are very animated, others remain stationary behind the podium. Some will not allow questions until after the lecture, others demand constant discussion and probing questions from students. Some are meticulous and organized, others scattered and absent-minded.

We occupy many statuses at the same time. I am a professor, but I am also a husband, son, nephew, uncle, father, friend, consumer, brother, second baseman, homeowner, neighbor, author, and jogger. Because each status has its own set of role expectations, my behavior is dictated to a large degree by the status that is most salient at the time. On the one hand, when I am playing softball, my status as husband or professor is not particularly relevant. On the other hand, if I want to play softball on my wedding anniversary, I may be in trouble!

Statuses often come in pairs or **relationships.** People engage in typical patterns of interaction based on the nature of their relationships. Employers are expected to interact with employees in a certain way, as are dentists with patients and salespeople with customers. In each case actions are constrained by the responsibilities and obligations associated with those particular statuses. We know, for instance, that lovers are supposed to interact with each other differently than with acquaintances or friends. In a parent-child relationship, both members are linked by certain rights, privileges, and obligations. Parents are responsible for providing their children with the basic necessities of life—food, clothing, shelter, and so forth. These expectations are so powerful that not meeting them may constitute the crime of negligence or abuse. Children, in turn, are expected to abide by their parents' wishes. Interactions within a relationship are a function not only of the personalities of the two people involved, but also of the *roles* they occupy.

The power of role expectations is felt most clearly when we occupy two conflicting statuses simultaneously. Sociologists use the term **role conflict** to describe such situations. People may feel frustrated in their efforts to do what they feel they're supposed to do when the demands of one role clash with the demands of another. A parent may have an important business meeting with out-of-town clients (status of business executive) at the same time her 8-year-old son is appearing in the school play (status of parent). Or a high school kid who works hard at his job at the local ice cream shop (status of employee) is frustrated when his buddies come and expect him to give them free ice cream (status of friend).

Micro-Macro Connection
Caring for Elderly Parents

Role conflict can also have devastating emotional and physical consequences often arising from larger, fundamental changes in society. For instance, the past several decades have witnessed a dramatic shift in the age structure of American society. More people are living into their 80s and 90s (see chapter 14), but at the same time couples are having fewer children (see chapter 8). The American family is expanding *vertically* (more generations living per family) and shrinking *horizontally* (fewer individuals per generation). What this means is that as life expectancy increases, there are fewer siblings around to share in caring for elderly parents (Sherman, Ward, and LaGory, 1988).

As a result, many people, particularly women in their 40s, 50s, and even 60s, are having to cope with the burden of caring for elderly parents in addition to the usual demands of work and family. More than 6 million elderly Americans now need help with such everyday basics as getting out of bed, eating, dressing, bathing, and using the bathroom (Beck, 1990). Given the high cost of nursing homes, many elderly parents end up moving in with their children. The typical pattern is that sons offer financial assistance, while daughters and daughters-in-law provide the time-consuming, hands-on care.

Almost every woman is going to have to take care of an aging parent or in-law at some point in her life (Lewin, 1989). A survey by the Travelers Corporation in 1985 found that about one out of every five female employees over the age of 30 is currently providing some care to an elderly parent (Lewin, 1989). As life expectancy increases, these caretaking responsibilities can last 10 years or more.

Meeting these obligations often comes at the expense of not living up to the expectations of other roles. Many women who provide care to elderly parents are forced to spend less time with their husbands and children, leading to resentment and frustration within their own families. Their occupational roles and financial well-being may also suffer. At a time when more families depend on two incomes for survival, many women have switched to part-time work, passed up promotions, or quit their jobs altogether, A study by the American Association of Retired Persons estimates that 14% of all part-time adult female workers had left their full-time jobs because of caregiving responsibilities. Of those not employed but who once had jobs, 27% had taken early retirement or simply quit (Lewin, 1989).

With these responsibilities come feelings of guilt, inadequacy, and resentment. One woman, who had quit her job to care for her mother, who had developed Alzheimer's disease, echoed the thoughts of many:

> I felt like I was going under. I couldn't do my job because I was pretty much in pieces. I was furious at my brother who didn't help at all. My 15-year-old daughter is mad at me because I am so engaged with my mother. My son has stopped visiting me. And the friends who had been wonderful and supportive through the birth of my babies and my divorce just faded away now that I need them the most. I am alternately so sad about my mother's decline that I can't stop crying and so enraged that my life is being messed up that I want to dump her. I used to think I was good at crises, but this just goes on and on, and I'm falling apart. (Lewin, 1989)

Groups

Sometimes networks of many interrelated statuses form into well-defined units called groups. A **group** is a set of people who interact more or less regularly with one another and who are conscious of their identity as a group. Families, clubs, and sports teams all constitute social groups. Groups tend to have a structure that defines the relationships between members, and each individual occupies some named position—father, president, treasurer, linebacker, and so forth.

A **primary group** consists of a small number of members who have direct contact over a relatively long period of time. Emotional attachment is high in such groups, and members have intimate knowledge of each other's lives. Families and close friends would be considered primary groups. A **secondary group**, in contrast, is much more anonymous and impersonal. The group is established for a specific task, such as the production or sales of consumer goods, and members are less emotionally committed to one another. Their roles tend to be highly structured. Primary groups may form within secondary groups, as when close friendships form among co-workers, but in general a secondary group is more formal and goal-driven.

Like societies, groups have a reality that is more than just the sum of the individuals who happen to be in them. A group can experience a changeover in membership without altering its basic structure. In primary groups such a change in membership cannot occur without some dramatic effect on the nature and identity of the group, such as when a family experiences a divorce or a death. Secondary groups, however, can endure relatively easily despite the fact that some individuals leave and new ones enter. In fact, the composition of the group might change completely, as when a high school senior class graduates, only to be replaced the following year by another group of students.

Groups by definition include some people and exclude others. Much of what we do and feel in our everyday lives revolves around our sense of group membership—our feelings of "us" and "them." The term **in-group** refers to the people who constitute the group to which you belong and with whom you identify. **Out-group** refers to people who don't belong. Group membership, then, can become a signifying feature of one's identity and a powerful force behind one's future actions and thoughts. For instance, a girl who is not a member of the popular clique at school but wants to be is likely to structure much of her daily activities around gaining entry into the group.

Social statuses such as race, gender, ethnicity, and religion can serve as important sources of a person's group identity. Although these attributes are not social groups in the strictest sense of the term, they function like groups in that members share certain characteristics and interests. For instance, members of a particular racial or ethnic group may organize into a well-defined unit to fight a political cause. The feelings of "we-ness" or "they-ness" that are generated by such group membership can be constructive or dangerous, encouraging pride and unity in some cases, anger and hatred in others.

Like statuses and roles, groups come with a set of general expectations that can shape the behavior of individual members. Actions within a group are judged according to a conventional set of ideas about how things *ought* to be. Hence, such family forms as single-parent households, homosexual parents, and childless couples may be seen by others as "abnormal" or "dysfunctional" only because they deviate from the traditional nuclear family.

Organizations

Organizations are larger, more complex networks of statuses. The American Medical Association, the International Brotherhood of Teamsters, the National Organization of Women, and the Catholic church are all examples of organizations. Organizations contain groups as well as individuals; some of these groups are transitory, some are more permanent. For instance, a university is composed of individual classes as well as more permanent groups like the faculty, administration, students, secretarial staff, maintenance staff, and alumni.

Formal organizations are often characterized by a *hierarchical division of labor.* Each person occupies a position that has a specific set of duties and responsibilities, and those positions can be "ranked" according to power and importance. At Ford Motor Company, for instance, assembly line workers do not make personnel or budgetary decisions, and the vice president in charge of marketing doesn't spray paint the underbodies of newly assembled automobiles. In general, people occupy positions in an organization because they have the skills to do the job that is required of them. When one can no longer meet the requirements of a certain job, that person will be replaced without seriously affecting the functioning of the organization.

Organizations are a profoundly common and visible feature of everyday social life. You cannot acquire food, get an education, pray, or earn a salary without coming into contact with or becoming a member of some organization. To be a full-fledged member of modern society is to be deeply involved in some form of organizational life (see chapter 9).

Social Institutions

When stable sets of statuses, roles, groups, and organizations form, they provide the foundation for addressing fundamental social needs. These enduring patterns of expectations are called **social institutions.** Key social institutions in modern society include the family, education, health and medicine, religion, the media, politics, and the economy.

Sociologists usually think of institutions as patterned ways of solving the problems and meeting the requirements of a particular society. The family helps regulate sexuality and the replacement of generations, and is the primary means by which young children are cared for. In the past, the family also was the primary institution responsible for socializing children into the culture. This function is now served by education, which creates new knowledge and trains individuals for future careers.

The institution of economy provides society with a system of common currency, an identifiable mode of exchange, and the production and allocation of resources. Political institutions, in the form of governments and legal systems, offer needed public services, a system of social control, and a system through which national leadership is established and changed. Finally, religion gives individuals a belief system and a network of personal support.

All institutions are interrelated. With the current debate over the state of the American health care system, people are becoming increasingly aware of its links to the economy and politics. Similarly, the family is intimately bound to economic, political, educational, and religious spheres.

To individual members of society, institutions appear to be natural and inevitable. Most of us could not imagine what life would be like without a family. Nor could we fathom what society would be like if there was no uniform way of establishing governments, a common currency, or a system of schools to educate our children. It is very easy, then, to think that institutions exist independently of people.

We each have a role to play, however, in coming up with collective solutions to our problems and contributing to maintaining or changing social institutions. Over the past several years, for instance, many countries have witnessed sweeping changes in the shape and content of their social institutions. In a few years Europe will undergo a significant alteration of the economic systems of many of its constituent countries by adopting a common form of currency. Travel and trade between and within these countries, as well as the behavior of individual consumers, will surely take on a different look. Although the effects of these changes will be felt on an international level, they are ultimately initiated, implemented, and, most important, experienced by individual people.

Culture

The most ubiquitous element of society is culture. Culture consists of both the material and nonmaterial products of a society. **Material culture** is the physical artifacts of society—buildings, inventions, food, technological products, artwork, writings, music—and often represents that society's adaptation to changing environmental conditions, as when new crops are cultivated to replace those harvested. Material culture can also bring about changes in the physical environment. For example, technological innovations create air and water pollution, which in turn create the need for further material developments.

Nonmaterial culture refers to the knowledge, beliefs, customs, values, morals, and symbols that are gathered over time and shared. In this sense, nonmaterial culture is a "design for living" that distinguishes one society from another. Like an owner's manual for social life, it tells us how our society works, how we are to conduct our everyday lives, and what to do if something breaks down.

In addition to providing practical information, culture gives us codes of conduct—the proper, acceptable ways of doing things. We usually don't think twice about it, yet it colors everything we experience.

Culture is particularly apparent when it is questioned or violated. Those who do not believe what the majority believes, value what the majority values, or obey the same rules the majority obeys are likely to elicit reactions from others in the form of punishment, treatment, or social ostracism. I will discuss this in more detail in chapter 4. Two key aspects of culture are thoroughly implicated in institutional, organizational, group, and individual behavior: values and norms.

Values

Perhaps no word in the English language carries more political baggage than *values*. Terms like *moral values, traditional values,* and *good ol' American values* are bandied about with reckless abandon. Sociologically speaking, a **value** is a standard of judgment by which people decide on desirable goals and outcomes (Hewitt & Hewitt, 1986). Success, independence, efficiency, and equality are seen as important values in this society because they represent general criteria on which our lives and the lives of others can be judged. Values justify the social rules that determine how we ought to behave. For instance, the law against murder clearly reflects the value we place on human life.

Values often come into conflict. The value of privacy ("stay out of other people's business") and the value of generosity ("help others in need") may clash when you are trying to decide whether to help someone who appears to need assistance. Sometimes the key values that characterize a particular social institution can come into conflict, causing widespread legal and moral uncertainty among individuals.

Micro-Macro Connection
Family Privacy and Parental Rights

One such dilemma involves what has come to be called "family values." *Family values* has long been a vague buzzword for crafty politicians. During the 1992 presidential election, debate over this term moved to the center stage of national politics. Despite the fact that no one could define what it meant, it *became* an issue.

While politicians may use the term ambiguously, sociologists are more likely to specify the values that pervade the institution of the family. As we look more closely into this area, we find serious contradictions. One "family value" that has always existed in some form or another is the ideal of family **autonomy** or privacy. American life is built on the assumption that what a family does in the privacy of its home is its own business. Whether members are treated lovingly or abusively has traditionally been left to the discretion of family members (see chapter 8).

The development of the ideal of family autonomy probably coincided, historically, with the separation of home and work and the growth of cities during the late 19th century (Parsons, 1971). The separation of home from public life reflected not only a growing set of new economic values but a technological shift toward self-sufficiency (Skolnick, 1987). Such products as the television, telephone, refrigerator, air conditioner, backyard swimming pool, and, more recently, the VCR, personal computer, and home shopping network have all increased the privacy and isolation of the American household by reducing the need to go elsewhere for entertainment, goods, or services. The familial institution has become increasingly self-contained. The large-scale commitment to this value has not been without its problems, however. The negative effects of *too much* privacy are only beginning to be realized. The value we place on the welfare of children has come into direct conflict with the value of family autonomy. At what point should a state agency intervene and violate the privacy of the family in order to protect the welfare of a child? When, if ever, should the sanctity of the family be sacrificed in the interests of saving a child from potential physical harm? Does it better serve society's interests to protect families or children?

In 1986 a 3-year-old child named Eli Creekmore was beaten and killed by his father in Everett, Washington. This tragic incident is not unique; thousands of children die at the hands of their parents each year in this country. What made this case particularly disturbing was that the child had been removed from his family because of documented child abuse and placed in foster care on two separate occasions prior to his death. Both times he was sent back home. On each occasion it was determined that, in the interests of protecting the family's right to remain intact and autonomous, it would be best if the child was returned to his parents. The case exposed a glaring problem in many child abuse laws: that they are written to protect the rights of parents and the sanctity of the family and not necessarily to protect the welfare of individual children.

We're horrified at the thought of a parent beating his or her child to the point of injury or death. But we're more horrified, it seems, at the thought of the state intervening into the private affairs of families. This value *defines* the American way of life. Severe physical punishment inflicted on children by their parents has become an issue of privacy, not an issue of violence. Consequently, the more this is tolerated by society, the more physical abuse of children there will be. From a sociological perspective, injuring children is simply the extreme outcome of widely practiced and accepted beliefs that parents have the right to punish their children as they see fit.

The state is more likely to violate the autonomy of a family when that family's *religious* or *cultural* beliefs and values conflict with those of the larger society. In 1990 a Christian Scientist couple from Massachusetts was convicted of involuntary manslaughter for refusing medical care for their 2-year-old son, who later died of an obstructed bowel (Margolick, 1990).

That same year a mother who had recently emigrated from China decided that her 7-year-old daughter, who suffered from crippling rheumatoid arthritis, would be better off with traditional Chinese therapies—herbs and meditation—than with conventional western medicine. When she rejected the pleas of her Connecticut physician to consent to surgery, the Connecticut Department of Children and Youth Services took the child into custody and charged the mother with criminal child neglect. Some months later a Federal judge ruled in her favor ("Does Doctor Know Best?" 1990).

These cases illustrate the profound effects of a clash of cultural and institutional values on the everyday lives of individuals. Situations like these pit the autonomy of the family against society's responsibility to protect the lives of children and the social value of the medical profession.

Norms

Norms specify what people *should* do and how they should pursue values. Norms are culturally defined rules of conduct. They tell us what is proper or necessary behavior within particular roles, groups, organizations, and institutions. Thousands of norms guide the minute and grand details of our lives, from the classroom to the dining room to the bedroom, from how we should act in elevators to how employees should address their employers.

Norms make our interactions with others reasonably predictable. We know that when we extend a hand to another person, that person will grasp it and a handshake will follow. But what if you held out your hand and didn't know if the other person was going to grab it or spit on it? Norms serve as the fundamental building blocks of social order. Without them, "living with others" in a relatively harmonious way would be utterly impossible (see chapter 4).

Creating Social Order: Three Perspectives

The question of what holds all these elements of society together and how they combine to create social order has concerned sociologists for many years. Three major theoretical orientations within sociology attempt to address this question: the structural-functionalist perspective, the conflict perspective, and symbolic interactionism. This book utilizes all three to examine the relationship between the individual and society.

The Structural-Functionalist Perspective

The structural-functionalist perspective emphasizes how a society is structured to maintain its stability. Society is like an organism. Just as the heart, lungs, and liver work in harmony to keep an animal alive, so too do social institutions work together to keep society alive, maintain social order, and allow us to live together.

According to sociologists Talcott Parsons and Neil Smelser (1956), institutions allow societies to attain national goals, adapt to a changing environment, reduce tension, and recruit individuals into patterned social roles. Economic institutions, for instance, develop ways of adapting to changing physical and human environments, to dwindling supplies of natural resources, or to competition from other societies. Likewise, educational institutions and the family train people for the future roles they will have to play to keep society going.

From the structural-functionalist perspective, if an aspect of social life does not contribute to society's survival—that is, if it serves no useful function—it will soon disappear. Things that persist, even if they seem to be disruptive, must contribute somehow to the survival of society. Take prostitution, for example. A practice so widely condemned and punished would appear to be dysfunctional for society. But prostitution has existed for as long as human civilization has existed. Functionalists suggest that prostitution satisfies sexual needs that may not be met through more socially acceptable forms such as marriage. A customer can have his or her physical needs satisfied without having to establish the sort of emotional attachment to another person that would destroy marriages, harm the institution of family, and ultimately threaten the entire society (K. Davis, 1937).

The Conflict Perspective

The structural-functionalist perspective focuses on the systematic usefulness of social arrangements without examining how those arrangements are created and maintained. According to the conflict perspective, some groups benefit more from existing arrangements than other groups.

Conflict sociologists see society not in terms of stability and agreement but in terms of conflict and struggle. They focus not on how all the elements of society contribute to its smooth operation, but on how these elements promote divisions and inequalities between groups. Social order, then, arises not from the societal pursuit of harmony, but from dominance and coercion. The family, government, religion, and other institutions maintain the power and privilege of some individuals or groups at the expense of others.

Conflicts can occur between different genders, races, ethnic groups, religions, or social classes. Karl Marx, perhaps the most famous conflict theorist, focused exclusively on economic arrangements. He argued that the foundations of all human societies are based on the ways those societies develop their primary mode of material production. The individuals or groups who control the means of production—land in an agricultural society, factories in an industrial one—have the power to create and maintain social institutions that serve their interests. Hence, economic, political, and educational systems in a modern society support the interests of those who control the wealth.

Marx believed that conflict between the "haves" and the "have-nots" is inevitable and creates a situation in which social order must be enforced by those in power. He said that this conflict is not caused by greedy, exploitive individuals; rather, it is a by-product of a system in which those who benefit from *structured* inequality are likely to act in ways that maintain it.

The Symbolic Interactionist Perspective

The structural functionalist and the conflict perspectives differ in their assumptions about the nature of society, yet both analyze society at the macro, or structural, level, focusing almost exclusively on societal patterns and the consequences they produce. Symbolic interactionism attempts to understand society and social structure through an examination of the personal day-to-day interactions of people as individuals, pairs, or groups.

These forms of interaction take place within a world of symbolic communication. The symbols we use—language, gestures, posture, and so on—are influenced by the larger context of a group or society (see chapter 5). Most human behavior is determined not by the objective facts of a given situation, but by the subjective meanings people attach to the situation (Weber, 1947). Society *emerges* from the interaction of individuals.

Conclusion

Living with others, as well as living within a social structure, influences many aspects of our everyday lives. But we must be cautious not to overstate the case. The fundamental elements of society are not merely the direct expressions of the personalities of individuals. We must also remember that people are more than "robots programmed by social structure" (Swanson, 1992).

The lesson I want you to take with you is that *the relationship between the individual and society is a reciprocal one.* One cannot be understood without accounting for the other. Yes, "society" touches our lives in intimate, important, and sometimes not altogether obvious ways. And yes, this influence is often beyond our immediate control. But society is not simply a "forbidding prison" that mechanically determines who we are and what we do (Berger, 1963). We as individuals can affect the very social structure that affects us. We can modify role expectations, create or destroy organizations, revolutionize institutions, and even alter the path of world history.

CHAPTER   HIGHLIGHTS

■ Although society exists as an objective fact, it is also a social construction that is created, reaffirmed, and altered through the day-to-day interactions of the very people it influences and controls.

■ Humans are social beings. We look to others to help define and interpret particular situations. Other people can influence what we see, feel, think, and do.

■ Society consists of socially recognizable combinations of individuals—relationships, groups, and organizations—as well as the products of human action—statuses, roles, history, culture, and institutions.

■ There are three major sociological perspectives. The structural-functionalist perspective focuses on the way various parts of society are structured and interrelated in order to maintain stability and order. The conflict perspective emphasizes how the various elements of society promote conflict and inequality between groups of people. Symbolic interactionism attempts to understand society and social structure through the interactions of people and how they subjectively define their worlds.

YOUR   TURN

Alcohol occupies an important but ambivalent place in American society. We decry its evils, yet we are encouraged to turn to it in times of happiness, sadness, disappointment, anger, and worry.

Behavior "under the influence" is an anatomical consequence of the presence of alcohol in the body. Among the physical effects are liver damage, vomiting, and hangovers. When a person's blood-alcohol level reaches a certain point, that person will have trouble walking and talking; at a higher level he or she will pass out.

But is the *social behavior* we come to expect from drunken people reducible to a chemical reaction in the body? The traditional explanation for drunken behavior is that the chemical properties of alcohol do something to the brain that reduces inhibitions. If this were true, though, drunken behavior would look the same everywhere. The fact is, social behavior under the influence of alcohol can vary from culture to culture. The way people handle themselves when drunk "is determined not by alcohol's toxic assault upon the seat of moral judgment, conscience, or the like, but by what their society makes of and imparts to them concerning the state of drunkenness" (MacAndrew & Edgerton, 1969, p. 165).

If you know people who grew up in a different culture (e.g., foreign students), ask them how people in their native countries behave when drunk. How do these behaviors differ from those you've observed here? You can also ask people from different races, ages, and social classes the same questions. Are there variations in the "drunken experience" even within this society? What do these differences illustrate about the norms and values of these different groups? Have them describe their first drunken experience. Are there similarities or differences in how people are introduced to alcohol?

You might also want to ask some young children to describe how drunk people act. Are there any similarities in the images they have of drunkenness? Where do you think their ideas about alcohol come from?

Use the results of these interviews to examine the role of social and societal influence on people's personal lives. Can your conclusions be expanded to other private phenomena such as sexual activity or religious experiences?

A SOCIOLOGICAL PORTRAIT OF IDENTITY

Take out your wallet. Even better, ask a friend for his or her wallet. Dump the contents out on the table. What can you tell about a person simply by looking at this collection of cards, photos, notes, etc.? More important, what can you tell about the larger society and the role it plays in our lives? Think of all the indicators of group or organizational membership that we have in our wallets. Think of the artifacts of friendships, families, and social class that we carry with us. If you've ever lost your wallet, you know the gnawing panic that results. To lose a wallet is to lose tangible evidence of your personal identity and your connections to the social structure. As you look at the wallet contents on these pages, reflect on the importance of groups, organizations, and institutions in your life.

❶ Depending on who you talk to, money is either "the root of all evil" or "what makes the world go 'round." There's no denying that money is vitally important in the lives of Americans. The entire structure of our society is built around it. But the money in our wallets has no intrinsic value. It is merely paper. It is valuable only because we, as a collective, agree to give it symbolic value. In fact, the dollar bill is one of the most internationally recognized symbols, readily accepted throughout the world.

We need identification cards to utilize the services of many of the organizations and groups to which we belong. Forget your membership card and you can't work out in your local gym; forget your meal card and you can't eat in your campus dining hall; forget your video club card and you can't rent that movie you were dying to see. Some office buildings, in the interest of security, have even issued identification cards with a magnetic strip that employees must swipe through a machine just to get into their offices.

Most of us carry a variety of credit cards for department stores or other retail outlets. But credit cards do more than simply enable us to make

purchases without having to pay with cash right away. They represent power, status, and prestige. Credit card companies have created a whole system of hierarchy and privilege. If you have a regular credit card, you're just a regular citizen; own a silver card and you have access to more privileges; a gold card puts you at the top of the heap, giving you even more opportunities. Other organizations have tried to use this status system. The VIP card ❷ you see here from a famous budget motel chain is a good example of this credit card irony.

Your driver's license ❸ is the most frequently asked-for identification card. What does this say about the cultural importance of automobiles in our lives? What are some of the reasons people ask to see our driver's licenses? The necessity of having this identification card has made many people who don't need or want to drive take a driving test.

The library card ❹, like many identification and credit cards, has a bar code on it. Magnetic strips and bar codes connect you to huge organizations of data banks that keep track of your credit worthiness and your record of payments (not to mention whether your have any over-due books). These data banks also sell your name to marketing organizations who profile your patterns of consumption—maybe not always accurately—for future marketing campaigns. The catalogs that multiply on your doorstep can probably be traced back to an identification strip on one of your cards.

The contents of a wallet reflect important sociological ideas. As you make your way through this book, notice how concepts like social identity, deviance, socialization, power, organizations, institutions, race, gender, class, and family can be "seen" by taking a peek inside your wallet. ■

I I
Constructing Self and Society

Part II examines the architecture of individuals and society: how reality and truth are constructed, how social order is created and maintained, how culture and history influence our personal experiences, how societal values, ideals, and norms are instilled, and how we acquire our sense of self. The tactical and strategic ways in which we present images of ourselves to others are also addressed. You will see how we define "acceptable" behavior and how we respond to those who "break the rules." The section closes with a look into how we form relationships, how we identify with groups, and how we cope with the organizational and institutional pressures of everyday life.

CHAPTER 3

Building Reality

Social Research and the Construction of Knowledge

- *The Social Construction of Reality*
- *Laying the Foundation: Symbolic Interactionism*
- *Building the Walls: Conflict and Power*
- *The Art of Social Research*
- *Conclusion*
- *Chapter Highlights*
- *Your Turn*

The year was 1897. Eight-year-old Virginia O'Hanlon became upset when her friends told her there was no Santa Claus. Her father encouraged her to write a letter to the *New York Sun* to find out the truth. The editor's reply, which included the now famous phrase "Yes, Virginia, there is a Santa Claus!"—has become a classic piece of American folklore. "Nobody sees Santa Claus," the editor wrote, "but that is no sign that there is no Santa Claus. The most real things in the world are those that neither children nor men can see" ("Is there a Santa," 1897).

In his book *Encounters With the Archdruid*, John McPhee (1971) examines the life and ideas of David Brower, one of America's most successful and energetic environmentalists. McPhee recalls a lecture in which Brower claimed that the United States has 6% of the world's population and uses 60% of the world's resources; and that only 1% of Americans use 60% of those resources. Afterward McPhee asked Brower where he got this interesting statistic:

> Brower said the figures had been worked out in the head of a friend of his from data assembled "to the best of his recollection." . . . [He] assured me that figures in themselves are merely indices. *What matters is that they feel right* [emphasis added]. Brower feels things. (p. 86)

What do these two very different examples have in common? Both reflect the fickle nature of "truth" and "reality." Young Virginia is encouraged to believe in the reality of something she cannot and will never perceive with her senses. She will certainly learn a different sort of truth about Santa Claus when she gets older, but for now she is urged to take on faith that Santa Claus, or at least the idea of Santa Claus, exists despite the lack of objective proof. Likewise, David Brower is urging people to believe in something that doesn't need to be seen. What's important is that the information "feels right," that it helps one's cause even if there is no hard evidence.

Such precarious uses of truth might appear foolish or deceitful. Yet much of our everyday knowledge is based on accepting as real the existence of things that can't be seen, touched, or proven—"the world taken-for-granted" (Berger, 1963, p. 147). Like Virginia, we learn to accept that things like electrons, the ozone layer, love, and God exist even though we cannot see them. And like David Brower, we learn to believe and use facts and figures provided by "experts" as long as they sound right.

How do we come to know what we know? How do we learn what is real and what isn't? You might think that studying reality ought to be confined to philosophy courses. You will see, however, that the way we distinguish fact from fantasy, truth from fiction, myth from reality is tied to interpersonal interaction, group membership, culture, history, and social institutions. In this chapter I examine how sociologists discover truths about human life through formal scientific research. To provide the appropriate context, it is necessary to present a sociological perspective on the nature of reality. How do individuals construct their realities? How is the process influenced by power, economics, and politics?

The Social Construction of Reality

In the previous chapter you learned that culture, social roles, groups, organizations, and institutions are human creations that provide structure to our everyday lives. These elements of society give us a distinctive lens through which we perceive the world. African Americans, for instance, are likely to see our criminal justice system as less "just" than whites do. In the American labor market, men still are likely to see open career paths whereas women see closed roads. Because of their respective occupational training, an architect, a real estate agent, a police officer, and a firefighter can each look at the same building and see different things: "a beautiful example of Victorian architecture," "a moderately priced fixer-upper," "an insecure house," or "a fire hazard." Ideas about truth and reality don't develop in a vacuum; rather they are generated and elaborated under specific social circumstances.

Reality is always a product of the culture and historical period in which it exists. If we change the culture or time frame, fundamental truths also change. In some cultures the existence of spirits, witches, and demons is a taken-for-granted part of everyday reality. It is hard for us to imagine that what we "know" to be true today—the laws of nature, the causes of certain diseases, and so forth—may not be true for everyone everywhere or may be replaced by a different truth tomorrow (Babbie, 1986). Think of all the people who once took for granted that the earth was flat or that cigarette smoking was harmless. Forty years ago a politician ranting about the "red menace" or the ever-present communist conspiracy would have been considered believable and rational. It is indeed possible that people 50 years from now may look back at the end of the 20th century and regard something that we consider to be our absolute truth as mistaken, misguided, or downright laughable.

The process through which reality is discovered, made known, reaffirmed, and altered by the members of a society is called the social construction of reality (Berger & Luckmann, 1966). This construction starts with the foundation that knowledge is a human creation. Most of us live our lives from the assumption that an objective reality exists independent of us. We assume that this reality is shared by others and can be taken for granted as reality. It doesn't have to be designated by a culture and verified over and beyond its simple presence; it's just there (Lindesmith, Strauss, & Denzin, 1991). Trees and buildings don't exist simply in our imagination. Yet there are times when what we define as real seems to have nothing to do with what our senses tell us is real.

Picture a 5-year-old child who wakes up in the middle of the night screaming that monsters are under her bed. Her parents comfort her by saying, "There aren't any monsters. You had a nightmare. It's just your imagination."

The next day the child comes down with the flu. The child wants to know why she is sick. The parents respond by saying, "You've caught a virus, a bug." "A bug? You mean like an ant or a beetle?" "No. It's the sort of bug you can't see . . . but it's there." Granted, viruses can be seen and verified with the proper equipment, but without access to such equipment the child simply takes the parents' word for it. In fact, most of us accept the reality of viruses without ever having seen them for ourselves. The child learns to accept the parents' claim that something that was "seen" is not real, while something that was not seen is real.

Hence, reality may be more a matter of agreement than something inherent in the world. Sociologists, particularly symbolic interactionists and conflict theorists, strive to explain the social construction of reality both in terms of its causes and its consequences. Their insights help explain many of the phenomena that influence our daily lives.

Laying the Foundation: Symbolic Interactionism

Symbolic interactionists believe that people act toward one another and interpret situations based on their definitions of reality, which are in turn learned from those around us. What we know to be real we share with other members of our culture. Imagine how difficult it would be to believe something no one else believed in. Psychiatrists use terms like *hallucination* and *delusion* to describe things experienced by people who see, hear, or believe things others don't.

Symbolic interactionism is an intellectual approach that examines how reality is related to language, how it generates expectations, and how it is protected in the face of contrary evidence. Before taking a look at some of those ideas, let's take a closer look at the process by which reality is created both individually and culturally.

The Stages of Reality Construction

According to some symbolic interactionists, reality is developed in three stages: externalization, objectivation, and internalization (Berger & Luckmann, 1966). These stages are not meant to imply that the creation of reality occurs in a neat progression. Instead they provide a general understanding of how the knowledge that guides our conduct is established and how it becomes a part of culture and common sense.

Externalization

The stage at which people construct a piece of cultural knowledge about some aspect of the world is called **externalization.** The process may be formal, as when sociologists develop systematic "theories" to explain a social phenomenon, or informal, as when someone suggests an explanation for why people act the way they do. Think of externalization as a sort of "fact marketing"—where people try to "sell" a particular explanation to the rest of us. For instance, until the late 18th century drunkenness was associated with demonic possession, weak will, or sin (Conrad & Schneider, 1980). Today, alcoholism is recognized as a disease by the medical community and the general public. Within academic disciplines like sociology externalized explanations for social events are usually subjected to logical scrutiny and research to determine their validity; in everyday life, however, they may be accepted as "the way things are" simply because of the perceived expertise, insight, or authority of the individual providing the information. The important point about externalization is that the ideas about why certain things happen are *fashioned by human beings.*

Objectivation

Externalization leads to the second and most crucial stage of reality construction. **Objectivation** occurs when the "facts" that were originally someone's ideas, speculations, or theories take on an objective reality of their own, *independent* of the people who first created them. It has become a self-evident fact in the minds of most that alcoholism is an illness. As this fact becomes part of the public consciousness and is used in day-to-day conversation, we collectively forget that somebody or some group initially thought it up. The idea becomes a reality that has always existed but was just waiting to be discovered. It becomes what "everybody knows" to be true.

The problem, however, is that rumors are sometimes communicated, externalized, and accepted as fact by the public *without* any connection between objectified knowledge and hard facts. We have all heard the stories of Halloween trick-or-treaters receiving apples filled with razor blades or candy mixed with pins. Each year parents are warned not to let their children eat anything that is unwrapped or homemade. Schools train children to inspect treats for signs of tampering. In some cities hospitals, police stations, and other municipal offices make themselves available to examine candy free of charge. California and New Jersey have even passed specific laws against food tampering, and some communities have even tried to ban trick-or-treating. A 1985 ABC News/*Washington Post* poll found that 60% of parents who planned to allow their children to go trick-or-treating were afraid of tainted candy. "Halloween sadism" has altered the meaning of Halloween and become a symbol for all that is wrong with this society.

The hard facts are that there have been only two child deaths attributed to Halloween sadism. In both these cases the treats were tainted by members of the child's family. Further investigations have concluded that the vast majority have been hoaxes (J. Best, 1990). We are left with objectified fact that has become an established part of our culture with little if any verifiable support.

Sometimes inaccurate research becomes objectified, exerting a powerful impact on the entire society. One such study forecasted a dramatic decline in the marriage prospects of well-educated women in their 30s (Bennett, Bloom, & Craig, 1986). The researchers pointed out that women who graduated from college were less likely to marry than women who never attended college. Because the number of women entering college was increasing, the proportion of women who would never marry would also rise. *Newsweek* ran a story—complete with a plummeting graph on the cover—declaring that successful single women in their 30s had only a 5% chance of ever getting married. By 40 their chances were 1%, meaning that, statistically, they were more likely "to be killed by a terrorist than find a husband." *Newsweek* said the figures "confirmed what everyone expected all along: that many women who seem to have it all . . . will never have mates" (Salholz, 1986, p. 55).

This finding, which was misinterpreted, exaggerated, and eventually omitted from the study by the researchers themselves, quickly entered the public consciousness and became objectified reality. *People* ran a story about famous women in their 40s who were still single, further perpetuating the perceived validity of this "cultural fact." Television talk shows dealt with the "stark reality" of grim marriage prospects as if they'd discovered a new terminal illness. Supermarkets across the country began offering "singles nights" in an attempt to conquer the statistical trend. In the process of objectifying this distorted piece of information a cultural value was being reaffirmed: that being married and having a satisfying family life was still an essential part of personal fulfillment for women who have established and maintained successful careers.

Internalization

The process through which people learn the objectified "facts" of a culture and make them a part of their own internal consciousness is **internalization**. Knowledge gains potency as it is handed down from generation to generation. Through the ordinary process of socialization (covered in depth in chapter 5), we are able to acquire knowledge without having to reconstruct the original process of formation: externalization and objectivation. To a child who hasn't yet been fully "socialized," certain "facts" about the world that are taken for granted by adults make little sense.

Take the common act of throwing and catching a ball. If you've ever been around 2- or 3-year-old children you know they have tremendous difficulty catching a ball thrown to them. Why? Certainly part of the reason has to do with undeveloped eye-hand coordination. But there is much more to it than that. If you watch them closely you will see that they cannot follow the flight of the ball very well. Adults have learned and therefore expect that a ball thrown in the air will eventually come down. We have internalized the laws of gravity and can anticipate the eventual fall of an ascending object and even estimate, with tremendous accuracy, where it will land. But small children haven't internalized such laws. They can't anticipate the trajectory of the ball, have no reason to expect that it will eventually come down, and therefore can't catch it.

Another example illustrates the institutional importance of internalizing a culture's reality. Each year educational tests are used to make crucial judgments about children in the American school system. When the reading tests used by the state of California were examined (Mehan & Wood, 1975), children were presented a word and a series of three pictures. They were told to mark the picture that "goes best" with the word. One item had the word *fly* followed by pictures of an elephant, a bird, and a dog. Many of the first-grade children marked the picture of the elephant. From an internalized, socially agreed-upon reality they were clearly wrong. But on closer inspection their answers made perfect sense from the children's perspective: They were all familiar with the Disney character Dumbo, the flying elephant. What was considered incorrect and a sign of incompetence from one perspective could be seen as accurate, even insightful, from the point of view of another.

The social construction of reality is a process by which human-created ideas become externally given realities handed down from generation to generation. They are so firmly accepted that to deny them is to deny common sense. We play by the rules so diligently and faithfully that we cannot imagine otherwise. Now let's look at some of the ways reality construction influences our everyday lives.

Figure 3.1   *Cross-Cultural Differences in Color Terms*

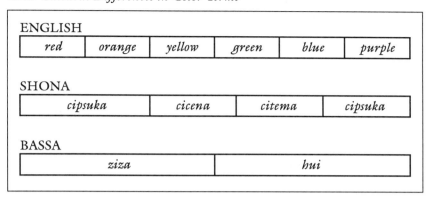

Source: Farb, 1983.

The Shape of Reality: Culture and Language

We live in a symbolic world and interact through symbolic communication (language). Language makes people, events, and ideas meaningful. In fact, reality is often determined by the language we speak (Sapir, 1949; Whorf, 1956). The use of words reinforces prevailing ideas and suppresses conflicting ideas about the world.

For instance, we all see the same colors because all colors exist in the physical world. Color consists of visible wavelengths that blend imperceptibly into one another (Farb, 1983). There are no sharp breaks in the color spectrum that distinguish, say, red from orange. But when we look at a rainbow we see six different colors: red, orange, yellow, green, blue, and purple. Not everyone in the world sees those same colors, though. People who speak non-European-related languages have different ways of partitioning the color spectrum. The Shona of Zimbabwe divide the spectrum into three colors: *cipsuka*, which is a bluish purple and a reddish orange; *citema*, which is a greenish blue; and *cicena*, which is a yellowish green. The Bassa of Liberia have only two color categories: *ziza*, or purplish blue-green, and *hui*, or yellowish red-orange (Gleason, 1961). These basic categories provide convenient labels from which people of these cultures can describe variants of color. When a Shona says "citema," others know immediately that she is referring to a greenish blue. For the Bassa, purple, blue, and green are different shades of *ziza*, just as pink is a shade of red in English (see Figure 3.1).

Language also reflects the phenomena that have practical significance for a culture. The Solomon Islanders have nine distinct words for "coconut," each specifying an important stage of growth, but they have only one word for all the meals of the day (M. M. Lewis, 1948). The Aleut Eskimos have 33 words for "snow" that allow them to distinguish between texture, temperature, weight, load-carrying capacity, and the speed at which a sled can run on its surface (E. T. Hiller, 1933). In Arabic there are approximately 6,000 words that denote the different shapes, functions, degrees of lineage, and attributes of a camel.

Much can be learned about a culture by looking at the categories and linguistic distinctions it makes for certain phenomena. Words reflect aspects of the world that are relevant and meaningful to people's lives. Think of all the English terms for one of the most important elements of our culture, money: *bucks, moolah, dough, boodle, dollars, sawbucks, C-spot, ten-spot, bills, greenbacks, bones, cash, scratch, long greens, simoleons, beans, dinero*. Then there are all the places where we can put our money: t-bills, certificates of deposit, money market funds, mutual funds, individual retirement accounts.

Anthropologist Benjamin Whorf (1956) points out that as people learn new languages they will come to think differently and therefore perceive reality differently. Imagine moving to a foreign country and never speaking English again. Not only would you have to master a different language, but eventually you'd also become a different person, perceiving the world in a way that is consistent with that country's linguistic version of reality.

A fascinating study carried out about 30 years ago illustrates how perceptions of reality can change as language changes. Anthropologist Susan Ervin-Tripp (1964) used as her subjects bilingual Japanese women living in San Francisco who had married American servicemen. The women spoke English with their husbands and children and Japanese with their Japanese friends. A bilingual interviewer carried on two discussions with each subject, one in English and one in Japanese. The two conversations were identical—same location, same interviewer, same topics. The only thing different was the language used. Ervin-Tripp found that the attitudes of the women changed when the language changed. In the English conversations, they saw things from an American perspective—the importance of independence, material wealth, and individual achievement. When speaking Japanese, however, their attitudes reflected the more traditional Japanese approach to life, which stresses community and family obligations. In the following example, one woman completed the same sentences in different ways:

"When my wishes conflict with my family's . . .

     . . . it is a time of great unhappiness." (Japanese)

     . . . I do what I want." (English)

"I will probably become . . .

     . . . a housewife." (Japanese)

     . . . a teacher." (English)

"Real friends should . . .

    . . . help each other." (Japanese)

    . . . be very frank." (English)

Such shifts did not occur when subjects were interviewed in one language but instructed to give responses typical of the other culture. Ervin-Tripp reported that these women became significantly "less Japanese" when they spoke English.

In addition to affecting perceptions of reality, language influences group identity and consequently our attitudes toward specific problems and processes (Sapir, 1929). The specialized language of a profession or other group, known as *jargon*, allows members to communicate with one another clearly and quickly. At the same time it forms boundaries and therefore mystifies and conceals meaning from outsiders (Farb, 1983). For instance, by using esoteric medical terminology when discussing a case in front of a patient, physicians define the parameters of their "in-group" and reinforce their image as highly trained experts.

Language is sometimes used to purposely deceive. A *euphemism* is an inoffensive expression that is substituted for one that may be offensive. On the surface such terms are used in the interests of politeness and good taste, like saying "perspiration" instead of "sweat." However, euphemisms shape perceptions. Political regimes routinely use them to cover up, distort, or frame their actions in a more positive light. Here are a few examples of euphemisms followed by their real meanings:

- *opposition research*—digging up dirt on an opposing candidate during an election.
- *plausible deniability*—engaging in an illegal or unethical act in a way that enables one's superior to claim a lack of knowledge of the act. This phrase was commonly used during the Iran-Contra hearings.
- *collateral damage*—civilian deaths during military combat.
- *radiation enhancement device*—neutron bomb.
- *peacekeeper*—MX missile.
- *ethnic cleansing*—deportation and massacre of Bosnians by Serbs in Bosnia-Herzegovina.
- *tactical redeployment*—retreat during battle.
- *Defense Department*—until 1947 called the War Department.
- *pre-dawn vertical insertion*—term used to describe the American invasion of Grenada in 1983.
- *economically nonaffluent*—poor.
- *revenue enhancement*—tax increase.

Language helps frame or structure social reality and give it meaning. Language also provides people with a cultural and group identity. We cannot be fully participating members of a group or a culture until we share its language.

Definition of the Situation

We do not respond directly and automatically to objects and situations; instead, we use language to define and interpret them and then act on the basis of those interpretations. Definitions of situations, however, need not coincide with objective reality. As discussed in chapter 2, a person will respond in an emergency situation only if he or she interprets it as such.

If you believe a person is cold and unfriendly you will act accordingly toward that person whether or not it is really true. During the Cold War many Americans saw the Soviet Union as the enemy and the Soviet people as evil and threatening. Today, the Soviet Union no longer exists and its people are no longer perceived as a threat. Whether they were ever truly a threat is significantly less important than our collective definition of them. People often go to great lengths to establish and preserve meaning even in situations that may in fact be meaningless (Watzlawick, 1976; McHugh, 1968).

Harold Garfinkel
Putting Meaning Into Meaningless Situations

Harold Garfinkel (1967) designed an experiment in which subjects were led to believe they were taking part in a study of a new approach to counseling. Each subject was paired with a person who was portrayed as a trainee counselor. The subject was escorted to a room and told to formulate a series of yes/no questions about a personal problem he or she had. The subject then asked the counselor the questions and received either a "yes" or "no" response. After each response, the subject was instructed to comment privately into a tape recorder about what he or she had learned.

The catch was that the answers provided by the "counselor" were completely random and had nothing at all to do with the content of the question being asked. In some instances subjects were given confusing and contradictory answers. A subject might be told "yes" in response to a question about whether someone in whom she or he had a romantic interest would make a suitable mate. But a short time later, when the subject asked whether to continue dating this person, the answer was no.

Although many subjects expressed tremendous frustration and anger, they kept struggling to find a pattern of meaning in the replies. Some subjects thought the counselor had learned something new about them between the two contradictory replies or had discovered some sort of deeper meaning (Wooton, 1975). If the counselor advised against continuing to date a desirable mate, the subject concluded that the counselor was telling him or her to "test" his or her love for the other person.

The subjects were always able to come up with a "sensible" explanation for the confusing responses they received. By showing how people can give meaning to an intrinsically meaningless situation, Garfinkel provided insight into the creation and maintenance of reality in everyday life.

One of the taken-for-granted assumptions we make in social interaction is that events are relatively orderly and predictable. Even confusing developments "make sense" on further examination. Once a definition has taken hold in our minds, it often becomes irrefutable.

Great Expectations: The Power of Self-fulfilling Prophecies

By acting on the basis of these definitions of reality we can often *create* the very conditions we believe actually exist. Such a phenomenon is called a **self-fulfilling prophecy**, which is an assumption or prediction that, purely as a result of having been made, causes the expected event to occur and thus confirms its own "accuracy" (Merton, 1948; Watzlawick, 1984).

In the late 1970s, newspapers on the West Coast began to publish stories of an impending gasoline shortage. People by the millions, fearful of being caught without fuel, started to hoard gas. Photos of long lines of people waiting hours to fill their tanks further increased the sense of panic and urgency. As a result, the gasoline reserves—which turned out not to be perilously low in the first place—were severely depleted, thereby bringing about the predicted shortage (Watzlawick, 1984). The mere belief in some version of reality creates expectations that can actually bring about a reality that never existed.

Robert Rosenthal and Lenore Jacobson
Pygmalion in the Classroom

Robert Rosenthal and Lenore Jacobson (1968) demonstrated the power of self-fulfilling prophecies in a classroom setting. They had spent much of their careers in education and had become increasingly concerned that teachers' expectations of lower-class and minority children were contributing to the high rates of failure among these students. Such ideas were not without support. In the early 1950s sociologist Howard Becker (1952) found that teachers in slum schools used different teaching techniques and expected less from their students than did teachers in middle-class schools.

Rosenthal and Jacobson's experiment took place in a public elementary school in a predominantly lower class but not impoverished community. At the beginning of the school year the researchers gave the students an intelligence test they called "The Harvard Test of Inflected Acquisition." They told the teachers that not only did this test determine intelligence quotients (IQs), but it could also identify those students who would make rapid, above-average intellectual progress in the coming year, whether or not they were currently "good" students:

Table 3.1   *Expectations and Educational Outcomes*

GAINS IN TOTAL IQ IN SIX GRADES:

	Control Group	"Academic Spurters"
First Grade	12.0	27.4
Second Grade	7.0	16.5
Third Grade	5.0	5.0
Fourth Grade	2.2	5.6
Fifth Grade	17.5	17.4
Sixth Grade	10.7	10.0

PERCENTAGES (%) OF FIRST AND SECOND GRADERS GAINING 10, 20, OR 30 IQ POINTS:

	Control Group	"Academic Spurters"
Gained 10 IQ points	49	79
Gained 20 IQ points	19	47
Gained 30 IQ points	5	21

Source: Rosenthal & Jacobson, 1968.

> As a part of our study we are further validating a test which predicts the likelihood that a child will show an inflection point or "spurt" within the near future. This test which will be administered in your school will allow us to predict which youngsters are most likely to show an academic spurt. The top 20 percent (approximately) of the scorers on this test will probably be found at various levels of academic functioning. (p. 66)

After the test was administered but before the school year began, teachers received the names of those students who, on the basis of the test, could be expected to perform well. In actuality, Rosenthal and Jacobson randomly picked these names from the class list. The test *did not* identify "academic spurters" as the teachers were led to believe. Any differences between these children and the rest of the class existed only in the head of the teacher.

A second intelligence test was administered at the end of the year. Those students who had been identified as academic spurters showed, on average, an increase of more than 12 points on their IQ scores compared to an increase of 8 points among the rest of the students. The differences were even larger in the early grades. First-grade spurters showed an average IQ increase of 27 points with almost half increasing by 20 points or more (see Table 3.1). Teacher subjective assessments, such as reading grades, showed similar differences. The teachers also indicated that these special students were better behaved, more intellectually curious, had greater chances for future success, and were friendlier than their nonspecial counterparts.

Rosenthal and Jacobson concluded that a self-fulfilling prophecy was at work. The teachers had subtly and unconsciously encouraged the performance they expected to see. Not only did they spend more time with these students, they were also more enthusiastic about teaching them, and unintentionally showed more warmth to them than to the other students. As a result, these students felt more capable and intelligent and performed accordingly.

Self-fulfilling prophecies not only influence our perceptions of reality but also allow us to create the reality we expect to see. Eventually these realities may become so powerful that we continue to believe them even in the face of apparently conflicting evidence.

Faith and Incorrigible Propositions

Some features of reality are grounded in physical evidence—fire is hot, sharp things hurt. But reality is often based not on hard evidence but on *faith*. Have you ever seen a magician saw a person in half and put him or her back together again? Your eyes tell you that this person's body, which was once whole, has now been severed. Your mind tells you that it is impossible for a person to be cut in half and live. You have faith in the fact that what your eyes are seeing is not real but a trick. You then ask the inevitable question: "How did the magician do it?" In searching for the answer, you are trying to prove the nonexistence of an event you have learned to believe cannot occur. You are trying to find evidence to reaffirm that your version of reality is right. It's this response that keeps magicians in business. If we believed that it was possible for people to be cut in half and then put back together there wouldn't be much interest in magic tricks.

Such assumptions about reality are articles of faith, so dear to us and so important to our lives that when something happens that questions some basic assumption (like an object disappearing into thin air), we are equipped to explain it away. Suppose you leave your house one morning with 75 cents in your pocket. When you arrive at your destination you have only 50 cents. Objectively, 25 cents has disappeared, but you "know better." Even though your eyes tell you that the money has disappeared, you have *learned to know* that this couldn't possibly have happened. Rather than abandon that belief, you come up with a series of "reasonable" explanations: "I must have miscounted," "A quarter must have fallen out of my pocket somehow," "Someone picked my pocket." To acknowledge the possibility that the money literally disappeared would be to challenge the reality on which your everyday life is based.

These unquestionable assumptions are called incorrigible propositions. An **incorrigible proposition** is a belief that cannot be proven wrong and has become so much a part of common sense that one continues to believe it even in the face of contradictory evidence. By explaining away contradictions with "reasonable" explanations we strengthen the correctness of the initial premise (Watzlawick, 1976).

Different cultures have different incorrigible propositions. Sociologists Hugh Mehan and Houston Wood (1975) examined the research of the anthropologist E. E. Evans-Pritchard (1937). Evans-Pritchard described an elaborate ritual practiced by the Azande, a small African society located in southwestern Sudan. When faced with important decisions—where to build a house, whom to marry, and so on—the Azande consult an oracle or a high spirit power. They prepare for the consultation by following a strictly prescribed ceremony. A substance is extracted from the bark of a certain type of tree and prepared in a special way during a seancelike ritual. The Azande believe that a powerful spirit enters the potion during this ceremony. They then pose a question to the spirit in such a way that it can be answered either yes or no. The substance is then fed to a chicken. The Azande believe that different reactions of the chicken to the ingested substance reflect different answers from the spirit. If the chicken lives, that signals a yes; if it dies, that means no.

Our Western belief system tells us that the tree bark obviously contains some poisonous chemical. Certain chickens are physically able to survive it, others aren't. But the Azande have no knowledge of the tree's poisonous qualities or of chicken physiology. In fact, they don't believe the tree or the chicken plays a part in the ceremony at all. The ritual that comes from gathering bark and feeding it to a chicken transforms the tree into the spirit power. The chicken lives or dies not because of a physical reaction to a chemical but because the oracle "hears like a person and settles cases like a king" (Evans-Pritchard, 1937, p. 321).

But what if the oracle is wrong? What if an Azande is told by the oracle to build a house by the river and the river overflows its banks, washing away the house? Evans-Pritchard observed several cases of Azande making bad decisions based on incorrect "advice" from the oracle. How can they reconcile these sorts of inconsistencies with a belief in the reality of the oracle?

To us the answer is obvious: There's no spirit, no magic, just the strength of the poison and the health of the chickens. We see these bad decisions as contradictions because we view them from the reality of Western science. We observe this ritual to determine if in fact there *is* an oracle, and of course we're predisposed to believe there isn't. We are looking for proof of the existence of something of which we are highly skeptical.

For the Azande, though, the contradictions are not contradictions at all. They *know* the oracle exists. This is their fundamental premise; just like our fundamental premise that things don't disappear into thin air. It is an article of faith that cannot be questioned. All that follows for the Azande is experienced from this beginning assumption. The Azande have ways of explaining contradictions to their truths, just as we do. When the oracle fails to provide them with the correct answer, they say, "A taboo must have been breached," or "Sorcerers must have intervened," or "The ceremony wasn't carried out correctly."

Protecting incorrigible propositions is essential for the maintenance of reality systems. By explaining away contradictions we are able to support our original assumptions and live in a coherent and orderly world.

Symbolic interactionism helps us to understand the importance of language, definitions of situations, self-fulfilling prophecies, and incorrigible propositions in forming and sustaining our everyday reality. What it doesn't address, however, is that certain people or groups of people are more influential in defining reality than others.

Building the Walls: Conflict and Power

Although the topic of institutional power will be discussed at length in chapter 10, it is important to note here that power, particularly economic and political power, has an important role in the construction of reality. Think of all the times you believed something just because someone with more influence, authority, or expertise—like a parent, an instructor, or a politician—told you it was true. From a conflict perspective reality is the product of social power imbalances.

In any modern society where classes, ethnic and religious groups, age groups, and political interests struggle for control over resources, there will also be a struggle for the power to determine or influence that society's conception of reality (Gans, 1972). Those who emerge successful gain control over information, define values, create myths, manipulate events, and influence what the rest of us take for granted. Conflict theorists argue that reality doesn't emerge simply out of social interaction but is based on the interests and visions of powerful people, groups, and organizations in society. People with more power, prestige, status, wealth, and access to high-level policy makers can make their perceptions of the world the entire culture's perception. In other words, "He who has the bigger stick has the better chance of imposing his definitions of reality" (Berger & Luckmann, 1966, p. 109). That "bigger stick" can be wielded morally, economically, or politically.

Moral Entrepreneurs

Certain groups have moral concerns they passionately want translated into the law. These **moral entrepreneurs** (Becker, 1963) need not be wealthy or influential individuals. Instead, by virtue of their initiative, access to decision makers, skillful use of publicity, and success in neutralizing any opposition, they are able to turn their interests into public policy (Hills, 1980). Just as a financial entrepreneur is in the business of selling a product to the public, the moral entrepreneur is in the business of selling a particular version of reality to the public. Groups that seek to outlaw pornography, sexual lyrics in rock music, abortion, gambling, and homosexuality, as well as groups that promote gun control, literacy, or support for AIDS research, are crusading for the creation of a new public conception of morality. For the moral entrepreneur the existing "reality" is not satisfactory: "He [sic] feels that nothing can be right in the world until rules are made to correct it. . . . Any means is justified to do away with it. The crusader is fervent and righteous, often self-righteous" (Becker, 1963, pp. 147-148).

Alcohol use is a prime example of a consumption habit that distinguishes one religious group or social class from another. In the early 20th century the actions of a small group of women, the Women's Christian Temperance Union, led to *Prohibition,* the criminalization of alcoholic beverages (Gusfield, 1963). This process symbolized the conflict between the values of rural middle-class Protestants and the values of immigrant, urban, lower-class Catholics (Gusfield, 1963). Alcohol consumption was part of the everyday lives of many new immigrant groups that settled in the industrial urban areas of the country. This lifestyle conflicted sharply with the native-born Protestant culture. Rural Protestants saw their status as endangered, and the issue of alcohol became a symbol for the conflict between very divergent lifestyles and worldviews.

The temperance movement was a symbolic crusade to try to maintain status in a rapidly changing society. This interpretation is supported by the fact that its advocates were less concerned with the enforcement of Prohibition laws than with their passage, which is why the amendment outlawing alcohol was eventually repealed. Issues of moral reform such as this are one way through which a group acts to preserve, enhance, and defend the dominance and prestige of its perception of reality within the total society (Gusfield, 1963).

The Economics of Reality

Various social institutions and the people who control them also play a significant role in shaping and sustaining perceptions of reality. Definitions of reality often reflect underlying economic concerns and interests. According to some conflict sociologists, dominant ideas that become socially "popular" reinforce the interests of the economic ruling class and allow it to control the activities of others.

Take mental illness, for example. The number of problems officially defined by the American Psychiatric Association as mental diseases and defects increases dramatically each year (Kirk & Kutchins, 1992; Szasz, 1990). The definition of what is and is not mental illness depends on the economic organization of society. We live in a society in which medical services are rarely paid by individuals out of their own pockets. Most of the money for health care comes from the federal and state governments or from private insurance companies. These parties will only pay for problems that are defined as medical illnesses. That's why insurance companies as well as the government have a lot at stake as to whether disorders such as alcoholism, gambling, depression, and cocaine addiction are formally defined as illnesses and therefore eligible to be covered by medical insurance.

Economic interests are frequently served by the manner in which language is used to define reality. In 1990 a law known as the Children's Television Act went into effect requiring local broadcasters to demonstrate their commitment to the educational needs of children in order to have their licenses renewed every 5 years (Andrews, 1992). The intent of the law was to improve the quality of children's programming. But instead of adding more educational programs, which are traditionally less lucrative, many stations kept the programs that were already in place and simply redefined *educational* and *informational*. A Detroit station, for example, considered the cartoon "Super Mario Brothers" educational because it taught children self-confidence. Another cartoon, "Yo Yogi," in which the main character captures a bank-robbing cockroach, was said to demonstrate the educational value of using one's head rather than one's muscles. It is no surprise that with hundreds of millions of dollars at stake, television companies would redefine reality in order to protect their financial interests.

The Politics of Reality

The institution of politics is also linked to societal definitions of reality. The essence of politics is to control public perceptions of reality so that people will do things or think about issues in ways that political leaders want them to. A political system influences people's decisions about what is moral and immoral and how people should or shouldn't act.

We tend to believe anything seen in print, confusing the amount of press devoted to a topic with the accuracy of the message. Politicians have capitalized on this human trait for years. "Mudslinging" has become as common an element of the American electoral process as stump speeches, debates, baby kissing, and patriotic songs. As the charges receive more attention and the public begins to believe them, they take on an objectified reality of their own. The actual validity of the claims becomes irrelevant as the accusation is transformed into "fact" and becomes solidified in the minds of the voting populace.

However, the relationship between politics and reality goes beyond the dirty campaigns of individual candidates. The social construction of reality itself is a massive political process. Governments live or die by their ability to manipulate public opinion so they can reinforce their claims to legitimacy. Information is selectively released, altered, or withheld in an attempt to gain public approval and support. Such shaping of reality is accomplished most notably through the media.

The Medium Is the Message

The mass media—television, radio, books, newspapers, magazines—are the primary means by which we are entertained (Ewen & Ewen, 1982). Furthermore, the messages we receive from the media, particularly television shows, reflect a core of dominant cultural values (Gitlin, 1979). The way characters are portrayed, the topics dealt with, the solutions imposed on fictional problems all link entertainment to the prevailing state of labor, societal tastes in consumption, the economic system, and the overall political structure.

The media are also our primary source of information about local, national, and international events and people and therefore play a key role in the American political system. The news, for instance, is the means by which political realities are disseminated to the public and is an essential tool in maintaining social order (Hallin, 1986; Parenti, 1986). News broadcasts tell us about things we cannot experience directly, making the most remote events meaningful (Molotch & Lester, 1974). The way we look at the world and define our lives within it is shaped and influenced by what we see on the news, hear on the radio, or read in our daily papers.

But what information do we get? Most of us assume that the stories we see are pure factual information, a reflection of the "world out there" (Molotch & Lester, 1975). The typical conception of the media's role in news production is that the media stand as reflectors of an objective reality consisting of knowably "important" events of the world. Armed with time and money, an expert with a "nose for news" will be led to occurrences that do indeed index that reality (Molotch & Lester, 1974, p. 105).

Like everything else, however, news is a constructed reality, a process through which occurrences and incidents are translated into news events (Molotch & Lester, 1974). Hundreds, perhaps thousands of potentially newsworthy events occur every day. Yet, if we're lucky, we'll see 10 of them on our favorite evening broadcast. These events exist as news not because of their inherent importance but because of the practical, political, or economic purposes they serve. The news is the product of decisions made by reporters, editors, network executives, and corporation owners, all of whom have their own interests, biases, and values (Molotch & Lester, 1974). The reality we receive from the media is thus an objectified, as opposed to objective, reality.

In China the flow of news information is clearly controlled by the powerful ruling group. Americans rail against such blatant and tyrannical censorship. "Freedom of the press" is a core American value, yet there are situations in which official censorship in this country is not only tolerated but encouraged.

Take the media coverage of the Persian Gulf War. Journalists were permitted to cover the war only if they were in organized "pools" escorted by military personnel (Pratkanis & Aronson, 1991). Reporters were never allowed unsupervised access to the battle lines or to the soldiers. Military escorts had the authority to stop any interview or photograph taking if they felt it endangered the operation. Any journalist who attempted to operate independently was subject to arrest. Reporters were completely dependent on official statements and government-issued videotapes. The public, while never being provided the full story, was told that such tight restrictions were necessary to ensure the physical safety of the war correspondents, protect the well-being of our soldiers, and promote the war effort.

It is not surprising that media reports during the war were congratulatory and optimistic: the low number of allied casualties, the spectacular success of the air campaign and ground attacks, the effectiveness of American high-tech weaponry, the Iraqi unwillingness to use chemical weapons, and so on. Press briefings gave the impression that allied forces were trying hard to maintain a high moral ground in the war (Lopez, 1991). Only after the war ended did we hear the other side of the story: the bombing of civilians, the destruction of electric, water, and sewage facilities in northern Iraq, the American casualties due to "friendly fire," the overstated effectiveness of Patriot missiles destroying Iraqi Scud missiles (Lopez, 1991). The official control of information allowed the public to define the war in terms that supported the military and the government.

For everyday news stories, such official censorship is usually unnecessary. Because of the economic pressures to attract audiences and keep their attention, TV networks and newspapers censor themselves (Bagdikian, 1991). Reporters are pointed toward particular stories, particular governmental activities, and particular foreign scenes. Other stories end up in the wastebasket or on the cutting-room floor.

The problem with the daily distillation of information is not so much what is false, but what is missing (Bagdikian, 1991). "What is not [shown] is hardly thought of at all in a world in which [the media] create reality as much as [they] record it" (Solomon, 1988, p. 124). We have no way of knowing what events have *not* been selected for inclusion in the day's news. Plausible alternatives are kept out of the public eye. As one media critic put it, "editors leave no blank spaces" (Cirino, 1973, p. 42).

Such economically and politically motivated selectivity becomes even more apparent when we consider that primary ownership of the media is in the hands of a small number of powerful individuals and organizations. Ten newspaper chains own more than half of all newspaper revenues in this country. Three television networks earn more than two thirds of total U.S. television revenues. Ten business and financial corporations control the three major television networks, 200 cable TV systems, 62 radio stations, 59 magazines, and 58 major newspapers (Parenti, 1986). Many directors of radio, television, and newspaper companies are also partners or directors of banks, big law firms, or other business organizations.

In addition, most journalists come from upper-middle-class families. Almost all have college degrees, and a majority have attended graduate school. Most newspeople earn a salary that puts them in the top 10% bracket (Parenti, 1986). Because common social class interests make for common political perspectives, there is a remarkable degree of ideological uniformity among those responsible for assembling and presenting the news.

In a complex society like ours, perceptions of reality and the phenomena we come to take as fact and truth are necessarily skewed and inextricably bound to incomplete, biased, and often inaccurate information. This is not to say that all the news we receive is knowingly misrepresented. On the contrary, reporters, editors, and producers are most likely presenting the news "as they see it." The problem is that "as they see it" is to some extent determined by their class background and political perspective. The definition of news, and consequently the creation of reality, is embedded in the broader political and economic structure of society. Parenti (1986) writes that our social institutions are

> the purveyors of [our] cultural myths, values, and legitimating viewpoints. To the extent that news producers—from publishers to reporters—are immersed in that culture, they may not be fully aware of how they misrepresent, evade, and suppress the news. . . . Devoid of the supportive background assumptions of the dominant belief system, the deviant view sounds just too improbable and too controversial to be treated as news, while the orthodox view appears as an objective representation of reality itself. (p. 240)

As the viewing public, our recourse is difficult because criticism of faulty policies requires good information that is frequently unavailable. The challenge we face is to recognize the processes at work in the social construction of reality and to take them into account as we make the decisions that affect our own lives. Fortunately we don't have to go it alone. One of the purposes of an academic discipline like sociology is to scientifically amass a body of knowledge that provides us with useful information on how our society works. This information is created through controlled social research.

The Art of Social Research

Research is all around us. Throughout our lives we are flooded with a sea of statistics that are supposedly the result of scientific research: which detergents make clothes brighter, which soft drinks are preferred by most people, which chewing gum is recommended by four out of five dentists. Many of the important decisions we make, from purchasing a car to voting for a candidate, are supported by some sort of research.

In addition, a significant proportion of our lives is spent "doing" research. Every time we seek out the opinions of others, gauge the attitude of a group, or draw conclusions about an event, we engage in a form of research. Say, for example, that you thought your test scores would improve if you studied with others. You then formed a study group. After the exam you compared your grade with the grade you received on the previous exam to see if there was any significant improvement. If there was, you would likely attribute your better performance to the study group.

Nature of Social Research

Although useful and common, personal research like this is fraught with problems. We may make inaccurate or selective observations, overgeneralize on the basis of a limited number of observations, or draw conclusions that protect our own interests (Babbie, 1992). Maybe your exam score would have improved even without the study group because you had a better understanding of the material this time and had a better sense of what the instructor expected.

In contrast to the casual way we carry out our personal research, sociological research is a systematic and careful process of collecting information. Observations across a variety of situations are methodically recorded; questions are designed and chosen in advance and asked in a consistent way of a large number of people; sophisticated techniques are used to ensure that the characteristics of the people in a study are similar to those of the population at large; computers are often used to generate statistics from which confident conclusions can be drawn.

Furthermore, sociological research is subjected to the scrutiny of colleagues who will point out any mistakes and shortcomings. Researchers are obligated to report not only their results but also the methods they used to collect data and the conditions surrounding the study. This allows other researchers to **replicate** a study—that is, perform it themselves to see if the same results are obtained. The more a particular research result is replicated, the greater its acceptance as fact in the sociological community.

Common Sense

A common criticism of sociology is that it is just a fancy version of common sense. Many people feel that social research tells us what we already know. A lot of the things we think are obvious, however, turn out not to be so straightforward on closer inspection.

Given what you see on television and in the movies, you might think that rape, assault, and murder occur only between total strangers. However, according to the Federal Bureau of Investigation (1991), approximately half of all murder victims were related to or knew their murderers. While people close to us provide a great deal of pleasure in our lives, they are also the ones who can frustrate and hurt us the most. Few people can make us as angry as a loved one.

Because of the high divorce rate in the United States, you might also think that people would be reluctant to get married. Sociological research has shown that this, too, is not the case. Close to 90% of Americans marry at least once by the time they're 40. In fact, about two thirds of divorced women and three fourths of divorced men eventually remarry (Cherlin, 1992). Although we have become increasingly likely to end a bad marriage, we still tend to place a high value on the institution of marriage itself. As you can see, common sense is sometimes misleading.

Empirical and Probabilistic Aspects

Sociological research, then, is a more sophisticated and structured form of the sort of individual inquiry we use every day. First and foremost, it is an empirical endeavor. **Empiricism** is the idea that questions about human behavior can be ascertained only through controlled, systematic observations in the real world. Great scholars can spend years thinking about human life and developing logical explanations about particular social phenomena. But for most sociologists determining the strength of an explanation depends on how much empirical support it has.

Another important characteristic of social research is that it is **probabilistic.** Philosophers have debated for centuries the question of why we do what we do. Are our actions always caused by forces beyond our control, or do we exercise complete free will and choose our own behaviors without any outside influence? Most sociologists believe that human behavior operates within laws of probability. Instead of claiming that X always causes Y, they are more likely to state that under certain conditions X will cause Y in most people. Whenever sociologists set out to find the reasons why people hold prejudiced beliefs, why some religious groups are more opposed to abortion than others, or why some countries have a higher birth rate than others, they are searching for the factors that would explain these phenomena most but not all of the time.

Several American sociologists in the 1920s found that rates of juvenile delinquency were much higher in certain areas of Chicago than others (Shaw, Forgaugh, McKay, & Cottrel, 1929). They believed that the disorganized state of inner-city neighborhoods was likely to cause some young people to become involved in criminal activity. It wasn't that these individuals were freely choosing to become delinquents or, for that matter, that they all would inevitably become delinquents by virtue of their residence; rather, some individuals under certain circumstances were likely to be influenced by powerful factors common to the inner city: lack of consistent role models, high population turnover, residential overcrowding, high rates of unemployment, urban decay, and so on. Social research doesn't attempt to predict behavior but instead attempts to identify what is most likely to influence that behavior.

Theories, Variables, and Hypotheses

In addition to being empirical and probabilistic, social research is purposeful. Unlike personal research, which may be motivated by a hunch, whim, or immediate need, most social research is guided by a particular theory. A **theory** is a set of statements or propositions that seek to explain or predict a particular aspect of social life (Chafetz, 1978). Theory does not mean, as is popularly thought, conjecture or speculation. Ideally, theories concern phenomena as they exist, not morality or ideological preference—that is, they deal with the way things are, not the way they *ought to be.* Some theories are highly general, attempting to explain the structure of entire societies; others are more modest, attempting to explain more narrowly defined behaviors (e.g., crime) among specific groups of people (e.g., juveniles). Travis Hirschi (1969) developed a theory of juvenile delinquency called "social control theory," in which he argued that delinquent acts occur when an individual's bond to society is weak or broken. These bonds are derived from a person's attachments to others who obey the law, the rewards one gains by acting nondelinquently, the amount of time a person engages in nondelinquent activity, and the degree to which a person is tied to society's conventional belief system.

The concepts found in theories are usually abstract and not amenable to empirical observation. You can't directly observe concepts like "social bonds," "conventional beliefs," or "attachments to others." Researchers must translate these concepts into observable **variables.** A variable is any characteristic, attitude, behavior, or event that can take on two or more values or attributes. For example, the variable "sex" has two categories: male and female. The variable "attitudes toward capital punishment" has categories ranging from very favorable to very unfavorable. The variable "social class" ranges from upper to lower.

In his survey of 1,200 boys in grades 6 through 12, Hirschi derived a set of measurable variables from his theoretical concepts. To determine the degree to which young people are attached to law-abiding others, he measured their attraction to parents, peers, and school officials. To determine the degree to which they derive rewards from acting nondelinquently, he asked them to assess the importance of things like getting good grades. To determine the proportion of their lives spent in conventional activities, he asked them how much time they spent in school-oriented activities. Finally, to determine their ties to a conventional belief system, he assessed their respect for the law and the police.

To test theories, sociologists must translate abstract theoretical propositions into testable **hypotheses.** A hypothesis is a researchable prediction that specifies the relationship between two or more variables. Hirschi hypothesized that high levels of attachments, commitments, involvements, and conventional beliefs are related to low levels of delinquency. The data he collected supported his predictions and therefore strengthened the power of his original theory.

The Modes of Research

Although the answers to important sociological questions are not always simple or clear, the techniques sociologists use to collect and examine data allow them to draw informed and reliable conclusions about human behavior and social life. The most common techniques are experiments, field research, historical analysis, and surveys.

Experiments

An **experiment** is typically a research situation designed to elicit some sort of behavior and is conducted under closely controlled laboratory circumstances. In its ideal form, the experimenter will randomly place subjects into two groups, then deliberately manipulate or introduce changes into the environment of one group of subjects (called the "experimental group") and not the other (called the "control group"). Care is taken to ensure that the groups are relatively identical except for the variable that the experimenter manipulates. Any observed or measured differences between the groups can then be attributed to the effects of the experimental manipulation (Singleton, Straits, & Straits, 1993).

Experiments have a significant advantage over other types of research because the researcher can directly control all the relevant variables. Thus, conclusions about one factor causing changes in another can be made more convincingly. The artificial nature of laboratory experiments, however, may make subjects behave differently than they would in their natural settings, leading some people to argue that experimentation in sociology is practically impossible (Silverman, 1982).

In order to overcome this difficulty, some sociologists have created experimental situations outside the laboratory. In 1979 Arthur Beaman and his colleagues (Beaman, Klentz, Diener, & Svanum, 1979) conducted an experiment to see whether self-awareness decreases the likelihood of engaging in socially undesirable behavior—in this case, stealing. He set up situations in which children arriving at several homes on Halloween night were sent into the living rooms alone to take candy from a bowl. They were first asked their names and ages and then told, "You may take one of the candies." For the experimental group, a large mirror was placed right next to the candy bowl so that the children couldn't help but see themselves. For the control group there was no mirror. Thirty-seven percent of the children in the control group took more than one candy, but only 4% of the children in the experimental group took more than one candy. The researchers concluded that self-awareness can have a significant effect on the honesty of our behavior.

Field Research

In **field research**, sociologists observe events as they actually occur, without selecting experimental and control groups or purposely introducing any changes into the subjects' environment. Field research can take several forms. In **nonparticipant observation**, the researcher observes people without directly interacting with them and without their knowledge that they are being observed. Sociologist Lyn Lofland (1973) studied how strangers relate to one another in public places by going to bus depots, airports, stores, restaurants, and parks and recording everything she saw.

Participant observation requires that the researcher interact with subjects. In some cases the researcher identifies himself or herself. Sociologists Irving Piliavin and Scott Briar (1964) were interested in the importance of demeanor in determining whether juvenile suspects would be apprehended by police. They rode around in the back of police cars and observed the interaction between officers and youths on the street. They found that juveniles who were noncooperative—those who acted nonchalantly, talked back to the officers, and displayed little remorse—were much more likely to be apprehended than those youths who were polite and cooperative.

In more delicate situations the researcher must conceal his or her identity. The researcher attempts to become a member of the group being observed and behave as naturally as possible.

In the mid-1950s a social psychologist named Leon Festinger set out to examine how groups protect their beliefs in the face of undeniable contradictory evidence (Festinger, Riecken, & Schacter, 1956). He chose to study a "doomsday cult" that had organized around the belief that a substantial chunk of the western hemisphere would be destroyed by a cataclysmic flood on December 21, 1955.

He knew that studying such a group would be quite difficult. Highly sensitive to the public's skepticism, members would probably be unwilling to answer an interviewer's questions about their activities and beliefs. Festinger believed that if he and his assistants presented themselves as researchers they would be perceived as a threat and denied access. So they decided to pose as individuals interested in joining the group. Eventually they became full-fledged members, participating in all the group's activities.

When the great flood didn't occur on December 21 the group had to find some way to reconcile their beliefs with the failed prophecy. As the fateful day was ending their leader began to make importance out of seemingly irrelevant recent news events. For instance, the Associated Press had reported that over the past few days earthquakes had occurred in Nevada, California, and Italy. The damage brought about by these disasters became "proof" to the group members that cataclysms were actually happening. Members claimed that because of the group's efforts their area had been spared from these upheavals.

Historical Analysis

Historical analysis relies on existing historical documents as a source of research information. Kai Erikson (1966) was interested in how communities construct definitions of acceptable and unacceptable behavior. In his book *Wayward Puritans,* he studied several "crime waves" among the Puritans of the Massachusetts Bay Colony in the late 17th century.

Erikson examined diaries, court records, birth and death records, letters, and other written documents of the period. Because a key piece of data was the number of criminal convictions, court records were an important source of information.

Piecing together fragments of information 300 years old was not easy. One problem Erikson faced was the fact that the Puritans didn't observe any consistent rules of spelling. A single name might be written in a number of different ways. The name of one gentleman was spelled 14 different ways! In some instances it wasn't clear whether two people with similar names were actually the same person. Erikson solved the problem by inspecting birth and death certificates and other records to distinguish one life span from another.

Erikson was able to draw some conclusions about the nature of human life and shifting cultural definitions of reality. He found that each time the colony was threatened in some way—by opposing religious groups, a crisis of faith in the authority of the community leaders, or the King of England's revocation of its charter—the numbers of convicted criminals and the severity of punishments significantly increased. Erikson believed that these fluctuations occurred because the community needed to restate its moral boundaries and reaffirm its authority.

Surveys

When it is impossible or impractical to carry out field observations, set up a controlled experimental situation, or use existing historical records, social researchers use the survey. **Surveys** require that the researcher pose a series of questions either verbally or on paper. The questions should be understood by the respondent the way the researcher wants them to be understood, and measure what the researcher wants them to measure. In addition, the respondent is expected to answer the questions honestly and thoughtfully.

All of us have had experience with surveys of one form or another. Every 10 years we are required to fill out questionnaires for the U.S. Census Bureau. At the end of some college courses you have probably filled out a course evaluation. Or perhaps you've been interviewed in a shopping mall or answered questions during a telephone survey.

Surveys typically utilize standardized formats. All subjects are asked the same questions in roughly the same way, and large samples of people are used as subjects. Sociologists Philip Blumstein and Pepper Schwartz (1983) undertook a massive study of intimate couples in America. They sent questionnaires to people from every income level, age group, religion, political ideology, and educational background. Some of their respondents lived together, others were married. Some had children, others were childless. Some were heterosexual, others homosexual. All couples filled out a 38-page questionnaire that asked questions about their leisure activities, emotional support, housework, finances, sexual relations, satisfaction, relations with children, and so forth. More than

6,000 couples participated. From these surveys Blumstein and Schwartz were able to draw conclusions about the importance of money, work, sexuality, power, and gender in couple's lives.

The Trustworthiness of Social Research

Most sociologists see research as not only personally valuable but central to human knowledge and understanding. However, as informed consumers we must ask: How accurate is this information? As I mentioned earlier, we tend to believe what we see in print. Unfortunately, much of what we read is either inaccurate or misleading. To evaluate the results of social research, we must examine the researcher's samples, indicators, values, and biases.

Samples

In determining the accuracy of published research, you must be aware of the people who participate as subjects in a given study. Frequently, researchers are interested in the attitudes, behaviors, or characteristics of certain groups—college students, women, Americans, and so on. It would be impossible to interview, survey, or observe all these people directly. Hence researchers must select from the larger population a smaller **sample** of respondents for study. The characteristics of this subgroup approximate the configuration of the entire population of interest. A sample is said to be **representative** if it is ensured that the small group being studied is typical of the population as a whole. For instance, a sample of 100 students from your university should include roughly the same proportion of first-year students, sophomores, juniors, and seniors that characterizes the entire school population. Sampling techniques have become highly sophisticated, as illustrated by the accuracy of polls conducted to predict election results.

In the physical sciences sampling is not an issue. Certain physical or chemical elements are assumed to be identical. One need only study a small number of test tubes of nitrogen because one test tube is the same as any other. Human beings, however, vary widely on every imaginable characteristic. One could not make a general statement about all Americans on the basis of interviewing one person. For that matter, one could not draw conclusions about all people from observing a sample consisting only of men, whites, or teenagers.

It is important to know who constitutes the sample of subjects in a research report. Samples that are not representative can lead to inaccurate and misleading conclusions. Note the sampling problems in the following letter to the editor from a small-town newspaper in the Midwest:

> I went to a restaurant yesterday for lunch. I began to feel guilty, when I reached into my pocket for a cigarette. . . . I was thinking of the government figures which estimated cigarette smokers at 26% of the population

of the United States. But everywhere I looked inside that room, people were smoking. I decided to count them.

There were 22 people in the room. . . . I was surprised to discover that the government's figures were an outright fabrication. . . . Seventeen people out of the 22 were cigarette smokers . . . that accounts for over 77% of the people in that restaurant . . . The government's figures are understated by 51% and just plain wrong! (*Greencastle Banner Graphic*, 1992)

This individual assumes that 22 people who frequented a small restaurant in a small, relatively poor rural town on a single day were an adequate representation of the entire population. Such a conclusion overlooks some important factors. Governmental studies show that the lower a person's income, the greater the likelihood that person will be a smoker. Furthermore, people in blue-collar or service jobs are more likely to smoke than people in white-collar jobs. Finally, the prevalence of smoking is higher in the Midwest than in other parts of the country (U.S. Department of Health and Human Services, 1988).

Indicators

One problem sociologists face when doing research is that the concepts they are interested in studying are usually difficult to see. What does powerlessness look like? How can you "see" marital instability? How would you recognize alienation or social class? Sociologists resign themselves to measuring **indicators** of things that cannot be measured directly. Researchers measure events and behaviors commonly thought to accompany a particular concept, hoping that what they are measuring is a valid indicator of the concept they are interested in.

Suppose you believed that people's attitudes toward abortion are influenced by the strength of their religious beliefs, or "religiosity." You might hypothesize that the more religious someone is, the less accepting he or she will be of abortion rights. To test this hypothesis you must first figure out what you mean by "religious." What might be an indicator of the strength of one's religious beliefs? You could determine if the subjects of your study identify themselves as members of some organized religion. Would this measure how religious they are? Probably not, because many people identify themselves as Catholic or Jewish but are not religious at all. Likewise there are people who consider themselves quite religious but don't identify with any organized religion. So this measure would focus on group differences but would fail to capture the intensity of a person's beliefs or the degree of religious interest.

Perhaps a better indicator would be some quantifiable behavior, like the frequency of attendance at formal religious services. Arguably, the more one attends church or synagogue, the more religious one is. But here too we run into problems. Church attendance, for instance, may reflect family pressure, habit, or the desire to socialize with others rather than religious commitment.

Furthermore, many very religious people are unable to attend services because they are sick or disabled.

Frequency of prayer might be a better indicator. Obviously people who pray a lot are more religious than people who don't pray at all. But some nonreligious people pray for things all the time. It is important to be aware of the fact that indicators seldom perfectly reflect the concepts they are intended to measure.

Surveys are particularly susceptible to inaccurate indicators. A loaded phrase or an unfamiliar word on a survey question can dramatically affect people's responses in ways unintended by the researcher. The National Opinion Research Center recently asked in its annual survey of public attitudes if the United States was spending too much, too little, or about the right amount of money on "assistance to the poor." Two thirds of the respondents said the country was spending too little. But when the word *welfare* was substituted for "assistance to the poor," nearly half of the respondents said the country was spending too much money (Kagay & Elder, 1992).

During the Watergate scandal, only 26% of respondents to a survey thought President Nixon "should be impeached." However, more than 50% of respondents felt he should be brought to trial before the Senate. These statements convey the same information; the only difference is that one statement uses the word *impeach*, which many people at the time incorrectly believed to mean a determination of guilt. Note how the wording of questions can change the nature of people's responses and therefore lead to very different conclusions about people's attitudes.

Values

In addition to samples and indicators, the researcher's own values, interests, and perspective can influence social research. Ideally, research is objective and nonbiased and measures what *is* and not what *should be*. The study of social events, however, is a process that can be understood only in the appropriate cultural, political, and ideological contexts (Ballard 1987; Denzin, 1989). Research is sometimes carried out to support a narrowly defined interest, as when tobacco companies fund studies on the relationship between smoking and cancer.

We must remember that sociologists are people too, with their own biases, preconceptions, and expectations. Our values determine from which vantage point information about a particular social phenomenon will be gathered (Eitzen & Baca-Zinn, 1991). If you were conducting research on whether the American criminal justice system is fair, would you seek out criminals, politicians, law enforcement personnel, judges, or victims? Each group will likely provide a different perception of the system. The most accurate picture of reality is likely to be based on the views of all subgroups involved.

Values can influence the questions that researchers find important enough to address in the first place (Reinharz, 1992). For instance, research on the family has historically reflected the interests of men by viewing the female-headed household as deviant and dysfunctional (Thorne & Yalom, 1982). Similarly, the male bias affects the questions that are researched in the study of women's work (Acker, 1978). The term *labor force* has traditionally referred to those working for pay and has excluded those doing unpaid work such as housework and volunteer jobs—areas that are predominantly female. Thus findings on labor force participation are more likely to reflect the significant elements of men's lives than of women's lives.

Despite these potential problems, social research remains an effective and efficient way of providing us with information about our world to help us make well-informed decisions at both the individual and societal levels. At the same time, we must be careful and critical consumers of such information, questioning how and from whom it was collected.

Conclusion

In this chapter I have described some of the processes by which reality is constructed, communicated, manipulated, and accepted. Reality, whether in the form of everyday observations or formal research, is ultimately a human creation. Different people can create different conceptions of reality.

This issue can be raised from a personal level to a global one. Every culture believes that its reality is the paramount one. Who is right? Can we truly believe that a reality in direct conflict with ours is equally valid? If everyone should have the right to believe what he or she wants, are we acknowledging the social constructive nature of reality or merely being tolerant of those who are not "smart enough" to think as we do? Do we have the right to tell other people or other cultures that what they do or believe is wrong only because it conflicts with our definition of reality? Exasperating and complex, these questions lie at the core of everyday life, international relations, and global survival.

CHAPTER HIGHLIGHTS

■ The social construction of reality (truth, knowledge, etc.) is the process by which reality is discovered, made known, reinforced, and changed by members of society.

■ Language is the medium through which reality construction takes place. It enables us to think, interpret, and define. Linguistic categories reflect aspects of a culture that are relevant and meaningful to people's lives.

■ As social beings, we respond to our interpretations and definitions of situations, not to the situations themselves. If people define situations as real, then the consequences of those situations become real.

- Not all of us possess the same ability to define reality. Individuals and groups in positions of power have the ability to control information, define values, create myths, manipulate events, and ultimately influence what others take for granted.

- The purpose of a discipline like sociology is to amass a body of knowledge that provides the public with useful information about how society works. This is done through systematic social research—experiments, field research, analyses of historical documents, interviews, and surveys.

YOUR TURN

The reality we take for granted is a social construction. This is particularly apparent when we look at the information presented to us as fact through published academic research, word of mouth, or the media. Reality is influenced by the individuals and organizations who are responsible for creating, assembling, and disseminating this information.

Choose an event that is currently making national headlines. It could be a story about the President or Congress, a major tragedy or disaster, or a highly publicized criminal trial. Over the course of a week analyze how this story is being covered by the following:

- your local newspaper

- the major national newspapers (*USA Today*, the *New York Times*, the *Washington Post*)

- weekly news magazines (*Time*, *Newsweek*, *U.S. News and World Report*)

- a local TV station

- the major networks (NBC, CBS, ABC, CNN)

Pay particular attention to:

- the amount of time or space devoted to the story

- the "tone" of the coverage (Is it supportive or critical? Purely factual or reflective of certain political opinions?)

Summarize your findings. What were the differences in how the story was covered (e.g., local versus national media, print versus electronic media, one TV network versus another)? What were the similarities?

Interpret your findings. What do these differences and similarities suggest about the people who run these organizations? Whose political or economic interests are being served or undermined by the manner in which the story is being presented to the public? Which medium do you think is providing the most accurate, objective coverage? Why?

CHAPTER 4

Building Order
Culture and History

- *Cultural Expectations and Everyday Norms*
- *Cultural Diversity and Cultural Conflict*
- *History: The "Archives" for Everyday Living*
- *Conclusion*
- *Chapter Highlights*
- *Your Turn*
- *VISUAL ESSAY Transforming a Cultural Tradition*

In Madagascar, the harvest months of August and September mark the *famadihana*—the "turning of the bones." Families receive messages from their dead loved ones, who may say they are uncomfortable or need new clothes. In an elaborate ceremony that includes feasting and singing, the family digs up the grave of the deceased. Widows and widowers can often be seen dancing with the bones of their dead spouses. The exhumed bones are then oiled and perfumed, rewrapped in a fresh burial shroud, and laid back onto the "bed" inside the family tomb (Perlez, 1991).

In the late 19th and early 20th centuries, dating and courtship in America was based on a ritualized system known as "calling." Although the process varied by region and social class, the following general guidelines were involved:

> When a girl reached the proper age or had her first "season" (depending on her family's social level), she became eligible to receive male callers. At first her mother or guardian invited young men to call; in subsequent seasons the young lady . . . could bestow an invitation to call upon any unmarried man to whom she had been properly introduced at a private dance, dinner, or other "entertainment." . . . Other young men . . . could be brought to call by friends or relatives of the girl's family, subject to her prior permission . . . The call itself was a complicated event. A myriad of rules governed everything: the proper amount of time between invitation and visit (two weeks or less); whether or not refreshments should be served . . . ; chaperonage (the first call must be made on mother and daughter . . .); appropriate topics of conversation (the man's interests, but never too personal); how leave should be taken (on no account should the woman accompany

[her caller] to the door nor stand talking while he struggles with his coat).
(B. L. Bailey, 1988, pp. 15-16)

How could anybody dig up the body of a dead relative? Why would young men and young women follow such elaborate rules just so they could go on a date? Such practices seem peculiar, silly, or backward to most of us, but to the people involved, they are or were simply the taken-for-granted "right" ways of doing things. Some of the things you do may even look silly to an outside observer. For instance, you may not think twice about eating a juicy steak, but someone from a culture that views cows as sacred may be horrified at the thought. You may routinely shave your face, legs, or armpits, but imagine what these practices would look like in a culture where such acts are blasphemous.

You may think bullfighting is "absurd," yet millions of Americans shell out money each year to watch men in brightly colored helmets and uniforms chase, throw, carry, and kick an object made out of the hide of a dead pig. You may pity the turn-of-the-century woman who squeezed her body into ultra-tight corsets in order to achieve the figure men admired (Ehrenreich & English, 1979). Yet many women today routinely use makeup, color their hair, have plastic surgery, and even starve themselves in the interests of becoming more attractive.

The legitimacy of certain practices and ideas can be understood only within the unique context of the group or society in which they occur. What is considered abnormal in one case might be perfectly normal, even necessary, in another.

Ancestor worship in Madagascar is a custom that has been around for hundreds of years, impervious to the arrival of Christian churches and western ideals. To the people who practice it, the ritual of burial and disinterment is more important than marriage. Life is seen as a mere transition. They believe that it is through one's ancestors that an individual is able to communicate with God. Consequently, the custom is quite rational and beneficial: Their own spiritual salvation depends on it.

Likewise, the practice of "calling" played an integral part in the culture of turn-of-the-century America. It maintained the social class structure by serving as a test of suitability, breeding, and background (B. L. Bailey, 1988). Calling enabled the middle and upper classes to protect themselves from what many at the time considered the "intrusions" of urban life and to screen out the effects of social and geographical mobility at the turn of the century. It also allowed parents to control the relationships of their children, thereby increasing the likelihood that their pedigree would remain intact.

These phenomena illustrate the important role played by culture and history in creating social order. Whether we're talking about our own ordinary rituals or those practiced by some distant culture, the normative patterns that mark the millions of seemingly trivial actions and social encounters of our everyday lives are what make society possible. They tell us what to expect from others and what others should expect from us.

We are products of the cultures and historical epochs in which we reside. This chapter looks at specific, taken-for-granted areas of our culture and compares them to others, past and present.

Cultural Expectations and Everyday Norms

From a very young age we learn, with a startling amount of accuracy, that certain types of shelter, food, tools, clothing, music, sports, and art characterize our culture and make it different from others. We also learn what to believe, what to value, and which actions are proper or improper in both public and private. Culture, whether material or nonmaterial, is a quiet guide. It is seldom advertised and so familiar that we usually are not conscious of its influential presence.

In common usage, the term *culture* is often evoked only when discussing something "foreign." We rarely feel the need to question why *we* do certain things in the course of our everyday lives—we just do them. It's *other* people in other lands whose rituals, beliefs, norms, and artifacts need explaining. What we fail to realize is that culture is "doing its job" most effectively when it is most invisible. Only in times of dramatic social change and moral uncertainty, or when circumstances force us to compare our society to another (e.g., when traveling abroad) do we become aware that we, too, are influenced by a set of cultural rules and values.

Sociologists and anthropologists usually speak of culture as a characteristic of an entire society. But culture can also exist in smaller, more narrowly defined units. Racial and ethnic groups, religions, and even geographical areas can each have their own distinct culture, or subculture.

Unique subcultures can also develop within large organizations. Consider life at a university. You are probably well aware of the material and nonmaterial culture that exists on your campus. Perhaps there is some landmark—a bell tower or an ornate archway—that is the defining feature of the university, or maybe there is an area or a piece of art that occupies a hallowed place in campus life. I'm sure you know what your school mascot is and what the school colors are. When you arrived on campus, you had to learn a tremendous amount of new information just to survive—how to register for courses, how to address a professor, where to eat and study, what administrators, faculty, and fellow students expect of you. You may have even been required to learn an entirely new vocabulary of terms that only students at your university understand. Just as you had to learn how to *be* a member of this society, you had to learn how to *be* a member of your university community.

Culture does more than provide individuals with lessons of social etiquette. It is also the fundamental means by which society is made relatively stable. Culture provides people with a common bond, a sense of shared personal experiences. That we can live together at all depends on the fact that we share a tremendous amount of cultural knowledge.

This knowledge allows us to predict, with a fair amount of certainty, what most people will do in a given situation. I can assume that when I say, "Hi, how are you?" you will say, "Fine." You probably would not go into some long-winded explanation, because that would violate the cultural rules. The actions of individuals are not simply functions of certain personality types or psychological predispositions; rather, they are a reflection of shared cultural expectations. We can learn how a society works by looking at the day-to-day social interactions of people within it. Culture provides us with information about which of these actions are preferred, accepted, disapproved, or unthinkable (McCall & Simmons, 1978).

You will recall from Chapter 2 that **norms** are the rules that govern the routine social encounters in which we all participate. They are the basis for an orderly society. Without norms, individual behaviors in any given situation would vary widely, and a lot more of our time would be spent trying to interpret others' behavior and frame our responses accordingly. Consider the unspoken norms that emerge in a situation we've all experienced, shopping at the supermarket:

> There is a customer role to be played in grocery stores. There generally is a standard of orderliness. Shoppers are not seen pushing each other out of the way, picking things out of each other's shopping carts, or sitting on the floor eating from a recently opened can. How does one "know" how the role of customer is to be played? Aside from the "No Shirt. No Bare Feet" sign on the door . . . there is no clear listing of shopping rules.
>
> Evidence of the implied existence of such rules can be found in the way people react to a fellow shopper dressed in a gorilla suit or to someone who violates the norms for waiting in line at the checkout counter. One may feel that rules are being broken when one finds oneself standing in line with melting ice cream behind a grandmother who takes out her grandchildren's photographs to show the clerk. Such behavior violates the norms of universalism (all customers are to be treated equally) and efficiency; the grocery store is not a context in which one shares one's private self with others, particularly anonymous others. (Kearl & Gordon, 1992, p. 274)

Although everyday norms like these are difficult to identify and describe, they reflect commonly held assumptions about conventional behavior: what is considered good and bad, moral and immoral, appropriate and inappropriate. Norms can be generalized in similar situations. You can be reasonably certain that grocery store behavior that is appropriate in Baltimore will be appropriate in Houston as well. The grocery store experience itself would be chaotic if there wasn't a certain degree of agreement over how we should act. Without such unspoken rules *every* situation would have to be interpreted, analyzed, and responded to as if it were an entirely new occasion. Social life would be utterly unmanageable.

Norms and Sanctions

Knowing what the cultural norms are is not enough to ensure that everyone will abide by them in the same fashion. Most norms provide only a *general* framework of expectations; rarely do they tell us exactly how to act and rarely are they obeyed by all people at all times. Furthermore, norms may be ambiguous or contradictory. It is no surprise, then, that behavior sometimes departs markedly from normative expectations. When this occurs, **sanctions** may be applied. A sanction is a social response that punishes or otherwise discourages violations of social norms.

Different norms evoke different sanctions when violated. **Mores** (MORE-ayz) are norms, sometimes highly codified and systematized into laws, that are taken very seriously by society. Violation of legal norms can elicit severe, state-sponsored punishment, such as serving time in prison for armed robbery. Other mores may be equally serious but are much less formally stated. Sanctions for violating these norms may be in the form of public ostracism or exclusion from the group, as when one is excommunicated for going against the moral doctrine of one's church.

The vast majority of everyday norms are relatively minor in comparison. These norms, called **folkways**, carry much less serious punishments when violated. For instance, if you chew with your mouth open and food dribbles down your chin, others might show outward signs of disapproval and consider you a "disgusting pig." This habit may impede future interactions with them and reduce the likelihood of future dinner invitations, but you won't be arrested or banished for doing it.

Sanctions not only punish an individual for violating a norm, but they also symbolically reinforce the values and morals of a given culture. When you violate a norm, you are not just challenging that specific norm; you are challenging the assumption we make that people will behave in predictable ways (see chapter 7).

According to the structural-functionalist perspective, each time a community moves to sanction an act, it restates where its normative boundaries are located (Erikson, 1966). In the process the rest of us are warned of what is in store if we, too, violate the norms. In the 17th century criminals and religious heretics were executed at high noon in the public square for all to see. The spectacle was meant to be a vivid and symbolic reaffirmation of the community's norms. Today, of course, such harsh sanctions are likely to be hidden from the public eye. However, the publicity surrounding them, as well as the visibility of less severe sanctions of norm violations, serves the same purpose: to declare to the community where the line between acceptable and unacceptable behavior lies.

By sanctioning the person who violates a norm, society informs its members of the type of person they *cannot* become and still live "normally" within its boundaries (Pfohl, 1985).

Emotions

To illustrate the enormous power of cultural norms I turn to a common area of social life: emotions. The norms that govern the expression of emotions do not exist in any explicit form, nor is there any severe, state-supported punishment awaiting violators. Yet they have important societal implications beyond the personal tastes, needs, and desires of individuals. People who instinctively hide or alter their emotions to fit the situation play a significant role in maintaining social order.

Take televised beauty pageants, for example. As the field of contestants is reduced to the final two, the camera focuses in on both of them. Usually they're standing on stage hugging one another in shaky anticipation of the final verdict. When the winner is announced, the runner-up is the picture of grace and charm, all smiles and congratulations. But we all know better. She has just lost the contest of her life on national television and has got to be sad, angry, or at the very least disappointed. Why does the runner-up suppress the urge to show her true emotions? Part of the reason is that she feels compelled to obey the cultural norms regarding the expression of emotions in that context. Imagine what would happen to the multimillion-dollar beauty contest industry if the losers suddenly began to display their bitterness and discontent on stage—arguing with judges, showing disdain for winners, and so forth.

We have many such unwritten rules about what is appropriate to feel, what is appropriate to display, and how intense the emotional display should be under specific circumstances. For instance, we're supposed to be sad at funerals, happy at weddings, and angry when we are insulted. We're supposed to feel joy when we receive good news, but not show too much of it if our good fortune is at someone else's expense. We're supposed to be mildly upset if we get a B− instead of a B+ in a course, but not sink into severe depression because of it. In extreme cases the violation of such norms can lead to grave sanctions, such as attributions of mental illness by others (Pugliesi, 1987; Thoits, 1985).

Micro-Macro Connection
Occupations and Emotions

Cultural norms about expressing emotions do more than just govern personal interactions. They are often linked to broader institutional concerns and needs. In her book *The Managed Heart*, Arlie Hochschild (1983) describes the *feeling rules* required by occupations in which employees have a great deal of contact with the public. To satisfy these rules, workers must either evoke or suppress their private feelings on demand. Flight attendants, for example, must constantly be good-natured in the face of unruly passengers and calm under dangerous conditions. They must make their work appear effortless and handle other people's feelings as deftly as their own. This is not just a matter of living up to social expectations; it is part of their job description. A "smile" becomes an economic asset and a public relations tool, reflecting confidence in the company and appreciation of the customers.

Likewise, doctors and nurses must control their emotions. They are trained to show kind concern for their patients and cannot show signs of disgust or alarm. Furthermore, they cannot become too emotionally involved with patients. Because they see pain, suffering, and death every day, however, it is difficult *not* to become attached to patients. Such emotional outlay would inevitably lead to "burnout," making effective job performance impossible. Doctors and nurses are more successful in their jobs when they are able to keep their emotions under control.

Other occupations may actually encourage excessive emotional display. In the world of professional sports, people tend to show emotions in more exaggerated forms than people in other occupations. Football players engage in elaborate dances when they score touchdowns. Hockey players scream and fight with opponents routinely. Baseball managers argue with umpires over controversial calls. Such displays are entertaining to the fans and keep them coming to the games, and thus have long-term financial value for the team organizations.

The larger occupational structure can determine the type of sentiments people feel, the magnitude of those feelings, and the way in which they can be "appropriately" shown. Such organizational control makes emotions a form of labor to be sold. Hochschild warns that such "emotional labor" will eventually take a heavy psychological toll on the workers who are required to put on cynical role performances as part of their everyday work lives. As a result, people will become increasingly estranged from their true feelings as the demands of their jobs continue to force them to adopt a display of emotions that reflect corporate needs and not their own (Hochschild, 1983).

If emotion norms vary across occupations, they likely vary across cultures as well. Evidence suggests that the *facial* display of emotions is universal (Ekman & Friesen, 1969). But while all people may experience anger, sadness, or joy, they express these feelings in different ways. The ancestor worshipers of Madagascar are supposed to show happiness when they dig up their deceased relatives' bones despite spontaneous feelings of sadness or even revulsion. The British are expected to "keep a stiff upper lip" in the face of adversity or tragedy. In Iran, grief and sorrow are shown much more openly and intensely than they are in the West. You may recall television images of mourners at the Ayatollah Khomeini's funeral screaming, wailing, and beating their heads in a display of grief. The crowd became so frenzied that the Ayatollah's body fell to the street and its burial shroud was torn to bits by the mourners.

Although it is not surprising that different societies or even different ethnic or religious groups within the same society express emotions differently, it is perhaps less obvious that the legitimacy and meaning of particular emotions are linked to larger societal concerns like politics and economics. Societies can shape or reject a variety of feeling states, often as a method of social control (Kearl & Gordon, 1992). Fear, for instance, may be used by some political and religious regimes to quell dissent and enforce obedience. Earlier in this century, in response to the increasing political and economic threat posed by African Americans, many white Southerners controlled blacks through the threat of lynching. Similarly, religious leaders will often use the fear of eternal damnation to ensure that their followers will cooperate.

Emotions such as guilt, anxiety, and shame wax and wane as political, social, or legal climates change. In the past, when communities were smaller and more interdependent, people were bound together by a high sense of common traditions, values, and goals (Toennies, 1887/1963). Everybody knew what everybody else was doing. Under such circumstances social behavior could be easily regulated by the threat of shame. If you broke the law or violated some norm of morality, you would bring humiliation upon you, your family, and the community at large.

As societies became more complex, such close ties began to disappear. Today, personal actions are less likely to be linked to intimate group membership. The political control of such behavior is more likely to be directed inward in the form of guilt and anxiety. For instance, if working mothers are implicated by politicians as contributing to the "breakdown" of the traditional family, more and more mothers will experience guilt when they seek employment outside the home (B. Berg, 1992). Likewise, more stringent restrictions on abortion would increase the anxiety experienced by women who are considering it.

Norms on expressing emotions give us a way to communicate and maintain social order. Although there are no laws against laughing at funerals, norms keep us in line by creating powerful cultural expectations that are difficult to violate.

Cultural Diversity and Cultural Conflict

As our population grows more ethnically and racially diverse, the likelihood of cultures clashing over folkways and mores escalates. Many of the difficulties and tragedies of contemporary society can be traced to a lack of awareness of differences in cultural expectations.

Several years ago, a Chinese immigrant living in New York bludgeoned his wife to death with a hammer after she had confessed she was having an affair. The facts of the case were clear. The man freely admitted he had killed his wife. Instead of being convicted of murder, however, the man was convicted of the lesser charge of second-degree manslaughter. He received a sentence of 5 years' probation.

The judge in the case said he treated the defendant lightly because of testimony that Chinese cultural attitudes toward adultery helped explain the crime. The defense attorney argued that the man did not intentionally kill his wife. Instead, the overwhelming sense of shame brought on by his wife's adultery put him in a frame of mind in which he could no longer control his actions. According to one anthropologist who testified in the case, adultery in

China is an "enormous stain" that reflects not only on the aggrieved husband, but also on his ancestors and all future generations of his family. The judge ruled that his actions, although tragic and unfortunate, were nonetheless understandable from the point of view of the man's culture (Bohlen, 1989).

An awareness of cultural differences can be crucial in understanding international relations. Edward Hall (1969), in his classic study of conceptions of space and territory, points out that perceiving the world differently leads to different definitions of what constitutes crowded living, interpersonal relationships, and even a different approach to both local and international politics. Knowing that Arabs find it acceptable to touch and breathe on one another during casual conversation and that Germans value privacy and distance would be an advantage in business or political negotiations (Karp & Yoels, 1985).

In sum, comparing our beliefs and behaviors to those of others sheds a great deal of light on the structure and process of society as well as the motivations behind individual behavior. We can also gain insight into why certain rituals, behaviors, and values exist in some cultures but not in others.

Health and Illness: A Reflection of Culture

Physical health is an area with which we are all familiar. While we know that people in some countries live longer and are more healthy than people in other countries, we usually don't associate health and illness with culture. In this section I describe medical treatment and the sick role, two facets that illustrate the enormous influence of culture in our lives and the conflict that can arise over cultural differences.

Medical Treatment

Medical beliefs and behaviors must be consistent with the prevailing cultural values of a particular society (Coe, 1978). Claims of illness are always subject to group or societal validation; that is, you can't claim to have a disease that doesn't exist in your culture.

The way doctors deal with patients and their ailments is also largely determined by cultural attitudes (Payer, 1988). Recall the discussion of the Azande in chapter 3. Because their everyday existence is tied to the supernatural, witchcraft, and sorcery, so too is their practice of medicine. The Azande "doctor" attempts to heal sick people by invoking the power of spirits. What is even more compelling, though, is that dramatic cultural differences in medical activity exist even when we compare societies that share many values, beliefs, norms, and structural elements.

In the United States medical treatment tends to derive from an aggressive, "can do" spirit. American doctors are much more likely than European doctors to prescribe drugs and resort to surgery (Payer, 1988). American women are more likely than their European counterparts to undergo radical mastectomies, deliver their babies by cesarean section, and undergo routine hysterectomies while still in their 40s. Americans see their bodies as machines that require annual checkups for routine maintenance. Diseases are enemies that need to be conquered (e.g., "beating" cancer).

In contrast, British medicine is much more subdued. British physicians don't recommend routine examinations, seldom prescribe drugs, and order about half as many X rays as American doctors do. British patients are also much less likely to have surgery. These practices influence the perceptions of patients. People who are quiet and withdrawn—which might be considered symptoms of clinical depression in the United States—tend to be seen by British psychiatrists as perfectly normal.

The French are keenly sensitive to bodily appearance, which is why physicians are more likely to treat breast and other types of cancer with radiation rather than surgery. The French believe that a patient's "constitution," or physical makeup, is as important in the onset of disease as germs and bacteria. They are more likely to prescribe vitamins to bolster the body than antibiotics to fight germs.

The choice of diagnoses and medical treatments is not a science. While scientific research can show us the risks and benefits of a certain course of action, the weighing of those costs and benefits is inevitably made on a cultural scale (Payer, 1988).

The Sick Role

In addition to determining the nature of illness, cultural attitudes determine what it means to be sick. Each society has a **sick role**, a widely understood set of rules about how we're supposed to behave when sick (Parsons, 1951). When you are sick, the illness is considered to be beyond your control, and you are excused from normal social role responsibilities. You are not expected to function in the same capacity you would if you are well.

The sick role entails certain obligations, too. For instance, its occupant is duty-bound to *want* to get better as quickly as possible, to seek technically competent help, and to cooperate in the process of recovery. The obligation to seek technical help is an explicit recognition of the power of the medical profession. In our culture expert assistance almost always involves following a doctor's instructions: medication, rest, exercise, drinking fluids, and so on. Most people in this culture do not go to witch doctors or exorcists for cures. For that matter, most are reluctant to use holistic healers, chiropractors, homeopaths, osteopaths, or any other alternative approach outside the purview of mainstream medicine.

Failure on the part of sick persons either to exercise their rights or to fulfill the obligations of the sick role may elicit sanctions from the group (Coe, 1978). For instance, those who do not appear as if they want to recover or who seem to enjoy being sick quickly lose certain privileges such as sympathy.

One may also give up legal rights by not seeking or following expert advice. Parents have been arrested for not acquiring traditional medical assistance for their sick children (see chapter 2). If you are hospitalized and your attending physician doesn't think you ought to be discharged, but you leave anyway, your records will indicate that you have left "A.M.A."—against medical advice. This designation protects the doctor and the hospital from any liability should your condition worsen.

The dimensions of the sick role are, of course, relative to the nature and severity of the illness (Segall, 1987). For certain illnesses we are entitled to stay in bed, free from all our usual obligations. For other illnesses we are expected to carry on with our usual activities. Compare the "rights" of a person with cancer to those of a person with a sore throat.

The sick role is influenced not only by the nature of the illness, but also by cultural factors. There is a practice found in parts of Japan, China, India, and Spain called the *couvade*. The word *couvade* comes from a French term meaning "cowardly inactivity." Among anthropologists it is used to describe a custom in which, during childbirth, the *father* experiences labor pains. In some instances he will lie down beside the mother and scream with pain as *she* is giving birth. Following the birth of the child, the mother is expected to return to work right away while the father goes to bed, sometimes for up to 40 days! It is the father, not the mother, who is relieved from ordinary social responsibilities and eligible for sympathy from the village.

In light of the fact that culture determines conceptions of illness and help-seeking behavior, it is reasonable to assume that subcultural beliefs among different ethnic groups within the same culture will also influence the sick role. One area where such differences can be seen is in the expression of pain.

Mark Zborowski
The Experience of Pain

On the surface it would appear that pain is physical and universal. But why do people with similar injuries react so differently to pain? Some individuals are better equipped to withstand pain than others, but this doesn't explain the cross-cultural differences. Sociologist Mark Zborowski (1952) investigated the meaning people attach to pain, the style of pain expression, and the future expectations derived from it. The groups he chose to study were Jews, Italians, and "Old Americans," whom he defined as white, native-born individuals, usually Protestant, whose grandparents were born in the United States and who did not identify themselves with any foreign group. He interviewed hospital patients from the selected groups, observing their behavior when in pain and discussing their cases with doctors and nurses.

Zborowski found that Jews and Italians tended to have very emotional responses to pain. This was consistent with the norms among these groups that allow for the open expression of feelings. Both groups felt free to talk about their pain, complain about it, and show their suffering by moaning, groaning, and crying. They complained a great deal, called for help frequently, and expected sympathy and assistance from others.

There were some differences. On the one hand, the Italian patients seemed to be concerned mainly with the immediacy of the pain experience and were disturbed by the actual pain sensation. On the other hand, the Jewish patients focused mainly on the symptomatic meaning of pain and on the significance of pain in relation to their health and welfare.

Among the "Old American" patients, Zborowski found little emotional complaining. They tended to be stoic in their attempts to minimize the significance of their experiences. Their complaints focused more on location and duration of the pain. They indicated there was no point in complaining because "it won't help anybody."

Zborowski noted that not all individuals from these three groups exhibited the same pain reactions. Nevertheless, he provided strong evidence that a purely physical and private experience like pain can be related to or dictated by one's subcultural expectations, which in turn can influence the sick role.

Age and Time

Another interesting area of human life that is very much dictated by culture is the conception of time. Time is the core system of all societies, organizing and synthesizing the activities of our everyday existence (E. T. Hall, 1983). Most of us think of time as uniform and unchangeable. After all, a minute is a minute no matter who you are or where you live.

Time, though, is a human construction. Some units of time, like days, months, and years, parallel natural events, like the movement of the earth and moon. Others, however, are clearly arbitrary. Seconds, minutes, and hours do not exist in nature. The appearance of the 7-day week has been traced to holy numbers, planets, and astrology (Zerubavel, 1985).

Although time is measured in absolute units, it is not perceived the same way in all situations. Think of how time flies when you're on an enjoyable date but drags on when you're in a boring class. The extra 5 minutes of sleep we desire after the alarm goes off in the morning is infinitely more valuable to us than 5 minutes stuck in traffic. In some situations time is structurally irrelevant. Las Vegas casinos, for example, have no windows and no clocks, and people gamble 24 hours a day.

It would be a mistake to assume that all members of a large complex society like ours share the same conceptions of time. Different regions have their own time rules. In some areas people are described as "laid back," in others they're "always in a hurry."

Conceptions of time are also tied to one's occupation. Work life is often synonymous with the amount of time you spend on the job. In most jobs people are paid by the hour. Workdays are punctuated by time demands or deadlines.

Time has become an economic commodity, something that can be exchanged for money, wasted, shared, or saved (Kearl & Gordon, 1992).

Contemporary life is almost completely organized around work time. In addition to working 40 hours a week, there is the time spent preparing for work, getting there, and getting back. So profound is work time that it has become a primary source of social identity. By spending 16 or more years in school we are investing in our own economic futures. Even when we enter the labor force, time becomes an investment, intimately tied to promotion and career development. Rules of seniority are based on the accumulation of time. People's statuses at work are likely to be derived from how many years they've been there. Over the course of our lives, many of the social roles we occupy have standardized timetables (Clausen, 1986). You're expected to finish your schooling, begin your career, maybe even get married and have a child within a culturally defined time frame. Violations of such time norms are quite visible, as when a 13-year-old or a 70-year-old enters college. There may be social sanctions for those who violate time norms. For instance, children under a certain age—depending on the state—are not allowed to marry. Conversely, we look askance at the unmarried 50-year-old who still lives at home with her or his parents.

Norms concerning the definition and use of time vary from culture to culture. There are no universal meanings for terms like *late, early,* or *on time.* Cultures differ in their orientations toward the future and the past. Phrases like "time heals all wounds" or "that's ancient history" are meaningful only within a culture that makes significant distinctions between the past and the future. To some people such phrases would make neither linguistic nor cultural sense. In many Arab societies there are only three sets of time: no time at all, now (which varies in duration), and forever (too long) (E. T. Hall, 1969). The Hopi of the American Southwest have no tenses in their language indicating past, present, or future (Whorf, 1956). For them time does not proceed in a linear fashion and is not perceived as a series of discrete instances. Life is cyclical, and events such as meals or ceremonies are not unique but are accumulated over time.

Americans are acutely sensitive to time and timing. Most of us own watches, and our days often consist of a series of precisely scheduled episodes. Your classes meet at specific times of the day. Perhaps you live in a dormitory where meals are served only at certain times. If you work, you have "hours" that you must keep or risk losing your job. A related American ideal is to be punctual or "on time." So valued are the rules of punctuality that if you violate them you are required to provide an apology and an explanation. While there may be individual differences, like the friend who is "always late," or situational differences, like arriving at a party "fashionably late," most of us subscribe to the notion that one *should* be on time if at all possible.

Other cultures place a very different value on punctuality. Psychologist Robert Levine studied time norms in Brazil. He notes that Brazilians have much more flexible conceptions of time and punctuality than Americans do (Levine &

Wolff, 1988). He wrote of an experience he had while he was a visiting professor at a university outside Rio de Janeiro:

> My class was scheduled from 10 until noon. Many students came late, some very late. Several arrived after 10:30. A few showed up closer to 11. Two came after that. All of the latecomers wore relaxed smiles. . . . Each one said hello, and although a few apologized briefly, none seemed terribly concerned about lateness. They assumed that I understood. . . .
>
> Back home in California, I never need to look at a clock to know when the class hour is ending. The shuffling of books is accompanied by strained expressions that say plaintively, "I'm starving. . . . I've got to go to the bathroom. . . . I'm going to suffocate if you keep us one more second." When noon arrived in my first Brazilian class, only a few students left immediately. Others slowly drifted out during the next 15 minutes. . . . When several remaining students kicked off their shoes at 12:30, I went into my own "starving/bathroom/suffocation" routine. Apparently for many of my students, staying late was simply of no more importance than arriving late in the first place. (pp. 78-79)

Such cultural differences in time are not merely amusing or trivial. They tell us a great deal about the nature and values of a particular society. Brazilians tend to believe that a person who is consistently late is probably more successful than one who is consistently on time. Lack of punctuality is a badge of success.

We tend to build ideas of national character around the pace of a particular culture's way of life. We admire the Germans and the Swiss because of their ability to "make the trains run on time." Some Arab and South American cultures may be characterized as "lazy" or "apathetic" because of their apparent disregard for timeliness. The Japanese are seen as aggressive, partly because their pace of life is quicker than ours and because they are "ahead of us" in other measurable ways (Levine & Wolff, 1988). Appreciating cultural differences in time sense becomes increasingly important as modern communications put greater numbers of people in daily contact.

Ethnocentrism

The crucial issue is not so much that people act and think differently; it is how we use this information. How do we feel about cultures, communities, or groups whose language, values, and practices are vastly different from our own?

Most American children are taught, explicitly or implicitly, that they live in the greatest country on Earth. They are taught to have pride in their religious, racial, or ethnic groups. But the belief that ours is the "best" means that others are "not the best." As a result, we evaluate other cultures in comparison to our own. The tendency to judge all other cultures by using one's own as the standard is called **ethnocentrism.**

Ethnocentrism exists because of the nature of human interaction itself. Much of our everyday lives is spent in groups and organizations. By their very character these collectivities are composed of individuals with some, though not necessarily all, shared interests. The same is true for larger cultures. To the extent that a majority of our time is spent with others "like us," our interactions with others "not like us" will be limited and they will remain "foreign" or "mysterious" to us. Similarity breeds comfort; difference, discomfort.

Another reason for the existence of ethnocentrism is the loyalty we come to develop to our particular culture. Not only are our interactions relatively limited to others in our communities, but we also come to feel good about belonging to them. Being a part of a group, organization, or culture that we feel positive about encourages a sense of loyalty, which in turn encourages ethnocentrism. Such loyalty obligates us to defend our culture (Charon, 1992). Different values, beliefs, and actions are not seen as merely different ways of thinking and doing but may be perceived as a threat to what we hold dear.

Such cultural loyalty is encouraged by ritual. Saying the Pledge of Allegiance at the beginning of the school day, playing the "Star-Spangled Banner" at sports events, and observing holidays such as Veterans Day and the Fourth of July all reinforce or demand some level of loyalty to American culture. These are the "sacred objects" of our society (Durkheim, 1915/1954). The same is true for other groups to which we belong. Religious artifacts and symbols, uniforms and team colors, and ethnic clothing all foster a sense of pride and identity and hold a community of similar people together, often to the exclusion of others.

Micro-Macro Connection
Transracial Adoption

Loyalty and pride in one's culture is an important issue in maintaining the uniqueness and vitality of the group. Such loyalty is likely to be felt most powerfully in the face of a perceived threat to the integrity and strength of the culture. Consider the issue of transracial adoption. The practice of families adopting children from a different racial group has generated heated debate between those who feel a child's racial and cultural identity are essential to the development of a positive self-image and those who feel race is irrelevant and ought to be minimized or ignored in the interests of finding a solid and loving home for a child.

Most transracial adoptions take place between white parents and minority children—African American, Hispanic, Asian. The assumption is that this child, who likely comes from a financially depressed and deprived background, will have new and precious opportunities in a more "advantaged" environment. Advocates argue that transracial adoption has the potential to transform a racially divided society into a racially integrated one. In the late 1960s, when transracial adoptions started to become more common, adoption agencies strongly encouraged white families to adopt children from other races. Today, organizations like the National Committee for Adoption have formally stated that because there are so many minority children waiting for adoption, permanency rather than racial matching should be of paramount consideration (Adamec & Pierce, 1991).

Transracial adoption has not been without its critics. In 1972 the National Association of Black Social Workers (NABSW) passed a resolution against the adoption of black children by white parents, which is still in effect today (F. J. Davis, 1991). They argued that transracial adoptions were harmful to black heritage and that in order to maintain the integrity of their culture blacks must be loyal to its uniqueness. They pointed out that a black child growing up in a white family, with its attendant white culture, will never learn about his or her own culture. White parents can never provide a black child with sufficient information about what it is like to be black in a predominantly white society. "The family is the critical center of social force. We cannot build strong families by transferring our children to another racial or ethnic group" (quoted in Adamec & Pierce, 1991, p. 298).

Considering the larger historical and political context, it is understandable why some groups fear that transracial adoption weakens their racial identity and culture. In the 1960s and 1970s nearly 30% of all Native American children were removed from their families and put up for adoption because social workers had deemed thousands of parents unfit due to poverty, alcoholism, and other problems. So devastating was the removal of these children that the Indian Child Welfare Act was passed in 1978, giving tribes special preference in adopting children of Native American heritage (Egan, 1993).

For African Americans, the civil rights movement of the 1960s instilled in them an unprecedented sense of pride in their racial identity. The 1970s marked the first generation of black parents in American history that was deeply committed to socializing their children to have positive racial self-concepts (Ladner, 1978). At a time when broad-based political power seemed to be within reach, the possibility that some black children were being raised as white was difficult to tolerate. If it was true that black children adopted by white parents had difficulty identifying with the black culture, then they would be less likely to support black political issues. In this sense, the potential loss of culture and racial identity could not be separated from broader political concerns.

The opposition to transracial adoption was quite effective. From the mid-1960s to the mid-1970s, when transracial adoption reached its peak, there were approximately 15,000 black children adopted by white parents (F. J. Davis, 1991). In 1971, 1 out of every 3 black children who was adopted was placed with a white family (Ladner, 1978). But by 1975 (the last year the government collected data on transracial adoption), adoptions of black children by white parents had disappeared almost completely (Adamec & Pierce, 1991; F. J. Davis, 1991). By 1987, 35 states had established policies against cross-racial adoption.

Were the fears of children losing their racial identities borne out? Research on this issue has been somewhat mixed. Some studies have shown that a relatively low percentage of young black children adopted by white families have problems with racial identity (e.g., Feigelman & Silverman, 1984). Several studies have found that preschool children involved in transracial adoptions are as well adjusted as children from same-race adoptions (Shireman & Johnson, 1986; Zastrow, 1977). One study that followed children of transracial adoptions from preschool age to adolescence found that despite periodic racial incidents of name calling at school and in other public situations, these older children were also quite well adjusted (R. Simon & Alstein, 1981).

Beyond the level of individual adjustment, though, the broader problem of the well-being of cultural heritage remains. There is some evidence that white adoptive parents are likely to minimize or ignore the racial identity of their children, considering parenthood and family more important than race (Ladner, 1978). In a study of 30 adolescent black children adopted by white parents, only 10 of them identified themselves as black, 6 said they were "mixed," and the rest tried to avoid a racial identity altogether by saying they were "human" or "American" (McRoy & Zurcher, 1983).

Not only does the issue of transracial adoption provide an interesting example of cultural loyalty and protection, it also shows conflicting institutional functions. Transracial adoption is as much about cultural conceptions of what the family's role in society ought to be as it is about race. Traditionally, one of the important functions of the family has been to offer unqualified emotional support, nurturance, and protection to its members. But the family is also supposed to provide its members with cultural instruction and a sense of racial, ethnic, or religious identity. The difficulty we face as a society in deciding which of these functions should take precedence is at the heart of the debate over transracial adoption.

History: The "Archives" for Everyday Living

Throughout this chapter I have addressed how the norms, values, and beliefs that make up a given culture affect people's everyday activities. The cultural diversity I have described has been *horizontal*—that is, differences between cultures at the same point in time. But we can also think of diversity *vertically*— that is, between past and present cultures in the same society.

Like culture, history is simultaneously ubiquitous and invisible. Just as culture tends to be equated with the foreign, history tends to be equated with the past. We rarely see the connection between our personal lives and the larger historical context in which we live. Instead, we often try to understand the thoughts and actions of people who lived in the past by a particular set of contemporary criteria. Abraham Lincoln, one of the most influential proponents of liberty and equality we've had in this country, once said, "There is a physical difference between the white and black races which I believe will forever forbid the two races living together on terms of social and political equality" (quoted in Gould, 1981, p. 35). Similar views were voiced by such important historical figures as Benjamin Franklin, Thomas Jefferson, and Charles Darwin. Such comments today would clearly and justifiably be taken as indications of a deeply held prejudice. However, we must understand such positions not as signs of personal bigotry but as reflections of the dominant belief system of the times. These individuals were expressing attitudes that were taken as undeniable truths by the scientific communities of their era. Innate "racial inferiority" was as much an established "scientific fact" then as the earth revolving around the sun is today.

Normative Variation Over Time

The norms, beliefs, and values that govern our everyday lives are likely to change over time. According to the Connecticut Department of Education, in 1940 the top disciplinary problems on high school campuses were talking, chewing gum, making noise, running in halls, cutting in line, wearing improper clothing, and not putting trash in the wastebasket. In the 1990s such activities are not likely to elicit harsh punishments from school officials, especially when they are compared to what are now considered to be the most common problems: drug abuse, alcohol abuse, vandalism, assault, teen pregnancy, suicide, gang warfare, rape, and arson.

Some behaviors that were wholly unacceptable in the past have now become commonplace. Premarital sex and women choosing *not* to be housewives do not incite the sort of moral outrage and suspicion they once did. On the other hand, many actions have become less acceptable, perhaps even criminal over time. There was a time when people could smoke cigarettes anywhere and anytime they pleased—in hospitals, supermarkets, restaurants, movie theaters. Now, with the increase in health awareness, smoking in public has been severely restricted and even outlawed in some cases.

Historical changes in the acceptance of certain behaviors involve more than just a societal realization of the danger of such behaviors. In fact, such designations are greatly influenced by cultural and economic concerns. Take, for instance, the criminalization of opium—the substance from which heroin is derived. During the 19th century, opium use was permitted without legal sanction and was commonly used for therapeutic purposes as a pain reliever, a cold medicine, and a cough suppressant (Inciardi, 1992). The typical "heroin addict" at the time was a white middle-class housewife.

By the early 20th century, however, things had changed considerably. There was a growing fear, particularly on the West Coast, of economic competition from Chinese laborers who had been "imported" to work on the railroads. Chinese immigrants became equated with opium use (Hagan, 1985). What followed must have made perfect logical sense at the time: If a despised group characteristically engages in a particular behavior, there must be something wrong with that behavior. A moral consensus soon emerged that focused on the presumed link between the Chinese and narcotics (Bonnie & Whitebread, 1974). It wasn't long before opium use became the dreaded Oriental Dope Problem. By 1914 tight legislative controls restricted the distribution of opium to authorized medical prescriptions only. By 1925 it was completely outlawed (Becker, 1963).

Childhood

We can also see evidence of historical variation in conceptions of different life stages such as childhood. In modern Western societies there is a widely held, unquestioned belief that children are fundamentally different from adults. We take for granted that children are innocent and are entitled to nurturance and protection. To some extent this belief is based on biological considerations. Young children are thoroughly dependent on adults for their survival. Infants cannot feed themselves or take care of themselves in any way. A 10-month-old child, left on its own, will surely die within days. It is not uncommon for a human to remain dependent on his or her parents for several *decades*. By contrast, other animal babies are much more self-sufficient. A newborn horse, for example, is able to gallop around when it is only a few minutes old.

It is not surprising, then, that we have laws protecting innocent and defenseless children from dangers like exploitation at work, pornography, neglect, and abuse. It seems inconceivable that the need to protect innocent children is not a fundamental value in all societies, present and past. However, the notion of children as a unique population is a relatively recent invention (Aries, 1962).

Until the end of the Middle Ages, children were seen as miniature versions of adults. If you look at paintings of the 15th and 16th centuries you will notice that the children depicted in family portraits look like shrunken replicas of their parents. Their clothes are the same and their bodily proportions are the same as those of adults.

This image goes beyond artistic representation. Because they were seen as miniature adults, they were expected to act accordingly. The notion that children deserve special protection and treatment did not exist at this time. Hence children could be and frequently were punished for social transgressions with the same severity that adults were (Aries, 1962).

This rather "unsentimental" treatment of children probably had something to do with demographic realities. Fatal disease in the Middle Ages was quite prevalent, and infant mortality rates were extremely high. Young children were not expected to live for very long. If one wanted only a few children, it was necessary to have many more in order to "hedge one's bets." As a result, parents couldn't allow themselves to get too emotionally attached to something that was seen as a probable loss. At that time, the death of a baby was probably not the emotional tragedy that it is today. In Spain, for example, when an infant died he or she was likely to be buried almost anywhere on the premises, like a pet cat or dog.

By the 18th century, perceptions of childhood were beginning to change. Children were now seen as innocent and in need of protection. Consequently, though, they were viewed as weak and susceptible to temptation. Along with the notion of protection came the notion of discipline, as parents taught their children to avoid the enticements of their social worlds.

Severe beatings of children in the name of discipline were common occurrences up until the late 18th century and occur in some areas of society even to this day. Such cruelty was often couched in religious terms. One Dutch theologian offered a theory that God had formed the human buttocks so that they could be severely beaten without incurring serious bodily injury (L. Stone, 1979). Heaven was sometimes described to children in Sunday school as "a place where children are never beaten" (Archer, 1985).

Definitions of childhood throughout history have been influenced by social institutions as well. Until the late 1800s, for instance, child labor was commonly practiced and accepted (Archer, 1985). Children worked as long and as hard as adults, sometimes even harder. Because of their small size, they were sometimes given difficult and hazardous jobs, like cleaning out the insides of narrow factory chimneys.

In addition, abandoned children were sometimes recruited by unscrupulous adults for use in robbery and prostitution. Some of them were physically mutilated so they could elicit more sympathy as beggars (L. Stone, 1979). Although there is little evidence of complete social approval or tolerance of these kinds of practices, it is clear that they weren't severely sanctioned either:

> Some had their teeth torn out to serve as artificial teeth for the rich; others were deliberately maimed by beggars to arouse compassion. . . . Even this latter crime was one upon which the law looked with a remarkably tolerant eye. In 1761 a beggar woman, convicted of deliberately "putting out the eyes of children with whom she went about the country" in order to attract pity and alms, was sentenced to no more than two years' imprisonment. (L. Stone, 1979, p. 298)

Only by the middle of the 19th century did the first child protection organizations emerge. In 1825, the first House of Refuge in America was founded, an institution whose purpose was to provide sanctuary to children who had been abused or neglected. In subsequent years many similar institutions were established.

Even these, however, were not totally sensitive to the welfare of children. Their purpose was not to protect but to prevent children from becoming economic burdens and threats to society. It was widely believed at the time that children who had bad childhoods would grow up to be bad adults. The value of removing children from their homes, then, was not to focus on abuse or neglect but to decrease the likelihood that negative parental influence would be transferred to the next generation. The House of Refuge sought to prevent the potential criminal tendencies of poor urban youths from ever surfacing by removing them from abusive home environments and placing them in institutions. Here they would share a "proper growing up" with other abandoned and neglected youths as well as delinquents who had violated the law (Pfohl, 1977).

The social value of children was also affected by major economic transformations in society (LeVine & White, 1992; Zelizer, 1985). The shift from a predominantly agricultural economy to an industrialized one in the 19th century revolutionized cultural conceptions. On the farm, families were bound together by economic necessity rather than emotions. Children were a crucial source of labor in the family economy and they were a source of financial support in old age (LeVine & White, 1992). Consequently, the birth of a child was hailed as the arrival of a future laborer who would contribute to the financial security of the family. In adoption practices, the most desirable child was the teenage male because of his potential value as a laborer (Zelizer, 1985).

With the advent of industrialization by the middle of the 20th century, however, children were no longer seen as economic necessities. The main source of income was now earned by the parents, or more accurately the fathers, outside the home. As a result, children became economically "useless," and people began to see them as downright costly to raise (LeVine & White, 1992). At the same time, though, their emotional importance was recognized. Today's parents are more likely to look to their children for intimacy and less likely to expect anything tangible in return. The contemporary social value of children is determined not by their labor potential but by the love and care they are thought to deserve. Hence the most desirable child for adoption today is the newborn baby.

Historical shifts in the definition of childhood can never be separated from larger political concerns, either. During World War II the government began a massive public relations program designed to lure women out of the homes and into the factories. Government motivational films convinced women that it was their patriotic duty to enter the labor force. Newsreels depicted formal child care centers as positive and nurturing environments for children. These nurseries also served as part of the nation's victory strategy by enabling mothers to join the workforce (Frank, Ziebarth, & Field, 1982).

After the war ended, however, the message was very different. Women were strongly encouraged to return to their "natural" domestic roles. Children needed their mothers at home. The phrase "8-hour orphan" was frequently used in government propaganda to describe the "horrible" experiences to which children of working mothers were subjected. Practically overnight, the political atmosphere had changed and with it the societal perception of childhood.

Today the economic and political realities of family life have again focused attention on the role of day care in children's lives (R. A. Thompson, 1991). Although most of us believe that parents are the ones who can provide the best care for their children, such arrangements are becoming increasingly difficult. The two-wage-earner family has become the norm over the past two decades (see chapter 8), and the number of working mothers has increased the need for affordable and effective organizational forms of child care. Today, more than half of the preschool-age children with working mothers in this society are in some form of day care, whether it's a private baby-sitter, day care center, or preschool. The rest are cared for by relatives (Lubeck & Garrett, 1990).

Concern over the long-term effects of day care on children has also grown. Research on this issue is mixed. According to one developmental psychologist, early and extended day care for children constitutes a "risk factor" for the development of insecure infant-parent attachments and contributes to the development of aggressiveness and noncompliance (Belsky, 1988). Another researcher has found that so-called latchkey children—those who are unsupervised by adults after school is out for the day—suffer from heightened rates of psychological disturbance, delinquency, and drug use (Galambos & Maggs, 1991). Yet others have found the negative effects of working parents to be overstated (e.g., Gottfried, 1991; Rodman, Pratto, & Nelson, 1985).

The belief that mothers who work create problems for their children is not so much a conclusion based on a body of research as it is a mismatch between the realities of contemporary family life and the social arrangements and expectations of past family patterns. The issue is best understood as a function of broader historical attitudes. According to several prominent sociologists, we could easily solve the "problems" created by working mothers if we, as a society, had the will to do so through government-supported child care services, workplace day care, after-school programs, lengthening the school day, or flexible work schedules for parents (Gerson, 1985; Skolnick, 1991).

More and more businesses are starting to implement some of these provisions (Spitze, 1988). In 1993 a comprehensive family leave bill was signed into law that guaranteed certain employees time off work to care for sick family members. How will these kinds of changes affect future conceptions of childhood and the family? While such innovations will no doubt help many families cope with the conflicting demands of work and child care, the institutional consequences may not be so positive. Some predict the social and economic gap will widen between families that are career-oriented and families that are child-oriented:

> Employers may make concessions to the fact that more workers have parental responsibilities by providing childcare during working hours, permitting flexible schedules, and granting workers leave to care for infants and sick children. But as long as there is another tier of workers who do not value these benefits, who will apply themselves instead to occupational and professional advancement, the "gains" made by parents will only serve to differentiate their work orientations from those of serious careerists. (Hunt & Hunt, 1990, pp. 272-273).

Conclusion

Over the span of a year or two, most cultures present an image of stability and agreement regarding the acceptability of certain behaviors. This agreement is illusory, however. From the perspective of a generation or even a decade, that sense of order is replaced by a sense of change (McCall & Simmons, 1978). Behaviors, values, beliefs, and morals fluctuate with startling frequency. Comparisons across eras, in addition to comparisons across cultures, can provide rich insight into shifting definitions of acceptability, the nature of everyday life, and ultimately large-scale social change and stability.

The cultural and historical underpinnings of our private lives help us see the relationship between the individual, society, and social order. While different cultures treat illnesses differently or define time differently, these practices also add continuity and order to social life.

To a single person, culture appears massive and unrelenting, but at the same time it cannot exist without people as a whole. Norms govern our lives, whether we live by them or rebel against them. To fully understand the relationship between the individual and society we must look beyond the fact that culture and history shape our lives; we must see them as human creations as well.

CHAPTER HIGHLIGHTS

■ Culture provides members of a society with a common bond, a sense that we see certain facets of society in similar ways. That we can live together at all depends on the fact that members of a society share a certain amount of cultural knowledge.

■ Norms—the rules and standards that govern all social encounters—provide order in our lives. They reflect commonly held assumptions about conventional behavior. Norm violations mark the boundaries of acceptable behavior and symbolically reaffirm what society defines as right and wrong.

■ The more ethnically and culturally diverse a society is, the greater the likelihood of normative clashes between groups.

■ Over the span of a few years, most cultures present an image of stability and agreement regarding normative boundaries. This agreement is illusory. Over a generation or even a decade, that sense of order is replaced by a sense of change.

YOUR TURN

The acceptability of certain acts or thoughts is *socially constructed*. We as a society decide what is and isn't appropriate, like how to shake hands, how close to stand to someone when conversing, and so forth. These norms form the basis of a taken-for-granted reality that underlies all we do but that remains largely unnoticed and unquestioned. These rules of conduct add predictability and order to our encounters with others. They are so common that they are noticed only when violated. The best proof of the existence of these norms lies in our reactions when they are violated.

The following is based on an exercise used by Jodi O'Brien at the University of Iowa. Choose an unspoken norm that lends order and predictability to daily social interactions. Here are some suggestions:

■ Make a purchase in a department store and offer to pay *more* than the listed price. Try to convince the clerk that you think the merchandise is worth the price you are offering.

■ Send a close family member a birthday card months away from his or her actual birthday.

■ Talk to yourself in a public place.

■ Stand or sit close to a stranger or stand *far* away from a good friend or lover during the course of an ordinary conversation.

■ Select an occasion—going to class, going on a date, going to the library—and dress differently than the expected "uniform." Treat your dress as absolutely appropriate to the circumstances.

■ Whenever someone says to you "See you later," ask him or her probing questions: When? Did you have some plans to get together later? What do you mean by "see"? and so on. Or when someone says, "How's it going?" ask: What do you mean by "it"? What do you mean by "going"?

■ In a restaurant demand to pay for your meal *before* you order it, or order dessert first, then the main course, then appetizers, then drinks.

It is particularly important that this behavior be neither flagrantly bizarre—like going to class dressed as a chicken—nor a violation of the law. Such acts do not address the power of the subtle, unspoken norms that make social life orderly. Also, do not do anything that might put you in danger. Finally, make sure the norm has something to do with keeping order in face-to-face interactions. For instance, coming to class 10 minutes late is a violation of a social norm, but it doesn't disrupt interactional order when it occurs. *Above all, remember to treat your violation as perfectly normal.* You must give the impression that what you are doing is perfectly acceptable and ordinary.

As you conduct your experiment, record your own feelings and reactions as well as those of the subjects. What were people's initial reactions? What did they do to try to "normalize" your behavior? How did you feel breaching this norm? Was it uncomfortable? If so, why? If possible, try to debrief your subjects afterward: Tell them what you were really doing, and then interview them regarding *their* interpretations of the experience. This will provide you with information on how people attempt to "explain away" unusual and strange circumstances and how they attempt to restore order to the situation. What are the implications of these sorts of "experiments" for an understanding of human behavior and the nature of social order in this society?

Altering a Cultural Tradition

PHOTOGRAPHS AND CONCEPT BY RUSSELL R. CHABOT

Norms add order and predictability to our everyday lives. In many common social situations the norms are so taken-for-granted, so obvious, that we don't even realize they exist until they are broken. Consider the funeral. Like many social traditions, funerals represent a public statement of how we do things in this culture. They are governed by a set of powerful rules that address everything from how we are supposed to dress to how we should express our grief. The ritual itself has some common, well-known elements, including embalming, an attendant religious service, public viewing in a funeral home, and the handling of the event by a professional funeral director.

The funeral you see here is quite different. It took place not in a funeral home but in the house that Bob (the deceased) and his wife, Nan, lived in for thirteen years. Note the informal dress of the mourners.

In typical funerals, caskets are treated with solemn reverence. Here Nan (behind the coffin box) violates this norm by inviting people to sign Bob's coffin Would you consider writing on a coffin disrespectful? Why or why not?

Guests were encouraged to bring their children, a segment of the population typically excluded from these events. How do you think most people in this society would react to this kind of funeral?

Here the mourners are standing in line waiting to pay their respects and, as they would discover, sign the coffin. By one estimate 500 people attended Bob's funeral. The local police even showed up with tow trucks, thinking it was a student party, as the semester had just ended at a nearby university.

While it is not uncommon to serve refreshments following a funeral, here people mingled, ate, and drank prior to the service. The scene looks more like a garden party or a wedding than a funeral. One guest was taken aback by the atmosphere, especially when, emerging from the house in grief, someone turned to him and said good naturedly, "Hey, you want a beer?"

Instead of clergy and a religious service, a storyteller talked about Bob's life. Others were then invited to tell stories of their own or say whatever they liked.

CHAPTER 5

Building Identity
The Social Construction of Self

My family once lived in a suburb just outside New York City. One day, when I was 9 years old, my parents sat me down and told me that due to financial concerns—that were beyond my understanding—we had to move. They had narrowed down our ultimate destination to two possibilities: Laredo, Texas, and Burbank, California. After some rather intense debate, they chose Burbank. And so we headed "out west" where from age 9 to age 18 I lived in the shadow of the entertainment industry with all its glamour, glitz, and movie stars. It wasn't long before I became a typical sun-worshiping, Frisbee-throwing California kid.

I often wonder how differently I would have turned out if my parents had chosen Laredo and I had spent my formative years in the middle of Texas instead of in the middle of Tinsel Town. Would I have a fondness for 10-gallon hats and snakeskin boots instead of tennis shoes and shorts? Would I have grown up with country music instead of the Beach Boys? Would I have a different accent? Would my goals be different? In short, would I *be* a different person?

Try to imagine what *your* life would be like if you had grown up under different circumstances. What if your father was a harpsichord enthusiast instead of a Cubs fan? What if your family was Jewish instead of Episcopalian? What if you had an older brother instead of a younger sister? What if you lived on a farm instead of in a big city? What if you were born in 1945 instead of 1975? Your tastes, preferences, and hobbies, as well as your morals, values, ambitions, and aspirations, would no doubt be different. But more profoundly, your self-concept, self-esteem, personality—the essence of who you are—would be altered.

Consider the broader social and historical circumstances of your life. What kind of impact might they have on the type of person you are? Talk to people who grew up in the 1930s and they will speak of the permanent impact the Great Depression had on them (Elder & Liker, 1982). Imagine spending your childhood as a Jew in Nazi Germany. That couldn't help but shape your outlook on life. The same can be said for growing up black in South Central Los Angeles in the 1990s, or white in Beverly Hills during the Reagan years. Today's ever-expanding communications technologies, including interactive and virtual-reality computers, information highways, video, and fax machines, will have an unmistakable impact on the kinds of adults you will see in the future (K. J. Gergen, 1991).

Becoming the person you are cannot be separated from the people, historical events, and social circumstances that surround you. In this chapter I examine the process of socialization: how we learn what's expected of us in our families, our communities, and our culture and how we learn to behave according to those expectations. The primary focus will be on the development of identity. Identity is our most essential and personal characteristic and consists of our sense of self, our gender, and our race and ethnicity. It thoroughly affects everything we do, feel, say, and think in our lives. Most people tend to believe that our self-concept, our sense of "maleness" or "femaleness," and our racial or ethnic identities are biologically or psychologically determined and therefore permanent and unchangeable. But, as you will discover, these characteristics are as much a product of our social surroundings and the significant people in our lives as they are a product of our innate traits and individual predispositions.

The famous developmental psychologist Jean Piaget (1954) once argued that a mature sense of self requires a recognition that one's thoughts, feelings, and perceptions are one's own. Very young children will frequently confuse the processes that go on in their own heads with some external reality, for instance, believing that nightmare monsters really exist.

From a sociological perspective, however, a mature sense of self entails recognizing that what we think and feel is *not* entirely our own. Our thoughts, perceptions, and self-concepts are produced in conjunction with larger social phenomena and are inextricably bound to the social institutions and cultural processes that make up our day-to-day existence. *Social structure* plays a key role in making us who we are.

The Social Construction of Human Beings

The question of how we become who we are has occupied the attention of biologists, psychologists, anthropologists, sociologists, philosophers, and novelists for centuries. Commonly, the issue is framed as an ongoing debate between *nature* (we are who we are because we are born that way) and *nurture* (we are who we are because of our environment). Are we simply a product of our genes and biochemistry, or are we somehow "created" by the people and the social institutions that surround us?

Most sociologists would argue that human beings are more than just a collection of the physical and psychological characteristics. That's not to say that inborn traits are of absolutely no importance. Certainly our physical attractiveness and strength, genetic predisposition to sickness, and so on, have some effect on our personal development. Furthermore, there's no arguing that our every thought and action is the product of a complex series of neurological and electrochemical events in our brains and bodies. Males and females obviously differ anatomically and hormonally and may even see the world differently as a result.

The issue is not so much whether these physiological events or innate differences exist; rather, it is whether they are *culturally defined* as significant. Society can magnify differences or cover them up. *We* collectively decide which physical traits are socially irrelevant (e.g., eye color), and which become embedded in our social institutions (e.g., sex and race), giving rise to different rights, duties, and expectations.

Who we become is not just a product of personal traits and experiences but is influenced by the behaviors and attitudes of significant people in our lives as well as cultural norms and values. As these things change, so do we. This is not an altogether comforting proposition. It implies that who we are may in some ways be "accidental," the shaky result of a series of social coincidences, chance encounters, decisions made by others, and political or historical events that are in large measure beyond our control.

Learning Who We Are: Socialization and Resocialization

The fundamental task of any society, be it industrial or agricultural, large or small, technologically advanced or simple, fascist or democratic, is to reproduce itself to create members whose behaviors, desires, and goals correspond to those that are deemed appropriate and desirable by that particular society. Through the powerful and ubiquitous process of **socialization** the needs of society become the needs of the individual.

Socialization is a process of learning. To socialize someone is to train him or her to behave appropriately. It is the means by which people acquire important social skills like driving a car, doing long division, speaking the language correctly, or using the little fork instead of the big fork at the right times. But socialization is also the way we learn how to perceive our world, how to interact with others, what it means to be male or female, how, when, why, and with whom to be sexual, what we should and should not do under certain circumstances, what our society defines as good and bad, and so on.

People often assume that socialization is synonymous with child rearing. It is true that the basic, formative instruction of life occurs early on. Young children must be taught the fundamental values, knowledge, and beliefs of their culture. Some of the socialization that occurs during childhood—often referred to as **anticipatory socialization**—is the primary means by which young individuals acquire the values and orientations found in the statuses they will likely enter in the future (Merton, 1957). Paper routes, Little League, dance lessons, dating, and so on give youngsters an opportunity to rehearse for the kinds of roles that await them in adulthood.

The socialization process does not end in childhood, however. In fact, it continues throughout our lives. Adults must be **resocialized** into a new set of norms, values, and expectations each time they leave behind old social contexts or roles and enter new ones (Brim, 1968; Ebaugh, 1988; Pescosolido, 1986; I. H. Simpson, 1979). For instance, we have to learn how to think and act like a spouse when we marry (Berger & Kellner, 1964), a parent when we have kids (A. Rossi, 1968), or a divorced person when a marriage ends (Vaughan, 1986).

For certain occupations, entrants must abandon their original expectations and adopt a more realistic view of that occupation. Police recruits must learn that deadly force is appropriate and sometimes necessary (Hunt, 1985). Many medical students' idealistic desires become more realistic as they confront the exhausting demands of their profession (Becker & Geer, 1958; Hafferty, 1991). Every new group we enter, every new friendship we form, every new life changing experience we have requires the formation of new identities and socialization into new sets of norms and beliefs.

Sometimes adult resocialization occurs forcefully and deliberately in order to meet larger organizational or societal needs. In prisons, mental hospitals, monasteries, military training camps, and other **total institutions** (Goffman, 1961), groups of individuals are cut off from the broader society and lead an enclosed, formally administered life. Previous socialization experiences are systematically destroyed and new ones developed to serve the interests of the institution. In an army boot camp, the individual must shed his or her identity as a civilian and adopt the new identity of soldier. He or she must learn to look, act, and think like a soldier and learn to see the world from the soldier's perspective. To aid in this transformation, recruits are stripped of old identity markers (clothes, personal possessions, hairstyle) and forced to take on new ones designed to nullify individuality (uniforms, identification numbers, similar haircuts).

Soon the individual learns to identify with the ideology of the institution. In the boot camp, the uniformity of values and appearance is intended to create a sense of solidarity among the soldiers and thereby make the military more effective in carrying out its tasks. Part of the reason there has been so much controversy over homosexuals in the military is that their presence allows a diversity of individual lifestyles into a context where, from an institutional perspective, similarity is essential.

We have seen situations where isolated resocialization can be tragically exploited. The 1978 mass suicide of 911 members of Jim Jones's People's

Temple in Jonestown, Guyana, and the 1993 armed standoff and subsequent destruction of David Koresh's Branch Davidian compound in Waco, Texas, are two noteworthy examples. Both Koresh and Jones told their followers that in order to achieve a better and more meaningful life they would have to sever all ties to their previous lives—values, relationships, emotional bonds, and so on.

The members abandoned their past "disreputable" selves so totally and were resocialized and indoctrinated by their leaders so completely that their ability to make decisions on their own behalf was impaired. By reducing the claims of competing roles and allegiances through isolation, Koresh and Jones succeeded in absorbing members within the boundaries of the group (Coser & Coser, 1993). When people are physically and emotionally cut off from their friends and family, they lose their personalities and can be influenced, cajoled, or threatened into doing virtually anything, even giving up their own lives.

Putting It into Context

What all types of socialization have in common—whether they occur in childhood or adulthood, whether freely chosen or forced, whether designed to teach specific skills or entire world views—is that none can take place in a social vacuum. Think about it: How could you know if you were attractive, smart, or funny unless there were people around to tell you so? Institutions such as the family and education and groups such as race and social class can exert considerable influence on our self-concept, our values, and our worldview.

The Impact of Social Institutions

In contemporary American society, the most powerful institutional agent is education. According to the functionalist perspective, the primary purpose of schools is the socialization of young people. Children formally enter the school system around age 5 when they begin kindergarten, although many enter earlier in preschool or nursery school. The "personalized" instruction of the family is replaced by the "impersonalized" instruction of the school, where the children will remain for the next 13 years or longer. No other institution has such extended and consistent access to a person's social growth. As a child learns to identify with school it becomes a key source of influence, rivaling only the family in importance.

Although schools are officially charged with equipping students with the skills they need to fulfill various roles in society (e.g., reading, writing, mathematics), they also teach students important social, political, and economic values. When elementary school students set up simulated grocery stores or banks, for instance, they are learning about the importance of free enterprise and finance in a capitalist society; when they hold mock elections, they are being introduced to a democratic political system.

Even more subtly, schools teach students what they can expect for themselves in the world. Ironically, the importance of individual accomplishment (e.g., grades) is stressed, but at the same time students learn their future success in society may be determined as much by *who* they are as by *what* they achieve. It is in school that children are first exposed to the fact that people and groups are ranked in society, and soon they get a sense of their own relative standing in the social hierarchy. There is ample evidence that teachers react to students on the basis of race, religion, social class, and gender (Wilkinson & Marrett, 1985). As a result, students get an early lesson about which opportunities will be open to them and which will be blocked.

Some conflict theorists contend that the school's agenda is even more narrowly defined. Early schooling is designed not so much to provide children with factual information and encourage creativity but to produce passive, nonproblematic conformists who will fit into the existing social order (Gracey, 1991). Rules against being late, talking out in class, or arguing with the teacher foster passivity and give students their first taste of formal evaluation and scrutiny by authoritative persons other than their parents. Obeying the kindergarten teacher today prepares the individual for obeying the high school teacher, college professor, and boss tomorrow.

Not all teachers and school systems are overwhelmingly dedicated to fitting every student into a passive role. Some teachers and alternative schools instill values that are at odds with existing social arrangements. The point is that because of the primacy of formal education in the everyday lives of most children, the institutional agenda of a particular school system can have important consequences for the types of people they will eventually become.

Another important institutional socializer is the media. As we saw in chapter 3, newspapers, magazines, television, and radio provide persuasive messages on the nature of reality. They also tell us the type of person we "should" be, from how we should perform our jobs to how different social classes live to what our intimate relationships and families are supposed to look like. The media teach us about prevailing American values, beliefs, myths, stereotypes, and trends (Gitlin, 1979) and provide an avenue through which to learn new attitudes and behavior (Bandura & Walters, 1963). Consider the role televised sports plays in teaching us certain cultural values (Gitlin, 1979). Television has reduced the sports experience to a sequence of individual achievements. During the 1994 NBA Championship between the Houston Rockets and the New York Knicks, for example, television announcers defined the series as a battle between two players, Hakeem Olajuwon and Patrick Ewing. It was touted as "the dream matchup." Much of the coverage focused on the comparative performances and personalities of these two players, reducing their teammates to supporting-cast members.

We have grown used to hearing descriptions like "best," "superstar," and "greatest of all time." Praise is heaped not only on individuals and the occasional "dynasty" team, but also on more specific actions: "best jump shot," "best backhand," "best at hitting with two outs and runners in scoring position," "best open field tackler," "best chip out of a sand trap." Such characterizations not only perpetuate the importance of individual achievement—a cultural value on which our entire social structure is based—but also give the impression that it is always possible to find something, however narrowly defined, at which one can be "best" (Gitlin, 1979).

The Role of Social Class

Social class also influences our socialization. Social classes consist of people who occupy similar economic positions of power, privilege, and prestige. We live in a society that is solidly structured along class distinctions (see chapters 10 and 11 for more detail). People's positions in the class system affect virtually every aspect of their lives, including political preferences, sexual behavior, church membership, diet, and life expectancy (Kohn, 1979).

Social Class and Socialization

Are children from different classes socialized by their parents to have different values and outlooks on life? According to sociologist Melvin Kohn (1979), the answer is yes. Kohn intereviewed 200 working-class and 200 middle-class couples who had at least one child of fifth-grade age. He found that the middle-class parents were more likely to value characteristics that promote self-direction and independence than were the working-class parents. Conversely, working-class parents were more likely to value characteristics that emphasize conformity to external authority.

Kohn felt these differences were consistent no matter what sex the child was or the size and composition of the family. Moreover, such differences are directly related to future goals. Working-class parents believed that eventual occupational success and survival depends on their children's ability to conform to and obey authority. Middle-class parents saw future success as stemming from assertiveness and initiative. Hence, middle-class children's feelings of control over their own destiny are likely to be much stronger.

Racial and Ethnic Identity

Although the issue of racial and ethnic inequality will be addressed at length in chapter 12, it is important to note here that in a race-conscious society like ours, racial and ethnic differences are widely believed to provide visible clues to other, less visible characteristics like temperament, intelligence, values, morality, sexuality, and tastes. A study by the National Opinion Research Center in 1991 found that three out of four whites believed that African Americans are more likely than whites to prefer living on welfare. Sixty-two percent thought African Americans were less likely than whites to be hardworking; 56% thought they were more violence-prone; and 53% felt they were less intelligent ("Whites retain," 1991). It is clear that we use racial and ethnic categories to impute traits to others (see chapter 6), but it is less clear how race and ethnicity are determined and how they help to form people's identities through socialization.

Beyond Biology: Race and Ethnicity

Race is a category of people labeled and treated as similar because of common biological traits, including skin color, texture of hair, and shape of eyes. We usually think of race as a fixed and immutable biological characteristic that can be easily used to separate people into distinct groups. Although the concept seems straightforward, it really isn't. Australian Aboriginals, for instance, have black skin and negroid facial features but have blond, wavy hair. The number of distinct races identified by scholars ranges from 4 to more than 30. There is no clear-cut, pure race. The diversity of physical traits *within* a racial group is often as great as the diversity *between* groups. Race is a social construction. The characteristics selected to distinguish one group from another have less to do with physical differences than with what *that particular culture* defines as socially significant.

Brazil historically has not had a rigid conception of race and thus has a variety of "intermediate" races. In fact, the designation of race is so fluid that parents, children, brothers, and sisters are sometimes accepted as representatives of very different races (Harris, 1964). In South Africa there are four legally defined races—black, white, colored, and Indian—but in Great Britain the term *black* is used to refer to all people who are not white. An African American visiting Tanzania is likely to be considered white by the African blacks there (Njeri, 1990).

In American society we tend to see race in categorical terms: black or white, red or yellow, brown or black. Even when there are ambiguities, such as mixed-race children, we still try to put people into specific categories. Often those categories have less to do with skin color than with dominant cultural beliefs about particular groups.

Micro-Macro Connection
The One-Drop Rule

In Langston Hughes's book *Simple Takes a Wife*, Simple has the following reaction to a story about a man who looked white but was officially declared "colored" by an Alabama court:

> . . . just one drop of black blood makes a man colored. *One* drop— you are a Negro! Now why is that? Why is Negro blood so much more powerful than any other kind of blood in the world? If a man has Irish blood in him, people will say, "He's *part* Irish." If he has a little Jewish blood, they'll say, "He's *half* Jewish." But if he has just a small bit of colored blood in him, BAM!—*"He's a Negro!"* . . . You can have ninety-nine drops of white blood in your veins down South—but if that other *one* drop is black, shame on

you! Even if you look white, you're black. That drop is really powerful. (Hughes, 1958, p. 201)

The United States still adheres to the *one-drop rule* for blacks but not for any other racial group (F. J. Davis, 1991). The term comes from a common law in the South during slavery that a "single drop of black blood" made a person black. According to the U.S. Census, to be considered black one only needs to have any known African black ancestry. Anthropologists call this a *hypodescent* rule, meaning that racially mixed people are always assigned the status of the subordinate group (F. J. Davis, 1991). Hence a person with seven out of eight great-grandparents who are white and only one who is black is still considered black.

Walter White, president of the National Association for the Advancement of Colored People (NAACP) from 1931 to 1955, was estimated to be no more than one-sixty-fourth African black. He had fair skin, fair hair, and blue eyes yet did not attempt to pass as white—something that would have made his life quite a bit easier at that time. The "race" that White represented was the social group with which he identified and *not* his genetic classification. This is why the black community became outraged when he married a white woman. He had crossed a major *social* barrier, if only a minute *color* barrier.

More recently a Louisiana woman found that although she had always considered herself white (she had twice married white men, and her parents and grandparents had blond hair and blue eyes), she was defined by the state of Louisiana as colored. State authorities had traced her ancestry back more than 200 years and found that her great-great-great-great-grandmother was black. She sued the state for $20,000, and the law that defined as black anyone whose ancestry was at least 3% black was eventually repealed (Jaynes, 1982).

The belief that a tiny amount of black ancestry could "contaminate" a person has been used to justify the exclusion and mistreatment of blacks through slavery and, later, segregation. Collective anxiety on the part of whites about the number of light-skinned blacks "passing" as white reached a peak in the early part of the 20th century. In the South there was tremendous fear, almost hysteria, over "invisible blackness." Showing a fondness for black culture or voluntarily associating with blacks was sometimes considered proof of blackness even in the absence of known black ancestry (F. J. Davis, 1991).

That this phenomenon is unique to blacks can be seen in the different reactions to mixed offspring found in other groups. Among Japanese Americans, for instance, mixed marriages were frowned on until recent years. A child who was predominantly Japanese with some white blood was considered white by the rest of the community and not fully admitted into the ethnic group. Among Orthodox Jews, a child born to a Jewish and non-Jewish parent is forbidden to claim a Jewish identity. Calling oneself "part Indian" is still less stigmatizing than calling oneself "part black" (Spickard, 1989).

The one-drop rule and the accompanying issue of racial identity has created racial tensions *within* the black community as well. Color divisiveness *among* blacks is seen by some within the black community as a worse problem than racial hatred expressed by whites. Light-skinned blacks are sometimes resented by darker-skinned blacks for using skin whiteners and hair straighteners to conform to white standards of beauty (F. J. Davis, 1991). The entertainer Michael Jackson has been severely criticized for removing most of his "black" physical features. Issues of personal identity, conflicting loyalties, and a marginal social status can make life miserable for blacks who appear white.

Although race is a meaningless category biologically speaking, it remains a crucial social category. Along with sex, it is the first thing we notice about one another (see chapter 6). Race is also important because of its connection to ethnicity. Ethnicity is a learned cultural heritage shared by a category of people. Your history, values, language, tastes, and habits may be more important indicators of your identity than skin color or other anatomical features (L. Williams, 1991a). Race and ethnicity need not be the same. For example, Caribbean blacks are quite different ethnically from African blacks.

The distinction between race and ethnicity is important at the level of individual identity. The debate over what constitutes a black identity was crystallized during the confirmation hearings on Judge Clarence Thomas's nomination to the Supreme Court in the fall of 1991. Some African Americans criticized Thomas for using his race selectively and playing down its importance until he was accused of sexual harassment by Professor Anita Hill. No one questioned Thomas's race, but many questioned his "blackness"—his ethnic loyalty—because he embraced conservative political attitudes and is married to a white woman. Said one observer of the Thomas-Hill hearings: "I saw a black woman, and a white man in black skin" (quoted in L. Williams, 1991a). Such a statement is interesting sociologically because it illustrates that one can be racially black but still have one's ethnic "blackness" called into question because one's beliefs, actions, and attitudes don't conform to those of most group members. To many, the very survival of the group depends on a shared ethnic identity.

Race and Socialization

The day after the Los Angeles riots in May 1992, students in my introductory class became embroiled in a heated discussion of the incident. One student, who was white, expressed concern that young children of all races will now grow up mistrusting or even hating the police. As a child she had been taught that the police were there to help people and that if she was ever in trouble or lost she could approach an officer for help. She never questioned whether or not they could be trusted. She then speculated how awful life would become for kids without the sense of safety and certainty she had been socialized to take for granted.

A few of the African-American students in class immediately pointed out to her that *their* socialization experiences had been quite different. Parents and others in their neighborhoods had taught them *never* to trust the police because officers were just as likely to exploit and harass them as to help them. They were taught to turn to neighbors if they ever needed help. To them the police were not knights in shining armor but bullies with badges. Although these two perspectives are not representative of *every* white or *every* African-American person in this country, the interchange illustrates the stark impact race can have on socialization.

For white children, the values they are taught when growing up are likely to mirror those of the wider society. Chances are that schools and religious institutions will reinforce the socialization messages expressed to them in their families, for example, "hard work will pay off in the long run."

For racial minorities, however, socialization occurs within a larger social environment that is often incompatible with realizing a positive self and group identity (Taylor, Chatters, Tucker, & Lewis, 1990). These children must become knowledgeable of the dominant white culture as well as their own simply to survive. African-American children must be socialized to deal with the realities of racism they will encounter every day (Staples, 1992). Childhood training frequently involves preparation for living in a society that has been and still is set up to ignore or actively exclude them. They must learn to deal with the personal and institutional prejudices that await them. They are more apt to be taught that "hard work" alone might not be enough to get ahead in this society.

The Socialization of Self

Whether a person is rich or poor, black or white, the most important outcome of the socialization process is the development of a sense of self. Self refers to the unique set of traits, behaviors, and attitudes that distinguishes one person from the next. Social scientists, however, have a more complex concept of what "self" is, and they take particular interest in the process through which a person develops a sense of self.

The Nature of Self

The **self** is both the active source of behavior and the passive object of behavior (G. H. Mead, 1934). As an active source, the self can initiate action that is frequently directed toward others. Curt and Mary are having dinner in a restaurant. Mary can perceive Curt, talk to him, evaluate him, perhaps even try to manipulate or persuade him to act in a way that is consistent with her interests. Mary also has a self that is a potential object of others' behavior: She can be perceived, talked to, evaluated, manipulated, or persuaded by Curt.

Mary can also direct these activities toward herself. She can perceive, evaluate, motivate, and even talk to *herself.* This is called **reflexive behavior.** To have a self is to have the ability to plan, observe, guide, and respond to one's own behavior (G. H. Mead, 1934).

Think of all the times you have tried to motivate yourself to act by saying something like, "All right, if I read 20 more pages of this boring textbook, I'll give myself a hot fudge sundae." To do this you must simultaneously be the motivator and the one being motivated; the seer and the seen.

At this very moment you are initiating an action: reading this book. But you also have the ability to be *aware* of your reading behavior, to observe yourself reading and even evaluate how well you are doing. This sounds like some sort of out-of-body experience, but it isn't. There is nothing more fundamental to human thought and action than the capacity for self-awareness. It allows us to control our own behavior and interact smoothly with other self-aware individuals.

The philosopher William James (1890) labeled the active source of behavior the "I" and the passive object of behavior the "me": "*I* perceive *me,*" or "*I* talk to *me.*" George Herbert Mead (1934) went one step further and described the "I" and the "me" as alternating phases of every action that involves the self. He felt that the "I" is the part of the self that responds directly to outside events. It is impulsive and not subject to control at first. The "I" can be seen in situations where we react spontaneously without assessing the possible consequences of our actions. You may have told yourself more than once: "It's such a beautiful day . . . the heck with studying for this stupid sociology exam, I'm going to the beach!"

The "me" represents society within the individual. It is the self-reflective, conventional aspect of the self that incorporates society's values, norms, ideals, and expectations. The "me" represents the internalization of the attitudes and group standards of others. If you reconsider your beach trip in light of its possible outcome, you are invoking the "me": "No, I'd better not go to the beach. I may fail the exam and the course."

According to Mead, the "I" and "me" are alternating elements of a constant process of thought and action. One moment we are responding directly to environmental stimuli. The next moment we direct our conscious attention inward and become aware of our conduct: "Wow, I can't believe how angry I am at Tom." This allows us to alter our behavior to bring it in line with social conventions ("I shouldn't be so angry at him . . . I'll apologize and act like everything's OK"). Then *this* behavior becomes the object of our own scrutiny ("I wonder if he thinks I'm still mad").

The ability to carry on this internal dialogue enables us to incorporate the perceptions and expectations of other people. The crucial aspect of the self is that it allows us to transform, modify, and control our behavior when we interact with people in various circumstances. As we become aware that different people expect different things, we can tailor our behavior to meet the demands of each situation.

The Acquisition of Self

The capacity for humans to control their own conduct rests on the development of the self. Because we can act toward ourselves as objects, we can imagine alternate lines of conduct and choose from among them. But how do we acquire a self? How is the newborn infant transformed into a self-aware, self-controlled member of society? Unlike other animals, human babies cannot care for themselves. Moreover, they possess no sense of self at birth, have no capacity for reflexive behavior, and lack the ability to consciously control their actions.

This is not to say that infants don't act. Anyone who has been around babies knows that they have a tremendous ability to initiate action ranging all the way from Kodak-moment cute to downright disgusting. They cry, eat, sleep, play with squeaky rubber toys, and eliminate waste, all with exquisite panache and regularity. They respond to the sounds, sights, smells, and touches of others from the very first days of life.

But this behavior is not characterized by the sort of self-consciousness that characterizes later behavior. Babies cannot say to themselves, "I can't believe how loud I can cry," or, "I wonder if Mom will feed me if I scream." As children grow older, though, they begin to exert greater control over their conduct. Part of this transformation is biological. As they mature they become more adept at muscle control. But physical development is only part of the picture. Humans must *acquire* certain cognitive capacities through interactions with others, including the abilities to differentiate between self and others, to understand and use symbolic language, and to take the roles of others.

The Differentiation of Self

To distinguish between oneself and others, one must be able to recognize oneself (Michener, DeLamater, & Schwartz, 1986). The first step in the acquisition of self, then, is learning to distinguish our own faces and bodies from the rest of the physical environment. Surprisingly, we are not born with this ability. Not only are newborns incapable of recognizing themselves, they also cannot even discriminate the boundaries between their bodies and the bodies of others. An infant will pull its own hair to the point of excruciating pain but will not realize that the hair it's pulling and the hair that it feels being pulled is the same hair.

With cognitive growth and social experience, the infant gradually recognizes itself as a unique physical object. Most studies in this area indicate that children usually develop this ability at about 18 months (e.g., Bertenthal & Fischer, 1978). If you make a large mark on a child's forehead with a washable marker, hold the youngster up to a mirror, and observe whether the child reaches up to wipe away the smudge, you can tell if the youngster knows that the image in the mirror is its own.

Language Acquisition

The next important step in the acquisition of the self is the development of speech (Hewitt, 1988). Mastery of the language is critical in a child's efforts to differentiate itself as a distinct social as well as physical object (Denzin, 1977). Most parents talk to their children from the start. Gradually, children learn to make sounds, imitate sounds, and use sounds as symbols for particular physical sensations or objects. The child learns that the sounds "Mama" and "Dada" are the sounds associated with two important objects in its life. Soon the child learns that other objects—toys, animals, foods, Aunt Donna—have unique sounds associated with them as well.

This learning process provides the child access into the preexisting linguistic world in which the child's parents and others live (Hewitt, 1988). The objects that are named are not only those that are recognized within the larger culture, but also those recognized within the family's particular social group (race, class, religion). The child learns the names of concrete objects (balls, buildings, furniture) as well as abstract ideas that cannot be directly perceived (e.g., God, happiness, idea). By learning that people and other objects have names, a child also begins to learn that there are many named ways in which these objects can be related to one another. Depending on who is talking to whom, the same person can be called several different names. The object "Daddy" is called, by various other people, "David," "Dave," "Dr. Newman," "Professor Newman," "Honey," and "Dummy." Furthermore, the child learns that different people can be referred to by the same name. All those other kids at the park have someone they also call "Mama."

Amidst these monumental discoveries young children learn that they too are objects that have names. When a child learns that others are referring to her when they use the word "Nancy," and that she too can use "Nancy" to refer to herself, it represents a significant leap forward in the acquisition of self. The child is now able to visualize herself as a part of the named world and the named relationships to which she belongs.

The self that initially emerges from this process is a rather simple one. "Nancy" is just a name associated with a body, which explains why very young children just learning to form sentences will refer to themselves by their name instead of the first-person pronoun (e.g., "Nancy is hungry" instead of "I am hungry"). A more sophisticated sense of self is derived from the child's ability to learn the *meaning* of this named object.

Children learn the meaning of named objects in their environment by observing the way other people act toward them. Children learn what "chair" means by observing people sitting in it. They learn that a "hot stove" is something to be avoided. Similarly, they learn the meaning of themselves by observing how people act toward them. People treat children in a variety of ways: care for them, punish them, love them, teach them. If parents, relatives, and other significant people perceive a child as smart, they will act toward him or her that way. Thus the child will eventually come to *believe* he or she is a smart person.

Sociologist Charles Horton Cooley (1902) referred to this process as the **looking-glass self.** We use the actions of others toward us as mirrors in which we see ourselves. How the child as-named-object is defined by others is linked to larger societal considerations as well. Every culture has its own way of defining individuals at various stages of the life cycle. As we saw in the previous chapter, children in past cultures were not always defined as a special subpopulation that requires nurturance and protection, but rather as miniature adults (Aries, 1962). They were expected to behave like adults and were held accountable for their actions just as adults would be. Hence a 5-year-old's self-worth might have been derived from how well he or she contributed economically to the family, not from how cute or playful he or she was.

Moreover, every society has its own standards of beauty and success. If thinness is deemed a desirable characteristic, a thin child is more likely to garner positive responses and develop a positive self-image than a child who violates this norm (i.e., an obese child).

The Development of Role Taking

Different people *expect* or *desire* different things from us. A child eventually learns to modify his or her behavior to suit different people. Four-year-old Robbie learns, for instance, that his 3-year-old sister loves it when he sticks green beans up his nose, but he also knows that Dad does not find this behavior at all amusing. So Robbie will avoid such conduct when Dad is around but will proceed to amuse his sister with this trick when Dad is gone. The ability to use other people's perspectives and expectations in formulating one's own behavior is called **role taking** (G. H. Mead, 1934).

Role-taking ability is developed gradually, paralleling the increasing matura-tion of linguistic abilities. G. H. Mead (1934) identified two major stages in the development of role-taking ability and, ultimately, in the socialization of the self: the play stage and the game stage. The **play stage** occurs when children are just beginning to acquire language. Most 3-year-olds are able to imitate the charac-teristics and behaviors associated with others in particular roles. They can play at being Mommy, a firefighter, a soccer player, an astronaut, and so on. This sort of play is marked by its transient, unorganized quality. Children at the play stage commonly drift from one role to another in no logical sequence. Mead pointed out that this trait is the definitive characteristic of childhood. You cannot count on a child. You cannot assume that what a child does now will determine what he or she will do a minute from now.

More important, role taking at the play stage is quite simple in form, limited to one other person at a time. Young children cannot see themselves from different perspectives simultaneously. They have no idea that certain behaviors may be unacceptable to a variety of people across a range of situations. They know only that this particular person who is in their immediate presence will not approve of this conduct. Children cannot see that Mom's disapproval of public nose picking reflects the attitudes of a larger group. This more sophisticated form of self-control develops at the next stage of the socialization process.

The **game stage** occurs when children first begin to participate in organized activities like school events and team sports. The difference between role taking at the play and game stages parallels the difference between childhood play behavior and game behavior. Play is not guided by a specific set of rules. There is no ultimate object of play, no clearly organized competition, no winners and losers. Children playing baseball at the play stage have no sense of strategy and may not even be aware of the rules and object of the game. They may be able to hit, catch, and throw the ball but have no idea how their behavior is linked to that of their teammates. If a little girl is playing third base and the ball is hit to her, she may throw the ball to the left fielder, not because this will help her team win the game but because that's where her best friend happens to be.

At the game stage children do have a sense of the object of the game. They realize that each player on the team is part of an organized network of roles determined by the rules of the game. They know they must continually adapt their behavior to the team's needs in order to achieve a goal. To do so, they must predict how both teammates and opponents will act under certain circumstances.

The ability to imagine the *group's* perspective characterizes the game stage of development. With regard to social behavior, not only does the child learn to respond to the demands of many people, but he or she can also respond to the demands of the community or even society as a whole. The perspective of society and its constituent values and attitudes is known as the **generalized other.**

To take the role of the generalized other is to perceive one's behavior from the point of view of the group, not just one particular person. "Mommy doesn't like it when I pick my nose in restaurants" (play stage) becomes "It is not acceptable to pick one's nose in public" (game stage). This ability is crucial because it makes it possible to resist the influence of specific people who happen to be in one's immediate presence. The boy who defies his peers by not joining them in an act of petty shoplifting is showing the power of the generalized other. During the game stage, the attitudes and expectations of the generalized other are incorporated into one's self-concept, forming the "me."

Real life is not that simple, though. The perspective of society is not the same for everyone. People from markedly different backgrounds are likely to internalize different sets of group attitudes and values. Granted, the generalized other becomes larger as a child matures, growing to include family, peer group, school, and finally the larger social community. But as societies themselves grow and become more complex, so does the generalized other.

Groups, organizations, and communities have their own sets of norms, values, and beliefs. A Catholic contemplating divorce, for instance, is taking the role of a different generalized other than an atheist contemplating divorce. Likewise, the social worlds and social standards of men and women are different, as are those of children and adults, parents and nonparents, middle-class and working-class people. As we move from one context to another, we adopt the perspective of the appropriate group and can become, for all intents and purposes, a different person. At work we behave one way, at church another, at a family reunion still another. We are as many different people as there are groups and organizations of which we are members. Because role taking is the process of imagining another person's attitudes and intentions and thereby anticipating that person's behavior, it is essential for everyday social interaction. Through it we are able to envision how others perceive us and what their response may be to some action we're contemplating. Hence we can select behaviors that are likely to meet with the approval of the person or persons with whom we are interacting and avoid behaviors that might meet with their disapproval.

By imagining others' reactions, we are able to "rehearse" social encounters prior to engaging in them. If we can predict their responses to our conduct, we are in a better position to devise a plan of action to meet both their expectations and our needs. Role taking is a crucial component of *self-control*. It is fundamental in the development of a social being who is capable of behaving in ways that conform to the wishes and expectations of others. Moreover, role taking becomes a means of *social control* to the extent that such behavior conforms to broader societal expectations. In this way it is the means by which culture is incorporated into the self.

The Self in Cultural Context

When we imagine how others will respond to our actions, we choose from a limited set of alternative lines of conduct that are a function of the wider culture. In the United States, the self is likely to incorporate key American virtues such as self-reliance and individualism. Hence personal goals often take priority over allegiance to groups (Bellah et al., 1985). Americans will readily change their group membership as it suits them—switching churches, leaving one employer for another, moving from neighborhood to neighborhood, and so on (Goleman, 1990). In most non-Western countries, however, the self is more likely to be *collectivist*, where personal identity is completely subsumed under group identity (K. J. Gergen, 1991). A high value is placed on preserving one's public image so as not to bring shame upon one's family, tribe, or community (Triandis,

McCusker, & Hui, 1990). Overcoming personal interests and temptations to show loyalty to one's group and other authorities is to be celebrated.

In individualistic cultures like ours, one's personal accomplishments are a key ingredient of one's self-concept. The amount of respect you deserve is determined in large part by your level of expertise. For example, a lecturer will be introduced to her audience as "a distinguished scholar, a leader in her field" along with a list of her scholarly achievements. In Asia, however, such pronouncements would be considered self-centered and egotistical. Asian lecturers usually begin their talks by telling the audience how little they know about the topic at hand (Goleman, 1990). Not only does this example show some interesting cultural differences in "appropriate" public behavior, it also illustrates vast differences in how people see themselves and the worlds they inhabit.

When we acquire a self, we are simultaneously acquiring a repertoire of behaviors that are culturally defined. Our cultural belief systems determine whether we see ourselves as a bundle of individual traits and accomplishments or as an extension of a dense network of social relations and group affiliations.

To fully understand how we become who we are, we must understand our position in the social structure. We must know the norms and values of our society, family, peers, co-workers, and so forth. We must know the attitudes taken toward us by people in socializing institutions. We must know that our race, social class, and religion set limits on the kinds of social relationships we can and will form and therefore limit our ability to take the roles of people who are different from us.

The Socialization of Gender

An analysis of socialization would be incomplete without examining the process by which we develop our gender. Gender, along with race and ethnicity, is one of the primary elements of our social being. Our everyday behavior, our tastes and desires, our experiences in intimate relationships, our health and well-being, our career choices, and our political beliefs are linked directly or indirectly to gender.

Sex Versus Gender

Before discussing how individuals acquire gender, it is necessary to distinguish between gender and sex. **Sex** is used to refer to a person's biological maleness or femaleness. **Gender** designates psychological, social, and cultural aspects of maleness and femaleness (S. J. Kessler & McKenna, 1978). This distinction is important because it reminds us that male-female differences in behaviors or experiences do not spring naturally from biological differences between the sexes (Lips, 1993). In addition, this distinction allows us to separate masculinity from maleness and femininity from femaleness, which makes it possible for people to deviate from cultural notions of gender without having any impact on their sex.

We usually think of sex as being determined at the time of conception. If you asked someone how to distinguish between males and females, the response would probably focus on observable physical characteristics—body shape, hair, voice, facial features, and so on. When scientists distinguish between the sexes, they, too, refer to physical traits: chromosomes (XX for female, XY for male), sex glands (ovaries and testes), hormones (estrogen and testosterone), internal sex organs (uterus and prostate gland), external genitalia (vagina and penis), reproductive capacities (pregnancy and impregnation), germ cells produced (ova and sperm), and secondary sex characteristics (hips and breasts, facial hair and deep voice).

These characteristics, and hence the two biological sex categories, male and female, are assumed to be universal, exhaustive (i.e., there's no third sex), and mutually exclusive (i.e., a person cannot be both or neither). There may be differences across time and cultures as to how we *expect* the two sexes to act and look, but no one would disagree that every society has some way of determining who *is* male and who *is* female. As a result, we cannot and perhaps should not be fully comfortable with any ambiguity:

> [People] are either one or the other, zero or 100 percent. We may modify our decision ("He is an effeminate man"), but we do not usually qualify it ("Maybe he is a man"). If we should have to qualify it, then we seek further information until the qualification is no longer necessary. (S. J. Kessler & McKenna, 1978, p. 2)

Yet things aren't always so clear cut. Hermaphrodites, for instance, are individuals in whom sexual differentiation is either incomplete or ambiguous. They may have the chromosomal pattern of a female but the external genitalia of a male, or they may have both ovaries *and* testicles. According to one prominent biologist, instead of two sexual categories, there are many gradations of sex running from female to male, and along that spectrum lie at least *five* sexes (Fausto-Sterling, 1993). In addition to males and females there are "true hermaphrodites," people who possess one testis and one ovary; "male pseudohermaphrodites," people who have testes and some aspects of female genitalia but no ovaries; and "female pseudohermaphrodites," people who have ovaries and some aspects of male genitalia but no testes.

It is interesting to note that the existence of hermaphrodites does not threaten the *cultural* reality of sex. Their conditions are usually defined by biologists as a combination of the two existing categories and not as a third, fourth, or fifth category unto itself. Furthermore, upon the diagnosis of hermaphroditism, a decision is always made to define the individual as either male or female. In societies with advanced medical technology, surgical and chemical means may be used to establish consistency between anatomy and the social label.

Our entire social structure is organized around the fact that there are two and only two sexes (Lorber, 1989). The male-female dichotomy in our culture is so essential to our way of life that those who challenge it are considered either crazy or cultural heretics who are being disloyal to the most fundamental of biological "facts." To suggest that the labels "male" and "female" are not sufficient to categorize everyone is to threaten the entire institutional order of social life.

Some cross-cultural evidence indicates that not every society subscribes to the "fact" that there are two and only two sexes. In traditional Navajo culture, one could be male, female, or *nadle*—a third sex assigned to those whose sex-typed anatomical characteristics were ambiguous at birth (M. K. Martin & Voorhies, 1975). Physically normal individuals also had the opportunity to choose to become *nadle* if they so desired. *Nadle* were allowed to perform the tasks of both men and women. Again we see that sexual characteristics need not be consistent with socially defined gender.

The traditional Mohave allowed men and women to cross sexes and genders. Boys who showed a preference for feminine toys, clothing, and activities would undergo a ceremony at puberty at which time they would become *alyha*. Henceforth they would adopt feminine names, perform female tasks, dress like women, and marry men. Mohave females who showed interest in a masculine lifestyle would become *hwame* at puberty. They would dress like men, hunt and farm, and assume paternal responsibility for children (M. K. Martin & Voorhies, 1975).

Among the Hua of Papua New Guinea, gender is thought to change throughout a person's life (Gailey, 1987). The Hua believe that women lose some of their femininity each time they have a child. After three births a woman has lost enough femininity to be allowed to participate in the discussions and rituals of men and share their higher status and authority. Men gradually lose their masculinity by giving it to young boys during developmental rituals. Consequently, older men come to acquire the same social status as young women (Gailey, 1987).

These cross-cultural examples illustrate that *our* beliefs about sex and gender are not held worldwide. Other societies exist where sex and gender are neither dichotomous nor permanent. Likewise, there are situations in U.S. society in which one's gender doesn't line up with one's sex. *Transsexuals*—those who have the normal biological characteristics of one sex but the gender identity of the other—will sometimes go so far as to have their biological sex altered through "corrective" surgery to bring it in line with their psychological gender. In other words, it's easier to alter their sex than to alter their gender.

To understand gender and the socialization process that creates it, we must understand it as a phenomenon susceptible to cultural definition like anything else.

The Societal Context of Gender

Gender is also a social role. Like other social roles, it implies a set of rights, expectations, obligations, and privileges commonly associated with that gender. In our society the gender dichotomy is a major way in which everyday life and larger social institutions are organized. Religious doctrines, for instance, frequently reinforce status and power differences between men and women. The traditional Judeo-Christian ideology incorporates beliefs that have historically given men special rights and privileges over women:

> Unto the woman [God] said, I will greatly multiply thy sorrow and thy conception; in sorrow thou shalt bring forth children, and thy desire shall be to thy husband, and he shall rule over thee. (Gen. 3:16)
>
> For a man . . . is the image and glory of God; but the woman is the glory of man. For the man is not of the woman, but the woman of the man. Neither was the man created for the woman, but the woman for the man. (1 Cor. 11:7-9)
>
> Blessed art Thou, oh Lord our God, King of the Universe, that I was not born a woman. (Orthodox Jewish morning prayer)

Other social institutions, too, afford different rights and privileges to men and women. The American political system has long excluded women from the highest levels of its decision-making process. Economic discrimination and exploitation in terms of both access to certain careers and low wages is well documented (see chapter 13). Family life has always been clearly delineated along gender lines, with men and women holding distinct and differently valued familial obligations.

Many of these institutions are in the process of changing, however. The last decade has seen more women's participation in the clergy, the paid labor force, and national politics. Marital and parental roles are slowly becoming more balanced. Yet while our society creeps forward toward gender equality, the impetus to keep the genders ideologically separate and their respective expectations different prevails.

Gender Differences

We live in a society in which virtually all institutions, organizations, and day-to-day interactions are built on fundamental differences between boys and girls, men and women, and masculine and feminine. Consider the gender distinctions in our language. Although English is not grammatically gendered as, say, French or Spanish, gender pervades the language, as in the traditional use of the inclusive male pronoun *he* and the generic *man* in referring to both genders. Such words make females appear as exceptions. Female terms are often created as mere extensions of existing male terms by adding an *ess* or *ette* (e.g., poet*ess*, steward*ess,* major*ette*) or by using the words *lady, female,* or *woman* as noun modifiers (e.g., *lady* doctor, *woman* lawyer, *female* engineer).

Even the use of nongendered terms like *congressperson* or *spokesperson* implies that the individual being referred to is female. The fact that women's job titles are modifications of traditional male terms reinforces the cultural belief that that occupation is still the man's domain with the woman being an exception to the rule. There's no need to call a man a *male* engineer or a *male* doctor because the terms themselves already imply a male occupant.

Our gender-biased vocabulary reflects and perpetuates underlying societal beliefs about the relative roles of men and women. To "mother" a child is to nurture, coddle, and protect that child; to "father" a child is simply to fertilize an egg. Similarly, a "governor" is an elected official who acts as the head of a state; a "governess" is one who cares for other people's children. In common usage, a "master" is one who rules over others; a "mistress" is a woman with whom a man has an extended extramarital affair (Richardson, 1987).

Men and women also differ in the ways they *use* language. Apparent gender differences in communication parallel gender differences in existing social arrangements. The common belief that women's speech tends to be more emotionally expressive than men's reflects a deeper cultural belief regarding the appropriate social roles and interpersonal obligations of males and females (Lakoff, 1973). One of the consequences of disclosing a great deal of information about yourself or openly showing your emotions is that it puts you in a position of relative powerlessness with regard to others (Blau, 1964). By linguistically overexposing themselves, women perpetuate the preexisting power differences that pervade gender relations. Indeed, some researchers (e.g., Kollock, Blumstein, & Schwartz, 1985) argue that certain gender-typed conversational behaviors, such as men interrupting more than women, are actually the result of power imbalances rather than inherent gender differences.

The Acquisition of Gender Roles

These sorts of gender distinctions are far from trivial and have serious educational, political, and economic implications. Different expectations create unequal opportunities. One's identity as male or female has a profound impact on one's self-development, determining paths chosen, decisions made, and treatment received at the hands of others.

How are all these ideas, expectations, and values transmitted to children? How do children come to *be* masculine or feminine in a way that is consistent with larger cultural dictates? The gender socialization process begins the moment a child is born. A physician, nurse, or midwife immediately starts that infant on a career as a male or female by authoritatively declaring whether it is a boy or girl. In most hospitals the infant boy is wrapped in a blue blanket, the infant girl in a pink one. From that point on the developmental paths of males and females diverge. The subsequent messages that individuals receive from families, books, television, and schools not only teach and reinforce gender-typed expectations but also influence the formation of their self-concepts.

Family

Parents are their children's first source of information about gender. If you asked parents whether they treated sons any differently from daughters, most would probably say no. Yet there is considerable evidence that what parents do and what they *say* they do are are two different things (Lips, 1993; Lytton & Romney, 1991; Renzetti & Curran, 1989). Gender-typed expectations are so ingrained in American parents that they are often unaware that they are behaving in accordance with them (Goldberg & Lewis, 1969; Will, Self, & Datan, 1976).

In one study, 30 first-time parents were asked to describe their recently born infants (less than 24 hours old). They frequently resorted to common gender stereotypes. Those with daughters described them as "tiny," "soft," "fine-featured," and "delicate." Sons were seen as "strong," "alert," "hardy," and "coordinated" (J. Z. Rubin, Provenzano, & Luria, 1974). Parents also tend to engage in rougher physical play with infant sons than with infant daughters and use different subtle tones of voice and pet names, like "Sweetie" versus "Tiger" (MacDonald & Parke, 1986; Tauber, 1979).

New parents, understandably proud of their new parental status, can be very sensitive about the correct identification of their child's sex. Even parents who claim to consider sex and gender irrelevant will nevertheless spend a great deal of time ensuring that their child has the culturally appropriate physical appearance of a boy or girl. This is not surprising given the centrality of sex and gender and the cultural distaste for ambiguity that I described earlier. Misidentifying the sex of their baby can be an embarrassing, even painful experience for some parents, which may explain why parents of a girl baby who has yet to grow hair (a visible sign of sex in this culture) will often tape pink ribbons to the bald baby's head.

Beyond its importance to parents, proper identification of babies has a lot to do with maintaining social order. When my elder son was an infant, I dressed him on several occasions in a pink, frilly snowsuit in order to observe the reactions of others. (Having a sociologist for a father can be rather difficult from time to time!) Invariably someone would approach us and start playing with the baby. Some variation of the following interchange inevitably ensued:

"Oh, she's so cute! What's your little girl's name?"

"Zachary."

"Isn't 'Zachary' a boy's name?"

"He's a boy."

At this point the responses would range from stunned confusion and awkward laughter to dirty looks and outright anger. Clearly they felt that I had emotionally abused my son somehow. I had purposely breached a fundamental gender norm and thereby created, in their minds, unnecessary trauma (for him) and interactional turmoil (for them). As you will recall from chapter 4, trouble-free social interaction, and ultimately social order, is predicated on everyone's adherence to the sort of taken-for-granted social norm that I had willingly and "disrespectfully" broken.

Both boys and girls learn to distinguish the female role from the male role and come to identify themselves "appropriately." According to most developmental psychologists, by the age of 3 or so most children can answer the question "Are you a boy or a girl?" accurately (e.g., Kohlberg, 1966). But to a young child, being a boy or a girl means no more than being named Bobby instead of Betty. It is simply another characteristic, like hair color or having 10 fingers. The child at this age has no conception that gender is a category into which every human can be placed (S. J. Kessler & McKenna, 1978).

At around age 5 the child begins to see gender as an invariant characteristic of the social world—something that is fixed and permanent. Likewise, there is a high degree of gender typing in their preferences for particular activities (Kohlberg, 1966). Children at this age express statements such as "men are doctors" and "women are nurses" as inflexible, objective "truths." Only later will the child be able to realize that gender roles are not as inflexible as once believed.

These early lessons of gender are provided by parents, siblings, and other significant people in the child's immediate environment. Often these individuals serve as observational models with whom the child can identify and ultimately imitate. Other times the lessons are more purposive and direct, as when parents provide their children with explicit instructions on proper gender behavior like "Big boys don't cry," or "Act like a young lady."

Evidence suggests that the instructions for boys are particularly rigid and restrictive during childhood (C. W. Franklin, 1988). Indeed, the social costs for gender-inappropriate behavior are disproportionately severe for boys. The "sissy" in American society will have much more difficulty during childhood than the "tomboy." This is clearly linked to the different social value ascribed to men and women and will be discussed in more detail in chapter 13.

As children grow older, parents tend to encourage more gender-typed activities. One study found that household tasks differ along gender lines. Boys were more likely to mow the lawn, shovel snow, take out the garbage, and do the yardwork, whereas girls tended to clean the house, wash dishes, cook, and babysit the younger children (White & Brinkerhoff, 1981).

Parents also influence their children's conceptions of sex and gender through the things they routinely purchase for them, such as clothes and toys. Not only do clothes inform others about the sex of an individual, they also send messages about how that person ought to be treated. Clothes direct behavior along traditional gender lines (Shakin, Shakin, & Sternglanz, 1985) and encourage or discourage certain gender-typed actions. Frilly dresses do not lend themselves easily to rough and dirty play. Likewise, it is difficult to walk quickly or assertively in high heels and tight miniskirts. Clothes for boys and men rarely restrict physical movement in this way.

Toys, too, serve to distinguish between the sexes. The toy industry has traditionally been built on a solid foundation of sex stereotypes. War toys, competitive games of strategy, and sports paraphernalia have been long-standing staples of the toy industry's boy market. The words *hero, warrior, battle,* and *speed* characterize boys' toys. Dolls, makeup kits, and toy kitchens continue to be profitable items for girls. The vocabulary of girls' toys consists of terms like *nurturing, love,* and *magic* (Lawson, 1993). Sex-specific toys foster different traits and skills in children and thereby serve to further segregate the two sexes into different patterns of social development. Boys' toys encourage invention, exploration, competition, and aggression. Girls' toys encourage creativity, nurturance, and physical attractiveness (C. L. Miller, 1987).

In some cases manufacturers have attempted—only half-heartedly—to blur the lines between boy and girl toys. The Hasbro toy company has tried to interest boys in troll dolls, which are traditionally popular among girls. What they came up with were old-fashioned action figures in the shape of a troll with names like "Troll Warrior" and "Battle Troll" (Lawson, 1993). Other companies have tried to sell girls on action figures and dinosaurs, which are typically the province of boys. But here, too, there is a drift into traditional sex stereotypes. Meritus Industries' "Darlin' Dinos," for example, are pink and have full heads of hair that can be combed. Mattel's "Wonder Woman" action figure fights not with swords or machine guns but with a wand that sprays bubbles.

Moreover, toy manufacturers are still quick to exploit the gender-distinct roles children are encouraged to pursue when they become adults. "My Bundle Baby," manufactured by Mattel, is a 10-inch infant doll in a padded pouch that can be worn around a child's abdomen. By pressing a button hidden inside the pouch, the child can feel the baby inside "kick" and can hear its heartbeat (Lawson, 1992). The "Judy" doll, manufactured by the Judith Corporation, looks like any other 11-inch doll except that she is pregnant. She comes with a distended tummy that, when removed, reveals the presence of a cute baby nestled comfortably inside the doll's plastic uterus. The baby can be bloodlessly removed and a flat, nonpregnant tummy inserted in its place. The advertisement reads, "Judy is more than a toy, she's a natural way for your child to learn while playing." Hence the Judy doll teaches young girls the cultural value of motherhood.

Media

Children receive gender lessons from other sources as well. Children's books, for instance, provide access to the world outside their immediate environment. Through them children learn what other little boys or girls do and what is expected of them. In the early 1970s, Lenore Weitzman and her colleagues studied the portrayal of gender in popular preschool books (Weitzman, Eifler, Hodada, & Ross, 1972). They found that boys played a more significant role in the stories than girls by a ratio of 11 to 1. Boys were more likely to be portrayed in adventurous pursuits or activities that required independence and strength; girls were likely to be confined to indoor activities and portrayed as passive and dependent.

The prevalence of gender stereotypes in children's books has decreased only slightly over the past several decades (S. B. Peterson & Lach, 1990). Males still tend to be portrayed as adventurous, competent, and clever, while females are depicted as fearful, incompetent, and dependent (A. J. Davis, 1984). In addition, recent attempts to neutralize the stereotypical portrayal of gender through nonsexist children's books have had little impact on the overall market (Giddens, 1991).

These images of males and females have a strong influence on children's perceptions and behaviors. One study found that children's own writing reflects the same sort of gender stereotypes that can be found in the books they read. Stories written by 180 youngsters in the first through sixth grades were examined. For both boys and girls there was a predominance of male characters. Male characters were depicted in stereotypically male occupations: doctor, astronaut, dentist, professor, police officer. Female characters were shown largely in female occupational roles: cook, teacher, babysitter, nurse (Trepanier & Romatowski, 1985).

Another important source of gender information is television. Although there are some notable exceptions (e.g., "Sesame Street"), most children's television shows continue to portray males and females in stereotypical gender roles (Signorielli, 1990). One study of children's programs broadcast on weekends and weekday afternoons found that male characters outnumbered female characters 3 to 1 (Barcus, 1978). Furthermore, male characters dominate the activities depicted and are more likely than female characters to be shown as holding positions of power (Nolan, Galst, & White, 1977).

The portrayal of gender on prime time television also remains rather traditional and stereotypical (Signorielli, 1990). From 1969 to 1985, prime time television was populated by two to three males for every female. Although fewer women are portrayed as housewives than in the past, close to half cannot be classified by occupation (Signorielli, 1990). Men tend to be portrayed as powerful and unemotional, while women express emotions much more easily and are significantly more likely to use sex and charm to get what they want. Physical attractiveness continues to be the preeminent quality for women on television (see also chapter 13).

Children who watch a lot of television are more likely to hold stereotypical attitudes toward gender, exhibit gender-related characteristics, and engage in gender-related activities (M. Morgan, 1987; Signorielli, 1990). In one study, girls who did not have stereotypical conceptions of gender to begin with showed a significant increase in sexist attitudes after 2 years of heavy television watching (M. Morgan, 1982). In another study, 4- to 6-year-old children refused to play with a particular toy after watching two Muppets on TV who said the toy was OK only for the other sex (Cobb, Stevens-Long, & Goldstein, 1982).

Schools

In addition to the family and the media, an important institutional setting for gender role socialization is the school. In school children learn the intellectual and social skills for roles played by adults of their gender (Grant, 1984). Like parents, however, teachers are likely to be unaware of the differential treatment they give to their male and female students. Many contemporary teachers still physically segregate boys from girls by, for example, asking them to line up by gender, pitting the boys against the girls in classroom competitions, or keeping them separated on the playground. It is not uncommon for teachers to ask boys to run the film projector or rearrange desks and ask girls to water the plants or dust the tables (Thorne & Luria, 1986). In fact, gender in schools has been found to account for more segregation than race (Schofield, 1982).

Teachers are also likely to treat their female students differently. One Washington, D.C., study found that teachers gave boys significantly more attention than girls in the form of assistance, praise, intellectual challenges, and punishment (Sadker & Sadker, 1985). This differential treatment is often reinforced by textbooks and other curricular materials that frequently consign women to stereotypical roles in American society (e.g., nurse, spouse) or ignore their contributions to the shaping of history.

The gender-differentiated socialization that occurs in education *extends* male experiences by encouraging curiosity, independence, and initiative, and *restricts* female experiences by discouraging exploration and stressing propriety (Block, 1983). The result is that both boys and girls acquire a sense of their relative social positions. When third graders were asked what they wanted to be when they grow up, boys typically identified such occupations as football player, spy, firefighter, and motorcycle racer. Girls' responses included mother, teacher, and "plain old woman" (R. Best, 1983).

Consequently, boys have higher expectations and higher self-esteem than girls, a gap that widens with each passing year in the school system. Around the ages of 8 and 9, about two thirds of both boys and girls report feeling confident and positive about themselves. By high school, however, the percentage drops to 29% for young women (Freiberg, 1991). As girls make the transformation from childhood to adolescence, they are faced with a conflict between the way they see themselves and the way others, particularly teachers, see them (Gilligan, 1990).

Similar gender-typed patterns continue through high school. Teenage boys derive their prestige almost exclusively from athletics. They are also likely to be encouraged by counselors and teachers to formulate ambitious career goals.

Prestige and popularity for teenage girls is more likely to come from their physical appearance and from having a boyfriend (Lott, 1987). As you might expect, girls' career aspirations tend to be lower than those of their male classmates (Bridges, 1988) despite girls' academic achievement, which is usually higher than that of boys.

College isn't much different. Most notably, the choice of major appears to be linked to gender. According to the National Center for Education Statistics, women dominate majors such as Art History, Education, Home Economics, Library Science, Nursing, and Social Work. Typically men's majors are Engineering, Military Science, Physics, Geology, Economics, Business, and Chemistry (Renzetti & Curran, 1989). College professors, like their elementary school counterparts, may treat men and women differently in the classroom as well. Disparaging comments about women, the use of sex-stereotyped examples, and the use of the generic "he" are some examples (R. M. Hall & Sandler, 1985).

Even as more and more colleges move to coed living arrangements, gender stereotypes persist. Anthropologist Michael Moffatt (1989) spent several years living among college students in a Rutgers University coed dorm. He concluded that the price women have had to pay for being treated as near-equals in this setting is that they must act more like men in order to be accepted. Here, too, the male standard of behavior predominates.

Conclusion

Becoming human is a complex, *social* process. Those intimate characteristics we hold so dear—our-self concept, our gender, and our racial and ethnic identity—are merely reflections of larger cultural attitudes, values, and expectations. Yet we are not perfect reflections. With all the powerful socializing institutions that pull our developmental strings, we continue to be and will always be individuals.

Sometimes we ignore our generalized others and strike out on our own with complete disregard for community standards and attitudes. Sometimes we form self-concepts that contradict information received from significant others. Sometimes we willingly violate the expectations associated with our gender or our race. Societal influence can only go so far in explaining how we become who we are. The rest—that which makes us truly unique—remains a mystery.

CHAPTER HIGHLIGHTS

■ Socialization is the process by which individuals learn their culture and learn to live according to the norms of that particular society. It is how we learn to perceive our world, gain a sense of our own racial and ethnic identity, and interact appropriately with others. It also tells us what it means to be a man or a woman, and what we should and should not do across a range of situations.

■ Socialization occurs within the context of several social institutions—schools, the media, and the family.

■ Socialization is not just a process that occurs during childhood. Adults must be resocialized into a new galaxy of norms, values, and expectations each time they leave or abandon old roles and enter new ones.

■ One of the most important outcomes of socialization for an individual is the development of a sense of self. The ability to modify our behavior to meet the expectations of other people and society in general rests on the development of the self.

■ Humans are not born with a self. To acquire a self, children must learn to recognize themselves as unique physical objects, master language, learn to take the role of others, and, in effect, see themselves from another's perspective.

■ We learn gender through socialization. Whereas sex refers to biological characteristics, gender designates the psychological, social, and cultural aspects of maleness and femaleness.

YOUR TURN

This chapter has focused on the construction of self and gender. Many social institutions assist in the process of socialization in ways that are sometimes not immediately apparent.

To see firsthand how this sort of socialization works, visit a local shopping mall. Most malls today have a children's clothing store. If yours doesn't, go to one of the large department stores and find the children's clothing section. Start with the infant clothes. Note the differences in the style, color, and texture of boys' clothes versus girls' clothes. Collect the same information regarding clothes for toddlers, preschool, and school-age children.

After collecting your "data," try to interpret the differences you noticed. Why do they exist? What do these differences say about the kinds of activities in which boys and girls are expected and encouraged to engage? For instance, whose clothes are "dainty"? Whose are "rugged"? How do these clothing differences reinforce our cultural conceptions of masculinity and femininity?

The next stop on your sociological shopping trip is the toy store. See if you can tell when you've entered the "boy" section or the "girl" section. How did you know? How did the toys differ? Note the differences in color, sound, and type of material used.

What sorts of interactions with other children do the toys encourage? Competition? Cooperation? Which sex's toys are designed for active play? Which encourage passive play? For what sorts of adult roles do the toys prepare children?

Finally, find a bookstore that has a children's book section. Are there "boy" books and "girl" books? How can you tell? What are the differences in the sorts of characters and plots that are portrayed?

Use your findings to discuss the role that consumer products play in socializing people into "appropriate" gender roles. Why is there so much sex-typing in these products? Are manufacturers simply responding to market demands (i.e., they make sex specific products because that's what people want), or do they have a role in creating those demands?

Multiracial Families

Photographs by Gigi Kaeser
Interview text by Peggy Gillespie

In a world of racial and ethnic chauvinism, multiracial families provide convincing evidence that races can co-exist not only in the same neighborhood but in the same home. Whether formed through marriage or by adoption, these families have become a common sight in America.

—Peggy Gillespie

With more and more children living in multiracial families, racial identity is fast becoming one of the most urgent and controversial issues facing families, schools, and the culture at large today. Traditional conceptions about what it means to be "black" or "white" or "Japanese" no longer apply as the boundaries between racial groups blur.

Peggy Gillespie, a member of a multiracial family herself, and Gigi Kaeser, a professional photographer, interviewed and took pictures of over 30 multiracial families as they investigated their unique challenges and concerns. The portraits and quotes you see here speak volumes about the changing but still troublesome role of race and racial identity in American society.

Penny Rhodes, Irv Rhodes, Caelah (23), and Lauren (16). (Caelah is Penny's daughter from her first marriage).

Irv *(Business Consultant)*: I grew up in a tiny town in Pennsylvania that was racially mixed, so I had friends who were black and white. . . . All the fathers were coalminers. It's harder to be a racist when everyone's poor and struggling together.

Penny *(Director of Human Resources)*: When you marry someone black, you cease to be the regular "white person" you were before. You become a witness to institutional racism.

Lauren *(student)*: It was strange when kids in kindergarten would ask me, "How come your father is black and your mother is white?" It shocked me at first. I had no clue that there was actually a big problem with it because my parents didn't tell me that it was unusual. . . . I had problems with my identity for awhile. When testing came in third grade, I checked the category "Black." Then in sixth grade, I told all the biracial kids to check the box marked "Other," because we weren't black and we weren't white.

Anne Nwokoye, Nkiruka Ramona (21), Ekene Annie Laurie (15), Ifeoma Justina (18)

Anne *(Office Manager of Everywoman's Center)*: When I was going to get married, my future husband wrote a letter to my mother . . . [and] told her he was a doctoral student and he laid out all his plans for what he was going to do in his life, and that he wanted me to be by his side. . . . [My] mother said, ". . . [His letter] was very nice but he . . . didn't say anything about being black." And I said, "Well, Nigerians wouldn't think of saying that." To Nigerians, race just isn't such a big issue.

After my husband and I separated in Nigeria, I returned to the United States with our daughters.... We are well-connected in the Nigerian community and the people in it treat us like family.

Ifeoma *(college student)*: It has been so hard to try and fit in with black Americans when you're not black American. I'm Nigerian and American, and there's such a cultural difference between a West African and a black American. . . . I'm definitely judged more harshly by black people than I am by white people. If it's known that you're mixed, you can be written off as not being dedicated to helping the black community — as not really being black.

Ravi Khanna, Lisa Khanna, Anjali (7), Shyam (5), Asha Devi (2 months)

Ravi *(Executive Director, Peace Development Fund):* I went to a Christian boarding school with lots of Westerners and exposures to many languages and cultures... I think I would have had difficulty marrying an Indian woman because ... it would have been very hard to adjust to a traditional Indian family, with arranged marriages and all that.... I see a lot of advantages to being in a multiracial family.... My hope is that the world will move towards more blending of cultures and races.

Norma Akamatsu, Ron Gatsik, Haru Akamatsu, Sarah (7)

Norma *(Social Worker/Psychotherapist)*: Ron [her Jewish husband] and I use the word "Jewpanese" to describe our family…. We haven't experienced much overt racism as a family. Before Sarah was born, at times when Ron and I would go to Stop and Shop, the cashiers would look at me and at Ron and then look at all of our stuff on the conveyor belt and ask, "Is this all together?"… I didn't see it as prejudice — it was just unfamiliarity.

Ron *(Psychiatrist)*: I grew up in a suburban New Jersey community across the Hudson from Manhattan, with significant black, Jewish, and other ethnic populations. But it wasn't until I left home, went off to college, and really got to know people from different places, backgrounds, and cultures that I began to change. I think the Civil Rights movement, the war in Vietnam, and the political work I was doing in these domains opened me up to the possibility of marrying outside of Judaism. Having fallen "head over heels" in love, hooking up with Norma was also a concrete manifestation of my politics, and a way of saying, "The world needs to change, and I need to change."

Norma and I celebrate Hanukkah and Christmas, meditate from time to time in the Tibetan Buddhist and Indian spiritual traditions, and try to foster an appreciation of "generic spirituality."

Prakash Laufer, Jody Wright, Olisa (13), Liina (8), Emily (2), Mahajoy (10)

Jody *(Co-Owner of Motherwear Catalog):* I considered adopting a child of a different race right from the beginning…. [Olisa's] birthmom is Filipino and her birth father is from Zimbabwe. Mahajoy's mother is also Filipino and her father is from Liberia. Emily is biracial too, but both her birthparents are American…. Liina, our biological daughter, asked me, "What does biracial mean?" I explained it to her and asked her how she felt about having sisters who were black. She said, "I don't know." It's just obvious to her. It's just the way the family is.

Prakash *(Co-Owner of Motherwear Catalog):* The best part of being a multiracial family is setting an example that it's a natural thing. . . . Diversity is much easier to talk about when people can see it in real families like ours.

Olisa: I hate the question, "What is it like to be in a multiracial family?" It's like being asked how I feel about living on Planet Earth when I've never lived anywhere else.

Tim Blake, Rob Ranney

Tim *(Early Childhood Educator)*: Someone once posed the question, "Is it easier being a gay couple or an interracial couple?" And we both agreed. It's much easier being a gay couple.

Rob *(Store Manager)*: Tim and I have been together for almost ten years. . . . For me, I've learned so much from getting involved with someone from a minority American culture. Tim hasn't learned an awful lot from me... there's no surprises there! But I've had a lot to learn about his history, language, culture, music, foods.... You can hide being gay almost anytime you need to by just taking your hands apart. Race is on your face. All the time.

CHAPTER 6

Building Image

Managing Individual and Institutional Identities

- *Forming Impressions of Others*
- *Impression Management: Actors on a Social Stage*
- *Social Structure and Impression Management*
- *Impression Mismanagement: Spoiled Identities*
- *Conclusion*
- *Chapter Highlights*
- *Your Turn*
- *VISUAL ESSAY A Sociological View of Bodies*

On Christmas Day, 1981, I met my soon-to-be wife's family for the first time. Entering this group of important strangers, I knew I had to be on my best behavior and try to say and do all the right things. I wanted to make sure the impression they formed of me was that of a likable fellow who would make a fine addition to the family.

As family members busily opened their presents, I noticed the wide and gleeful eyes of my wife's 14-year-old sister as she unwrapped what was to her a very special gift: her very own basketball. Being the youngest in a family of eight kids, she didn't have much she could call her own, so this was a significant moment for her. She had finally broken away from a life filled with hand-me-downs and communal equipment. She hugged that ball as if it were a puppy.

I saw my chance to make the perfect first impression. *I'm not a bad basketball player*, I thought to myself. *I'll take her outside to the basketball hoop in the driveway, impress her with my shooting skills, become her idol, and win family approval.* "Hey, Mary," I said, "let's go out and shoot some hoops." After we stepped outside I grabbed the new ball from her. "Look at this," I said, as I flung it toward the basket from about 40 feet away! We both watched as the ball arced gracefully toward its destination, and for a brief moment I actually thought it was going to go in. But that was not to be.

As if guided by the taunting hand of fate, the ball struck an exposed bolt that protruded from the base of the supporting pole of the hoop. There was a sickeningly loud *pop*, followed by a hissing sound as the ball fluttered to the ground like a deflated balloon. It sat there lifeless, never having experienced the joy of "swishing" through a net. For that matter, it never even bounced on the ground in its short-lived inflated state.

For a few seconds we both stood numb and motionless. Then I turned to apologize to the 14-year-old girl whose once cheerful eyes now harbored the kind of hate and resentment usually reserved for ax murderers. In a flash she burst into tears and ran into the house, shrieking, "THAT GUY popped my ball!" It was hardly the heroic identity I was striving for. As the angry mob poured into the backyard to stare at the villainous and still somewhat unknown perpetrator, I became painfully aware of the fragile nature of the self-images we try to project to others.

We all have been in situations—a first date, a job interview, meeting a girlfriend or boyfriend's family for the first time—in which we are compelled to "make a good impression." We want to present a favorable image of ourselves so that others will make positive judgments of us. This phenomenon, referred to as **impression management**, is not only an important and universal aspect of our personal lives, but a key element of social structure as well.

In this chapter I examine the social creation of images. How do we form impressions of others? What do we do to control the impressions others form of us? I also discuss broader sociological applications of the principles of impression management. What are the institutional motivations behind individual impression management? How do groups and organizations present and manage collective impressions? How is impression management linked to social order? Finally, what happens when impression management fails and images are spoiled as mine was in the above story?

Forming Impressions of Others

As discussed in chapter 5, an important acquisition in the development of self is the ability to role-take—to look at yourself through the eyes of another person. Only when we acquire this ability can we control our behavior to meet the expectations of others. In order to take someone else's role, we must categorize and define that person based on the information available to us. When we first meet someone, particularly someone we don't know very well, we form an immediate impression based on observable cues (Pryor & Ostrom, 1981). These cues consist of social group characteristics (age, race, sex), physical attributes, and verbal and nonverbal expressions.

Social Group Membership

Age, sex, race, and, to a certain degree, ethnicity can usually be determined by looking at a person's physical features. Religion and social class are less obvious.

These attributes help us form an initial assessment of the identities of other people. As you saw in the previous chapter, our socialization experiences provide us with a sense of the cultural significance of being male or female, young or old, black or white, upper class or working class, and so on. Moreover, we have learned to expect certain things from certain types of people. For instance, if *all* you know about a person is that she's female, you're likely to assume that she's probably compassionate, emotional, and nurturant. Likewise, if *all* you know about a person is that he or she is 85 years old, you might predict that this person has low energy, poor memory, and conservative political attitudes. Such predictions are rarely completely accurate. Nevertheless, we begin social interactions with these culturally defined conceptions of how people from certain social groups are likely to act, what their tastes and preferences might be, and even what values they are likely to hold.

This information provides the initial backdrop to all social encounters between people who have little if any prior knowledge of one another. It is so pervasive and so quickly processed that we usually notice it only when it *isn't* there. Imagine how difficult it would be to form a friendship or even carry on a conversation if you didn't know whether you were dealing with someone of the same or opposite sex.

From a person's readily observable social characteristics, we form a preliminary judgment of that individual as a representative of a group about whom we have already formed certain behavioral expectations. These expectations need not be positive or negative. When this information is the only thing we know about an individual, we structure our impressions around it.

Looking at Individual Attributes

Impressions based on social group membership are not final. We must be prepared to confirm or modify our impressions based on additional information unique to that particular person (Berndt & Heller, 1986). To do this, we assess other characteristics that are easily perceivable: physical appearance, clothing, and so on.

Physical Appearance

A quick glance at the latest magazine or television advertisements attests to the enormous importance of physical appearance in American society. Everywhere we turn, it seems, we are encouraged to believe that if our skin isn't free of blemishes, if we are too short, if we are over- or underweight, if our hair isn't stylish, if our clothes don't reflect the latest fashion trend, we have fallen short of the important cultural standard of attractiveness. We say that beauty is only skin deep, but do we really mean it? Although we readily acknowledge that using a person's physical attractiveness to form an impression is shallow and unfair, we do it anyway.

Research shows that physical appearance dramatically affects our perceptions and judgments of others. In our culture, being physically attractive often indicates the presence of other positive characteristics. Attractive men are perceived to be more masculine and attractive women more feminine than their unattractive counterparts (Gillen, 1981). We assume that physically attractive people possess other desirable traits like sensitivity, kindness, strength, and sexual responsiveness (Dion, Berscheid, & Walster, 1972). The impressions adults form of young children are heavily influenced by the child's physical attractiveness (Clifford & Walster, 1973; Dion, 1972). Even research on juries suggests that attractive people are treated better (e.g., receive shorter jail sentences) than unattractive people (Stewart, 1980).

Physical appearance has considerable impact on our own feelings of self-worth as well. According to one study, 85% of women and 72% of men are dissatisfied with at least one aspect of their looks (cited in Goleman, 1991a). Such dissatisfaction can have long-lasting effects. People who don't like the way they look report higher levels of overall unhappiness than people who are satisfied with their appearance (Berscheid & Walster, 1974).

So important is the ideal of physical attractiveness that a psychiatric diagnosis called *body dysmorphic disorder* has become more common over the last 10 years (Goleman, 1991a). Psychiatrists estimate that between 2 and 10% of the population have this "disorder." These individuals are so self-conscious about their looks that their lives are constricted in some significant way, from feeling inhibited during lovemaking to becoming homebound or suicidal.

Assessments of our own physical attractiveness cannot be separated from other societal factors such as the cultural importance of gender. In our society physical appearance is a more crucial determinant of self-worth for women than it is for men. It also plays a significant role in defining cultural ideals of femininity. Throughout history different parts of the female anatomy have been used to symbolize a woman's femininity and sexuality. Consider a young woman's breast development: "Parents and relatives mark their appearance as a landmark event, schoolmates take notice, girlfriends compare, boys zero in; later a husband, a lover, a baby expect a proprietary share. No other part of the human anatomy has such semipublic, intensely private status" (Brownmiller, 1984, pp. 40-41).

Given the amount of social attention, it is not surprising that many women are self-conscious about their breasts. It's estimated that at least 150,000 women a year in the United States undergo breast implant surgery (S. M. Wolfe, 1991). Although some of these procedures are performed for medical reasons, the vast majority—upward of 80%—are performed for cosmetic reasons. In the early 1990s, breast implants ranked second only to liposuction (a procedure that siphons away body fat) as the most popular form of cosmetic surgery (L. Williams, 1992a).

But gender differences in the importance of physical appearance are not limited just to individual parts of the anatomy. The cultural norms used to evaluate overall female beauty continue to be so narrow and unrealistic that many women have a sense of perpetual deficiency as a result (Schur, 1984). Women have more money, political clout, and legal recognition today than ever before, but they are continuously encouraged to define themselves almost exclusively in terms of their physical appearance. At the individual level such an emphasis devalues a person's other attributes and accomplishments; at the institutional level it feeds the nation's economy by sustaining several multibillion-dollar industries, including advertising, fashion, and cosmetics (Schur, 1984).

Micro-Macro Connection
Obesity

The negative effects of a lack of physical attractiveness on impression formation are perhaps felt most strongly by those whose body size does not meet cultural standards of acceptability. The phenomenal growth and success of the diet "industry"—low-calorie foods, dieting books, weight-loss organizations, and so forth—provides clear evidence of the obsession with weight in this country. Those who are noticeably overweight tend to be evaluated quite negatively (Allon, 1982; English, 1991).

Fatness carries tremendous symbolic meaning in this society and deeply affects a person's sense of identity and the impressions formed by others. An overweight person may be judged by others as lacking in willpower, self-indulgent, personally offensive, and even morally and socially unfit (Millman, 1980). The following story appeared several years ago in newspapers across the country:

> UPI reports that majorette Peggy Ward will be barred from Friday's football game. The reason? Ms. Ward is 1½ pounds overweight. She is 5 foot 4 and 127½ pounds. This weight exceeds the guidelines established by the band director. The school superintendent supports the band director, but Ms. Ward is fighting back by fasting to make the limit in time for the game. But the event has been psychologically costly for the majorette. "The pressure and intense publicity surrounding the controversy apparently became too much at one point for Ms. Ward, who telephoned her mother . . . in tears and asked to be taken home from school." (cited in E. E. Jones et al., 1984, p. 1)

Obesity can even affect economic opportunities. In high-visibility occupations such as modeling, public relations, and sales, overweight people often are regarded as unemployable based on the belief that they will project a negative image of the company. In one California city, hiring policies once specified that teachers could not be more than 25% overweight (Laslett & Warren, 1987).

While our society's distaste for obesity applies to everyone, it is again felt particularly strongly by women. Cultural standards have idealized increasingly thinner female bodies since the 1920s (Freedman, 1986). In one study 70% of college women felt they were overweight, although less than 40% actually were (T. M. Miller, Coffman, & Linke, 1980). Furthermore, women are becoming weight conscious at increasingly younger ages. A 1987 survey of 500 elementary school children found that more than half the girls thought they were too fat, even though only 15% were actually heavier than the norm (Goleman, 1991a).

These are not merely the trivial misperceptions of individual women. Unnecessary concern over weight shows how powerful cultural beliefs are in the formation of self-concepts. At best, the failure to meet broad cultural standards of thinness can generate antagonism toward one's own body and lowered self-esteem. At worst, it can lead to life-threatening eating disorders (Chernin, 1981). And, of course, female weight concern has macro-level implications because of the role it plays in supporting the many large businesses that sell weight-loss products and programs.

Clothing and Body Adornment

The way people dress and decorate their bodies also provides information important in forming impressions. It communicates feelings, beliefs, and group identity to others. We make assessments of ethnicity, social class, age, cultural tastes, morality, and political attitudes on the basis of people's clothes, jewelry, hairstyles, and so on. A common T-shirt can

> speak over the din of a concert, a party, or a sport event. It can carry a concise and lucid message in ways body and behavior cannot. . . . The tee shirt is the modern equivalent of the poster in prerevolutionary France, wall graffiti in Latin America, or the flaming cross in antebellum South. . . . The wearing of brand names, of exotic place names, of expensive tee shirts . . . [says] to all who will look that the wearer is well located in the class system. (Young, 1993, pp. 147-148)

The emphasis on clothing and body adornments can be found everywhere. Business people are acutely aware of and usually conform to a rigid corporate dress code. The staffs of most high profile politicians now include fashion consultants who advise them about the right clothes or haircut for particular occasions. And, as you are well aware, appropriate fashion styles make up a significant element of the student culture on most college campuses (Moffatt, 1989). In short, Americans tell one another who they are and what they stand for by what they wear.

Clothing and body adornment are important in understanding the nature of impression formation because, unlike age, race, gender, and, to a certain extent, physical attractiveness, they can be *purposely* managed and manipulated to influence the impressions others form of us. Hence people can use their mode of dress to convey to others the impression that they have the status to be worthy of respect or, at the very least, attention (Lauer & Handel, 1977). Rappers and punk rockers use clothing and hairstyle as an expression of social rebellion. Children often signal their entry into the world of adolescence by wearing the clothing of their peers and refusing to wear the clothing chosen by their parents (G. P. Stone, 1981).

Verbal and Nonverbal Expressions

Another important piece of information we use in forming impressions of others is what people express to us verbally or nonverbally. Through talk, movement, posture, and gestures people provide cues about their values, attitudes, sentiments, personality, and past history (G. P. Stone, 1981). Most of us are quite proficient at "reading" even the subtlest nonverbal messages. We learn early on that a raised eyebrow, a nod of the head, or a slight hand gesture can mean something in a social encounter. So important is this ability that a deficiency in it is considered by some psychologists to be a learning disability akin to severe reading problems (Goleman, 1989).

As we obtain information from others in order to form impressions, we also selectively communicate information about ourselves to them. This is done through physical expressions such as a shaky voice, flushed face, and trembling hands, which are difficult to control, or through words, which can be purposely used to express certain emotions, desires, attributes, or attitudes.

We can strategically furnish or conceal information. On a first date, you might hide the fact that this is the first date you've had in 2 years. On the same date, however, you may casually drop a line about your family's vacation home in Aspen. In both cases you've attempted to communicate information that will maximize your perceived desirability in this person's eyes. People form impressions of others and *manage* impressions of themselves at the same time. The ability to manage impressions is the defining feature of human interaction.

Impression Management: Actors on a Social Stage

Social encounters flow more smoothly when people are able to achieve some sort of agreement in defining the situation at hand. What also needs to be negotiated, however, are the identities of the people involved. Individuals must decide what sort of self-image they want to present and what sort of image they will allow the other person to claim in a social encounter. Erving Goffman (1959a), the sociologist most responsible for the scholarly examination of impression management, portrays everyday life as a series of social interactions in which a person is motivated to "sell" a particular image to others. Various people occupy various identities: student, sibling, child, employee, wealthy person, trusted friend, future lawyer. As a general rule, the more important an identity is to an individual's overall self-concept, the more time he or she will spend on activities expressing that identity (McCall & Simmons, 1978). For instance, if you aspire to be a marriage counselor, you may spend a great deal of time listening to people's problems or commenting on people's relationships.

The primary goal of impression management is to project a particular identity that will increase the likelihood of obtaining favorable outcomes from others in particular social situations (E. E. Jones & Pittman, 1982; Stryker, 1980). This sometimes requires advertising, exaggerating, or fabricating your positive qualities and concealing behaviors or attributes that you believe others will find unappealing.

Goffman argues that impression management is not used just to present false or inflated images of ourselves. Many attributes we possess are not immediately apparent to others or may be misinterpreted. Imagine yourself taking the final exam in your sociology course. You look up from your paper and make brief eye contact with the instructor. Suddenly you become acutely aware that you are being watched. You are not cheating, but you think the instructor may interpret your wandering eyes as an indication of cheating. What do you do? Chances are you will consciously overemphasize your noncheating behavior by *acting* as though you're in deep thought or by glancing at the clock, in order to maintain your "law-abiding" image.

Obtaining favorable outcomes through impression management is usually associated with social approval—that is, being respected and liked by others. However, different circumstances may require projecting different identities (E. E. Jones & Pittman, 1982). Perhaps you've been in situations where you tried to appear helpless in order to get someone else to do a task you really didn't want to do, or maybe you tried to be as powerful and fearsome as you could to intimidate someone into doing something. Perhaps you "played dumb" to avoid challenging the status of a superior (Gove, Hughes, & Geerkin, 1980). As social beings we have the ability to tailor our images to fit the requirements of a particular situation.

Normative Constraints on Impression Management

Individual impression management is linked to social structure by a set of powerful but unspoken cultural norms (Crittenden & Wiley, 1985). Self-promotion may help us present ourselves in the most favorable light, but too much self-promotion can have decidedly negative consequences. The brazen self-promoter or braggart often is perceived as a socially inept individual with suspicious motives. We are culturally obligated to inject *some* modesty into the statements we make about ourselves. Under certain conditions, such as performing an act of extreme bravery, an individual's interests might best be served by *not* accepting personal credit for positive outcomes (Bradley, 1978).

Cultural norms define what attributes are valued. In a culture that values mental prowess over physical agility, impression management strategies are likely to demonstrate intelligence rather than strength. These norms cannot be separated from broader socioeconomic factors. In a capitalist society like ours, workers must be careful to communicate supportive attitudes and respectful demeanor to their superiors or risk losing their jobs (Welsh, 1984). The importance we attach to weekends, holidays, vacations, and all those times when we can "act naturally" illustrates the extent to which the economic structure constrains the rest of our lives.

Altercasting

In addition to managing our own impressions, we must also decide what sort of identity we will allow others to claim. Sometimes we find ourselves in situations where it is to our advantage to place the other person in a particular identity. Using verbal strategies to impose a certain image on others is called **altercasting** (Weinstein & Deutschberger, 1963).

We cast others into roles that are to our advantage. The applied identity then forces people to act "voluntarily" in ways that are consistent with our interests. Saying "After all the things I've done for you, the least you could do is let me borrow your car," immediately places on the recipient of the comment the identity of "obligated friend" and compels him or her to reciprocate a favor. Similarly, when a teacher tells a student, "I know you can do better," the student is compelled to live up to an identity of competence.

The use of altercasting is demonstrated in a study by sociologist Philip Blumstein (1975) on social interaction in a dating situation. Women in the study were instructed to claim a "healthily assertive" identity by altercasting their dates into a submissive role. They would say things like, "I've been dating this one guy, but we broke up because he would never let me have any say about what we do. You wouldn't treat me that way, would you?" Or, "I like guys who don't come on like they own me, but let me take some initiative." While some of the men rejected the attempts, most allowed their dates to claim the assertive identity by presenting themselves in a way that was consistent with the identity into which they had been cast (e.g., "Sorry I've been so pushy. Whatever you say goes").

This research has obvious implications for interpersonal power relations and the means by which people can manipulate the behavior of others. It also sheds light on the strength of particular identities that make up one's self-concept. Most of the men who resisted the altercasting attempts had indicated earlier in the study that dominance was an important aspect of their own self-concept. The men who rated dominance as unimportant were more likely to accept the submissive identity. Blumstein concluded that we tend to reject altercasting attempts that threaten an identity that is central to our overall self-concept.

Dramaturgy: Social Interaction as Theater

"All the world's a stage, and all the men and women merely players. They have their exits and their entrances, and one man in his time plays many parts," wrote William Shakespeare in *As You Like It*. The process of impression management can be examined as a series of calculated "performances." Goffman (1959a) argues that people in everyday life are like actors on a stage. The study of social interaction as theater is called **dramaturgy.** The "audience" consists of people who observe the behavior of others, the "roles" are the images people are trying to project, and the "script" consists of our communications with others. The goal is to enact a performance that is believable to a particular audience and that allows us to achieve the goals we desire. Every aspect of social life can be examined dramaturgically, from the ritualized greetings of strangers to the everyday dynamics of our family, school, and work lives.

Front Stage and Back Stage

A key structural element of dramaturgy is the distinction between front stage and back stage. In the theater, front stage is where the performance takes place. In contrast, back stage is where makeup is removed, lines are rehearsed, performances are rehashed, and people are able to fall "out of character."

In social interaction, **front stage** is where people maintain the appropriate appearance as they interact with others. In a restaurant, front stage is the dining room where the customers (the audience) are present. Here the servers (the actors) are expected to present themselves as upbeat, happy, competent, and courteous. **Back stage**, however, is the region where people can knowingly violate their impression management performances. In the restaurant back stage is the kitchen area where the once courteous servers now shout, shove dishes, and even complain about or make fun of the customers.

The barrier between front and back stage is crucial to successful impression management because it blocks the audience from seeing behavior that would ruin the performance. During a therapy session (front stage), psychiatrists usually appear extremely interested in everything their patients say and show considerable sympathy for their problems. At a dinner party with colleagues or at home with family (back stage), however, they may express total boredom and disdain for the patients' disclosures. If patients were to see such back-stage behavior, not only would the performance be disrupted, but the psychiatrist's professional credibility and reputation would suffer as well. One study found that beneath their mask of neutrality, many psychiatrists report harboring strong and professionally inappropriate feelings, including hatred, fear, anger, and sexual arousal, toward their patients (Goleman, 1993).

Props

Successful impression management also depends on the control of identity objects, called *props* in the environment. In the theater, props must be handled deftly for an effective performance. A gun that doesn't go off when it's supposed to or a chair that collapses can destroy an entire play. The same is true in social interaction. For instance, you might make sure your school books are in clear view and beer bottles disposed of as you prepare for an upcoming visit from your parents. Similarly, you may spend a great deal of time setting a romantic mood for a dinner date in your apartment—the right music, the right lighting, pictures of former lovers hidden from view, and so on. Clearly, the mishandling of these props can severely disrupt the performance and, ultimately, the impression you wished to convey.

Social Structure and Impression Management

Up to this point I've described dramaturgy and impression management from the point of view of individual people driven by a personal desire to present themselves in the most favorable light possible. But people do not exist in a social vacuum. The impressions people manage are also motivated by the social groups, organizations, and institutions to which they belong.

The Effect of Social Groups and Institutions on Impression Management

A person's social group identity influences immediate expectations and impressions. If expectations can be self-fulfilling, then social group membership may also influence the sorts of images people with particular attributes *present* in social interaction.

Gender

Expectations based on gender are so powerful that they can define people's behavior and determine the impressions they manage. If people want to be judged positively by others, they may be forced to present themselves in ways that are consistent with the stereotypical characteristics believed to be appropriate for their gender (Crittenden, 1991; Spence, Deaux, & Helmreich, 1985). Women are more likely to present images of themselves as weak or dependent, whereas men are more likely to project power and competence (Gruber & White, 1986; Instone, Major, & Bunker, 1983; P. Johnson, 1976). The following situation pairs a stereotypical female with a stereotypical male:

> She cannot change a tire, understand algebra, read a legal document, carry a suitcase, or order wine. Her classic male counterpart, of course, rushes in to fill the breach. His vanity is touched by the indispensability of his contributions to her survival in the world. [She] influences the male to expend

energy on her behalf; to do things for her that she would like to have done. She accomplishes this at the small cost of being considered totally incompetent by her vain and dedicated [partner]. (E. E. Jones & Pittman, 1982, p. 248)

Such images, of course, depend on the perceived expectations of others. In a study by von Baeyer, Sherk, and Zanna (1981), female subjects played the role of job applicants who were to be interviewed by a male "employer" who they thought held either traditional or nontraditional views of women. The women who believed their interviewer held traditional views of women were much more likely to present themselves in a stereotypically feminine way. They wore more makeup and clothing accessories, talked less, made less eye contact, and gave more traditional answers to questions about marriage and children than the women who saw their interviewers as nontraditional. Another study found that men were likely to present themselves in a strong, independent, stereotypically masculine way in order to conform to what they thought were the expectations of others in the study (Eagly, Wood, & Fishbaugh, 1981).

From a conflict perspective, these impression management tactics are likely to be influenced by a social structure in which men and women have traditionally been assigned different positions of power (Howard, Blumstein, & Schwartz, 1986). Hence, as women gain more power and as gender stereotypes lose their legitimacy, the images people present of themselves in social situations might also change.

Race and Ethnicity

Like gender, people of racial or ethnic minorities are often forced to present self-images that are consistent with the expectations or stereotypes of others (Lyman & Douglass, 1973). In a society where race is a primary source of inequality, living up (or down) to such expectations may be one of the few means by which people can participate actively in public life while retaining their own cultural identity. Individuals from oppressed groups may appear to fit common racial or ethnic stereotypes in public (front stage), but an analysis of private (back stage) behavior often indicates a keen awareness of the roles they have been forced to play and suggests that impression management is an important survival tactic.

Sociologist Reyes Ramos (1990) describes the strategies, or *movidas*, that Mexican Americans use in dealing with the dominant white culture in their daily lives. He tells of an encounter he observed between an elementary school principal and the Mexican-American father of a fourth-grade boy who had allegedly broken a school window. The father appeared extremely nervous and stupid. He spoke in broken English and acted as though he didn't understand the situation very well. Ramos had seen this man interact competently and speak perfect English in other situations. When he asked why he had presented himself in such a way, the father replied:

> Oh, I was pulling a *movida*. I came on like the dumb Mexican, all lost and confused. You know how that guy thinks of us most of the time. Besides, had I come on straight, he might have held me responsible for the broken window Freddy broke. I am not about to pay for a window my boy broke by accident. (p. 94)

Social Class

Social class can also influence impression management. For instance, some working-class youths, frustrated by their lack of access to the middle-class world and their inability to meet the requirements of "respectability" as defined by the dominant culture, may present themselves as malicious or dangerous in order to gain attention or achieve status and respect within the context of their group (Campbell, 1987; A. K. Cohen, 1955).

Conversely, those who occupy the dominant classes of American society receive the most attention (Derber, 1979). People cater to them in restaurants, shops, and other public settings. In addition to monopolizing the formal attention-getting roles in politics and in the workplace, they are also advantaged in claiming attention in ordinary interaction. Attention can be "purchased" through impression management. By displaying the symbolic props of material success—large homes, tasteful furnishings, luxury cars, expensive clothes—upper-class individuals can attract the attention of others and thereby reinforce their own sense of worth and status.

In the world of work, occupational status is often exploited as a means of getting attention. Bank presidents and chief executive officers need not disclose their high status because it is already known to people with whom they interact regularly. Their occupational status is a permanently recognized "badge of ability" (Derber, 1979, p. 83). Other people, however, must consciously advertise their occupation to receive the attention to which they feel they are entitled. For example, physicians may wear beepers and white coats outside their work environment to communicate their high-status identity to others. For business executives or other professionals, this information surfaces in conversation through blatant or subtle verbal disclosures.

Because of the primacy of work in American society, those who have no way of exhibiting an occupational badge or whose occupation is seen as inferior find their social worth constantly in question, particularly in interactions with high-status others. They must resort to alternative strategies, like talking constantly or shifting the conversation to a topic about which they have some expertise, simply to prevent others from withdrawing attention and to reduce the fear that they might be completely disregarded (Trudgill, 1972).

Institutions

Within certain institutional contexts, elements of impression management are sometimes determined by larger structural needs. Politicians, for instance, must be prepared to use impression management to get a certain result on an opinion poll or a vote at the next election. They must present an image that will appeal to the public, even if it's not an image they particularly like.

Political impression management continues past election day. The president, with the help or hindrance of the media, must play simultaneously to an external and internal audience (P. Hall, 1990). The external audience is composed of foreign allies and adversaries who must be convinced of his authority and his ability to fulfill commitments. The internal audience is the voting public, whom he must impress through the portrayal of "presidential character": good health, appropriate holidays and recreation, a stable home and family life, and so forth.

If you have ever seen a political party's national convention, you have witnessed the careful and strategic staging of an event designed to manage the image of a particular candidate. Gala political occasions like these are ideologically oriented toward the promise of a prosperous culture and a better society (Mayo, 1990). If the attention of the audience depended solely on the speeches of the politicians, conventions would be a dismal failure. The props must be cleverly and meticulously controlled. The design of the political scene is an attempt to create an unreal environment, emphasizing massiveness, ornateness, and formality (Mayo, 1990). Music, balloons, lighting, colors, even individual delegates are all transformed into stage props that must be tactically crafted to project to the nation images of a candidate and his party that are patriotic, unified, organized, and effective, even when they aren't.

Impression management plays a prominent role in the socialization process found within many occupations as well (Hochschild, 1983). If you've ever worked as a salesperson, you know the economic importance of presenting yourself as knowledgeable, trustworthy, and, above all, honest. Medical school students must learn how to manage their emotions in front of patients and present the image of a "competent physician." New teachers must learn what images are most effective in getting students to comply. Here's how one teacher described the importance of impression management:

> You can't ever let them get the upper hand on you or you're through. So I start out tough. The first day I get a new class in, I let them know who's boss. . . . You've got to start off tough, then you can ease up as you go along. If you start out easy-going, when you try to be tough, they'll just look at you and laugh. (Goffman, 1959a, p. 12)

Collective Impression Management

Successful impression management is not a concern with just one individual at a time. Images of *sets* of individuals must also be managed. We often find ourselves in situations that require a "couple" image, a "group" image, or an "organizational" image of some sort. These impressions are more complex than individual ones and often require the help and cooperation of others in preparing and maintaining the desired impression.

Teamwork

Goffman uses the term **performance team** to describe sets of individuals who intimately cooperate in staging a performance that leads an audience to form an impression of one or all of the team members (Goffman, 1959a). For example, parents often work together as a team in presenting a united front and an image of authority to their children. Team members are highly dependent on one another and must show a fair amount of trust and loyalty because each member has the power to disrupt or "give away" the performance at any moment. Individuals who cannot be trusted—like small children or people who are emotionally unstable—must not be chosen as teammates.

One of the most obvious teams is the married couple. Couples frequently find themselves in public situations where they must create or sustain a collective impression for others. Whether the couple is entertaining friends at home, attending the office holiday party, or dining at a restaurant, their behavior is witnessed by an audience. The couple is socially obligated to present a believable and cooperative image, particularly if the audience does not know them very well.

As you well know, nothing is more uncomfortable than being present when a couple is fighting, bickering, or putting each other down. We, as the audience, feel as if we are watching something not meant for our eyes. Cultural norms dictate that couples are supposed to convey the message that all is well between them, even if all isn't well. If the teamwork is cohesive and the performance believable, a couple can give the impression that they are happy and content even if they have had a bitter fight moments before going out in public. You can see how the cultural value of marriage—and, by extension, the institution of family—is publicly reinforced by the ability of couples to project contented images of their relationship.

Like individual impression management, successful teamwork depends on maintaining the boundary between front and back stage. This boundary is especially fragile and always in danger of being breached by poor teamwork. Team members must trust each other to be loyal to the performance (Goffman, 1959a). In addition, the intrusion of third parties can also expose the back-stage aspect of impression management. For instance, young children who can speak but are not yet schooled in the social conventions of everyday interaction represent a particular peril to successful front-stage teamwork. Imagine a dinner guest being informed by a precocious 4-year-old that "Mommy and Daddy wanted someone else to come over, but she couldn't come. So they invited you." From the dramaturgical perspective, children are not trustworthy performance teammates. They are often too honest to maintain a particular front. They are naturally inclined to let audiences back stage, thereby disrupting both the order of the situation and the identities the actors have attempted to claim.

The ability to go back stage periodically is critical to the maintenance of a sound team relationship. Not only does it give the team a place to rehearse public performances, but it also provides a refuge from public scrutiny. For married couples, tensions can rise if they must constantly be "on" for an audience and never have the opportunity to go back stage. This is precisely why it is so difficult for a couple to have out-of-town guests stay with them for a long period of time, or to live with one or the other partner's parents. There is no back stage, no chance for privacy, no place to go to escape the demands of audience expectations.

We often find ourselves in situations where we must depend on others for the successful performance of the roles we play. Without teamwork many performances would fail, interactions would fall apart, and, ultimately, society would be threatened (Henslin, 1991). Successful teamwork may also have financial implications. Some professions require individual and team impressions to be managed with finesse so that clients do not become embarrassed, humiliated, or threatened (e.g., Henslin & Biggs, 1978).

Organizational Impression Management

Organizations must carefully manage their impressions, particularly if they depend on public approval for their survival (S. J. Taylor & Bogdan, 1980). Individual impression management and organizational impression management are governed by the same principles (Hochschild, 1983). Take, for instance, the management of physical space. The walls of a hospital are usually lined with soothing paintings designed to calm, not agitate. Children's wards are often filled with colorful images of familiar cartoon characters. Airplanes are meticulously designed to manage a collective impression that distracts passengers from the potential danger:

> The Muzak tunes, the TV and movie screens, and the smiling flight attendants serving drinks are all calculated to "make you feel at home." Even fellow passengers are considered part of the stage. At Delta Airlines, for example, flight attendants in training are advised that they can prevent the boarding of certain types of passengers—a passenger with "severe facial scars," for example. The instructor elaborated: "You know, the other passengers might be reminded of an airplane crash they had read about." The bearer of a "severe facial scar," then, is not deemed a good prop. His or her effect on the emotions of other money-paying passengers might be all wrong. (Hochschild, 1983, pp. 51-52)

For some organizations, collective impression management is the defining feature of the services they provide. Organizations with a dubious history or a negative public perception must be acutely vigilant of the images they present to the public. One obvious example is the funeral industry.

Ronny Turner and Charles Edgley
Mortuary Performances

Perhaps no other industry is as concerned with public image as the funeral industry. Even the use of the term *funeral director* instead of *undertaker* attests to the importance of performance and impression management. Funeral directors must present themselves as sincere, sympathetic, and understanding. Because of the extreme emotions involved in their work, every aspect must be tightly controlled down to the last detail. The American funeral industry has long been the focus of stinging attacks regarding issues of fraud and financial exploitation (e.g., Mitford, 1963).

Ronny Turner and Charles Edgley (1976) observed funeral services, interviewed directors, and studied the manuals of 15 mortuaries in three cities. They examined the manner in which mortuary employees manage the circumstances of the funeral ritual in order to establish the legitimacy of their work. The director, for instance, must stage the performance so that the grieving family and friends will attribute dignity, respect, and sincerity to the mortuary. The images and impressions that are formed must be favorable ones. Turner and Edgley write: "A successful funeral is a sequence of activities performed by the funeral director and his staff that are later seen by the bereaved as a respectful, appropriate tribute to the life and memory of the deceased" (p. 287).

The maintenance of a separate and completely hidden back-stage area is essential to the performance. The preparation room is physically separated from the public areas of the funeral home. Here the corpse is prepared for the funeral. The procedures used—washing, shaving, slicing, powdering, embalming—would shock the friends and family of the deceased. Jokes, racial slurs, sexual comments, insults, and other activities that are clearly unacceptable front stage are commonplace back stage. The "casket" becomes the "stuffing box"; the "dearly departed" becomes the "cold one"; "embalming" becomes "pickling," and so on.

Such back-stage behavior, while seemingly distasteful and inappropriate, is not meant to be callous. It may be an institutionalized means by which employees manage stress and psychologically distance themselves from a potentially repulsive and gloomy aspect of their occupation. Similar lightheartedness can be found among medical students who, in the course of their clinical training, must observe the dissection of cadavers (Hafferty, 1991). By going back stage, one is able to maintain composure in highly emotional situations, thereby protecting the stability of the overall occupational structure.

You can see how witnessing the preparation of the body for the funeral would destroy the front-stage impression so essential to the industry. The body is *never* touched by mortuary personnel in front of family and friends. The deceased is transformed from an object back stage to a respected human being front stage.

As for the management of the setting, funeral homes always present themselves as warm, soothing places with white columns, lots of flowers and grass, and meticulous indoor decorations. Black is never seen. Many hearses are now gray, white, or blue instead of the traditional black. The chapel, where the memorial service is held, is designed to pull off a successful performance. Here, music is tactfully used to set the mood.

The orderliness of life and death is maintained through successful individual and organizational impression management. For their part, the audience actively participates. The family has no intention of going back stage; they want little if any knowledge of bodily preparations or other arrangements. They too have a stake in impressions being maintained and the event flowing smoothly.

Impression Mismanagement: Spoiled Identities

Impression management is important but precarious for individuals, teams, and organizations. We sometimes fail miserably in our attempts to project favorable images of ourselves to others. We may mishandle props, blow our lines, allow the audience back stage, or otherwise destroy the credibility of our performances. Some of us manage to recover from ineffective impression management quite well, while others suffer an extended devaluation of their identities. What happens when impression management is unsuccessful? What do we do to overcome such interactional mishaps that allow us to regain identities and restore social order?

Embarrassment

A common emotional reaction to impression mismanagement is embarrassment. Embarrassment is the spontaneous feeling we experience when the identity we are presenting is suddenly and unexpectedly discredited in front of others (Gross & Stone, 1964). An adolescent boy trying to look "cool" in front of his friends may have his tough image shattered by the unexpected arrival of his mother in the family station wagon. We see embarrassment in the fixed smile, the nervous hollow laugh, the busy hands, and the downward glance that conceals the eyes from the gaze of others (Goffman, 1967).

Embarrassment can come from a multitude of sources: lack of poise (e.g., stumbling, spilling a drink, inappropriate bodily display), intrusion into the private settings of others, dressing improperly for a particular social occasion, and so on. In the story at the beginning of this chapter, my claim to be a friendly and desirable person was thoroughly discredited by a single errant and embarrassing basketball shot.

Embarrassment is sociologically important because it can be contagious and therefore has the potential to destroy the orderliness of a social situation, debilitating everyone involved. Imagine being at your graduation ceremony. As the class valedictorian is giving the commencement address, a gust of wind blows her note cards off the podium. As she reaches down to collect them, she knocks over the microphone and tears her gown. In front of hundreds of people she stands there, flustered, not knowing what to say or do. The situation would be uncomfortable and embarrassing not only for her, but for you and the rest of the audience as well.

Because social interaction is a joint venture, the people involved—the embarrassed person and those who recognize the embarrassment—must somehow deal with it so that order can be restored. A continuous state of embarrassment is disruptive for all concerned; hence it is in everyone's best interest to cooperate in eliminating it. To respond to such an act may be as embarrassing as the original episode itself, so we may pretend not to notice the faux pas to prevent calling excess attention to it (Lindesmith, Strauss, & Denzin, 1991). By suppressing signs of recognition we make it easier for the person to regain composure (Goffman, 1967). A mutual commitment to supporting others' social identities, even when those identities are in danger, is a fundamental rule of social interaction.

There are times, however, when embarrassment is used strategically to disrupt another person's impression management. Practical jokes, for instance, are intentional attempts to cause someone else to lose identity. On a more serious note, embarrassment or the threat of embarrassment can be used by groups and organizations as a form of behavioral control to encourage a preferred activity or discourage behavior that may be damaging to the group (e.g., hazing). In this way embarrassment reasserts the power structure of a group or organization, since only certain people can legitimately embarrass others. A low-status employee has much less freedom to embarrass a superior than vice versa.

For groups and organizations, embarrassment not only affects public image, but it also may have severe economic and political consequences. Most governments and large corporations have public relations departments that carefully manage the corporate image by controlling the damage of negative publicity (E. Gross, 1984). Many of America's most successful companies have had to deal with tarnished images due to insensitive, negligent, or criminal behavior: Union Carbide and the chemical disaster in Bhopal, India; A. H. Robins and the injuries caused by the Dalkon Shield birth control device; Eli Lilly and the violent side effects of the drug Prozac; Dow Chemical and the lingering health effects of the defoliant Agent Orange used during the Vietnam War; Rockwell, GTE, General Electric, and other military contractors guilty of overcharging the government for supplies, and so on.

Sometimes all it takes is a rumor to cause massive corporate embarrassment. In 1993 a rash of reports surfaced around the United States from people who claimed to have found hypodermic needles and syringes in cans of Diet Pepsi.

Investigators eventually found the claims to be unsubstantiated. Nevertheless, stores in many parts of the country began to pull the product off their shelves or offer refunds to worried customers. Even the Food and Drug Administration advised consumers to buy Pepsi in glass or plastic bottles. The phenomenon was a public relations nightmare for Pepsi. Facing severe financial losses, the company mounted a massive and expensive media campaign that included TV commercials, talk show appearances, full-page newspaper ads, and a toll-free consumer hotline to counteract the embarrassment and costly fallout of a spoiled public image.

Like individuals, organizations must constantly deal with actual and potential failures in impression management. While organizations and governments can enlist the aid of experts to help them overcome the debilitating effects of negative images, individuals are left to their own devices to restore their tarnished identities.

Repairing and Overcoming Spoiled Identities

When inappropriate identities are established or appropriate ones lost, successful impression management becomes impossible (E. Gross & Stone, 1964). On an individual level, the knowledge that one is being evaluated negatively can produce discomfort strong enough to impede thought, speech, and action. An analysis of our everyday reactions to embarrassment and identity spoilage reveals a great deal about social order and the structural requirements of role performances.

The major responsibility for restoring order lies with the person or group whose actions disrupted things in the first place. The embarrassment that results from failure in claiming an identity is not a trivial matter. Social life requires that we protect each other so that we can carry on the business of living (L. H. Lofland, 1971). Moral imperative obligates us to save identities and situations that are being threatened. The two main ways of preserving social order in such cases are aligning actions and intentional identity transformations.

Aligning Actions

When events occur that damage one's claimed identity, this signals a need for an **aligning action** (Stokes & Hewitt, 1976). An aligning action brings back into order a situation that has become disordered and restores the image that has been disrupted as a result of the unwelcome event. Sometimes this can be done easily and quickly. If you step on a person's foot while standing in line at a cafeteria, a simple apology may be all that's needed to bring order back. By apologizing you acknowledge the wrongfulness of the act and send the message that you are not ordinarily a breaker of such social norms. If you don't offer an apology, your identity will remain forever suspect. Other situations, however, call for more detailed repairs to take place in the form of an account or a disclaimer.

Under certain circumstances we may be called on or anticipate being called on not only to apologize, but also to explain our motives (C. W. Mills, 1940; M. Scott & Lyman, 1968). To do this we often use an **account,** a verbal statement designed to explain unanticipated, embarrassing, or unacceptable behavior. Accounts can take two forms: excuses and justifications.

When a person provides an *excuse,* he or she acknowledges the wrongfulness of the act but denies responsibility. The person is saying, "I know what I've done looks bad, but for the following reasons you should not consider me blameworthy." Perhaps the individual will cite events beyond his or her control (e.g., "I was late for the wedding because there was a lot of traffic on the highway") or blame others (e.g., "I spilled my milk because so-and-so pushed me").

Justifications entail an admission of responsibility but also contain a persuasive attempt to define the behavior as appropriate under the circumstances. Justifying an act asserts its acceptability despite claims to the contrary and attempts to neutralize threats to one's identity by trying to convince others that the act shouldn't be considered threatening. Such verbal strategies are not limited to "embarrassing" acts. There are several justifications that people often use for rather serious "offenses" (Sykes & Matza, 1957). Such tactics include denying that anyone was hurt by the act ("Yeah, I stole the car, but no one got hurt"), claiming that the victim deserved to be victimized ("I beat him up, but he had it coming"), or claiming higher, unselfish motives ("I stole food, but I did it to feed my family").

To illustrate the role accounts play in warding off threats to identity, Diana Scully and Joseph Marolla (1984) interviewed 114 convicted rapists to see what sorts of accounts they used to explain themselves and their violent actions. Although some of the men admitted they had raped their victims, many either denied they were guilty or defined their actions as essentially "nonrapes." They attempted to justify their behavior by presenting the victim in a light that made *her* appear responsible, regardless of their own actions. Some of the men defined women as seductresses, claiming that they said no when they meant yes or that they actually enjoyed it, and by stating that nice girls don't get raped. These justifications are buttressed by the cultural view of women as sexual commodities. Accounts are an important factor contributing to cultural environment that trivializes and sometimes even condones rape.

To be acceptable, accounts must fall within the range of believable explanations within a given society. Like reality, accounts are embedded in the "everybody knows" assumptions of a culture. Citing "family problems" as a cause of one's depression and listlessness can work as an excuse only if the audience understands what that implies. Accounts linguistically reinforce cultural or group boundaries by reflecting shared expectations. In some societies, like the Azande discussed in chapter 3, there is no conception of coincidence or chance. It is unlikely that an Azande would explain an identity-threatening, disruptive act as "accidental."

Some accounts may be so overused that they are immediately considered unreasonable even if they are true (e.g., "The dog ate my homework"). Others are deemed illegitimate because the seriousness of the infraction exceeds the credibility of the account. If you cite blocked vision as the reason you ran over a neighbor's tomato plant with your car, that account might be accepted. However, if you ran over the neighbor's child, such an account would fall far short of acceptability.

The acceptability of accounts is specific to particular groups or situations. A group is able to maintain the loyalty of its members in part because it provides a context in which they can *talk* about the reasons for their conduct and have their reasons confirmed by others. For instance, if you didn't do your homework, "I was hungry, so I went for pizza" may be a legitimate excuse among your friends but would fail if you tried to use it with your instructor (Bernstein, 1990).

The legitimacy of accounts can be linked to larger structural or institutional concerns too. A company president who explains the low salaries he or she pays by citing market pressures and profit margins may be supported by business colleagues but scorned by his or her employees.

From both a societal and individual perspective, accounts help redefine or repair failed interactions or spoiled identities. They are institutionalized mechanisms through which people or groups are expected to provide some explanation for behavior that does not meet acceptable community or societal standards.

Another type of aligning action, the **disclaimer**, is a verbal assertion given *before the fact* to forestall any complaints or negative implications (Hewitt & Stokes, 1975). If we think something we are about to do or say will threaten our identity or be used by others to construct a negative judgment of us, we may employ a disclaimer. Phrases such as "This may sound crazy to you, but . . ." or "I probably don't know what I'm talking about, but . . ." or "This may sound racist, but . . ." introduce acts or expressions that ordinarily might be considered undesirable. Hence a person claiming to be nonracist feels he or she can go ahead and make a racist statement, and a self-proclaimed nonexpert can pretend to be an expert as long as a disclaimer is provided.

The anticipatory nature of disclaimers not only requires knowledge of the potential wrongfulness or harmfulness of an act or statement, it also illustrates the important role impression management plays in everyday life. At the individual level, disclaimers keep others from making negative judgments and destroying public images. At the corporate level, they can protect an organization financially, ethically, and legally, as in television messages that warn "The following may not be suitable for young children" or in warning labels on dangerous products.

Accounts and disclaimers are an important link between the individual and society. Such strategies are the means by which people "take account" of their culture (Hewitt & Stokes, 1975). In repairing threatened interactions or forestalling possible threats, people explicitly define the relationship between their questionable conduct and prevailing cultural norms. Through these tactics we bring our problematic conduct into line with prevailing normative expectations. We publicly reaffirm our commitment to the social order that our conduct has violated and thereby defend the sanctity of our social identities and the "goodness" of society.

Cooling Out

Everyone who bears witness to a spoiled identity has a stake in repairing the situation. However, there are times when socially undesirable acts are so major or happen with such frequency that aligning actions are no longer effective. Others may cease to help violators restore spoiled identities and may in fact *deliberately* destroy the identities of those who fail repeatedly and glaringly.

One such technique is called **cooling out** (Goffman, 1952). The term comes from con artists who "cool the mark out," or make the victim of a con feel like she or he hasn't been conned. In the context of social interaction, cooling out means gently persuading someone who has lost face to accept a less desirable but still reasonable alternative identity. People engaged in cooling out seek to *persuade* offenders to change, rather than force them. It is an attempt to minimize distress. The challenge, though, is that the offender must not be aware that he or she is being persuaded.

Cooling out is a common element of social life. Consumer complaint personnel, coaches, doctors, and priests all have cooling out as their major function. Cooling out also plays a major part in informal relationships. A partner who terminates a dating or courting relationship might persuade the other person to stay a "good friend," thereby gently pushing the person into a lesser role without completely destroying his or her identity.

Some individuals are involuntarily placed in the "cooler" role not because of their job or relationship, but because of who they are. Women, for instance, must constantly deal with the unsolicited comments and advances of men in public situations (Snow, Robinson, & McCall, 1991). Most women who have been in bars or nightclubs have faced the problem of unwanted male attention. In an attempt to escape from the encounter without disrupting the orderliness of the situation, women may offer polite excuses, advertise their unavailability, or otherwise "let him down easily." Successful, trouble-free public life for women is contingent on their ability to cool men out. For their part men, too, are obligated to respond to the cooling-out lines in a cooperative manner, leave the encounter without too much fuss, and preserve the order of the situation.

Cooling out is often motivated by institutional pressures. Consider the environment of higher education. The aspirations of many people in American society are encouraged by open-door admissions policies in some universities and most community colleges (Karabel, 1972). When there is a widely held cultural belief that higher education is linked to higher employment opportunities and that anyone can go to college, more and more people will enter the system. Discrepancies, however, inevitably arise between people's aspirations and their ability to succeed. If educational institutions adopted a "hard response," and simply kicked unqualified students out of school, the result would likely be widespread public pressure and anxiety over the system itself.

Hence, most community colleges opt for the "soft response" of cooling out the unqualified student (B. Clark, 1960). A counselor may direct a poor student toward an alternative major that would be easier but is still portrayed as "not that different" from the student's original goal (e.g., nurse's aide instead of registered nurse), or the counselor might encourage the student to seek employment after graduation rather than transfer to a four-year university. The student is being gently persuaded to redefine himself or herself.

The important sociological consequence of this process is that the aspiration-ability discrepancy is masked, minimizing stress on the individual and on the system. Society is thereby able to continue to encourage maximum effort without any major disturbances from unfulfilled expectations. By cooling out "failed" students, society is able to avoid massive public discontent with the entire institution of education.

Institutional cooling-out processes like these are inherent in an educational system that doesn't have clear selection criteria. In the United States, acceptance into college is based on achievement (tests, grades), aptitude (standardized test scores), and personality traits (interviews, letters of recommendation). In contrast, educational selection in Japan is based on a single criterion: achievement on grades and exams. Selections are made upon admission to senior high school. National universities do not allow any exceptions. Because career paths are clearly and quickly defined, Japanese higher education has no need for an institutionalized cooling-out process (Kariya & Rosenbaum, 1987).

Stigma

Impression management failure can result from either transitory discrediting events or serious and extended ones. People may attempt to recapture spoiled identities, be subtly encouraged to take on new ones, or be forcibly pushed into less desirable ones. The assumption is that the identity of a valuable or competent person has suddenly been tarnished and he or she is now looked upon in a less than favorable light, which ultimately can be corrected.

In some situations, though, a person's identity can be *permanently* spoiled in the eyes of others. For this individual social interaction is not a process to be used for significant personal gain, but an obstacle to overcome or avoid. And the impression management task is not so much to recapture a tarnished identity but to successfully minimize the social damage it may cause. Such permanent identity spoilage is called **stigma.** A stigma is a deeply discrediting characteristic widely viewed as an insurmountable obstacle that prevents competent or morally trustworthy behavior (Goffman, 1963). According to Goffman, there are three types of stigma: defects of the body (e.g., scars, blindness, paralyzed or missing limbs), defects of character (e.g., dishonesty, weak will, radical beliefs inferred from a known record of mental illness, imprisonment, or substance abuse), and membership in particular social groups such as certain races, religions, or ethnicities that are devalued in society.

Stigma is a social construction. Each society creates its own hierarchies of desirable and undesirable traits. Sometimes the motivation is clear, as when an individual is stigmatized as a "hardened criminal" for repeatedly breaking society's laws. Other times the designation of a stigma seems rather arbitrary. For instance, in our culture the use of one mechanism to compensate for a sensory deficiency (eyeglasses) is far less stigmatizing than the use of another (hearing aid).

The nature of stigma can vary across time and culture. Being a Christian in the 1990s is very different from being one in A.D. 10, and being a Christian in the United States is different from being one in the Middle East (Ainlay, Becker, & Coleman, 1986). Obesity is stigmatized in contemporary Western societies but was seen as desirable, attractive, and symbolic of status and wealth in the past (Clinard & Meier, 1979).

Some stigmatized attributes have remained remarkably stable in the face of major social changes. While divorce has become more commonplace and even acceptable in contemporary society, divorced *people* often still feel discredited in the eyes of others (Gertsel, 1987). Many divorced people believe they are perceived as failures and are targets of informal sanctions like exclusion, blame, and devaluation. Some even come to believe that their married friends and acquaintances see them as misfits who could not maintain a stable marriage.

Once recognized, stigmas spoil the identities of individuals regardless of other attributes those individuals might have. As a result, interactions between the stigmatized and the nonstigmatized—called **mixed contacts**—are often uneasy. We have all felt uncomfortable with people who are "different" in appearance or behavior and are subsequently stigmatized by others. Stigma initiates a judgment process that colors impressions and sets up barriers to interaction (E. E. Jones et al., 1984).

Whether intentional or not, nonstigmatized individuals often pressure stigmatized people to conform to the inferior identities being placed on them. A person in a wheelchair who is discouraged from undertaking certain activities or a blind person who is dissuaded from venturing out of the house alone is never given the chance to develop those skills and is subsequently kept dependent.

The anticipation can lead stigmatized and nonstigmatized people to arrange their lives so as to avoid mixed contacts (Goffman, 1963). Research shows that people terminate interactions sooner, are more inhibited, and are more rigid

Table 6.1

Perceptions of Interaction Partners by "Stigmatized" Individuals (Ratings made on 14-point scales; the higher the number, the higher the level of that attribute)

Dimension	Type of Disability	
	Allergy (nonstigmatized)	Scar (stigmatized)
Tenseness	2.37	8.00
Attractiveness	8.62	6.37
Patronization	1.87	4.12

Source: Kleck & Strenta, 1980.

when interacting with a physically disabled person than with a physically normal person (Kleck, 1968; Kleck, Ono, & Hastorf, 1966). Such discomfort probably stems from uncertainty as to what behavior is appropriate. On the one hand, the nonstigmatized may fear that if they show direct sympathy or interest in someone's condition they will be regarded as rude or intrusive. On the other hand, ignoring it may make the interaction artificial or create impossible demands (Michener, DeLamater, & Schwartz, 1986). Goffman argues that people with stigmatizing conditions usually have some sense that others are evaluating them negatively, whether in the form of disgust, anger, or pity.

In one study a group of subjects was led to believe that a large scar applied to their faces with stage makeup stigmatized them in the eyes of people with whom they were to interact. Another group was led to believe that their interaction partners knew they had a mild allergy—a nonstigmatizing condition (Kleck & Strenta, 1980). Actually, the interaction partners had no knowledge of either condition: They weren't told of the allergy, and no artificial scar had been applied. Nevertheless, the "facial scar" subjects who *thought* they were being stigmatized perceived their partners as more tense, more patronizing, and less attracted to them than did the "allergic," nonstigmatized subjects (see Table 6.1). Videotapes of the interactions showed no evidence of stigmatization in the actual conversations. Hence people who *believe* they are stigmatized perceive that others are relating to them negatively.

Whether their perceptions are accurate or not, people with stigmatizing conditions are often motivated to use drastic coping strategies to manage the stigma and establish the most favorable identity possible. One strategy is to hide the stigmatizing condition as completely as possible. People who are hard of hearing, for instance, may learn to read lips or otherwise interact with people as if they can hear; those with bodily stigmas may opt for surgical remedies.

Michael Petrunik and Clifford Shearing (1983) studied the coping strategies used by people who stutter. They observed and took part in weekly therapy groups over a period of 13 years. In addition they conducted in-depth interviews with stutterers, their families and friends, speech therapists, and other medical practitioners. Common public reactions to stutterers include pity, condescension, ridicule, and impatience. Some stutterers hide their stigma by avoiding speaking situations or by not using particularly troublesome words. Others structure situations so that someone else does the talking. For example, in a restaurant stutterers may encourage others to order first. As soon as an acceptable item is mentioned, they simply duplicate the order by saying, "Me too" or "Same here."

Of course, not all stigmas can be hidden. Some individuals must manage their stigmas in ways that minimize the degree to which they intrude on and disrupt the interaction. One tactic is to boldly call attention to their condition by mastering areas thought to be closed to them, such as when an amputee goes mountain climbing, or by organizing a movement to counter social oppression, such as demanding legislation outlawing discrimination against the handicapped. Others will use self-deprecating humor to relieve the tension felt by the nonstigmatized. Still others may try to focus attention on attributes that are unrelated to the stigma. A person in a wheelchair may carry around esoteric books in a conspicuous manner to show others that he or she can perform well in other areas.

Some stigmatized individuals, particularly those whose conditions are not immediately observable, use a policy of selective disclosure and concealment. Couples who are unable to have children feel the stigmatizing effects of this breach of family norms. Sociologist Charlene Miall (1989) interviewed and surveyed 70 infertile women to see if they felt stigmatized by others. Nearly all the respondents categorized infertility as something negative, an indication of failure, or an inability to function "normally." Furthermore, most of the women regarded infertility as a discreditable attribute and were concerned that an awareness of their problems would cause others to view them in a new and damaging light.

Consequently, most of these women engaged in some form of informational control to manage the stigma and thereby manage the impressions others formed of them. Many simply concealed the information from everyone except medical personnel and infertility counselors. Others used medical accounts, saying "It's beyond my control." Some disclosed the information only to people they felt would not think ill of them. Some even used the disclosure of their infertility to gain control of the situation by deliberately shocking their "normal" audience (Miall, 1989).

Just as aligning actions and cooling out maintain social order, so do coping strategies used by stigmatized individuals. By successfully managing their stigmas in public interactions, they are able to avoid the embarrassment of indelicate questions and gain acceptance. The interaction becomes smooth-flowing. The nonstigmatized also benefit because they are saved from facing the true pain and injustice suffered by stigmatized people, thus alleviating their own sense of discomfort and guilt.

The power of stigma to determine the course of one's social life is rooted not in the nature of the characteristic itself, but in the public's fear of things that are unknown or different. Certain characteristics—serious physical illnesses, for example—elicit fear because their cause is unknown or unpredictable (S. Sontag, 1979).

The fear that excludes stigmatized individuals from everyday encounters doesn't disrupt just the orderliness of social interactions. What we don't see we don't know, and what we don't know we don't trust. If nonstigmatized individuals do not interact with stigmatized people, perceptions will continue to be distorted and negative (F. X. Gibbons, 1986).

Overcoming the problems created by stigma cannot be accomplished solely through individual impression management techniques. Improvements can be accomplished only at the societal level through the alteration of cultural beliefs about the nature of stigma (Link, Mirotznik, & Cullen, 1991). As long as we hold stigmatized individuals solely responsible for overcoming their condition, social problems will continue to be perceived only in individual terms.

Conclusion

People consciously manufacture images of themselves that allow them to achieve some desired goal. There's no denying that most of us go through life trying to create the impression that we're attractive, honest, competent, and sincere. To that end we carefully manage our appearance, present qualities we think others will admire, and hide qualities we think they won't. When caught in an act that may threaten the impression we're trying to foster, we will strategically use statements that disclaim, excuse, or justify it. At times we will even force other people into identities that suit our needs and interests (i.e., altercasting).

What does all this say about the nature of society and the people within it? Chances are that after reading this chapter you have an image of human beings as cunning, manipulative, and cynical play-actors whose lives are merely a string of phony performances carefully designed to fit the selfish needs of the moment. If you act one way with your friends and another way with your parents, which is the real you? The impression manager comes across as someone who consciously and fraudulently presents an inaccurate image in order to take advantage of a particular situation. Even the person who seems not to care about his or her appearance may be consciously cultivating the image of "not caring."

Are we simply creatures of appearance who freely change our images to suit the expectations of a given audience, or is there something more stable that characterizes us across all situations? It is true that we are creatures of appearance. Others form impressions based on how we look and the information we selectively provide. People cannot get into our heads. What good is it to be a terrific person if no one knows it?

If you are aware that the impression you are managing is *not* you, then you must have some knowledge of what *is* you, and what you are may, in fact, transcend the demands of particular situations. Is there a basic, pervasive part of our being that allows us to choose from a repertoire of identities the one that best suits the immediate needs of the situation?

As you ponder these questions, realize that the answers you come up with not only indicate your feelings about impression management but also reflect your beliefs about the nature of individuals and the role society and others play in our everyday lives.

CHAPTER HIGHLIGHTS

■ A significant portion of social life is influenced by the images we form of others and the images others form of us.

■ Impression formation is based initially on our assessment of social group membership (race, gender, etc.), personal attributes (e.g., physical attractiveness), and verbal and nonverbal messages.

■ While we are gathering information about others to form impressions of them, we are fully aware that they are doing the same thing. Impression management is the process by which we attempt to control and manipulate information about ourselves to influence the impressions others form of us. Impression management can be both individual and collective.

■ Impression *mis*management can lead to the creation of damaged identities that must be repaired through aligning actions and cooling out in order to sustain social interaction.

YOUR TURN

In this chapter we have examined the importance of impression management. For most of us, impression management is a tool we use to present ourselves as likable people. Occasionally, however, our attempts fail. Survey several friends or classmates and have them describe their most embarrassing moment. What were the circumstances surrounding the incident? What were the identities they were trying to present? How did the attempt to claim this identity fail? What were their immediate physical and behavioral reactions to the embarrassment? What did they do to try to overcome the embarrassment and return order? Did they offer some sort of account? Were the consequences of the failed impression management temporary or permanent? What did the witnesses to the embarrassing incident do? Did their reactions alleviate or intensify the embarrassment?

Once you've gathered a substantial number of stories (about 12 or 15), see if you can find some common themes. What are the most frequent types of embarrassing situations? What are the most frequent reactions? Sociologists Edward Gross and Gregory Stone wrote, "In the wreckage left by embarrassment lie the broken foundations of social transactions." What do you suppose they meant by that? Discuss the sociological importance of embarrassment (and, more important, the reactions to embarrassment) in terms of the maintenance of interactional and social order.

A Sociological View of Bodies

The impressions we form of others are often made on the basis of physical appearance. As you well know, the way we look is a prime obsession among Americans today. "Making a good impression" typically means conforming to a generally held cultural conception of attractiveness or desirability. However, in recent years, more and more Americans have discovered that they can use their bodies as vehicles for creating all sorts of images of themselves. Modes of body adornment once considered characteristic of society's fringe element have now become part of mainstream American culture. In the

following visual essay I will examine one such practice, tattooing, which has witnessed dramatic shifts over the past decade in both cultural acceptability and the types of people who wear them.

Although bodily adornment is usually thought to be the province of women, the tattoo has always been different. Tattoos originated in this country with men--mostly in the military--who either used them as identifiers of their masculinity and patriotism, or to remind them of home (girlfriends, mother). Tattoos have traditionally been the perfect way for men to act in accordance with the cultural belief that they be "strong and silent": they create an image of toughness without the need for behavioral or verbal support.

But tattoos have always done more than simply provide visible symbols of masculinity. The practice of tattooing has developed into a common art form with its own community, journals, and standards of excellence. For some people, like the man pictured here, tattoos transform the body into a walking, breathing work of art.

Tattoos are used to send all sorts of messages about personal identity ...

They can be the means through which one expresses one's spirituality,

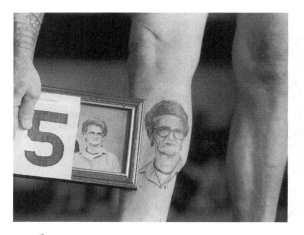

devotion to family (this man has a tattoo of his mother on his leg),

Violence (this man tattooed the logo from the 1970s cult movie "Clockwork Orange"),

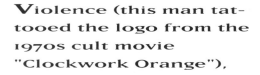

or rebelliousness.

Sometimes tattoos are used to send political messages. In an attempt to "reclaim" her body, this woman had the word "rape" tattooed on her stomach after she had been raped. She wanted to show that the crime, like the tattooed word, leaves a permanent mark on the victim.

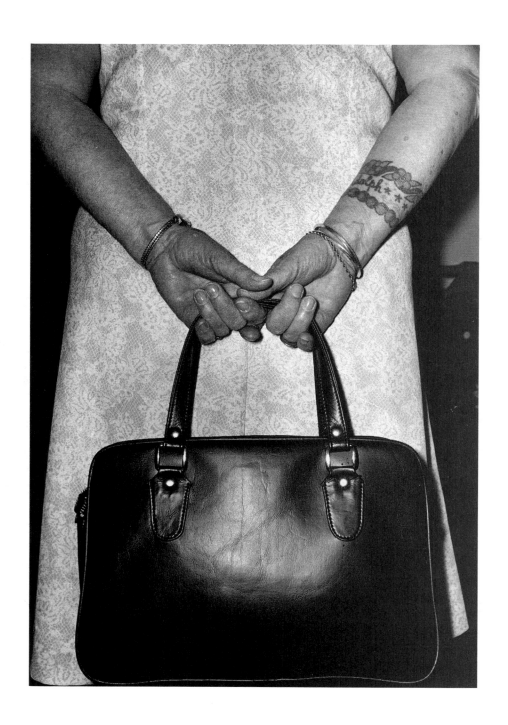

In the 1990s, the tattoo has shed its image as a badge of masculinity or a subcultural oddity and has become a popular and common fixture on the landscape of American culture. Celebrities have achieved public notoriety because of tattoos. Indeed, tattoos can now be seen on people from virtually every segment of the population.

Children emulate adult tattoo-wearers through use of "temporary tattoos."

Constructing Difference

Social Deviance

In 1936 a 29-year-old woman named Gladys Burr was diagnosed as psychotic. Later that year she was also declared mentally retarded and shortly thereafter was committed to the Mansfield Training School for the Retarded in Connecticut. From the beginning of her stay there, she never felt that she deserved to be institutionalized. She wrote several letters to state officials asking that they reconsider her placement, but to no avail (Brooke, 1985). Little note was taken of the fact that she had completed 2 years of high school and a 3-month business course.

Six months after being committed, doctors declared her "cured," and several intelligence tests revealed her IQ to be in the normal range or slightly above. Despite these developments, which would seem to indicate that she did not need to be institutionalized, Gladys Burr remained in a series of state-run hospitals, training centers, and group homes until her release in 1978—42 years after her initial commitment! In 1985, after a prolonged legal battle, she was awarded $235,000 in compensation and damages. She died in 1990.

Why did this happen? How could she have failed to persuade the authorities that she was normal? According to Burr's lawyer, the reason was clear and simple: They forgot about her. In large bureaucracies such as state mental health systems, someone is bound to be overlooked or ignored every once in a while. It's obvious that she had somehow fallen through the cracks.

But perhaps something more was going on—something about the way people perceived Burr and the impressions they formed of her. As you know, people respond to other people based on their expectations of them. Could it be that because Gladys was authoritatively pronounced "psychotic" and "mentally retarded" she could not convince people otherwise?

We may never know in Gladys Burr's case. But what we do know is that such labels and what they imply in people's minds can overshadow everything else about a person. Gladys had been officially tagged a deviant by others and publicly degraded. From that point on, nothing she did or said could overcome that label.

Being denied one's freedom for 42 years as a result of a designation of deviance is an extreme and rare occurrence. Keep in mind, though, that the process of affixing deviant labels and judging people on the basis of them can be found not only in systems like mental hospitals and criminal courts but in social interchanges as well. Perhaps there have been times in your life when you acquired some sort of reputation that you could not shed.

In this chapter I focus on several questions that have been addressed by many sociologists but are still met with widespread disagreement: What is deviance? How do people become deviant? Who gets to define what is and is not deviant? What are the consequences of being identified as deviant by others?

Defining Deviance

For the most part, deviance refers to socially condemned behavior: the violation of some agreed-upon norm that prevails in a community or in society at large. Staring at a stranger in an elevator, driving over the speed limit, talking to yourself in public, wearing clothes that are outlandish, robbing a bank, or intentionally taking someone's life can all be considered deviant acts.

The determination of which behaviors or characteristics comprise deviant activity, however, is more complex. We usually assume that there is some agreement regarding what and who gets defined as deviant. For instance, no one would challenge the notion that child abuse is bad and that child abusers ought to be punished. But the level of agreement within a given society over what is deviant—what specific acts *constitute* child abuse—is subject to much variation, disagreement, and even overt conflict. What is a method of discipline to one parent is a form of abuse to another.

To make the issue more complex, some functionalist sociologists (e.g., Durkheim, 1958; K. Erikson, 1966) argue that deviance is not always bad for society and may actually serve a purpose. As you recall from chapter 4, norm violations help define the moral boundaries that distinguish right from wrong, increase feelings of in-group togetherness for those who unite in collective opposition to normative threats, and encourage society to revise itself and respond to new concerns. At the surface level, acts of deviance are disruptive and generate varying degrees of social disapproval, but at a deeper level, they can contribute to the maintenance and continuity of every society.

Before examining the social implications of deviance, let's look at two different approaches on defining it: absolutism and relativism.

Absolutism

According to **absolutism,** there are two fundamental types of human behavior: that which is inherently proper and good, and that which is obviously improper, immoral, evil, and bad. The distinction is clear and identifiable. Deviance is a malfunction, a potentially destructive force that society needs to eliminate or, at the very least, keep under control.

The absolutist believes that there is or should be agreement as to the basic goals people ought to pursue. No normal, decent person would willingly violate norms and participate in a deviant lifestyle, be it violent crime, drug use, or nontraditional sexuality. Consider the following letter to the editor from an irate citizen protesting the discussion of homosexuality in a college English course:

> Homosexuality is one of the most vile blasphemies against God. . . . [I]t is not society that is sick, it is those whose life-styles debase the sacred purpose of the sex act. Homosexuality is not part of the "total human experience" which a healthy, well-balanced human being can ever accept. The practice of homosexuality is an abomination of the natural order. . . . It is not love; it is undisciplined lust, drawing man down to the level of animals. (quoted in Hills, 1980, p. 9)

This absolutist definition of deviance does not allow for alternative conceptions of right and wrong. Behavior that does not fit the tight values of the absolutist is self-evidently "sick," "disturbed," or "detestable." Deviance is not something in which a healthy, well-adjusted person would engage; rather, it is seen as comparable to malignant cells in an organism, something to be eliminated, treated, and contained (Hills, 1980). It matters little whether the source of the behavior lies in the individual's own makeup or in the environment within which he or she lives.

An absolutist definition of deviance implies something about the person committing the act as well. To many people, deviant individuals are morally, psychologically, and even physically different from ordinary, conforming people. The attribute or behavior that serves as the basic reason for defining a person as deviant in the first place is pervasive and essential to his or her entire character (Hills, 1980). Every aspect of that person's personality is somehow tied to this characteristic. Respectable, conventional qualities become insignificant. It doesn't matter, for instance, that the "sexual deviant" has an otherwise ordinary life, that the "schizophrenic" has recovered, or that the violent act of the "murderer" was completely atypical of the rest of his or her life.

In short, the deviant act or trait becomes a sort of moral identity, signifying a judgment about the overall worth of the individual (J. Katz, 1975). Being defined as deviant means being identified as someone who cannot and should not be treated as an ordinary human being. Often this sort of absolute disapproval has less to do with specific offending acts than with the kind of person one is thought to be (Schur, 1984).

This is where the absolutist approach runs into some problems. Absolute beliefs about deviants and deviance are often guided by powerful and emotionally laden stereotypical imagery. If you ask someone to imagine what a typical drug addict looks like, chances are the response will describe a dirty, poor, strung-out young man living on the streets and resorting to theft to support his habit. The image probably wouldn't be of a middle-class alcoholic housewife or a clean-shaven, hardworking physician hooked on prescription drugs, even though these groups constitute a higher percentage of drug addicts than any other in American society (Hills, 1980). Likewise, the image of the typical rapist is usually that of a psychotic stranger lurking in the bushes or masquerading as a door-to-door salesman, and not a classmate, fellow employee, dating partner, or longtime family friend, even though these types of people account for the majority of rapes committed in this country (Warshaw, 1988).

When absolute beliefs about what deviants look like are held by people within the criminal justice system—police, judges, attorneys, juries—decisions about whom to apprehend, their guilt or innocence, and the severity of their punishment reflect these biases as much as they reflect the nature of the act committed. In other words, stereotypical conceptions of race, age, religion, gender, physical appearance, and so on can influence a person's chances of being processed through the system and "becoming" a deviant. Sociologists William Chambliss and Richard Nagasawa (1969) compared the arrest rates of white, African-American, and Japanese-American youths in Seattle, Washington. They found that ethnic stereotypes led police to overestimate the involvement of African Americans in criminal activities and underestimate the involvement of Japanese Americans. Similarly, Mary Cameron (1964) found that of a sample of women arrested for shoplifting in Chicago over a 3-year period, 11% of whites were formally charged with a crime, compared to 58% of African Americans. Once arrested, African Americans and Hispanics are less likely than whites to be freed on bail and more likely to receive longer prison sentences if found guilty (Lizotte, 1978). Table 7.1 shows the black/white disparity in arrests, convictions, and length of sentence across the entire United States. Such biases can distort the official records regarding who makes up the population of deviants in this country and can reinforce public perceptions of what deviants look like (Archer, 1985; Pfohl, 1985; Reiman, 1990).

No matter what the behavior, oversimplified images of the typical deviant will always fall short of accounting for *every* individual. The vast majority of African Americans do not commit crimes, and the majority of Italians are not involved in the Mafia. Nevertheless, the degree to which images like these are *thought* to characterize an entire group is important insofar as it determines individual and

Table 7.1 *Racial Differences in Arrests, Convictions, and Length of Sentence*

Proportion of Total Population:	Whites(%) 80.3	Blacks(%) 12.1
Arrests:		
All offenses	69.0	29.0
Violent crimes	53.6	44.8
Property crimes	66.4	31.3
Drug crimes	58.1	41.0
Convictions:		
All offenses	52	47
Violent crimes	50	48
Property crimes	57	42
Drug crimes	43	56
Length of sentence (in months):		
All offenses	51.9	65.4
Violent crimes	88.0	98.4
Property crimes	27.4	24.1
Drug crimes	70.0	89.4

Source: U.S. Bureau of Justice Statistics, 1993.

societal responses. If affluent housewives or businesspeople who abuse drugs are *not* considered drug addicts, they will never be the focus of law enforcement attention, collective moral outrage, or public policy.

Relativism

An absolutist definition of deviance can lead to narrow and often inaccurate perceptions of many important social problems. For the relativist, complex societies consist of different groups with different values and interests. Sometimes these groups agree and cooperate to achieve a common goal, as when all segments of society join together to fight a foreign enemy. But more often than not there is conflict and struggle between groups to realize their own interests and goals. In **relativism,** life cannot be seen in terms of absolute right and wrong. Deviance is not a property inherent in any particular act, belief, or condition; instead, it is socially created by collective human judgments and ideas. Like beauty, deviance is in the eye of the beholder.

Deviance is a phenomenon that fluctuates with some frequency. We can have as much or as little deviance as we want depending on what we choose to count as deviant. Consider definitions of acceptable sexuality. Homosexuality was once culturally defined as a sinful crime punishable by death. By the mid-20th century, it was considered a sickness requiring psychotherapeutic treatment (Conrad & Schneider, 1980). Today, despite the continuing debate over its causes, public sentiment has become considerably less stigmatizing, although intolerance has grown again in some circles with the advent of AIDS.

Despite the ever-changing nature of conceptions of deviance, *every* society identifies certain individuals and certain behaviors as bothersome and disruptive and therefore justifiable targets of social control, be it treatment, punishment, spiritual healing, or correction. Who or what gets designated as deviant depends on the values, morals, and norms of each society.

To fully understand the societal and personal implications of deviance designations, we must look at how these definitions are created and perpetuated. From a relativistic approach, one of the key factors in determining the deviant nature of an act is who is doing the defining. If it is true that an act is deviant only because someone sees it that way, then the definition starts to look rather arbitrary. One person's crime becomes another person's act of moral conscience; one group's evil is another group's virtue; one culture's freedom fighter is another culture's terrorist. When we try to see certain acts from another group's perspective, even our most solidly held ideas about deviance become perplexing:

> Is, for example, the leader of loose-knit bands of hit-and-run killers of British soldiers a "homicidal maniac," a "crazed cult killer," or a "bandit"? Or is George Washington a revolutionary hero? Is Nat Turner, who executed Virginia slave owners and their families in 1830, in the same category? Is the Jewish terrorist in Palestine in 1948 distinguishable from the Palestinian terrorist in Israel in 1978? (Lauderdale, 1980, p. 5)

Definitions of specific phenomena as deviant are relative to particular social, community, or group standards and settings. When one community's standards are different from another's, conflict is likely to ensue. For example, the sacramental use of peyote—a cactus that contains the hallucinogenic substance mescaline—has been a part of the religious rituals of certain Native American groups for centuries. In 1990 the Oregon State Supreme Court ruled that the First Amendment's protection of free exercise of religion required state law to exempt the use of peyote for religious purposes.

The U. S. Supreme Court later overturned this ruling, stating that governmental policies and laws must be upheld even if it is to the disadvantage of some religious groups. Justice Antonin Scalia, in defending the criminalization of this religious practice, stated that it was an "unavoidable consequence of democratic government [which] must be preferred to a system in which each conscience is a law unto itself" (quoted in Greenhouse, 1990). Thus, although those who used peyote in this manner didn't consider themselves deviant—from their perspective they were conforming perfectly to the dictates of their religion—they were defined and treated that way by the dominant culture.

While the absolutist approach assumes that certain individual characteristics are typical of all deviants, the relativist approach acknowledges that there is no typical deviant. In fact, the same objective act committed by two different people may be defined very differently. Certain people are able to resist attempts to define their actions as deviant. For example, street prostitutes are regularly harassed, arrested, and jailed by the police. In the 1980s, however, Sydney Biddle Barrows, a wealthy descendent of an original Plymouth colonist, established a high-class brothel as a business enterprise and became known as the "Mayflower Madam." Instead of spending time in prison for breaking the law, she made the talk-show circuit and wrote a best-selling book. Clearly her socioeconomic status and pedigree influenced public definitions regarding the deviant nature of her activities. When she did it, somehow it wasn't so bad.

Immediate situational circumstances can also influence definitions of deviance. Drinking liquor in a bar is more acceptable than drinking in your college classroom; drinking on the weekend is more acceptable than drinking during the week; drinking in the evening is more acceptable than drinking in the morning.

Even acts of extreme violence may be defined as acceptable under certain circumstances. Killings committed under the auspices of the government—shooting looters during a riot, killing enemy soldiers during wartime, or capital punishment—fall outside the category of behaviors deemed deviant and problematic in society. Likewise, killing another individual in self-defense is not defined as murder and may be seen by the general public as necessary, even rewardable behavior (Ben-Yehuda, 1990). So even the act of purposely taking a human life is tolerated by certain groups or cultures under certain conditions (E. Goode, 1984).

Micro-Macro Connection
Mercy Killing

In the United States, the right to die has become as strident a rallying cry as the right to life. To some people the right to die with dignity is the most fundamental and inalienable of all human rights. But what about helping another person commit suicide or, in the extreme, taking the life of a person who is terminally ill or suffering? Are these acts of deviance or acts of compassion? Murder or mercy killing?

Over the last decade or so we have witnessed a tremendous increase in controversial ethical and legal battles over this issue. All one has to do is pick up the newspaper to read about a family fighting to take a loved one off of life-support equipment, or a husband putting his wife "out of her misery" because he can't stand to see her suffer any longer. One of the most highly publicized cases was that of Roswell Gilbert. In March of 1984 Gilbert, then 76 years old, fatally shot his wife, who suffered from Alzheimer's disease, in their Fort Lauderdale condominium. Gilbert was arrested, convicted of murder, and sentenced to life imprisonment. In 1990 his sentence was commuted to 5 years. Some felt he acted out of love for his wife; others thought he was a cold-blooded killer.

In 1991 Derek Humphry, founder of the Hemlock Society, wrote a controversial book called *Final Exit*. The Hemlock Society is an organization committed to protecting and promoting people's right to die a dignified death. This book, unlike others on the topic that offer philosophical arguments in favor of euthanasia or mercy killing, provides practical, step-by-step guidance for those who wish to assist others in committing suicide. It gives advice on choosing the most efficient and painless technique, finding a physician who will help, skirting the law, acquiring, storing, and using lethal drugs, and taking care of life insurance policies and other financial considerations. Humphry even provides a checklist of things one ought to attend to before dying and a table showing lethal dosages of common and readily available prescription drugs. Despite the vociferous opposition to the publication and sale of the book, it remained on the *New York Times* best-seller list for several weeks.

One of the most notorious figures in recent years has been Dr. Jack Kevorkian. Kevorkian, a retired Michigan physician, invented and, at the time of this writing, continues to use a machine that allows people to inject lethal doses of drugs into themselves. On June 4, 1990, he wrote a letter to the *New York Times* in which he talked freely about helping a woman suffering from Alzheimer's disease kill herself the day before. Desiring a gentle and certain death, she had sought out Kevorkian and his machine. On several occasions Kevorkian has been arrested and charged with first-degree murder. In 1994, he was tried and found not guilty.

To the absolutist there is no controversy in any of these cases. Life is absolutely sacred. A person purposely taking the life of another person, even if motivated by love and sympathy, is and always will be a murderer. A person who writes a book on how to do it is an accomplice to murder. To the relativist, however, taking account of situational circumstances means that different audiences will define these acts differently. In fact, the situational circumstances are the *only* relevant piece of information. The value of life itself must be weighed against other values like the personal freedom to be active, freedom from suffering, and control over one's life (Finlay, 1985). Allowing a suffering, terminally ill person to live would be the moral equivalent of a crime. Putting an end to his or her misery would be the acceptable thing to do under certain circumstances.

The controversy over mercy killing goes beyond the moral and ethical debate over individual actions and definitions of deviance. The issue is intimately tied to the broader structure of the medical profession and its place in society. The mere consideration of mercy killing is only possible because of recent technological developments in medicine. Because people can be kept alive artificially for indefinite periods of time, the very definition of death is now more problematic than it was in the past (Finlay, 1985). Answering the question of when a person ought to die is relevant only if medical technology is sophisticated enough to allow physicians to intervene and keep that person alive.

How the controversy over mercy killing is ultimately resolved will in turn have a dramatic impact on the practice of medicine. Fifty years ago, a doctor's task was clear: Keep the patient alive as long as possible. Today, things are not so simple. Imagine how the profession would have to change if mercy killing ever became a viable and legally acceptable solution to the problem of human suffering. The practices and beliefs underlying the entire medical establishment—from the training of medical students to the structure of hospitals to the role of health and life insurance—would have to change.

In the Netherlands a law has recently been enacted that legalizes physician-assisted suicide. According to the law, a physician can help a patient die if the following strict guidelines are met: The patient must make the decision voluntarily after being informed of all alternatives, the patient's condition must be "unbearable" and "hopeless," the physician must consult a colleague, and the procedure must be documented and subjected to a professional investigation (Simons, 1993). Dutch physicians must now make decisions not only on how to keep their patients well, but also on how to let them die. It will be interesting to see over the next several years how Dutch institutions accommodate such dramatic changes.

In sum, to a relativist, *who* commits the act, *who* labels it, and *where* and *when* it occurs are as important in determining its deviant nature as *what* is committed. Some people have the wherewithal to avoid having their acts defined as deviant. Definitions of deviant behavior change over time, and certain acts are acceptable to some audiences and not others.

The Elements of Deviance

Given the complex and controversial issues covered so far, the general definition of deviance we're left with goes something like this: **Deviance** is the behavior (how people act), ideas (how people think), or attributes (how people appear) of an individual or group that some people in society find offensive, wrong, immoral, sinful, evil, strange, or disgusting. This definition consists of three elements (Aday, 1990).

First, there must be some sort of behavioral *expectation*—a norm that defines appropriate, acceptable behavior, ideas, or characteristics. The expectations may be implicit or explicit, formal or informal, and more or less widely shared.

Second, deviance implies that there is some *violation* of the normative expectations. As we will see, the violation may be real or alleged; that is, an accusation of wrongdoing may be enough to give someone a reputation of deviance.

Finally, there must be an individual, group, or societal *reaction* to the deviance. If it is not known, the act, belief, or attribute in question never gets defined as deviant. If it is known, the reaction is likely to lead to some sort of response: avoidance, criticism, warnings, punishment, or treatment. The reaction may accurately reflect the facts or bear little resemblance to what really happened, as when people are punished and ostracized for acts they did not commit.

Labeling Deviance

Now that you have a sense of the socially constructed nature of deviance designations, let's discuss how people become deviant. I should note that the question of *how* people become deviant is different from the question of *why* people commit deviant acts. Most theories assume there is agreement as to what acts are deviant and proceed directly to an examination of the characteristics of people who commit them.

Sociologist Robert Merton (1957) argues that people are likely to commit deviant acts if they experience a contradiction between the culturally defined goals that we are all socialized to strive for (e.g., wealth and success) and access to the legitimate means by which they can achieve those goals (e.g., education, good jobs, and family influence). If you come to believe that being wealthy and achieving the "American Dream" is an important goal, but you have no money, no employment opportunities, and no access to higher education, Merton argues that you will be inclined to achieve the goal of success through *illegitimate* means like theft or the sale of illegal goods and services. In this sense, the person who sells illegal products to get rich is motivated by the same desires as the person who sells real estate to get rich. Other people who lack access to the legitimate means reject the desire to achieve the culturally defined goals of wealth and success and retreat from society altogether. According to Merton, vagrants, chronic drunks, drug addicts, and the mentally ill fall into this category.

Another sociologist, Edwin Sutherland (Sutherland & Cressey, 1955), argues that individuals *learn* deviant patterns of behavior from the people with whom they associate on a regular basis. Deviant behaviors are learned within the context of primary groups: friends, family members, peers. Through our associations with these influential individuals we learn not only the techniques for committing deviant acts (like how to pick a lock or how to snort cocaine), but also a set of beliefs and attitudes that justify or rationalize the behavior (Sykes & Matza, 1957). In order to commit deviant acts, we must learn how to perceive those acts as normal.

Theories like these are useful in explaining why some people engage in deviant acts while others don't, but they bypass the question of why certain acts committed by certain people are considered deviant in the first place. To find the answer, we must examine the social and interpersonal processes through which acts, attributes, and beliefs are defined as deviant (e.g., Becker, 1963; Lemert, 1972). Such an approach, often called *labeling theory*, doesn't analyze what causes people to commit deviant acts. Instead, it attempts to explain how cultural and individual perceptions create and sustain deviant identities. According to this theory, deviance is the consequence of the application of rules and sanctions to an offender. A deviant person, then, is not someone who is fundamentally different from a nondeviant, but someone to whom the label "deviant" has been successfully applied (Becker, 1963).

The primary concern is not what causes people to deviate in the first place, but what happens to a person—like Gladys Burr—*after* being identified as deviant by others. Although there are situations where deviant labels can be used for therapeutic purposes, such as the retention and use of the "alcoholic" label by members of Alcoholics Anonymous (Trice & Roman, 1970), labeling theorists usually assume that labels are harmful. The process of being singled out, defined, and reacted to as deviant changes a person in the eyes of others and consequently will have important life consequences for that individual. It may alter his or her self-concept, taint face-to-face interactions with nondeviants, and increase the probability that the behavior itself will be stabilized or made worse (Archer, 1985).

The Dramatization of Evil

The historical roots of this concern over the effects of labeling date back to a book written in 1938 by sociologist Frank Tannenbaum called *Crime and Community*. Tannenbaum was primarily interested in male juvenile delinquents, although his ideas can be applied to many different deviant groups. He believed that most acts of delinquency—breaking windows, petty theft, truancy, and so on—are a normal part of adolescent street life. Kids engage in these activities for fun, adventure, and excitement. The community at large, though, is likely to see such activities as evil or a nuisance and may demand some sort of control over the situation (i.e., punishment). As the behavior becomes more visible and frequent, the situation gradually becomes redefined. There is a shift from the definition of specific acts as "evil" to a definition of the individual as "evil." Once this occurs, *all* of the boy's acts become suspect. His companions, hangouts, speech, clothes, conduct, and everything about him becomes an object of scrutiny and further proof of his delinquent nature. From the community's point of view, the basically "good" individual who used to do mischievous things has now become a bad and useless human being.

Because first impressions are important in determining how others see us and, consequently, how we see ourselves, this "delinquent" label can have a tremendous impact on the young boy's life. What concerned Tannenbaum in particular was the effect the label would have on the boy's self-concept. The boy is likely to be overwhelmed by the community reaction and begin to think of himself as the type of person who would do such things. Over time the label becomes a self-fulfilling prophecy. The juvenile becomes bad because he is *defined* as bad by others.

We see evidence of this phenomenon in the school environment. When an act of theft or vandalism is committed on campus, the first person to be suspected is the kid or kids with the bad reputation. And if this person does something good or charitable, his or her ulterior motives are immediately called into question.

Tannenbaum called this process the *dramatization of evil*, and it plays a greater role in the making of a criminal than perhaps any other experience. By altering the individual's self-concept, the reactions of others, no matter how compassionate the intent, may perpetuate the deviance they seek to get rid of by trapping him in a role from which he cannot escape. He now lives in a different world. He has been "tagged" (Tannenbaum, 1938).

The Stickiness of Labels

Like stigmas (see chapter 6), deviant labels are difficult to overcome and can impede social life. The person who is labeled a deviant acquires a devalued social identity. In the eyes of others, the person who steals *is* a thief, the person who kills *is* a murderer. To possess a deviant identity is to be differentiated from those considered "normal." Subsequently the motives, actions, and character of the "deviant" are assumed to be typical of others who possess the label. The criminal is "cold-blooded and ruthless," the mental patient is "dangerous," the alcoholic is "weak-willed," the prostitute is "dirty and immoral."

It is one thing to violate a social norm, but it is something else entirely to be *socially defined* as a deviant. The label does more than mark you as someone who has committed some deviant act. It suggests that you are someone who is habitually given to certain kinds of undesirable behavior and who can be *expected* to behave in this way in the future. It influences the kinds of feelings others have and behaviors others direct toward you: rejection, suspicion, withdrawal, fear, mistrust, and hatred (A. K. Cohen, 1966).

Richard Schwartz and Jerome Skolnick
The Criminal Applicant

Deviant labels can impair the individual's eligibility to enter a broad range of socially acceptable roles, such as employment and marriage. Richard Schwartz and Jerome Skolnick (1962) constructed an interesting experiment to see if deviant labels restrict people's life chances. Posing as representatives of an employment agency, they prepared four fictitious employment folders. In all the folders their "client" was described as a 32-year-old single male with a high school education and a record of successive short-term jobs as a kitchen helper, maintenance worker, and handyman.

The folders differed only in the applicant's past record of criminal court involvement. The first folder indicated that he had been convicted and sentenced for assault. In the second, he had been tried for assault but found innocent. The third folder also showed that he was tried and acquitted, but included a supportive letter from the judge certifying the finding of not guilty and reaffirm-

Figure 7.1   *Legal Stigma*

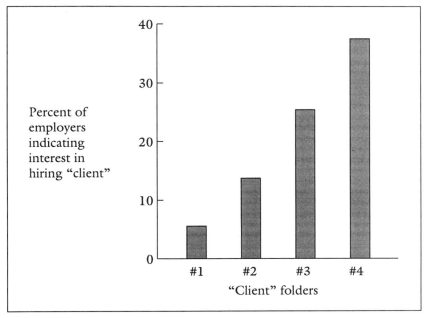

Source: R. D. Schwartz & Skolnick, 1962.

ing the legal presumption of innocence. The fourth made no mention of any criminal record, implying that the "client" had never been involved in the court system (R. D. Schwartz & Skolnick, 1962).

The researchers contacted a hundred potential employers who were randomly divided into four groups of 25. Each group received one folder. The employer was asked whether he or she could use the man described in the folder. To ensure the reality of the situation, the employers were not told that they were part of a study.

Of the 25 employers who received folder 4 (no record), nine (36%) indicated an interest in hiring him. Of those who received folder 3 (acquittal plus letter from judge) six (24%) showed an interest in hiring the man. Three of the 25 (12%) potential employers who read folder 2 (acquittal) showed an interest. Finally, of the 25 employers who received folder 1 (convicted and sentenced for assault), only one (4%) expressed any interest in hiring the man (see Figure 7.1).

The study showed that employment opportunities are severely restricted by the presence of a deviant label. Similar stigmatizing effects of deviant labels have been found in other countries (Buikhuisen & Dijksterhuis, 1971) and for other offenses like marijuana possession (Erickson & Goodstadt, 1979) and drunk driving (Boshier & Johnson, 1974).

Why would such apparent discrimination occur? From the point of view of the potential employer, there are certainly justifiable reasons for refusing to hire ex-convicts. While they may have paid their debt to society, this is no guarantee of future legal behavior. Americans have become increasingly distrustful of our criminal justice system. There is a widespread belief among the public that prisons do not rehabilitate but actually make convicts *more* deviant by teaching them better ways of crime and providing social networks to criminal activity on the outside (R. Johnson, 1987).

It is impossible to know just how many ex-convicts actually commit crimes after their release. We do know that a great many of them return to prison. It is estimated that approximately two-thirds of all adult inmates in the United States have been in prison before (Petersilia, 1985; U.S. Bureau of Justice Statistics, 1983). Of the more serious crimes, roughly 35% of convicted robbers, 43% of convicted burglars, and 22% of people convicted of homicide are convicted of second crimes (Wallerstedt, 1984).

Although stigmatization due to fear of future criminal activity may be justifiable, rational, or understandable, it doesn't account for the findings of the above studies, which show that a mere *charge* of criminal activity conjures up suspicions of tainted character and is often sufficient to prevent an employer from hiring someone. The labeling process is powerful enough, even in the absence of wrongdoing, to produce a durable loss of status for the individual. Not only does this challenge the important legal contention that one is "innocent until proven guilty," it also suggests that the negative effects of being labeled a criminal cannot be reduced simply by diverting offenders away from prison (Erickson & Goodstadt, 1979).

Labels, once affixed, become all-encompassing, acting as a filter for incoming information. Others tend to interpret subsequent actions with the label in mind, seeking out behavior that supports the label and explaining away behavior that seems out of character. For someone who has a record of past criminal activity, every act might be interpreted as an expression of his or her criminal tendencies. This process is particularly apparent for people labeled "mentally ill."

The Social Construction of Mental Illness

In the minds of most people, mental illness is akin to a physical disease that can be effectively controlled or cured only through medical treatment. Psychiatric "symptoms," however, are also violations of social norms. That is, the behaviors that characterize mental illnesses—hearing voices, talking to oneself, inappropriate display of emotions, and so on—conflict with socially appropriate conduct. To understand the phenomenon of mental illness, we must examine the cultural and interpersonal contexts within which the purported biochemical, genetic, and psychological processes take place. As a labeling theorist would point out, an identity as a "mentally ill" person does not exist independent of the reaction of others.

Thomas Scheff (1966) was one of the first sociologists to propose a theory of mental illness that takes account of social as well as individual processes. Although this theory has been criticized by both psychiatrists (e.g., Torrey, 1988) and sociologists (e.g., Gove, 1982), it sheds important light on how people labeled as mentally ill may be forced into a deviant role by the responses of others.

Residual Rule Breaking

According to Scheff, all cultures have a variety of terms for categorizing behaviors that violate norms. Murder, assault, drunkenness—these categories are relatively well defined and agreed upon by members of society. However, there are other violations for which the culture does not provide explicit names: the positioning of one's body with regard to another, the expression of appropriate emotions, gestures, and so on. There are no formal rules for these actions, yet the person who does the "wrong" thing somehow makes us uncomfortable and leads us to form certain impressions about him or her: strange, weird, dangerous.

Scheff calls these violations **residual rule-breaking behaviors.** In the past or in different cultures, residual rule breaking might have been attributed to witchcraft or demonic possession. Today, these activities may be labeled as psychiatric symptoms indicative of underlying mental illness. The diagnosis depends on such factors as the identity of the rule breaker, the particular rule broken, the amount of strange behavior a community will tolerate, alternative explanations that might rationalize the behavior, and the social context within which the rule breaking takes place (Cockerham, 1992).

Like other labeling theorists, Scheff is not concerned with what initially causes residual rule-breaking behaviors. He states that they can arise from genetics, biochemistry, physiology, psychological peculiarities, or environmental stresses. His point is that the behaviors elicit negative social reactions from others. Long-term mental illness is more than just a physical or psychiatric disease. It is a social role that may or may not have identifiable medical sources.

Although there is no way to get an exact estimate, the rate of unrecorded residual rule breaking is probably extremely high. Most residual rule breaking goes undiagnosed or is of transitory significance. Many people who are withdrawn, fly off the handle easily, or hear voices are not labeled as mentally ill either by themselves or by others (Scheff, 1966). In 1962 a group of sociologists and psychiatrists led by Leo Srole devised a method to examine the prevalence of untreated mental illness. They interviewed a sample of people in New York City concerning behaviors and experiences that psychiatrists would consider symptoms of mental problems: anxiety, depression, obsessive thoughts, and so forth

(Srole et al., 1962). A panel of psychiatrists then rated the questionnaires from zero (no symptoms) to six (incapacitating symptoms). The panel found that only 20% of the respondents were sufficiently free of symptoms to be considered normal. The other 80% had at least one psychiatric symptom, and of those, 24% could be considered impaired because of mental illness. In a 1994 survey, more than 8,000 Americans between the ages of 15 and 54 participated in structured psychiatric interviews. Results showed that close to 50% of them have experienced a mental disorder at some point in their lives (R. C. Kessler et al., 1994).

These findings have been used to support the argument that the country needs more psychiatric treatment facilities. For Scheff, such a high frequency of undiagnosed mental illness speaks volumes about the sociological nature of mental illness and our ability to explain away or rationalize some residual rule breaking to avoid formally labeling others as mentally ill. Sometimes we say the violation is just an eccentricity; other times it is accommodated by the person's family and friends. Many families have a monumental capacity to overlook or minimize evidence of disturbance (Jackson, 1954; Yarrow, Schwartz, Murphy, & Deasy, 1955). They may say, "There's nothing really wrong," "It's a physical problem," or "She's under a lot of stress at work these days." People rely on these tactics so they can live with or manage problematic behavior (Lynch, 1983).

All this suggests that individual normality, as well as abnormality, is socially constructed. The people in one's immediate circle can and often do have tremendous influence over the determination of deviance. Those who can't take full responsibility for maintaining normality must have it done for them.

The Stereotyped Imagery of Madness

If most people who engage in residual rule breaking are not recognized as mentally ill, how do we account for the small percentage who go on to receive the formal label? The answer lies in the nature of societal reaction. Reactions to residual rule breaking are shaped by shared conceptions of insanity and normality. At a very young age we learn the stereotypes of madness through the wacky antics of such cartoon characters as Daffy Duck and Krazy Kat. These stereotypes are continually reaffirmed through social interaction (Scheff, 1966). Our language is filled with words and phrases that reflect images of madness (e.g., "weirdo," "bananas," "He's crazy," "You must be nuts").

The news media add details to support such stereotypes. Representations of mental illness emphasize its bizarre aspects, perpetuating the belief that crazy people look and act differently from "normal" people. News accounts of violence frequently begin with phrases like "so-and-so, who has a history of mental illness . . . ," or "so-and-so, a former mental patient . . ." It's highly unlikely that a story would begin with the statement: "Mr. John Smith, an ex-mental patient, was elected director of the Collegetown Glee Club." Such portrayals force the reader or viewer to infer that murder, rape, or other types of violence occur more frequently among former mental patients than among the general population, when in actuality the number is lower than one would think (Winick, 1982). This selective reporting confirms the public stereotype that mentally ill people are violent and lack self-control.

What makes these portrayals all the more influential is that most of us, because we lack direct exposure to the mentally ill, must rely on them as the sole source of information. When the rule-breaking behavior of an individual becomes a public issue, these stereotypes become the guiding imagery for action (Scheff, 1966). If you think all crazy people are potentially violent, and I act in a way that is consistent with your stereotype of a crazy person (e.g., talking to myself), you may assume that I may become violent at any moment. You are then more likely to consider me mentally ill and avoid me or, in the extreme, contact psychiatric authorities. So powerful are these cultural images of insanity that people will sometimes seek psychiatric help voluntarily if they observe themselves persistently acting in such a manner (Thoits, 1985).

Entering and Exiting the Mentally Ill Role

If the residual rule breaker is labeled and placed under the care of psychiatric authorities, he or she may eventually come to accept the role imputed to him or her (Scheff, 1966). The rule breaker will *become* the mental patient. How does this happen?

As discussed in the previous chapter, people can be subtly encouraged to take on particular identities and act in ways that are consistent with the expectations of others. People who are labelled "mentally disturbed" are apt to be confused and highly receptive to the cues they receive from those around them, particularly when they are first labeled (Scheff, 1966). Hence they are likely to accept the deviant label and act as they think a mentally ill person is supposed to act. Instead of saying, "I'm a normal person who occasionally does weird things," he or she says, "I'm crazy. I do weird things because I'm mentally ill."

Ordinarily, patients who display "insight" into their conditions are rewarded by mental health personnel. Trouble can be avoided if one plays the role of mental patient. Conversely, denying the label or trying to shed it too quickly can be met with punishment and trap the patient in a vicious cycle. If patients refuse to accept the label ("There's nothing wrong with me"), the staff may interpret it as another symptom of the illness: denial. The implicit message seems to be "You're not sane until we say you are."

Psychiatric staff members can sometimes deflate patients' self-images of sanity by compelling them to face the "reality" of their illness (Goffman, 1959b). In fact, the social environment of a mental hospital is set up to deny any image of sanity the patient might have. The patient soon realizes that it makes no sense to stake a claim in an identity that will be discredited by the psychiatric staff.

Adoption of the mentally ill role becomes the most efficient way of coping with a demoralizing situation (Goffman, 1959b).

Even after one is declared "cured," it is often difficult to resume a nondeviant role. Although there is mounting evidence that community reactions to former mental patients are not as negative as they once were (Cockerham, 1992; Torrey, 1988), some of these individuals may still experience varying degrees of discrimination, abuse, and suspicion. A significant proportion of the public still sees former mental patients as dangerous and is reluctant to interact with them (Link et al., 1987).

David Rosenhan
Being Sane in Insane Places

In 1973 sociologist David Rosenhan designed a clever study to examine the difficulty people have shedding the "mentally ill" label. He was particularly interested in how staffs in mental institutions go about processing information about patients in light of their diagnosed condition. He decided that the best way to get this information was from the inside through participant observation. Rosenhan and seven associates had themselves committed to different mental hospitals by complaining that they were hearing voices (a symptom commonly believed to be characteristic of schizophrenia). The staff did not know the pseudopatients were actually part of a field experiment. They assumed they were patients like any other and had no reason to believe the reported symptoms were fake.

Beyond the alleged symptoms and a falsification of name and occupation, the important events of the pseudopatients' life histories were presented as they had actually occurred. Furthermore, prior to the study, Rosenhan instructed them to act completely normal upon admission into the hospital. That is, they were not to act "crazy" in any way. In fact, Rosenhan told them that acting normal was the only way they could get out.

Despite the fact that they did nothing out of the ordinary, the pseudopatients remained hospitalized for an average of 19 days, from a low of 9 days to a high of 52. Their sanity was never detected except, ironically enough, by the *actual* patients in the hospitals. All of Rosenhan's associates retained the deviant label even after being discharged. Their schizophrenia was said to be "in remission," implying that it was dormant and could possibly resurface. At no time during their stay in the hospital was the legitimacy of their schizophrenic label ever questioned. It was simply assumed that they *were* schizophrenic; after all, why else would they have heard voices?

Everything they did and said was understood from this premise. Normal behaviors were overlooked entirely or profoundly misinterpreted. Minor disagreements became deep-seated indicators of emotional instability. Boredom was interpreted as nervousness or anxiety. Even the act of writing on a notepad was seen by the staff as a sign of some deeper psychological disturbance.

Furthermore, even though there was nothing "pathological" about the pseudopatients' past histories, these records were reinterpreted to be consistent with the schizophrenic label. One patient, for instance, had a close relationship with his mother but a remote one with his father during early childhood. As he matured he became closer to his father while his relationship with his mother became more distant. He had a warm and loving relationship with his wife and children, although there were occasional fights and friction. In short, there was nothing particularly unusual about this person's history. But notice how this history was translated into something troubled and psychopathological by the attending psychiatrist:

> This white 39-year-old male . . . manifests a long history of *considerable ambivalence in close relationships,* which began in early childhood. A warm relationship with his mother cools during his adolescence. A distant relationship to his father is described as becoming very intense. *Affective stability is absent.* His attempts to control emotions with his wife and children are punctuated by angry outbursts and, in the case of the children, spankings. And while he says that he has several good friends, one senses considerable ambivalence embedded in those relationships also [emphasis added]. (Rosenhan, 1973, p. 253)

Just as behavior was interpreted in light of the label, the facts of this man's past were distorted to achieve consistency with what was generally believed to be true about the family dynamics of schizophrenics. Rosenhan didn't conclude that the staffs at these hospitals were incompetent or dishonest. In fact, he argues that there was no conscious effort to misconstrue the evidence to fit the label. They were doing their jobs effectively. He reasoned that the labels were so sticky that they profoundly affected the way information was processed and perceived. Had the same behaviors been observed in a different context, without the perceptual effects of the preexisting label, they no doubt would have been interpreted in an entirely different fashion.

Mental illness must be understood as an interactional as well as a medical phenomenon. The actual or imagined reactions of others can determine a mental patient's self-image, create "deviant" patterns of behavior, and lead to social rejection after the illness is "cured." Although it may be true that some mental illnesses are caused by biological or chemical processes, such conditions are considered disorders in the first place because their symptoms violate the norms of everyday life. Whatever psychological distress may actually be present, the *labeling* of mental illness necessarily involves an interpretation.

Consider two people, person A and person B, who are suffering from an incapacitating depression in which they display identical symptoms. They are overwhelmingly sad, can't eat, can't sleep, and are unable to carry out their customary roles in life. Person A's wife has just died, he's unemployed, the bills are piling up, and he sees no likelihood of a change in his circumstances. Person B shows all the same symptoms of depression as Person A, but no one can figure out why. He has a satisfying and high-paying job and a loving wife and family.

On the one hand, Person A probably would not be considered mentally ill because his depression has a logical and culturally acceptable explanation. On the other hand, Person B is likely to be regarded as sick because his social circumstances do not explain his problems. Clearly, then, the diagnosis of mental illness in these cases is not just a matter of brain chemistry but is dependent on a process of social interpretation (Turner & Edgley, 1983).

The Role of Power

Because deviance is socially defined, the behaviors and conditions that come to be called "deviant" can at times appear somewhat arbitrary. Often the definition of deviance is a form of social control exerted by more powerful people and groups over less powerful people and groups. Let's examine this process from a conflict perspective. Prior to the 17th century, people who were "insane" were not necessarily separated from the general population. Like poor people and other "undesirables," they freely roamed the countryside. Responsibility for their care rested with the family or the local community. Madness at the time was a public matter, out in the open and part of everyday life. As long as the people weren't dangerous, they weren't considered particularly troublesome.

As cities began to grow, so did the population of roaming vagrants and mad people. Their presence and visibility became increasingly annoying and bothersome to the rest of the population. In 1657 King Louis XIII of France issued a royal decree forbidding all people from begging on the streets of Paris. It wasn't long before the French army began to hunt down street people and herd them into an institution euphemistically called the Hôpital Général (Foucault, 1965). There, mad people were confined with beggars, vagabonds, street thieves, the poor, the unemployed, and anybody else who could not support himself or herself. It is estimated that at its peak the hospital held 1% of the entire population of Paris (Conrad & Schneider, 1980).

The General Hospital wasn't the kind of hospital we have today. There were no medical treatments, doctors, nurses, or medical equipment. It was more like a pauper's prison that symbolically represented society's distaste for idleness and laziness. More important, it served the interests of the growing ruling class of landowners, merchants, and businesspeople. In periods of economic prosperity, the inhabitants of the hospital provided a limitless pool of cheap labor. In slow economic times, the hospital reabsorbed these individuals so they wouldn't be a nuisance to the more affluent citizens.

As capitalism began to flourish and the need for a competent workforce increased, the ruling class thought it best to separate the hospital inhabitants who could work from those who couldn't (i.e., the insane). A more specialized institution, the madhouse, was established to house only the insane. This separation occurred not to provide the insane with more effective psychiatric treatment but to protect others from the "contagion" of madness (Foucault, 1965). Their presence disrupted the reserve labor pool, so they had to be segregated. The madhouse quickly grew in popularity, evolving into the more humanitarian insane asylum of the 19th century and the more therapeutic mental hospital of the 20th century. Thus, a new deviant category (the insane) and a new way of dealing with them (confinement in specialized institutions) were created by the state primarily for economic and social reasons (Chambliss, 1974).

Conflict theorists also point out that it is often in the interest of powerful groups to foster a belief that society's rules are under attack by deviants and that official action against them is needed. It is argued, for instance, that the contemporary criminal justice system works to ensure that the offender who winds up in prison is a member of the lowest socioeconomic class (Reiman, 1990). Poor people are more likely to get arrested, be formally charged with a crime, have their cases go to trial, get convicted, and receive harsher sentences. This imbalance is not simply the result of prejudice against the poor. If that were the case, the situation would be relatively easy to deal with. Instead, it occurs because poor individuals happen to commit acts that fit commonly held definitions of what a crime is. As a result, these individuals become "typical criminals."

The Social Reality of Crime

One of the most important constructed realities is that which determines what we regard as legal or illegal behavior. A popular conception of the law is that it exists to protect the best interests of the people. Certain acts are defined as crimes because they offend the majority. We come to trust our legal institutions—legislators, courts, and police—to regulate social behavior in the interest of the common good.

From a conflict perspective, however, the law is not a mechanism that merely protects good people from bad people; it is a political instrument used by specific groups to further their own interests, often at the expense of others. The law is created by economic elites who control the production and distribution of major resources in society (Chambliss, 1964; Quinney, 1970). Law is, of course, determined by legislative action. But legislatures are greatly influenced by these powerful segments of society via lobbying groups, political action committees, individual campaign contributions, and so on (see chapter 10). Acts that conflict with the economic or political interests of the groups who have the power to influence public policy are more likely to be addressed. An early example of how power structures can influence the social reality of crime was the creation of vagrancy laws in the 14th and 15th centuries (Chambliss, 1964). During this period the Black Death decimated Europe's labor force. The lack of an adequate pool of labor forced landowners to pay higher wages for "free" labor and made it more difficult to keep workers bound to their land as serfs.

Vagrancy laws were created that made it illegal for someone unemployed to refuse work if it was offered and prohibited them from fleeing employment when they had accepted it. (It would be like someone offering you a job for $1 an hour that you were required by law to take.) These laws were designed to force laborers to accept employment at a low wage in order to provide the landowner with an adequate supply of labor at a price he could afford (Chambliss, 1964). A new category of criminal conduct was established that clearly supported the interests of wealthy landowners.

In addition to influencing the creation of laws, power also affects public *ideas* about crime. Through mass communication, dominant groups expose the public to ideas that force us to look at crime in ways that are favorable to them. The selective portrayal of crime plays an important role in shaping public perceptions of the "crime problem" and therefore its "official" definition. When politicians talk about fighting America's crime problem, or when news shows report an increase in crime rates, they are almost always referring to street crimes (illegal drug use, robbery, burglary, murder, assault, etc.) rather than corporate crimes, governmental crimes, or crimes more likely to be committed by people in positions of power:

> Press coverage focuses public attention on crime in the streets with scarcely a mention of "crime in the suites," downplaying such . . . crimes as briberies, embezzlements, kickbacks, monopolistic restraints of trade, illegal uses of public funds by private interests, occupational safety violations, unsafe consumer goods, and environmental poisonings. (Parenti, 1986, p. 12)

Furthermore, how crime is defined and reported is largely determined by the race and social class of the victim and victimizer. Affluent victims receive more press coverage than poor victims, leaving the public with the impression that most crime victims are from middle- and upper-class backgrounds. Conversely, racial minority and low-income lawbreakers are more likely to be publicized as criminals than are corporate leaders whose law-breaking activity may actually be more harmful to the common good (Parenti, 1986).

Such exposure creates a certain way of perceiving crime that *becomes social reality*. We accept the objectified fact that certain people or actions are a threat to the well-being of the entire society and therefore a threat to our own personal interests. Thus the enactment and enforcement of laws against some acts and not others represent not only a legal victory but a victory in the struggle to control social reality.

White-Collar Crime

We take for granted that street crime is our worst social problem and that white-collar crime is not as dangerous or as costly (Reiman, 1990). However, the threat posed by the typical criminal is not the greatest threat to which we are exposed. Unsafe work conditions, dangerous chemicals in our air, water, and food, faulty products, unnecessary surgery, and shoddy emergency medical services put us in constant and imminent physical and economic danger:

> Every year roughly 28,000 deaths and 130,000 serious injuries are caused by dangerous products. At least 100,000 workers die from exposure to deadly chemicals and other safety hazards. Workplace carcinogens are estimated to cause between 23 and 38 percent of all cancer deaths. . . . Fraud costs the nation's businesses and individuals upwards of $100 billion each year. The Senate Judiciary Committee has estimated that faulty goods, monopolistic practices and other such violations cost consumers $171 to $231 billion. . . . The dollar cost of corporate crime in the United States is more than 10 times greater than the combined total from larcenies, robberies, burglaries and auto thefts. (Mokhiber, 1989, p. 14)

The individuals responsible for these activities rarely show up in police or prison records. Although antitrust violations, false advertising, price fixing, unfair labor practices, embezzlement, and fraud cost society more money and pose a greater danger to the public safety than ordinary street criminals, the people who commit these white-collar crimes seldom receive heavy punishment (Reiman, 1990). Their offenses tend not to be treated as "real" crimes. Furthermore, large corporations that commit such crimes usually go through less visible civil procedures than embarrassing criminal trials.

In 1992 the U.S. Justice Department accused Teledyne, Inc., of systematically falsifying tests on an electrical component used in the construction of sophisticated weapons and spacecraft. The suit asserted that Teledyne was essentially selling the government a $6 part for $20. It was estimated that these practices, which went on for about 7 years, defrauded the government of about $250 million (Stevenson, 1992).

Three years earlier Teledyne pled guilty to overcharging the Defense Department. Twice before their shipping operations had been suspended by the Pentagon because of overcharging. Despite all this, the company continues to do business with the government today. If you had stolen $250 million dollars from a bank, would you be allowed to carry on with life as usual or do business with the very company from which you had stolen?

A 1984 fire in a coal mine operated by Utah Power and Light resulted in the deaths of 27 miners. A subsequent investigation found 34 obvious safety violations that directly caused the deaths. The owners of the company were not charged with murder, negligent homicide, involuntary manslaughter, or any other crime. Instead, the Federal Mine Safety and Health Administration imposed a fine of $111,470 on the power company—about one-third the maximum penalty possible, or about $4,200 per death (B. A. Franklin, 1987).

Activities like these take place every day without much public outcry, moral panic, or legislative action. Yet at the same time massive law enforcement efforts are directed at "typical" street criminals like street beggars, thieves, and drug dealers.

The War on Drugs

As you're well aware, the United States has been in an ill-defined and undeclared but highly publicized "war" for many years: the War on Drugs. There is a widespread feeling on the part of the public that many of our social ills are created by the moral failure of a specific group of individuals: drug users and drug dealers. They are the enemy, they are destroying our country, and they need to be stopped (E. Goode, 1989).

Many sociologists argue that antidrug campaigns and legislative activities in the United States are motivated more by economic and political interests than by a genuine concern for the health and welfare of vulnerable members of society (E. Goode, 1989). The so-called Drug War is a political gold mine. Capitalizing on the "drug menace" as a personal and societal threat is a common political tactic in our society (Ben-Yehuda, 1990). Drug scares are attractive to the media and to the population at large because they tend to focus on a foreign menace supplying the drugs and portray the vulnerable youth of the country as victims (P. Morgan, Wallack, & Buchanan, 1988). It is relatively easy to generate moral panic from phrases like "Drugs destroy young minds" or "Drugs destroy the future of our country." Indeed the term *drugs* itself is an easy and safe scapegoat on which to focus collective hatred.

The Drug War is also big business. More than $60 billion is spent each year at all levels of the criminal justice system to fight the drug menace (Gottfredson & Hirschi, 1989). Law enforcement and some political groups portray the drug problem as ever worsening, but the facts suggest that America's drug problem is being blown out of proportion. National statistics indicate that, due to the aging of the American population, the rate of both illegal and legal drug use has been steadily declining since the mid-1970s (Gottfredson & Hirschi, 1989). A survey of 12th graders from 1975 to 1991 showed a decrease in lifetime drug use starting in 1983 (see Figure 7.2).

When we hear the phrase "the War on Drugs," we all know that the drugs in question are the *illegal* ones: marijuana, crack, heroin, cocaine, and so forth. The assumption is that illegal drugs are the most dangerous substances and the ones that must be eradicated. However, the difference between legal and illegal drugs is not necessarily a function of their relative danger. The National Commission on Marijuana and Drug Abuse defines a drug as any chemical that affects the structure and function of a living organism (cited in Fine, 1990). Such a definition would include alcohol, nicotine, caffeine, and perhaps even salt and sugar. These substances, even though they can be harmful, are either completely legal or legal under certain age restrictions.

Figure 7.2   *Lifetime Drug Use by 12th Graders*

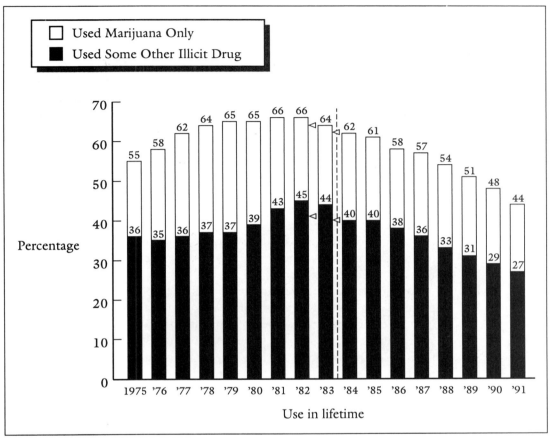

Notes: Use of "some other illicit drug" includes any use of hallucinogens, cocain, and heroin, or any use that is not under a doctor's orders of other opiates, stimulants, sedatives, or tranquilizers.

Δ shows the percentage that results if nonprescription stimulants are excluded.

The dashed vertical line indicates that after 1983 the shaded and open bars are defined by using the amphetamine questions that were revised to exclude nonprescription stimulants from the definition of "illicit drugs."

Source: National Institute on Drug Abuse, 1992.

Tobacco, for example, is a clearer health risk than either alcohol or marijuana but is rarely discussed in terms of drug abuse. Cigarettes are estimated to cause 85% of all cases of lung cancer, adding up to about 130,000 deaths a year. In addition, they are purportedly linked to approximately 60,000 deaths by emphysema and 100,000 deaths due to heart disease each year (Reiman, 1990). Knowing the hazards of cigarette smoking has not prompted our society to outlaw them entirely, as it has outlawed marijuana smoking and cocaine use.

The legality or illegality of a drug may be more a function of who uses it than how dangerous it is. Marijuana and crack are sold by "pushers"; cigarettes and alcohol are sold by "businesspeople." You will recall from chapter 3 that addiction to opium was not defined as a problem until it became associated with Chinese immigrants rather than middle-class housewives.

Why don't abusers of legal drugs elicit the same frenzied, warlike public reaction as "illegal" drugs? One reason is that substances like tobacco and alcohol represent multi-billion-dollar industries. Criminalizing tobacco would certainly destroy the economies of several states. Another reason has to do, again, with public perceptions of "typical" drug addicts. They are assumed to be irresponsible and dangerous and to look dirty and unkempt. But society does not stigmatize and scorn "respectable" people addicted to legal substances.

To the extent that the public is convinced of the importance and urgency of the drug problem, law enforcement officials will use these perceptions and any other tactic to ensure the public good, even if such measures cross the line of ethics and individual, constitutional rights. Police don't harass people addicted to prescription drugs, ransack their homes, or develop creative ways of apprehending and arresting them.

Consider a law enforcement method called the "drug courier profile." The profile is a set of characteristics that are innocent in and of themselves, but when used together they serve as clues to identifying drug smugglers in public facilities such as airports, train stations, bus depots, and interstate highways. Officers look for people who are obviously in a hurry, have bought a one-way ticket or paid for the ticket with cash, have changed travel plans at the last minute, are the first to get off the plane, or fly to or from Miami or Detroit or any other city with heavy drug traffic. The Supreme Court ruled in 1989 that such factors, as well as a person's physical appearance, can amount to a "reasonable suspicion" that allows law enforcement officers to stop and interrogate people who fit the profile. It is estimated that hundreds of people are stopped each week as they are boarding, arriving, or simply passing through an airport (Belkin, 1990).

Other people who fit the "drug swallower profile" have been forcibly taken to local hospitals to be X-rayed to see if they had swallowed pouches filled with drugs. In 1990, 348 people were X-rayed in New York, Miami, and Houston. Of those, 161 (or 46%) were found to be carrying drugs (Belkin, 1990). The Drug Enforcement Administration says that such a success rate justifies the practice. In other words, in the interests of curtailing drug traffic it is worth the price of wrongly accusing and inconveniencing innocent people if guilty people are caught in the process.

Critics argue that the success of the practice is not the issue. They suggest that stereotypes, particularly racial ones, are a key element of the drug courier profile. In December of 1989 the *Mississippi Sun Herald* examined police files on people stopped and searched on a major interstate highway. Of 57 stops, 55 involved Hispanics or African Americans who drove cars with Texas or Florida license plates. A Rutgers University statistician found that on a stretch of the New Jersey Turnpike, only 4.7% of all traffic consisted of late-model cars with out-of-state license plates driven by African-American men. However, more than 80% of the cars that were stopped and interrogated on the highway fit that description (cited in Belkin, 1990).

The Medicalization of Deviant Behavior

Given the fact that deviance designations are related to the economic and political power arrangements in society, how does a particular way of thinking about deviance become dominant? In chapter 3 I described the actions of moral entrepreneurs—people or groups of people who crusade to have their versions of reality accepted by society at large. Moral entrepreneurs are interested in a single issue, be it abortion, drunk driving, child abuse, or offensive art. Occasionally, however, certain industries or institutions become particularly influential in constructing an entire belief system that proposes causes and solutions to a wide range of social problems. Instead of fighting for one particular issue, some groups fight for an entire worldview.

Perhaps the most obvious and powerful force in defining deviance today is the medical establishment. The field of medicine has been extremely successful in presenting a conception of deviance that equates it with illness. Each time we automatically refer to bizarre or troublesome behavior as "sick," we help to perpetuate the perception that deviance is diseaselike. As a consequence, many physicians, psychologists, psychiatrists, therapists, insurance agents, and the entire pharmaceutical industry benefit from a medicalized view of deviant behavior.

Medicalization, or the "medical model," is the definition of behavior as a medical problem or illness and the mandating or licensing of the medical profession to provide some type of treatment for it (Conrad, 1975). Conduct that was once categorized simply as misbehavior is now redefined as psychiatric diseases, disorders, or syndromes. Between 1952 and 1986 the number of mental disorders recognized by the American Psychiatric Association increased from 110 to 210 (*Harper's Magazine*, 1986). To accommodate the growing number of "illnesses," the number of psychiatric professionals and the number of people seeking psychiatric help have almost tripled over the last two decades. The U.S. government has estimated that the economic cost of mental health care is close to $55 billion a year (Kirk & Kutchins, 1992). Experts estimate that between 20 and 33% of Americans suffer from some sort of mental disorder (Robins & Regier, 1991). Along with alcoholism, drug addiction, and mental illness, these disorders now include overeating, undereating, learning disabilities, shyness, violence, child abuse, and excessive gambling, shopping, and sex.

Why has the medical view of deviance become so dominant? One reason is that medical explanations of troublesome social problems and deviant behaviors are appealing to a society that craves quick, simple, scientific answers. It is comforting when a researcher tells us that violence is the result of a dysfunction in the brain; it then becomes a problem of defective, violent *individuals*, not of the larger societal context within which such acts take place. Likewise, it is a relief when our doctor or therapist tells us our anxiety, depression, crabbiness, and insecurity will vanish if we take a drug like Prozac, an antidepressant introduced in 1988 that to date has been taken by more than 10 million people worldwide (Angier, 1993). By looking inside the individual, we are spared the difficult task of looking at the structure of our society. The depressed person is the problem, not us.

The medicalization of deviance also appeals to our humanitarian values. The designation of a problem as an illness removes legal and moral scrutiny or punishment in favor of therapeutic treatment (Zola, 1986). The alcoholic is no longer a sinner or a criminal but a victim, someone whose behavior is beyond his or her control due to an "illness." Children who have trouble learning in school aren't disobedient and disruptive, they are "sick." If people are violating norms because of a disease that has invaded their bodies, they should not be held morally responsible. Medicalization creates less social stigma and condemnation of people labeled deviant.

Despite its enormous appeal, our tendency to medicalize deviance has serious social consequences (Conrad, 1975). These include the use of medicine as a means of social control, the individualization of complex social issues, and the depoliticization of deviance.

Medicine as a Means of Social Control

The medical profession is a powerful establishment. To become a physician, one must undergo years of rigorous training and be licensed by the profession's governing body. Because special expertise is acquired in this area, we assume that admission into the ranks must be carefully controlled. Physicians enjoy a tremendously high status in American society. "Plumber's orders," "accountant's orders," or even "sociologist's orders" do not carry the same influence and authority that "doctor's orders" carry. Consequently, physicians are able to claim jurisdiction over the label of illness and anything to which the label can be attached, regardless of whether or not they can deal with it effectively (Friedson, 1970).

Decisions regarding diagnosis and treatment of a host of problems are almost completely controlled by the profession. The consequences of these decisions reach far beyond the health and well-being of an individual patient. Plastic surgeons have helped define or at least perpetuate cultural standards of beauty. Any psychiatrist who prescribes drugs for a person's emotional suffering alters our cultural conceptions of what conditions we need not tolerate. Organ transplants have redefined our notions of death and dying (Zola, 1986). The more behaviors that are defined as illnesses, the larger the legitimate domain of the profession:

> The increasing acceptance of technical [medical] solutions . . . results in
> the withdrawal of more and more areas of human experience from the
> realm of public discussion. For when drunkenness, juvenile delinquency . . .
> and extreme political beliefs are seen as symptoms of an underlying illness
> or biological defect the merits of such behaviors or beliefs need not be
> evaluated. (Reynolds, 1973, p. 200)

Defining a problem as medical removes it from the public arena and places it
where only medical people with medical expertise can talk about it (Conrad,
1975). In addition, medicalizing deviance allows and justifies certain intrusive
procedures to be performed on individuals not only in the name of "treatment"
but also in the interests of the common good. When health professionals attempt
to eradicate a disease or a behavior, we all supposedly benefit. No other
profession has such extensive access to a person's body or mind as physical and
psychiatric medicine (Conrad, 1975). According to one critic, there may be a
larger, more sinister motive behind the use of medical techniques to shape and
control the behavior of deviants:

> [A]uthorities have moved beyond clubs, bullets, and eavesdropping devices
> and are resorting to such things as electroshock, mind-destroying drugs,
> and psychosurgery. Since the established powers presume that the present
> social system is virtuous, then those who are prone to violent or disruptive
> behavior, or who show themselves to be manifestly disturbed about the
> conditions under which they live, must be suffering from *inner* malfunc-
> tions that can best be treated by various mind controls. (Parenti, 1988,
> pp. 150-151)

Individualizing Complex Social Issues

Our society often emphasizes the individual over the social system. Depression,
alcoholism, eating disorders, and so on are "diseases" that lie within the person
rather than in the relationship between the person and his or her social world.
Hence they can be remedied only through actions aimed at the individual
(Kovel, 1980). Instead of seeing certain deviant behaviors as symptomatic of a
faulty social system—blocked economic opportunities, neighborhood decay,
repressive social institutions, or unattainable cultural standards—we see them as
expressions of individual traits or shortcomings.

Individualistic medical explanations of deviance are not necessarily wrong.
Many violent people *do* have brain diseases, and some schizophrenics *do* have
chemical imbalances. But when we focus exclusively on these explanations, the
solutions we seek address the perpetrator alone to the exclusion of everything else.

Consider the problem of hyperkinesis, or attention deficit hyperactivity
disorder. A child who is "hyperactive" is difficult to deal with at home and in the
classroom. He or she fidgets and squirms, has difficulty remaining seated, can't
sustain attention in tasks or play activities, can't follow rules, talks excessively,
and is easily distracted (American Psychiatric Association, 1987).

Forty years ago these children were considered bad or troublesome and would have been subjected to punishment or expulsion from school. Today, however, most hyperactive behavior is diagnosed as a symptom of a mental disorder and drugs are prescribed to treat it. It is estimated that between 750,000 and one million children in the United States are taking drugs to curb their overactivity or inattentiveness ("More children taking," 1988). Despite occasional adverse side effects, the drugs are generally successful in quieting the unruly and annoying behavior (Whalen & Henker, 1977). In this sense, the medicalization of hyperactivity is useful. As Conrad (1975) writes, everyone involved benefits from the medical diagnosis and treatment of the problem:

> Both the school and the parents are concerned with the child's behavior; the child is very difficult at home and disruptive in school. No punishments or rewards seem consistently to work in modifying the behavior; and both parents and school are at their wits' end. A medical evaluation is suggested. The diagnoses of hyperkinetic behavior leads to prescribing . . . medications. The child's behavior seems to become more socially acceptable, reducing problems in school and at home. (p. 19)

But are we ignoring the possibility that these actions may be an adaptation to the child's social environment? Hyperactive behavior may be a response to an educational system that is set up to discourage individual expression (Conrad, 1975). Narrowly defined norms of acceptable behavior make it difficult if not impossible for children to pursue their own desires and needs. Consequently, the illness label conveniently diverts attention away from the school system as a potential cause or contributor to the problem and focuses attention exclusively on the individual child.

I'm not suggesting that all children who are diagnosed with attention deficit hyperactivity disorder are disruptive because they are bored in school or because their individual creativity has been discouraged. The point is that from an institutional perspective, the labeling of disruptiveness as an individual disorder serves the interests of the school system by protecting its legitimacy and authority. The institution could not function if disruptiveness were tolerated (Tobin, Wu, & Davidson, 1989). When unruly behavior is translated into a sickness, medical remedies (i.e., drugs) become a convenient tool for enforcing conformity and upholding the values of the system. If our educational institution promoted and encouraged free individual expression instead of obedience and discipline, overactivity wouldn't be considered disruptive and wouldn't be a problem in need of a solution.

Depoliticizing Deviant Behavior

The process of individualizing and medicalizing social problems depoliticizes deviant behavior. The legitimacy of disruptive or threatening behaviors and statements is automatically destroyed when they are seen as symptoms of individual defects or illnesses. One need not pay attention to the critical remarks of an opponent if that opponent is defined as mentally ill. If we want to consider a person insane, we need not 'drive' him mad; we can simply 'declare' him mad (Szasz, 1984, p. 158). Historically, political opposition has often been quelled by the tactical use of medical labels. Political dissidents in totalitarian countries are often declared mentally ill and confined to hospitals in an attempt to quiet dangerous political criticism (Medvedev & Medvedev, 1971).

Such practices are not found only in foreign countries. In 1945 the famous American poet Ezra Pound, who was living in Italy, was brought back to the United States to stand trial for treason. He was accused of making anti-American radio broadcasts from Rome during World War II, but the court, prosecution, and defense, together with several psychiatrists, agreed that he was mentally unfit to stand trial. He was committed to St. Elizabeth's Mental Hospital in Washington, D.C., where he remained for the next 13 years. Although some have argued that this was done to help Pound avoid an almost certain prison sentence, others suggest that declaring him "mentally ill" not only punished him for subversive conduct but was used to discount statements he had made that attempted to undermine the United States' war effort.

Nor is the political use of medicalization restricted to past history. A *Dallas Morning News* investigation discovered that high-ranking military commanders have tried to discredit and intimidate subordinates who report security and safety violations or military overpricing by ordering them to undergo psychiatric evaluations or by sending them to a mental ward (Timms & McGonigle, 1992). One West Point cadet spent a month in a psychiatric ward for reporting widespread illegal drug use at the academy. He observed that there were officer patients in the ward who had objected to Army policy and who were involuntarily receiving electric shock treatments. A chief petty officer in the Air Force contends that his forced hospitalization was part of a retaliation for reporting payroll abuses at Dallas Naval Air Station. He insightfully describes the power of medical labels to discredit his political criticism: "What happened was nobody would speak to me. Let's face it. After someone has gone to a mental ward, you kind of question what's going on. It was a nice ploy, and it worked. What they did was totally neutralize me" (quoted in Timms & McGonigle, 1992).

Portraying deviants as sick people who must be dealt with through medical therapies is a powerful way for dominant groups in society to maintain conformity and the status quo. The seemingly merciful medical labels serve not only to reduce individual responsibility, but also to reduce the likelihood that such potentially contagious political behavior will be taken seriously (Hills, 1980).

Conclusion

When we talk about deviance, we usually speak of extreme forms: crime, mental illness, substance abuse, and so on. These activities are indeed troublesome, but for most people they remain comfortably distant phenomena. I think most of us would like to cling to the belief that deviants are "them" and normal people are "us."

The lesson I want you to take away from this chapter (and previous ones as well) is that the issue of deviance is, essentially, an issue of social definition. As a group, community, or culture, we decide which differences are benign and which are devalued. Standards and expectations change. Norms come and go. The consequence is that each of us could be considered deviant to some degree by some audience. We have all broken unspoken interactional norms; many of us have even broken the law. To a lesser degree, we are all potential Gladys Burrs who can be erroneously labeled deviant and treated unfairly as a result. Given the right—or wrong—circumstances, all of us run the risk of being negatively labeled or acquiring a bad reputation.

This chapter has examined deviance as both a micro- and macro-sociological phenomenon. While sociologists are interested in the broad social and political processes that create cultural definitions of deviance, they are also interested in how these definitions are applied in everyday life. Societal definitions have their most potent effect when expressed on a face-to-face level. We can talk about powerful institutions like medicine creating definitions of deviance that are consistent with broader political or economic interests, but if these definitions aren't accepted as appropriate to some degree by most of us, they will be ineffectual. Again, we see evidence of the sociological imagination, the complex interplay between individuals and the culture and community within which they live.

CHAPTER HIGHLIGHTS

■ According to an absolutist definition of deviance, there are two fundamental types of behavior: that which is inherently proper, good, and acceptable, and that which is inherently improper, bad, and unacceptable.

■ In contrast, a relativist definition of deviance suggests that deviance is not a property inherent in any particular act, belief, or condition. Instead, it is a definition of behavior that is socially created by collective human judgments. Hence, like beauty, deviance is in the eye of the beholder.

■ According to conflict theory, the definition of deviance is a form of social control exerted by more powerful people and groups over less powerful ones.

■ The labeling theory of deviance argues that deviance is a consequence of the application of rules and sanctions to an offender. Deviant labels can impede everyday social life by forming expectations in the minds of others.

■ The medical profession has had a great deal of influence in defining and explaining deviant behavior. Medicalization is the depiction of deviance as a medical problem or illness and the mandating or licensing of medical professionals to provide some kind of treatment for it.

Y O U R   T U R N

People's perceptions of deviant acts and individuals are a crucial element of our understanding of deviance. From a conflict perspective, these perceptions are usually consistent with the goals and interests of those in power. But what exactly are people's perceptions of deviance?

Retype the list below and make copies. Find 20 to 30 people who would be willing to read the list and answer a few questions. Try to get an equal proportion of males and females and younger and older people. Have each person rank the following "deviant" acts in order from 1 to 15, with 15 being the most serious and 1 the least serious. Do not define for them what is meant by "serious."

☐ _____ catching your spouse with a lover and killing them both

☐ _____ employee embezzling company funds

☐ _____ armed robbery of a supermarket

☐ _____ forcible rape of a stranger in a park

☐ _____ selling liquor to minors

☐ _____ killing a suspected burglar in one's home

☐ _____ practicing medicine without a license

☐ _____ soliciting for prostitution

☐ _____ hitting your child

☐ _____ selling cocaine

☐ _____ manufacturing and selling cars known to have dangerous defects

☐ _____ forcible rape of a former spouse

☐ _____ being drunk in public

☐ _____ killing a person for a fee

☐ _____ fixing prices of machines sold to businesses

After the volunteers are finished, ask them how they decided on their selections. What criteria did they use for judging the seriousness of each act? Where did their perceptions come from? Why do they think the "less serious" acts on the list are against the law?

After collecting all of your data, compute the average ranking for each of the 15 items. The larger the average score, the more the perceived seriousness of that act. Which acts were considered the most serious and which the least serious? Was there a fair amount of agreement among the people in your sample? Were there any differences between the ratings of men and women? Between older and younger people? Using the conflict perspective discuss the role these perceptions play in the nature and control of deviance.

[NOTE: The 15 items in this exercise are adapted from P. Rossi, E. Waite, C. E. Bose, and R. E. Berk, "The seriousness of crimes: Normative structure and individual differences," American Sociological Review, 39, 224-237, 1974.]

Graffiti:
Social Deviance or Art Form?

Photographs and concept by James Prigoff

Most people would consider graffiti an ugly and harmful form of deviant expression that wantonly defaces property. Yet the deviant nature of graffiti is a matter of human judgment and evaluation. As you will see in the following pages, the identity of the individual or group responsible for creating graffiti may be more relevant to it being called "deviant" than the painted drawings or words themselves.

Mural by Omega in Psycho City, 1991, San Francisco. Artists are: Omega, Hex, Raevyn, Crayone, Picasso, Toons, Benz, & Ink.

Lask with his mural "Wine," 1985, Staten Island, New York.

Spraycan Art by H. Chalfant and J. Prigoff (New York: Thames & Hudson, 1987).

The world of the graffiti writer is a diverse sub-culture with its own well-defined language, roles, and standards of excellence. New York-style graffiti, and its artistic outgrowth, spraycan art, which originated in the train yards of New York City in the 1960s, has come to communicate everything from simple group identity and political ideology to messages about power, anger, and rebellion.

Phresh with his mural "Stop in the Name of Crime," © 1984, Oakland, California

"**I**'m not out here to change the world. I just say what's on my mind. I see the whole city as my canvas. Wherever there is a wall, I just love to paint it."

-- Carlos "Dzine" Rolon, one of six artists featured in a graffiti artists' show in a museum in Patterson, New Jersey

These murals were done by Chico on the Lower East Side, New York City.

"**I** write my name up there and then maybe paint a lit-tle extra picture around it and -- KA POW! -- I'm famous. It's a real rush."

-- Alex Alvarez, graf-fiti artist

"Hmm…looks like vandalism to me," painted by Apolonari, in Oakland, California. *Spraycan Art.*

"**W**hen you have a can in your hand you can communicate with anyone anywhere."

"**K**ids call it tagging. To most adults, it is nothing but ugly, hostile graffiti, as unavoidable as a scream . . . insistent and rude as rap from a boom box. . . . Whatever else it is, this is lettering on public display, far different from the dismal sprawlings on a public toilet. This is script as stylized as the uniform of teen urban life -- the bandanna, the baseball hat worn backwards, the Raiders' football jacket."
-- Richard Rodriguez, author of *Days of Obligation: A Conversation with My Mexican Father* and an editor of *YO!* (Youth Outlook), a newsletter for teens

Neon at the Oakland Amtrak line.

Is graffiti always deviant? What is the difference between the graffiti sprayed on a garbage truck, a commissioned mural carrying the name of a political candidate during a campaign, and a soft drink advertisement painted on the side of a city bus? Who gets to write and draw on public property?

On this sanitation truck, "youth without permission practice their calligraphy and design capability." *-- James Prigoff, photographer and co-author of* Spraycan Art.

Corporate "graffiti": A Pepsi ad completely covers this San Francisco city bus.

Jerry Brown commissioned Frame, a spraycan artist, to paint his name and a mural on this bus to advertise his presidential candidacy in 1991.

Sometimes as a form of deviant behavior becomes more common and sophisticated it becomes part of the mainstream culture. Here you can see how a graffiti artist who was once considered the prototypical urban vandal is now recognized and celebrated by the commercial art world. His work has been featured in San Francisco art shows and galleries.

"Twist" is the tag of artist Barry McGee. Twist's "throw-ups" (large names written in bubble or block letters) abound in San Francisco.

Now accepted as an artist, Twist had his work displayed in the San Jose Art Museum in 1994. He also had a one-man show at the Yerba Buena Gardens, San Francisco.

Twist has become well-known in San Francisco for his social-commentary murals.

ities and private groups still try to fight graffiti, while conflicting messages are sent by mainstream culture. Here we see that graffiti, once the visual scourge of neighborhoods, has become another weapon in the financial arsenal of the corporate world.

The city of Los Angeles uses fierce football heroes in its campaign to stop graffiti.

Chrysler created its own "graffiti" altered ad for its Plymouth Neon. The ads started out with a plan white background, an image of the car, and the simple message "Hi." In subsequent weeks, advertisers added letters, graffiti-style, to spell out "Hip" and "Chill." The outcry from anti-graffiti organizations prompted the public relations manager for the Chrysler corporation to issue a formal statement: "We don't promote or condone graffiti or the destruction of property. . . . The campaign [has been] very successful. It's given the car a personality."

CHAPTER 8

Building Social Relationships

Intimacy and Family

- *The Irony of Intimacy: Desires and Difficulties in Family Relationships*
- *The History of Intimacy and Family*
- *The Culture of Intimacy and Family*
- *Family and Social Structure*
- *Intimacy as a Personal Construction*
- *Terminating a Relationship: Uncoupling*
- *Family Violence*
- *Conclusion*
- *Chapter Highlights*
- *Your Turn*
- *VISUAL ESSAY Mothers, Materials, and Means*

So far, the 1990s have been a strange and highly public decade for family and intimate relationships in the United States. Over the past few years a number of events have aroused controversy and challenged social norms and values. Some people see these events as the demise of the "traditional" family; others see them as a sign of the redefinition of family in light of changing societal circumstances:

- Fictional representations of family took on new meaning. Former Vice President Dan Quayle attacked the television sitcom character Murphy Brown for undermining "traditional family values" by deciding to become a single mother. Former President George Bush spoke of wanting an American family that looked a lot more like the Waltons than the Simpsons.

- Celebrities such as Jack Nicholson, Eddie Murphy, and Warren Beatty, as well as one-fourth of all single American women between the ages of 18 and 44, became unwed parents.

- The relationship between one of the country's most acclaimed filmmakers, Woody Allen, and his well-known actress partner, Mia Farrow, went up in flames after the disclosure of his affair with her adopted daughter and amid accusations that he sexually abused one of their other children.

- Antioch College of Ohio instituted a sexual offense policy requiring students in sexual situations to obtain clear verbal consent for *every* sex act, from kissing to intercourse.

■ A survey found that over one-fourth of sixth graders in New Haven, Connecticut, are sexually active.

■ A Virginia woman made national headlines for weeks after slicing off her husband's penis after he had allegedly and repeatedly raped her. That same year 3 to 4 million women were battered by their husbands.

■ A 12-year-old boy hired a lawyer to sue his negligent parents for "divorce" and initially won, only to have the decision reversed on appeal.

■ A court ruled that a 2½-year-old girl be removed from the parents with whom she had lived since birth and placed in the custody of her biological parents. The court decided that the parental rights of the biological father, who did not know he was the father at the time the baby was put up for adoption, could not be cut off unless there was powerful evidence of unfitness.

■ Several cities passed domestic partnership laws granting homosexual and cohabiting couples some of the same legal rights previously reserved for married couples. But in Richmond, Virginia, a mother lost custody of her 2-year-old son because she was a lesbian.

■ Scientists at George Washington University successfully cloned human embryos, raising the futuristic possibility that one day couples can have identical twins of different ages.

Intimate and family relationships have certainly come to the forefront of the nation's consciousness. While the public debates over some of these issues have sometimes bordered on the ridiculous, the fact is that people have begun to question what terms like *family* and *intimacy* mean and what is in store for them in their own lives.

Of all the social relationships in our private spheres, the most important are those we have with family and intimate friends. Perhaps no facet of human existence is more familiar to us or occupies more time, effort, and emotion. Most of us spend our childhood and adolescence in some kind of family, go through the sometimes painful rituals of dating, fall in love, and become spouses, parents, and grandparents. Many of us have also seen the dark side of these relationships, too: divorce, abuse, and violence.

Like every other aspect of our individual lives, family relationships can be understood only within the broader social context. We often fail to realize that laws, customs, and social institutions regulate what we can and can't do with our partners, potential partners, parents, and children (Cherlin, 1978). This chapter takes a sociological peek into the private and public aspects of intimate relationships and family. Specifically, it explores the role these relationships play in our daily lives. How has this role changed over time? How do societal factors like institutions, gender, race, and social class affect our perceptions of intimacy and family? How are these relationships established? How are they ended? And why is the family environment the setting for so much violence and abuse in today's society?

The Irony of Intimacy: Desires and Difficulties in Family Relationships

Intimate relationships, whether they are between lovers, friends, or family, are the standard against which many of us judge the quality and happiness of our lives (Campbell, Converse, & Rodgers, 1976). We spend a tremendous amount of time worrying about present relationships, contemplating new ones, obsessing over past ones, or fretting over the fact that we are currently unattached. Indeed, the search for intimacy and romance has become one of the prime obsessions of the nineties. Popular magazines, self-help books, advice columns, supermarket tabloids, and television talk shows overflow with advice, warnings, and pseudoscientific analyses of every conceivable aspect of a relationship: finding the right mate, achieving sexual satisfaction, maintaining relationships, raising well-adjusted children, resolving conflict, ending relationships, readjusting, and so on.

Ironically, at a time when we hunger for closeness and will sometimes pay tidy sums of money to get it, our intimate lives are fraught with difficulty. In our complex, urban, and industrial society, we have become less integrated and connected to others. Between 1970 and 1990, the number of American adults living alone almost doubled; single people now make up about one-fourth of the U.S. population (U.S. Bureau of the Census, 1990a). The structure of American households has also diversified, as shown in Figure 8.1.

Some sociologists talk about how our culture's emphasis on individualism has taken away our sense of community, diminishing our ability to establish intimate ties and making it easier for us to walk away from family relationships that we see as unfulfilling (Bellah et al., 1985; Sidel, 1986). The high value contemporary society places on individual achievement and success sometimes makes family relationships seem expendable. In a national poll, 25% of Americans said that for $10 million they'd abandon their entire family (J. Peterson & Kim, 1991).

For those of us who do establish relationships, more problems await. Experts project that about one out of every two marriages that begins this year will eventually end in divorce (Martin & Bumpass, 1989). Every day in this country, four women are killed by their spouses or lovers; and in any given year more women are abused by their husbands than get married in the same period. One in seven Americans claims to have been sexually abused as a child and one in six claims to have been physically abused (cited in Coontz, 1992). Half of all children will spend a part of their childhood in a single-parent home. The number of families living in poverty has grown substantially since the early 1970s, with single-mother households representing the poorest of all family types.

Many functionalist sociologists have voiced concern over the current state of the American family. The family, they argue, has lost many, if not all, of its

Figure 8.1   *Diversity of American Households in 1994*

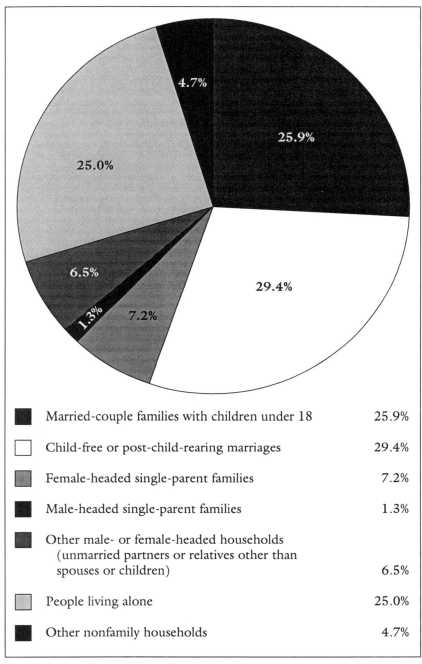

■	Married-couple families with children under 18	25.9%
□	Child-free or post-child-rearing marriages	29.4%
▨	Female-headed single-parent families	7.2%
■	Male-headed single-parent families	1.3%
▨	Other male- or female-headed households (unmarried partners or relatives other than spouses or children)	6.5%
▨	People living alone	25.0%
■	Other nonfamily households	4.7%

Source: Lamanna & Riedmann, 1994.

traditional functions (Lasch, 1977). Historically, the family was the center of many important activities. It was where children received most of their education and religious training. It was where both children and adults could expect to receive emotional nurturance and support. It was the institution that regulated sexual activity and reproduction. And it was also the economic center of society, where family members worked together to earn a living and support one another financially.

But as our economy shifted from a system based on small, privately owned agricultural enterprises to one based on massive industrial manufacturing, so did the role of the family. Economic production moved from the home to the factory, and families became more dependent on the money that members earned outside the home. The teaching of skills and values that were once a part of everyday home life began to take place almost exclusively in the schools. Even the family's role as a source of emotional security and nurturance has disappeared as it has become less able to shield its members from the harsh realities of modern life (Lasch, 1977).

For all these reasons many people in this country, from research scholars to politicians to everyday individuals on the street, are concerned about the survival of the American family. To understand the complex role of family relationships in the larger social structure and in the private sphere, we must learn more about the dominant historical and cultural settings in which these relationships take place.

The History of Intimacy and Family

We are the products of history, both our own and that of our society. Because our lives are shaped by the events that take place around us, it is not surprising that history influences our perceptions of family as well. While anxiety over the role of the family is particularly acute today, each succeeding generation of Americans from the time of the Puritans to the late 20th century has been concerned about a "crisis of the family" (Hareven, 1992; Skolnick, 1991).

Beliefs about the strengths and weaknesses, successes and failures of the family are usually based on a comparison to families of the past. As anxiety over the future of the American family escalates, calls for a return to the "good ol' days" of family life become louder. The belief in a lost "golden age" of family has led people to depict the present as a period of rapid decline and inevitable family breakdown (Coontz, 1992; Hareven, 1992; Skolnick, 1991).

But what about the family of the past? How golden was the golden age of family? According to sociologist William Goode (1971), the traditional family of the past that we speak so fondly of and want to re-create never existed. He calls our idealized image of the past "the classical family of Western nostalgia":

It is a pretty picture of life down on grandma's farm. There are lots of happy children, and many kinfolk live together in a large rambling house. Everyone works hard. Most of the food to be eaten during the winter is grown, preserved, and stored on the farm. . . . The family has many functions; it is the source of economic stability and religious, educational, and vocational training. Father is stern and reserved and has the final decision in all important matters. . . . All boys and girls marry, and marry young. . . . After marriage, the couple lives harmoniously, either near the boy's parents or with them. . . . No one divorces. (p. 624)

Like most stereotypes, this one is not altogether accurate. Because 19th-century adults had a shorter life expectancy than adults today, children were actually *more* likely to live in a single-parent home at that time due to the death of a parent (Kain, 1990). Although more than 20% of American children live in poverty today, about the same proportion lived in orphanages at the turn of the century, and not just because their parents had died. Many were there because their parents simply couldn't afford to raise them. Rates of alcohol and drug abuse, school dropouts, and domestic violence were all higher a century ago than they are today (cited in Coontz, 1992).

Perhaps the most pervasive myth is that of the **extended family**—several generations living under the same roof. Today's more isolated **nuclear family**, consisting only of mother, father, and children, is often compared unfavorably to the image of the huge, happy family of the past with its massive and perpetually available support network. Research shows, however, that despite images of families with lots of grandparents, aunts, uncles, and other relatives living together, the American family has always been fairly small (Blumstein & Schwartz, 1983; W. J. Goode, 1971; Hareven, 1992). There is no strong tradition in this country of extended families. In fact, the highest proportion of extended family households ever recorded in this country was only around 20% between 1850 and 1885 (Hareven, 1978). Because people didn't live as long as they do today, most died before ever seeing their grandchildren. Even in the 1700s the typical family consisted of a husband, a wife, and approximately three children.

When households of the past *were* large, it was probably due to the presence of nonfamily members in the house: servants, apprentices, boarders, and visitors. The reduction in household size over the last several centuries was not due to a decline in the number of extended relatives, but to a decrease in nonfamily members, a reduction in the number of children in a family, and an increase in young adults living alone (Kobrin, 1976).

As people immigrated to the United States from countries like China or Italy that *did* have a tradition of extended families, their first order of business upon arrival was to surrender their extended families so they could create their own households. Reducing the size of their families was seen as a clear sign that they had "become" Americans. Large, multigenerational families simply didn't make economic sense anymore. Being geographically mobile with a family of 12 would be next to impossible.

In addition, it's not at all clear that today's family is as isolated as some people make it out to be. More Americans than ever have grandparents alive, and the ties between grandparents and grandchildren may be stronger than ever. Today, most adults see or talk to a parent on the phone at least once a week (Coontz, 1992). Extended family members may not live under the same roof, but they do stay in contact and provide advice, emotional support, and financial help when needed (Cicirelli, 1983).

Another oft-cited indicator of the demise of the American family that is based on mythical conceptions of the past is the current high divorce rate. Most of us assume that the divorce rate in this county was always very low until it accelerated with unprecedented speed during the 1960s and 1970s and has remained perilously high ever since. To many observers it seemed that the intact middle-class lifestyle depicted in 1950s television shows like "Ozzie and Harriet," "Father Knows Best," and "Leave It to Beaver" had crumbled away forever. The rise in the divorce rate was attributed to the free love movement of "swinging singles, open marriages, alternative lifestyles, and women's liberation" (Skolnick, 1991). True, this era was a revolutionary period in American history. Norms governing all aspects of social life were certainly changing.

What these conclusions overlook, however, is the longer historical trend in American divorce. People were comparing divorce rates in the 1960s and 1970s to the abnormally low rate of the 1950s—the so-called baby boom years. From this narrow perspective the divorce rate did, indeed, shoot up. But by looking at the trends over the century we find a pattern that leads to some very different conclusions. Divorce in this country had been increasing steadily since 1900. It rose sharply right after World War II due most likely to short courtships before the young men shipped out and the stress of separation, and then dropped just as sharply during the 1950s. The high divorce rates of the 1960s and 1970s, then, represented a return to a national trend that had been developing since the turn of the century (see Figure 8.2).

Furthermore, the rate of "hidden" marital separation a hundred years ago was probably not that much less than the rate of "visible" separation today (Sennett, 1984). For financial or religious reasons, divorce was not an option for many people a century ago. A significant number turned to the functional equivalents of divorce—desertion and abandonment—which have been around for centuries. Although the divorce rate may have been lower in the past, families found other ways to break up.

In sum, the image of a warm, secure, stable family life in past times is at odds with the actual history of the American family (Skolnick, 1991). We have a heritage of challenge and crisis. By glorifying a mythical and idealized past, we artificially limit ourselves to an inaccurate image of what we think a "normal" family ought to look like.

Figure 8.2

Historical Trends in American Divorce (Annual divorce rate, United States. For 1920-1988: divorces per 1,000 married women aged 15 and over; for 1860-1920: divorces per 1,000 existing marriages.)

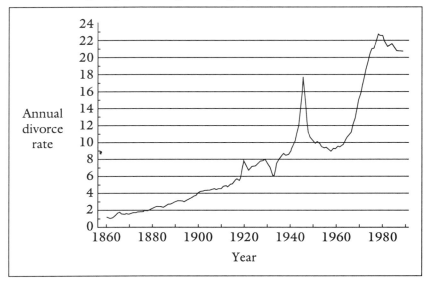

Source: Cherlin, 1992.

The Culture of Intimacy and Family

Family attitudes and behaviors are also influenced by culture. Families can be found in every human society, and they are all designed to address similar societal needs: regulating sexual behavior, creating new members of society to replace those who die, and protecting and socializing the young. The way families go about meeting these needs—their structure, customs, patterns of authority, and so on—differ widely across cultures.

Consider **monogamy**, the marriage of one man and one woman. Most of us take for granted that this relationship is the fundamental building block of the family. Some people may have several spouses over their lifetimes, but they are only allowed one at a time, and some families do exist without a married couple. But there is no denying that the monogamous marriage is an integral part of our *image* of the family.

Monogamous marriage continues to be the only adult intimate relationship that has achieved large-scale societal legitimacy in American society. It is still the one relationship in which sexual activity is not only acceptable but expected. Monogamous marriage, like the family in general, is an institution, a patterned way of life that includes a set of commonly known roles, statuses, and expectations:

People know about it; they can describe it; and they have spent a lifetime learning how to react to it. The *idea* of marriage is larger than any individual marriage. The *role* of husband or wife is greater than any individual who takes on that role. (Blumstein & Schwartz, 1983, p. 318)

No other relationship has achieved such status. Despite its current state of disrepair and public concern with its disintegration, monogamous marriage remains the pinnacle of committed intimacy. It is the cultural standard against which all other types of intimate relationships are judged. For instance, the campaign to legally recognize permanent homosexual relationships is, in essence, a campaign to elevate those unions to the status of marriage.

It is hard to imagine a society that is not structured around the practice of monogamy, but there are many cultures that allow an individual to have several husbands or wives at the same time. This type of marriage is called **polygamy**. Some anthropologists estimate that about 75% of the world's societies prefer some type of polygamy, although not everyone has the resources to have more than one spouse (Murdock, 1957). Even in the United States, certain groups practice polygamy. Approximately 50,000 members of a dissident Mormon sect in Colorado, Utah, and Arizona live in households made up of a man with two or more wives (D. Johnson, 1991).

Cultures differ in other taken-for-granted facets of family life. Take living arrangements, for example. In our society, families tend to be **neolocal**—that is, we expect young married couples to establish households separate from their respective families when financially possible. Cross-culturally, however, this arrangement is somewhat uncommon. Only about 5% of the world's societies are neolocal (Murdock, 1957). In most societies married couples either live with or near the husband's relatives (**patrilocal residence**) or the wife's relatives (**matrilocal residence**).

The belief that husbands, wives, and children ought to live together is not found everywhere either. Among the Kipsigis of Kenya, for instance, the mother and children live in one house while the father lives in another. The Kipsigis are polygamous, so a man might have several homes for his several wives at one time (Stephens, 1963). Among the Thonga of southern Africa, children live with their grandmothers once they stop breastfeeding. They remain there for several years and are then returned to their parents. On the traditional Israeli kibbutz, or commune, children were raised not by their parents but in an "infants' house," where they were cared for by a trained nurse (Nanda, 1994).

Child-rearing philosophies vary cross-culturally as well. As I discussed in chapter 4, most Americans believe that young children are inherently helpless and dependent. We feel that if parents attend to the child's drives and desires with consistency and affection, that child will learn to trust them, adopt their values, develop a sturdy self-concept, and turn out to be a well-rounded, normal individual. In contrast, the traditional Japanese parent views the young infant not as dependent and helpless, but as a willful creature whose natural instincts need to be tamed (Kagan, 1976). Any excitement on the part of the child must be suppressed. In the highlands of Guatemala, parents believe that their child's personality is determined by the date of birth. The parents are almost entirely uninvolved in the child's life, standing aside so he or she can grow as nature intended. Despite these dramatic differences, most children in all three cultures grow up equally well adapted to their societies.

Our conception of family does not exist everywhere. Each society adopts a family structure that suits its needs. The point is that whatever a given culture decides to define as the legitimate characteristics of a family has important consequences for people's lives within that culture.

In our society the *official* definition of family, as used by the U.S. Census Bureau, is "two or more persons, including the householder, who are related by birth, marriage, or adoption, and who live together as one household." If we accept this narrow definition, and all that it implies, then other living arrangements—homosexual relationships, nonmarital cohabitation, and group living—cannot be considered families in the strict sense of the word. They become deviant lifestyles that require condemnation, alternative arrangements that require tolerance, or sociological curiosities that require explanation.

On a personal level, things like inheritance rights, insurance coverage, eligibility to live in certain apartment complexes, savings from joint tax returns, and even visitation rights in prisons and hospital intensive care units are determined by marital or family status. If job-related benefits, like spousal coverage on an insurance policy and bereavement leave, are available only to "married couples," then members of other kinds of relationships will not be eligible.

In 1990 a woman whose lesbian partner had died of cancer charged AT&T (her deceased lover's employer) with discrimination for refusing to pay her the same death benefits it would have paid to a surviving spouse. In her suit she claimed that her relationship was as much a marriage as any heterosexual union. She and her lover had even formalized their relationship in a 1977 ceremony where they exchanged vows and rings in the company of parents and friends. They bought a house together and raised her children from a previous marriage together. AT&T said its benefits were for legal spouses only, and since the law did not recognize homosexual unions, neither did the company (Lewin, 1990).

Most Americans still perceive homosexual unions as a threat to the "family" (Weston, 1991). Voters in several areas of the country (e.g., Colorado and Cincinnati, Ohio) have recently passed bills limiting the rights of homosexuals. Nevertheless, there have been some noteworthy changes. In San Francisco, gay couples can now register their relationships with the city and declare that they have "an intimate, committed relationship of mutual caring," that they live together, and that they agree to be responsible for each other's basic living expenses. Similar laws have been enacted in cities such as West Hollywood, California, Ithaca, New York, and Madison, Wisconsin. The city of Seattle,

Washington, extends full medical, dental, and life insurance benefits to the domestic partners of city workers. In addition, several large corporations, including Sony Music Company, Ben & Jerry's Homemade, Inc., Lotus Development Corporation, Apple Computer, Inc., and the University of Chicago, now grant "domestic partners" the same benefits traditionally granted to spouses such as health insurance, pension benefits, employee discounts, and health club membership (J. L. Griffin, 1993).

Cohabitors have also faced difficulty in having their relationships culturally legitimated. While public attitudes have grown more tolerant of unmarried adults living together (Spanier, 1989), the law has been slower to adjust. In 1986 a state appeals court in St. Louis ruled that a couple could be ousted from their jointly owned house, citing an ordinance prohibiting an unmarried man and woman from living together. The court stated, "There is no doubt that there is a *governmental interest* [emphasis added] in marriage and in preserving the integrity of the biological or legal family." ("Court rules city," 1986).

Family and Social Structure

Definitions and perceptions of intimate and family relationships are affected by the larger social structure. The political and economic institutions that shape society influence and are influenced by the actions of individuals within family relationships.

Politics

Many of today's most pressing political issues—affordable child care, parental leave, abortion, homelessness, poverty—are fundamentally family problems. For example, abortion didn't become a significant political issue until the late 1960s when it became part of the larger movement for women's rights and reproductive freedom. Later the right-to-life movement framed the abortion debate not only as a moral and political issue, but also as a symbolic crusade to define (or redefine) the role of motherhood and family within the larger society (Luker, 1984). *Family* has taken on enormous symbolic importance in social life and has become a highly emotional political buzzword.

Over the past two decades many politicians have defined as one of their primary goals the restoration of "traditional family values." What exactly "traditional" means is never made clear. In a definitional sense, "traditional family" is used to refer to persons living together who are related by blood, marriage, or adoption. Presumably, however, the term has more to do with the nature and structure of family authority, the moral obligations of parenting and marital commitment, and the legitimate boundaries of sexual expression (Hunter, 1991). Conservative critics deplore not only the greater visibility of cohabiting and homosexual couples but also the increasing numbers of working mothers and rising rates of divorce. Despite all the political rhetoric, however, wives and mothers still remain in the workplace, divorce rates continue to be high, sex has not been confined to marriage, and gays have not returned to the closet (Skolnick, 1991).

Economics

The world of economics has obvious implications for the family as well. Economic factors are involved in virtually every aspect of family life, from the amount of money coming in to the day-to-day management of finances and major purchasing decisions. It is no surprise that money matters are closely related to feelings of satisfaction within intimate relationships. When couples are disappointed with the amount of money they have or how it is to be spent, they find *all* aspects of their relationships less satisfying (Blumstein & Schwartz, 1983).

It is crucial to see such financial problems not as private troubles, but as an issue directly linked to larger economic patterns. Consider the relationship between work and family. Many contemporary economists say that in order to sustain a viable national economy, we as a nation must "tolerate" a certain amount of unemployment (see Lekachman, 1991). While this may make good financial sense, it says nothing about the lives of those people who are without sufficient income to support their families.

At the global level, the competitive pressures of the international capitalist marketplace have forced many businesses and industries to make greater use of so-called disposable workers—those who work part-time or on temporary contract—in order to maintain profits. These jobs offer no benefits and no security and therefore import instability directly into family life (Kilborn, 1993b; Uchitelle, 1993).

Another corporate response to growing international competition and reduced profits is to reduce costs by cutting salaries, laying off workers, or encouraging early retirement. Some businesses cut costs by relocating either to other countries or to other parts of the United States, where they can pay lower wages (see chapter 10 for a more detailed discussion). For instance, there are more than 1,100 U.S.-owned manufacturing plants, including those run by Ford, General Motors, RCA, and Zenith, located in northern Mexico (Baca-Zinn & Eitzen, 1993). While the companies obviously benefit, the displaced American workers do not.

The demands of industrial economies can strain and disrupt families. Financial uncertainty makes a stable family life very difficult. It is nearly impossible to sustain a supportive, nurturant family environment without adequate income or health insurance. When economic foundations are weak, the emotional bonds that tie a family together can be stretched to the breaking point (Newman,

1988). In an effort to improve their personal financial situations, most families today, by necessity, consist of two working partners.

Micro-Macro Connection
The Dual-Earner Couple

One of the most significant economic facts to emerge in the late 20th century is that in most families both partners must work. The financial strains of modern living make it virtually impossible for young couples today to survive on one income. In 1990, 54% of families with at least one child under the age of 6 had two working parents. That figure is up from 32% in 1976. Of those families with children between the ages of 6 and 10, 68% consist of an employed mother and father (U.S. Bureau of the Census, 1991a). The dual-earner family is now the most common American family type.

Most dual-earner couples work not because they want to but because they have to. The image of the traditional family where Mom stays home to raise the kids simply cannot work for most people given the economic realities of modern society. Only about 14% of American families include married couples that have only one worker outside the home (Kain, 1990).

Nevertheless, society, for the most part, is still built around the outdated belief that only one partner in a couple should be working. Hence things like affordable child care and maternity and paternity leave are woefully inadequate to serve the needs of most young working couples who are just beginning their families. Even those couples in which both partners have successful careers must come to grips with both the external demands of the organization that employs them and the lack of a model for creating and sustaining their own family relationships (Hertz, 1986). The dilemma is felt most strongly when parenting and work responsibilities come into conflict.

Let's look at the 1992 case of a 32-year-old Minnesota woman. She was fired from her job as an accounting clerk at a computer company because she had to stay home from work frequently to care for her sick baby, who had a series of illnesses including pneumonia, influenza, and pinkeye. The company stated that she missed almost half the work time from January to May of 1990. The State Commissioner of Jobs and Training said she was not eligible for unemployment benefits because she had "voluntarily" put family interests ahead of her employer's interests, thus amounting to misconduct (Lewin, 1991). Her husband was unable to care for the child, and all her nearby relatives worked. In addition, she said, most day care providers do not accept sick children and the cost of bringing somebody into the home to care for the child was far too expensive. Eventually an appeals court overturned the denial of benefits, ruling that her absenteeism was beyond her control and therefore did not amount to misconduct.

This case illustrates the profound problems individuals can face when their intimate lives clash with larger political and economic priorities. Society has been slow to come to terms with the realities of family life in the nineties, such as increases in female-headed households and women entering the paid labor force.

As recently as 1990, only 52% of the nation's largest companies had some form of maternity leave guaranteeing that an employee would not lose her job (Aldous & Dumon, 1990).

In 1993 President Clinton signed into law a bill that guarantees workers up to 12 weeks of unpaid sick leave per year to care for a new child or a sick relative. While this law represents a noteworthy shift in the government's position on the dual-earner family, it has some important qualifications that seriously limit its applicability to a significant proportion of the population. First of all, the law covers only workers who have been employed continuously for at least one year and who work at least 25 hours a week. As a result, temporary contract workers would not be eligible. In addition, the law exempts companies with fewer than 50 workers; hence, only about 40% of the American workforce is covered. Some critics even fear that companies with exactly 50 employees might be motivated to dismiss a single employee to avoid the requirement. Finally, the law allows an employer to deny leave to any employee who is in the highest paid 10% of its workforce, if allowing that person to take the leave would create "substantial and grievous injury" to the business operations.

By comparison, the United States' two major economic competitors, Germany and Japan, have family leave policies with no such conditions. Each country guarantees a minimum of 3 months of *paid* family leave to *all* employees regardless of the size of their employer. Additional unpaid leave is available if it is needed (Shanker, 1990). In Sweden, pregnant women are given 8 weeks of paid leave *before* the baby is born, and either parent can remain at home for up to 9 months after the child is born while drawing 90% of his or her salary (Kamerman, 1985; Sidel, 1986). Swedish parents are allowed to take time off, with pay, to care for sick children up to the age of 12 (B. Cohen, 1991).

Gender

We cannot talk about cultural and structural influences on the family without discussing the role of gender. Gender roles in the family are certainly changing. But men and women are still likely to enter relationships with vastly different expectations, desires, and goals. Gender explains a variety of phenomena in intimate relationships, such as the way people talk to one another, how they express themselves sexually, and what they feel their responsibilities are. As a result, gender influences how men and women go about creating, maintaining, and thinking about family relationships.

It is often argued that the traditional gender-role socialization of women emphasizes sensitivity, the expression of affection, and the revelation of weakness, whereas men are taught to be competitive, strong, and emotionally inexpressive. Research has consistently shown that women have more close friends than men and are more romantic in their intimate relationships (Perlman & Fehr, 1987). Furthermore, there is a great deal of support for the contention that women are more concerned about, attentive to, and aware of the dynamics of their relationships than men are (e.g., Fincham & Bradbury, 1987; Rusbult, Zembrodt, & Iwaniszek, 1986). They even think more and talk more about their relationships than men do (Acitelli, 1988; Holtzworth-Munroe & Jacobson, 1985).

Ironically, such attentiveness and concern do not necessarily mean that women get more out of those relationships than men. In fact, the opposite may be true. According to one sociologist, every marriage actually contains two marriages: "his" and "hers"—and "his" seems to be the better deal (Bernard, 1972). Married men derive more satisfaction from marriage than married women do (Skolnick, 1981). Marriage even seems to benefit men's health and well-being. Married men get sick less, live longer, and have fewer emotional problems than single men (Ross, Mirowsky, & Goldstein, 1990).

But for women, the opposite is true. Because of the continued pressures of gender-typed family responsibilities, women are more likely than men to experience the stresses associated with parenthood and running the house. Three times as many married as single women show signs of anxiety, depression, and emotional distress (Carr, 1988). Wives are more likely to suffer some loss of identity when they marry. Not only do most women still change their names upon marrying, but their careers often become secondary to that of their husbands. In most states, husbands still have the legal right to decide where the couple will live after marriage (Renzetti & Curran, 1989).

Social Diversity

Another influential factor in people's family lives is their membership in important social groups. Ethnic, religious, and social class differences in family structure, sexual division of labor, child rearing, and so on have been well documented (e.g., L. Rubin, 1976; Shon & Ja, 1992; Staples & Mirande, 1980). Compared to African-American and Hispanic families, white families tend to have a higher household income, fewer children, and a higher proportion of two-parent groups (Baca-Zinn & Eitzen, 1993). African-American and Hispanic families, however, have greater access to emotional and economic support from extended family and friendship support networks than do white families (Taylor et al., 1990; Vega, 1990).

The increasing ethnic diversity of the American population is likely to alter our conceptions of the "typical" family in the years to come. Whether American families in the future become more similar or more diverse depends on whether the formation of families across racial, religious, or social class lines becomes more common than it is today.

Unlike some countries such as India and Pakistan, where marriages are arranged by families with little thought given to the compatibility or shared affection of the partners, the choice of marital partners in the United States is supposedly more open and a matter of personal preference. Most of us assume that we have the freedom to become attracted to whomever we please, and that love is all that is needed to establish a fulfilling, long-lasting relationship. But our intimate choices are far from free and private. The choices we make regarding whom to date, live with, or marry are governed by two important social rules that limit the field of eligible partners: exogamy and endogamy. **Exogamy** specifies that an individual must marry outside certain groups. In almost all societies, exogamy rules prohibit people from marrying members of their own nuclear family—siblings, parents, and children. Rules of exogamy extend to certain people outside the nuclear family to include cousins, grand-parents, and, in some states, stepsiblings.

Less obvious are the rules of **endogamy**, which is marriage within one's social group. The vast majority of intimate relationships in this country occur between people from the same race, religion, and social class. While these similar backgrounds increase the likelihood that the two people will share common beliefs, values, and experiences, rules of endogamy reflect our society's tradi-tional distaste for relationships that cross group boundaries.

Religion

Today, approximately 20% of all marriages occur between people of different religions (Glenn, 1982). Most religions actively discourage interfaith marriages out of a concern that such marriages may weaken people's religious beliefs and values, lead to the raising of children in a different faith, or take religion out of the family entirely. Religious leaders are often concerned about the bigger problem of maintaining their ethnic identity within a diverse and complex society (M. M. Gordon, 1964).

Among those religions whose numbers are already small, the phenomenon of interfaith marriage is particularly urgent and troublesome. It is more than just an individual violation of group identity. It is perceived as a dangerous and ever-growing force that threatens to destroy a culture and heritage. For instance, it is estimated that about 25% of American Jews marry non-Jews, up from 6% in the early 1960s (Gruson, 1985). Many Jewish leaders fear that the outcome of this growing trend will be not only the shrinking of the Jewish population, but also the erosion and perhaps extinction of an entire way of life. They believe that the survival of American Jewry itself depends on maintaining the integrity of traditional Jewish values and institutions. Interfaith marriage is not just a matter of individual prerogative but a shirking of one's responsibility to the larger group.

Race

The United States has a particularly strong aversion to relationships that cross racial lines. Although not always enforced, laws forbidding marriage and sexual contact between whites and other racial groups—Asian Americans, African Americans, and Native Americans—existed in most states until 1967 when the Supreme Court ruled that they were unconstitutional (Spickard, 1989). Usually, the interracial marriages would simply be declared null and void, but in certain cases couples were imprisoned, sometimes for 2 years or more.

While still infrequent—they constitute a little over 1% of all marriages—interracial marriages have more than tripled since 1970, according to the U.S. Bureau of the Census (Wilkerson, 1991a). However, we still experience massive discomfort over the thought of interracial relationships. Some couples, fearful of family ostracism, never tell their own parents that they are married and have children. Others suffer blatant indignities such as being spat on or refused services. According to one researcher, "Interracial relationships have not passed the 'no blink' test. It's clear that the majority of whites are not prepared to accept this as just another couple. The minimum you get is a look and a stare" (quoted in Wilkerson, 1991a). One in five whites still believes interracial marriage should be illegal. Sixty-six percent said they would oppose a close relative's marriage to a black person. Only 4% said they would favor it.

Social Class

People also tend to marry within their social classes (Carter & Glick, 1976). Even if two individuals from different races or religions marry, chances are they will have similar class backgrounds. Certainly some people do marry others from different social classes, but the classes tend to be adjacent ones, for instance, an upper-class woman marrying a middle-class man. But marriages that take place between people of vastly different class rankings are quite rare. The reason is that individuals from similar social classes are likely to share values, tastes, goals, expectations, and educational background.

Our education system plays an important role in bringing people from similar class backgrounds together. Neighborhood high schools tend to be homogeneous in social class, and students tend to rank themselves according to their parents' socioeconomic status. College continues class segregation. People from upper-class backgrounds are considerably more likely to attend costly private schools, whereas those from the working class are most likely to enroll in community colleges. These structural conditions increase the odds that the people whom you meet and form intimate relationships with will come from a similar class background.

The role that social class plays in people's intimate lives is particularly apparent when we look at differences in family functioning. In many ways all families must face the same issues: work, leisure, child rearing, and interpersonal relations (L. Rubin, 1976). But beneath the similarities we see dramatic differences in how these issues are handled. Because of heightened concern over class boundaries, ancestry, and maintenance of prestige, upper-class parents exert much more control over the dating behaviors of their children than lower-class parents (Domhoff, 1983; M. K. Whyte, 1990). Upper-class families are also better able to use their wealth and resources in coping with some of the demands of family life. Finding adequate child care arrangements will probably not pose much of a dilemma to parents who can afford a full-time, live-in nanny. The picture for working-class families, though, is quite different.

Lillian Rubin
Working-Class
Families

To examine class differences in family life, sociologist Lillian Rubin (1976) conducted in-depth interviews with 50 working-class families. For purposes of comparison she also interviewed 25 professional middle-class families. The differences she found give a personal face to the effects of social class on family life in American society. Among the differences she discovered were that working-class people are more likely than middle-class people to marry early, have large families, have premarital pregnancies, and experience marital unhappiness and divorce.

Working-class youth, living in the confined space of their parents' homes, must often forego college and make significant economic contributions to the family. For them, marriage often represents an attractive escape from the hardships and restrictions of their lives with their parents. The women Rubin interviewed were almost unanimous in their beliefs that many of the troubles in their marriages came from marrying too early. Many expressed hope that their daughters would not make "the same mistake" they had made.

Another noticeable characteristic of working-class marriages is that there tends to be a severe split between masculine and feminine cultures. Working-class couples tend to be more traditional in their perceptions of gender roles. Working-class wives seem to be more willing than middle-class wives to grant legitimacy to their husbands' authority. Furthermore, Rubin found that there was little communication between husbands and wives, especially regarding personal or emotional matters:

> They talk *at* each other, *past* each other, or *through* each other—rarely *with* or *to* each other. He blames her: "She's too emotional." She blames him: "He's always so rational." . . . The problem lies in the fact that they do not have a language with which to communicate, with which to understand each other. (p. 116)

In perhaps the most telling illustration, Rubin asked the wives what they valued most in their husbands. The professional middle-class subjects tended to focus on such issues as intimacy, sharing, communication, and the comforts and prestige that their husbands' occupations provided them. Working-class wives were more dismal in their assessments, focusing on the *absence* of such problems as unemployment, alcoholism, and violence. As one 33-year-old housewife put it:

> I guess I can't complain. He's a steady worker; he doesn't drink; he doesn't hit me. That's a lot more than my mother had, and she didn't sit around complaining and feeling sorry for herself, so I sure haven't got the right.
> (L. Rubin, 1976, p. 93)

This is not to say that working-class women are not concerned with the emotional side of their marriages. When the material aspects of life are problematic, they become dominant, all-consuming issues that require immediate solutions. Thus to understand the private experiences of intimacy, we must take into consideration the position of a particular family in the larger structure of society.

Intimacy as a Personal Construction

With all these historical, cultural, and social forces in mind, let's turn to how individuals go about constructing and maintaining intimate and family relationships. As you will recall from chapter 3, society would be impossible if people didn't come to some agreement about the meanings they give to the symbols, objects, and events in their day-to-day lives. The same is true for intimacy. What we choose to call an intimate relationship and how we choose to act within that relationship depends not only on the values of our culture, race, religion, and social class, but also on our own personal definitions of the situation at hand.

Relationships as Negotiated Realities

During the initial stages of a relationship, we devote a great deal of energy to trying to figure out just exactly what sort of situation it is. "Is this relationship going to lead to marriage or is it just a temporary fling?" "Is he Mr. Right or just a good friend?" A little uncertainty may be tolerable or even enticing at first, but eventually we want some clear definition of the relationship. Sometimes we will directly confront the issue and ask our partners straight out, "Do you love me? Do you want a serious relationship?" Barring such boldness, we may drop subtle hints, look for little clues, or consult third parties to assist us in defining the situation.

Even marriages must be interpreted by those involved. "Becoming" a spouse requires more than saying "I do." We must learn to act and think like a married person in a way that conforms to cultural expectations. Because marriage is an institutionalized form of intimacy, we can anticipate what it will be like long before we are actually in one. We come equipped with information from our parents' marriage and from the images of marriage we see in the media.

But the unique qualities and expectations both partners bring with them means that each relationship will be experienced differently. Spouses must create a new identity for themselves as a *couple* and, through interaction with each other, reinforce this identify (Berger & Kellner, 1964). The new identity imposes new obligations on the husband and wife. They are now a social unit in the eyes of others and of society. They must think of themselves as a couple and organize their activities accordingly (Berger & Kellner, 1964).

This process is not without its difficulties. Because no couple exists in a social vacuum, the presence of old friends serves as a constant reminder of past single lives and roles. Picture the stereotypical image of the newlywed husband who has trouble adjusting to his new married identity and continues to spend a great deal of time with his single friends, much to the dismay of his wife. To aid in the transformation, then, couples often call on other groups to assist in codefining the new reality. They may associate only with people who strengthen their new definition (e.g., other married couples) and avoid those who may weaken or threaten the new reality.

Eventually people involved in a relationship create a consistent pattern of interaction, a set of habits, rules, and shared worldviews. As one partner's definitions of reality correlate with the definitions of the other, the couple develops a **private culture,** which is their own unique way of dealing with the demands of married life (Blumstein & Kollock, 1988). The private culture includes things as mundane as a weekly dinner schedule or a Sunday-morning-newspaper-reading-breakfast-in-bed-ritual, or as serious as whether the relationship will be one of dominance or equality and how household finances will be handled. Some rituals and habits disappear as the composition of the family changes (e.g., the arrival of children), while others persist and are passed on to future generations.

The private culture is important not only because it indicates a high level of commitment on the part of the people involved, but because it identifies the relationship's boundaries, marking the line between insiders and outsiders. Tangible or intangible symbols of the relationship, including pet names, significant songs, important dates, favorite places, memorable events, and souvenirs, emerge to set this union apart from others. Mishandling any of these symbols—forgetting an anniversary, throwing away a little gift given on a first date, performing some act of affection with someone else—may be disastrous. It is not just the trinket that is being thrown away, or the date that is being forgotten, it is the relationship that these things symbolize that has seemingly lost its value and is being cast aside.

The Formation of Love Relationships

How do people construct their intimate relationships? There is something vaguely vulgar about trying to scientifically study how romantic relationships develop. Love can't be examined in a laboratory. A universal process of falling in love can't be discovered or described because it differs for everyone. Yet, by detaching ourselves from the romantic poetry of intimacy we can gain insight into the social forces that determine to whom we are attracted, how relationships become more serious, and what keeps us together once a relationship begins.

Sociologists have developed several ways of describing how intimate relationships develop. Two of them will be described here: the stage model and the social exchange model.

The Stage Model

Sociologist Ira Reiss (1960) argues that the development of intimate relationships takes place in a series of stages: rapport, self-disclosure, mutual dependency, and need fulfillment. We proceed through these stages in order. For instance, before we disclose intimate information about ourselves, we must first achieve a certain level of rapport and compatibility with that person.

You will recall that a society's "rules of endogamy" increase the likelihood that people will develop relationships with others who are similar to them in terms of social class, race, and religion. These characteristics act as filters when two people first come into contact. People tend to make instant judgments about another person's potential as a romantic partner on the basis of them. Once they have interacted a few times, however, other factors come into play.

When two people first meet, their conversation tends to be somewhat superficial as they attempt to establish rapport or a general sense of compatibility (e.g., "My favorite ice cream flavor is vanilla swiss almond, I like to jog, and my favorite group is R.E.M."). At this stage, interaction may be complicated by deliberate impression management. Individuals may try to present values, opinions, or biographical information they think the other person will find appealing. They don't want to say or do things that will upset, anger, or repel him or her. However, as people grow more comfortable and trusting of one another, the disclosures become more intimate and revealing, and therefore more risky.

The next stage of relationship development, **self-disclosure**, is characterized by our willingness to reveal personal pieces of information about ourselves: problematic events in our past history, the depth of our feelings toward the other person, our fears and vulnerabilities. Such self-disclosures not only convey information, but they are also a symbolic gesture meant to tell the other person that "I feel close enough to you to share this with you. I trust you not to laugh, belittle, or devalue what I am going to tell you." Research has shown that the greater the level of self-disclosure between partners, the greater their satisfaction in the relationship (Altman & Taylor, 1973; Hendrick, 1981).

Self-disclosure is governed by a clear set of social norms and expectations. One important but often unspoken expectation is that the intimate self-disclosure should be reciprocated (Derlega, Harris, & Chaikin, 1973). We provide more and more intimate facts about ourselves in hopes that our partner will do the same. When people complain about communication problems in their relationships, they are usually referring to an imbalance in the nature and amount of information partners are sharing with each other.

Reciprocity is particularly important when one discloses one's affection. People often go through a great deal of strategic maneuvering before telling their partners how they feel about them. Say you've been involved in a terrific relationship with someone for about 6 months. You think you love him or her, and you think he or she loves you, but neither of you has said anything yet. You are at a restaurant having a romantic meal when you decide to do it. You say something like, "There's something I want to tell you. We've been seeing each other for several months now and it's been fantastic . . . really special. I hope it has been fantastic for you, too. Well—" (beads of sweat are forming on your forehead and your hands are beginning to shake) "—I just wanted you to know that . . . ahem . . . that, well, I LOVE YOU."

Phew! You did it. Your partner looks up from his or her fettucine alfredo. Your eyes meet. In these few seconds of silence you try to decipher his or her reaction. You're undoubtedly anticipating some kind of reciprocation, right? You're thinking to yourself, *Tell me you're head over heels in love with me too.* Imagine your horror if, instead, he or she says, "That's nice . . . hey, are you going to eat your asparagus?"

This response is not only tremendously embarrassing but emotionally devastating because there has been a clear violation of the norms of interaction. We expect such disclosures to be met with similar levels of disclosure (Cunningham, Strassberg, & Haan, 1986). When they aren't, we are forced to acknowledge that our definition of the situation does not conform to that of the other person.

Self-disclosure is a hazardous affair. When our partners do not disclose enough, we never know what they are truly feeling. But because we don't want to appear pushy by constantly asking for feelings and reassurances, we resign ourselves to quiet suffering. In the absence of clear information, we frequently let our imaginations run wild. We find ourselves attributing feelings we *think* our partner has. We scrutinize every sentence, every gesture, for some shred of evidence that will tell us what this other person is feeling.

Disclosing too much, too quickly, though, can also be problematic (Altman & Taylor, 1973). Those who tell everyone, even complete strangers, every intimate detail of their lives and feelings have not learned the importance of timing and have cast the recipient into the uncomfortable and perhaps unwanted role of trusted confidant.

When a relationship moves beyond the point of self-disclosure, partners enter the next stage: mutual dependency and need fulfillment (Reiss, 1960). The lives of the individuals involved become more intertwined. People get used to doing things that require the presence of the other person—an audience for their jokes, a confidant for the expression of their fears and wishes, a partner for their sexual experiences (Reiss & Lee, 1988). They begin to depend on each other to meet their emotional, interpersonal, sexual, or economic needs (Kelley et al., 1983).

A clear sign of this mutual dependency comes from people outside the relationship. Partners often don't consider themselves a couple until they are publicly recognized as such by their friends and peers. When this happens, the couple is bound by a new and complex set of social expectations: They might be issued joint invitations to social gatherings, be expected to accompany each other to public events, or be expected to know each other's whereabouts at all times.

The power that these expectations have over how we act and think reinforces the contention that emerging personal relationships develop within a social context. Intimacy is not just a phenomenon that occurs between the two people involved. Other people react to the relationship and can either validate it or disapprove of it.

The Social Exchange Model

Another perspective on the development of intimate relationships is the social exchange model (Blau, 1964; Emerson, 1962; Homans, 1961; Z. Rubin, 1973; Thibaut & Kelley, 1959). Reiss's stage model simply identified the steps in a process of relationship development. The exchange approach uses the principles of economics to explain why we are attracted to some people and not others and why we pursue and remain in some relationships and avoid or leave others.

This perspective assumes that humans are motivated by a desire to maximize rewards, the same force that drives economic marketplaces. Rewards can assume many forms: money, desired goods and services, attention, status, prestige, and approval from others. At the same time we are also motivated by a desire to minimize costs. Humans will choose a particular line of action over other alternative lines of action if it produces the best profit (rewards minus costs).

When applied to intimacy, this fundamental premise implies that those relationships which are the most "profitable" to both partners will be the most satisfying and the most likely to last. Intimate relationships provide obvious rewards like love, sexual gratification, warmth, desirable characteristics of the other partner, and companionship. But there are certain costs as well, including time and effort spent trying to maintain the relationship, undesirable characteristics of the other partner, and conflict. Research has consistently shown that couples who indicate high levels of happiness are those in which partners are providing each other with many rewarding experiences and few costly ones (Birchler, Weiss, & Vincent, 1975; Rusbult, 1983; Vincent, Weiss, & Birchler, 1975).

Unlike economic exchanges, in which the rewards and costs are objective, the rewards and costs in the intimate marketplace are matters of subjective definition. A characteristic that one person finds rewarding (e.g., sensitivity) may be costly to another (e.g., wimpiness). Even so, such preferences are embedded within the larger society's definitions of desirability. As long as there are generally agreed-upon standards of a person's worth, our preferences and our relationships will share some features of the marketplace (Z. Rubin, 1973).

It is also important to consider people's expectations. These expectations are derived from past experiences (Thibaut & Kelley, 1959). We judge the attractiveness of the outcomes we receive in present relationships by comparing them to outcomes we have received in previous ones. If our present relationship exceeds our expectations—that is, it is "better" than any relationship in which we have been involved before—satisfaction is likely to be high. On the other hand, if our present relationship doesn't provide us with what we have come to expect—the conversations aren't as interesting, the sex isn't as good, we aren't treated as nicely—we probably won't be very happy.

We also compare the attractiveness of a present relationship to the kinds of profits we think we *could* receive in an alternative relationship (Thibaut & Kelley, 1959). This sort of comparison determines whether we will stay in a relationship. If an individual perceives there to be available alternative relationships that would be *more* rewarding than the present one, he or she will be less likely to remain. But when people feel as if there are few or no alternatives they tend to stay in their relationships, even if they are unsatisfying (J. H. Berg & McQuinn, 1986).

Expectations shed light on the curious and sometimes inexplicable things people do in their intimate relationships. I'm sure you've seen people who remain in relationships that to outside observers seem undesirable or unrewarding. If, as social exchange theorists argue, people form and maintain relationships only if they are profitable, this would make no sense. But we must take into consideration that person's expectations and perceptions of alternatives. If a woman receives certain necessary resources from her obnoxious, beer-swilling partner (e.g., financial support) but feels that she can't get those resources elsewhere, she may stay in the relationship out of necessity. If a man has had a history of bad relationships, his expectations may be quite low to begin with, so he may be satisfied in a relationship that appears intolerable to others.

Subjective judgments of how much profit is to be derived from a relationship and how well it compares to past experiences and perceived alternatives are not made by one partner alone. It takes two to make a relationship work, and that means the other partner is also interested in maximizing rewards and minimizing costs. Relationships work best when there is **equity**; that is, when both partners are deriving benefits from the relationship that are *proportional* to what they are investing into it. The presence or absence of equity has profound effects on the satisfaction felt by individuals as well as the stability of the relationship itself (Hatfield et al., 1985; Utne et al., 1984).

An investment is anything one contributes to the relationship such as time, money, interest, or personal characteristics like good looks or a sense of humor (R. Brown, 1986). Investments reflect what we think we have to offer. They create feelings of entitlement or deservedness. When a friend says, "You deserve better than her," or "You're entitled to some happiness," there is an implicit statement of equity involved: "Given what you have invested or what you have to offer, in all fairness you should be receiving greater benefits." The actual existence of inequity is perhaps less important than an individual's perception that it exists.

Not every relationship is perfectly equitable. When things become disproportionate, feelings of unfairness result. There are two types of inequity: underbenefited (i.e., one feels one is not getting from the relationship what one feels one deserves) and overbenefited (i.e., one feels one is getting too much for what one has to offer). Each kind threatens the stability of the relationship.

Social psychologist Elaine Hatfield (Hatfield, Walster, & Traupmann, 1978) interviewed 537 college men and women who were dating someone either casually or steadily. She asked them whether they expected to be with their partners after 1 year and after 5 years. Those who felt their relationships were perfectly equitable were much more likely to think the relationships would last. Interestingly, the overbenefited subjects were just as doubtful as underbenefited subjects about the future prospects of their relationships. Presumably, the underbenefited felt they would do better in the future, while the overbenefited didn't expect their luck to last. A follow-up study 3 months later indicated that the equitable relationships were, in fact, more likely to be intact.

Both types of inequity are uncomfortable and motivate individuals to restore either actual or psychological equity (Brehm, 1992). The underbenefited partner may attempt to restore equity by reducing his or her investments or by demanding more from the partner. If I feel I am being underbenefited, I may decide not to do as many chores around the house, or I may stop showing my partner any affection. If that fails, I may start to demand more benefits or more investments from my partner: "Do you think you could start showing some appreciation for what I do around here, or at least start doing some of this stuff yourself?" The overbenefited partner may come to feel guilty for getting *more* than he or she feels is deserved. This person may try to increase his or her contributions (e.g., do more around the house) or increase the benefits enjoyed by his or her partner (e.g., shower the partner with gifts).

The problem with these strategies is that they can backfire. For instance, my reduction of contributions to the relationship may be met by a similar reduction on the part of my partner. Or, my partner may take advantage of my attempts to increase his or her benefits. So individuals will often resort to attempts to restore equity psychologically, to convince themselves that, although it seems otherwise, equity does in fact exist (Brehm, 1992). On the one hand, I may talk myself into believing that my partner is a special person who deserves more than I do. Perhaps she has had terrible experiences in the past and deserves to be treated well in this relationship. On the other hand, if I am the overbenefited partner, I may convince myself that because of some particularly noble quality I possess, I deserve the favorable inequity.

Inequity is fairly obvious when the imbalances are in the area of household tasks, financial contributions, or outward displays of affection. But it is more difficult to identify when there is an imbalance in feelings, or emotional investments. We all know of relationships in which one partner is more in love than the other partner. Situations where emotional attachment is out of balance could create serious and potentially dangerous power differences in relationships. The person who loves less or does not express unconditional affection has the upper hand in the relationship because the other person will suffer more should the relationship end (Blau, 1964). The individual who loves less can thus dictate the terms of the relationship and can, if so inclined, exploit the other by making heavy demands. The partner who loves more has more interest in maintaining the relationship and may be forced to put up with a lot in the process.

When attempts to overcome inequity fail, relationships are likely to end. The ending of a relationship, just like its beginning, requires certain identity transformations on the part of the participants and takes place within a social context that includes friends, families, and others who have an "interest" in the relationship.

Terminating a Relationship: Uncoupling

Most of us have experienced the termination of a dating relationship or have seen the end of a marriage, either our own or that of someone close to us. As I mentioned earlier in this chapter, it is estimated that roughly one out of every two marriages that begins this year will end in divorce at some point in the future. Such a high probability of divorce terrifies people who are about to enter a "lifetime" relationship and distresses those already married who want some sense of permanence for their children (Blumstein & Schwartz, 1983). Divorce has become a prevalent feature of family life in this society.

Although the endings of relationships are common, they are not the sort of thing that many of us prepare or train for. Prenuptial agreements may spell out in advance the settlement conditions *if* a marriage were to end, but they address only the economic and legal facets of breakups, not the emotional, interpersonal, and social ones.

The "spoiling" of a close relationship can be emotionally devastating. It can create deep wounds akin to those associated with the death of a loved one (McCall, 1982). We may experience a wide range of emotions, including anger, bitterness, sadness, self-pity, self-doubt, guilt, and shame. When a relationship ends, so do the benefits, the private culture, and the need fulfillment that came with it. We lose the partner on whom we came to depend, and we lose contact with friends and acquaintances whom we came to know through that partner.

The ending of a relationship also requires a transformation of identity. Becoming an ex-spouse or ex-lover means exiting one social role and entering another (Ebaugh, 1988). People whose relationships have ended must remove themselves from the norms and expectations associated with the old role and learn new ones. They must begin to see the world from a single person's perspective and not the couple's perspective. In addition, the entire history of the relationship requires redefinition. Those once pleasant rituals of the private culture become annoying habits in retrospect. The good times get reinterpreted as something bad; the bad times are seen as more typical and indicative of the eventual breakup. Further complicating the process of role exit is the social stigma associated with the termination of an intimate relationship. Like most things in our achievement-oriented society, relationships—particularly marriages—tend to be viewed in success/failure terms. Although studies consistently show a clear decline in disapproval of divorce as a general category, disapproval of divorced *individuals* continues (Gertsel, 1987). These individuals may come to feel demoralized and rejected by married friends and experience diminishing self-esteem. The stigmatizing effects of divorce illustrate, again, the social nature of intimate relationships. Friends and family close to the couple can increase feelings of stigma by passing judgment and taking sides.

Going Public

There is no single pattern in the ending of a relationship. Each individual, each situation is different. Nevertheless, there is a common problem faced by all people ending a relationship: how to break the news to one's partner and one's community.

While the breakup of any intimate relationship is, in the overall scheme of things, a collective act, most are initiated by one or the other person (McCall, 1982; Vaughan, 1986). Disclosing to one's partner the desire to end a relationship is particularly difficult because this society has no norms governing such situations. Although we may want to be tactful, sensitive, and considerate, more often than not we end up being the opposite:

> The truth is, we don't know how to tell our partners we no longer want to be with them. There is no good way, no kind way, no easy way to do it without hurting the other person. Often, we are in such pain ourselves as we consider taking our leave that we act out of frustration rather than rationality, hurting others despite our wish to be humane. (Vaughan, 1986, p. 296)

Because the termination of a relationship is such an unpleasant experience, most people resort to indirect methods, such as making the partner's life so miserable that he or she decides to end the relationship. To confront the partner directly is to risk being the bad guy, the person responsible for the destruction of a once loving relationship.

Role exit from an intimate relationship also involves adjustment and adaptation on the part of people outside the relationship (Ebaugh, 1988). The ending of a relationship is a complex process that must be executed under its own set of interactional norms as well as the watchful eyes of others. Not only do ex-partners feel compelled to reinterpret the past and explain the breakup to themselves, but they are also obligated to provide coherent stories or accounts to others. Friends, relatives, co-workers, and other interested parties typically want to know whom to blame, who to help, and whose side to take (Gertsel, 1987).

Partners may at first actively suppress information about the true status of their relationship, engaging in a collaborative cover-up (Vaughan, 1986). Eventually the private wish to terminate becomes a public one. At this point the front-stage image of solidarity is undeniably broken and the relationship is thoroughly spoiled. Even the partner who did not initiate the breakup generally finds public disclosure of the initiator's wish too damaging and dishonoring to continue the cover-up (McCall, 1982).

The explanations offered by each partner will almost certainly be different because of their distinctive perspectives on the termination process (McCall, 1982). Both people face touchy situations. The partner who did not initiate the breakup may seek sympathy. Perhaps he or she tries to play the "victim" but doesn't want to admit that his or her "market value" has plummeted in someone's eyes.

The initiator of the breakup is likely to face a tough audience (Vaughan, 1986). He or she must frame the partner and the relationship in a way that justifies the termination. The initiator may feel compelled to provide accounts that forestall any possibility that the person receiving the information will define him or her as the blameworthy party.

Finally, the failure of a relationship has institutional implications by threatening the ideal cultural images of love and romance (Blumstein & Kollock, 1988). A breakup calls into question the entire moral code of intimacy. Friends may begin to question the stability of their own relationships. The disengaging couple is socially obligated to inform others that although commitment to this particular relationship has deteriorated, commitment to the *idea* of relationships has not. Such commitment is reflected in the high percentage of people who remarry after divorce.

Remarriage and the Reconstituted Family

When you add to the high divorce rate the fact that more and more people are delaying marriage, choosing to remain single, or cohabiting instead of marrying, it might appear as though people have lost faith in the institution of marriage. However, it is estimated that more than 90% of today's young adults will marry at some point in their lives (Norton, 1987). Half of all marriages today involve at least one partner who was previously married (Bumpass, Sweet, & Castro Martin, 1990). Overall, four out of every five divorced individuals in this country are likely to remarry (Norton, 1987). These statistics suggest that although people are quite willing to escape a bad marriage, they have not necessarily given up on marriage.

Although they are common, remarriages are not without their problems. The divorce rate for remarriages is actually higher than the rate for first marriages (Cherlin, 1978). This may be due to the fact that remarriage is an incomplete institution. Remarriage disrupts the conventional family structure so that the traditional roles, relationships, and norms no longer apply. We have no set of institutional expectations for relationships between former and current spouses, between stepparents and stepchildren, between step- and half-siblings, and with extended kin (Ahrons & Rodgers, 1987). Laws and customs have been slow to catch up. For instance, do stepchildren have legal claims to their stepparents' property? Do incest rules apply to stepsiblings? An increasing number of people are finding themselves in a marital structure quite different from the kind with which they are familiar (Goetting, 1982).

The family relationships produced by remarriage can be complex and confusing (S. M. Jones, 1978). Consider the knotty but not uncommon situation of one family:

> When Ellen was eight and David ten, their parents separated. They continued to live with their mother, Nancy, spending weekends and vacations with their father, Jim. Two years after the divorce their father married Elaine, who was the custodial parent of her daughter, Jamie, aged six. Ellen and David lived in a one-parent household with their mother for three years, at which time their mother remarried. Their new stepfather, Craig, also had been divorced, and he was the joint-custodial parent of two daughters, aged six and eleven. His daughters spent about ten days each month living in his house. Within the next four years, Ellen and David's father and stepmother had two children of their own, a son and a daughter. When Ellen and David are 15 and 17, their family looks like this: They have two biological parents, two stepparents, three stepsisters, a half-brother and a half-sister. . . . They have two sets of stepgrandparents, two sets of biological grandparents, and a large network of aunts, uncles, and cousins. (Ahrons & Rodgers, 1987, p. 279)

Remarriage is particularly difficult when children are involved. When a new parent enters the former single-parent family, the entire system may be thrown out of balance. Rules and habits change and, for a time, confusion, resentment, and hostility may be the norm. While conflict is common in all types of families, issues like favoritism, divided loyalties, the right to discipline, and financial responsibility are particularly likely to occur in the reconstituted family.

The high divorce rate of remarriages and the frequency of conflict within reconstituted families are not simply an outgrowth of people's psychological inability to sustain intimate relationships, as some analysts have claimed. It is the fact that remarriages are not fully institutionalized that makes them susceptible to failure. The lack of clear role definitions, the absence of established societal norms, and the increased complexity of the family structure itself increase the likelihood of tension and turmoil.

Perhaps in the future, as our culture develops standard ways of defining and coping with these families, remarriage might become more institutionalized and less problematic. But as long as parents and children are separated from one another and as long as other adults (i.e., the one who marries a remarried spouse) are expected to take on parental role responsibilities without being able to legitimately expect the rewards (e.g., the loyalty and love of someone else's child), there will continue to be a great deal of tension and confusion. The structure of reconstituted families continues to grow more complex, making the lack of institutional guidelines even more serious.

Family Violence

Throughout this chapter I have discussed the vital role of family and intimacy in our everyday lives. These relationships, it seems, are the places to which we ought to be able to escape when life becomes overwhelming. Now matter how lousy your day was or how much you hate your job, you can still look forward to spending the evening with your loved one. At least you'll get some much needed nurturance, warmth, and compassion from him or her, right? Certainly you won't get screamed at, emotionally belittled, punched in the face, or have your life threatened simply because you came home too late or said the wrong thing at the wrong time.

But that is precisely what awaits a large number of people, particularly women and children, in this country. Nothing is more opposed to our image of the loving family than the idea of domestic violence. The tragic irony is that, outside of wars and riots, the home—that loving place that nourishes us when the outside world has sucked away our life energy—is the most violent place in American society.

Although it would be comforting to believe that domestic violence is rare and occurs only in families where there is a "sick" parent or spouse, the fact is that it happens with alarming frequency and is likely to be committed by people we would otherwise consider normal. Spouse abuse and child abuse are found in every class, race, and religion. Domestic violence is not a deviant aberration, it is a fundamental characteristic of the way we relate to one another in family settings.

It has been estimated that some form of intimate violence occurs in at least one out of every four marriages in this country (Straus, Gelles, & Steinmetz, 1980). Half of the victims are beaten at least three times a year. There are more than two million *reported* cases of child abuse each year, and in a given year 1,300 children will die of abuse or neglect (Gelles & Cornell, 1990). Because of the private nature of this violence and the desire of family members to keep it hidden, all of these figures are almost certainly underestimates.

Public Tolerance of Domestic Violence

To understand why there is such a high frequency of domestic violence in this country, we must look at public perceptions and attitudes toward it. In a national survey, one in four wives and one in three husbands said that hitting a partner was "necessary, normal, or good." When the same sample was asked about "slapping or spanking" a 12-year-old child, the figure rose to about 75% (Straus, Gelles, & Steinmetz, 1980).

While being violent with a stranger in public has clear, definite, and punishable consequences, being violent with a family member in the privacy of one's own home has few. People hit their "loved ones" simply because they can (Gelles & Straus, 1988). Traditionally we have perceived domestic violence, particularly wife abuse, as somehow less bothersome and more tolerable than other types of violence.

Psychologists Lance Shotland and Margaret Straw (1976) performed an experiment that involved staging what appeared to be heated altercations between a man and woman as they emerged from an elevator. They set up two scenarios that were identical except for one important detail. In the first, the woman, who is the object of the man's verbal and physical threats, shouts, "Get away from me! I don't even know you!" In the second (with identical actors and identical behaviors), she says, "Get away from me! I don't know why I ever married you!"

In the first situation, bystanders intervened 65% of the time (that is, they attempted to stop the apparent fight). In the second, bystanders intervened only 19% of the time. Clearly the second case was being defined by observers as a domestic dispute between spouses, conjuring up a different set of norms that stopped them from "getting involved" in the private affairs of a couple. The perception of an intimate relationship prevented most people from seeing the incident as a potentially violent and dangerous situation.

Similar perceptions exist at the organizational level. Police departments have historically been reluctant to get too involved in domestic disputes. Some have arrest policies called "stitch rules," which specify how serious an injury a victim must sustain, measured by how many stitches are required, to justify an arrest of the assailant (Gillespie, 1989). One study found that the majority of domestic disputes and family violence incidents reported to the police resulted in no arrest; either the police did nothing or the offender was referred to other agencies (Bell & Bell, 1991). Given this sort of response, it is not surprising that only about 15% of battered women ever contact the police (Straus & Gelles, 1986).

But things are starting to change. Many police departments around the country have revised their unspoken "hands-off" policies toward domestic violence cases. In Indianapolis, where the number of domestic violence cases doubled between 1990 and 1991, officers are now required to make an arrest even if they don't directly witness the assault. In addition, officers must have 30 hours of in-service domestic violence training each year. In other cities, domestic violence victims are prohibited from dropping assault charges once they are filed.

Putting Family Violence Into a Cultural Context

Individual-level factors such as economic frustration, stress, and alcohol and drug use are frequently implicated as major causes of domestic violence. To some analysts batterers are either psychopaths or people who are just plain prone to violence. But to fully understand domestic violence, we must take a look at some important characteristics of our society.

We live in one of the most violent industrialized countries on earth. The United States is fundamentally committed to the use of violence to achieve desirable changes (Straus, 1977). It is in our streets, our schools, our movies, our television shows, our toy stores, our spectator sports, and our government. It's even in our everyday language: we *assault* problems, *conquer* fears, *beat* others to the punch, *pound* home ideas, and *shoot down* opinions (Ewing, 1992). For many, violence is the appropriate means by which to resolve certain problems. It is not surprising, then, that such cultural patterns of violence would spill into the American family.

We also live in a society dominated by and built around the interests of men. Men occupy the high-status positions, exercise decision-making and political power, tend to be dominant in interpersonal relationships, and occupy the roles society defines as most valuable (Frieze et al., 1978). Domestic violence not only is a consequence of male domination, it reinforces it:

> The act of violence is many things at once. At the same instant it is the individual man acting out relations of sexual power; it is the violence of a society— a hierarchical, authoritarian, sexist, class-divided . . . crazy society—being focused through an individual man onto an individual woman. . . . These acts of violence are like a ritualized acting out of our social relations of power: the dominant and the weaker, the powerful and the powerless . . . the masculine and the feminine. (Kaufman, 1987, p. 1)

Male dominance has a long and infamous history (Gelles & Cornell, 1990). Roman law, for instance, justified a husband's killing of his wife for reasons such as adultery, drinking wine, and other so-called inappropriate behaviors (Steinmetz, Clavan, & Stein, 1990). The "rule of thumb" in English common law recognized a husband's right to beat his wife with a stick that was no bigger than the circumference of his thumb.

We have long believed that if a man's home is his castle, what goes on inside the castle walls should be shielded from public or governmental scrutiny. This is not merely a vestige of medieval life. Several years ago a Boston woman called the police to report that her husband had beaten her and then pushed her down the stairs. The officer on duty answered, "Listen, lady, he pays the bills, doesn't he? What he does inside his home is his business" (quoted in Straus, Gelles, & Steinmetz, 1980).

If it is true that some men beat their partners because they feel that such behavior is appropriate, then some wife beaters are not psychotic, deranged, "sick" individuals, but men who believe that male dominance is their birth right. Men who assault their wives are actually living up to cultural prescriptions that are cherished in Western society—aggressiveness, male dominance, and female subordination (Dobash & Dobash, 1979).

This makes the problem of domestic violence all the more insidious because it represents an extreme extension of norms dictating suitable spousal treatment. There is a deeply entrenched cultural tendency to perceive domestic violence as "normal" violence, as something that, while not necessarily desirable, is not surprising or unexpected either. As a result, much of the research in this area has focused on the *victim's* response to the situation.

Responses to Abuse

One question that has captured the attention of many marriage and family researchers is: Why do women stay in abusive relationships? During the 1960s the masochism thesis—that is, women liked being humiliated and hurt—was the predominant reason offered by psychiatrists (e.g., Saul, 1972). Even today, many psychiatrists believe masochism, or self-defeating personality disorder, as it is now called, should be a "legitimate" medical explanation for women who stay in abusive relationships. Other contemporary explanations focus on the woman's character flaws, such as weak will or pathological emotional attachment.

All of these wrongly focus on the victim while paying little attention to her social situation. The social exchange model can help us better understand this phenomenon of victim blaming. In a culture that is still reluctant to punish abusers, it is not surprising that many women perceive there to be no alternatives available and feel physically, economically, and emotionally trapped in their relationships. For instance, women who are unemployed are significantly less likely to leave an abusive marriage than women who are employed and therefore have their own source of income (Strube & Barbour, 1983). The cultural context of abusive relationships can even affect the perceptions of the victims. Kathleen Ferraro and John Johnson (1983) were participant observers at a shelter for battered women in the Southwest. They gathered information from 120 women, ranging in age from 17 to 68, who came to the shelter over the span of a year. From this information they identified several common techniques battered women use to justify or neutralize the violence their partners direct toward them and that may actually inhibit a sense of outrage and efforts to escape the abuse. Some women had convinced themselves that they must endure the abuse while helping their "troubled" partners return to their "normal," nonabusive selves. Others claimed that their abusive partners were "sick" and that their actions were beyond their control; their partners were also victims. Finally, many women blamed themselves, taking the responsibility away from their spouses.

Conclusion

Intimate relationships form the center of our personal universes. But while they are the principal source of identity, happiness, and satisfaction for many, they are also the source of tremendous anguish and suffering for others.

Furthermore, we have seen that family is a public as well as a private institution. True, most intimate and family behavior occurs away from the watchful eyes of others; only we have access to our thoughts, desires, and feelings regarding someone with whom we are intimately involved. But other people do care about what goes on in our relationships. People around us, the government, even society as a whole, have a vested interest in what happens in our intimate lives.

The social institutions and culture that make up our society also shape the very nature and definition of "family." Today the boundaries of that definition are being pushed by rapidly increasing numbers of "nontraditional" families: dual-earner couples, single-parent households, cohabitation, voluntary single-hood, same-sex marriages, and so on.

Every relationship, whether it violates or conforms to current social norms, reflects the dominant ideals and beliefs about what a marriage or a family ought to look like. Each relationship is unique. However, this uniqueness will always be bounded by the broader constraints of our cultural, group, and institutional values.

CHAPTER HIGHLIGHTS

■ In this culture, intimate relationships are the standard against which we judge the quality and happiness of our everyday lives. Yet in a complex, individualistic society like ours they are becoming more difficult to establish and sustain.

■ Many people in this society long for a return to the "golden age" of the family. But our image of the family of the past is largely a myth.

■ Although the monogamous marriage is the only sexual relationship that has achieved widespread cultural legitimacy in this society, other forms of intimacy (e.g., extra- and premarital sex, polygamy) are considered legitimate in other societies.

■ Although we like to think that the things we do in our family relationships are completely private experiences, they are continually influenced by large-scale political interests and economic pressures. Furthermore, our choices of romantic partners are governed to some degree by cultural rules that encourage us to form relationships *within* certain social groups and *outside* others.

■ Intimate relationships are ongoing systems of negotiation. The meaning of a relationship must be defined by those within it. Eventually couples develop their own private culture and their own unique way of dealing with the everyday demands of married life.

■ The social exchange model of relationship development utilizes economic principles—rewards, costs, profits, investments, equity—to explain why we form and maintain relationships with some people and not others.

■ Like the beginnings, the endings of relationships (e.g., divorce) also occur within a cultural, historical, and community context. The high rate of remarriage after divorce indicates that Americans still view the *institution* of marriage as desirable.

■ Instead of viewing domestic violence (spouse abuse and child abuse) as a product of "sick" individuals, sociologists are likely to view it as the product of a culture that tolerates violence in a variety of situations, traditionally grants men authority over women in family roles, and values family privacy and autonomy over the well-being of individual members.

YOUR TURN

There is no universal definition of "family." Our ideas about what a family is lie in sharp contrast to those of people in other cultures. Within our culture, there is also tremendous debate over what a family is and who gets to be defined as a family.

With so much disagreement, it would be interesting to find out how people actually define a family. Go to a spot on campus where there is a lot of foot traffic and ask passersby for their definition of the word *family*. See if you can find any patterns in their responses. Is there a tendency to focus on blood relations or is the emotional component of family more important? Is the presence of children necessary to be considered a family?

To delve deeper into the diversity of family definitions and experiences, pose the following questions to several friends or classmates. Try to talk to people from different racial, ethnic, religious, gender, and age groups:

■ How many brothers and sisters do you have?

■ If they are younger, did your parents expect you to help take care of them?

- Did you share a room with any of them while you were growing up?
- How many different houses did you live in while growing up?
- How often do you see your grandparents?
- Did you ever have grandparents or other relatives live in your house?
- Do you address your relatives by family terms ("Uncle Bob," "Aunt Beth," "Grandpa," "Grandma") or by first name?
- Do you expect to help support your parents when you are older?

Examine the various responses. How do you explain these differences? What do people's responses say about the structure of their families?

Mothers, Materials, and Means

Photographs and text by Dona Schwartz

Societies generate cultural norms and values, ideal standards against which individuals measure the performance of their own lives. In complex societies such as ours, a dominant culture exists alongside subcultures that may be based on region, ethnicity, race, class, or gender. Both cultural and subcultural ideals play a powerful role in individuals' conduct and the satisfaction they derive from their daily lives.

As a visual sociologist and mother, I have become especially interested in the ways in which women of different social class backgrounds experience motherhood. I suspected at the outset that mothers' everyday lives would bear little resemblance to the cultural stereotypes I encountered on television and in magazines. I wanted to find out if other women shared the white middle-class ideal I carry around in my head. And I wanted to understand how their individual life circumstances affect the way they approach the challenging job of mothering.

I located and began photographing several women. One of them, Kristi, was raised in a middle class suburb. After graduating from college she became acquainted with a man serving time in prison. After his release, Kristi became pregnant with his child. Because he was involved with several other women, she didn't consider marriage. Without a steady income or an apartment, Kristi felt she couldn't adequately care for her baby, so she gave Joslyn up for adoption. When Joslyn's father failed to sign the consent papers, Kristi was compelled to bring her baby home. Several years and a prison sentence later, Joslyn's father came to visit. Kristi got pregnant again and a baby boy, Gideon, joined the family. Kristi receives welfare payments of $532 per month, $100 in food stamps, and $30 in WIC coupons. Her days revolve around the care of her two children. On her refrigerator a note reminds her to take time out for herself, a luxury she can ill afford.

Kristi and her children all share a bedroom in their four-room apartment; Kristi and Joslyn share a bed. Since she's up early every morning with Gideon, the kids' 9:00 bedtime suits Kristi, too.

Joslyn and Gideon entertain one another while Kristi puts away laundry after a trip to the laundromat.

Kristi can't afford a car or insurance so she depends on public transportation or close friends to get around.

When Kristi shops for groceries she buys no more than what she can carry home on the bus while toting the baby and keeping an eye on Joslyn.

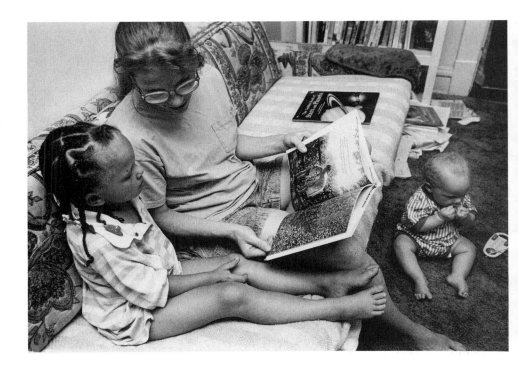

Kristi makes regular trips to the library to pick out books to read to Joslyn and Gideon. She squeezes outings to the library or the park, picnics, or visits from Joslyn's playmates into the daily routine of feeding, bathing, and napping.

Joslyn helps her mother prepare dinner by grinding some spinach for Gideon.

Each morning Christee wakes, dresses, and feeds her four children and prepares them for the day. Each contributes to the pandemonium by asserting his or her own special demands. McKeever insists on wearing shorts to preschool; Cullen must have his breakfast seated on the kitchen counter, and baby Hennessey refuses his breakfast altogether.

After graduating from college, Christee moved to St. Paul, Minnesota, to take a job as an occupational therapist. She met her husband, a bank vice president, at a friend's wedding, and soon after the birth of their first child she quit working. Like Kristi, she has chosen to stay at home with her children, but her husband's salary provides the family with a large, well-furnished house and two cars. Christee's children attend private schools; she can afford a nanny. Despite these significant advantages, transporting children, running errands, and attending school meetings consume Christee's days. She is able, however, to reserve some time for herself: she goes to exercise classes, lunches with friends, and does community volunteer work.

With their lunches packed and books gathered, Christee loads the children into the minivan and drops them off at three different schools. Left behind, Hennessey accompanies his mother on the series of errands that follow.

Christee plays an active role at her children's schools. As part of the task of organizing a birthday party for McKeever's preschool teacher, she creates a booklet of birthday wishes made from drawings collected from all the schoolchildren.

Keeping the house supplied with groceries for a family of six occupies much of Christee's time. Having someone to care for the children at home makes shopping less of an ordeal.

Extracurricular activities round out the children's days. The three eldest take Suzuki piano lessons, a teaching method that requires the active participation of a parent. Karate, swimming lessons in the summer and skiing in the winter, academic tutoring, and French lessons keep Christee on the road so much that she added a car phone to the minivan mobile command center.

Cullen's tenth birthday party included sledding, pizza and ice cream sundae construction, ghost stories, and a sleepover.

CHAPTER 9

Building Social Structure

Groups, Organizations, and Institutions

- *Groups and Everyday Life*
- *Individual Lives and the Structure of Organizations*
- *Individuals, Organizations, and Institutions*
- *Conclusion*
- *Chapter Highlights*
- *Your Turn*

In the early morning hours of May 21, 1992, two buses carrying members of the California Angels baseball team were on their way from New York to Baltimore for a weekend series with the Orioles. The players and coaches had just settled in for the 2-hour trip when they were jolted from their seats as one of the buses careened out of control, crashed through a guard rail, and landed on its side in a ravine. Fortunately, only a few of the players and coaches were injured. As the shock of this potential disaster faded, baseball fans and sportswriters began to wonder what would have happened had all or most of the team been severely injured or killed.

The incident brought to light a little-known rule euphemistically called the "rehabilitation plan." Since 1965, major league baseball has had a procedure for immediately replacing teams that lose players due to some tragedy. If a few players are disabled or killed, a team supplements its roster by promoting minor league players. However, in the event of a wide-scale tragedy, that is, when a team loses six or more players to death or disability, the plan goes into effect. The team would be allowed to select replacement players through a draft from healthy teams. The league president would decide how many players each remaining team could "protect" from being drafted (Eskenazi, 1992).

Other professional sports leagues have similar disaster plans. The National Basketball Association, for instance, has a plan that goes into effect if five or more players on a team die or are dismembered. Remaining teams could protect up to five of their players. The rest would be available for a draft. The National Football League has two plans, one for a disaster and one for a near-disaster. A near-disaster is defined as the loss of fewer than 15 players in one accident. The team would be required to replace these players through the signing of free agents—players who are not, at the time, under contract with another team. But if a quarterback is among those lost, the team would be allowed to draft up to two replacement quarterbacks from other teams. If more than 15 players are lost, the team decides whether to cancel the rest of the season. If it decides to continue, the near-disaster plan goes into effect. If it cancels, the disaster plan goes into effect, and the team would be able to draft players from other teams the following year (Eskenazi, 1992).

What do all these arrangements have to do with the creation of social structure? They illustrate an important theme of this chapter: that groups, organizations, and institutions are something more than the people who happen to make them up. They usually don't cease to exist if their constituent members are lost. The California Angels would have continued even if that accident had been much worse.

Even though groups, organizations, and institutions exist at a level above that of the individual, they are still human creations. One of the great sociological paradoxes of human existence is that we are capable of producing a social structure that intrudes on virtually every aspect of our daily lives. We then experience this structure as something other than a human product. It is ironic that in a society that so fiercely extols the virtue of rugged individualism and personal accomplishment, we spend most of our lives either within or responding to the influence of larger structural entities. From the warm intimacy of our families to the cold depersonalization of massive bureaucracies, social structure is a fundamental part of our existence. This chapter focuses on our relationship with the social structure we create and maintain. This focus will require an examination of the structure not only from the individual's perspective, but also from the macro-sociological perspective of the organizations and institutions themselves. Many important social issues look quite different depending on the perspective we use to understand them.

Groups and Everyday Life

As discussed in chapter 2, groups are collections of individuals with shared interests that have a lasting identity and some form of organization. Groups provide us with a sense of belonging. The relationship we have with social groups is a reciprocal one: While groups can determine the actions and thoughts of individuals, those individuals can in turn exert tremendous influence on the groups to which they belong.

Group Effects on Individuals

One of the ways in which groups influence individual action involves the norms that develop within a group. Perhaps you've expressed an opinion or engaged in some behavior that met with disapproval from your friends or classmates. Or maybe you expressed an unpopular political sentiment in class or dated someone your friends despised. If so, you certainly know the discomfort of standing out and violating the group's standards. Think of how others in the group showed their disapproval. Did they try to persuade you to think or behave otherwise, or did they simply ignore you and make you feel like an outcast?

By nature, groups pressure their members to conform. Whenever a member says or does something that is out of line with group norms, other members may increase their communication with that person in an effort to change her or his mind (Rodin, 1985). If majority members lack the capability or desire to apply pressure to the person who is out of line, they may simply reject him or her either blatantly or subtly (Schacter, 1951). Rejecting the "deviant" is a means of reestablishing equilibrium within the group and ensuring that its values and perceptions remain dominant. In so doing the group not only rids itself of a "troublemaker," it also reinforces the goodness of its beliefs.

Group Decision Making

Group structure also influences the way members think and make decisions. We have all had the experience of trying to come to a decision or solve a problem within a group setting. Maybe you were a member of the planning committee for the school prom or for the homecoming game festivities. Or maybe you've been in a club that had to come up with a budget. It would seem that a group of people working together would make effective, rational decisions. After all, there would be many viewpoints expressed so the potential consequences of all options could be explored and the relative value of each could be weighed. The group would be able to take advantage of the special expertise or knowledge of each member so that the best decision is ultimately reached.

Group decision making doesn't always function so smoothly, however. Sometimes not all opinions are heard, or one or two people dominate the discussion. Or sometimes pressures to reach agreement and maintain good feelings lead the group to adopt a faulty decision that is promoted by a powerful and vocal individual whom the rest of the group members don't want to cross. All of these conditions are likely to create a situation in which a compromise is reached that satisfies no one.

Psychologist Irving Janis (1991) uses the term **groupthink** to describe a mode of thinking within a group whereby pressures to achieve a unanimous decision overwhelm individual members' motivation to weigh alternatives realistically. In an effort to achieve consensus, maintain good feelings among the group, or appease a leader, critical thought, the weighing of pros and cons, and a discussion of all alternatives are neglected. Janis argues that groupthink is likely to occur when there is a crisis situation, when the group is tight-knit, when the members are insulated from the criticisms of qualified outsiders, and when there is a powerful leader who actively promotes his or her favored solution. The group then comes to an unwise decision that might have been avoided had there been more discussion.

Some of the worst political decisions in history may have resulted from the harmful consequences of groupthink. President John F. Kennedy's failed Bay of Pigs invasion in 1961, Richard Nixon's Watergate cover-up, and Ronald Reagan's Iran-Contra scandal are examples of situations in which a small group of presidential advisers suppressed their desire to disagree in order to give the illusion of unanimity and cohesiveness within a group. One of the most striking and tragic cases of groupthink occurred in 1986 when the ill-fated decision to launch the space shuttle *Challenger* was made.

Gregory Moorhead, Richard Ference, and Chris Neck
The Challenger *Disaster*

On January 28, 1986, the space shuttle *Challenger* was launched from Kennedy Space Center in Florida. The temperature that morning was in the mid-20s, well below the lowest temperature at which the rocket booster engines had been tested. Seventy-three seconds after lift-off the shuttle exploded, killing all seven passengers—six astronauts and one civilian.

The Presidential Commission investigating the incident concluded that flawed decision making during meetings the night before was the primary contributing cause of the accident. How could such smart, well-intentioned people make such a disastrous decision? Researcher Greg Moorhead and his colleagues (Moorhead, Ference, & Neck, 1991) reviewed the notes of these meetings to see if groupthink had played a part. The meetings took place throughout the day and evening of January 27. Those involved—known as "The Level I Flight Readiness Review Panel"—consisted of NASA representatives from the Johnson Space Center in Houston and the Kennedy Space Center in Florida, and engineers from Morton Thiokol Inc. in Utah (manufacturers of the crucial O-ring seals). At 8:45 P.M. the Morton Thiokol engineers on the panel, fearful of a malfunction under untested temperatures, recommended not to launch. Usually such expressions of doubt would have been enough to postpone the mission. But their warnings went unheeded and, through the ensuing discussions, the fateful decision to launch was made.

Was groupthink responsible? One of the conditions under which groupthink occurs is that the group is close and highly cohesive. The people on this panel had worked together for many years. They knew each other quite well and had worked their way up the ranks of the space program together. There was a high level of esprit de corps between them.

A second condition is that there is a group leader (or leaders) who energetically states and defends his or her position. In this case two top-level managers from NASA actively promoted their pro-launch opinions in the face of any opposition. They had a preferred decision in mind and engaged in actions designed to promote it rather than critically weigh the alternatives. They tended to focus on supportive information and ignore any information that may have reflected negatively on their position. In addition, they constructed elaborate rationalizations that discounted the earlier warnings, ultimately convincing themselves and the rest of the panel that the engineers' data were inconclusive.

Finally, groupthink is likely to occur when those promoting the opposing position are effectively neutralized. The Morton Thiokol engineers who made the negative recommendations were not even present or consulted when the final decision to launch was made. Neither did the panel seek the opinions of others outside the group who may have had expertise in the area. Curiously, the role the engineers played was quite different from their role in past launch-readiness meetings. Ordinarily they would be called on to prove with 100% certainty that the shuttle was ready. The slightest doubt would be sufficient to postpone the project. In this case, however, the engineers were forced to show beyond all doubt that the booster rockets were unsafe. That is, they were told to prove with 100% certainty that the rockets would fail. Without the appropriate data— remember, the engines had not been tested at temperatures this low—they could not prove conclusively that a failure would occur. Hence their objections were dismissed.

Other external circumstances enhanced the groupthink effect. The panel was under strong pressure from the public and the government to launch on time. A delay would have been a public relations disaster. The launch had already been postponed once, and the window of opportunity for another launch was closing fast. Panel members feared that further delays could actually affect future congressional funding for the entire space program. Under such pressures to make a decision quickly, the groupthink effect was magnified.

The decision to launch the Challenger can be classified as a groupthink situation. This analysis has important implications for all group decision-making situations. If there is a strong desire to achieve consensus around a position by an authoritative leader, rational decisions may be next to impossible. In our attempts to belong and to be trusted and liked, we may sacrifice reason in order to conform to the group. Powerful pressures and norms induce members toward agreement and away from rational debate.

Social Dilemmas: The Effects of Individuals on Groups

We can see that the structure of a group sometimes leads individuals to make terrible decisions. It is also the case that private decisions made at the individual level can lead to disaster for an entire group or community. We often take for granted that groups of individuals with common interests will attempt to further those common interests. Let's say members of a group want to make sure that their neighborhood is free of crime. It follows logically that each individual would, as a rational person, act to achieve that objective. For instance, everyone would volunteer at some point to "patrol" his or her street at night, or they might chip in money to improve street lighting.

In actuality, though, the opposite appears to be true (Cross & Guyer, 1980; Messick & Brewer, 1983; Olsen, 1965). People often do not voluntarily act to achieve the common objective unless there is some sort of coercion or other device to force their behavior. Instead, they will act to ensure their own personal interests, such as not donating money for a new street light under the belief that others will do so. Such a phenomenon is known as a **social dilemma** (Messick & Brewer, 1983). When each person in a group pursues his or her own self-interests, the result may be ruin for everyone. If each person individually comes to the decision not to donate money, the new street light never gets purchased, and everyone suffers.

The phenomenon of social dilemmas illustrates how individual actions can have important, even disastrous, consequences for larger collectivities. Major social problems like pollution can be understood as stemming, at least in part, from the decisions made by people acting in their own interest as opposed to the collective interest. If I fling one bag of trash onto the highway, it doesn't seem so significant or destructive. But, of course, when a significant number of people do the same, it becomes destructive. Moreover, if we think of nations as individual actors and the planet as the group, many situations of resource depletion that have national and international significance, including inadequate recycling, failure to conserve energy, and species extinction, can be understood from this perspective. Two types of social dilemmas are the tragedy of the commons and the free-rider problem.

The Tragedy of the Commons

The term *commons* was originally used to describe the pasture ground that was often located in the center of New England towns where herders brought their animals to graze. The land was a public good available to anyone. Used in moderation by everyone, the commons works. The grass will be allowed to regenerate, resulting in a perpetual supply of food for the herds (Hardin & Baden, 1977).

However, each herder is aware that it is to his or her personal benefit to increase the size of his or her herd and let the animals eat as much as they want. While each animal represents a profit, the cost of grazing them is shared by all the herders. Responding to such an incentive, each herder rationally decides to increase his or her herd. When this occurs, the commons begins to deteriorate. The process continues because no single herder will find it beneficial to reduce the size of his or her herd when others aren't reducing theirs. When all the herders allow their growing herds to eat as much of the grass as they want for as long as they want, the grass will never be allowed to regenerate. The tragic conclusion is that the commons will collapse and the herds that grazed on it will be destroyed because the short-term needs of the individual overshadowed the long-term collective needs of the group.

In this illustration, the common resource was grass, and the group was relatively small. However the "tragedy of the commons" model can be applied to any situation where common resources can be used by a number of people and are available to all: air, food, fuel, water, and so on. The situation becomes particularly dangerous when the group adopts a crisis mentality.

You probably recall the destructive floods that took place in several Midwestern states during the summer of 1993. When a river overflowed its banks in Des Moines, Iowa, it wiped out a filtration system and made the municipal water system unsafe. People were unable to use running water for weeks and were without drinkable water for longer than that. In order to restore full water service, the system had to be refilled with clean water. To accomplish this, local officials asked everyone to voluntarily refrain from using water in their homes and businesses for a few days. The situation was urgent. Without full water pressure in the city's water pipes, not only were residents without regular water service, but fire engines weren't able to use hydrants.

If everyone did as they were asked and refrained from using water, the system would have been replenished and everyone would have had water within a couple of days. For some individuals, however, the temptation to use water secretly in the privacy of their own homes was too hard to resist. So many residents violated the city's rules that the resumption of full water service was delayed for many more days (Bradsher, 1993). As a result of individuals seeking their short-term benefits, the entire community suffered.

Why do such dilemmas occur? Part of the problem is a lack of communication and a lack of trust among individual members of a group or community. I may want to conserve water by using it sparingly, but if I think that my neighbors are hoarding, I, too, will hoard to make sure I don't go without. Hence I am induced to follow a line of action that results in a positive outcome for me but that may eventually have negative outcomes for the group or community. In the end we will all be worse off than if we had ignored our individual self-interest in the first place. In dire circumstances immediate gratification is enticing. A "sensible" strategy—that is, one of moderation and conservation—is quite easy to abandon at the first sign of someone else satisfying his or her short-term gains.

The problem is made worse by the fact that individuals are fooled into thinking that meeting their individual needs will not have an effect on the entire group. "Is the cost of my using an extra gallon of water really going to harm the community?" From my point of view the answer is no. The dilemma arises, however, when everyone, or at least a substantial number of people, arrives at the same conclusion. As we collectively ignore or downplay the consequences of our actions, we collectively overuse the resource and pave the way for disasters that none of us has caused individually (Edney, 1979).

The Free-Rider Problem

Social dilemmas can also occur when people refrain from contributing something to a common resource when the resource is available anyway. To put it another way, why pay for something you can use for free? For example, it is irrational, from an individual's point of view, to donate money to public television. I can enjoy "Sesame Street" and "Masterpiece Theater" without paying a penny. My small, personal donation wouldn't be more than a tiny drop in public television's budgetary bucket and would have no noticeable impact on the entire amount needed to run a network anyway. From my perspective, there is no incentive for me to incur any costs when I don't have to. If everyone acted this way, however, we would all keep our money, but we'd eventually lose the resource. If public television depended solely on voluntary donations—corporate grants and sponsorships actually keep it going—it would have disappeared a long time ago.

Sociologists sometimes refer to this situation as the **free-rider** problem (Olsen, 1965). As the term implies, a free rider is the individual who acquires a good or service without risking any personal costs or contributing anything in return. Free ridership can be seen in a variety of everyday activities, from reading a magazine at a newsstand without buying it, to photocopying a chapter from a book without buying the book. We all enjoy the benefits our tax dollars provide us—police, firefighters, smooth roads, and other municipal services. But if taxes were voluntary, would anyone willingly pay for these services?

In a study of the 1979 Three Mile Island accident, which damaged a nuclear power plant, 87% of the local residents who were worried about the safety of the plant and who were opposed to restarting it never contributed any time or money to the numerous community groups that had been organized to represent their interests. One of the reasons they offered for free riding and not getting involved was the belief that enough people were already involved to make their participation unnecessary (Walsh & Warland, 1983).

We can see evidence of the free-rider problem at the institutional level as well. People often talk about children as a vital resource on whom the future of the country and the planet lie. The care and education of these children can be seen as a public resource. All of society benefits when children are in good physical, social, and psychological health. Yet most members of society are not willing to pay for the services necessary to ensure the well-being of children. It is difficult to convince people that increasing their taxes to improve schools, raise teachers' salaries, or hire more social workers will benefit them in the long run.

Solving Social Dilemmas

Social dilemmas can be solved or at least decreased in several ways (Messick & Brewer, 1983). Establishing communication between individuals helps because it allows people to know what others are up to. When individual actions are identifiable, feelings of personal responsibility are likely to increase (Edney & Harper, 1978). However, this is not very practical when the group or community is quite large, like an entire country, for instance.

Another solution is to use coercion through restrictive rules or laws to prevent people from seeking their self-interested goals. Paying taxes is one example. Some companies are union "closed shops," meaning that in order to work there an employee *must* join the union and pay union dues. Without this requirement, individual employees would be able to enjoy the benefits provided by the union—higher wages, better working conditions—without having to pay anything for them.

The city of Des Moines used a form of coercion to ensure compliance with its water use rules. Realizing they couldn't count solely on the integrity of the citizens, city officials set up an emergency hotline where people could call and anonymously turn in violators of the water rules. When identified, a work crew would go to a home or business and check for unauthorized water use. If the crew found the water meter running, a valve at the curb would be turned off for a week. No appeals were allowed and water users were never told who turned them in. In addition, the offenders' names and addresses were immediately made known to reporters under Iowa's open records rules, and spread across the state by newspapers, radio, and television (Bradsher, 1993).

Individual Lives and the Structure of Organizations

Organizations are another defining structural feature of a complex society. We are all, to varying degrees, organizational creatures. We're born in them, educated in them, spend most of our adult lives working for them, and will most likely die in them (E. Gross & Etzioni, 1985). Think about all the things you do in the course of a typical day that are touched by some larger organizational system. Organizations design, produce, and market the alarm clock that wakes you up, the sheets and pillow cases you sleep on, the toothpaste you sleepily use, the showerhead that jolts you into consciousness, the clothes you put on, the coffee you can't begin the day without, the newspaper you read, the car you drive, the computer you use at work, the bed you return to, and so on.

Organizations are responsible for the food that graces your table. The farm where the food is produced is probably a huge organization, as are the unions that protect the workers who produce the food and the transportation companies that bring it to your local stores. And all this is controlled by a vast network of financial organizations that sets prices and by governmental agencies that ensure the food's safety.

In order to prepare the food that is produced, delivered, and sold, you have to use products made by other organizations: a sink, a refrigerator, a microwave, a stove. To use those appliances you have to make arrangements with other organizations like the Department of Water and Power, the Gas Company, and the Electric Company. And in order to pay these bills, you have to use still other organizations: the U.S. Postal Service, your bank, and credit companies.

Where does the money to pay the bills come from? Most likely your job. If you are employed, you probably work for yet another organization. When you receive a paycheck, the Internal Revenue Service and the Social Security Administration step in to take their share.

Now think of the car you use to get to that job. It was no doubt manufactured in a huge corporation and sold to you by a local dealership. The fuel that makes it run is produced by huge multinational corporations. The roads you travel to get to your destinations are built and maintained by massive organizations within the state and federal governments. You can't even drive unless you are covered by insurance, which is available only through an authorized company.

What if things aren't going well? Say you get sick, or you have an accident, or you have a dispute with someone else. Here, too, organizations come into play. You have to make use of hospitals, insurance companies, police departments, and courts.

You get the picture? Life in a complex society is a life touched by public and private organizations at every turn. One of the most important types of organizations you must deal with every day is the bureaucracy.

Bureaucracies: Playing by the Rules

In a large, complex society like ours, things must be done in a formal, planned, and unified way. Let's take a closer look at the production and delivery of food. Because most of us don't grow our own food, we are dependent on others to provide it for us. With a population of 250 million people there must be some systematic way of getting food to our tables. The people responsible for producing it can't make decisions on what to grow and when to grow it informally and spontaneously. The people responsible for selling it to us can't make its availability random and unpredictable. Imagine how chaotic your life would be if you didn't know when your local supermarket would be open or what sorts of foods would be available for purchase. What if one day it sold nothing but flour, the next day only plums, and the day after just packaged lunch meats?

In a small-scale community where people grow their own food and the local Mom and Pop grocery store provides everything else, this might not be such a problem. The interactions between employees and customers are quite personal and friendly. If you want a certain kind of food, all you have to do is ask for it. We often look with fondness and nostalgia at such remnants of "the good ol' days." Such an arrangement can't work in a massive society. There has to be a relatively efficient and predictable system of providing products and services to large numbers of people. The tasks that need to be done just to keep that system going are too complex for a single person to know: accounting, sales, marketing, research and development, public relations, insurance, maintenance, shipping and receiving, and so on. This is what makes bureaucracy necessary.

A **bureaucracy** is a large hierarchical organization that is governed by formal rules and regulations and that has a clear specification of work tasks. According to the famous 19th-century sociologist, Max Weber (VAY-ber) (1946), a bureaucracy is the most efficient means of managing large groups of people. Weber felt that in a bureaucracy all decisions are made purely on the basis of what will accomplish the organization's goals. Today, however, we tend to see bureaucracies as impersonal, rigid machines that trespass into our personal lives. Bureaucracies conjure up images of rows of desks occupied by faceless workers, endless lines and forms to fill out, and frustrations over "red tape." Indeed the word *bureaucrat* has taken on such a negative connotation that to be called one is the highest order of insult.

Characteristics of Bureaucracies

Bureaucracy refers to a specific type of organization with certain important characteristics. First of all, the bureaucracy has a clear-cut **division of labor**, which is carefully specified by written job descriptions and the degree of authority given to each position. The term means that people can specialize in a certain task and become more skilled at it. The bureaucracy theoretically becomes more efficient because it employs only specialized experts in each position with every one of them responsible only for the effective performance of his or her narrowly defined duties (Blau & Meyer, 1987). The division of labor is such a common characteristic of large organizations that most of us couldn't imagine things otherwise.

The division of labor enables large organizations to accomplish larger goals than would be possible if everyone acted independently. Tasks become highly specific, sometimes to the point where it is illegal to perform someone else's task. For instance, hospitals are highly complex bureaucracies made up of many different groups: nurses, doctors, administrators, orderlies, food service workers, janitors, and patients. The responsibilities of each are highly specialized and restricted. Orderlies don't prescribe drugs, nurses don't perform surgery, doctors don't help patients with their insurance forms. While everyone plays an important role in keeping the hospital going so that sick people can get better, they must sacrifice the freedom to do any task they want in the interests of efficiently meeting the organization's goals.

Not only are tasks divided in a bureaucracy, they are also ranked. The second major characteristic of a bureaucracy is a **hierarchy of authority** (Weber, 1946). Most bureaucracies are organized in a pyramid shape with a few people at the top who have a lot of power and many at the bottom who have virtually none.

People at one level are responsible to those above them but can exert authority over those below.

Authority tends to be attached to the position and not to the person occupying the position. This ensures that the bureaucracy will not stop functioning in the event of a retirement or a death. It also means that authority is supposed to be honored despite the personal characteristics of the person occupying the position. In the highly bureaucratized military, you must obey the orders of your superior despite any personal feelings you have about that individual.

When President Bill Clinton took office in 1993, he automatically became the Commander-in-Chief of the military. Because of his lack of military service, many in the armed forces resented him. Some high-ranking military officials privately expressed their mistrust of him. And yet those officers never questioned their obligation to follow his directives. In other bureuacracies, such obedience might not be as strict. Nevertheless, a bureaucracy requires some sort of chain of command. Not only does this allow some people to control others, it also justifies paying some people higher salaries than others.

Bureaucracies are also governed by an elaborate system of formal and explicit rules and regulations. Such a system is designed to make sure that a particular task is done the same way by each person occupying that position. With a system of rules people don't have to reinvent the wheel each time a problem arises. The rules can govern everything from personal appearance and simple tasks like filing documents to complex issues like financial or political decisions of international significance.

Furthermore, the rules carefully specify the relationships between various positions in the bureaucracy. Officials are supposed to perform their tasks impartially and impersonally. In the bureaucracy there is no place for the expression of strong feelings about superiors, subordinates, or clients. Ironically, the very factors that make the typical bureaucrat unpopular with the public—an aloof attitude, lack of genuine concern—actually allow the organization to run more efficiently. We want the person administering our driver's license examination to acknowledge us and care about us, but to do so would seriously impede the smooth functioning of the entire system. Think of how you'd feel if the person in front of you in line at the Department of Motor Vehicles engaged in excessive chitchat with the clerk behind the window or if the road-test examiner decided to stop for a cup of coffee with the person who was taking his or her driver's test before you.

Your university is a clear example of a bureaucracy. There is a definite division of labor that involves janitors, secretaries, librarians, coaches, professors, and administrators. The tasks people are responsible for are highly specialized. Professors in the Spanish Department don't teach courses in biology. For that matter, sociology professors who teach social deviance probably don't teach demography.

Although the power afforded different positions varies from school to school, all universities have some sort of hierarchy of authority. Usually this hierarchy consists of students at the bottom (sorry!), followed by staff employees, part-time instructors, professors, and department chairs. At the administrative level there are associate deans, deans, vice presidents, and ultimately the president of the university and the board of trustees. In addition the university is governed by a strict set of rules regarding when and how students can register for classes, when grades must be turned in by the professor, graduation requirements, and university policies. Strict adherence on the part of university employees to these rules and policies, sometimes to the chagrin of the frustrated student who can't register for the one class he or she needs to graduate, is likely to give the university its final bureaucratic characteristic: impersonality.

Problems of Bureaucracies

Although he stressed the functional necessity of bureaucracies in complex Western societies, Weber warned that they could take on a life of their own, becoming "iron cages" for those within them. He feared that bureaucracies might one day become so efficient and powerful in controlling people that, once established, the momentum of bureaucratization would be irreversible. Weber worried that bureaucracies might come to dominate every part of society, locking people into a system where their only movement was from one de-humanizing bureaucracy to another.

In a classic bureaucracy the emphasis on conformity and routine inhibits the rational exercise of judgment. Bureaucratic life is precise. Personal discretion is minimized. People are expected to arrive at work at a given time, perform a predetermined set of activities, rest at a certain time, and resume work until the day is over. In some companies, one shift of workers will replace another so that work can continue uninterrupted around the clock. Many bureaucracies are designed like machines, and the people within them are expected to behave as if they were parts of a machine. The mechanistic definitions of job responsibilities often encourage organizational members to adopt mindless, segmented attitudes about their jobs: "I do what I'm told," "It's not my responsibility."

As workers are fit into roles that completely determine their duties, responsibilities, and rights, they often become rigid and inflexible and are less concerned with the quality of their work than with whether they and others are playing by the rules. Hence, people emerge who are oriented more toward conformity than toward problem solving and critical thinking. They are the source of frustrating red tape, procedures and practices that often seem designed to *prevent* things from happening (G. Morgan, 1986).

Weber's fears have been largely realized. The bureaucratic model pervades every corner of modern society. The most successful bureaucracies not only dominate the business landscape, they have come to influence our entire way of life. Take, for instance, large fast-food restaurant chains. It is difficult for most of us to imagine what life would be like if we weren't able to go to the drive-thru and grab a quick bite to eat on the run. More than providing convenience, these restaurants have become a key piece of American culture. One fast-food corporation that has been particularly influential is McDonald's.

George Ritzer
The
McDonaldization
of Society

Sociologist George Ritzer (1993) uses the McDonald's restaurant chain as a metaphor for describing some of the harmful effects of bureaucratization on society. McDonald's, Inc., earns between $800 and $900 million in profits each year. Tens of thousands of McDonald's restaurants can be found in every corner of life: from airports, shopping malls, and college campuses across the United States to the main thoroughfares in major foreign cities such as London, Paris, Moscow, and Beijing. Its phenomenal success has spawned countless other fast-food chains that emulate its model: Kentucky Fried Chicken, Taco Bell, Domino's Pizza, Long John Silver's, and so on. McDonald's fast-food formula has also influenced other types of businesses, among them Toys "R" Us, *USA Today*, Econo-Lodge motels, Pearle Vision Centers, Jiffy Lube, and Blockbuster Video.

But the success of McDonald's is more than just a story about hamburgers, profits, and business savvy. McDonald's has become a sacred institution, occupying a central place in popular culture. As you know, the "golden arches" of McDonald's are probably one of the most identifiable symbols in society today. They're everywhere. When we're not driving past them in town or on an interstate highway, we see them on television. A 1986 survey found that 96% of schoolchildren were able to identify Ronald McDonald (Greenhouse, 1986). McDonald's appeals to us in a variety of ways:

> The restaurants themselves are depicted as spick-and-span, the food is said to be fresh and nutritious, the employees are shown to be young and eager, the managers appear gentle and caring, and the dining experience itself seems to be fun-filled. We are even led to believe that we contribute, at least indirectly, to charities by supporting the company that supports Ronald McDonald Houses for sick children. (Ritzer, 1993, p. 6)

According to Ritzer, McDonald's has been so successful primarily because it fits Weber's model of the classic bureaucracy. It has a clear division of labor and a uniform system of rules that make it highly efficient and predictable. No matter where you are, you know what to expect when you go into a McDonald's. The filet-o-fish sandwich in Phoenix tastes the same as the one in Brussels. If you've ever watched the workers behind the counter, they each have specialized tasks that are narrowly defined:

> By combining twentieth-century computer technology with nineteenth-century time-and-motion studies, the McDonald's corporation has broken

the jobs of griddleman, waitress, cashier and even manager down into small, simple steps. . . . The corporation has systematically extracted the decision-making elements from filling french fry boxes or scheduling staff. . . . They relentlessly weed out all variables that might make it necessary to make a decision at the store level, whether on pickles or on cleaning procedures. (Garson, 1988, p. 37)

McDonaldization will continue to thrive for several reasons. First, it is impelled by economic interests. Profit-making enterprises will go on emulating the McDonald's bureaucratic model because it leads to higher profits and lower costs. When McDonald's offers greater efficiency and therefore higher profits through the increased use of nonhuman technology or the uniformity of its product, others quickly follow suit.

Second, McDonaldization has become such a culturally desirable process that many enterprises pursue it as an end in its own right. We live in a culture that treasures efficiency, speed, predictability, and control, and we seek these things out whether or not economic gains are involved. Our desire for these values often blinds us to the fact that fast foods, as well as their domestic equivalent, microwave foods, actually cost us more than if we had prepared the meals ourselves. For many people the commitment to McDonald's is more emotional than economic. We all have memories of McDonald's: It's where we went after Little League games, it's where we hung out as teenagers, it's where we stopped on the way to the hospital for the birth of a first child, and so on. Because of the hallowed place it occupies in our society, people are willing to overlook its disadvantages.

Finally, McDonaldization parallels other changes occurring in society. With the increasing number of dual-earner couples, and therefore the increasing number of workers in general, there is less likely to be someone in the family who has the time or the desire to buy the ingredients, prepare the meal, eat it, and clean up afterward. Furthermore, a society that emphasizes mobility is one in which the fast-food mentality will thrive.

But there is a downside to this model. While the efficiency, speed, and predictability of McDonaldized systems may be appealing and comforting to some, the system as a whole has made social life more homogeneous, more rigid, and less personal. The "fast food" model has robbed us of our sponteneity. Our creativity and desire for uniqueness have been reduced, trapping us in Weber's "iron cage"—a bureaucratic culture that requires little thought and leaves virtually nothing to chance.

The Hierarchical Makeup of Organizations

Given the previous descriptions, you might think that everyone within a bureaucracy feels alienated, depersonalized, or perhaps even exploited. But a person's experience in a large bureaucracy depends in part where he or she fits in the overall hierarchy of the organization. While some people are dehumanized by their place in the hierarchy, others may actually benefit from theirs.

The Upper Echelons

People at the top of large organizations have come the furthest, are the fewest in number, and get the most out of their position. One interesting and disturbing characteristic of American executives is that they tend to be extremely *homogeneous*; that is, they are similar to one another in terms of relevant social characteristics (DiMaggio & Powell, 1983; Kanter, 1977; W. H. Whyte, 1956). They are almost exclusively male, white, and middle or upper class. In addition, their educational, social, and familial experiences are remarkably similar (Kanter, 1977; C. W. Mills, 1956). This homogeneity is due not only to historical prejudices in hiring and promotion practices, but also to the nature of top-level jobs.

The higher one's place is in the bureaucracy, the more ambiguous one's job description becomes. Upper-level executives don't have clearly bounded jobs with neatly defined responsibilities. The executive must be prepared to use discretion and be flexible enough to deal with a variety of different problems at all times. New issues continuously arise that require quick judgment and decisive action. Ironically, however, while discretion is the defining feature of an executive's position, the bulk of his or her time is not spent in making major decisions, creating, and planning, but in attending meetings, writing memos, responding to phone messages and faxes, and participating in company-related social gatherings.

The role of the executive is, by nature, a vague one. There are no clear-cut criteria to evaluate whether a person is performing her or his job effectively. Things like sales and production records or profit margins can provide only indirect indicators of an executive's competence. When asked what makes an executive effective, top-level employees identified such vague factors as the ability to communicate and winning acceptance as the most important criteria (Kanter, 1977).

In such an environment, rapid communication, common language, and common understanding are important. Executives are therefore forced to spend a great deal of time with other executives whom they have come to trust and with whom they can communicate most smoothly and readily.

The best way to ensure acceptance and ease of communication is to limit top-level jobs to people who are similar to one another, who have had similar experiences, and who come from similar backgrounds. This is why many male executives report feeling uncomfortable communicating with women: "You never knew where you stood. They changed their minds all the time; I never knew what they'd do from one minute to the next" (Kanter, 1977, p. 58).

The result is a closed circle of executives who resemble one another but who are insulated from the rest of the organization. The structure of their occupational roles makes it more comfortable to try to exclude people seen as different. From this perspective it is easy to see why racial and ethnic minorities and women have been traditionally excluded from high-level positions in bureaucratic organizations.

There is a self-fulfilling prophecy embedded in all of this as well. The more closed and exclusive the network of executives, the more difficult it is for "outsiders" to break in. Their very difficulty gaining access to the top level of the organization is then perceived as a sign of their incompetence and an indicator to the insiders that they were right to close their ranks in the first place.

The Middle Ground

The view from the middle is quite different. The middle is in some ways the most discouraging part of an organization (Kanter & Stein, 1979). While those at the top set the organizational agenda and dictate policy, and those at the bottom solely follow orders and directives from above, it is the people in the middle who provide the essential link between the two. They are caught between those below, whose cooperation they need, and those above, who selectively grant them the authority to implement organizational policy. Hence middle-level employees are sometimes trapped in a world of conflicting role expectations.

Often the morale of people in the middle is sustained by the belief that they have a shot at the top. If I believe that in the future I will be promoted, my boring and unfulfilling job as a middle-level manager will hold different meaning for me than if I expect to remain in the same position forever (McHugh, 1968). It becomes a step on the ladder of success, a necessary but temporary stage in my upward mobility. Unpleasant tasks may be minor inconveniences, but they are the price I have to pay. This hope of future promotion may drive people in the middle to concentrate on accumulating bits of status and privilege and make enough of an impact to gain recognition from those above.

For many middle-level employees, however, the hope of upward mobility is just that, hope. Because of the pyramid structure of most bureaucracies, the vast majority of middle-level employees will not move up. Many simply fail in the increasingly competitive push for advancement into the upper echelons of the organization. Others are stuck in jobs that provide little or no opportunity for advancement. While some people are able to develop a comfortable niche in the middle (Kanter & Stein, 1979), others are likely to harbor a bitterness that creates feelings of alienation and anger and may manifest itself in attempts to retaliate and punish the company.

Because of the structure of most large organizations, middle-level managers are forced to become powerless and cautious in their approach to their jobs. They are in the frustrating position of being helpless in terms of overall policy established by those above them, while also being responsible for the results produced by those below them. Unwilling to jeopardize the limited privileges they have attained, middle-level managers often become controlling, coercive, and demanding in their relationships with the people they supervise, ruling their narrow domain with an iron hand:

> Getting everything right, and demanding that subordinates do the same, is the response of those who lack other ways to impress those above them or to secure their position; and in turn, they demand this kind of ritualistic conformity from subordinates, like a school teacher more concerned about the neatness of the paper than its ideas. (Kanter & Stein, 1979, p. 95)

For some people in the middle, membership in the organization *becomes* their life, often to the detriment of other roles and relationships. Almost four decades ago sociologist William H. Whyte (1956) described how the personal lives of rising young executives were often overshadowed by their desire to succeed in the corporate world. Large organizations instilled in their employees a corporate social ethic, a belief that "belongingness" to the group was the ultimate need of the individual. Such beliefs encouraged total commitment to the organization, making a person's private life irrelevant for smooth organizational functioning. They knew that the organization rewarded those who sacrificed everything else to become "good team players."

Whyte's depiction of the private costs of organizational life ring true today. Organizations still value team players, middle-level employees who place organizational interests above their own (Jackall, 1988). To be a good team player one must avoid expressing strong political or moral opinions, sacrifice one's home life by putting in long hours, and be forever obedient to one's superiors. Being seen as a loyal and effective group member and sticking to one's assigned position are also important. A good team player is not a prima donna. Striking, distinctive characteristics, such as being abrasive, pushy, or not knowing when to back off, are dangerous in the bureaucratic world. According to one study, one of the most damaging things that can be said about a middle-level manager is that he or she is brilliant. This usually signals a judgment that the individual has publicly asserted his or her intelligence and is perceived as a threat to others (Jackall, 1988).

Interestingly, while organizations still value the social ethic and the ideal of team play, individuals today seem to be less willing to sacrifice their personal lives and beliefs for the organization. Two sociologists, Paul Leinberger and Bruce Tucker (1991), interviewed the sons and daughters of the original "organizational men" that Whyte interviewed more than 30 years earlier. They found that these individuals were very different from their parents in their values and attitudes. They tended to be individualists, more inclined to pursue self-fulfillment than a feeling of belongingness to the organization. Given recent social trends, this is not surprising. In an era when corporate mergers, relocations, and periodic layoffs are commonplace, the concept of organizational loyalty has become all but extinct.

Although there is little desire to go back to a past when middle-level employees sacrificed everything for their career aspirations, Leinberger and Tucker point out that today's cultural emphasis on individualism has created other problems such as feelings of isolation, the inability to commit to others, and the absence of a sense of community.

Lower Echelons

A discussion of the everyday experience of bureaucracy would be incomplete without discussing what it looks like from the bottom. The bottom consists of those who stand lowest in the organization's hierarchy. They are paid the least, valued the least, and considered the most expendable (Kanter & Stein, 1979). The real sign that you are at the bottom is the degree to which you are controlled by others. People at the bottom don't have the right to define their occupational tasks themselves. They have little discretion, little autonomy, little freedom, and little influence. In the university bureaucracy, for example, students usually don't have much say over the content of their courses, the curriculum of their major, or the requirements necessary for graduation.

Most American corporations are still organized in terms of ideas developed in the early 1900s. The fundamental principle is that a highly specific division of labor increases productivity and lowers costs. Hence the low-level work tasks in a bureaucratic organization are usually subdivided into small parts that can be performed repetitively by unskilled workers. This structure provides management with the maximum control over workers' jobs while the workers themselves become "an indistinguishable swarm" (Kanter & Stein, 1979, p. 178).

Often technological advancements coincide with the subdivision of low-level jobs and a decrease in the skill levels required to do them (Hartmann, Kraut, & Tilly, 1989). In the insurance industry, the skilled work of assigning risks and assessing people's claims has been increasingly incorporated into computer software programs. What once required a great deal of human judgment and discretion is now almost completely routinized. Less skilled, less experienced, and lower paid clerks can now perform the work once performed by skilled workers and professionals (Hartmann, Kraut, & Tilly, 1989).

This process, called **deskilling,** creates jobs that require obedience and passivity rather than talent and experience. Deskilling provides the organization with clear financial benefits but creates low levels of job satisfaction among the employees. Dull and repetitive tasks that offer little challenge, such as assembly-line work, account for a substantial amount of discontent experienced by workers at the bottom of large bureaucracies (U.S. Dept. of Health, Education and Welfare, 1973).

In one study assembly-line workers in textile and automobile plants were compared to skilled technicians in the chemical industry. Because the skilled workers had jobs that involved the exercise of judgment and initiative, they were much less alienated and found their jobs much more rewarding than the assembly-line workers (Blauner, 1964).

Attempts at enriching the otherwise dull work lives of people at the bottom have been somewhat successful. Workers at the Motorola Company had to assemble a portable telephone beeper that consisted of 80 small parts. In the traditional way, each worker made a small change and passed the unit on to the next worker. In the revised procedure, each worker assembled an entire unit, and the worker's name appeared on the completed beeper. Although the assembly costs were higher, the company claimed that the quality of the product was also higher and absenteeism and turnover rates were lower (cited in Gross & Etzioni, 1985).

Without such workplace innovations, the task facing many workers at the bottom is to make their occupational lives tolerable by exerting some kind of control over the work they do. It would appear, from the previous discussion, that the top-down flow of authority in bureaucratic organizations would make such a task relatively impossible. In reality, though, lower-level employees are not completely powerless and can be somewhat autonomous, even creative, in their positions.

For one thing, the sheer size of large corporations makes it next to impossible for middle- and upper-level managers to supervise directly and therefore exert continuous authority over lower-level workers. This creates substantial opportunities, even in the most highly structured and repetitive jobs, for workers to exert some control over their work. Workers can either redefine the immediate nature of their tasks or willingly and secretly violate the expectations and orders of superiors.

For instance, in one study of machine operators it was found that while management saw the workday composed of distinct periods marked by check-in time, lunch break, and check-out time, the workers created their own way of dividing up the day (Roy, 1959). There was coffee time, peach time, banana time, fish time, and Coke time. During banana time, one worker would steal a banana out of the lunchbox of another and cry out "Banana Time!" The person from whom the banana was stolen would always make a fuss, but he would continue to bring one each day. Little games like this relieved boredom and made the workday more tolerable.

In sum, lower-level workers are not necessarily powerless automatons whose lives are totally structured from above. In fact, the authority of middle-level managers is thoroughly dependent on their subordinates' willingness to cooperate and abide by management's directives. Worker resistance can be disastrous for the manager and for the organization as a whole (Armstrong, Goodman, &

Hyman, 1981). People who don't care about the organization because they feel it doesn't care about them can allow mistakes to go through, put in the minimum amount of time possible, or engage in deliberate sabotage. When organized, lower-level workers can actually exert tremendous influence over the policies of a company through strikes, slow downs, and collective bargaining arrangements (see chapter 15).

Creating Organizational Reality

Organizations are more than just structure, rules, policies, goals, job descriptions, and standard operating procedures. Like society as a whole, they have their formal, structural characteristics, which are created, maintained, and changed through the everyday actions of their members (G. Morgan, 1986).

The language of an organization is one of the ways it actually creates its own reality. At one level, new members must learn the jargon of the organization in order to survive within it. To function within the navy system, a recruit must learn the meaning of a dizzying array of words, phrases, acronyms, abbreviations, slang, sounds, and symbols that are unintelligible to outsiders (Evered, 1983). More important, language helps to generate and maintain the organization by marking boundaries between insiders and outsiders. Corporate slogans like "Quality is job 1" (Ford), "Progress is our most important product" (General Electric), and "No surprises" (Holiday Inn) communicate the values around which organizations build and symbolize important aspects of the corporate philosophy (G. Morgan, 1986). In some organizations new members are told stories about the founding of the organization, its charismatic leaders, or some other significant event that becomes a metaphor for the culture of that organization.

One would assume that the success of an organization depends on the degree to which its culture is learned and accepted by all involved. In other words, the organizations that work well are those in which everyone internalizes the same rules, values, and beliefs. But we must distinguish between the formal structure of an organization and the actual day-to-day activities within it. Whatever the official rules, beliefs, and values of the organization, people have their own ideas and may develop their own informal structure within the larger formal structure of the organization (Meyer & Rowan, 1977).

Restricting output is one such norm that frequently emerges in factory settings (P. Thompson, 1989). Employees collectively decide, implicitly or explicitly, not to produce as much as they are physically capable of producing. This informal system of productivity norms develops partly out of a mistrust in management and the belief that increased productivity would result in higher expectations, not higher rewards (Roethlisberger & Dickson, 1939). Those who produce too much or who work too quickly are considered "rate busters," deviants within the factory subculture.

Restricted output can also be seen in the college classroom. Most instructors will tell their students that classroom discussion is important and may even use it as a criterion for assigning a final grade. Yet rarely does every student, or even a majority of students, in a class participate. Most college students know that there will inevitably be a small group of people—perhaps 3 or 4 in a class of 40—who can be counted on to respond to questions asked by the professor or comment on any issue raised in class. These students relieve the remainder of the class from the burden of having to talk in class (Karp & Yoels, 1976).

But such a contribution is not without its costs. While these talkative students are carrying the discussion for the entire class, they tend to be disliked by others. There is a strong norm among many students that people shouldn't talk too much in class (Karp & Yoels, 1976). Many feel they must restrict classroom participation so they won't appear so eager to please the instructor. Talking too much in class is a form of linguistic rate busting. It upsets the normative arrangement of the classroom and, in the students' eyes, may increase the instructor's expectations, thereby hurting everyone in the long run. Other students indicate their annoyance by audibly sighing, rolling their eyes, rattling their notebooks, or openly snickering when a classmate talks too much.

At a higher level, an organization may substitute, for its formally stated goals, others for which it was not originally created (E. Gross & Etzioni, 1985). Most organizations are established to serve a specific purpose. But some organizations often displace their original goals with the informal goal of maintaining their own well-being.

Consider social welfare agencies that seek to rehabilitate the blind. Their stated goal is to help blind people become independent, functioning members of society. While the vast majority of blind people are old or severely handicapped in other ways, agencies pay little attention to these people. Instead, they prefer the "desirable" blind—young people who have employment prospects—because it is easier to raise money for them (R. Scott, 1967). However, there aren't enough "desirable" blind people to go around, so agencies are forced to compete with one another to get clients. They then attempt to keep their blind clients dependent on the agency, rather than make them independent, self-sufficient members of society. So while the formal goal of the organization is to help people, the more immediate goal is to survive.

One of the fascinating ironies of large organizations is that if everyone followed every rule exactly and literally, the organization would self-destruct. The goal of the highly bureaucratized criminal court system is to ensure justice by punishing those who have violated society's laws. Each person accused of committing a serious crime is constitutionally guaranteed a trial by a jury of his or her peers. The jury trial is the epitome of justice and has been played out in movies and television with such frequency that we all know what it looks like even if we haven't directly experienced it ourselves. The typical image most of us have of the justice process is one of a combative struggle between the state's prosecuting attorney and the attorney for the accused.

However, the day-to-day operations of the criminal court system bear little resemblance to this common media image. Public defenders, district attorneys, private attorneys, and judges actually work closely together to move offenders through the system in an orderly fashion (Sudnow, 1965). Only a tiny percentage of criminal cases—between 10 and 20%—ever go to trial (D. C. Gibbons, 1992). The rest are either dismissed or, more commonly, plea bargained. A plea bargain is an arrangement where in exchange for a less severe punishment the accused pleads guilty to a less serious crime.

If judges and attorneys followed the procedural rules of their jobs to the letter and provided all their clients with their constitutional right to a jury trial, the system would break down. The courts, already overtaxed, would be incapable of handling the volume of cases. The informal system of plea bargaining has taken root, allowing the courts to continue functioning. Those individuals who exclusively play by the rules, like the young idealistic public defender who wants to take all of his or her cases to trial, are subject to informal sanctions by judges and superiors such as inconvenient trial dates or heavier case loads.

In sum, organizational life is a combination of formal structural rules and informal patterns of behavior. Codified rules are sometimes violated and new, unspoken ones created instead. Stated organizational goals often conflict with the real ones. Although there may appear to be a clear chain of command, the informal structure—friendships, coalitions, and so on—often has more of an impact on how things are done.

Understanding the influence of organizations on our everyday lives tells only part of the story. Organizations themselves exist within a larger structural context, acting as a sort of liaison between people and major social institutions. Norms in a university classroom setting adapt to immediate organizational demands but are also governed by even larger institutional expectations of "teachers" and "students."

Individuals, Organizations, and Institutions

Social structure consists not only of social groups and formal organizations but of major social institutions as well: economics, government, religion, health care, education, and family. As you recall from chapter 2, institutions are stable sets of statuses, roles, groups, and organizations that provide the foundation for behavior in certain major areas of social life. They are patterned ways of solving the problems and meeting the needs of a particular society.

We have already seen how the private experiences of individuals, such as socialization, impression management, and the formation of intimate relationships, take place within a broader institutional context. In a complex society, much of our behavior is institutionalized—that is, governed by the common, taken-for-granted expectations associated with various social roles (Berger & Luckmann, 1966). The actions of parents and children within a family, teachers and students in a classroom, representatives in Congress, and workers and supervisors in a factory are examples of institutionalized behavior. Much of what occurs in these settings is fairly repetitive and predictable. If problematic situations arise—a death in the family, a breakdown of factory machinery, a national political crisis—there is usually a precedent or at least some agreement on how people ought to act.

Institutions are more than just systems of routine behaviors. Each individual is unique and brings a personal touch to institutional behavior. Some parents are more strict than others in raising their children; some factory supervisors are more flexible than others; some students talk and argue in class; some legislators are more active than others in trying to change laws. Institutionalized behavior is always a combination of the structurally defined expectations of a social position and the characteristics of the particular person occupying it (Zucker, 1991).

Individuals aren't the only ones influenced by large social institutions. Organizations, too, must operate within an institutional context. Individuals comprise groups, groups comprise organizations, and the structure of these organizations exerts tremendous influence over our day-to-day experiences. But this is only part of the picture. Some social phenomena can be understood only if we take a step back and treat organizations and institutions as the objects of analysis.

Organizational Networks Within Institutions

Like individual people, organizations are born, grow, become overweight, slim down, migrate, form relationships with others, and die. They interact with one another, too, cooperating on some occasions and competing on others depending on the prevailing economic and political winds. While we can talk about a hierarchy of people or groups within an organization, we can also talk about a hierarchy of organizations within an institution. As with people, some organizations are more powerful than others and can dictate the manner in which others live their lives. When giant corporations like General Electric, Microsoft, Coca-Cola, and IBM change their operations or come up with an innovative new product, it immediately influences the practices of other organizations throughout their respective industries. If one of these titans decides to downsize or expand its operations, the effects are felt throughout the entire financial community.

But even powerful organizations like these cannot stand alone. As with people, organizations need to be connected to other organizations. Massive networks of organizations are linked by common goals and needs. The networks are often so complex that organizations from very different fields find themselves dependent on one another for survival. Our experiences with major institutions, then, are often mediated by organizations.

Consider the American health care system. All of us have had experience with health care in some form or another. Often our contact with it occurs within an organizational setting such as a hospital. Think about the vast network of organizations necessary for a single hospital to operate. First of all, it is tightly linked to all the other hospitals in the area. A change in one, such as a reduction in the number of patients treated or the opening of a new state-of-the-art trauma center, would quickly have consequences for all the others. The linkage between hospitals makes it possible for equipment, staff, and patients to be transferred from one hospital to another when necessary.

The hospital must also be linked to formal socializing organizations like medical schools, nursing schools, and teaching hospitals. It couldn't function if it didn't have connections to organizations responsible for the professional training of its staff. These organizations, in turn, are usually affiliated with larger universities, thus expanding the links in the network.

To survive financially, the hospital must also have connections to funding organizations. Hospitals have traditionally been owned and operated by a variety of governmental, religious, nonprofit, and for-profit organizations. They must operate under a set of strict regulations, which means they must also be linked to the city, state, and federal governmental agencies responsible for certification such as the Joint Commission on Accreditation of Hospitals (Perrow, 1986). Add to these the links to the medical equipment industry, the drug industry, insurance companies, the legal profession, charities, and patients' rights groups, and the system becomes even more complex.

When you consider that each of these parts of the health care system is a part of its own complex bureaucratic network, it begins to boggle the mind. Despite its size and importance, in the end it is people who make the whole system work and who can change it. As of this writing, there is an ongoing debate at the highest levels of government about how to change the nation's health care system. If changes occur, the whole institutional network will sink or swim on the actions of the individual people who represent business, medical, governmental, and consumer interests.

To have a sociological imagination—to fully understand how our lives are affected by social forces—we have to know something about how the organizations to which we belong affect one another and how they are influenced by the larger institutional context in which they exist.

Institutional Pressures Toward Similarity

If you think about how many varieties of organizations there are in the world, it is tempting to focus on their diversity. Some are large, others small. Some are formal and complex, others informal and simple. Some have a pyramid-shaped chain of command, others are more egalitarian (E. Gross & Etzioni, 1985). Sociologists have long been interested in the unique ways different organizations adapt to changing political, economic, cultural, or environmental circumstances. However, organizations seem to be more similar than different and even tend to imitate one another's actions as they become established in a particular institution (DiMaggio & Powell, 1983).

Organizational similarity is not really that surprising. Because of the nature of the problems organizations in the same industry have to address, they come to adopt similar methods of dealing with them. There isn't much difference in the ways NBC, ABC, and CBS go about trying to attract viewers. As you well know, the perceived success of a certain type of television show, such as the miniseries or the reality-based docudrama, creates an avalanche of similar shows on other networks (Gitlin, 1979).

What *is* surprising is the fact that the imitated practices are not necessarily more effective. As once innovative new strategies spread throughout the industry, there comes a time when they no longer improve the organization's performance. Viewers eventually get sick of "real life" cop shows or emergency rescue shows. The net effect of the imitations is to lessen diversity within the industry. In short, instead of adjusting directly to changes in the social environment—such as the shifting tastes of the television viewing public—organizations end up adjusting to what other organizations are doing (DiMaggio & Powell, 1983).

The tendency for organizations to emulate one another is heightened in times of institutional uncertainty (DiMaggio & Powell, 1983). When new technologies are poorly understood, when there are dramatic changes in the physical environment, or when local, state, and federal governments create new regulations or set new agendas, there is apt to be some confusion about how things ought to be done. Just as individuals look to one another to help define ambiguous situations and determine an appropriate course of action (see chapter 2), so do organizations. Take changes in the field of higher education, for instance. The pool of potential college students—18-year-old high school graduates—has been decreasing over the last several years because of a drop in the birth rate in the mid-1970s. In addition, costs of college tuition have been steadily increasing. Many colleges and universities across the country are being forced to address the problem of how to attract more students. The problem is particularly acute among private colleges that depend on tuition money.

Such was the case at the university where I teach. As enrollment shrank, administrative panic began to set in. An outside consultant was called in to design a new marketing strategy for the school. I was one of several professors asked to meet with the consultant and provide him with information about the school and what it was like to teach here. He had some clear strategies for "packaging" the school's image to make it more attractive to prospective students despite the high cost. The ideas sounded interesting: redesigned brochures, a new recruitment video, state-of-the-art bulk mailing techniques, and so on.

After our meeting I asked him how many other schools he worked for. He said between 15 and 20, several of which were schools like mine competing for the same shrinking pool of students. Although he was quick to point out that each school's situation was unique, he admitted that many of the "novel" strategies he advised us to use were things other universities were already using. We were addressing a new and uncertain dilemma by replicating the practices of other organizations in the network.

Organizations also resemble one another because those who run them, particularly professionals, tend to come from similar training backgrounds. In many institutions the professional career track is so closely guarded that the individuals who make it to the top are virtually indistinguishable from one another (DiMaggio & Powell, 1983). Medical schools are important centers for the development of organizational norms among doctors. Furthermore, the fact that most doctors belong to the American Medical Association creates a pool of individuals with similar attitudes and approaches across a range of organizations. When these doctors become administrators, they will likely bring this common approach to running a hospital.

Certain organizational forms dominate not necessarily because they are the most effective means of achieving goals, but because social forces like institutional uncertainty and the power of professions to provide individuals with a single normative standard create pressures toward similarity. Such similarity makes it easier for organizations to interact with one another and to be acknowledged as legitimate and reputable within the field (DiMaggio & Powell, 1983). But it is not without its costs. When organizations replicate one another, institutional change becomes difficult, and the iron cage of bureaucracy becomes harder to escape. Moreover, when organizations model each other they may imitate responses that are inadequate, harmful, or maybe even catastrophic. One such situation involves the AIDs epidemic.

Micro-Macro Connection
The AIDS Epidemic

We usually don't think of the spread of deadly diseases as an organizational or institutional issue. Epidemics occur because people infect one another with a disease that has no cure. AIDS (acquired immunodeficiency syndrome) is a deadly infectious disease that has reached epidemic proportions. By 1991 more than 125,000 people, mostly men between the ages of 25 and 44, had died from it (U.S. Bureau of the Census, 1992a). AIDS has become the leading cause of death among this segment of the population in close to 40% of America's large cities.

Although the epidemic was first identified in 1981 (Shilts, 1987), it really wasn't taken that seriously by the government or the scientific community until several years later. By the time President Ronald Reagan first spoke of the disease publicly—in 1985, after actor Rock Hudson's death—more than 20,000 people

Table 9.1   *AIDS Cases, Deaths, and Government Expenditures, 1984-1991*

	Cases	Deaths	State Expenditures (in millions)
1984	4,442	3,266	NA
1985	8,215	6,404	9.6
1986	13,150	10,965	27.5
1987	21,109	14,612	66.7
1988	30,754	18,248	156.3
1989	33,638	25,045	247.0
1990	41,616	26,389	278.9
1991	43,672	19,718	330.6
Total (as of 1991)	199,516	126,827	

Source: U.S. Bureau of the Census, 1992a.

had already died from it (Shilts, 1987). That year the federal government allocated only about $100 million for AIDS research; the total provided by the states for research, patient care, and education amounted to about $9 million (see Table 9.1).

In contrast, 10 years earlier President Gerald Ford authorized $135 million dollars for a nationwide inoculation program against the swine flu. By the time that program ended, only 107 cases of swine flu had been reported, and 58 people had died from it (Eitzen & Baca-Zinn, 1989).

Today, of course, AIDS funding is in the billions and the disease is recognized for what it is: a chronic, deadly virus that has infected more than a million people and will be a part of the human condition for a long time to come (Fee & Fox, 1992). All state governments, including the District of Columbia, now provide funds for AIDS treatment and research. Virtually every public school system and every university has a form of AIDS awareness education. Why did it take so long for the magnitude of the epidemic to be recognized by the public, the government, and the scientific community?

Part of the reason was the stigmatized identity of the majority of the victims—gay men, intravenous drug users, and so on. Fear, hostility, and discrimination certainly prevented massive public outcry and a quick and effective response from the scientific community. To many citizens AIDS was self-inflicted, the product of unnatural and repugnant behavior. Images of rampant promiscuity among the gay male population only added to the widespread rejection of homosexuality and, therefore, shaped the unsympathetic public response to AIDS. Even among the scientific community in the mid-1980s there was little prestige to be gained in studying a "homosexual disease" (Fee & Fox, 1992; Shilts, 1987).

Sociologists Charles Perrow and Mauro Guillen (1990) argue that this explanation is insufficient. They point out that if intolerance were all that mattered, the repression of homosexuals and intravenous drug users would have been fiercer than it had been and wouldn't have required an epidemic to increase it. These individuals are not executed or placed in concentration camps as a matter of public policy as they are in some countries such as Cuba (Perrow & Guillen, 1990). Certainly discrimination exists in this country. But it is not officially and overtly sanctioned. Furthermore, public health and government officials have gone to great lengths to reassure the gay community that everything possible is being done for them.

Perrow and Guillen say that there is a more pervasive, although not immediately apparent, explanation: organizational failure. The organizational structure that was set up at the time—the government, medical research firms, hospitals, and so on—was ill equipped to deal with the AIDS epidemic. Inaction, slowness, and outright denial became the normative responses that organizations copied from one another.

Ironically, the essential facts about the disease—that it is a blood-borne virus infecting men and women whether gay or straight, that it can be passed on by a mother to her unborn child, and that it can be prevented by relatively cheap measures (e.g., condoms)—were well known early on. Yet for several years, the government, the medical community, and even the gay community mounted no public education campaign. In those early years, most of the at-risk population was visible, accessible, and geographically concentrated in small areas of major cities such as New York and San Francisco. It would have been relatively easy and cheap to implement a massive educational effort to stop the spread of the disease (Perrow & Guillen, 1990). But 2 years after the epidemic began the total of the government's attempts to prevent the spread of AIDS among gay men was two sentences of guidance: "Sexual contact should be avoided with persons known or suspected to have AIDS. Members of high-risk groups should be aware that multiple sexual partners increase the probability of developing AIDS" (Shilts, 1987, p. 242).

Budget considerations played a major role in the federal government's response to AIDS. These budgetary decisions were politically as well as economically motivated. There is no denying that feelings about gay people and IV drug users influenced the government's response. The Reagan administration aligned quite clearly with religious, conservative groups such as the Moral Majority. Had this epidemic affected nonstigmatized citizens, there is little doubt that it would have been fought with greater resources and less government denial (Perrow & Guillen, 1990).

The response of the medical community was also ineffective. All bureaucratic organizations fail to some degree, but the American health care system is particularly prone to failure. The United States spends more money on health care but gets less results in terms of good overall health statistics than any industrialized country (Perrow & Guillen, 1990). It is a system characterized by fragmented services, poor leadership, and a complacent public. AIDS came along at a time of high inflation and massive federal cutbacks in health care services. With reduced revenues, hospitals had a hard time dealing with the surge of AIDS patients that began knocking on their doors in the mid-1980s.

Part of this problem is institutional. American medicine's emphasis of treatment over prevention (see chapter 4) has made hospitals the major focus of our health care system. Because controlling costs is the chief goal of health policy and treating AIDS patients is costly, it is not surprising that the response to this epidemic was inadequate. Some hospitals with special "AIDS units" experienced a mass defection of non-AIDS patients who went elsewhere. For others that admitted large numbers of AIDS patients, the resulting shortage of beds meant jammed emergency rooms and long waiting periods. This had an economic effect on the entire community. Many business owners, for example, pointed to the lack of hospital bed space as a reason for moving their companies to other cities, thereby reducing the number of jobs available in the community.

In addition, the process of reviewing and publishing medical research in the most prestigious scholarly journals may have also delayed public acknowledgment of the seriousness of the epidemic. These journals are the primary means by which information is disseminated in the medical community. Also, publishing articles in these journals is the primary means by which individual researchers can enhance their reputations. The process of reviewing, revising, and publishing, however, can take up to a year and virtually all journals have an iron-clad rule about the secrecy of material that is being considered for publication: If there is any leak whatsoever to the popular press about the research, the journal will not publish the article (Shilts, 1987).

These operating procedures delayed the publication of information about the disease. The first article on AIDS appeared in June 1981 in the *Morbidity and Mortality Weekly Report*, a newsletter published by the Centers for Disease Control (CDC) that is far less prestigious but has a much shorter publication time than the top journals. Even when the article was published, the CDC dropped all references to homosexuality from the title and placed it inconspicuously on the second page of the report, not wanting to offend homosexuals or inflame prejudice against them, (Shilts, 1987).

The many organizations that comprise the nation's blood industry were also slow to respond. There was no national program for testing blood or screening blood donors until several years after the epidemic began. As early as July of 1982, the CDC warned the blood industry of their suspicion that the disease was transmitted through blood and asked that blood banks not accept blood from high-risk groups. It also recommended that the Public Health Service test all blood.

The opposition to such recommendations was strong. The gay community strongly opposed screening for high-risk groups on civil rights grounds and the fear of further discrimination against gays. The blood industry, fearing for its own livelihood, continued to deny there was any danger (Perrow & Guillen, 1990). As late as 1984, the Red Cross refused to acknowledge that AIDS could be transmitted through blood transfusions. Blood banks finally began screening the blood supply in March of 1985. However, it wasn't until July of that year that they bothered notifying the donors that they were infected. Many people continued to pass on the virus unknowingly to others. By 1989 several thousand blood transfusion AIDS cases had been reported, and hundreds of lawsuits had been filed against the blood banks.

The National Hemophilia Foundation found that AIDS conflicted with its goals and weakened its ability to do its job. Hemophiliacs lack the substance that clots blood. A blood-clotting product made of donated blood increased the life span of many hemophiliacs to near normal up until 1985 when blood screening was finally in place. Because of the lack of screening, the infection rate of hemophiliacs who received blood transfusions prior to 1985 ranged from 65 to 95% (Perrow & Guillen, 1990).

In sum, the AIDS crisis is tied to organizational failure. The federal, state, and local governments failed to fund education and research, the research community failed to respond quickly enough, the health care system failed to respond effectively enough, and the blood industry failed to insure the safety of their product. To make matters worse, organizations replicated each other's ineffectiveness and inaction. The sad conclusion is that the magnitude and seriousness of the epidemic could have been avoided had the organizational response been different.

Conclusion

More than three centuries ago, John Donne wrote, "No man is an island, entire of itself; every man is a piece of the continent, a part of the main." The same can be said of contemporary social life. We are not isolated individuals whose lives are simply functions of personal characteristics and predispositions. We are *social* beings. We are part of aggregations of other social beings. We have a powerful need to belong to something larger than ourselves. As a result, we constantly affect and are affected by our associations with others, whether face-to-face or in well-structured groups, massive bureaucratic organizations, or all-encompassing social institutions.

Throughout Part II of this book I've discussed the relationship between the individual and society in terms of how society and culture affect everyday experiences and how those experiences help to construct and maintain social order. The development of self and self-controlled behavior, the influence of cultural norms, responses to deviance, and so on are all topics that provide insight into how we are able to live together in a relatively orderly and predictable way. In this chapter, however, we see that the social structure, although created and maintained by the actions of individuals, is more than just the sum of those actions. Organizations interact at a level well above the individual; institutions are organized in a massive, global system.

Social structure is bigger than us, exerts enormous control over our lives, and is an *objectified* reality that appears to exist independent of us. But it cannot exist *without* us. I'm reminded of a skit from the old British comedy show "Monty Python's Flying Circus," in which a high-rise apartment building stood erect only because its inhabitants believed in it. When they doubted its existence, it began to crumble. Like this building, social structure requires constant human support. Once we as a society are no longer able to sustain our organizations or believe in our institutions, they fall apart.

CHAPTER HIGHLIGHTS

■ By nature, groups exert pressures on individual members to conform to the group norms. But private actions and personal decisions can also have an impact on an entire group or community (e.g., social dilemmas).

■ By virtue of living in society, we are all organizational creatures. We are born in organizations, educated in them, spend most of our adult lives working in them, and will probably die in them.

■ A common form of organization in American society is the bureaucracy. A bureaucracy is a large hierarchical organization that is governed by a system of rules and regulations, has a clear specification of work tasks, and has a well-defined division of labor.

■ The everyday experience of bureaucratic organizations is determined by where one fits into the hierarchical structure. Bureaucracies look very different depending on whether one is situated at the top, middle, or bottom.

■ Organizations are more than structures, rules, policies, goals, job descriptions, and standard operating procedures. Each organization, and each division within an organization, develops its own norms, values, and language.

■ Organizations exist within highly interconnected networks. In times of institutional or environmental uncertainty, organizations tend to imitate one another, adopting similar activities, policies, and goals.

YOUR TURN

One of the major criticisms of contemporary society is its routine and over-whelming, sometimes dehumanizing, way of life. To see such routinization firsthand, visit several fast-food restaurants close to your home (McDonald's, Taco Bell, Kentucky Fried Chicken, Long John Silver's, and the like). Observe the overall structure of the establishment. How is the work area situated in regard to the customer area? Are the cooking facilities hidden from public view? Note the number of employees and the gender configuration of the staff. Observe the way the customers are processed. Can you detect a "script" that the employees follow? How do they address customers? How are orders filled? Is there any room for "ad-libbing"? Does each worker seem responsible for a single task (grilling burgers, bagging french fries, operating the cash register, cleaning tables)? Do male employees seem to work in different areas than female employ-ees? Is there an apparent hierarchy among the workers? What is the manager's role?

Compare your findings across the different restaurants you observed. How much similarity in routine is there? Does there seem to be a common procedure that is characteristic of all fast-food restaurants, or does each restaurant have a unique way of running? How do things like diversity and creativity fit into the procedure?

Drawing from this chapter's discussion of the features of bureaucracies and the notion of McDonaldization, discuss how the systems employed in these restaurants maximize efficiency at the cost of dehumanizing the people involved, both workers and customers.

III

Social Structure and Everyday Life

Up to this point you have learned how our social lives are constructed and ordered. But this is only part of the picture. What does social life look like from the top down? Once the architecture is constructed and in place, what influence does it exert on our everyday lives? In answering this question we investigate the various sources of structural inequality in society: social class, race and ethnicity, gender, and population trends. These facets of society seem ominous and impenetrable. However, you will see that our lives don't completely fall under the control of the social structure. The small acts of individual people can sometimes change an entire society.

CHAPTER 10

The Architecture of Stratification
Class, Power, and Inequality

High in the crow's nest of the luxury liner *Titanic*, lookout Frederick Fleet peered into the dazzling night. It was calm, clear, and bitterly cold. There was no moon, but the cloudless sky blazed with stars. The Atlantic Ocean was like polished plate glass; people said later that they had never seen it so smooth.

> Suddenly Fleet saw something directly ahead, even darker than the darkness. At first it was small, . . . but every second it grew larger and closer. Quickly Fleet banged the crow's nest bell three times, warning of danger ahead. (Lord, 1956, quoted in Sidel, 1986, p. xiii)

The iceberg Fleet saw drew closer and closer. At the last second the ship steered clear of it, and for a brief moment it seemed that disaster had been avoided. However, the grinding sound that seemed to come from somewhere deep inside the hull of the vessel indicated that the ship had, in fact, struck the deadly iceberg.

The *Titanic* was the most magnificent vessel of its time. It had every amenity and comfort: Turkish baths, the finest orchestras, intricately tiled walls, the best cuisine. What it didn't have were enough lifeboats. There was only room for 1,178 out of the 2,207 passengers and crew members on board. Over the next 2½ hours on that cold April night in 1912, as the "unsinkable" ocean liner was engulfed by the frigid waters of the north Atlantic, more than 1,500 people lost their lives.

All this is fairly well known. What is less well known is that some of the passengers actually had much better survival chances than others. The percentage of people saved from the wealthy first-class deck (over 60%) was much higher than the percentage saved from the second-class deck (36%), which was higher than the percentage of the lowest, or "steerage," class passengers who were saved (24%). The figures were even more striking for women and children, who, by virtue of chivalrous tradition, were entitled to be spared first. Ninety-seven percent of the women and children in first class and 89% of those in second class survived. However, only 42% of the women and children in steerage were saved (W. Hall, 1986).

One of the reasons so many of the wealthier passengers survived was that access to the lifeboats was from the higher first- and second-class decks. The locked doors and other barriers that kept the third-class passengers from venturing up to the upper decks during the cruise were not removed when disaster struck. In addition, there is evidence that little effort was made to save the people in steerage. Some were even forcibly kept down by sailors standing guard.

For the passengers on the *Titanic*, social inequality meant more than just differences in the comfort of their accommodations or the quality of the food they ate. It literally meant life or death. This situation, while much less graphic, is not all that different from what we face in today's society. While those at the top have easy access to various "lifeboats" in times of social or economic disaster, others face locked gates, segregated decks, and policies that make mere survival exceedingly difficult (Sidel, 1986).

The next several chapters will examine the various aspects of social inequality. In this chapter I examine the issues of class and stratification. Why does inequality exist? How is it related to power, and how is that power expressed at the individual and institutional levels? Finally, what does inequality look like at the global level? In subsequent chapters I explore other facets of inequality such as poverty, race, gender, and population processes.

Before I begin, let me point out that the approach of these chapters is more top-down than the previous ones, as I examine the larger social structures and institutions that create and perpetuate inequality. Keep in mind, however, that individuals both create these social structures and live under their influence. Inequality, as well as the power of social structure, is often felt most forcefully and reinforced most effectively in the chain of day-to-day interactions that constitute our ordinary private experiences (Collins, 1981). People bring with them into all social encounters different levels of conversational, emotional, physical, institutional, and cultural resources that create and enforce the status differences between them. Although social inequalities exist at a level "above" the individual, they are not fixed and unyielding. They ultimately derive from the actions of real people.

The Nature of Stratification and Inequality

Inequality is woven into the fabric of all societies through a structured system of stratification. **Stratification** is a ranking of entire groups of people that perpetuates unequal rewards and life chances in a society. Just as geologists talk about strata of rock that are layered one on top of another, the "social strata" of people are arranged from low to high. All societies, past and present, have had some form of stratification, although each may vary in the degree of inequality.

One of the most persistent historical forms of stratification was slavery. **Slavery** was an economic form of inequality in which some people were legally the property of others. One could become a slave in a variety of ways: through birth, military defeat, falling into debt, or, as in the United States, capture and commercial trade (Kerbo, 1991). Because slaves were considered possessions, they were denied the rights and life chances other people took for granted.

In some societies today, such as India and Pakistan, stratification is created by a **caste system** in which heredity ensures that a person of one caste cannot become a member of another caste. One's caste, which determines one's lifestyle, prestige, and occupational choices, is fixed at birth and cannot be changed. Cultural rules specify that people should take the occupation of their parents and marry within their caste (Weber, 1970). The rights and duties associated with membership in each caste are clear. In India, "untouchables"—members of the lowest caste—are required to hide or, if that's not possible, bow in the presence of anyone from a higher caste.

Another form of stratification is the **estate,** or **feudal, system**, which develops when high-status groups own land and have power based on their noble birth (Kerbo, 1991). In medieval Europe the highest "estate" in society was occupied by the aristocracy, who derived their wealth and power from large-scale land holdings. The clergy formed the next estate. Although they had lower status than the aristocracy, they still claimed considerable status because the Church itself owned a great deal of land and exerted influence over people's lives. The last, or "third," estate were the commoners: serfs, peasants, artisans, and merchants. Movement between estates was possible although infrequent. Occasionally a commoner might be knighted or a wealthy merchant might become an aristocrat. Estate systems were most commonly found in preindustrial societies.

Stratification systems in contemporary industrialized societies are likely to be based on social class. Throughout this book I have talked about the effects of social class on a variety of experiences—socialization, deviance, family, and so forth. But social class is more than a characteristic that distinguishes one group's pattern of behavior from another's. It is a means of ranking people or groups that determines access to important resources and life changes. **Social class** refers to any group of people who share a similar economic position in society based on their wealth and income. Closely related to the concept of class is social status. In chapter 2, I defined status simply as a social position. But with regard to stratification, **social status** refers to the prestige, honor, respect, and lifestyle associated with different positions or groups in society (Weber, 1970). Social status is obviously correlated with wealth and income but can also be derived from achieved characteristics such as educational attainment and occupational prestige, and from ascribed characteristics such as race, ethnicity, gender, and family pedigree. Hence it is possible for a person's class ranking to be different from his or her status ranking. For instance, the occupational prestige of high school teachers is far higher than that of carpenters, plumbers, and mechanics (J. A. Davis & Smith, 1986), yet teachers' incomes are often substantially lower. Organized criminals may have a lot of money but lack status—that is, prestige and honor.

Class systems are different from other systems of stratification in that there are no *legal* barriers to **social mobility,** the movement of people or groups from one class to another. In practice, however, mobility between classes may be quite difficult. Much as we'd like to believe otherwise, the opportunities to move from one class to another are not available to all members of society. Often the families we are born into exert as much or more influence on our class standing as our personal achievements. Likewise, race and gender have historically determined a person's access to educational, social, and employment opportunities.

Structural Functionalism

Sociologists have long been interested in figuring out *why* societies are stratified. From a structural functionalist perspective, the answer lies in a society's inevitable need for order. Because social inequality is found everywhere and is apparently unavoidable, it must somehow be necessary for societies to run smoothly.

As with bureaucracies, the efficient functioning of society requires that various tasks be allocated through a strictly defined division of labor. If the tasks associated with all social positions in a society were equally pleasant, equally important, and required the same talents, it wouldn't make any difference who got into which position. But functionalists argue it *does* make a difference. Some positions are more important than others and require greater talent and training, such as teaching and medicine. Society's dilemma is to make sure that the most talented people perform the most important tasks. One way to ensure this is to assign higher rewards—better pay, greater prestige, more social privileges—to some positions in society so that they will be attractive to the people with the necessary talents and abilities.

Presumably, if these talented people were not offered sufficiently high rewards, there would be no reason for them to take on difficult and demanding tasks associated with those important positions. Why would people go through the agony and costs of many years of medical school if there weren't some promise of compensation and high prestige? Those who rise to the top are seen as the most worthy and deserving because they are the ones who can do the most good for society (K. Davis & Moore, 1945).

But the functional importance of a position is not enough to warrant a high place in the stratification system. If a position is easily filled, it need not be heavily rewarded, even though it is important (K. Davis & Moore, 1945). Imagine what our society would be like if there weren't people who removed our trash. Not only would our streets be unsightly, but our collective health would suffer too. Therefore garbage collectors serve a vital social function. They don't get paid very much, however, and trash removal certainly isn't a highly respected occupation.

Why aren't garbage collectors higher up in the hierarchy of occupations? According to the structural functionalist perspective, it is because there is no shortage of people who have the skills needed to collect garbage. Physicians also serve the collective health needs of a society, but because of the skills and training needed, society must offer rewards high enough to ensure that qualified people will want to become doctors.

The structural functionalist perspective gives us important insight into how societies ensure that all positions in the division of labor are filled. Every society, no matter how simple or complex, differentiates people in terms of prestige and esteem and possesses a certain amount of institutional inequality. Critics argue that this explanation doesn't address the fact that stratification can be unjust, divisive, and a source of social *dis*order (Tumin, 1953).

One look at the salary structure in our society reveals that many highly rewarded positions are not as functional as positions that receive smaller rewards. Entertainers and professional athletes are among the highest paid people in American society. A champion heavyweight boxer, for example, can make several million dollars for a few minutes' worth of punching someone else's face. Comedians like Bill Cosby and singers like Barbra Streisand are among the wealthiest of Americans. You might say that their careers serve important social functions by providing the rest of us with a recreational release from the demands of ordinary life, and there's no denying that the best entertainers and athletes have rare skills indeed. However, it seems that society probably can do without another record album, TV show, starting pitcher, or heavyweight prizefighter more easily than it can do without competent physicians, scientists, computer programmers, teachers, or even trash collectors.

Furthermore, the functionalist argument that there are only a limited number of talented people around to occupy important social positions is probably overstated. Many people have the talent to become doctors. What they lack is access to training. Why is it that some people—women and racial minorities—are paid less for or excluded entirely from certain jobs? The debates over equal employment opportunity (see chapter 12) and comparable worth (see chapter 13) are essentially debates over how the functional importance of certain positions is determined.

Finally, when functionalists claim that stratification serves the needs of society, we must ask whose needs? A system of slavery obviously met the needs of one group at the expense of another. In a class-stratified society, those individuals who receive the greatest rewards can make sure they continue receiving such rewards. Over time, the competition for the most desirable positions will become less open and less competitive. The offspring of "talented"—that is, high status—parents will inevitably have an advantage over equally talented people who are born into less successful families. Social background and not personal aptitude may become the primary criterion for filling important social positions (Tumin, 1953).

Conflict Theory

Conflict theorists argue that social inequality is neither necessary nor a source of social order. They see it as a reflection of the unequal distribution of power in society and as a primary source of conflict, coercion, and unhappiness. Stratification ultimately rests on the unequal distribution of resources—some people have them, others don't. Important resources include money, land, information, education, health care, safety, and adequate housing. Those high in the stratification system can control the resources because they are able to set the rules that limit challenges to their positions by others. A system of stratification allows members of the dominant group to use those in subordinate positions as consumers, renters, employees, and so on, thereby reinforcing their own superiority over others.

Stratification virtually guarantees that some groups or classes of people (those who have less) will always be competing with other groups or classes (those who have more). The stratification system serves the interests of those at the top and not the fundamental survival needs of the entire society. The dominant classes can manipulate the economic and political system to maintain advantages over others and to protect their interests. What the conflict perspective gives us that the structural functionalist perspective doesn't is an acknowledgment of the interconnected roles economic and political institutions play in creating and maintaining a stratified society.

The Marxian Class Model

According to Karl Marx and Friedrich Engels (1848/1982), societies are divided into conflicting and stratified classes on the basis of two criteria: ownership of the **means of production**—land, commercial enterprises, factories, and wealth—and the ability to purchase and control the labor of others. Marx and Engels felt that in modern societies, two major classes emerge: **capitalists** (or bourgeoisie), who own the means of production and are able to purchase the labor power of others, and **workers** (or proletariat), who neither own the means of production nor have the ability to purchase the labor power

Table 10.1   *Marxian Model of Class*

	Control labor of others	Do not control labor of others
Own means of production (land, factories, etc.)	CAPITALISTS	PETITE BOURGEOISIE
Do not own means of production	WORKERS	WORKERS

of others. Workers, instead, must sell their own labor power. Some workers, including store managers and supervisors, may control other workers, but their power is minimal compared to that exerted over them by those in the capitalist class. Marx and Engels supplemented this two-tiered conception of class by adding a third, the **petite bourgeoisie,** which is a sort of transitional class of people who own the means of production but don't purchase the labor power of others. This class would consist of self-employed skilled laborers and business-people who are economically self-sufficient but don't have a staff of subordinate workers (Robinson & Kelley, 1979). (See Table 10.1.)

Capitalists have considerable sway over what will be produced, how much will be produced, and who will get how much of it. Such influence allows them to control other people's livelihoods, the communities in which people live, and the economic decisions that affect the entire society. In such a structure there is an inevitable tendency for the rich to get richer, to use their wealth to create more wealth for themselves, and to act in ways that will protect their interests and positions in society.

Ultimately, the wealthy gain the ability to influence important social institutions: the government, the media, the schools, and the courts. Those in power have access to the means necessary to create and promote a reality that justifies their exploitive actions. This version of reality is so influential that even those who are harmed by it come to accept it. Marx called this phenomenon **false consciousness.** False consciousness is crucial because it is the primary means by which the powerful classes in society prevent protest and revolution. As long as large numbers of poor people continue to believe in the American Dream—that wealth and success are solely the products of individual hard work and effort rather than structured inequalities in society—resentment and animosity toward the rich will be minimized because the inequalities will be perceived as fair and deserved (Robinson & Bell, 1978).

Other Conflict Models of Class Stratification

For Marx, economic inequality was the only important factor in creating a system of class stratification. If private ownership of property were ever to be abolished, all other forms of inequality and conflict would disappear. He was not interested in the power and authority relations between workers and those who directly controlled them.

In Marx's time, the mid-19th century, ownership of property and control of labor in a capitalist system were synonymous. It made sense to lump all those who didn't own productive resources into one class and all those who did into another. However, the nature of capitalism has changed a lot since then. Today corporations have become much larger and more bureaucratic with a long, multilevel chain of command. Ownership of the largest corporations often lies in the hands of stockholders who have no connections at all to the everyday workings of the business. Thus ownership and management are separated. The powerful people who run businesses and control workers on a day-to-day basis are frequently not the same people who own the businesses.

As a result, other sociologists (e.g., Dahrendorf, 1959) have argued for an explanation of class stratification that focuses primarily on different levels of authority. What's important is not just who owns the means of production, but whether some people are able to exercise authority over others. Class stratification need not be based solely on the ownership of material wealth.

Authority is the possession of some status or quality that compels others to obey (Starr, 1982). A person with authority has the power to order or forbid behavior in others (Wrong, 1988). Such commands don't require the use of force or persuasion, nor do they need to be explained or justified. Rulers have authority over the ruled, as do teachers over students, employers over employees, and parents over children. These authority relationships are not fixed, of course: Children fight with their parents, students disagree with their teachers, and workers protest against their bosses. But while the legitimacy of the authority may sometimes be called into question, the ongoing dependence of the subordinates maintains it. The worker may disagree with the boss and the student may disagree with the teacher, but the boss still signs the paycheck and the teacher still assigns final grades.

According to Ralf Dahrendorf (1959), social classes are distinguished on the basis of their relations to authority. Whereas Marx lumped all those who didn't own the means of production in the same worker class, Dahrendorf lumps together all those who exert authority over others, whether or not they own the means of production, into the **command class** (Robinson & Kelley, 1979). The command class includes not only capitalist owners but all levels of managers and supervisors as well. On the other end are members of the **obey class,** workers who are subject to the authority of others but exercise none themselves. Finally, there is what Dahrendorf called the **classless group,** self-employed people who

Table 10.2   *Dahrendorf Model of Class*

	Exercise authority	Do not exercise authority
Own means of production	COMMAND CLASS	CLASSLESS GROUP
Do not own means of production	COMMAND CLASS	OBEY CLASS

Table 10.3   *Wright Model of Class*

	Exercise authority	Do not exercise authority
Own means of production	CAPITALISTS	PETITE BOURGEOISIE
Do not own means of production	MANAGERS	WORKERS

neither exercise authority nor are subject to it. The Dahrendorf model is shown in Table 10.2.

Like Marx, Dahrendorf believed that relations between classes inherently involve conflicts of interest. By emphasizing authority, Dahrendorf argues that stratification is not an exclusively economic phenomenon but derives from the social relations between people who possess different degrees of power.

Sociologist Erik Olin Wright (Wright, 1976; Wright et al., 1982; Wright & Perrone, 1977) has developed a model of class stratification that synthesizes the ideas of Marx and Dahrendorf, incorporating both the ownership of means of production and the exercise of authority over others. The capitalist and petite bourgeoisie classes in the scheme are identical to Marx's. What is different is that the class of people who do not own society's productive resources (Marx's worker class) are divided into two classes, managers and workers (see Table 10.3).

Wright's approach gives us a sense of the complexities of conflict and social class that Marx's and Dahrendorf's do not. We can see that social class is not simply a reflection of income or the extent to which a group exercises authority over another. Lawyers, plumbers, and cooks, for instance, may own their own businesses and hire assistants (which would place them in the capitalist class), work for a large company without any surbordinates (placing them in the worker class), work for a large company and have subordinates (placing them in the manager class), or work alone (placing them in the petite bourgeoisie class) (Robinson & Kelley, 1979).

Class conflict is also more than just a clash between rich and poor. There are, in fact, multiple lines of conflict—economic, political, administrative, or social. Some positions, or what Wright calls *contradictory class locations*, fall between two major classes. These positions make it difficult for individuals to identify with one side or the other. Managers and supervisors, for instance, often must struggle over where their allegiances should lie. They can ally with workers because both are subordinates of capitalist owners. Yet because they can exercise authority over some people, they also share the interests and concerns of owners.

Class Societies

What makes the concept of class even more complex is the fact that when most of us think of social class in our everyday lives, it is not in terms of broad occupational classes like capitalists, petite bourgeoisie, managers, and workers. We are more likely to define class in crude relative terms (i.e., from upper to lower) using a combination of such outward signs as speech patterns, mannerisms, and style of dress (Domhoff, 1983).

Contemporary sociologists usually compile information on quantifiable factors like income, wealth, occupational status, and educational attainment in order to rank people. While this is certainly a clearer and more systematic way of defining class than relying on outward appearances, the boundaries between classes still tend to be rather fuzzy. Some have argued that there aren't any discrete classes with clearly defined boundaries at all, but rather a socioeconomic continuum on which to rank individuals (Blau & Duncan, 1967).

Nevertheless, class designations remain a part of everyday thinking and social research. The "upper" class is usually thought to include owners of vast amounts of property and other forms of wealth, owners of large corporations, top financiers, and members of prestigious families. The "middle" class is likely to include managers, supervisors, executives, small business owners, and professionals (e.g., lawyers, doctors, teachers, engineers). The "working" class includes industrial and factory workers, office workers, clerks, and farm and manual laborers. Finally, the "poor" consist of people who work for minimum wages or are chronically unemployed. They are sometimes referred to as the "underclass." These are the people who do society's dirty work, often for very low wages (Walton, 1990; Wright et al., 1982).

Class stratification is most vivid when we consider the income gap between the highest and lowest paid people. In 1990 the income of the top 20% highest paid American families accounted for almost half of all before-tax income in the United States, the highest since World War II. That same year the income of the 20% lowest paid families accounted for less than 5% of before-tax income, the lowest in more than 25 years (U.S. Bureau of the Census, 1992a). Since 1990, the highest paid 1% of American families have seen their pretax incomes grow by 77%, while the lowest paid 20% of families have seen theirs *decrease* by 9% (Nasar, 1992). While an additional two million children fell into poverty during the late 1980s and early 1990s, the number of millionaires increased by 1400%, from 4,414 to 63,642 (Farhi, 1992).

Even more striking are the disparities in wealth, which include ownership of durable consumer goods like cars, houses, and furniture plus financial assets like stocks, bonds, savings, and life insurance. Here the wealthiest Americans—the top one half of 1% whose average annual wealth topped $8.85 million—control 35% of the entire nation's wealth. This tiny group of "super rich" owns over 60% of all corporate stock in this country, 58% of unincorporated businesses, 77% of the value of all trusts, and 62% of state and local bonds.

"Class" implies more than just economic position. People's social class standing provides them with an understanding of the world and where they fit into it. A description like "middle class" or "working class" may not mean much when applied to a single person. It does tell us something, however, about the broader system of stratification and how people are clustered at different levels of comfort, status, and control over their lives (Ehrenreich, 1989). "Class" is also a statement about culture that defines an entire way of life:

> It's composed of ideas, behavior, attitudes, values, and language; class is how you think, feel, act, look, dress, talk, move, walk; class is what stores you shop at, restaurants you eat in; class is the schools you attend, the education you attain; class is the very jobs you will work at throughout your adult life. Class even determines when we marry and become mothers. . . . We experience class at every level of our lives; class is who our friends are, where we live . . . even what kind of car we drive, if we own one. . . . In other words, class is socially constructed and all-encompassing. (Langston, 1992, p. 112)

Thus when we talk about social class, we are making broad generalizations about large groups of people regarding what they look like and how they live. Class is a statement about self-worth and the quality of one's life (Langston, 1992). It determines your life chances, including access to education, high-paying jobs, life expectancy, physical health, and treatment by the criminal justice system (Della Fave, 1980; Reiman, 1990). Research shows that those at lower levels of the stratification system are more likely to die prematurely as a result of homicide, accidents, or inadequate health care than are people at higher levels

(Kearl, 1989). The death rate for Americans with family incomes of less than $9,000 a year is three times higher than that of people with family incomes of more than $25,000 a year (Pear, 1993a). As you recall from chapter 7, working-class and poor people are significantly more likely to get arrested, get convicted, go to prison, and receive the death penalty than are upper-class people (Reiman, 1990).

Class Consciousness

To fully understand the phenomenon of class in American society, it is important to go beyond differences in objective economic conditions and life chances. We must look at people's *subjective* beliefs about what class they belong to and their feelings and attitudes about social stratification.

Marx felt that **class consciousness**—people's awareness of their true class identity—would eventually create a revolutionary movement on the part of the proletariat to eliminate class differences. It's not surprising that, traditionally, there has been a pronounced reluctance on the part of Americans to recognize class differences and to identify themselves in terms of class (Domhoff, 1983; Langston, 1992). The willingness of people to place themselves in social classes would, in itself, be an open recognition of class inequalities, something American society is not *supposed* to have. Some sociologists have concluded that Americans aren't particularly class conscious: They don't recognize the class system, they don't think of themselves in terms of class membership, and they don't define their lives in class-related ways (e.g., Hurst, 1979).

Research suggests that Americans *are*, in fact, acutely aware of class distinctions and are quite willing to identify their position within the class system. Sociologists Mary and Robert Jackman (1983) asked a national sample of more than 1,900 American adults the following question: "People talk about social classes such as the poor, the working class, the middle class, the upper-middle class and the upper class. Which of these classes would you say you belong to?" (p. 14).

They found that all but 3.5% of the sample identified themselves with one of the class categories provided. As you might expect, people found it difficult to identify themselves in terms of either extreme. Only 7.6% perceived themselves as poor, and a little more than 9% perceived themselves either as upper-middle or upper class. The vast majority of people considered themselves either working class (36.6%) or middle class (43.3%) (see Table 10.4). This wasn't just a matter of people identifying themselves with a particular class because they were forced to give an answer. About 80% of the respondents indicated that they felt strongly about their class identification.

People's perception of where they are in the system affects their beliefs about the nature of inequality. Those at the lower end are likely to see stratification as unfair (Robinson & Bell, 1978) and may even express animosity toward those

Table 10.4   *Class Identification by Race and Sex*

	Poor	Working	Middle	Upper-middle	Upper	Other[a]	No social classes	Don't know	Not ascertained	Total *N*
Total sample	7.6%	36.6	43.3	8.2	1.0	1.3	0.5	1.5	0.2	1,914
Whites	4.8%	35.8	46.4	9.0	1.0	1.1	0.5	1.3	0.2	1,648
Blacks	27.7%	41.5	22.1	1.5	1.5	2.6	0.5	2.6	0.0	195
Other[b]	14.1%	39.1	32.8	7.8	0.0	1.6	0.0	3.1	1.6	64
Men	5.4%	41.4	40.5	8.5	1.1	1.4	0.9	0.5	0.4	802
Women	9.2%	33.1	45.2	8.0	0.9	1.2	0.2	2.2	0.1	1,112

[a]This category includes identification with two classes (e.g., "poor and working," "working and middle") and irrelevant responses.

[b]This category includes Asian Americans, Hispanic Americans, and Native Americans.

Source: Jackman & Jackman, 1983.

above them (Halle, 1984). However, upper-class people are likely to see stratification as a hierarchy of positions in which opportunities for success and advancement are equally distributed. One of the ideological cornerstones of middle- and upper-class America is the belief that all people are created equal and that social class should not impede a person's progress in everyday life. In other words, *your* ambition, effort, and intellect alone are responsible for your success.

Susan Ostrander
Upper-Class Consciousness

To more closely examine the issue of class consciousness, sociologist Susan Ostrander (1980) conducted in-depth interviews with 38 upper-class women in a large midwestern city. These women belonged to distinctly upper-class clubs, lived in the wealthiest areas of the city, had husbands who worked in the top echelons of business, and had children who attended private schools. They showed an obvious sense of "we-ness," a sense of belonging, and a feeling of cohesiveness with other wealthy individuals. Their daily activities, which included volunteer and charity work, were clearly organized around class-related behaviors and values. Nevertheless, when asked directly whether they considered themselves upper class, they quickly rejected the use of the term with comments like:

> I hate [the term] upper class. It's so *non*-upper class to use it. I just call it "all of us," those of us who are well-born.

> I hate to use the word "class." We're responsible, fortunate people, old families, the people who have something.

> I wouldn't classify anyone as upper class, just as productive, worthwhile people.

We're not supposed to have layers [in our society]. I'm embarrassed to admit to you that we do, and that I feel superior at my social level. I like being part of the upper crust.

Ostrander concluded that class consciousness is not a matter of how people identify themselves, but a matter of how people act. Despite an unwillingness to call themselves upper class, the activities of these wealthy women clearly indicate that they are. The implications of such unwillingness to place oneself in a class position are profoundly important. If there is a reluctance among those at the top to acknowledge that a class structure exists, then any strategy to eliminate class inequality will be seen as unnecessary and receive little attention.

Downward Mobility and the Disappearing Middle Class

In discussing the American class system and class consciousness, it is tempting to focus attention on the very top or the very bottom, overlooking the vast chunk of the population that falls somewhere in the ill-defined middle (Ehrenreich, 1990). Those who are neither exceedingly wealthy nor destitute are experiencing increasing economic instability in today's society.

The term *middle class* has become particularly important in defining American culture: its moods, political direction, lifestyles, values, habits, and tastes. During the first half of the 20th century, middle-class parents were more strict with their children than were working-class parents. Child development experts advised all parents that the key ingredient in bringing up a child was a firm hand and strong discipline. By the 1960s, however, middle-class parents had become more permissive. Now the experts were advising parents to be warm and affectionate while giving their children "room" to explore and grow (Goleman, 1991b). In short, the middle class is taken as a social norm against which every other class is measured and judged. It is a universal class, a class that represents everyone (Ehrenreich, 1990).

Given the lofty cultural status of the middle class in American society, two recent scholarly examinations of this class, Katherine Newman's *Falling From Grace* and Barbara Ehrenreich's *Fear of Falling*, have portrayed the experiences of this segment of the population in terms of metaphorical tumbles. The metaphors are apt given the increase in what sociologists term *downward social mobility* among members of the middle class. Instead of playing out the American Dream and rising through the class structure via hard work and perseverance, many are falling and falling hard. They are losing their jobs, struggling to make ends meet, and confronting the sort of prolonged economic hardship that in the past had been confined to the poor.

The Fall of the Middle Class

The traditional pattern of mobility in this country has always been that present generations of people would exceed the standard of living of previous ones.

Table 10.5   *Median Household Income: 1989 to 1991**

	1989	1990	1991
All Households	$31,750	$31,203	$30,126
White	33,398	32,545	31,569
Black	19,862	19,462	18,807
Asian and Pacific Islander	39,654	40,068	36,449
Hispanic origin (of any race)	24,078	23,270	22,691

* in 1990 dollars

Source: U.S. Bureau of the Census, 1992a.

Nothing was more typically American than the expectation that children, once grown and in careers of their own, would eventually surpass their parents' financial well-being and quality of life. But today many young people are coming to the realization that their lives will probably be worse than that of their parents. A *Newsweek* poll in 1991 showed that only 62% of Americans are satisfied with their current standard of living, the lowest level since 1963 (M. Levinson, 1991).

These subjective reports of dissatisfaction are bolstered by government statistics that show that median family income declined by more than 5% between 1989 and 1991 (U.S. Bureau of the Census, 1992a) (see Table 10.5). Between 1973 and 1991, the average hourly wage for nonsupervisory workers decreased 13% after adjusting for inflation (Levinson, 1991). Between 1963 and 1978, only 23% of the new jobs that were created paid poverty-level wages; however, during the 1980s and early 1990s, more than half of the new full-time jobs that were created were unskilled, unstable positions paying below the poverty line (Harrison & Bluestone, 1988; J. E. Schwarz & Volgy, 1993).

Not only are people earning less, but what they do earn can't buy what it used to. In 1985 the National Association of Homebuilders determined that a family needs an income of approximately $37,000 to afford a median-priced home. The median family income that year was $27,735, almost $10,000 short (cited in Ehrenreich, 1990). More than half of all families today can't afford to buy a home (Gergen, 1991).

Downward Mobility and Self-Concept

So unexpected and "foreign" is downward social mobility to most middle-class Americans born after the Great Depression that anthropologist Katherine Newman (1988) likens it to living in a different culture. She conducted anthropological field interviews with 150 "downwardly mobile" people in a variety of settings. She discovered that in the face of downward mobility, people lose their feelings of security and find themselves suddenly powerless and unable to control the direction of their lives. The experience of the downwardly mobile middle class is quite different from that of the officially poor. These are people who once had it made. They have skills, education, and years of steady work experience. Many are homeowners. But the American Dream has become a nightmare. As a result, they must contend not only with the financial hardships but with the psychological and social consequences of "falling from grace."

Nowhere are the consequences of downward mobility more striking than in the unique problems of identity. At one time the downwardly mobile *were* successfully middle class. They enjoyed the trappings and apparent stability of a reasonably comfortable life. They became accustomed to power, to deference, and to the middle-class norms of consumption. But they have lost all that and must now venture out into a work world that offers no autonomy, no authority, and no feelings of self-importance (Newman, 1988). They are caught between two selves, one highly valued, the other not. Consequently, many continue to cling to previous occupational identities:

> Even after hundreds of interviews fail to rescue them from a bottom-level job, after the family home has been sold to pay off debts, after the sense of self-assurance fades to be replaced by self-recrimination, the torture of two selves endures. For the kids' sake, for the [spouse's] sake, or simply for the sake of one's own sanity, it is hard to ditch yesterday's honored identity in order to make room for today's poor substitute. (Newman, 1988, p. 10)

In other areas of life, society has institutionalized some of the roles that result from dramatic changes in personal circumstances: the ex-spouse, the ex-alcoholic, the retiree (Ebaugh, 1988). But there are no guidelines for the downwardly mobile to assist them in shedding the old self; there is no legitimate role for the ex-breadwinner. Without a coherent identity they have lost their place in the social landscape. Although a massive loss such as General Motors laying off 29,000 workers in 1986 may create feelings of collective tragedy and allow one to attribute cause for the downward mobility to external forces, it is little solace to the person who has lost not only a career and a lifestyle, but a valuable identity as well.

Downward Mobility and the Family

Downward mobility wreaks havoc on the institution of family by destroying the economic foundations of life and stretching emotional bonds to the breaking point (Newman, 1988). The reduction in income has far-reaching social and economic consequences, from residential moves to inferior housing. It means drastically less money for recreation and leisure and more pressures due to inadequate time and finances. The sudden financial strain also causes social dislocation through the loss of familiar friendships and emotional support networks.

Women are particularly vulnerable to downward mobility. Some plunge due to the loss of a job. But for most the main cause is divorce. In the United States, divorced men experience an average 42% *increase* in their standard of living; divorced women (and their children) experience a 73% *decrease* (Weitzman, 1985).

Despite the increased participation of women in the paid labor force, most women still subordinate their careers to that of their husbands (Weitzman, 1985). Hence, marriage gives men the opportunity to build and enhance their earning capacity, but for women marriage is more likely to be a career liability.

A divorced woman faces a world in which her earning capacity is less than a man's simply because she is a woman (see chapter 13 for more details). If she did not work outside the home during her marriage, she also must deal with the toll those years away from her career path have taken on her ability to earn a living. Even today marriage still imposes disadvantages on a woman's employment prospects. This is particularly true if she is awarded custody of minor children. After a divorce men become single and women become single parents (Weitzman, 1985). This responsibility further restricts a woman's job opportunities by limiting her work schedule and job location, her availability to work overtime, the freedom to take advantage of special training, travel, and other opportunities for advancement.

Children are hard hit by downward mobility as well. Their values and future plans are threatened. Once "invincible" parents become mere shells of their former middle-class selves. The parental authority that sprang from their financial control disappears. A 15-year-old woman describes the sad transformation of the father she once idolized after he lost his job as a successful show business promoter:

> He just seemed to be getting irrational. He would walk around the house talking to himself and stay up all night, smoking cigarettes in the dark. . . . All I perceived is that somebody who used to be a figure of strength was behaving strangely: starting to cry at odd times . . . hanging around the house unshaven in his underwear when I would bring dates home. . . . In the absence of any understanding of what was going on, my attitude was one of anger and disgust, like "Why don't you get your act together? What's the matter with you?" (Newman, 1988, p. 96)

For some children, downward mobility makes economic stability a doubtful concept. As children become adults, many cannot trust the appearance of success because they fear failure may be lurking around the corner: "The higher they climb, the more urgently they sense they are about to fall" (p. 142).

The problems of economic instability are not unique to people at the very bottom of the stratification system. Today, more and more people are having difficulty making ends meet. With so many different types of people from different status backgrounds and circumstances suffering financially, we can no longer contend that they have only themselves to blame.

Stratification and Power in Everyday Life

Through class and status inequality, social stratification creates an unequal distribution of power. **Power** can be defined as the capacity to follow a line of action despite interference or resistance from others (Weber, 1968). More important, power is the ability to intentionally influence others to act in a way that is consistent with one's wishes (Wrong, 1988), or even to change their beliefs, emotions, behaviors, and identity.

Those who own businesses, who are highly educated, who occupy prestigious positions in society, and who are connected to one another through upper-class social and family ties have the ability to make major decisions that profoundly influence the lives of others. If you work for General Motors and the board of directors decides to discontinue a line of trucks manufactured at your plant, you may be out of a job. Similarly, if the owner of the computer software company where you work decides to move the office from Los Angeles to Phoenix because it's not as expensive to run a business there, you might be forced to relocate. Compare the effects of these high-level decisions to the decisions made by ordinary people. If you buy a Ford instead of a Chevrolet or decide to move across the country, those actions will have virtually no effect on the lives of your superiors.

Power is rarely absolute, though. It's not very often that someone or some group or organization has total control over all aspects of your life. Even in the most lopsided power relationship, the person or group in the disadvantaged position is still able to influence the behavior of superiors: workers strike, peasants revolt, children manipulate their parents by giving them the silent treatment. In some situations the outward signs of a power relationship obscure a much more complicated scenario. The office secretary, for instance, wields a tremendous amount of hidden power by controlling the flow of information to his or her boss, managing the boss's public impressions, and making sure the entire office runs smoothly. While a doctor's *formal* power over nurses is undeniable, many nurses learn how to take the initiative and make recommendations to doctors in a way that appears deferential (Stein, 1967).

Power is felt most forcefully in the multitude of interactions that characterize our lives (Collins, 1981). When we first hear the word *power*, we think of it in terms of orders, threats, and coercion. But *noncoercive* forms of power are much more common. These can be seen in the subtle gestures that signal power and assert dominance (Henley, 1977). Nonverbal gestures, the use of time and space, and conversational behaviors are rarely recognized as activities that are derived from the political, economic, and family structures that determine our lives. The humiliation of being powerless is felt when people are ignored or interrupted, are intimidated by another's presence, are afraid to approach or touch a superior, or have their privacy freely invaded by another. These often unnoticed details of ordinary social encounters—the signs and symbols of dominance, the subtle messages of threat, or the gestures of submission—can reveal a great deal about one person's power over another and that person's place within the larger stratification system.

Power and Role Taking

As discussed in chapter 5, a key element in the development of the self is mastering the ability to take the role of others. It is something we all must learn to do in order to be functioning members of society. But from an institutional perspective, some roles command more respect than others, and some people face much less pressure to engage in role taking than others.

People in superior positions have the "luxury" of being insensitive and indifferent to the desires of subordinates. Therefore they will not find it necessary to take the role of people who are less powerful. In the political arena, low-level White House staffers must have thorough knowledge of the President's likes and dislikes in order to avoid a misjudgment of his conduct that might get them into trouble. The President, however, doesn't have to conform his behavior to the wishes and desires of underlings. This is not to say that he is necessarily mean or inconsiderate of his staff. It simply means that the institutionalized structure of the situation does not require such awareness to flow from top to bottom.

The less powerful a person is in any sort of relationship, the more dependent he or she is on that relationship (Emerson, 1962). If a less powerful person has a greater stake in the continuation of a relationship, then he or she must be more aware of the more powerful person's preferences and interests. Powerless individuals thus use role taking as a management strategy (Thomas, Franks, & Calonico, 1972).

Common sense suggests that people who have greater knowledge and experience would be better role takers (e.g., parents should be more sensitive to their children's views than vice versa). However, given the conditions of power and dependence, this is not the case. The same goes for other institutional contexts. First-year college students are much more aware of actions and interests of upper-class students than vice versa. Low-level employees must be sensitive to the behaviors and preferences of their superiors in order to achieve occupational success and mobility. It could even be argued that powerless nations must have heightened sensitivity to the activities of more powerful neighboring countries. I have heard some Canadians complain that they are "required" to know virtually everything about the United States—its culture as well as its economic and political systems—whereas most people in the United States tend to be rather oblivious to even the most accessible elements of Canadian society and culture.

Hurry Up and Wait

In chapter 4 I described the social norms that govern the use and perception of time. While time is experienced under rather strict cultural guidelines, it is also profoundly influenced by power. At the interpersonal level, time can be used as a means of social control. If you have ever been to summer camp, either as a camper or a counselor, you know how tightly time is controlled. Most camps schedule events throughout the day, keeping campers' free time to an absolute minimum. This reduces the likelihood of them getting into trouble. All parents know the importance of controlling when their children eat, sleep, and play. Children's time is of no significance. They are made to do things when it is convenient for their parents.

In short, powerful people have the ability to control the timing, length, and nature of interactions. The powerful share as little of their time with the powerless as possible, while the powerless must give up time as the powerful demand it (Henley, 1977). Waiting, an element of social life known by us all, is an important means by which power can be created, maintained, and legitimated (B. Schwartz, 1973). The least powerful people in society can be approached at will, while the most powerful can be seen only "by appointment." If you have ever been kept waiting in a doctor's office past the scheduled time of your appointment, you are aware of the frustration that comes from knowing that your time is being defined as less important than the doctor's.

Waiting is experienced differently by different social classes. The organizational lives of poor and working-class people are filled with waiting—in hospital emergency rooms, for unemployment or welfare benefits, for food stamps, in courts, in long check-out lines at discount stores. What's more, because of the nature of their jobs, they are often unable to take time off to acquire certain services that aren't available during nonworking hours, like going to the bank or to the gas company.

Some of the waiting is caused by a demand for goods and services that are in limited supply. You may be forced to wait for a rare part for your foreign car because it is not kept in stock and must be obtained elsewhere. In other situations, though, waiting may be used strategically and purposely to express power and keep others in their place. To be kept waiting is to be provided a message that your time (and therefore your social worth) isn't as valuable as the time and worth of the person imposing the wait. Waiting provides a sense of subordination. To the powerful person, the fact that others are willing to wait for him or her merely serves to reinforce the sense of importance and domination associated with his or her position.

Strength in Words

Power is also expressed in the way people talk to one another. Because we live in a symbolic world, the terms we use to refer to ourselves and others provide a great deal of information about who and what we think we are. The fact that an uncle calls me Davey is irritating not because I don't like the name, but because it doesn't fit with my professional self-concept. The terms we use to address others—Ms., Ma'am, Sir, Mr., Doctor, Senator, and so on—may on the surface appear simply to be forms of etiquette. On closer inspection, however, the norms that govern the use of such terms reflect underlying power differences.

Forms of address are governed by the relative status differences of the individuals involved. The conversations that take place between friends or siblings are commonly marked by the mutual use of informal terms like first names or nicknames. When status is different, though, the lower-status person is often required to use terms of respect and formal pronouns like sir or ma'am. In the South in years past, every white person had the privilege of addressing any black by first name and receiving the respectful form of address in return. These differences are clearly institutionalized in some languages. In Spanish, *tu* is the familiar word for "you," which is used when talking to a subordinate or to a status equal. *Usted* also means "you," but it is the formal version used when one is addressing a status superior.

Conversational style is also affected by power differences. Ordinarily, conversations are organized to ensure that one speaker talks at a time and that speakers trade off. Speakers are usually expected to respect and obey the rules of taking turns or risk some form of informal punishment. For instance, the person who always butts in and never lets another get a word in edgewise will soon gain a reputation as ill-mannered and uncouth.

The power derived from differences in social status gives certain people more freedom than others to violate and ignore these rules. To interrupt someone in midsentence is not only rude but a clear expression of power, for it immediately makes the other person stop talking. Often politicians in debates will attempt to gain the upper hand by frequently interrupting their opponents, thus preventing them from getting their message across unchallenged.

Sociologists Peter Kollock, Phil Blumstein, and Pepper Schwartz (1985) examined taped conversations between intimate partners in heterosexual, gay male, and lesbian couples to see if positions of power influenced people's conversational behavior. They were particularly interested in such conversational norm violations as interrupting, talking over the other person, and monopolizing the conversation. They found that regardless of the sexual composition of the couple—the factor that in past research had been used to explain differences in conversational behavior—people in positions of power interrupted more, overlapped their partners more, and talked for longer periods of uninterrupted time than those people with less power. In other words, power can create a conversational division of labor.

The interpersonal expression of power is embedded in the very structure of a stratified society. The power we see in conversations, role taking, the use of time, and so on is a product of the macro-level forces of culture and social institutions. Hence stratification systems persist and acquire legitimacy when a large majority of the people in the society reproduce the unequal distribution of power, wealth, and prestige in their everyday activities.

The Impact of Institutional Power

Beliefs and actions are not the only factors that maintain stratification. Inequality also shapes the nature of social institutions and the way those institutions interact. It is produced and reproduced in families, economic relations, political activity, and the educational system. Once established and in place, practices and programs are supported by those individuals, groups, and organizations that benefit from them. Wealthy school districts are likely to acquire and retain more innovative and expensive educational programs than are poorer districts. Those at the top of the class structure are both the architects and the products of the institutional expectations that eventually become a taken-for-granted part of our society (Powell, 1991).

Institutional power is often established through the structure authority relations that exist between people. Institutional authority is based on dependence and legitimacy. Legitimacy rests on the belief that you *should* obey the directives of an authority; dependence is based on the undesirable consequences that await you if you don't.

Dependence is directly related to the unequal distribution of economic resources described earlier. Such inequalities enable certain individuals or groups to exercise tremendous power over others. If I control something you need to survive or have become accustomed to, our relationship can easily become one of exploitation. I may force you to act as I wish by dangling before you the resources you need. Dependence is built into many institutional roles: Children depend on parents for their physical needs, employees depend on employers for their financial needs, students depend on teachers for their educational needs.

The crises that sometimes lead people to consult professionals—doctors when we're sick, lawyers when we're in legal trouble, accountants when we have money problems—create greater possibilities for dependence than other authority-subordinate relationships. In a large complex society, professionals often act as gatekeepers between people and the benefits they desire or the penalties they fear (Starr, 1982). Teachers certify those who are eligible to graduate from school; judges determine who will and will not go to prison. The authority of professionals is enhanced by our need for them.

The dependency, power, and trust that exist between clients and professionals is influenced by one's position in the larger class system. On the one hand, wealthy individuals are likely to see professionals under voluntary conditions and are more likely to pay for sessions in private settings. Furthermore, they are likely to share the same beliefs and values as the professionals they consult. On the other hand, when poor or working-class people encounter professionals it is more likely to be involuntary or take place in public institutions.

Legitimacy refers to the generally acknowledged *right* to command and the acknowledged *obligation* to obey (Wrong, 1988). It is the source of the command rather than its content that endows it with legitimacy. By nature of their institutional positions, generals, presidents, queens, kings, and other leaders can issue commands that will be obeyed by others simply because of who they are. The norms that grant one person legitimate authority over another are shared by the larger community and culture to which the two people belong. Because legitimacy is culturally derived, it represents the incorporation of larger societal ideals into power relationships. Legitimate authority allows an individual to exert influence in those areas of life where the people involved agree that such influence is proper and right (Huston, 1983). The costs of disobeying legitimate authority are socially prescribed and enforced by the community. It would come as no surprise if your boss fired you for consistently disobeying his or her commands. You may think your boss is a dolt, consider the commands unreasonable, or feel the reaction was extreme, yet you still would acknowledge that the boss certainly had the right to respond that way.

Legitimate authority is often based on perceived competence, such as when you obey the directives of someone because you believe in his or her expertise to decide on a line of action that is in your best interest (Wrong, 1988). "Doctor's orders" is the prototype of legitimacy derived from cultural definitions of competence. The doctor who tells a patient, "Stop smoking or you will die within a year," is not threatening to kill the patient, nor is he or she appealing to the patient's sense of moral obligation to obey. He or she is simply saying, "I'm the expert here. I have been trained to identify causes of illness. I have the appropriate credentials. Hence I am qualified to tell you how you can become healthier."

At the structural level, institutionalized authority is a defining characteristic of professions. A **profession** is an occupation that requires extensive training and that is governed by a code of ethics. Professionals become powerful because we depend on their knowledge and competence. They are able to claim authority not necessarily because of their personal charm and intelligence, but because they are members of a social group that has had its competence legitimated by the culture (Starr, 1982). If they violate the standards of the community, as when a physician or lawyer commits malpractice, their authority becomes illegitimate.

The phenomenon of power and waiting is more than just an individual tactic for gaining the upper hand over someone. It often derives from structural conditions that characterize the profession. Because a significant number of people fail to keep their appointments, for instance, doctors overbook—that is, schedule several people at the same time. The waiting room is an institutionalized response to a common problem in the profession. That most of us quietly tolerate waiting says more about the power behind the profession than the power of that individual physician.

Professionals not only advise us to act in certain ways, they also provide a collective interpretation of reality. The church, for instance, makes authoritative judgments about the nature of the world. In a highly specialized society, different professional communities come to rule different aspects of reality, such as the structure of the atom, the elements of the law, the nature of the universe, or the process of disease (Starr, 1982). Such authority is so extensive that it transcends individual people, residing in cultural objects like the Bible, dictionaries, maps, mathematical tables, or written laws.

The power derived from authority is a key feature of institutional relationships. Even more important, many historical battles for freedom and justice revolve around the issue of legitimate authority. Slavery was "justified" by slave owners with the argument that whites, by virtue of their race, had legitimate authority over blacks. Similarly, the historical subordination of women in families as well as in the workforce has long been justified by the argument that men are physically, genetically, and maybe even spiritually endowed with legitimate authority. Mutinies, revolutions, and movements for change are challenges to conceptions of legitimate authority.

One of the longest-running debates among sociologists is how institutional power and authority are distributed within our economic and political systems. The two main perspectives of this question focus on the power of interest groups and the power of a small ruling class.

The Pluralist Perspective

Institutional power and authority are most apparent in the political sphere. From an early age we learn about the democratic character of the American political system. We are taught that we have a government "of, by, and for the people," and we learn to favorably contrast our system of government with that of others. Our political system is one in which the will of the majority always prevails, in which there is equality for everybody under the law, and in which policy decisions are made to maximize the common good. Even schoolyard disputes are often settled by the democratic declaration, "Majority rules!"

At the heart of **pluralism**—or the pluralist perspective—is the notion that power in American society is evenly distributed among a number of interest groups (Dahl, 1961). These groups represent a variety of constituencies from all corners of society: farmers, women, laborers, business and industry, gun owners, religious, racial, age, or ethnic groups, and so on. These groups, although they are made up mostly of "ordinary" Americans, have access to government officials because of their numbers. They compete with one another to influence political decisions. Those groups that are well organized are able to neutralize attacks on their interests.

Because their interests are narrow, no single group is concerned with all issues of national policy. Hence no group is capable of dominating at all times. In this way, power is constantly shifting and, in the long run, is balanced. On occasion diverse interest groups will even form curious alliances when some common interest is threatened, as when radical feminists and fundamentalist Christians fight together against the "evils" of pornography.

According to sociologist David Riesman (1950), the federal government in a pluralist society is a *neutral* body that is responsive to all groups and dominated by none. The president and congress simply make decisions based on the wishes of a particular interest group that happens, at that point in time, to have the largest amount of support from the people. In this way the political system is democratic. Decisions of national and international significance are made in the interests of those groups that have the most popular support. People are free to join or otherwise support the groups that promise to best represent their interests. Power, then, is ultimately in the hands of the people.

Although Riesman felt that interest groups fit into a democratic system of government by representing the needs of the people, he could not have foreseen the enormous power and influence these groups have attained in their own right. While they certainly ensure that a variety of interests will be represented at the highest levels of the government, it's not clear whether the average citizen has much influence over them or is able to have his or her interests represented by them.

The most common type of interest group on the political landscape today is the **political action committee** (PAC). PACs are organizations formed to represent narrowly defined special interests, including big business (tobacco growers, banks, real estate, electronics, construction), professions (teachers, lawyers, physicians), labor unions (autoworkers, teamsters, sheet metal workers, postal workers), or ideological positions on single issues (gun control, human rights, Social Security, abortion).

PACs were born out of political necessity in the 1940s. When labor unions were prohibited from spending union treasury money on candidates for federal office, they came up with the idea of pooling donations and presenting that money to the candidates. The idea caught on with business and ideological groups. By 1974 there were approximately 500 PACs. Today there are close to 5,000 PACs representing both ends of the political spectrum from environmentalists to the National Rifle Association (Makinson, 1993).

PACs are allowed to collect funds from their members and make contributions much larger than those allowed to individual contributors. The amount of money PACs spent on political campaigns increased from under $20 million in 1974 to over $160 million in 1990 (Makinson, 1993). Although financial contributions made by PACs have dropped slightly in recent years, these interest groups still exert tremendous control over candidates and the entire electoral process. That PACs have influenced the way our government makes decisions is undeniable. In the early 1980s, for instance, 92% of Congress members who received contributions from PACs supporting the construction of a nuclear breeder reactor voted for it. Only 29% of those who received no contributions did so (Green, 1984). In 1982 a PAC called the National Automobile Dealer's Association opposed a bill that would have required used-car dealers to tell prospective buyers about known defects in their cars. The association distributed campaign contributions in excess of $840,000 to senators and representatives. Eighty-five percent of those who received these contributions voted against the legislation. And in 1988, $8.4 million was given to candidates for the House of Representatives who were running *unopposed* (Eitzen & Baca-Zinn, 1991).

Political ideology doesn't stand in the way of PACs' attempts to buy influence and ensure access to elected officials. Common Cause, a reform group that frequently criticizes the influential power of PACs, studied seven Senate races in 1988. They found that 274 PACs gave money to *both* Democratic and Republican candidates in the same races. Federal Express Corporation, for instance, contributed to all 14 candidates in these races (Minzesheimer, 1989). What seems to matter to PACs is not the candidate's political affiliation but his or her power to affect legislation.

How accurate is it to describe the American political system as pluralistic? Compared with many other nations, the United States does have well-established formal rules to put "the little guy" on equal footing with the rich and powerful. After all, a poor person's vote counts as much as a wealthy person's. But the everyday experiences many Americans have with the political system have led them to doubt its "democratic" character. Many people feel that government and the political power that comes with it has been concentrated in the hands of a very few people who are primarily concerned with their own interests and not the interests of the people.

The Ruling-Class Perspective

According to sociologists G. William Domhoff (1983) and C. Wright Mills (1956), political and economic power rest not in the hands of competing interest groups but in the hands of a small, socially cohesive **ruling class.** They feel that pluralism is a myth, reflecting what we might *like* American society to be and not what it really is. Instead of the United States being a pure democracy, they argue that it is a society dominated by a small group of people—men and, in very rare cases, women—who hold the highest political and economic positions in the country.

Influential interest groups do exist, but only at a secondary level of power. The real power to make decisions of local, national, and global significance is at a level above and beyond their reach. It is the ruling class alone that makes economic and policy decisions that chart the course of American society.

Composed of rich businesspeople and their families, America's ruling class is an exclusive group that occupies the highest levels of status and prestige. As evidence of their existence, social registers are maintained in many major American cities. These registers are telephone book–like volumes that contain information about America's elite. Individuals and families are listed in them by virtue of their family pedigree and their economic standing. Furthermore, the American ruling class is perpetuated through a set of clubs, resorts, charitable and cultural organizations, and social activities that provide members with a distinctive lifestyle and perspective on the world that distinguishes them from the rest of society.

More important, the ruling class is able to run the political and economic institutions in this country by controlling the executive branch of government, both major political parties, large corporations, the majority of privately held corporate stock, the media, universities, councils for national and international affairs, and so on (Domhoff, 1983). Hence members of the ruling class enjoy political and economic power to a degree not available to other classes. They can work in a number of ways to ensure that their interests are met.

First of all, they may directly participate in national government. Pierre Du Pont of Delaware, John D. Rockefeller IV of West Virginia, and John Danforth of Missouri are heirs to immense fortunes and have served or are serving as U.S. senators or representatives. Perhaps the most obvious example of the meshing of economic power and political aspirations came in 1992 with the presidential campaign of H. Ross Perot. The Texas multibillionaire made no bones about the fact that he intended to use his tremendous financial resources to try to get elected.

A second way the ruling class can participate in the political process is by making financial contributions to the campaigns of politicians who support their interests or who are sympathetic to their views. Because successful campaigns cost so much money to run, candidates for office often must mold their views to be consistent with the views of those providing financial support. The idea that a small group of privileged people is able to dominate politics and the economy violates our country's fundamental pluralistic values. Keep in mind, however, that the existence of an American ruling class doesn't necessarily imply that other classes in society are totally powerless (Domhoff, 1983). Even the most powerless people can develop the capacity to disrupt the system. Under certain circumstances the voting masses have placed legislative restraints on the actions of the ruling class. "Ruling class" doesn't necessarily mean total control and domination. Instead, it refers to the ability to set the terms and define the rules under which other groups and classes must operate.

You can see how this approach echoes some of the general notions of the conflict perspective described earlier: that political power in a stratified society is based on the unequal distribution of wealth, information, and other resources. Implicit in this explanation of society's political and economic power structure is the notion that those with wealth and authority can structure other social institutions to ensure that their personal interests are met and that the class itself endures. Like other social structures, the names and faces of the ruling class may change, but the institutions that perpetuate it stay virtually intact over time.

Wealth, Class, and Education

Consider the role of the educational system. Many members of the ruling class spend their childhoods in private schools, their adolescence in boarding schools, and their college years in heavily endowed private universities (Domhoff, 1983). The educational system not only plays a key socializing role (see chapter 5), but also an important role in perpetuating or reproducing the American class structure. For working-class and poor kids, schools teach them their place in authority relationships so that they will be prepared for the subordinate work positions they will occupy in the future (Bowles & Gintis, 1976).

Schools provide very different lessons for children of the ruling class. Elite private schools have been called "educational country clubs" where children from families like the Rockefellers, Kennedys, and Vanderbilts go to get socially polished for admission to exclusive colleges (Cookson & Persell, 1985). In addition to the standard curriculum, these schools teach "vocabulary, inflection, styles of dress, aesthetic tastes, values and manners" (Collins, 1971).

In boarding schools, required attendance at school functions, participation in esoteric sports such as lacrosse, squash, and crew, the wearing of school blazers or ties, and other "character building" activities are designed to teach young people the unique lifestyle of the ruling class. In many ways, boarding schools function like total institutions (Goffman, 1961), isolating members from the outside world and providing them with routines and traditions that are highly effective agents of socialization.

Peter Cookson and Caroline Persell (1985) studied more than 60 elite boarding schools in the United States and Great Britain. They accumulated hundreds of hours of interviews and conversations with prep school heads, teachers, students, and alumni and distributed questionnaires to thousands of students and teachers. They observed classes, assemblies, chapel services, sports contests, cultural events, meals, and other school activities and were given access to catalogs, curriculum listings, brochures, SAT scores, and grade point averages.

The researchers found that the philosophies, programs, and lifestyles of boarding schools help transmit power and privilege. The schools act as gate-keepers into prestigious universities. After attending these universities, boarding school graduates connect with one another in the financial and governmental world. The prep school experience forms an everlasting social, political, and economic bond. Institutional and interpersonal ties exist at the highest levels of business, finance, and government. Said the director of development at Choate, an elite prep school in Connecticut:

> There is no door in this entire country that cannot be opened by a Choate graduate. I can go anywhere in this country and anywhere there's a man I want to see . . . I can find a Choate man to open that door for me. (quoted in Cookson & Persell, 1985, p. 200)

The privileged social backgrounds that are produced and maintained through the elite educational system are similar to one another but highly *un*representative of the American population as a whole. This standing practically guarantees that members of the ruling class who occupy key political and economic positions will form a like-minded, cohesive group that bears little resemblance to the majority of Americans whose lives depend on their national and international decisions.

Class Connections

The homogeneity of the ruling class provides members not only with opportunities for social contacts, but also with opportunities for the sharing of knowledge and mutually beneficial financial and governmental activities (Eitzen, Jung, & Purdy, 1982). Retired government leaders are often appointed to corporate boards. Government officials frequently call on business leaders for advice. Persons of wealth are routinely invited to become U.S. ambassadors. Former cabinet members become highly paid business consultants. Top corporate executives are often given cabinet posts or other advisory positions within the government. Such traffic in personnel has become so heavy that Congress recently had to pass a law setting time limits and restricting permissible contact between ex-government officials and their successors.

Members of the ruling class often act as **corporate interlocks,** serving on the boards of directors of several large corporations simultaneously (Useem, 1978). In a study by a senate subcommittee on governmental affairs, of the top 245 large corporations in the United States, 123 were interlocked through at least one common board member with an average of 62 of the remaining 122 corporations. For instance, Morgan Bank shared directors with such corporations as Ford, Eastman Kodak, IBM, Procter and Gamble, Sears Roebuck, General Motors, General Electric, Bethlehem Steel, and Prudential Insurance (U.S. Senate Committee on Governmental Affairs, 1978).

Although people are forbidden by law to serve on the boards of competing corporations, say Ford and General Motors, for instance, corporate interlocks still can have a substantial impact over the economy and subsequently our personal lives. Interlocks reduce competition among corporations in general, provide a means of sharing information about corporate plans and operations, provide a sense of unity among top corporate officials in the economy, and help provide a common approach in corporate dealings with the government.

These individuals are also in a position to exercise influence over several major firms simultaneously. Because credit is a crucial resource for most large corporations, for instance, the inclusion of a banking executive on their boards of directors can help ensure adequate financing in the future (Useem, 1978).

A relatively small number of corporate giants with various ties among themselves have come to dominate the economy. Through this domination they have obtained tremendous political influence. What is important about this inner circle from an institutional perspective is that instead of being concerned with the interests of a single organization, these companies are unified in their concern for the long-term interests of business as a whole. They come together as a community, sharing similar values and goals (Domhoff, 1983). When individual members of this inner group find their way into positions of political influence, they can speak for the interests of the entire corporate world, rather than the narrowly defined interests of one corporation.

Global Stratification

Because of their access to economic and political resources, the members of the American ruling class are able to go outside our country's borders to pursue their financial interests, if domestic opportunities aren't promising. They can invest their money in more lucrative foreign corporations or, with assistance from the government, establish their businesses or factories abroad.

The perpetuation of the American class structure must be understood within the context of a *global* system of inequality. Now more than ever, our everyday lives have become a product of both local and global events. The next time you stroll through a shopping mall, notice all the products that are made in other countries: clothes, shoes, food, cooking utensils, computers, stereo equipment, sporting goods, toys, and so forth. Sitting in my office, I see that my telephone, radio, and computer were made in Japan, my watch in the Philippines, my stapler in Great Britain, my calculator in Taiwan, my shoes in Korea, my pants in Hong Kong, my water in France, my picture frame in Thailand, and my briefcase, paper clips, and tea kettle in China.

If a product wasn't made in another country, chances are some of its component parts were (e.g., computer chips). Almost 40% of all the parts used in American manufacturing are imported from foreign countries (Cetron, Rocha, & Luckins, 1988). The production of the Ford Escort, for example, involves parts assembled in 16 countries on three continents (Braun, 1991). When you think of the enormous number of international transactions and interactions that must take place for all these things to arrive in your local stores, you get a good sense of how interdependent the world has become.

The trend toward globalization may have brought the world's inhabitants closer together, but it has not occurred evenly or fairly. Because different nations have differing amounts of power to ensure that their interests are met, there exists a global stratification system that produces inequalities in wealth and standards of living between the industrialized, developed countries of the world and the less developed, so-called Third World countries.

In 1987 the average per capita income in the developed countries of western Europe, the United States, Canada, and Japan was $14,670 (the figure for the United States was $18,530). By contrast, in the less developed countries of South America, Asia, and Africa, which comprise 60% of the world's population, the average person earns only $290 a year. Similar inequalities between countries can be found in rates of infant mortality, illiteracy, life expectancy, and access to safe water (Schor, 1991). Wealthy countries, which account for about 20% of the world's population, consume 85% of the world's supply of paper, 79% of its steel, and 80% of all commercial energy (Kerbo, 1991; Schor, 1991).

Structured inequalities exist not only within national boundaries, but within a worldwide system of stratification. Because of their access to better technology, wealthy nations are able to produce higher quality goods at lower prices compared to poor nations (D. A. Smith, 1993). This allows them to have a more favorable balance of trade and ultimately leads to greater control of the world's financial resources (Wallerstein, 1974). As with domestic stratification, a global class system exists that is based on differing *national* interests. Like powerful elite groups, it is in the interests of powerful nations to retain their favored positions while keeping other nations in their place.

As the gap between rich and poor nations continues to grow, so does the gap between rich and poor people. I described earlier the widening income gaps in the United States. Such inequalities are even worse in poor countries. In 1950 in Mexico, the richest one-fifth of the population had an average income 10 times that of the poorest one-fifth. Today the ratio is more than 20 to 1. In Latin America, only 10% of the farmers own 90% of the farmland (Kerbo, 1991).

Global stratification has been made more complex by the growth of massive multinational corporations. Economic globalization has meant that countries all over the world are connected by social, political, and economic processes that have made national boundaries all but irrelevant. Some of the largest American corporations, such as Exxon, IBM, Mobil, and Dow Chemical, have branches or production facilities in other countries and earn well over half of their revenues from foreign sales (Braun, 1991). At the same time, foreign firms and individuals have increasingly invested in American companies. These multinational corporations do not fall under the governance of any one country. Their decisions reflect corporate goals and not necessarily the well-being or interests of any particular country.

From a functionalist perspective, it would seem that an American company locating a factory in a poor country would yield benefits for everyone involved.

The host country benefits from the creation of new jobs and a higher standard of living. The corporation, of course, benefits from increased profits. And the country in which the corporation is based benefits from lower consumer prices for the products manufactured abroad. Furthermore, the entire planet benefits because these firms have allegiances to many different countries and therefore might be inclined to exert pressure on them to settle their political differences without violence.

Multinational corporations are a valuable part of the international economy. However, conflict theorists argue that while the short-term effects of multinationals may be beneficial, they can actually perpetuate or even worsen global stratification. One common criticism of multinationals is that they exploit local workers and communities. The employees who work in foreign plants or factories work under conditions that we wouldn't tolerate in this country. The most obvious condition is the wage they earn. Whereas the hourly wage of an auto worker in the United States is over $20, the wage of a worker in Taiwan or South Korea is less than $3 (Braun, 1991). Also, occupational safety requirements, such as protection against dangerous conditions or substances, and environmental regulations that drive up the cost of products in this country sometimes don't exist in other countries. Hence local workers might become sicker and the environment more polluted as a result of less regulated manufacturing processes (Satchell, 1991).

In addition, the money these corporations earn is rarely reinvested into the host country. Eighty-five percent of the profit from exported products ends up in the hands of the multinational corporations, bankers, traders, and distributors rather than staying in the host country (Braun, 1991). Brazil is one of the world's largest agricultural exporters. But while the amounts of fruits, vegetables, and soybeans it shipped abroad over the past several decades grew considerably, the number of Brazilians who are undernourished grew from one-third to two-thirds of the population during the same period of time (Braun, 1991).

It would be an overstatement to say that all multinationals are hard-hearted organizations that don't care about the physical well-being of workers abroad, nor about the financial well-being of workers at home whose jobs are exported to other countries. From their perspective, relocating manufacturing facilities in another country where labor is less expensive is a necessary response to global economic pressures. But those processes that drive corporate decisions do sometimes drive individuals out of work. Say companies like Dole or Del Monte abandon their production facilities in Hawaii because the unionized workers there had managed to raise their minimum wage to $3.25 an hour. If the firms then move to the Philippines, where the same work can be done for $1 a day and where workers can be exposed to harmful chemicals, we all suffer (Braun, 1991).

Whether you think multinational corporations are beneficial or harmful, one thing is clear: As long as foreign investment continues to benefit these corporations, and as long as multinationals continue to be a key component in the push of many developing countries toward modernizing their economies, they will be here to stay. Global stratification will continue to be the defining feature of the world society, and it will become increasingly difficult for ordinary citizens to avoid being influenced by the economic and political processes that play themselves out on the international stage.

Conclusion

In chapter 1, I pondered the question of how free we really are to act as we wish. I described some of the personal, interpersonal, and structural considerations that limit or constrain our choices. In this chapter we have seen that this fundamental issue is affected by social stratification and inequality. Certain groups of people have a greater capacity to control their own lives than others. Your position in the stratification system can determine not only your ability to influence people and exert authority, but a whole host of life chances as well, from financial stability to housing, education, and health care. The unequal distribution of resources, most notably wealth, at both the national and international levels has created a seemingly indestructible culture of haves and have-nots.

Power and inequality are also obvious in the social institutions and political decision-making processes that guide our existence and in the relationships between countries in the global marketplace. These processes might seem distant from your private experiences. But it is in the minute details of our lives that power and inequality derived from these processes touch us tangibly and personally. Our routine interactions sometimes reflect the constraints as well as the privileges that are bestowed on us by virtue of our social positions; our access to jobs and careers sometimes reflects economic processes at the international level.

That profound imbalances in wealth, power, and prestige are the defining feature of this society is nothing short of ironic given how loudly and frequently we sing of our cultural commitment to the values of equality and justice. Nevertheless, our system is set up, by and large, to promote, enhance, and protect the interests of those who reside at or near the top of the stratification system. Authority, wealth, and influence grant rights unseen and unknown to the vast majority of people who have fewer structural advantages.

C H A P T E R   H I G H L I G H T S

■ Stratification is a ranking of entire groups of people, based on race, gender, or social class, that perpetuates unequal rewards and life chances in society.

■ The structural-functionalist explanation of stratification is that the stability of society depends on all social positions being filled—that is, there are people around to do all the jobs that need to be done. Higher rewards such as prestige and large salaries are afforded to the most important positions, thereby ensuring that the most qualified individuals will occupy the highest positions.

■ Conflict theory argues that stratification reflects an unequal distribution of power in society and is a primary source of conflict and tension.

■ Social class is the primary means of stratification in American society. Contemporary sociologists are likely to define one's class standing as a combination of income, wealth, occupational prestige, and educational attainment.

■ Social class is more than an economic position; it is a way of life that affects how we experience every facet of our lives. The middle class has been particularly influential in defining American culture and its moods, politics, lifestyles, and tastes.

■ Stratification is most vividly felt in the everyday expression of interpersonal power: role taking, conversation, and the use of time and space.

■ Sociologists are also concerned with how power and authority are distributed within our economic and political institutions. The pluralist perspective, which emphasizes the role of competing interest groups, and the ruling-class perspective, which emphasizes the role of a small group of wealthy individuals, are two competing explanations of institutional power.

■ Stratification exists not only among different groups within the same society, but also among different societies within a global community. Wealthy nations are better able to control the world's financial resources than poor nations.

YOUR TURN

Social stratification can be based on more than just individual achievement. Your family can determine your access to certain opportunities and life chances. Furthermore, the American dream of upward mobility—enjoying a quality of life superior to that of your parents—is becoming for many a nightmare of downward mobility.

To understand how your life has been and continues to be influenced by the lives of people in your family, construct a family tree. You may need to ask your parents, grandparents, and other relatives about distant ancestors. Go back as far into the past as you can. For each person in the tree, identify his or her occupation and the highest level of education achieved. Is there a pattern of upward or downward mobility in your family? To what extent has family helped or hindered individuals' mobility? Is there a career legacy that has been handed down from generation to generation? How do the occupational and educational paths of men and women differ in your family? What are your own career aspirations? How do they compare to those of your ancestors? If you have or expect to have children, what are your career and educational aspirations for them? Does your family experience support the contention that social class is "hereditary"?

STRATIFICATION THROUGH THE URBAN LENS

Photographs and concept by Camilo José Vergara

Since the riots of the 1960s, American cities have experienced profound transformations, best revealed in the spatial restructuring of their ghettos and the emergence of new urban forms. . . . [T]he power of the physical surroundings to shape lives, to mirror people's existence and to symbolize social relations has been ignored."

—Camilo José Vergara

It is easy to think of poverty as a fixed characteristic of people or places. However, poverty is a social process, one that can be seen in the way neighborhoods change over time. Photographer Camilo José Vergara uses a method called "rephotography"--the process of photographing the same site over a period of years--to document the effects of urban change on people's lives.

Empty lots scatter across once busy urban downtown Detroit. Most of the skyscrapers are empty or almost empty. Many are ruined.

A church con-
gregation
holds a yard
and barbecue
sale for the
homeless on
the East Side
of Detroit.

Here we see the deterioration of a busy Detroit neighborhood into vacant lots, or what Vergara calls "green ghettos." "During the decade beginning in 1968, the year after 'the riot,' the city lost 208,000 jobs, one-third of its total employment. By 1990 about a million people lived in the city, nearly half the 1950 population, and of those, one-quarter were on welfare. At the same time, well over 10 percent of the city's 140 square miles of land was vacant" (Vergara, 1994).

This scene of a
clapboard house
amidst a field of
wildflowers could
be in rural
Indiana, but it is
in fact a residen-
tial location in
the city of
Detroit.

(October 1987) The Thirteenth Avenue Presbyterian Church was constructed in Newark, New Jersey, in 1888. It served as Newark's oldest black congregation between 1910 and 1967.

(February 1990) By the 1970s, after more and more congregation members left the neighborhood, the church was disbanded. Over the years, its walls were weakened by scavengers, or "brickeaters." In 1987, what was left of the old building was occupied by squatters.

Entrance to the Thirteenth Presbyterian Church surrounded by townhouses, February 1992.

(October 1992)   Now townhouses occupy the site, and all that remains of the Romanesque brickwork is a curved section serving as a memento of an elegant past.

The U.S. post office is the main symbol of the federal government in American cities. But where you might expect classical buildings patriotically decorated with eagles and images of the Pony Express, here in the ghetto there are instead concrete blocks, high fences, and the windows are covered by iron gratings.

Fortification epitomizes the ghetto in America today. . . . Buildings grow claws and spikes, their entrances acquire metal plates, their roofs get fenced in, and any additional openings are sealed, cutting down on light and ventilation."

--Camilo José Vergara, 1994

Many commercial establishments in ghettos are heavily fortified. Locked grates around this hairstyling salon on Chicago's South Side render these alluring pictures difficult to comprehend.

At this nursing home in Detroit an iron gate and barbed wire separate the inhabitants from the neighborhood, and vice versa.

View along Charlotte Street, South Bronx, March 1981. Although running only 3 short blocks, Charlotte Street was the most famous ghetto street in the country; with great fanfare, Jimmy Carter (1977) and Ronald Reagan (1979) each visited this national symbol of "urban decay."

The same forces of abandonment that can open the way for urban decay can also free land for new homes. Under the leadership of churches, community organizations, and private developers, many such ghettos have kicked out the dependent poor and refused to admit the enterprises that serve them (e.g., homeless shelters, methadone clinics, prisons, and incinerators). Instead they focus on attracting working families, keeping out drug dealers, and building guarded enclaves.

Here is Charlotte Street in August 1989, part of a "reclaimed ghetto." Photographer Vergara asks: Are such efforts leading to the elimination of ghettos or toward the creation of mini-cities of exclusion within a larger urban wasteland?

The Architecture of Stratification

Poverty

The following story appeared in the *Washington Post* on December 12, 1991:

> A homeless man who spent the night huddled under a blanket a block from the White House was found dead yesterday morning, the second such death on a District street in five weeks. . . . News of the second death spread quickly among advocates for the homeless, many of whom have been predicting a bleak winter for the indigent. The District has cut money for the homeless drastically this year—$3 million compared to $8 million last year—and the number of shelter beds has been reduced from 1770 to 1200. Said a woman who worked nearby, "You see it on the news and you read about it, but when you actually see one of them pass on, it's a whole new insight. It was horrible and ugly. People shouldn't have to die like that." (Escobar, 1991, p. D6)

A few weeks later, on Christmas Day, after visiting a soup kitchen in Washington, D.C., Patrick Buchanan, who was running for President at the time, had this to say in response to a question regarding what he would do about the problem of homeless people sleeping on the streets:

> I would put them up for the night, and if they kept doing it I would pick them up for vagrancy and lock them up. . . . We also have a right—especially women and kids—to streets that are safe and free from fear. We've got to take the streets back. ("Buchanan talks tough," 1991, p. A4)

These two events underscore quite graphically the strange paradox we have in our country regarding the issue of poverty. Poverty is a social problem that is becoming larger and more deadly with each passing day. And, as the number of people who are hungry, homeless, and sick increases, poverty is also becoming a more visible part of our everyday lives. In a 1989 survey, 51% of the respondents indicated that they had seen homelessness firsthand, up from only 36% in 1986 (Oreskes & Toner, 1989). But even though the problem is undeniably getting worse, public attitudes toward poverty and poor people frequently remain indifferent or even hostile.

Chapter 10 introduced you to the structural inequalities of American society and the world and how these inequalities provide some nations and people with a disproportionate amount of wealth, power, and privilege. In this chapter I examine the bottom of the social stratification system. What is poverty? How is it officially defined by the government? What are some of the everyday consequences of being poor? What are the cultural and institutional forces that perpetuate poverty?

✳What Poverty Is

Poverty is a word that has become all too common in the English language. Politicians typically include it in their laundry lists of issues they say they plan to address if elected. Social researchers devote their careers to examining and explaining whom it affects and why it occurs. People point to it as the major cause of other social problems like violent crime and drug abuse.

But what exactly is poverty? In common usage, poverty is usually conceived in subsistence terms as the lack of sufficient money to ensure adequate functioning. Sociologists, though, often make a distinction between absolute and relative poverty. **Absolute poverty** refers to the minimal requirements necessary to sustain a reasonably healthy existence. **Relative poverty** refers to one's position with regard to the living standards of the majority in any given society (Giddens, 1991). Absolute poverty means not having enough money for adequate food, clothing, and shelter, but relative poverty is more difficult to define. It is based on relevant comparisons regarding the quality of life in a society and therefore reflects culturally defined aspirations and expectations. An annual family income of $5,000, which would constitute abject poverty in our country, is perhaps five times *higher* than the average income in many developing countries. Life in an American slum might be considered luxurious compared to the plight of tens of millions of starving people in other parts of the world. In Bangladesh, for example, 55% of the population are without access to health facilities, 51% are without access to safe water, and overall life expectancy is only about 51 years (Institute on Hunger and Development, 1992).

Drawing the Line

The U.S. government has its own absolute definition of poverty, which it uses to identify those who need assistance. The official **poverty line** identifies the amount of yearly income a family requires in order to meet its basic needs. The

Figure 11.1   *Historical Trends in Poverty Rates in the United States*

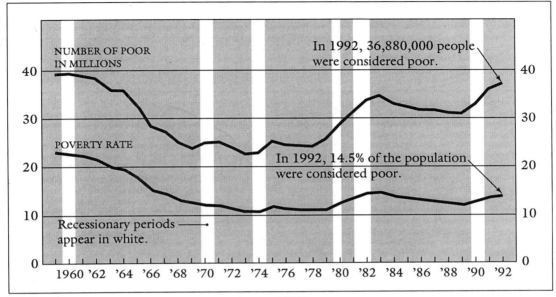

NUMBER OF POOR IN MILLIONS

In 1992, 36,880,000 people were considered poor.

POVERTY RATE

In 1992, 14.5% of the population were considered poor.

Recessionary periods appear in white.

Source: "America's poor showing," 1993.

figure is adjusted each year to account for inflation. In 1960 the official poverty line for a family of four was an annual income of $3,000; in 1993 it was $14,763.

To measure the success of its efforts to relieve poverty, the government also tracks the official **poverty rate,** the percentage of Americans whose income falls below the poverty line. In 1960 the poverty rate in this country was over 22%. It reached a low of 11.4% in 1978 and has been gradually climbing ever since. Today, approximately 36.9 million Americans (14.5% of the population) fall below the official government poverty line (U.S. Bureau of the Census, 1993, reported in "America's poor showing," 1993) (see Figure 11.1).

The government bases its definition of poverty on pretax money income only and does not include food stamps, Medicaid, public housing, and other noncash benefits (Renwick & Bergmann, 1993). The cutoff line itself is computed from something called the Thrifty Food Plan established by the U.S. Department of Agriculture. This plan is the cost of a subsistence diet, which is the bare minimum a family would need in order to survive. The plan does not identify a healthy, nutritious diet, but one on which people are likely to become malnourished if it becomes long term (Beeghley, 1984).

In the early 1960s an obscure civil servant working for the Social Security administration took the Thrifty Food Plan and multiplied it by three, since research at the time showed that the average family spent one-third of its income on food each year. The resulting amount was adopted in 1969 as the government's official poverty line. The line does vary according to family size and region and is adjusted annually for inflation, but the formula itself and the basic definition of poverty have remained the same (DeParle, 1990; Ruggles, 1990).

The Face of Poverty

The poverty line and the national poverty rate are useful statistics for policy makers, economists, and sociologists. But when used to describe national trends in poverty, they obscure important differences among subgroups of the population. Although two out of every three poor people in this country are white, the poverty rate for non-Hispanic whites—that is, whites of European descent—(9.6%) and Asian Americans (12.5%) is considerably lower than that for Hispanics (29.3%) and African Americans (33.3%). Southern states have the highest rate of poverty (16.9%) and the Northeast has the lowest (12.3%). Finally, poverty is higher in rural areas (16.8%) than in cities (13.9%) (U.S. Bureau of the Census, 1993, cited in "America's poor showing," 1993).

The face of American poverty has changed over time. Although racial and ethnic minorities have consistently been rated among the poorest Americans, other groups have seen their status change, some for better, some for worse. Take the elderly, for example. Before Social Security was instituted in 1935, many of the most destitute Americans were those over 65. As recently as 1970, 25% of Americans over the age of 65 fell below the poverty line. Today, only about 12% of the people in this age group are poor (see Figure 11.2 and chapter 14).

Taking their place, however, are women and children. In 1992 the poverty rate for families headed by a single mother was 34.9% compared to 11.7% for all other families. While families headed by women account for about 13% of nonpoor families, they account for 53% of poor ones. Perhaps the most striking feature about the increase of women in poverty is that they are largely people who were not born into poverty but were instead forced into it by unemployment, illness, and especially divorce (Sidel, 1986).

Compared to the decrease in the number of elderly poor, the poverty rate for children under the age of 18 was almost 22% in 1992 (Figure 11.2). While children under 18 represent 26% of the American population, they constitute 40% of those living in poverty. A study in 1988 of eight industrialized countries (the United States, Canada, Australia, Germany, Norway, Sweden, Switzerland, and the United Kingdom) found that the United States had the highest proportion of children living in poverty (Smeeding, Torrey, & Rein, 1988). Most poor children live in single-parent families. The Census Bureau estimates that about 60% of children born in 1983 will spend some part of their childhood in a single-parent home. Others feel the figure is closer to two-thirds (Hofferth, 1983). Whichever is correct, it is clear that a significant proportion of the current

Figure 11.2   *Historical Trends in Poverty Rate by Age*

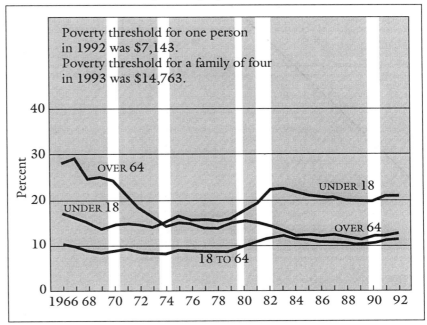

Poverty threshold for one person
in 1992 was $7,143.
Poverty threshold for a family of four
in 1993 was $14,763.

Source: "America's poor showing," 1993.

generation of American children will spend some part of their lives financially
impoverished.

The Poor and the Near-Poor

Many policy makers, sociologists, and concerned citizens question whether the
poverty line provides an accurate cutoff point between the poor and the
nonpoor in this country. On the one hand, if families actually need an income
higher than the official poverty level just to survive, then the line is being set too
low, *under*estimating the amount of poverty in the country. On the other hand,
if families can meet the minimum requirements to support life on less than the
official poverty level, then the line is being set too high and the extent of poverty
will be *over*estimated.

Several things have changed since a family's basic needs were last defined in
the early sixties. By 1990, for instance, food costs had dropped to one-sixth of
the average family's budget because the price of other things, such as housing
and medical costs, had inflated at much higher rates (Cloward & Piven, 1993).
Today, most people spend almost half their income on housing alone (Ruggles,
1990). In addition, there were fewer dual-earner or single-parent families in the

past, meaning that fewer families had to pay for child care at that time. In short, today's family has many more expenses and therefore probably spends a *greater* proportion of its total income on nonfood items. The consequence is that the official poverty line, based on outdated spending patterns, is probably too low and therefore underestimates the extent of poverty in this country.

Interestingly, while the government is likely to downplay the problem of poverty or even claim that the poverty rate is *over*estimated (see DeParle, 1990), at the same time it seems to agree implicitly that the poverty line is too low. The Census Bureau defines as **near-poor** individuals or families who earn between 100 and 125% of the poverty line, resulting in an overall "near-poverty" rate of about 18%. Families are eligible for food stamps if they earn up to 130% of the poverty line. Pregnant women and children younger than the age of six are eligible for Medicaid if their families earn up to 133% of the poverty line (DeParle, 1990).

Deciding who is and isn't officially poor is not just a matter of semantics. When the poverty line is too low, we fail to recognize the problems of many families who do not have enough money to survive but who earn more than what the government thinks is sufficient and hence are *not* officially defined as poor. A needy family making slightly more than the poverty line still may not qualify for a variety of public assistance programs such as housing benefits, education aid, or Aid to Families With Dependent Children. As a result, their standard of living may not be as good as that of a family that earns less and therefore qualifies for these programs.

In addition, the poverty line income does not by any means define a comfortable standard of living. Consider the $14,763 pretax poverty line income for a family of four in 1993. Is that enough to meet a family's costs? Let's calculate a minimum subsistence budget for a hypothetical family with two preschool children. They live in a working-class neighborhood. Both parents are employed. According to recent estimates of food costs (Renwick & Bergmann, 1993), that family would have to spend a minimum of about $350 a month on food. A decent two-bedroom apartment in this neighborhood would rent for no less than $350 a month. Utilities—gas, electric, water, sewage, telephone—add up to about $170 a month. If this fictitious neighborhood has no public transportation and the family must own a car, count on $100 a month in transportation and insurance costs. What about health care? According to the National Health Care Expenditure Survey, the average monthly medical expenses for a family of four are roughly $100 (Renwick & Bergmann, 1993). Because both parents work, full-time day care for the two children would cost about $500 a month (Renwick & Bergmann, 1993). Clothing runs about $100 a month if we include the purchase of clothes and shoes as well as the costs of doing laundry at a laundromat. The cost of personal care and miscellaneous items—haircuts, toiletries, shaving cream, toothpaste, sponges, house cleansers, diapers for the children—would be about $50 a month.

The total comes out to about $1,720 a month, or $20,640 a year—and we haven't even taken out taxes yet or allowed for other incidental costs like furniture, household repairs, and entertainment. This amount is almost $6,000 *above* the official poverty line. And it might even be a somewhat conservative estimate: Others have calculated the minimum amount of money needed by a family of four to be closer to $22,000—50% higher than the current poverty line (Ruggles, 1990; J. E. Schwarz & Volgy, 1993).

You might think that with two working adults, earning $22,000 a year might not be so difficult. But at the current minimum wage, which is $4.25 an hour, two adults working full-time would make only $17,680. Obviously, minimum wage is not intended to bring a worker's income above the poverty line. The family that makes $17,000 or $18,000 a year is not officially considered poor but doesn't earn enough to adequately meet its expenses and provide a comfortable life for its members.

Life on the edge of poverty is precarious. Imagine being a poor single mother with a sick child. One trip to the doctor might cost an entire week's food budget or a month of rent. If you depend on a car to get to work and it breaks down, a few hundred dollars to fix it might mean not paying the electric bill that month and having less money for other necessities.

In sum, in addition to the 36.9 million officially poor Americans, there are a significant number of others whose income places them in the category of near-poor. That is, their incomes are too high to be officially poor, but so low that any slight drop—caused by the loss of a job, a serious illness, disability, or some other major unforeseen expense—would send them into poverty. The near-poor are a huge but largely unnoticed segment of the population. It has been estimated that about one-quarter of Americans hovering above the poverty line will fall below it at some point in their lives.

Although calls for a revision of the poverty line can be heard from economists and advocates for the poor, we must realize that there are institutional obstacles to doing so. Think of the implications of raising the poverty line and therefore dramatically increasing, by perhaps tens of millions, the number of officially poor people in this country. A sudden increase in the poverty rate not only would bring the obvious political costs to whatever administration happens to be in office, but would certainly bring on the demand for increased spending on social welfare programs, something few people in government are willing to consider given the ongoing public pressure to reduce government spending.

❀ The Consequences of Poverty

Poverty, of course, is more than just a phenomenon of income figures, statistical rates, and political liabilities. It is a predicament with immediate, sometimes life-threatening consequences. You've heard the old saying, "Money can't buy happiness." The implication is that true satisfaction in life is more than just a matter of having a lot of money. Yet such a saying provides little solace to those people who can't pay their bills, don't know where their next meal is coming from or if their job will exist tomorrow, suffer from ill health, or have no home. One of the most striking features of poverty in the United States is that it goes beyond simply not having enough money, to pervading every aspect of an individual's life. The entertainer Pearl Bailey perhaps summed it up best: "I've been rich and I've been poor. Rich is better."[7]

The Growing Problem of Homelessness

The most publicly visible consequence of poverty is homelessness. No one knows for sure exactly how many homeless people there are in the United States. Estimates range from 600,000 to 3 million. In the past homelessness was unseen and was confined mostly to skid-row areas of large cities or in hobo villages aside train tracks. The typical street person was an unemployed, alcoholic male over the age of 50. Today, however, only about one in five homeless people fits this stereotype. The rest are families, single parents, young adults, adolescents, or children (Siwek, 1992). In fact, entire families constitute 43% of the homeless population nationwide. In New York City these families make up 75% of all homeless people ("A growing percentage," 1993).

Furthermore, homeless people today aren't just found in skid-row sections of major cities. We see them in suburban parks, in train and bus stations, in abandoned buildings, and on the sidewalks of trendy neighborhoods. Shelters are available, but they are few and far between, overcrowded, and plagued by drugs, violence, and crime. In rural areas homelessness is just as prominent though much less visible. Here homeless people might sleep in sheds, barns, and cars or temporarily with family or friends (Fitchen, 1992a).

The Institutional Causes of Homelessness

In a national poll conducted in 1989, 82% of the respondents believed that homelessness was the fault of mental hospitals for releasing patients who couldn't lead normal lives. Drug and alcohol abuse was blamed by 90% of the sample (cited in A. B. Johnson, 1990). Certainly mentally ill and drug-addicted people are the most noticeable and disturbing of the homeless population; maybe that's why people are so quick to identify these factors as the prime causes of homelessness.

These results reflect a common but largely inaccurate perception about the nature of homelessness: that all homeless people are mentally ill. Such a belief is appealing because it suggests that individuals are responsible for their own fate and explains why an affluent society like ours cannot provide something so simple and basic as housing for all its citizens (A. B. Johnson, 1990). Further-more, if the homeless *are* all crazy, we have an obvious solution: Treat and cure their mental illness, and the problem of homelessness will go away.

But there is a great deal of evidence that the number of mentally ill homeless people has been grossly exaggerated (A. B. Johnson, 1990). Sociologist David Snow and his colleagues conducted a field study of homeless people in Austin, Texas, over a 20-month period (Snow et al., 1986). They found that, contrary to the commonly cited statistic that 50-90% of the homeless are mentally ill, the figure was actually closer to 15%. In addition, only 10% of the homeless in the study had any previous history of psychiatric hospitalization. The authors concluded that far from being mentally ill, homeless people were caught in low-paying, dead-end jobs without much hope of advancement. They were unable to build up enough money to cope with disasters like illness, fire, or eviction. When the money ran out, they were forced to leave their homes. Although some found less expensive housing, most could not.

The most obvious and important reason for homelessness, then, is an institutional one: the national decline in affordable housing (P. Rossi, 1988). During the 1980s most of the country's largest cities experienced massive reductions in low-income housing ranging from 12 to 58%. In the nation as a whole, half a million units of low-income housing are lost every year to condominium conversion, abandonment, arson, and demolition. In Boston between 1982 and 1984, over 80% of housing units that were renting for $300 or less disappeared, while those going for $600 or more doubled. Between 1981 and 1986 federal support for low-income housing dropped from $28 billion to $9 billion (Kozol, 1988).

Compounding the problem are zoning laws that prevent the construction of multifamily dwellings in "fashionable neighborhoods." Many residents in these neighborhoods fear a decrease in their property values should low-income residents move in. As one high school teacher in suburban Chicago put it, "People want to do something about [homelessness], but not if it's on their doorstep" (quoted in Oreskes & Toner, 1989).

Economic forces have also diminished the family's ability to absorb homeless relatives. Suppose you found out that a close family member had lost all his or her money and did not have a place to live. You probably would try to assist that person, either with financial help or even making room in your own home, right? In 1987, 2.6 million extremely poor adults aged 22 to 59 were living in their parents' homes; an additional 677,000 were living with siblings or grandparents (P. Rossi, 1988). But how would you feel if you had to pay that person's expenses or share a home with him or her for several years? Research shows that the average length of tolerance is about 4 years (P. Rossi, 1988); after that people tend to wear out their welcomes. Furthermore, as economic conditions force more families to slip into poverty or near-poverty themselves, fewer have the resources to support an additional member. Poverty not only undermines people's abilities to survive on their own but also makes it difficult for family members to help them.

Public Attitudes and Intolerance

A fair amount of evidence suggests that the public's tolerance of homelessness is wearing thin (Smolowe, 1993). What sympathy and benevolence there was during the seventies and eighties has seemingly given way to a tide of frustration and animosity as more and more cities impose harsher restrictions on homeless people in an effort to reduce their visibility and force them to go elsewhere (Wilkerson, 1991b).

In July of 1991, the city of Atlanta passed a law authorizing the arrest of anyone loitering in abandoned buildings, sleeping on park benches, or engaging in "aggressive panhandling." That same year the District of Columbia closed two emergency shelters and announced plans to eliminate half of the beds in the remaining shelters. Voters there repealed a 1984 law that required the city to shelter all people in need. In San Francisco, city planners "sleep-proof" benches (e.g., by nailing pieces of wood to the bench so people can't lie down) to discourage homeless people from sleeping in bus shelters (Smolowe, 1993). Santa Barbara, California, banned homeless people from sleeping on public streets, beaches, or sidewalks. This measure left the homeless with one place to sleep—a public lot surrounded by trees where they are kept out of sight of downtown businesses. Said the president of Santa Barbara's Chamber of Commerce:

> Our goal is to make things as uncomfortable for them as we can so they can move on. When you look at these characters sitting out in the middle of the day when everybody else is working just to survive, you don't get a lot of sympathy. (quoted in Wilkerson, 1991b, p. 10)

This sort of municipal intolerance is not universal. In 1993 a federal judge declared as unconstitutional the city of Miami's practice of arresting homeless people for "harmless, involuntary, life sustaining acts" in the city's streets and parks. The ruling prompted the city to impose a 1% tax on restaurant meals to finance programs for the homeless such as medical treatment, job training, low-cost housing, and temporary shelters (Rohter, 1993). It's estimated that the program will generate about $7.5 million in its first year.

But such policies are rare, and increasing citizen apathy and a decline in political concern have further contributed to the persistence of the problem. A *New York Times*/CBS News Poll in 1992 showed widespread indifference to the homeless despite the fact that increasing numbers of people have personally seen homeless people in their communities or on their way to work. Fifty-five percent of the respondents said that most people have become so used to seeing the homeless that they are no longer upset by the sight (Steinfels, 1992). Another survey found that 87% of the respondents felt that the unwillingness of homeless people to work was at least partly to blame for the problem of homelessness (see Table 11.1) (Oreskes & Toner, 1989).

The growing public intolerance and resentment of homelessness may be more the result of feelings of frustration and powerlessness than callousness.

Table 11.1   *Public Perceptions of the Causes of Homelessness*

	Amount of Effect on Homelessness		
	A lot	Some	Hardly any
Reason:			
Local government failing to take care of people in need	30%	52%	14%
Homeless people being unwilling to work	37%	50%	11%
Mental institutions releasing patients who aren't able to live normal lives	44%	38%	12%
The domestic policies of the federal government	24%	52%	18%
Alcohol and drug abuse by the homeless	50%	40%	7%

Source: Oreskes & Turner, 1989.

Such is the paradox of the sociological imagination. The frustration may indicate that some people are abandoning individualistic explanations of homelessness, talking instead about the root causes of poverty: lack of affordable housing and a changing economy that has all but eliminated entire classes of well-paying, low-skilled jobs. Yet such institutional causes are commonly seen as problems far beyond the reach of the individual citizen, who may be quite concerned about the problem but who feels a kind of "compassion fatigue" and hopelessness.

Health Issues

Related to homelessness and poverty is the problem of physical health. It's estimated that about 12% of the general population is in poor health. That figure rises to 32% for the poor and 44% for the homeless. Poor people, and in particular homeless people, are more likely to suffer from such medical problems as trauma, infection, chronic disease, and malnutrition (Siwek, 1992). In addition, poor people go to the hospital more often and stay longer than others. For families with incomes under $14,000 the hospitalization rate in 1989 was 131 per 1,000; for families with incomes over $50,000 the rate was 72 per 1,000; and the poorer group spent twice as many days in hospital as the affluent group (National Center for Health Statistics, cited in Colburn, 1992).

At the same time, the medical treatment received by poor people is generally worse than it is for others. About 30% of poor people have no medical insurance (U.S. Bureau of the Census, 1990b). A 1991 report by the Center for Health Policy Studies at Georgetown University found that hospital patients without medical insurance die at up to three times the rate of similar patients with insurance ("Uninsured hospital patients," 1991). Poor people also die younger. At age 25, women with incomes above $50,000 can expect to live 4 years longer than women with incomes below $5,000. For men, it is 10 years. Advances in medical technology that have increased life expectancy affect mainly the middle and upper classes, not the poor (Colburn, 1992; Pear, 1993b).

The infant mortality rate, an important indicator of the general health of a population, has also been increasing in this country, particularly among the poor. Among industrialized nations, the United States ranks 18th in infant mortality. Countries like Japan, Sweden, Great Britain, Finland, Spain, Singapore, and Hong Kong have significantly lower infant mortality rates. Some 700 babies who are born in the United States each day suffer from low birth weight, which is mainly due to the mother's poor health and a lack of prenatal care. Seventy-two of those babies will die before one month; 110 will die before their first birthday. Incidentally, our national infant mortality rate masks discrepancies between subpopulations. Nonwhite infants are twice as likely to die in the first year of life as white ones (J. L. Brown & Pizer, 1987). Some of the poorer areas of the United States show higher rates of infant mortality than less-developed countries like Cuba, Jamaica, Panama, and Costa Rica (J. L. Brown, 1987).

Hunger and Malnutrition

One of the crucial reasons why poverty adversely affects physical health is poor nutrition. There seems to be a clear link between income and the nutritional value of one's diet. The Agriculture Department has found that while the average weekly grocery budget rose slightly in middle- and upper-income households during the eighties, food spending fell 13.1% in the nation's poorest households (O'Neill, 1992). Poor people simply cannot afford the sorts of healthy foods available to more affluent individuals and therefore don't have the luxury of choosing food items that are nutritionally sound.

This society's heightened concern with diet over the past several years has only amplified the disparity between the rich and the poor. The more health concerns shape the country's most expensive cuisine and the higher the prices rise on "healthful" vegetables, pastas, fish, and other fat-reduced food products, the more healthful eating drifts beyond the reach of poor people (O'Neill, 1992).

Interestingly, throughout history the foods that characterized upper- and working-class lifestyles have completely reversed. Anthropologist Nan Rothschild (1990) studied excavations in New York City that helped reveal the way of life in the 18th century. She found that wealthy areas could be identified by the remains of heavy meat bones, while poorer neighborhoods were indicated by cheap vegetables and fish. By 1984, however, that pattern had completely reversed. Apparently, in contemporary society, the lighter the food one eats, the higher one's status. Because of poor grocery distribution in low-income neighborhoods, fresh fruits and vegetables in these neighborhoods are typically more expensive than those in suburban stores, driving healthy foods further beyond the reach of the poor.

Dietary concerns have become one of the great dividers between poor people and the rest of society. As one senior vice president for a market research firm in New York put it: "When I hear the words, 'I don't care if it's good for me or not,' I know that I am talking to somebody poor. Almost nobody above the poverty level says that anymore" (cited in O'Neill, 1992, p. C6).

Poverty not only affects the quality of food but the quantity as well. For the vast majority of Americans concerned with weighing *too much*, the reality of not having enough to eat is a distant one. When most of us hear the word *hunger* we are likely to conjure up images of famine-ravaged countries in sub-Saharan Africa or destitute villages in Latin America or Southeast Asia where naked, dusty children, stomachs bloated with the telltale signs of malnutrition, plead for scraps of food. In 1985, the United Nations World Food Council estimated that more than 500 million people worldwide were undernourished, despite the fact that annual food production is adequate to feed every person on earth. Every day more than 40,000 children throughout the world die from hunger-related causes (N. A. Lewis, 1988).

A common misconception we have about hunger is that there isn't enough food to feed people because of natural factors such as droughts and soil erosion. But the world food shortage is only partly caused by environmental conditions. Politics and economics play an even bigger role. Many developing countries, like India and Brazil, export huge amounts of food while millions of their people are starving or malnourished. In an attempt to modernize, they often spend a disproportionate amount of money on building up cities and industrializing their economies. As a result, farmers in rural areas aren't provided the incentives to grow as much food as they could. In some areas, civil wars and border disputes also take up a significant proportion of revenue that might otherwise go to domestic food production. Ethiopia, for instance, spends 42% of its budget on defense (Matthews, 1989). Corrupt governments and warring factions sometimes prevent food supplies from reaching the neediest people.

Whatever its cause, as long as the image of hunger remains a foreign one, we can continue to convince ourselves that it is a distant tragedy, one that we can comfortably address from afar with benefit concerts and charity events. But while the calamity of world hunger can never be understated, sooner or later we will be forced to acknowledge the magnitude of the problem in this country. No one can agree on the figures, but estimates on the hungry population in the United States range from 5 million to 30 million (Barringer, 1992).

The Psychological Impact of Poverty

Even if a poor person has a home to live in and doesn't suffer from ill health or hunger, the consequences of poverty can still be psychologically damaging. How do poor people adapt to a society that measures its members' worth in terms of occupational achievement and accumulated wealth? Feelings of self-worth tend to be based on one's ability to amass and consume material goods. According to Thorsten Veblen (1899/1953), the wealthy do not acquire wealth in order to consume goods conspicuously; rather, they consume goods in order to display their accumulation of wealth to others. Poor and working-class people are unable to indicate their social worth to others because by and large they have no goods to display. A special governmental task force on work in America once found that lower-class, blue-collar workers have

> an almost overwhelming sense of inferiority: the worker cannot talk proudly to his children about his job, and many workers feel they must apologize for their status. Thus the working-class home may be permeated with an atmosphere of failure—even of depressing self-degradation. (cited in Neubeck, 1986, p. 176)

Richard Sennett and Jonathan Cobb
The Hidden Injuries of Class

Sociologists Richard Sennett and Jonathan Cobb (1972) interviewed working-class men to examine the lives and conflicts of people near the bottom of the occupational scale. These men were employed and not officially poor. However, their economic situations were sufficiently insecure to create in them the sorts of identity conflicts experienced by many poor people. Listen to how one garbage collector defined his failures as being the result of his own inadequacies:

> Look, I know it's nobody's fault but mine that I got stuck here where I am, I mean . . . if I wasn't such a dumb———. . . no, it ain't that neither . . . if I'd applied myself, I know I got it in me to be different, can't say anyone did it to me. (p. 96)

To survive in this perceptual world of failure and self-blame, these people must somehow defend themselves and restore dignity and value to their lives. They begin to define their work as meaningless and irrelevant to their core identity and perceive it as a *sacrifice* they make for their families rather than a reflection of self-worth. Instead of focusing on the dreariness of their dead-end jobs or the insignificance of their work performance, working-class men come to view their work self-righteously as a noble act of sacrifice, thus providing an alternative source of esteem. The meaningless work *becomes* meaningful insofar as it is seen as a means to achieve a future goal for one's family. A bricklayer put it simply: "My job is to work for my family" (p. 135).

Defining a job as sacrifice solves the problem of powerlessness in several ways. First, in return for their sacrifice, working-class men can demand a position of power within their own families: "In exchange for my sacrifice, you will obey and respect me." Second, framing degrading work as sacrifice allows these men to slip the bonds of the present and orient their lives toward the future, something that gives them a sense of control they can't get through their jobs.

Ironically, framing work as sacrifice causes other hidden injuries. Most American parents want for their children what they themselves could not attain.

They are more than willing to work two or even three jobs, go without many of life's luxuries, and even forego medical care or insurance in order to give their children more. Even upper- and middle-class parents want to see the struggles of their adult lives redeemed through sacrifice for their children.

However, there are differences in the nature of the sacrifice between upper-class and working-class parents. The balancing act of working-class parents is much more treacherous. On the one hand, they want to spend time with the children and show concern for them. On the other hand, they know that the only way they can provide a "good home" for their family, which, in turn, will give their own lives greater meaning, is to work longer hours at an unfulfilling job and be absent from home more frequently. Unfortunately, from the perspective of the child, parental absence is precisely what constitutes a "bad home."

In addition, it is more difficult for working-class parents to sacrifice "successfully." Upper-class parents make sacrifices so that their children will have a life *like* theirs. Working-class parents sacrifice so that their children will *not* have a life like theirs. Their lives are not a "model" but a "warning." Hence the sacrifice does not end the conditions that made the parents prey to feelings of shame and inadequacy in the first place. The danger of this type of sacrifice is that if the children *do* fulfill the parents' wishes and rise above their quality of life, there is the possibility that the parents may become a "burden" to them.

The everyday experience of class goes well beyond financial stability or instability. People who struggle to make ends meet are caught in a vicious trap. Their work offers no glory or pride—as culturally defined—unless framed as future- and family-oriented sacrifice. But by making such sacrifices, other painful wounds are opened up, including resentment, hostility, and shame.

✳ Why Poverty Persists

Now that we have a sense of what poverty is and how it affects individuals, let's take a look at it from a more macro-sociological perspective. As I mentioned in the previous chapter, every society has a system of stratification, meaning that there will always be a group of people at the top and a group at the bottom. Even in the best of times, our prosperous country has had a sizable population of poor people. Why is that? On the surface this seems like a profoundly silly question. Everyone knows there is poverty because some people don't have enough money to sustain a stable standard of living.

The more sociologically relevant question is, Why is it that in such an affluent country, poverty for millions of people is a permanent fixture on the social landscape? To explain the persistence of poverty we must look at the structural role poverty plays in larger social institutions as well as the dominant cultural beliefs and attitudes that help to support it.

The Institutional Functions of Poverty

In chapter 10, I discussed the structural functionalist assertion that stratification and inequality are necessary because they ensure that the most qualified and valuable people in society will occupy the most prestigious and most highly rewarded positions. Social conditions exist and persist only if they are functional to society in some way. But functional for whom? If you were to survey people on the street and ask them if poverty was a good or bad thing, they would all, I'm sure, say "bad." No one is going to sing the virtues of poverty and its accompanying manifestations—hunger, homelessness, unemployment, and so on.

 Yet, according to sociologist Herbert Gans (1971), we must face the fact that within a free market economy and competitive society like ours, poverty plays a necessary *institutional* role. While functionalism has often been criticized for its propensity to justify the status quo, Gans combines it with conflict thinking to link poverty and class. To that end, he identifies several economic and social "functions" played by poverty that benefit all other classes in this society.

Economic Functions

Economically, the existence of poverty benefits the rest of society in a variety of ways. There is no question that our economic system *depends* on a large poor population. First, poverty provides a ready pool of low-wage laborers who are available to do society's "dirty work." Poor people will work at low wages primarily because they have little choice. They will do the dangerous, undignified, or menial jobs that others won't do but that are necessary to keep businesses running, such as housekeeping, hospital cleaning, garbage collection, and manual labor. When large numbers of poor people compete for scarce jobs, business owners have the luxury of paying low wages.

Poverty also creates occupations and services that either serve the poor or protect the rest of society from them: police officers, penologists, social workers, lawyers, pawnshop owners, and so on. Drug dealers and loan sharks depend on the presence of a large population of poor people willing to utilize their services.

On an organizational level, the welfare system supports a vast network of private sector businesses that make enormous profits by providing the system with a wide range of goods and services. When you hear people use the term *welfare dependency*, they are probably referring to the alleged long-term reliance of some welfare recipients on programs like Aid to Families With Dependent Children or food stamps. But we can also talk about people or organizations whose livelihood depends on the existence of a vast welfare system.

For instance, everyone who works in the system needs to have an office or clinic space in which to work, as well as supplies, equipment, and furnishings. Bankers, real estate developers, office system suppliers, computer manufacturers, and the construction and building industries profit each time a new welfare office, mental hospital, jail, unemployment office or public housing project for the poor is needed (Bedard, 1991). Some government assistance programs provide things to poor people that must be purchased from private industry. For instance, approximately one-third of all the infant formula manufactured in this country is purchased by the U.S. Department of Agriculture for its Women, Infant, and Child (WIC) nutrition program. In 1988, this amounted to half a billion dollars' worth of sales for the infant formula industry (Novac, 1988).

Another economic function of poverty is that poor people purchase goods and services that would otherwise go unused: secondhand goods, day-old bread, fruits, and vegetables, deteriorated housing, dilapidated cars, incompetent physicians, and so forth. Consider the following example of a company benefiting from its ability to sell a faulty product to the poor:

> At regular intervals, pineapple juice canneries must clean out the pipes that carry the juice from the crushing to the canning rooms. To do this, a salt solution is forced through the pipes and then flushed out before the new canning process starts again. A few years ago, one large cannery went through this cleaning operation and began running juice again before it was discovered that the pipes had not been totally purged of the salt solution. But, by that time, thousands of gallons of pineapple juice, all of it slightly salty, had already been processed and canned.
>
> The cans were sold, unlabeled, at a very low price to a food distributor who specializes in handling off-brand and reject merchandise for sale in poor neighborhoods and communities. The distributor put labels on the cans and retailed them for about half the usual price for that size, making a very good profit for himself. Across the label was printed "No Sweetener Added," certainly an accurate statement of the juice's condition (Jacobs, 1988, pp. 123-124).

Clearly, this merchandise would have had little or no monetary value outside the poverty market.

Social Functions

The poor also serve several less obvious social functions. They act as a visible reminder to the rest of society of the "legitimacy" of the conventional values of hard work, thrift, and honesty. Although the poor are just as moral and law abiding as anyone else, they are more likely to get caught and punished when they participate in deviant acts (Reiman, 1990). They lack the political and cultural power to correct the stereotypes others have of them as being lazy, dishonest, or promiscuous. As a result, they provide "living proof" that moral deviance does not pay.

Furthermore, poverty guarantees the status of those who are not poor. The poor provide a reference point against which others can compare themselves. Charity events allow upper- and middle-class people to symbolically demonstrate their concern and philanthropy and reinforce their feelings of moral superiority. Finally, the poor provide the manual labor that enables societies to produce many impressive achievements, from railroads to national parks.

It's easy to dismiss the functionalist explanation of poverty as cold and heartless. We certainly don't want to admit that poor people and the welfare system allow the rest of us the opportunity to live comfortable and pleasant lifestyles. Yet this explanation is quite compelling. Just as society needs talented people to fill its important occupational positions, it also needs a stable population of poor people to fill its "less important" positions. After all, *someone* needs to clean toilets or work the night shift at McDonald's. What would society be like if there was full equality? Who would do the dirty work?

If we are truly serious about getting rid of poverty, we must find alternative ways of performing the functions it currently fulfills. This will assuredly come at a cost to those of us who are now able to take advantage of its presence. Poverty will be eliminated only when it becomes *dys*functional for people who aren't poor.

The Ideology of Competitive Individualism

Poverty also exists because of cultural beliefs and values that support the economic status quo. An important component of this value system is the belief in competitive individualism (Feagin, 1975; M. Lewis, 1978; Neubeck, 1986).

As children, most of us are taught by our families and schools that nobody deserves a free ride. The way to be successful is to work hard, have a willingness to strive for goals, and compete well against others. Those who work hard should be rewarded with success. In this way we are fully responsible for our own economic fates. Stories of people like Abraham Lincoln and Henry Ford reinforce the notion that anybody can be successful if he or she simply has the desire and puts in the necessary effort.

The belief in competitive individualism is fostered by the economic socialization children receive in school. Sociologists Scott Cummings and Del Taebel (1978) surveyed children from grades 3 through 12 to see how they learned about economic life and stratification in this country. They found that early on young people begin to articulate the idea that private ownership and individual productivity are necessary components of a smooth-flowing economy. As one ninth grader put it:

> People that own their own businesses will work harder because they want to make more money; if no one can own anything they aren't going to work so hard and so nobody will make much money and then the economy falls apart. (Cummings & Taebel, 1978, p. 205)

Cummings and Taebel discovered that while younger children enthusiastically support the idea that the government ought to do more to help poor people, by the 12th grade many of them have come to hold the individual responsible for his or her own economic destiny. Character flaws and motivational deficiencies are often seen as the causes of poverty and economic insecurity. You can see how their responses clearly support the belief of competitive individualism:

People are rich because they have the know-how and the opportunity, and to an extent most of them are wealthy because of some type of motivation that causes them not to settle at one step or one degree; they wanted to reach higher heights. . . . People are poor because they are not educated enough to know that there is something for them out there; that they can make money. . . . They are ignorant and uneducated; a lot of them just don't care . . . they're happy the way they are . . . if you really want to have some money, you can get it no matter how poor you have been. (Cummings & Taebel, 1978, p. 207)

This shows the dark side of competitive individualism. In a truly fair competition there will always be people who win and people who lose. And so it follows that economic success is due completely to individual effort and competitive abilities. When we internalize the belief in competitive individualism, we are also adopting an explanation of why rewards are distributed unequally and why there is poverty. If people who are financially successful deserve to be there because of their individual hard work and desire, then the people who fail and are suffering financially must equally deserve their plight due to a *lack* of hard work and desire.

Such a belief system doesn't take into consideration that the competition itself is perhaps not fair. Opportunities to learn a trade, skill, or profession are assumed to be available to everyone. Every person is supposed to have the chance to "be all that he or she can be." As we saw in chapter 10, however, the system may be rigged to favor those who already have power and wealth.

Competitive individualism allows us not only to explain inequality but also to maintain our belief that the world is a fair and just place (Lerner, 1970). We have an intense need to believe that we live in a world where good things happen to good people and bad things happen to bad people. People will get what they deserve: If you work hard, good things will happen to you. When used to explain poverty, this future-oriented belief often gives way to a past-oriented belief that people deserve what they get. If a poor person is suffering, he or she *must have done something* to deserve it, and that "something" is either a lack of ability, a defective trait, or a lack of desire to succeed. People get unequal rewards because some are born smarter, stay in school longer, or work harder.

The belief in competitive individualism gives people the sense that they can control their own fate. Furthermore, people will tolerate a system of tremendous inequality if they are able to convince themselves that the inequality is just and fair, that those who are suffering deserve their fate (J. Huber & Form, 1973). Because we are all supposedly created equal, no one should be inhibited from exercising his or her ambitions to the fullest extent (M. Lewis, 1978). Individual opportunity is the presumed birthright of every American. So while grudgingly acknowledging the existence of unequal outcomes, Americans can justify the situation by emphasizing equal *chances*. To take or not to take advantage of these chances is up to the individual. In this way the cultural ideology of poverty both explains and justifies the system of stratification. That people tend to focus on the individual traits of poor people ignores the impact of social structure on personal achievement and mobility.

Joan Huber and William Form
Why the Rich Are Rich and the Poor Are Poor

The ideology of competitive individualism is not equally accepted by all Americans, according to sociologists Joan Huber and William Form (1973). Wealthy and middle-class individuals see themselves as deserving of their status. They are likely to explain their wealth and poverty in individualistic terms such as personal characteristics like ability, thrift, or effort. The poor, however, are more likely to emphasize structural forces in their lives, such as the failure of private industry to provide sufficient jobs or the failure of society to provide adequate schooling (see also Feagin, 1975). In other words, the belief in competitive individualism should be most attractive to those receiving the highest rewards from the stratification system.

To test their hypothesis, Huber and Form interviewed 107 poor, 200 middle income, and 47 rich individuals in Michigan. They bluntly asked their subjects, "Why are rich people rich and why are poor people poor?" They found that about twice as many rich people as poor people cited personal attributes as the cause of both wealth and poverty. Here is a response typical of those offered by the wealthy subjects:

> If you have to generalize, it's the self-discipline to accumulate capital and later to use that capital effectively and intelligently to make income and wealth. The poor? I don't think the average person on the lower economic scale wants to assume the responsibilities and obligations necessary to become rich. He doesn't want to be bothered. . . . The rich acquire wealth by their own effort. The poor lack the ability to rise above their class situation. There's no lack of opportunity but lack of ability. (p. 102)

Compare this response to one made by a poor subject in the study:

> The rich stepped on other people's toes to acquire what they got or they were born with it. The poor? It was handed down through the family. . . . They lacked opportunity. (p. 103)

Higher-income respondents were also more likely to think that poor people don't work as hard as rich people and to believe that a lack of motivation accounted for their lack of success. The great majority of poor people felt that they worked just as hard as anybody else even though their rewards have been low. They tended to think that the opportunity structure in society prevented them from becoming successful. Such perceptions have enormously important implications for governmental policy. If those in power tend to believe that poor people lack motivation, then poverty programs will focus on reducing people's dependence on government subsidies and not on reducing poverty itself (Morris & Williamson, 1987).

The Culture of Poverty

If it is true that poor people perceive the causes of poverty very differently from those who are better off, can we then say that poor people have their own belief system—a unique "culture"—that influences their lives and persists over generations? A variation of the belief in competitive individualism is the argument that the poor as a group possess beliefs, norms, values, and goals that are significantly different from the rest of society and that perpetuate a particular lifestyle and keep them poor.

Oscar Lewis (1968), the chief proponent of this **culture of poverty** thesis, maintains that poor people, resigned to their position in society, develop a unique value structure to deal with the improbability that they will become successful in terms of the values and goals of the larger society. This culture is at odds with the dominant middle-class culture because it downplays the importance of self-discipline and hard work. While it may keep people trapped in what appears (to the outside observer) to be an intolerable life, it nevertheless provides its own pleasures. Street life in the ghetto is exhilarating compared to a world where jobs are dull, arduous, and difficult to obtain and hold (P. Peterson, 1991). It is more fun to hang out, tell exaggerated stories, and exhibit one's latest purchases and conquests than it is to work and struggle in the "conventional" world. It is this extreme "present-orientedness"—the inability to live for the future (Banfield, 1970)—and not the lack of income or wealth that is the principal cause of poverty. The culture of poverty is an adaptation and reaction of the poor to their position in a stratified society (O. Lewis, 1968).

Once the culture of poverty comes into existence, it perpetuates itself. This way of life is remarkably persistent: You can take the child out of the ghetto, but you can't take the ghetto out of the child. Furthermore, it is passed down from generation to generation. By age six or seven, most children have absorbed the basic values and attitudes of their subculture, rendering them unable to take advantage of any opportunities that may present themselves later in life. Others have argued that a poor family that has had a history of welfare dependence will tend to bear children who lack ambition, a solid work-ethic, and self-reliance (Auletta, 1982).

It would seem that to generate a persistent culture of poverty, there must be a large group of *permanently poor* in this society. Government statistics show that this isn't the case. Only a little over half of the individuals living in poverty in a given year are found to be poor the next, and considerably less than one half remain poor over many years (Duncan, 1984; Sherraden, 1988). Between 1969 and 1978, only 2.6% of poor people were "persistently" poor, meaning they were in poverty for 8 years or more, and only 0.7% were poor for the entire period (Duncan, 1984). In short, people tend to move in and out of poverty, making it difficult to sustain a single, long-standing, poverty-based lifestyle and value system.

Contrary to popular belief, not all poor people are on welfare. In 1990 only about 42% of persons below the poverty level received cash assistance like Aid to Families With Dependent Children, and about 49% received food stamps (U.S. Bureau of the Census, 1990b). Most people are only welfare dependent for about 2 years at a time (Bedard, 1991). As in poverty, there is a great deal of movement in and out of welfare, making it difficult to sustain a tradition of dependence across generations.

Critics of the culture of poverty approach also contend that the behavior of poor people is largely due to institutional impediments such as a tradition of racial or ethnic prejudice and discrimination, residential segregation, limited economic opportunities, and occupational obstacles against advancement (Wilson, 1980). Any cultural values that exist must emerge from specific social and historical circumstances that reflect one's class, race, and ethnicity. Consider poverty among racial minorities. In a racially stratified society, the economic class position of individual minorities is heavily influenced by their racial history. The African-American experience, for example, still bears the mark of slavery and Jim Crow laws.

Despite the lack of supportive evidence, the culture of poverty explanation remains popular. Many people strongly believe that the poor live by a different set of moral standards and therefore will remain in poverty. Like competitive individualism, this ideology protects the nonpoor, the larger social structure, and the economic system from blame. Today, the argument that hard work is the tried and true way from poverty to wealth dominates much of the debate over poverty and government assistance. Many feel our welfare system makes the problem worse by breeding a cycle of dependency. After all, if poverty *is* a "way of life," then some sort of massive redistribution of wealth that would give poor people enough money to raise them out of poverty is not the answer; changing their troublesome culture is. Says one sociologist sarcastically, "By liquidating the lower-class culture we can liquidate the lower class, and, thereby, bring an end to poverty" (Ryan, 1976, p. 123).

The Clinton administration has proposed that the way to end poverty is to replace the current welfare system with a system of "workfare." The idea is to force welfare recipients to work by placing a 2-year limitation on public assistance and by making schooling, job search, and training programs mandatory. In 1992 New Jersey enacted welfare reform that denies additional benefits to mothers for any children born after the mothers are already on welfare. It also eliminates benefits for able-bodied recipients whose youngest children are older than 2 and who refuse to work or take part in a job-training program. The clear assumption underlying these reform measures is that the behavior of poor people is the source of the problem and therefore should, in the interests of society, be modified.

An Institutional View of Poverty

The overarching goal of welfare reform is a good one: to reduce poverty. And where "workfare" programs are being tested—in California, for instance—they are showing moderately encouraging results in making some individuals less reliant on government assistance (Passell, 1993). From a sociological perspective, however, these programs overlook important institutional factors that may in the long run make them ineffective. As long as we affix the blame for poverty on the poor people themselves—their aberrant subcultural values, reproductive habits, and lack of effort, skill, and intelligence—the structural causes of poverty will remain unchallenged and unchanged.

Work and Occupational Structure

We need to consider the overall structure of occupations in this country. The United States has what is called a **segmented labor market,** meaning that the economy is divided into two job sectors that have different characteristics and payoffs (D. M. Gordon, Edwards, & Reich, 1982). The primary sector includes large bureaucratic organizations with relatively stable production and sales. Jobs in this category require high-level skills, are highly paid, provide good benefits, and have good working conditions. Within this sector there are both upper-tier jobs (high-status professionals and managers) and lower-tier jobs (such as white-collar clerical and blue-collar skilled workers). These lower-tier jobs tend to be rather monotonous and mobility is limited. But because they are likely to be unionized, they still tend to be relatively secure.

The secondary sector is composed of marginal firms where product demand is unstable. The welfare of these companies springs directly from the well-being of primary companies (Braun, 1991). As a result, the jobs here, which include low-level clerical and unskilled blue-collar occupations, have considerably lower pay, far less job security, poorer working conditions, and fewer prospects for advancement. The secondary sector is particularly vulnerable to business slowdowns and technological changes that can lead to abrupt and widespread unemployment. For instance, many of the factory jobs that most Americans in the past could reasonably expect to get even if they weren't well educated or well trained are disappearing as companies automate, move their facilities elsewhere, or simply go out of business. As the economic system expands and contracts, so does unemployment, particularly in the secondary sector. In the process these business cycles produce and maintain poverty.

Unemployment is the key element in all of this. As with official definitions of poverty, the official definition of "unemployed" also underestimates the magnitude of the problem. According to the Bureau of Labor Statistics, in order to be officially considered unemployed you must be out of work, must be available for work, and must have actively sought work in the past 4 weeks (Herbert, 1993).

On average, somewhere between 8 million and 9 million people fall into this category.

But this figure doesn't account for the millions of "discouraged" workers who want a good job but have become so disheartened that they've stopped looking. In addition, there are some 30 million people—over a quarter of the U.S. labor force—who are employed in part-time or temporary jobs. A substantial proportion of them would prefer permanent full-time jobs but cannot find them. These workers are six times more likely than full-time workers to receive minimum wage and much less likely to receive health and pension benefits (Cloward & Piven, 1993). And what about the large, unmeasurable group of "underemployed" who are working in jobs for which they are overqualified, like college graduates and other professionals who deliver pizza or drive cabs to make ends meet?

There is little reason to think that a substantial number of unemployed poor people, who might be on welfare and who probably have few marketable skills, can become self-sufficient when growing millions of currently employed people cannot. When the labor market is saturated with people either looking for work or seeking to improve their employment situation, and when the only jobs that are available are low-paying ones, mandatory job-training programs and limitations on benefits will not be very effective in reducing dependence on welfare (Cloward & Piven, 1993). One study found that none of these programs succeed in raising earnings more than $2,000 above what recipients receive in welfare payments. Only a handful of people in welfare-to-work programs achieve a stable source of income and job-related benefits that adequately cover medical expenses. Not surprisingly, a substantial number of people who find jobs end up reapplying for welfare because they cannot survive on their earnings (Cloward & Piven, 1993).

The American occupational structure has an impact on communities as well. Where jobs are scarce and prospects for industrial development are low, pockets of poverty will exist. For instance, it is doubtful that a corporation will open a manufacturing facility in a run-down area of a large city that has a high crime rate. The movement of manufacturing jobs out of the inner city and to the suburbs or overseas leaves residents isolated and without any realistic prospects for work (Wilson, 1987).

Most people in the inner city don't have the resources to live in the areas where the jobs are, so those who want to work must find a way to get there. If public transportation is unavailable, the cost of purchasing and operating a car might be too much (Kasarda, 1989). Ironically, the stability of the inner city is further undermined when those people who *do* have job skills and who can serve as positive role models—teachers, professionals, merchants, and the like—move out of the neighborhood and into areas where the jobs are located. The urban poor become isolated from the rest of society economically, socially, and geographically.

In rural areas, because of the loss and downsizing of manu... tend to be low-paid, part-time, and temporary. What makes i... is that poor people from urban areas, squeezed out by high rents... end up in rural towns where the subsequent competition for a sh... of jobs becomes even tighter. Also, the housing market is worse... Approximately 42% of the rural poor currently spend more tha... income on housing (Fitchen, 1992b).

In sum, the institutional structure of employment in the United States has had a dramatic impact on poverty. Millions of good jobs no longer exist, and the ones that remain offer little security. You can see how broad economic processes that no single individual or group caused or controls significantly affect the livelihood of American workers and thereby perpetuates poverty (Granovetter & Tilly, 1988). The problems are not likely to disappear without major changes in the American occupational structure and the nature of jobs that are created in the future.

Education

In a society where status is usually based on credentials, chances of success in life are strongly determined by educational attainment (Jencks et al., 1979). You are probably taking this class and reading this book because you assume that getting a college education is a prerequisite for having a successful career. But although education is necessary for all of us to get ahead, it is not equally available to all segments of the population.

As addressed in chapter 10, the probability of getting a good education is closely tied to family and class background. In poor neighborhoods, where children seldom have the opportunity to interact with people in middle-class, professional jobs, they have little understanding of the relationship between schooling and career success (Wilson, 1987). Poverty also adversely affects the development of linguistic, educational, and job-related skills necessary for the world of work in the mainstream economy. Teachers become frustrated and do not teach; children become cynical and do not learn. Children from the lowest 10% in socioeconomic status are only one-twelfth as likely to complete college as the highest 10%, averaging about 5 fewer years of education (Bowles & Gintis, 1976).

In the Chicago school system, of the 39,500 students who enrolled in the ninth grade in 1980, only 18,500 (or 47%) graduated 4 years later; of these, only about 6,000 (15%) were capable of reading at or above the national 12th-grade level. Of the 25,000 African-American and Hispanic students who were enrolled in these segregated, nonselective schools, only 2,000 (or 8%) both completed high school and could read at or above a level considered average for the rest of the country (Wilson, 1987).

Like elite private schools, poor public schools serve to legitimate inequality. For many people, the worst schools can produce feelings of powerlessness that continue throughout their lives (Bowles & Gintis, 1976). Discipline and hierarchy, two crucial requirements for a free market economy, are taught early on in the education system. Poor children's prior socialization—their manner of speech, dress, and action—do not fit with those of the teacher and the school administration at large, and so they are subtly made to feel inadequate. The "successful" students in these schools are the ones who learn to submit to authority. Instead of developing as competent, hopeful members of society, many poor young people become resigned to their fate.

The educational deck clearly seems to be stacked against poor people. With very few exceptions, the quality of elementary and high school education for the poor is inferior to the quality of education available to children in the middle and upper classes. Even if they graduate from high school, most poor children cannot afford to attend college. Those who do are more likely to attend community colleges or state universities that lack the quality and prestige of their more expensive counterparts (A. M. Cohen & Brawer, 1982).

When we look at the institutional causes of poverty, we see that the personality or "cultural" traits often associated with poverty—low ambition, not subscribing to the ethic of hard work, inability to plan for the future—might be better understood as *consequences* of poverty rather than causes of it. As long as the structural obstacles to stable employment, adequate wages, and a decent education continue to exist, so will the characteristic hopelessness associated with poverty.

Conclusion

This chapter has examined the dark side of the American Dream. In a society presumably founded on the assumption of equality, we have seen that powerlessness, degradation, and disadvantage are common elements of everyday life for millions of people. It's rather shocking that in a country as wealthy as this one, a comfortable and stable life is well beyond the reach of tens of millions of people. The constant images we see of wealth and power remind poor, working-class, and, for that matter, downwardly mobile middle-class people that they are outsiders who can only watch and long to be part of that golden world (Sidel, 1986).

Culture and social institutions justify and perpetuate social inequality, but there is also the personal side. We speak of the poor as if they are an unchanging and faceless group to be pitied, despised, or feared. To talk of "the poverty problem" is to talk about some depersonalized, permanent fixture on the American landscape. But poverty is people. It's people standing in soup kitchen lines and welfare lines. It's people living in rat-infested projects. It's people sleeping on sidewalks. It's people struggling to acquire things the rest of society takes for granted. It's people coming up short in their quest for the American Dream.

For those of us fortunate enough never to have been hungry or homeless or on welfare, these are easy issues to ignore. When we cross the street to avoid coming face-to-face with a "street person," we are engaging in a futile attempt to return the problem of poverty to its once comfortable home of concealment. As long as poverty remains invisible, it remains someone else's problem. As long as poverty is seen as the "fault" of poor people, it remains someone else's responsibility. And as long as it remains someone else's problem and someone else's responsibility, it becomes virtually impossible to ignite the kind of public compassion necessary to solve it.

CHAPTER HIGHLIGHTS

■ The face of American poverty has changed somewhat over the last several decades. Single mothers and their children have seen their economic status deteriorate while that of people over age 65 has improved somewhat.

■ The official poverty line, the dollar cutoff point that defines the amount of income necessary to provide minimal subsistence living, may actually be set too low, thereby underestimating the proportion of the population that is suffering financially.

■ Poverty persists because in a free market and competitive society it serves economic and social functions. In addition, the ideology of competitive individualism—that to succeed in life all one has to do is work hard and win in competition with others—creates a belief that poor people are to blame for their own suffering. Finally, poverty receives institutional "support" in the form of segmented labor markets and inadequate educational systems.

■ Traits commonly associated with poor people—low ambition, failure to subscribe to the ethic of hard work, inability to plan for the future, and so on—might be better understood as the consequences of poverty rather than the causes of it.

YOUR TURN

Economic stress is no longer a way of life only for people who fall under the official poverty line. Even people whose income is well above the poverty line find that their ability to make ends meet has been steadily deteriorating.

Imagine a family of four living in your hometown. Suppose that both parents work, one child is 7 years old and in elementary school, the other is 3 and must be cared for during the day.

Make a list of all the goods and services this family will need to function at *a minimum subsistence level*—that is, the poverty line. Be as complete as possible. Consider food, clothing, housing, transportation, medical care, child care, entertainment, and so on.

Estimate the minimum monthly cost of each item. If you currently live on your own and must pay these expenses yourself, use those figures as a starting point (but remember this is for a family of four). If you live in a dorm or at home, ask your parents (or anyone else who pays bills) what their expenses are for such goods and services. Call the local day care center to see what they charge for child care. Go to the local supermarket and compute the family food budget. For those expenses that aren't divided on a monthly basis (e.g., clothing, household appliances), estimate the yearly cost and divide by 12.

Once you have estimated the total monthly expenses, multiply by 12 to get the family of four's subsistence budget. If your estimate is higher than the government's official poverty line (around $14,763), what sorts of items could you cut out of the budget for the family to be defined as officially poor and therefore eligible for certain governmental programs? By cutting expenses from your minimal subsistence budget you will get a good sense of what poverty is like.

Describe the quality of life of this hypothetical family that makes too much to be officially poor and too little to sustain a comfortable life. What sorts of things are they forced to do without that a more affluent family might simply take for granted (e.g., annual vacations, a second car, eating out once a week)? What would be the impact of poverty on the lives of the children? How will the family's difficulty in meeting its basic subsistence needs translate into access to opportunities (education, jobs, health, etc.) for the children later in life?

[NOTE: This exercise is adapted from M. V. Miller, "Poverty and its definition," in R. C. Barnes & E. W. Mills, Techniques for Teaching Sociological Concepts, Washington, DC: American Sociological Association, 1985.]

CHAPTER 12

The Architecture of Race
Racial and Ethnic Inequality

On the night of October 15, 1992, something important happened in this country that went largely unnoticed. And the fact that no one noticed it—or at least that no one commented on it publicly—is more remarkable than the event itself.

That night millions of Americans huddled in front of their television sets to watch a political debate between the three major candidates for the office of President of the United States. George Bush, Bill Clinton, and Ross Perot stood center stage, waiting for the moderator to begin the proceedings. The debate itself was not the remarkable event. What *was* remarkable was the identity of the moderator. ABC correspondent Carole Simpson, an African-American woman, was controlling an event that would help determine the election of one of these men to the highest office in the land.

If you had told an abolitionist in the 1860s or even a civil rights worker in the 1960s that someday an African-American woman would be the moderator at a national political event of this magnitude, he or she might have laughed in your face. Even 10 or 15 years ago it probably would have been inconceivable. But there she was, firing questions, interrupting candidates, and effectively running the show. She wasn't "black news correspondent Carole Simpson," she was just "news correspondent Carole Simpson."

It made me think about the tremendous gains that African Americans and other racial groups have made economically and educationally over the past decades. The number of middle- and upper-class African Americans, Asian Americans, and Hispanics has increased significantly. Some of today's highest paid entertainers and athletes are African American. An African American sits on the Supreme Court. An African American has served as the head of the Joint Chiefs of Staff, the highest military official in the country. There are more Hispanics and Native Americans in elected offices than ever before. Asian Americans have achieved tremendous economic and educational success.

Yet as I watched Simpson that night, my mind kept pulling me back to a different reality. Despite progress, blacks, Hispanics, and Native Americans remain the poorest and most disadvantaged of all groups in this country. Almost half of all black babies are born into poverty, compared to fewer than one in eight white babies (Edelman, 1988; Morganthau, 1992). Only about half of all Hispanic students complete high school and one-quarter of all Hispanic families have zero net wealth (Blackwell, 1990).

I thought of specific events that also belied the image of racial progress. There were, of course, the 2 days of riots in Los Angeles in the spring of 1992 and the accompanying violence that erupted in neighborhoods all over the country.

I thought of the 16-year-old African-American boy who went into the all-white Bensonhurst section of Brooklyn in 1989 to inspect a car for sale there and ended up being beaten to death by a pack of white youths.

I thought of many college campuses that in the past few years have experienced a flurry of incidents stemming from long-dormant racial hatred. In the fall of 1990, 10 black law students at Yale University received anonymous "nigger" notes in their dormitory mailboxes after a reported rape. At the University of Connecticut, a group of white students taunted and spit at Asian-American students who were on their way to a dance. At Olivet College, a small, quiet campus in rural Michigan, a racial brawl ensued following a rash of rumors about black men and white women. Students at the University of Wisconsin held a mock slave auction.

How far have we really come? Which is the real United States? Is it the one that Martin Luther King, Jr., dreamed about in 1963, a place where race, religion, and ethnicity were losing their status as major criteria for judging the content of one's character? Or is it the one perpetually torn apart by economic inequality, prejudice, and hatred?

In the previous two chapters I examined America's class stratification system. But social class isn't the only thing that influences social status and life chances. Chapter 12 focuses on another important determinant of social inequality: race and ethnicity.

Through the Years: Stories of Oppression and Inequality

Conflict over racial and ethnic identity is a worldwide issue that won't go away. It seems as though hostility of one group for another is among the most universal of human feelings (Schlesinger, 1992). Even today, when people from every corner of the globe are linked technologically, economically, and ecologically and mass migrations mix people from different races, religions, and cultures in unprecedented numbers, racial and ethnic hostilities are at an all-time high (Barber, 1992).

Look at the front page of the newspaper and you will see stories of conflict and violence between blacks and whites in South Africa, Jews and Palestinians in Israel, Serbs and Muslims in Bosnia, English-speaking Canadians and French-speaking Canadians in Quebec, Tamils and Sinhalese in Sri Lanka, Azerbaijanis and Armenians in the former Soviet Union, and Chinese and Malays in Malaysia. In Romania and Hungary, Gypsies are openly despised. Some Romanians and Hungarians even favor their mass extermination, stereotyping them as lazy, unclean, dishonest, and criminal (Kamm, 1993). In Great Britain, France, and Germany, loud and sometimes violent resentment is directed toward immigrants from Africa, Eastern Europe, and Asia. Racial and ethnic hatred around the world has cost the lives of literally millions of people. In 1991 alone there were more than 30 wars in progress, most of them ethnic, racial, tribal, or religious in character (Barber, 1992).

Our own racial and ethnic tensions might seem rather tame in comparison. In general, Americans of different racial and ethnic backgrounds get along with one another pretty well. Yet racial and ethnic problems have been and continue to be divisive and destructive. They have been a defining feature of the American social landscape from the very beginning.

In 1835 the French scholar Alexis de Tocqueville (1835/1969) wrote that racial conflict perpetually haunts the American imagination. More than a century later, Gunnar Myrdal, the Swedish economist, saw that America's racial problems were a severe threat to our collective definition as a people. He observed that despite the "American Creed"—our stated values of liberty and equality—white Americans could not treat other racial groups as their equals (Myrdal, 1944). Even as the 20th century winds down, we still can't seem to decide the place that racial and ethnic diversity ought to have in our society. To understand race relations in American social life today, we must learn about the historical background of the groups that have experienced oppression.

A glance at the history of America reveals that our story is not just one of freedom, justice, and equality, but one of conquest, discrimination, and exclusion. Racial and ethnic inequality has manifested itself in such phenomena as slavery, the seizure of vast tracts of land from Native Americans and Mexicans, Jim Crow laws, the exclusion of Chinese and Japanese workers in the 19th century, widespread economic, educational, and political deprivation, the violent and nonviolent protests of the civil rights movement, and hate crimes in the late 20th century. Along the way it has affected people's access to the basic necessities of life, including housing, health care, family stability, and occupations. For some racial inequality has served as a rallying cry and a source of solidarity for the oppressed; for others it has served as a justification for that very oppression.

Every racial or ethnic minority has its own story of persecution. When they first arrived in significant numbers in the United States, white European immigrants—Irish, Italians, Poles, Jews, Greeks—were all objects of varying degrees of hatred, suspicion, and discrimination. Jews, for instance, were refused admission to many American universities until the middle of the 20th century. The National Origins Act of 1924 placed restrictions on immigration from southern Europe—mainly Greece and Italy—up until the 1960s. Newspaper want ads from the 19th century routinely carried the message "No Irish need apply."

Because these groups were the same race as the dominant white Protestants, however, they were able eventually to overcome most of these obstacles and gain entry into mainstream society. But for people of color, namely Native Americans, Hispanics, African Americans, and Asian Americans, racial equality and destigmatization have been more difficult to achieve.

Native Americans

The story of Native Americans has been one of racially inspired massacres, the takeover of their ancestral lands, confinement on white-run reservations, and unending governmental manipulation. Successive waves of westward expansion in the 18th and 19th centuries pushed them off any land white settlers considered desirable. Native Americans "started off with everything and have gradually lost much of what they had to an advancing alien civilization" (U.S. Commission on Civil Rights, 1992). Furthermore, a commonly held European belief that Native Americans were "savages" who should be displaced to make way for white civilization provided the ideological justification for conquering them.

Despite their history of severe oppression, though, Native Americans have shown a remarkable ability to endure and in some cases promote their own economic interests. In the Pacific Northwest, for instance, some Indian tribes have been successful in protecting their rights to lucrative fishing waters (F. G. Cohen, 1986). Elsewhere, organizations have been formed to advance the financial concerns of Native Americans in industries like gas, oil, and coal where substantial reserves exist on Indian land (Snipp, 1986).

Hispanic Americans

The history of Hispanics, particularly Mexican Americans, has also been one marked by hostility and oppression. When the United States expanded into the southwest, it was into areas that had already been settled by Mexicans. After a war that lasted from 1846 to 1848, Mexico lost half of its national territory, including what is now Arizona, California, Colorado, New Mexico, Texas, Nevada, and Utah, as well as parts of Kansas, Oklahoma, and Wyoming.

In theory, Mexicans living on the American side of the new border were to be given all the rights of U.S. citizens. In practice, however, their property rights were violated and they lost control of their mining, ranching, and farming industries. The exploitation of Mexican workers coincided with a developing economic system that was built around mining and large-scale agriculture, activities that demanded a large pool of cheap labor (Farley, 1982). Today, the per capita income for Hispanics is approximately half that of whites (U.S. Bureau of the Census, 1992c). Nevertheless, in some areas of the country, Hispanics have become quite successful. Cubans, for example, have achieved substantial economic and political power in a number of cities in south Florida.

African Americans

African Americans have historically been the most visible target of racial hostility. From 1619, when the first black slaves were sold in Jamestown, Virginia, to 1865, when the 13th Amendment was passed outlawing slavery, several million blacks in this country endured the brutal reality of forced servitude. Even after slavery was abolished, the conditions of life for blacks in this country showed little improvement. The laws of the land, popularly known as Jim Crow laws, established rigid lines between the races. In 1896 the Supreme Court ruled that segregation was constitutional. Unequal access to public transportation, schools, hotels, theaters, restaurants, campgrounds, drinking fountains, the military, and practically every other aspect of social life continued until the middle of the 20th century.

Although blatant discrimination has declined in the last four decades and economic and political advances have been made, the quality of life for most African Americans remains far below that of whites. In 1990 the per capita income for African Americans was $9,017 compared to $15,265 for whites. According to a 1992 survey, over half of African Americans think that the quality of their lives has gotten worse over the last decade (Morganthau, 1992).

Asian Americans

Asian Americans have experienced treatment that calls into question the American declaration that all people are created equal. The Chinese were brought to this country in the second half of the 19th century as laborers to work on the expanding railroad system. Although the Chinese, and later the Japanese, population in this country was not very large, anti-Asian sentiment began to grow. Asians were seen by working whites as economic competitors for the scarce jobs that existed. As a result, laws were passed that put limits on and even prohibited Asian immigration. These attitudes culminated in the internment of hundreds of thousands of Japanese Americans following the bombing of Pearl Harbor in 1941.

The irony of race for Chinese, Japanese, Koreans, Vietnamese, Cambodians, Laotians, and other Asian groups is that they are often perceived as "model minorities" or "America's greatest success story." Large numbers of Asian-American students are enrolled in the top colleges and universities in this country (Brand, 1987). The median income for Japanese and Chinese Americans is actually higher than that of the population as a whole (U.S. Bureau of the Census, 1992a).

But the expectations and resentment associated with being the "model minority" can be just as confining and oppressive as those created by more negative labels. During the mid-1980s some university administrators openly worried about what they perceived as the overrepresentation of Asian students among their student bodies. The University of California Berkeley, Stanford University, and Brown University used discriminatory quotas or increased the English language proficiency requirements for admission to limit the enrollment of Asian American applicants. At the University of California, alone, Asian enrollment dropped 21% from 1983 to 1984 (Takagi, 1990). A report by the Federal Civil Rights Commission found that Asian Americans still face widespread discrimination in the workplace and are often victims of racially motivated harassment and violence (Dugger, 1992).

Opportunities to achieve "life, liberty, and the pursuit of happiness" have always been distributed along racial and ethnic lines in this country. Although some groups have been able to transcend the status of "despised minority," others continue to suffer.

One Culture, One People? Assimilation Versus Multiculturalism

Racial and ethnic hostility promises to be one of the most important global issues of the 21st century. We have seen ethnic tensions shatter existing national boundaries in countries such as Yugoslavia and the former Soviet Union. In the United States, we are in a period of unprecedented ethnic diversity (see Table 12.1). Soon the presumption that the "typical" American is someone who can trace her or his descendants to Europe will be a thing of the past.

Over the past decade there has been a 38% increase in residents for whom English is a foreign language (Barringer, 1993b). It is estimated that at least 5% of the total kindergarten through 12th-grade population in this country speak no English at all. In states such as New York and New Mexico, the figure may be as high as 25%. In one elementary school in Brooklyn 40% of the children are immigrants whose families speak any one of 26 languages (Leslie, 1991). Schools in Arlington, Virginia, now need to offer bilingual education or other language support for children in as many as 100 different languages. What effect will these changes in racial and ethnic configuration have on our personal lives, our culture, and our social institutions?

Table 12.1   *Expected Changes in Racial and Ethnic Composition of U.S. Population in the Future*

	1990	2010
White	80.3%	79.6%
Black	12.1%	13.6%
Hispanic origin	9.0%	13.2%
Asian or Pacific Islander	2.9%	5.9%
Native American, Eskimo, or Aleut	0.8%	0.9%

Note: Figures do not add up to 100% because a Hispanic person can be of any race.

Source: U.S. Bureau of the Census, 1991b, 1992d.

The "Melting Pot"

One of the bedrock goals of the American value system has always been the ultimate assimilation of racial and ethnic groups into mainstream society. **Assimilation** is the process by which members of minority groups change their ways to conform to those of the dominant culture. I can recall as a child learning of 19th-century descriptions of America as the great "melting pot," a place where immigrants of varied racial and ethnic backgrounds willingly and happily blended to create a brand-new national identity. Most people believed that opportunities for inclusion into the larger society as well as high-paying, stable jobs could come about only if people from different cultures gradually lost their differences and adopted the lifestyle of the majority.

It sounded good, particularly when the image of full assimilation was spiced with stories of my own grandparents who arrived in this country as penniless immigrants but worked hard and eventually "became" proud Americans. However, the inherent trap of assimilation is that while it may signal an ethnic or racial group's inclusion into mainstream society, it also means that the only way for a group to transcend its status as a disliked minority is to conform to the dominant—in our society, Anglo-American—way of life.

Assimilation has sometimes been systematically forced upon certain groups whose beliefs conflict with the dominant white culture. Native Americans, for instance, were forced to abandon a lifestyle that was built on values unacceptable to whites. When blacks were brought to America as slaves, they were forced to take new names, families were split apart, and they were forbidden to practice any of the traditions of their native cultures.

Multiculturalism and Social Institutions

In contrast to the melting pot model, many people today feel that the maintenance of a pluralistic or multicultural society—where groups maintain not only their ethnic identity, but also their own language, art, music, food, literature, and religion—enriches American civilization. With the massive influx of foreign-born, non-English-speaking people into this country, it has become especially difficult to think of America as one culture and Americans as one people.

Many of our social institutions are struggling with the question of how to represent the different histories and cultures of all these diverse groups. In the educational system, the traditional emphasis on the history and culture of white European civilization is now being attacked as anglocentric, racist, and incomplete. Over the past 25 years, most universities have created what are known as ethnic studies programs: African-American Studies, Latino/Latina Studies, Asian Studies, Native American Studies.

Multiculturalism has also become an issue in the workplace. Employers are finding that they need assistance managing an ever-expanding, diverse workforce in which members of minority groups and immigrants now hold a significant proportion of the jobs (L. Williams, 1992b). Only a few years ago the idea of adjusting to ethnic and racial diversity in the workplace was being dismissed by employers as irrelevant to production and profit and as threatening to the white male workforce. Today, however, more employers view diversity as good business. Companies that set aside time and money and hire expensive consultants to cultivate diversity hope that there will be fewer costly lawsuits over unfair treatment and a more tolerant and innovative work environment. Employers are being taught how to accommodate cultural differences. For instance, a manager may be encouraged to realize that an Asian employee's reluctance to give an oral presentation at a staff meeting is motivated by that individual's adherence to cultural norms of modesty and not by professional inadequacy (L. Williams, 1992b).

The increasing diversity of the population not only will have an impact on people's ideas about what it means to be American and who can call themselves American, but it will also shape our relations with one another and our social institutions.

Racial and Ethnic Relations

Given our long history of racial inequality, it is likely that the increasing size of racial and ethnic minorities, the growing influx of non-English-speaking immigrants, and the subsequent heightened competition and conflict over scarce economic resources will perpetuate our society's racist past. **Racism** is a principle of social domination by which a group seen as inferior or different is exploited, controlled, and oppressed psychologically, socially, politically, and economically by another group (Blauner, 1972). Racism can be manifested at the personal level through individual attitudes and behavior, at the cultural level in our language and collective ideologies, and at the macro-structural level in our social institutions.

Personal Racism

Personal racism is the expression of negative feelings toward certain racial or ethnic groups by individual people. This is the most obvious form of racism and includes the use of derogatory names, biased treatment during face-to-face contact, avoidance, and threats or acts of violence. Personal racism receives the most media attention when it is violent and brutal, such as racially motivated hate crimes or the organized hatred of white supremacist groups. However, subtle forms of personal racism, like the high school guidance counselor who steers minority students away from "hard" subjects toward those that do not prepare them for higher paying jobs, are much more common. Whether blatant or subtle, personal racism rests on two important psychological constructs: stereotypes and prejudice.

Stereotypes

The word stereotype was first used by the political commentator Walter Lippmann in 1922. He defined it as an oversimplified picture of the world, one that satisfies our need to see our social environment as a more understandable and manageable place than it really is. It is the overgeneralized belief that a certain trait, behavior, or attitude characterizes all members of some identifiable group. Casual observations easily refute the accuracy of common racial or ethnic stereotypes. Not all African Americans are on welfare, not all Jews are greedy, not all Italians belong to the Mafia, not all Asian Americans are excellent students, and so on. Overgeneralizations like these can never be true for *every* member of that group.

Yet despite their obvious inaccuracy, stereotypes remain a common part of our everyday thinking. We all know what the stereotypes are, even if most of us choose not to express them. Today it seems clear that stereotypes aren't the irrational beliefs they were once thought to be. The modern view of stereotypes is that they are *natural* categories and an essential, universal aspect of human thought (Hamilton, 1981). Our brains have a tendency to divide the world into hard and fast categories: black and white, strong and weak, them and us (Rothenberg, 1992). By allowing us to group information into easily identifiable categories, stereotypes make the processing of information and the formation of impressions more efficient. As we saw in chapter 6, our lives would be utterly chaotic if we weren't able to quickly categorize people in terms of sex, race, age, ethnicity, and so on.

In short, it is unrealistic to condemn stereotypical thoughts. We all have them, we all know them, and we all must employ stereotypes to organize the "kaleidoscopic flow of events" around us (McCall & Simmons, 1978, p. 110). Stereotypes, in and of themselves, are inescapable.

Nevertheless, stereotypes must be learned. One of the most potent sources of racial and ethnic stereotypes is the media. Television, films, and literature provide large audiences with both real and fantasized images of people, events, and situations. In so doing, they offer representations of racial, religious, and ethnic groups that impersonally form the basis of many people's attitudes and beliefs. Consider the skewed images of certain ethnic groups served up on television: the savage Indian, the Jewish-American Princess, the lazy Mexican, the obnoxious Japanese tourist, the fanatic Arab terrorist, and so on.

Although all racial and ethnic groups suffer from stereotypical media portrayal, most of the attention focuses on African Americans. Early television shows of the 1950s, including "Amos 'n Andy" and "The Beulah Show," depicted blacks either as lazy clowns, opportunistic crooks, or happy, docile servants. Most blacks realized, even then, that the rest of the country was receiving inaccurate and dangerous images of them. Henry Louis Gates (1992) recalls what it was like in the early 1950s:

> I can remember as a child sitting upstairs in my bedroom and hearing my mother shout at the top of her voice that someone "*colored . . . colored!*" was on TV and that we had all better come downstairs at once. And, without fail, we did, sitting in front of our TV, nervous, full of expectation and dread, praying that our home girl or boy would not let the race down. (p. 311)

Television representations have not always been blatantly negative. "Sanford and Son," "Good Times," "What's Happening," and the other so-called ghetto sitcoms of the 1970s tried to represent blacks more positively by showing slums and housing projects as places where people could lead happy, loving, even humorous lives. When American society itself could not achieve social reform through civil rights, television solved the problem by inventing symbols of black success and racial harmony (Gates, 1992). Shows like "Julia" or "I Spy" in the 1960s, "Roots" and "The Jeffersons" in the 1970s, and "Benson," "A Different World," and "The Cosby Show" in the 1980s and 1990s seemingly overcame these harmful stereotypes by depicting blacks as strong, smart, and successful.

But critics have charged that these portrayals are also fantasies that may be just as harmful to African Americans as the negative stereotypes of the 1950s. They feel that the characters in these shows, which were designed to overcome past images and tell America that blacks can be "just like" whites, amounted to what some call the "white Negro" in television. The message seemed to be that the more black characters resembled whites, the more acceptable they would be to the viewing audience. If one worked hard and had the right values and aspirations, everything would be OK, thus reaffirming hard-core middle-class values and the American Dream. The George Jefferson character from "The Jeffersons" began his TV existence as the working-class neighbor of Archie Bunker. But through dogged commitment to the American values of hard work and determination, he and his family were able to "move up" into the new black upper class and, not surprisingly, into a white neighborhood.

Such representations feed the cultural belief that blacks are personally responsible for their poor social conditions, with little or no acknowledgment of the structural reality most black people face that restricts life opportunities. Once we come to believe that "anyone can be successful"—like Cliff and Clair Huxtable on "The Cosby Show"—we are provided the luxury of seeing no need to change societal conditions. To no surprise, "Cosby" was one of the most popular television shows in South Africa during the 1980s (Gates, 1992).

In the past, when all blacks were represented in demeaning or peripheral roles, we could believe that American racism was indiscriminate, affecting every black person (Gates, 1992). However, the social vision of shows like "Cosby," which reflects the integration of blacks into the upper middle class, throws the blame for black poverty back onto the impoverished. White America was exposed to the idealized image of the black American while, at the same time, the social and economic conditions of the average black were bleaker than they had been in years. The underlying message is that racism will end when blacks become as successful as whites (Jhally & Lewis, 1992).

Prejudice and Discrimination

When stereotypes are used to form a set of rigidly held, unfavorable attitudes, beliefs, and feelings about members of a racial or ethnic group, they constitute **prejudice** (Allport, 1954). In one study a group of whites was shown a photograph of a white person holding a razor blade while arguing with a black person on a New York subway. They were shown the picture for a split second and then asked to write down what they saw. More than half of them saw the *black* man holding the razor against the *white* man's throat (cited in Helmreich, 1992). The belief that all blacks are violent was so powerful that it distorted people's perceptions.

Prejudiced beliefs like this would be of little significance if they weren't linked, from time to time, to discrimination. **Discrimination** refers to the unfair treatment of people based on some social characteristic such as race, sex, or ethnicity. The 1964 Civil Rights Act prohibits discrimination or segregation on the grounds of race, color, religion, or national origin. This act has produced tremendous progress in American race relations. Nevertheless discrimination, ranging from hate-inspired violence to avoidance, suspicions of wrongdoing, and denied privileges, still exists.

In 1993 the Denny's Restaurant chain agreed to a settlement with the U.S. Justice Department regarding allegations of discrimination against black customers. Customers claimed that Denny's required black customers to pay a cover charge or pay in advance for meals, refused to honor its free Birthday Meal offer to blacks, subjected blacks to racially derogatory remarks, and threatened and/or forcibly removed black customers. The company denied the charges but agreed to provide racial sensitivity training to its employees and managers, post notices of its policy of nondiscrimination in its restaurants, and include 20 blacks in its television and newspaper ads ("Denny's Restaurant hit with discrimination suit," 1993).

Most of the time discrimination is much more subtle; in fact, the person engaging in it may not even realize he or she is doing so. Psychologists Carl Word, Mark Zanna, and Joel Cooper (1974) created an experimental situation in which white subjects were led to believe they were interviewing applicants for a team position in a group decision-making experiment. Their behavior was secretly being observed by the researchers. The applicants, who were really confederates of the researchers, were both black and white.

The results showed that the interviewers treated black applicants very differently from white ones. For instance, they placed their chairs at a significantly greater distance from the black interviewees. They leaned forward less and made less eye contact with the black applicants. In addition, they ended the interview sooner and tended to trip over their words.

In a second experiment Word, Zanna, and Cooper sought to determine the effect such behavior would have on the applicants. The interviewers were now confederates of the experimenters. These new interviewers were trained to mimic the behaviors found among interviewers in the first experiment. This time, applicants who encountered the less "friendly" behavior—that is, reduced eye contact, greater physical distance, and so on—performed less adequately and showed less composure during the interview than others.

These experiments illustrate the process by which racism operates, even in people who are not self-consciously racist. We are generally so unaware of our own nonverbal behavior that if we unwittingly give off signs of our dislike, we don't interpret others' subsequent behavior as reactions to our nonverbal cues. Rather, we attribute it to some inherent trait in them. We may unknowingly create the very actions that we use as evidence of some flaw or deficiency in that group.

As such behavior becomes common among large numbers of people, prejudice and discrimination become mutually reinforcing. If one group is defined as inferior by another and treated that way, the resulting discrimination in the form of denied access to jobs and inferior education becomes self-fulfilling in that it will produce the very inferiority that the group was believed to possess in the first place.

Micro-Macro Connection
Class, Race, and Discrimination

Some sociologists have argued that discriminatory treatment, as well as the unequal economic, social, and political status of some racial groups, is more a function of social class than of race (e.g., W. J. Wilson, 1980). If this were true, the lives of middle- and upper-class members of racial minorities should be relatively free of discrimination. Yet this is far from the case. For many highly successful black professionals, lack of respect, faint praise, low expectations, shattered hopes, and outright exclusion are common features of their career lives (Cose, 1993).

Sociologist Joe Feagin (1991) conducted in-depth interviews with 37 middle-class black Americans to determine the extent of discrimination directed against them in public situations. These 37 people, who were all college educated and held professional or managerial jobs, reported a total of 62 discriminatory incidents in public places like hotels, jewelry stores, and restaurants. The incidents consisted of avoidance, poor service, closer scrutiny, verbal epithets, "hate stares," and police threats and harassment.

The events disturbed the subjects not only because of the racist attitudes that lay behind them but also because they had come to believe that their upward social mobility protected them from such treatment. A 28-year-old New York lawyer sums up such experiences this way:

> When I walk into a store they don't see my Princeton undergraduate degree, my Harvard law degree, my associate law status. They see a black man. Credentials do not make your blackness invisible no matter how impressive they may be. (quoted in L. Williams, 1991b)

Feagin concludes that the stigma of color is still very important in the lives of African Americans, including affluent ones. They remain vulnerable targets of deprivation and discrimination. This modern form of racism within public, economic settings is rooted in deep racial prejudices:

> Blacks are seen as shoplifters, as unclean, as disreputable poor. No matter how affluent and influential, a black person cannot escape the stigma of being black even while relaxing or shopping. (quoted in L. Williams, 1991b)

The days of "No Negroes" and "No Coloreds" may be gone, but the expressions of personal racism described here serve as a constant reminder that, as the 20th century draws to a close, African Americans, as well as other racial minorities, are still being stereotyped, prejudged, and discriminated against on the basis of their race. Taken as individual incidents, racial slurs, "hate stares," and poor service in restaurants may seem to be just trivial inconveniences. However, these forms of discrimination reflect the reality to which racial and ethnic minorities of all classes are exposed on a daily basis.

What whites may see as "minority paranoia" is a response to discrimination and humiliation that has accumulated over the years and has become part of everyday life. Hence African Americans, Hispanics, and others are forced, structurally, to bear the burden of all sorts of discrimination. One woman interviewed by Feagin pointed out that whenever she leaves her home she must put on her "shield" and be prepared for the insults and discrimination she expects to receive in public places.

From the point of view of those discriminated against, subtle forms of personal racism are harder to fight than the overt bigotry of the past. If you are excluded from a job because you're Asian, or denied membership in a club because you're Jewish, you can fight to open those doors. Today, some people have made it through these doors (Blauner, 1992), but once inside, they have found there are still barriers to overcome.

A New Form of Racism

The nature of public attitudes toward racial and ethnic groups has changed, prompting many sociologists to rethink their ideas of what constitutes personal racism. Attitudes toward the principle of racial equality and the rejection of absolute segregation in schools, housing, and jobs have improved markedly over the past three or four decades (Schuman, Steeh, & Bobo, 1988). These improvements suggest that traditional racism may no longer be as prevalent a factor in American social life as it used to be.

But if the *principle* of equal opportunity now enjoys support, this does not appear to be the case regarding concrete efforts to change the racial status quo (McClendon, 1985). For instance, while most whites feel that schools should be integrated and that people of all races should have equal opportunities to enter any occupation, overwhelming majorities in national surveys oppose special government economic assistance to minorities and government efforts to desegregate schools, such as court-ordered busing. And as recently as 1988, only a slim majority of whites favored legislation to prevent racial discrimination in the sale or rental of housing (Schuman, Steeh, & Bobo, 1988).

This paradox has led some to argue that a new form of racism has emerged (Sniderman & Tetlock, 1986). **Symbolic racism** is linked to the traditional forms of personal racism by common negative feelings toward certain groups. This form of racism is not expressed directly but rather indirectly through opposition to programs that seek to improve the status of minorities in society (McClelland & Auster, 1990). The symbolic racist would tend to disagree strongly with a statement like "Black people are not generally as smart as white people," but at the same time would likely agree with a statement like "Blacks are getting too demanding in their push for equal rights." They justify their opposition to government programs specially designed to help minorities on the grounds that they violate the cherished principle that one's achievements should be based on merit. What complicates the situation even more is that this type of personal racism is often expressed by people who consider themselves liberal, unbiased, and nonprejudiced. They are likely to

> sympathize with the victims of past injustice; support public policies that, in principle, promote racial equality . . . ; identify more generally with a liberal political agenda; regard themselves as non-prejudiced and non-discriminatory; but, almost unavoidably, possess negative feelings and

beliefs about Blacks [and other racial groups]. (Gaertner & Dovidio, 1990, p. 271)

The feelings experienced are not hate or hostility but discomfort, uneasiness, and sometimes fear, which tend to motivate avoidance rather than outright destructive acts. Symbolic racists are people who maintain that it is wrong to discriminate against a person because of his or her race but who nonetheless cannot entirely escape the cultural forces that give rise to racist beliefs in the first place.

You can see how symbolic racism can be more insidious than overt personal racism. Social and legal pressures can have a significant impact on traditional expressions of bigotry; however, such techniques cannot alleviate symbolic racism because these people already subscribe to egalitarian, nondiscriminating values. They are acutely aware of the social undesirability and the unfairness of their feelings, but they hold them anyway.

The changing face of racism has serious societal consequences as well. When racism exists but remains hidden, people are tempted to assume that it has disappeared, forestalling the perceived need for political or social action to help groups who have traditionally been the objects of discrimination. Most whites in our country believe that the socioeconomic status of blacks has vastly improved and see no need to continue federal programs to assist them (Kluegel & Smith, 1986). Many whites now believe that the only reason so many blacks are unsuccessful is that they aren't committed to "white" values—hard work, individualism, delayed gratification, and so on. Although these beliefs are more subtle than overt acts of bigotry, they have the same effect by promoting prejudice toward individuals on the basis of stereotypes.

The Cultural Ideology of Racism

If I stopped here in my discussion of racism and its constituent elements, you might be inclined to consider it a phenomenon of individuals that could best be stopped by changing the way people think and act. But the sociologically important thing about racism is that it exists not just in individuals' minds and actions but in a cultural ideology that both justifies the domination of some groups over others and provides a set of social norms that prescribes differential treatment for these groups (O'Sullivan See & Wilson, 1988). From a conflict perspective, the cultural ideology of racism that exists in our language and in our prevailing collective beliefs maintains racial and ethnic inequality.

Racism in Language

If we accept that the dominant white culture in this country is racist, then we would expect that language—the transmitter of culture—to be racist as well (Moore, 1992). Certainly racial slurs and derogatory words reflect underlying racism. But racism doesn't just lie in spoken or written language. As recently as 2 or 3 years ago, American Sign Language relied on visual stereotypical representations as signs for certain racial and ethnic groups. For instance, the sign for "Japanese" was a twisting of the little finger next to the eye. The sign for "Negro" was a flattening of the nose. The sign for "stingy" was derived from the sign for "Jewish" (stroking an imaginary beard). Such signs have fallen out of polite usage with increased sensitivity to their harmful effects (Senior, 1994).

What is particularly important about language is the extent to which the seemingly neutral or even positive content of our everyday words perpetuates racism. Consider the use of common terms to refer to diverse ethnic groups. Today we use the general terms *Native Americans* or *Asian Americans* to refer to a variety of peoples whose traditions and lifestyles are quite different from one another. Similarly, *Hispanic* refers to all people whose backgrounds are from such culturally diverse areas as Mexico, the Caribbean, Central America, and South America.

When the first Europeans "discovered" Africans, they were quick to label them all "black" (Omi & Winant, 1992). Not only did this term mask the fact that they came from a variety of different cultures, it also maximized the perceived differences between "black" Africans and "white" Europeans (Fairchild, 1985). Furthermore, the word *black* capitalizes on a large set of negative connotations within the English language. For instance, good guys wear white hats and bad guys wear black hats. Among the definitions of *black* in *Webster's New Universal Unabridged Dictionary* are soiled and dirty, thoroughly evil, wicked, gloomy, marked by disaster, hostile, and disgraceful. The definition of white, on the other hand, includes fairness of complexion, innocent, favorable, fortunate, pure, and spotless.

The pervasive "goodness" of white and "badness" of black affects children by the age of 4 and provides white children with a false sense of superiority (Moore, 1992). Children know the difference between a black lie, which is harmful and inexcusable, and a white lie, which is small, insignificant, and harmless. A black mark on your academic record certainly will not help your chances of getting into medical school. Black cats crossing your path are bad luck. Black magic is sinister and devilish. The black sheep of the family causes everyone else shame and embarrassment by not conforming to generally accepted standards of behavior. To be blackballed or blacklisted is to be ostracized and identified as undesirable. Blackmail is a powerful way to force someone into an act he or she would rather avoid (Moore, 1992).

More important are the political implications of racist terminology. Terms like *culturally deprived, economically disadvantaged,* and *underdeveloped* mislead and distort our awareness of social phenomena. To apply the label "culturally deprived" to a Hispanic person, for instance, is to symbolically reinforce the belief that the only culture that really matters is the dominant white one. Even a term like *minority* influences racial perceptions. While people of color are a statistical minority in this country, they are the vast majority worldwide. In South Africa, blacks comprise about 70% of the population but still suffer widespread discrimination. By using the term *minority* we lose sight of this larger global reality. Similarly, the use of the term *nonwhite* to describe people of color implies that white is the standard against which all others are measured.

In 1992 we celebrated the 500th anniversary of Columbus's voyage to the Americas. Most of us were taught that this event was a positive step toward the creation of a civilized New World. Every 5-year-old in the country has been taught that Columbus "discovered" America in 1492. According to *Webster's Unabridged Dictionary*, to "discover" is to find something that was previously unknown or to gain sight of something previously unseen. Hence, a continent inhabited by millions of people for thousands of years cannot, logically, be "discovered." Nevertheless, we continue to use this term, ignoring the perspective of Native Americans who are likely to see this event not as the dawning of the civilized New World, but as the first step toward their subjugation and annihilation.

Certain adjectives that are usually used in a positive context convey something very different when applied in a racial context. You will often hear blacks described on television or in newspapers as "intelligent" or "bright and articulate." While such descriptions may be well meaning, they imply that the person in question violates preconceived notions about the intellect and speaking abilities of "most blacks." That a person feels compelled to use such qualifying adjectives illustrates how deeply embedded racist beliefs can be.

Racist language is just a small part of the overall problem of racist ideology in American society. It seemingly pales in comparison to more visible issues like racial violence and economic discrimination. We must remember, however, that language filters our perceptions. It affects the way people think from the time they first learn to speak. Efforts are being made today to address the issue of language and its crucial role in maintaining racism and oppression. People are becoming more aware of the capacity of words to both glorify and degrade others (Moore, 1992).

The Myth of Innate Racial Inferiority

The cultural ideology of racism is also supported by theories positing innate racial or ethnic inferiority. These theories have long been used to explain why certain racial groups, as a whole, lag behind whites in such areas as educational achievement and financial success. They combine with the belief in competitive individualism (see chapter 11) to provide "scientific" justification and a seemingly intellectual climate for the perpetuation of all forms of prejudice and discrimination.

Appeals to biology and nature have been used throughout history to define the existing stratification system as proper and inevitable (Gould, 1981). In the

18th and 19th centuries no one doubted the correctness of natural racial rankings: Indians below whites, and blacks below everyone else. Even some of our historical idols—Abraham Lincoln, Thomas Jefferson, Charles Darwin—held beliefs about the "natural inferiority" of some races that were common knowledge at the time, but would be considered bigoted or racially insensitive today.

The approval given by scientists to conventional racial rankings arose not from objective data and careful research but from a shared worldview, a cultural belief that expressed the "goodness" of racial stratification. Such beliefs were then twisted into independent, "scientific" support. Scientists, like everybody else, have attitudes and values that shape what they see. This is not the result of outright dishonesty or hypocrisy; rather, it is the way human minds work and the generally accepted knowledge of the day.

From a functionalist perspective, cultural beliefs about innate racial inferiority provide advantages for the dominant group. These beliefs discourage subordinate groups from attempting to question their disadvantaged status. In addition, they provide moral justification for maintaining a society in which some groups are routinely deprived of their rights and privileges. Whites could justify the enslavement of blacks, and Nazis could justify the extermination of Jews and other "undesirables," by promoting the belief that those groups were inherently subhuman.

Ironically, cultural beliefs about natural racial inferiority need not be based on biological characteristics in order to benefit the dominant group. The most disadvantaged minority in Japan, for instance, are the Burakumin. The Burakumin, who represent about 2% of the Japanese population, are biologically, religiously, and ethnically indistinguishable from other Japanese, but a national poll found that more than two-thirds of Japanese people consider the Burakumin a different race (Hane, 1982). Their low status probably dates back to the 17th century, when their occupations consisted of killing and dealing with the remains of dead animals, which violated Buddhist principles. These jobs were necessary for society but considered so degrading that only "subhuman" outcasts would do them, forever contaminating those who engaged in them.

The innate inferiority of the Burakumin is beyond question to most Japanese. They are widely believed to be mentally inferior, aggressive, impulsive, and dirty (Neary, 1986). They fill the functional role in Japanese society of the out-group that can be looked down upon. Before marriage or hiring a new employee, some Japanese will have a detective agency check the background of a person for Burakumin ancestors. Like disadvantaged ethnic or racial groups in the United States, the Burakumin suffer the highest rates of poverty and psychological problems and the lowest rates of educational attainment in Japanese society.

Races do differ in obvious, visible ways: skin color, anatomical structure, and so forth. But despite energetic searches over the centuries, the link between "inferior" race-based genes and intelligence, creativity, or other valued abilities has not yet been found (Hacker, 1992). Comparing racial groups on, say, intelligence, and discovering that one group performs better on average than the other overlooks the range of differences within and between groups. Many African Americans are more intelligent than the average white; many whites are less intelligent than the average Native American. Variations like these are difficult to explain genetically.

It makes more sense to argue that if certain races or ethnic groups do better in some areas than others, it is because they grew up in environments that prepared them for these endeavors. The importance of one's learning environment in affecting intelligence was illustrated several years ago by the finding that IQ scores for some groups have been rising for the past 50 years (cited in Goleman, 1984). Early tests of Jewish, Chinese, and Italian immigrants showed these groups to be far below average in intelligence. Their grandchildren, however, have average or above average IQ scores (Sowell, 1977). Such a large difference over the span of two generations cannot be explained by heredity.

Nevertheless, the idea that racial inferiority is innate is appealing. If observable, physical differences between races are inherited, why not differences in social behavior, intelligence, the ability to rule, and so on? Like the belief in competitive individualism, the belief in innate racial inferiority places the blame for suffering and economic failure on the traits of the individual rather than on the society in which that individual exists.

Racism flourishes in a culture that has an ideology which creates and maintains racial inequality. That racism can exist well above the level of personal attitudes indicates that it won't disappear by simply reducing people's prejudices and stereotypes. This point becomes particularly important when we examine racism at the structural level of social institutions.

Institutional Racism: Building Injustice Into the System

Institutional racism consists of established laws, customs, and practices that systematically reflect and produce racial inequalities in society, whether or not the individuals maintaining these practices have racist intentions (J. M. Jones, 1986). Because Native Americans, African Americans, Hispanics, and other groups have historically been excluded from key positions of authority in social institutions, they often find themselves victimized by the *routine* workings of such structures. Institutional racism is the established and customary means by which some groups are kept subordinate (Eitzen & Baca-Zinn, 1989).

Institutions have a permanent, inevitable quality. Once they are in operation, it is extremely difficult to change them except through massive, sometimes revolutionary means. A society can be racist even if only a minority of its members are racist. Because it is a built-in feature of social arrangements, institutional racism is much more difficult to detect than acts of personal racism. For example, when granting home mortgage loans, many banks use ZIP codes to mark off the neighborhoods they consider high risks—that is, where property values are low and liable to drop even further once minorities take over. Although this practice, called "red-lining," is considered a "good" business policy and is not intentionally racist, the consequences of using it make it racist because these high-risk neighborhoods tend to be inhabited predominantly by people of color. Institutional racism is difficult to address because there is no individual "bad guy," no identifiable bigot who is the source of intentional hate-motivated discrimination.

Likewise, people in neighborhoods where hazardous waste treatment plants or other sources of industrial pollution exist are disproportionately exposed to unhealthful effects of air pollution, water pollution, and pesticides. The decisions on where to place such facilities are often based not on race but on factors like the cost of land, population density, and geological conditions. However, these decisions have the effect of discriminating against certain groups when the plants are built in predominantly minority areas. A study of toxic emissions along the lower Mississippi River by the Environmental Protection Agency showed that 9 out of the 10 major sources of industrial pollution in Louisiana are in predominantly black neighborhoods. In the town of Carville, an area that is 70% black, 353 pounds of toxic material per person per year is released into the environment. That compares to an average 105 pounds in the rest of the state (Cushman, 1993).

Racism in one institution tends to be accompanied by racism in another. For instance, the traditional exclusion of certain racial and ethnic groups from the upper levels of education will affect their economic opportunities, which in turn will affect their access to other basic necessities like quality health care and housing. I described in chapter 11 how poverty has become geographically concentrated, leaving poor communities more isolated and without access to the institutions, resources, and values necessary for success in modern society (Wilson, 1987). Residential segregation based on class and race is so high in this society that one sociologist refers to the situation as "American apartheid" (Massey, 1990).

Although white attitudes toward neighborhood integration have become more favorable over the years and laws have been established to prevent housing discrimination, levels of black and Hispanic residential segregation remain quite high in urban areas where poverty is most severe: New York, Chicago, Philadelphia, Detroit. All of these cities have seen a dramatic increase in their Hispanic and black populations and an accompanying decrease in the white population (Kasarda, 1985). But if laws prohibit it and personal racism has eased, why does residential segregation still exist? Certainly the distribution of races in a whole city involves more than just individual bigotry and personal discrimination.

Diana Pearce
Institutional
Racism and
Real Estate

Sociologist Diana Pearce (1979) was interested in how a structural phenomenon like residential segregation in neighborhoods is maintained. She randomly selected about a hundred real estate agents in the greater Detroit area to be in her study. Each agent was visited at different times by a white couple and a black couple who were looking to purchase a house. The couples were similar in terms of education level, occupation, income, family size, and the type of house they wanted. The agents were unaware that the couples were trained and paid accomplices of the researcher.

Pearce found that the chances of actually seeing a house on the first visit to the real estate agent were one in four for the black couples and three in four for the white couples. Even when the black couples were shown homes, they were shown fewer than the white couples. The efforts of the black homeseekers to see homes were not met with strong, blatant refusal. Instead they were met with reasonable sounding excuses like "I don't have the key" or "I need to make an appointment ahead of time." Finally, when black couples were shown homes, they were subtly "steered" into poorer neighborhoods. This lack of overt insult and mistreatment masks the discriminatory treatment to which the black home-seekers were subjected.

Pearce concluded that such practices were not isolated instances of personal racism; in fact, they occurred in a variety of different communities across the entire metropolitan area. There seems to be a high level of consensus in the real estate field about what the racial composition of Detroit neighborhoods ought to be. This study shows that racism embedded in an entire industry can be manifested at the personal level. But the fact that the actions of these agents were "typical" of all agents characterizes their practices as institutional racism.

Economics

Institutional racism is readily apparent throughout our economic institutions. Let's look at participation in the labor force. Despite recent advances, workers from racial and ethnic minorities tend to be concentrated in lower paying jobs. While African Americans make up 10% of the entire American workforce, they make up 31% of nursing aides and orderlies, 25% of all taxi drivers, 25% of hotel maids, and 22% of janitors and cleaners (National Committee on Pay Equity, 1992). They are severely underrepresented in the fields of law (3.2%), medicine (3%), and engineering (3.2%) (Hacker, 1992). Only about one-quarter of Hispanics have managerial, technical, and administrative jobs compared to one-half of non-Hispanic whites (Valdivieso & Davis, 1991). In the micro-electronic manufacturing industries of Silicon Valley, people of color comprise 26% of the total workforce, but 80% of the lower paying production jobs (Hossfeld, 1990).

Because minorities are occupationally concentrated in these kinds of jobs and geographically concentrated in poor inner city neighborhoods, they are particularly vulnerable to economically motivated business processes such as plant shut-downs, the automation of lower-level production jobs, and corporate reloca-tions. For instance, when a factory in a predominantly black or Hispanic section of an inner city moves to an all-white suburb, current minority employees will be adversely affected because they will tend to face greater problems securing housing in the new location, or will face higher transportation costs in commut-ing to the new work location (Squires, 1980). It is no surprise that the rate of unemployment for people of color is twice as high as that of whites (U.S. Bureau of the Census, 1991c).

We can see evidence of institutional racism in common employment policies, too. If you've ever worked in a job for a long period of time, you know that continuous service is rewarded with certain privileges and benefits. People who have worked at a company the longest tend to get the higher salaries, even though their jobs might be no more demanding than those of more recent hirees. Moreover, they have better job stability because seniority rules usually include a "last hired, first fired" provision.

Again, there is nothing inherently discriminatory about seniority rules. Most of us think it is perfectly fair that people who have been with a company longest ought to be entitled to certain benefits as a result. However, seniority rules become institutionally racist when they are applied to jobs for which only whites had been hired in the past. If a company has only recently begun hiring Asian Americans or Hispanics and finds itself in the position of having to lay off workers, the newest employees, who also happen to be a higher proportion of minorities, will be the first to lose their jobs.

In addition, members of racial and ethnic minorities remain marginal partici-pants in the economy as owners of their own businesses. Loan companies usually demand a credit history, some form of collateral, and evidence of potential success before they will lend money to prospective businesses. These are stand-ard practices, but when they are applied to members of groups who may have a poor credit rating because of past exploitation and no collateral because of poverty, they serve to perpetuate the racial stratification. It is true that poor people are greater credit risks and that businesses in poorer communities must pay more for insurance because of the greater likelihood of theft or property damage. But it is also true that the higher costs of doing business not only make it more difficult for members of minorities to start their own businesses, but also hurt consumers in these areas who must pay higher prices for goods and services.

At an even broader level, market pressures also perpetuate institutional racism. Racial and ethnic discrimination in business settings is sometimes diffi-cult to overcome precisely because it may occur for reasons other than personal hatred. On the surface you would think that discrimination would be self-destructive for employers. A company that refuses to hire Hispanics, for instance, not only is losing out on a broader pool of labor, but also is running the risk of driving away a group of potential customers. As customers and prospective employees drift to nondiscriminatory companies, you would think that the discriminating ones would eventually be driven out of business (Sunstein, 1991, p. 22).

In light of this, the fact that racial discrimination continues to exist in business situations is puzzling. However, if we look at it not as a problem of personal racism, but as a function of the competitive, profit-driven nature of the economic marketplace, then it starts to make sense. Businesses are sometimes pressured into racial discrimination by catering to customer tastes. A few years ago, the Cracker Barrel restaurant chain adopted a policy that known homosexual employees were to be fired. Although public pressure eventually forced them to reverse this policy, their rationale was that homosexual waiters were driving customers away. It wasn't that they had anything against homosexuals, the company contended, it was simply a business decision.

An employer who is intent on introducing norms of equality into the workforce may actually be financially punished for doing so. From his or her point of view "discrimination is in fact neutral, a quite ordinary form of profit-maximization through catering to consumer demand" (Sunstein, 1991, p. 25). As long as the economic marketplace is driven by consumer preferences that happen to be racist, institutional discrimination will continue.

Through such business practices, the disadvantage of certain groups becomes self-perpetuating. Members of racial minorities are often ambivalent about entering occupations previously closed to them (Pettigrew & Martin, 1987). For instance, relatively few African Americans are likely to invest in the lengthy education needed to become a doctor as long as white patients remain uneasy about being treated by African-American doctors. But with few African-American-doctors in practice, white people may never have the chance to learn tolerance and acceptance. The result is a further perpetuation, perhaps even an increase, in discriminatory hiring practices.

There are, of course, exceptions. We all know of situations where members of a racial or ethnic minority invested a great deal of themselves in a profession that treated them inhospitably. In general, however, the discouraging reception for most perpetuates the exclusion of these groups from certain sectors of the economy (Sunstein, 1991).

Interestingly, just as racist actions may be motivated by economic forces and not personal prejudice, so are *nonracist* actions. Network television, in the 1990s, has more series than ever featuring black characters. At one point in 1993, the Fox network had nine black-oriented series. On the surface this appears to be a sign that the entertainment industry is finally attempting to eradicate a long tradition of racial inequality. On closer inspection, though, it appears that this trend is really being driven by economic considerations. A recent Nielsen study showed that black households average 70 hours a week of television watching compared with 47 hours in nonblack households (Hammer, 1992). The decision to represent more blacks on television is a financially motivated one, reflecting the industry's need to cater to the perceived tastes of the viewership, whoever that viewership happens to be.

As long as individuals are motivated to maximize their own interests (and profits), they are likely to adapt to market tastes. To the extent that those tastes reflect underlying prejudice, discrimination will continue. This functionalist explanation of institutional racism is important because it enables us to see why discrimination is so difficult to end. The problem is not individual bigotry; it is that mistreatment has been built into the system so effectively that it is sometimes difficult to see, let alone remove.

Education

In 1954 the U. S. Supreme Court ruled, in *Brown v. Board of Education of Topeka,* that racially segregated schools were unconstitutional because they were inherently unequal. A recent study by the Harvard Project on School Desegregation, however, found that 66% of all African-American public school students and 74% of Hispanic students still attend predominantly minority schools, defined as those schools with more than 50% of their enrollment made up of either African-American or Hispanic students (Celis, 1993). The percentage rises to 94% in the nation's large inner cities. These figures represent the highest rates of school segregation reported in the last 25 years.

The racial mix of the classroom has important implications for the quality of education. These groups continue to have significantly lower educational attainment than whites. Where over 20% of whites complete 4 or more years of college, only 10.7% of blacks and 8.6% of Hispanics do so (U.S. Bureau of the Census, 1991c). As a result, lower educational achievement interacts with other economic forces to present a major barrier to social advancement for minorities.

Schools in poor communities lack the financial and therefore educational resources that more affluent communities have (see chapter 11). In 1989 the city of Chicago spent $5,000 for each student in its secondary schools. This compares to $9,000 in some of the wealthy suburbs a few miles to the north (Kozol, 1991). While these differences are a function of the value of property in these communities and not race per se, the consequences are nonetheless linked to race because of the high concentration of racial and ethnic minorities in poor school districts. Furthermore, these districts face increasing financial pressures because of reductions in federal assistance programs. The rising cost of higher education also reduces the number of minority students who are able to attend college.

Lack of money isn't the only problem. Common practices within the educational system itself may perpetuate institutional discrimination. According to the National Coalition of Advocates for Students, poor, black, or Hispanic children are more likely to be physically punished, suspended, expelled, or forced to repeat a grade than white students. These forms of treatment go beyond personal mistreatment and humiliation because they all increase the likelihood that a child will drop out of school (Eitzen & Baca-Zinn, 1991).

Consider also the common use of standardized intelligence tests (IQ, SAT, etc.). Many elementary and secondary schools use IQ tests as the basis for **tracking** students, that is, assigning them to different educational programs based on their intellectual abilities. In principle, tracking allows every student to receive an education consistent with his or her talents. In practice, however, students from privileged backgrounds are likely to be placed in higher tracks, while those from less privileged backgrounds, who are disproportionately members of minority groups, are likely to be placed in lower tracks (Bowles & Gintis, 1976; Oakes, 1985).

IQ tests supposedly measure innate intelligence. Many educational experts agree, though, that these tests are culture-bound, tapping an individual's familiarity with a specific range of white, middle-class experiences rather than indicating innate intelligence (Curran & Renzetti, 1990). Here is a typical IQ question:

Tennis is to racquet as baseball is to:

    a. club

    b. strike

    c. bat

    d. home run

This question does not measure mental skills like insight or creativity; instead, it measures a specific piece of knowledge that must be learned from the environment. To the extent that a child's environment does not include such knowledge—that is, he or she has never been exposed to tennis or baseball—that child will not be able to answer this question, and the IQ score will suffer (Goleman, 1984). This doesn't mean that the child is less intelligent, only that he or she hasn't had the social experiences necessary to answer the question correctly.

Imagine taking an IQ test consisting of questions that reflected the experiences of a culture about which you knew very little. The specific group from whose culture the test items are developed will probably score significantly higher than you on these tests. One researcher developed an intelligence test based on knowledge found within Chicano culture (Ramirez, 1988). Among the questions included were:

That part of the southwestern United States from which it is believed the Aztecs migrated before they settled in Mexico City is:

    a. San Diego

    b. Aztlan

    c. Colorado

    d. Santa Barbara

Chicano term for the police:

a. la migra
b. la chota
c. el gabacho
d. el pachuco

When administered to white and Chicano college students, Chicanos scored significantly higher on average than whites: 93.3 out of a possible 140 points compared to 36.4 for the white students. (The correct answer to both questions, by the way, is "b.")

In sum, the irony of institutional racism, whether economic or educational, is that while it may not be the result of conscious bigotry on the part of individual people and therefore not motivated by outright personal hatred, it is likely to be more harmful in the long run and more difficult to stop. If tomorrow all Americans were to wake up with all hatred, prejudice, and animosity toward other groups gone from their hearts and minds, institutional racism would still exist:

> All that is needed for job opportunities to remain unequal is for employers to hire those with the most conventional training and experience and to use machines when they seem more . . . economical than manual labor. All that is needed to ensure that poor children get an inferior education is to continue . . . using class-biased tests, . . . rewarding children who conform to the teachers' middle-class concepts of the "good student," and paying disproportionately less for education. In other words, all that is needed to perpetuate discrimination in the United States is to pursue a policy of "business as usual." (Eitzen & Baca-Zinn, 1989, pp. 218-219)

Overcoming Institutional Racism

Clearly, then, overcoming institutional racism will take more than the good will of individual people. The most obvious and far-reaching structural solution to the problem of institutional racism is a governmental policy referred to as **affirmative action.** Affirmative action is a program that seeks out members of minority groups for educational or occupational positions from which they had previously been excluded. The assumption is that organizations will not change racist policies unless they are punished for not doing so. Another assumption is that past discrimination has left certain people ill equipped to compete as equals today.

Contrary to popular belief, the goal of affirmative action is not to enact hiring quotas. Employers are not compelled to hire unqualified persons or compromise standards to meet these goals. They are simply required to gather all relevant information on all qualified applicants and to interview minority candidates and make sure they have access to job information. Government agencies and private

Figure 12.1   *Trends in Black to White Earnings Ratio, 1953-1985*

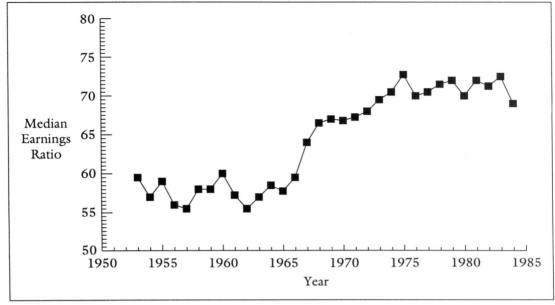

Source: U.S. Commission on Civil Rights, 1986.

firms doing business with the government, for instance, are required to publicly announce job openings at least 45 days prior to the cutoff day for applications (Cherry, 1989). Quotas are only a last resort, reserved for situations in which firms are not making good-faith efforts to seek out *qualified* minority candidates. If a firm announces a job opening in newspapers that reach only the white community, or uses discriminatory procedures to eliminate minorities from employment, the government can then impose quotas.

Affirmative action policies have been used successfully in several areas of social life. Cities have been ordered to bus children to other school districts to eliminate school segregation. Businesses, unions, universities, and local governments, accused of discrimination in hiring or admission, have been sued under the 1964 Civil Rights Act. In part, because of such action, people of color now hold a greater percentage of management, white-collar, and upper-level blue-collar jobs than ever before. Minority employment among firms doing business with the government grew by 20% between 1974 and 1980 (Pear, 1983). Wages and salaries relative to those of whites have also improved. Figure 12.1 shows the change in the earnings ratio between blacks and whites from 1953 to 1985.

Despite such advances, affirmative action came under fire starting in the 1980s. Critics argue that the constitutional protection of each person's right to life, liberty, and property means that all groups, including those whose rights have never been violated or neglected, must have their opportunities safeguarded and must be treated equally. Hence *any* preferential treatment of a group, even one whose rights have been historically unrecognized, amounts to a form of "reverse discrimination" that usually claims white males as its victims. Not only is this unfair, they suggest, but it will also create a "white backlash" and undermine the main goal of the policy, which is to reduce prejudice.

The catalyst for these criticisms was a case that went to the Supreme Court in 1978. A white male student named Alan Bakke was twice denied admission into a California medical school. He claimed that less qualified applicants had been accepted under a special admissions program that saved 16 out of 100 places for minorities. The Supreme Court ruled in favor of Bakke, although it also stated that race or ethnicity could be used as one of several factors in evaluating applicants. The court reversed itself a year later, however, when it ruled that private employers could legally give special preference to black workers to eliminate "manifest racial imbalance" in jobs traditionally restricted to whites.

After more than two decades of affirmative action, many whites have come to believe that enough has been done and now the deck is stacked against *them*. There has never been greater disagreement about whether past discrimination entitles racial and ethnic minorities to preferential treatment in education or hiring. In a 1991 survey, 72% of whites felt that qualified blacks should not receive preference over equally qualified whites in such matters as getting into college or getting jobs (Fineman, 1991).

Even some members of the African-American community argue that affirmative action is a mixed blessing and may actually hurt those groups it is intended to help (Loury, 1985). For instance, black students attending predominantly white universities often find that many of their white classmates assume they were admitted because of affirmative action and not their intelligence. According to some, many of the continuing problems blacks face today are a product of the cultivation and exploitation of the status of "victim." Programs like affirmative action simply reinforce inferiority and encourage blacks to claim victimization (Steele, 1990).

In a society with a tradition of inequality, what is the best way to establish institutional and personal equality? Is it necessary to discriminate in the opposite direction to "make things equal," or is it enough simply to treat people equally from this point on?

Imagine a fictitious final game of the NCAA Basketball Championship Tournament between University A and University B. The rules of the game clearly favor University A. They are allowed five players on the court, while Team B is allowed only four. Team A gets four points for every basket made, while Team B gets two. Team A is given two points for each free throw made, team B gets one. Team A is allowed to physically impede the progress of the opposing players without being called for a foul, and so on.

At halftime Team A leads Team B by a score of 70 to 15. During halftime the NCAA Rules Committee, responding to pressure from the referees, the fans, and players from both teams, decides that the current rules have made the game completely unfair and have harmed the interests of Team B. The committee declares that the second half of the game will utilize a new system of rules that makes the game more just. Each team has the same number of players on the court and receives the same number of points per basket. The inequality of the game has been successfully eliminated, and fairness rules the day.

But there's a slight problem. The score is still 70 to 15! In other words, just because opportunities have been equalized doesn't mean that disadvantages of the past have been entirely erased. Such is the problem we face today. We can legislate hiring or admission polices that do away with unfair advantages to *any* group, but does that address a long history of exclusion? For a long time to come, members of certain groups will continue to be underrepresented in traditionally white positions. Is it possible to achieve complete equality without forcing those who have benefited historically to give up some of their advantages? The answer to this question is complex, controversial, and emotionally charged and will have a great impact on the nature of American race relations as we enter the 21st century.

Conclusion

On April 16, 1963, Martin Luther King, Jr., allowed himself to be arrested and jailed for leading a civil rights demonstration in Birmingham, Alabama. Birmingham at the time was perhaps the most thoroughly segregated city in the country. Not only were blacks subjected to daily doses of fear, violence, and humiliation, they also had to constantly fight what Dr. King called "a degenerating sense of nobodiness." Torn between the brutal reality of a racist society and a fierce optimism for the future, he wrote from his jail cell:

> Let us all hope that the dark clouds of racial prejudice will soon pass away
> and the deep fog of misunderstanding will be lifted from our fear-drenched
> communities and in some not too distant tomorrow the radiant stars of
> love and brotherhood will shine over our great nation with all of their scin-
> tillating beauty. (King, 1991, p. 158)

Some 30 years later Dr. King's words continue to fall on deaf ears. Our society—and most societies around the globe—still struggle with the debilitating effects of personal and institutional discrimination based on race, religion, and ethnicity. In the United States, lynchings and state-supported segregation have given way to a quiet, almost polite racism that resides not in bloodshed and flagrant exclusion but in the day-to-day workings of our social institutions.

With a few exceptions, minority groups still suffer noticeable disadvantages in economics, education, politics, employment, vulnerability to crime, health care, and so on. Three decades after racial segregation was ruled unconstitutional, the complete integration of such fundamental social institutions as public schools, government, and business remains largely unachieved. When opportunities to learn, legislate, and make a living are unequally distributed according to race, *all* facets of life remain unequal.

One reason why race relations are so problematic today is that public debate over the issue confuses the various types of racism. While one person might use "racism" to refer to personal forms of bigotry, another might use it to refer to broader forms of institutional racism. Different types of racism require different solutions. We cannot put an end to economic deprivation or massive residential segregation by trying to convince people not to hold sterotypical beliefs about other groups.

I realize this chapter has been rather depressing. After reading it, it's hard to imagine a multiracial society without racial stratification. We must remember, however, that differences do not have to imply inequality. The transformation from difference to disadvantage is a social construction. We as a culture have decided that some differences should be irrelevant while others should be the primary criterion for making social and legal distinctions between groups of people. Because we construct these differences, we can tear them down.

CHAPTER HIGHLIGHTS

■ The history of race in American society is an ambivalent one. Our famous sayings about equality conflict with the experiences of most racial and ethnic minorities: oppression, violence, and exploitation. Opportunities for life, liberty, and the pursuit of happiness have always been distributed along racial and ethnic lines.

■ American society is built on the assumption that different immigrant groups will ultimately assimilate, changing their way of life to conform to that of the dominant culture. But the increasing diversity of the population has shaped people's ideas about what it means to be an American and has influenced our relationships with one another and with our social institutions.

■ Personal racism is manifested in the form of bigotry, prejudice, and individual acts of discrimination.

■ Racism can also be found in a language and cultural ideology that justifies a set of social norms prescribing differential treatment of certain groups.

■ Institutional racism exists in established institutional practices and customs that reflect, produce, and maintain racial inequality. Institutional racism is more difficult to detect than personal racism, hence it is more difficult to stop. Because such racism exists at a level above personal attitudes, it will not disappear simply by reducing people's prejudices.

Y O U R   T U R N

In this chapter I examined the personal and institutional forms that racism takes. A curious and disturbing feature of prejudice is that many of our beliefs and attitudes about other racial or ethnic groups are formed without any direct contact with members of those groups. The media—most notably television—play a significant role in providing the public with often inaccurate and oversimplified information about racial and ethnic groups that indirectly shapes public attitudes.

For one week, observe several prime time television shows that feature prominent African-American, Hispanic, and Asian characters. The shows can be either comedies or dramas. Note the number of characters on each show that are people of color. Pay particular attention to the way the characters are portrayed. What is their apparent social class standing? How does their behavior conform to common stereotypes associated with members of these groups? How frequently do they refer to their own race? Do the plots of the shows revolve around what you might consider "racial" themes? That is, how often does the issue of race come up during the course of the show?

Interpret your observations sociologically. What are the implicit messages communicated by the portrayal of racial/ethnic minorities? Are characters who *do not* act in stereotypical ways conforming instead to a white, middle-class standard? If so, how will this ultimately affect public perceptions of race?

CHAPTER 13

The Architecture of Gender

Women, Men, and Inequality

- *From Objectification to Victim Blaming: Sexism at the Personal level*
- *The Ideology of Sexism*
- *Institutional Sexism*
- *Conclusion*
- *Chapter Highlights*
- *Your Turn*

At a women's rights convention held in Seneca Falls, New York, participants created a modified version of the Declaration of Independence. They called it the Declaration of Sentiments and Resolutions. Here are some excerpts from that document:

> We hold these truths to be self-evident: that all men and women are created equal. . . . The history of mankind is a history of repeated injuries . . . on the part of man toward woman, having in direct object the establishment of an absolute tyranny over her:
>
> - He has compelled her to submit to laws, in the formation of which she had no voice.
> - He has monopolized nearly all profitable [occupations], and from those she is permitted to follow, she receives but a scanty remuneration. He closes against her all the avenues to wealth and distinction which he considers most honorable to himself.
> - He has endeavored, in every way that he could, to destroy her confidence in her own powers, to lessen her self-respect, and to make her willing to lead a dependent and abject life.
>
> In view of their social degradation and in view of the unjust laws above mentioned, and because women do feel themselves aggrieved, oppressed, and fraudulently deprived of the most sacred rights, we insist that they have immediate admission to all the rights and privileges which belong to them as citizens of the United States.

The women who wrote this declaration were not the bra burners of the 1960s, the women's libbers of the 1970s, or the radical feminists of the 1990s. They were participants in the first meeting in support of women's rights ever held in our country—in 1848!

Many of us are inclined to believe that the battle against sexual inequality is a relatively recent phenomenon that emerged along with the civil rights movement of the 1960s and the so-called sexual revolution of the 1970s. We tend to think that women of the past were either content with their second-class status or unaware that it could be otherwise. As you can see from the above declaration, though, early American women were anything but passive, ignorant victims of discrimination. They were as angry, humiliated, and frustrated by social mistreatment as many women are today. The purpose of their struggle—to overcome economic, legal, and social inequality—was as relevant and urgent in 1848 as it is in the 1990s.

Along with racial and class inequality, sexual inequality has been a fundamental part of the historical development of our national identity. It has influenced the lives and dreams of individual people, shaped popular culture, and created and maintained social institutions. Chapter 5 discussed how we learn to become boys and girls, men and women within the appropriate social and cultural context. Being placed in a category based on your gender affects everything you do in life. But gender is more than just a source of personal identity that sets societal expectations; it is a major criterion for the distribution of important resources in most societies. Therefore, gender is perhaps the most important determinant of stratification worldwide.

In this chapter I explore the lives and experiences of women living in a society constructed by and for men. Several important questions are addressed: What is sexism? How is it expressed and felt at the personal level? How is it supported by cultural beliefs and symbols? At the institutional level, how is sexism related to family and work roles? What are its legal and economic consequences?

From Objectification to Victim Blaming: Sexism at the Personal Level

What do you think of when you hear the word *sexism?* The husband who won't let his wife work outside the home? The construction worker who whistles and shouts sexual comments at female passersby? The office worker who tells lewd jokes about women around the water cooler? It is all those things, but sociologically speaking, **sexism** refers to a system of beliefs and behaviors by which a group of people are oppressed, controlled, and exploited because of presumed gender differences (Anderson & Collins, 1992; Rothenberg, 1992). In a male-dominated society, or **patriarchy,** cultural beliefs and values give higher prestige and importance to men than to women. Sexual inequality exists throughout society, from the perceptions, thoughts, and social interactions of men and women to the organization of social institutions. Above all, sexual inequality provides men with privileged access to socially valued resources and furnishes them with the ability to influence the political, economic, and personal decisions of others.⌋

In chapter 12, I discussed the differences between personal and institutional racism. A similar distinction can be made between personal and institutional sexism. At the personal level, sexism refers to attitudes and behaviors communicated in everyday interaction. Research on sex stereotypes, for instance, has consistently shown that women are perceived as more passive, emotional, easily influenced, and dependent than men (Broverman et al., 1972; Tavris & Offir, 1984). Others have noted the myriad ways personal sexism can be expressed, both overtly and subtly, in micro-level interactions such as physical domination, condescending comments, sabotage, and exploitation (Benokraitis & Feagin, 1993). Such attitudes and behaviors not only place women in a lower status position vis-à-vis men, but also channel them into unequal social opportunities.

Men aren't the only ones who can be personally sexist. Certainly many women dislike men, judge them on the basis of stereotypes, hold prejudiced attitudes toward them, and even discriminate against them socially or professionally. We must keep in mind, though, that male sexism occupies a very different place in society than female sexism. The balance of power in this society has historically allowed men as a group to subordinate women socially and sometimes legally to protect their own interests and privileges. Because men tend to dominate this society, male sexism has more cultural legitimacy and more serious consequences than female sexism.

Consider the following quote from a female newspaper columnist:

> By whistling and yelling at attractive but insecure young men, we women may actually help them feel better about themselves, and give them new appreciation of their bodies. Some might say women were descending to the level of mail street-corner oafs, but I'm willing to take that risk. If, with so little effort, I can bring joy to my fellow man, then I am willing to whistle at cute guys going down the street. (Viets, 1992)

These actions don't sound so bad, do they? If you're a man, being whistled at or receiving sexual comments might be downright flattering. So why do women get so upset when such behavior is directed toward them? The answer simply is that this behavior means different things to men and women.

Verbal harassment might be an enjoyable, esteem-enhancing experience for men because it doesn't have the weight of a long tradition of subordination and objectification attached to it, nor is it linked in any way to the threat of violence. In other words, a whistle is just a whistle. Their entire worth is not being condensed into a crude assessment of their physical appearance. To women who must still fight to be taken seriously in all areas of their social, private, and professional lives, however, whistles and lewd comments reinforce their lowly status in the stratification system. These actions serve as a reminder that their social value continues to be based primarily on their looks. Men have the luxury of knowing that, for them, this will never be so.

Sexism and Social Interaction

Social interaction has always been a more perilous venture for women than men. Sex-role stereotypes put them at a disadvantage in any exchange with men. Communication is one area of social interaction that clearly shows the effects of sexism. Women and men carry on conversations in different ways (Parlee, 1989; Tannen, 1990). For instance, women are more likely than men to use a questioning intonation at the end of a statement like, "She's a good professor, don't you think?" They are also more likely to use modifiers and hedges like "sort of" and "kind of," and be excessively polite and deferential in their speech (Lakoff, 1975). Such techniques may make the speaker sound less powerful and therefore call into question the credibility and qualifications of women who happen to occupy positions of authority. Imagine if your math professor said, "The answer to the problem is 3X + Y, isn't it?" or if your boss said, "We're going to pursue the Johnson account, is that OK?"

The implicit, nonverbal messages of social interaction—body movements, facial expressions, posture—also have more serious implications and consequences for women than for men. Recall from chapter 6 that nonverbal cues play an important role not only in preserving social order but in providing people with information about their social worth. Nonverbal behavior also serves to keep women "in their place." Because they are socialized to be passive in most situations, women are likely to be targets of mild forms of interactional social control. For instance, the fact that men can more freely touch women than vice versa serves as a reminder that women's bodies are free property for everyone's use:

> I have seen women swung painfully dizzy at square dances, chased by playful gangs of men and thrown in water, carried, spanked, or dunked at the beach, all clearly against their will. The cheek- and hair-patting, chin-chucking, and bottom patting and pinching continue as part of many women's daily experiences. (Henley, 1977, pp. 121-122)

In addition, women's bodily demeanor must be restrained and restricted (Henley, 1977). Femininity is gauged by how little space women take up; masculinity is judged by men's expansiveness and the strength of their gestures. What is considered "ladylike"—crossed legs, folded arms—is also a closed expression of submission. Men's freedom of movement—feet on the desk, legs spread, straddling a chair—conveys power and dominance. Such interactional norms place women who are in authoritative positions in a no-win situation. If, on the one hand, they meet cultural definitions of femininity by being passive, polite, submissive, and vulnerable, they fail to meet the requirements of authority. If, on the other hand, they exercise their authority by being assertive, confident, dominant, and tough, their femininity is called into question (J. L. Mills, 1985).

Sexual Violence

The epitome of sexual domination expressed at the personal level is, of course, rape. Forcible rape is the most frequently committed but least reported violent crime in America today. A study funded by the U.S. Department of Health and Human Services found that 683,000 women had been raped in 1990, a figure more than five times as high as the 130,260 sexual assaults officially reported to the police that same year. In addition, it is estimated that at least 12.1 million women have been the victims of forcible rape at least once in their lives (cited in Johnston, 1992). More than 70% of the women surveyed in this study said they were concerned about their families discovering they had been raped, and about two-thirds worried that they might be blamed. Rape also has one of the lowest conviction rates of any violent crime: Only about 1 in 150 suspected rapists is ever found guilty (Renzetti & Curran, 1989).

According to conflict theorists, sex stratification has long distorted our society's understanding of rape. Throughout history women have been viewed socially and legally as the property of men, either fathers or husbands. In the past, rape was seen as a crime against men or, more accurately, against men's property (S. Griffin, 1986). Any interest a husband had in his wife being sexually assaulted reflected a concern with his own status, the loss of male honor, and the devaluation of his sexual property.

According to some feminist theorists rape, and the threat of rape, has been used throughout history to keep women in their place (Brownmiller, 1975). The existence of rape limits women's freedom, denies them the right of self-determination, makes them dependent on men, and subordinates and oppresses them (S. Griffin, 1986). All forms of oppression, whether they are against blacks in South Africa, peasants in South America, or women in the United States, employ the threat of violence to ensure compliance (Sheffield, 1987). The subordination of women depends on the power of men to intimidate and punish sexually.

The fear of rape goes beyond simply making life uncomfortable for women. It also affects them economically by restricting opportunities. Women may avoid some neighborhoods where there is affordable housing because of potential danger. If a woman has a job that requires night work, she may be forced to buy a car to avoid walking at night or utilizing public transportation. The threat of sexual assault limits where and when she is able to work, thereby limiting her money-earning choices and perhaps keeping her financially dependent on others.

Women are also harmed by the larger cultural ideology surrounding rape and rapists. I think most of us are inclined to believe that men who rape must be insane. The stereotypical image is of the sex-crazed stranger hiding in bushes or in the back seat of a parked car. He is the wild-eyed psychopath bent on harming and humiliating women because of some deep-seated psychological defect. All one has to do to avoid being raped then is to avoid strange guys.

There is little evidence that rapists as a group are any more disturbed or crazy than nonrapists (S. Griffin, 1986; Warshaw, 1988). In fact, most rapists are quite "normal" from usual societal standards. Furthermore, most are not strangers but friends or acquaintances of their victims (Warshaw, 1988). But when rape is perceived as the result of a small number of defective strangers, it doesn't have any effect on the dominant culture and established social arrangements (Hills, 1980). In other words, it's not the fault of society, it's the fault of flawed individuals who can't abide by society's rules. This may explain why date or acquaintance rape, marital rape, and other forms of sexual violence that don't fit the typical image have, until quite recently, been ignored or trivialized.

The crime of rape must be examined within the broader cultural context that encourages certain types of behavior between men and women. Rape then becomes less an act of deviance and more an act of overconformity to cultural expectations; less an act of defective individuals and more an act of "normal" men. As one author wrote, rape is the "All American Crime," involving precisely those characteristics traditionally regarded as desirable in men: strength, power, domination, and control (S. Griffin, 1989).

Rape and other forms of sexual domination are an integral part of a culture that perpetuates the power of men over women (Hills, 1980). To no surprise, then, the legal response tends to be consistent with men's interests by focusing on women's complicity or blameworthiness. Unlike any other crime, victims typically must prove their innocence rather than the state proving the guilt of the rapist. This is partly because the definition of rape is based on a traditional model of sexual intercourse—vaginal-penile penetration—rather than the violent context within which the act takes place. Rape is still largely viewed in terms of women's sexuality rather than men's coercion (Sheffield, 1987).

The exclusive focus on the sexual component of the crime requires that information about the circumstances of the act and about the relationship between the people involved be taken into consideration. Victims must provide some evidence that they were "unwilling" and tried to resist. No other crime requires that the victim prove lack of consent. People aren't asked if they wanted their car stolen or if they consented to being robbed.

If women cannot prove that they resisted, consent is presumed. Anything short of vigorous and repeated resistance calls the *victim's* motives into question. In the fall of 1992 in Austin, Texas, a man forcibly entered a woman's apartment. The woman fled and locked herself in the bathroom. He broke down the door, held a knife to her, and demanded sex. Fearing for her life, not only because of the knife but also because of the chances of contracting a sexually transmitted disease, she begged the man to put on a condom. He agreed and went on to assault her for over an hour. The next day he was arrested for burglary with intent to commit sexual assault. In a sworn deposition he admitted that he had held a knife to her and had had sex with her. The grand jury originally refused to indict the man because the victim's act of providing a condom was taken to mean consent. Only after widespread public outrage was the man tried, convicted, and sentenced to 40 years.

Not only are women sometimes accused of not doing enough to stop rape, they are occasionally suspected of actually doing something to invite or "precipitate" it (Amir, 1971). Many people regard situations in which a woman places herself at risk—by hitchhiking, acting seductively, wearing provocative clothing, or telling dirty jokes—as a form of victim-precipitated rape. Historically, jurors in rape trials have used such thinking in their deliberations. Accused rapists have been acquitted in cases where victims had been raped during beer drinking parties, had willingly entered a car with several men, had hitchhiked, or had gone dancing with the men who ultimately assaulted them (Wood, 1975).

Consider this statement by a California Court of Appeals in overturning the conviction of a man who had been convicted in a lower court of picking up and raping a hitchhiker:

> The lone female hitchhiker in the absence of an emergency situation, as a practical matter, advises all who pass by that she is willing to enter the vehicle with anyone who stops and in so doing advertises that she has less concern for the consequences than the average female. Under such circumstances it would not be unreasonable for a man in the position of the defendant here to believe that the female would consent to sexual relations. (quoted in Hills, 1980, p. 65)

Even some sociologists subscribe to the notion that women sometimes precipitate their own victimization. In 1971 Menacham Amir undertook a study of 600 rape victims and 1,200 offenders in the Philadelphia area. He concluded that about one out of every five rapes he examined was victim-precipitated. He defined victim precipitation as those situations in which the victim had actually agreed to have sex with the offender or had been thought to have agreed to this by the offender, but had changed her mind before the act or had not reacted "strongly enough" when the suggestion of sex was first made. He also categorized as victim-precipitated those rapes that were preceded by "risky situations marred with sexuality," such as a woman using indecent language or behaving in a way that could be construed as a sexual invitation.

Research indicates that such beliefs are common among the public, further perpetuating the cultural belief that women provoke rape. One survey of 400 teens (Goodchilds et al., 1988) found that approximately half of the boys and about 30% of the girls felt it was acceptable for a man to force sex on a woman when

- she is going to have sex with him and changes her mind;
- she has "led" him on;
- she gets him sexually excited;
- they have dated for a long time; or
- she lets him touch her above the waist.

In another study, 200 male and 200 female college undergraduates were given a list of statements and asked to indicate the extent to which they agreed with them (Barnett & Feild, 1977). Fifty-nine percent of the men and 38% of the women agreed that women provoke rape by their appearance. Forty-one percent of the men and 27% of the women agreed that women should be held responsible for preventing their own victimization. And 32% of the men and 8% of the women felt that it would do some women good to get raped.

The important sociological point of these findings is that many men and even some women don't always define violent sexual assault as wrong and think it is what men are supposed or expected to do under certain circumstances. These views have become so entrenched in this culture's view of rape that many women have internalized the message, blaming themselves for their own victimization. Outside of fear, self-blame is the most common reaction to rape and is more frequent in occurrence than anger (Janoff-Bulman, 1979). When rape victims say things like, "I shouldn't have walked alone," "I should have locked my windows," "I shouldn't have worn that dress to the party," they are at least partly taking the blame for a crime they didn't commit.

The crucial consequence of victim blaming is that women must bear most if not all of the responsibility for preventing rape. I frequently pose this question to students in my classes: What can *people* do to stop rape from occurring? Their responses always contain things like: Don't hitchhike. Don't walk alone at night. Don't get drunk at parties where men are present. Don't initiate sex play. Don't engage in foreplay if you have no intention of "going all the way." Don't miscommunicate your intentions. Don't wear provocative clothing. Don't accept invitations from strangers. Note how these suggestions focus exclusively on things that *women* should avoid in order to prevent rape and say nothing about the things *men* can do to stop it.

I don't mean to imply that one ought to ignore this advice. It certainly makes sense, given the violent nature of today's society, to communicate intentions clearly and not to put oneself in dangerous situations. The implication of such instructions, however, speaks volumes about the nature of rape and the place of women in this society. Confining discussions of rape prevention to women's behavior suggests that if a woman doesn't take these precautions, she is "inviting trouble." And "inviting trouble" implies that violent male behavior either is a natural response or is likely to happen if certain things aren't done to discourage it. Hence, a woman cannot dress the way she wants, walk where and when she wants, talk to whom she wants, or change her mind about having sex.

Without a fundamental restructuring of society, no significant reduction in rape is likely to occur. Such a change would require a transformation of male-female relationships and childhood socialization, as well as a more equitable sharing of political and economic power. The recent increase in attention paid toward rape, particularly toward acquaintance or date rape, is a first step toward a shift in public awareness. Myths are being debunked, the sexual exploitation of women in the media is being protested, and the rules governing admissible evidence in rape trials are being changed. However, as long as a deeply ingrained sexist ideology that objectifies women and glorifies male assertiveness continues to exist, so too will sexual violence.

The Ideology of Sexism

The domination of one group over another is always endorsed by a set of beliefs that explains and justifies that domination. With racism, it is the belief in innate racial inferiority; with sexism, it is the belief that biology is destiny, which leads to the subsequent cultural devaluation of women.

Biology Is Destiny

The unique physiology and biological functioning of women have been used for centuries to advance the view that women's disadvantaged status in society is a function of their anatomy (Holstrom, 1982). For 19th-century physicians, few facts were more incontestable than the fact that women were the products and prisoners of their reproductive systems. Women's place in society was thought to be linked to and controlled by the existence and function of the uterus and ovaries (Scull & Favreau, 1986). Everything "abnormal" about women could be explained by their reproductive anatomy: the predominance of the emotional over the rational, the capacity for affection, the love of children and aptitude for child rearing, the preference for domestic work, and so on (Ehrenreich & English, 1979; Scull & Favreau, 1986).

Scholars at the time warned that young women who studied too much not only were struggling against nature but would badly damage their reproductive organs and perhaps even go insane in the process (Fausto-Sterling, 1985). The exclusion of women from higher education was not only justifiable but necessary for health reasons and for the long-term good of society.

Such beliefs about the undesirable effects of women's biological functioning are not just a thing of the past. Many contemporary physicians and psychiatrists argue that the normal biological process of menstruation predisposes women to certain personality disorders. In 1993 the Board of Trustees of the American Psychiatric Association debated the merits of whether a psychiatric diagnosis called "premenstrual dysphoric disorder" ought to be included in its official manual of mental disorders. (At the time of this writing it appears in the manual as a "proposed category in need of further investigation.")

There is no denying that women around the world recognize irritability, moodiness, and other symptoms related to menstruation. The issue, however, is whether these symptoms ought to be labeled as a medical problem (Lander, 1988). To do so fosters a belief that women's bodies are weak and in need of medical attention and allows for the selling of drugs to healthy women (C. A. Bailey, 1993).

Functionalist sociologists have also used the observable physical differences between men and women as the basis of their explanation of sexual inequality. The fact that men tend to be physically stronger and that women bear and nurse children has created many culturally recognized and necessary sex-segregated roles, especially at work and in the family (Parsons & Bales, 1955).

This specialization of roles is the most effective way to maintain societal stability. By giving birth to new members, by socializing very young children, and by providing affection and nurturance, women make invaluable contributions to the reproduction of society. The common occupations that women have outside the home—teacher, nurse, day care provider, maid, social worker, and so on—tend simply to be extensions of their "natural" tendencies.

Men's physical characteristics better suit them for the roles of economic provider and protector of the family. Because they are assumed to be "naturally endowed" with traits like strength, assertiveness, competitiveness, and rationality, they are best qualified to enter the serious and competitive world of work and politics (Kokopeli & Lakey, 1992). As one social scientist matter-of-factly put it, men inevitably occupy the most prestigious positions in society because they possess more testosterone—the hormone associated with aggression—and therefore have a competitive advantage over women in the occupational marketplace (Goldberg, 1974). In short, men are assumed to be the natural power wielders and societal leaders. One study, however, has found that the higher the level of testosterone in men, the *lower* their occupational status (Dabbs, 1992).

But by depicting masculinity and femininity as natural, biological phenomena, functionalists confuse sex with gender. Their message is simple and clear: Nature cannot change, so we ought not try to change it. The assumption that gender is unchangeable overlooks the wide cultural and historical variation in conceptions of masculinity and femininity. You will recall from chapter 5 that traits can be modified or completely changed by cultural circumstances.

Margaret Mead
*Sex and
Temperament*

The famous anthropologist Margaret Mead (1963) believed that masculine and feminine characteristics were based not on biological sex difference but on cultural conditioning. She set out to support her theory by studying three cultures in New Guinea. Among the mountain-dwelling Arapesh, men and women displayed similar attitudes and actions. They showed traits we would commonly associate with femininity: cooperation, passivity, sensitivity to others. Mead described both men and women as being "maternal." These characteristics were linked to broader cultural beliefs about people's relationship to the environment. The Arapesh didn't have any conception of "ownership" of land, so there were never conflicts over possession of property.

South of the Arapesh were the Mundugumor, a group of cannibals and headhunters. Here, too, males and females were similar. However, both displayed traits we, in the West, would associate with masculinity: assertiveness, emotional inexpressiveness, insensitivity to others. Women, according to Mead, were just as violent, just as aggressive, and just as jealous as men. Both were equally virile, without any of the "soft" characteristics we associate with femininity.

Finally, there were the Tchambuli. This group *did* distinguish between male and female traits. However, their gender expectations were the opposite of what we have here. Women were the ones who were dominant, assertive, and managerial; men were submissive, emotional, and seen as inherently delicate.

Mead's work is important because it shows that definitions of the natural tendencies of men and women vary from culture to culture. Women need not be the nurturers of children; men need not be the aggressors. Both engage in behaviors different from those in western cultures yet are still considered men and women.

In sum, the functionalist rationale for sexual inequality is difficult to justify. Technological advances, including bottled baby formula and contraceptives that reduce women's childbearing and child-rearing responsibilities, and improved mechanization that lessens the need for sheer physical strength, have made the biological imperative for gender-based role responsibilities obsolete (Gough, 1971). Nevertheless, as long as people *believe* that gender-linked roles and societal contributions are determined by nature, they will continue to accept sexual inequality in opportunities, expectations, and outcomes. If it is "natural" for women to play nurturant, weak, and dependent roles, then structurally limiting them to such positions is neither unfair nor oppressive.

The Cultural Devaluation of Women

If biology is *not* destiny, then we must look to culture to explain the unequal treatment of women. Anthropologists agree that despite cross-cultural differences in gender expectations, most societies devalue women to some extent (Stockard & Johnson, 1992). In some societies the extreme consequences of female devaluation can literally be fatal.

In Bangladesh, land laws dictate that a family's property can be passed down only through males. A daughter's inheritance automatically goes to her husband upon marriage. Daughters are an economic liability and are discriminated against daily. Families short on food will commonly see to it that the male children are well fed, often at the expense of female children. Nationwide, girls get 16% less food than boys. As a result, girls grow up sicker. Many female babies are so undernourished that they die within the first year (Bryjak & Soroka, 1992).

The cultural devaluation of women can have even more violent consequences. One of the most pernicious forms of wife abuse—known locally as "bride burning" or "dowry deaths"—takes place in India (Heise, 1989; Van Willigen & Channa, 1991). Dowry was traditionally a cultural institution that referred to the gifts that a woman received from her parents upon marriage. Even though it was officially banned in 1961, dowry is still an essential part of premarital negotiations and now refers to the wealth that the bride's family pays the groom. In many cases it has become a get-rich-quick scheme for men and their families. Young brides who, by custom, live with their new husband's parents, are commonly subjected to severe abuse if promised money is not paid. Sometimes dowry harassment ends in suicide or murder. In 1992, 4,785 wives were killed by their husbands for not providing adequate dowries (Gargan, 1993). Often the husband and his family try to disguise the murder as an accident by setting the wife on fire and then claiming she died in a kitchen mishap. In the city of Bombay, 19% of all deaths among women 15 to 44 years old are due to "accidental burns" (Heise, 1989).

In our society the cultural devaluation of women is not usually so life-threatening. Here devaluation is manifested in beliefs that women are less capable than men in performing many tasks outside the home (Wagner, Ford, & Ford, 1986). People still find female doctors or dentists unusual and debate the role of female soldiers in combat. The controversy in both the Episcopal and Catholic churches over whether or not women should be ordained as ministers illustrates the depth and intensity of people's feelings about gender-appropriate career pursuits. Female devaluation, however, is not just a matter of men subjugating women. Women also come to expect certain things in their lives that affect not only the perceptions of others but their self-perceptions as well.

Moreover, the qualities we consider feminine are usually seen as less socially valuable than those considered masculine. For a boy to be called a girl is the ultimate schoolyard insult because it implies weakness, frailty, and lack of ability. Even today, many men can be easily whipped into anger by accusations of femininity, as when drill sergeants or football coaches call their male soldiers or players "girls" or "ladies" to draw out their aggressiveness.

The devaluation of women, and therefore all things "feminine," even influences the cultural value of certain emotions. We think of love as involving emotional expressiveness, verbal self-disclosure, and affection (Cancian, 1987). Clearly these are qualities associated with women. The desirable masculine traits—independence, competence, emotional inexpressiveness—usually imply the antithesis of love. It is no coincidence, then, that our society tends to glorify instrumental, rational achievement and downplay emotional expression as overly sentimental and foolish. When we think of love in such a way, men's power over women is strengthened because women are encouraged to specialize in and be emotionally responsible for romantic relationships, while men are expected to specialize in work activities that are more highly regarded in society.

Sexism and Cultural Symbolism

An explanation of sexist ideology wouldn't be complete without some mention of the cultural images that contribute to the subordination and devaluation of women. In large part, these images come from the media. You saw in chapter 5 how the media portrayal of men and women contributes to early gender socialization. But these images can also be dangerous and demeaning, as women are underrepresented and, more important, misrepresented in the media (Cantor, 1987).

A glimpse at the portrayal of women in advertising, fashion, television, music videos, and films today reveals that the image of the modern woman is a dual one (Sidel, 1990). On the one hand, there is the successful woman of the nineties: the perfect wife/mother/career woman, the triumphant professional who leaps gracefully about the pages of fashion magazines. Like the popular television character Murphy Brown, she is outgoing, bright, attractive, and assertive. No occupation is beyond her reach: She can be a lawyer, doctor, politician, executive, police officer, or entrepreneur.

On the other hand, there is the stereotypical image of the exhibited woman. She is the seductive sex object displayed in beer commercials, magazine advertisements, soap operas, and the swimsuit issue of *Sports Illustrated*. According to a recent study by the National Commission on Working Women, television continues to present stereotypes that show women as shallow, vain, and materialistic characters whose looks still count for more than their brains (cited in Sidel, 1990). The sex object is the most dangerous media image of all because conventional beauty is her only attribute: "Women are constantly exhorted to emulate this ideal, to feel ashamed and guilty if they fail, and to feel that their desirability and lovability are contingent upon physical perfection" (Kilbourne, 1992, p. 349).

It is no surprise, then, that beauty pageants, the epitome of the exhibition of women, continue to be popular in our country. An estimated 55 million people, 75% of whom are women, tune in each year to watch the Miss America Pageant (Sidel, 1990). Many women watch these shows to find out what an attractive female is supposed to look like (Freedman, 1986). In 1987, 80,000 women competed in local and state pageants for a shot at the title of Miss America.

The image of beauty presented by the exhibited woman is artificial and largely unattainable. For instance, the body sizes of the winners of the Miss America Pageant have been steadily decreasing over the past 20 years, reaffirming the cultural value of thinness (Garner et al., 1980). Women are encouraged to view themselves as in constant need of alteration, improvement, and disguise. Hence they will not hesitate to go to great lengths to change their faces and bodies (Kilbourne, 1992). Any doubt that such images have an effect on the activities and self-concepts of young women is quickly dispelled by the statistics on eating disorders in America and the number of school-age girls who diet.

It is conservatively estimated that one in five young American women today has an eating disorder. A recent survey of students in Chicago area schools found that more than half the fourth-grade girls were dieting and three-quarters felt they were overweight (cited in Kilbourne, 1992). A *Glamour* magazine survey in 1984 found that over 75% of the respondents considered themselves over-weight. What is more telling is that nearly half of the women in this survey, who were in reality *under*weight, reported feeling too fat and wanting to diet. Sticklike standards of beauty have become an ideal many young women are ready to starve for to attain (cited in Kilbourne, 1992).

These media messages are confusing and can be, as in the case of eating disorders, lethal. Young women today not only must achieve at unprecedented levels, but they also must look sexy doing it. These images create the illusion that success or failure is purely a personal, private achievement, and ignore the complex social, economic, and political forces that continue to operate and prevent real-life women from achieving the kind of success the artificial media images seem to enjoy so easily.

Institutional Sexism

The subordination of women that is part of the workings of social institutions (or **institutional sexism**) has far greater consequences for women as a group. As we have seen throughout this book, the experiences of individuals must always be located within an institutional structure. The law, the family, and the organization of work all have a role in producing gender stratification (M. Brinton, 1988). These institutions have historically been developed by men, dominated by men, and interpreted by men. The only institutions in which women have had a central role is the family, but as we will see that role has traditionally been a subordinate one (Acker, 1992). When sexism in social institutions becomes part of the ongoing operation of large-scale organizations, it perpetuates and magnifies women's structural disadvantages, making social equality all the more difficult to attain.

Not only are social institutions sexist—in that women are segregated, exploited, or excluded—they are also gendered. In other words, institutions and organizations themselves are structured along gender lines. Most bureaucracies in institutional areas like business, politics, and the military operate according to masculine principles:

> This "masculine ethic" elevates the traits assumed to belong to men . . . to necessities for effective organizations: a tough-minded approach to problems; analytic abilities to abstract and plan; a capacity to set aside personal, emotional considerations in the interests of task accomplishment; a cognitive superiority in problem-solving and decision making. (Kanter, 1975, p. 43)

Successful leaders and organizations are usually portrayed as aggressive, goal-oriented, competitive, and efficient, all characteristics we associate with masculinity in this society. Rarely are prosperous businesses or efficient departments in the military described as supportive, nurturant, cooperative, kind, and caring (Acker, 1992).

Sexism and the Law

Historically women have been denied many of the legal rights that men take for granted. In 1894, for instance, the U.S. Supreme Court heard the case of Belva Lockwood, who was denied a license to practice law even though the state of Virginia permitted any "person" licensed as an attorney in any other state to practice there. The court ruled against Lockwood, stating that the word *person* meant "male" (Renzetti & Curran, 1989).

In the past, when women got married, they lost many of the legal rights they enjoyed as single women: legal title to their property, the right to execute contracts, and so forth. Husbands could chastise their wives, force them to stay at home, and even rape them without legal sanction. Such laws were based on the English common law doctrine of "coverture," under which a married woman's legal identity was submerged into that of her husband (Baron, 1987).

We don't have to go back a century to find attempts at limiting the legal rights of women. In 1981 a bill called the Family Protection Act was introduced in Congress. Although the bill was never passed, its objective was to dismantle many of the legal achievements of the women's movement. Among its proposals were eliminating federal laws supporting equal education, forbidding the "intermingling of the sexes in any sport or other school-related activities," requiring marriage and motherhood to be taught as the proper career for girls, denying federal funding to any school using textbooks portraying women in nontraditional roles, repealing all federal laws protecting battered wives from their husbands, and banning all federally funded legal aid for any women seeking abortion counseling or divorce (Faludi, 1991). In addition, through an extra tax on spouses who file separate income tax returns, the bill encouraged a family structure with a working husband and nonworking wife (Ruether, 1980).

To counteract this long history of legal inequality, Congress has passed many laws aimed at improving the situation of women in this society. The 1964 Civil Rights Act focused on sexism in employment. The 1974 Educational Amendments Act focused on gender equality in education. Obstacles to equality have been removed in other areas like housing, the granting of credit, and hiring practices (Eitzen & Baca-Zinn, 1989). The 1993 Family Leave Act guarantees some working mothers (as well as fathers) up to 12 weeks of unpaid sick leave per year to care for a new child or a sick relative.

But these laws haven't been entirely successful. Occupations are still highly segregated along gender lines; female workers still earn a fraction of what male workers earn; college athletic budgets are still highly skewed toward men's sports; and a woman's right to control her own body through legal abortion continues to be challenged.

Even laws explicitly designed to protect women's rights have created unforeseen disadvantages. Since 1970, most states have adopted "no-fault" divorce laws. These laws eliminated the requirement that one partner be found guilty. Instead, marriages are declared unworkable and are terminated. The laws also redefined the responsibilities of husbands and wives. The husband was no longer automatically considered the head of the household and the wife was no longer considered solely responsible for the care of the children. Financial awards—alimony and child support—are based on the spouses' ability to work. If neither spouse is unable to work, courts usually assume that both are equally capable.

Although written to make the termination of marriages more fair, these laws have actually increased the number of women who become poor after a divorce (Arendell, 1984; Weitzman, 1985). As we discussed in chapter 10, divorced husbands typically experience an increase in their standard of living, while divorced wives suffer a decrease. In California, for instance, after no-fault divorce laws were enacted, only 13% of mothers with preschool children received spousal support (cited in Tavris, 1992). The situation for divorced women, particularly older women, was so bad that the California legislature had to pass the Displaced Homemakers Relief Act, which required judges to consider the future earning potential of each spouse before awarding a settlement.

Not all legislation aimed at giving women equal legal rights has met with public approval. In 1982 the Equal Rights Amendment, which would have made unconstitutional state and federal laws that treated men and women unequally, was defeated. The defeat of ERA is a classic example of how powerful the control of perceptions of reality and definitions of situations can be. The amendment consisted of a single sentence: "Equality of rights under the law shall not be denied or abridged by the United States or any State on account of sex." Opponents claimed the amendment would destroy American life by, among other things, integrating public bathrooms, forcing women to fight in the military, and destroying the family. One group called the amendment one of "the most destructive pieces of legislation ever to pass Congress," and referred to feminists as "moral perverts" and "enemies of every decent society" (Spretnak, 1982).

Sexism and the Family

Much of the sexual inequality found in the law revolves around the traditional family role of women as the producer and socializer of children. Women have always retained the responsibility of reproduction; it is one of the few areas in society where women can exert tremendous societal influence (Rowland, 1990). Motherhood has always been considered the pinnacle of a woman's social identity and her God-given and socially expected duty. However, while this role can be the source of pride, joy, and a sense of accomplishment, it can also be the source of pain, exploitation, and discrimination.

Reproductive Technology and Fetal Rights

Although the institution of family is idealized in our society, reproduction is relatively invisible and devalued until it fails to function, and then it is likely to become the focus of criticism (Acker, 1992). Traditionally, the only reproductive issue facing women was choice: the right to have or not to have children. Thirty years ago, feminists fought to protect women's right to have children by opposing organized efforts at the forced sterilization of some women. Later, they fought to ensure women's right *not* to bear children by fighting for universal access to contraception and abortion.

Today the issue of reproductive choice is much more complicated. Technological developments like in vitro fertilization and surrogate motherhood have allowed thousands of infertile women to conceive children. Although access is limited primarily to the affluent, these procedures have the potential of increasing the reproductive choices and opportunities available to women (B. K. Rothman, 1987; Rowland, 1990).

Ironically, such advances, coupled with our culture's inability to accept infertility, make it increasingly more difficult for women to choose *not* to have children and may in fact actually take away their reproductive control. Increased technological intervention into the processes by which women conceive has allowed the male-dominated medical profession to control the reproductive process (Rowland, 1990; Woliver, 1989).

Men tend to benefit professionally and economically from these developments. Because of the cultural value placed on children, research into the area has faced virtually no criticism and has been allowed to expand with little community debate (Rowland, 1990). After all, who would criticize research that could provide infertile couples with the miracle of a baby? Unfortunately, women are the ones who serve as experimental subjects. Their bodies become "uterine environments" within which "harvested" eggs can be planted. Women must also face the emotional and physical risks, which include infection, painful side effects, permanent physical injury, or the heartbreak of failure. As one critic put it: "Who invented it, who manufactured it, who licensed it, who dispenses it? But who dies from it?" (quoted in Rowland, 1990, p. 351).

Furthermore, when women are pregnant they often find that their rights are considered secondary to those of their unborn children. The contemporary debate that pits fetal rights against women's rights illustrates the growing public desire to place women's reproductive capacities under outside governmental control. In this way, pregnant women are denied the rights of bodily integrity and self-determination that all competent adults in this society are granted (Tavris, 1992).

The growing sentiment in this country is that women should have a moral, societal, and legal responsibility to insure a healthy birth. Consider several recent court cases:

- In Washington, D.C., a judge ordered a pregnant woman seriously ill with cancer to undergo a cesarean section against her wishes and those of her husband, her parents, and her doctor, in order to save the life of her 25-week-old fetus. She and the fetus died during the procedure, which was performed quickly, before her lawyers could appeal.

■ In Wisconsin, the U.S. Court of Appeals upheld an automotive battery plant's "fetal protection policy," which barred fertile women from higher paying, more prestigious jobs in the factory because they might be exposed to lead, which might cause birth defects. Many of the women barred from these jobs were in their late 40s and had no intention of having any more children. No female employee, exposed to lead in the factory, had ever shown any ill effects. This decision was ultimately overturned by the U.S. Supreme Court.

■ A pregnant woman in Wyoming was arrested for endangering her unborn child when she arrived drunk at a hospital for treatment of injuries inflicted by her abusive husband. The charges were dropped but were to be reinstated if the child was born with any alcohol-caused defects. No charges were filed against the husband (Pollitt, 1990).

Cases like these, as well as increasing public concern over the prenatal behavior of pregnant women, show the extent to which society has come to define women as *the* major threat to the health of their newborns. Consequently, women's behavior has become the most urgent political target in the fight to protect children.

Focusing solely on pregnant women allows us to ignore other dangers and other threats to the well-being of children that lie outside the mother's body: poverty, inadequate health care, poor housing, environmental hazards, racism, and so on. One in five pregnant women today lack access to any sort of prenatal health care (Pollitt, 1990), yet such facts are overlooked in the pursuit of fetal rights. Controlling the behavior of mothers allows the government to appear concerned about babies without having to spend any money, change any priorities, or challenge any vested interests (Pollitt, 1990). But as we become more obsessed with pregnant women's behavior, the health and well-being of American children continues to decline. Like poverty, homelessness, and crime, the health of children is construed as a matter of freely chosen *individual* behavior: "We have crime because we have lots of bad people, poverty because we have lots of lazy people . . . and tiny, sickly, impaired babies because we have lots of women who just don't give a damn" (Pollitt, 1990, p. 243).

Once a problem is defined this way, coercion and punishment come to be seen as justifiable and necessary responses. I'm not suggesting that using drugs or smoking cigarettes while pregnant is a good thing to do. But the problem of infant sickness must be placed in the larger institutional context:

> The concept of fetal rights . . . posits a world in which women will be held accountable, on sketchy or no evidence, for birth defects; . . . in which courts, employers, social workers and doctors—not to mention nosy neighbors and vengeful male partners—will monitor women's behavior. It imposes responsibilities without giving women the wherewithal to fulfill them, and places upon women alone duties that belong to both parents and to the community. (Pollitt, 1990, p. 251)

Housework and the Domestic Division of Labor

A woman's important role in the family is not solely her ability to produce new family members. In most families she is the key to the household's smooth functioning. One of the major consequences of the Industrial Revolution of the late 19th and early 20th centuries was the separation of work and home. Prior to industrialization, the nation's economy was primarily agricultural. People's lives centered around the farm, where husbands and wives were partners not only in making a home but in making a living (Vanek, 1980). The farm couple was interdependent; each needed the other for survival.

Women therefore played a crucial role in the family economy by producing the basic necessities. It was taken for granted that women provided for the family along with men (Bernard, 1981). Although the relationship between husbands and wives on the farm was never entirely equal—wives still did most if not all of the housekeeping and family care—complete male dominance was offset by women's indispensable contributions to the household economy (Vanek, 1980).

With the advent of industrialization, things began to change. New forms of technology and the promise of new financial opportunities and a good living drew men away from the farms and into cities and factories. For the first time in American history, the family economy was based outside the household. Women no longer found themselves involved in the day-to-day supervision of the family's business as they had once been. Instead, they were consigned to the only domestic responsibilities that remained: the care and nurturance of children and the maintenance of the household. Since this work was unpaid and since visible goods were no longer being produced at home, women quickly found that their work had no place in an industrial economy (Hareven, 1992).

The devaluation of women's work is also the result of the difference in power between the public and private spheres (Sidel, 1990). As long as men have a monopoly over the public sphere, they will wield greater economic and political power within society and also be able to translate that power into authority at home. "Women's work" within the relatively powerless private sphere will continue to be hidden, free, and of little social value.

If a woman were to be paid for all her labor as mother and housekeeper according to the actual pay scales for the jobs she does—chauffeur, nurse, day care worker, maid, cook, therapist—her yearly salary would be over $50,000, substantially more than the salaries of most male full-time workers. In 1990 unpaid household work was equal to about 44% of the gross national product, or over $1 trillion (Strong & DeVault, 1992). However, because societal and family power are a function of who earns the money, such work does not afford women the prestige it might if it were paid labor. It's not that housewives don't work, it's that they work outside the mainstream economy in which work is strictly defined as something one is paid to do (Ciancanelli & Berch, 1987; Voyandoff, 1990).

Despite significant shifts in attitudes toward gender roles and the accelerated entry of women into the paid labor force, housework continues to be predominantly female. Dana Hiller and William Philliber (1986) interviewed 489 married couples about their housework experiences. Despite the fact that 69% of the wives in the sample worked outside the home, they found that their marriages were still heavily colored by traditional expectations about each spouse's respective responsibilities. Husbands were still perceived as the primary wage earners, and wives were expected to be in charge of the housework. Over 70% of the sample felt that wives should be primarily responsible for such tasks as cooking, cleaning, washing clothes, ironing, food shopping, and taking care of the children.

Other research has consistently shown that women spend about 50 hours a week doing housework, while men contribute a maximum of about 11 hours (Cowan, 1991; Levant, Slatter, & Loiselle, 1987). Moreover, the housework men do tends to be quite different from the work their wives are doing:

> They take out the garbage, they mow the lawns, they play with children, they occasionally go to the supermarket or shop for household durables, they paint the attic or fix the faucet; but by and large, they do not launder, clean, or cook, nor do they feed, clothe, bathe, or transport children. These . . . most time-consuming activities . . . are exclusively the domain of women. (Cowan, 1991, p. 207)

One could argue that traditional gender disparities in household responsibilities actually reflect an equitable, functional, interdependent division of labor. That is, the husband works in the paid labor force and supports the family financially, while the wife takes care of the household work and child care. Each person provides essential services in exchange for those provided by the other.

If this were the case, you would expect housework to be shared equally if both partners work full-time, right? Research in this area, though, indicates that the gender discrepancy in housework responsibilities does not diminish when women work full-time. Although employed wives do spend less time on housework than housewives—on average, around 20 hours less a week—their husbands do not "pick up the slack" (Blumstein & Schwartz, 1983; Geerken & Gove, 1983; J. N. Morgan, 1978). Working women continue to have almost exclusive responsibility for housework and end up working what amounts to two full-time jobs. Even if a husband is unemployed, he does much less housework than a wife who puts in a 40-hour week. Interestingly, this is the case even among couples who profess egalitarian, nonsexist values. Husbands who say that all the housework should be shared still spend significantly less time doing it than their wives (Blumstein & Schwartz, 1983).

The fact that housework is still predominantly women's work, no matter what her or her spouse's employment status, gives us some sense of how pervasive and powerful our sexist ideology continues to be. The aversion to housework on the part of men may be so intense that it can sour a relationship. The more housework married men do, the more conflict there is in the marriage (Blumstein & Schwartz, 1983). Such a pattern may serve as a significant barrier to the reorganization of gender roles within the family.

Sexism and the Economy

Family obligations that keep women out of the paid labor force or restrict their opportunities once they enter it work to promote economic inequality (Acker, 1988). Economic well-being influences many aspects of a person's life, including political power, access to education, relationship satisfaction, and physical and emotional health.

Women have historically been prevented from taking advantage of the occupational opportunities and rewards to which most men have had free access. Today women continue to have much less earning power in the American labor market than men (Blood, Tuttle, & Lakey, 1992). About two-thirds of all poor people in this country are women. Institutional sexism is most vividly felt within the work sphere, for that is where discrimination can be measured in dollars and career mobility.

The unequal economic status of women not only results from personal expressions of sexism but is tied to larger economic structures and institutional forces. The standard assumptions that drive the typical workplace often work against women. Think of the things you have to do in order to be considered a good worker by your boss. You may have to work extra hours, travel to faraway business meetings, go to conferences, attend training programs, be willing to work unpopular shifts, or entertain out-of-town clients. These activities assume you have the time and the freedom from familial obligations to do them. Because women, especially mothers, still tend to have the lion's share of responsibility at home, they will have more difficulty making time for these activities and therefore will be less able to "prove" to management that they are good, committed employees. Because of the built-in assumptions about what one needs to do to get ahead, women are less likely than men to possess the qualities commonly associated with an "ideal worker."

Sex Segregation in the Workplace

Women have made remarkable progress in overcoming traditional obstacles to employment. Today, almost 70% of all women between the ages of 18 and 64 work in the paid labor force (Baca-Zinn & Eitzen, 1993). Close to half of all American workers today are female (Reskin & Padavic, 1994). Moreover, over the past several decades women have increased their representation dramatically in male-dominated fields like engineering, medicine, law, and administration (Reskin & Hartmann, 1986). The representation of women in skilled trades has increased by over 80% (Sidel, 1986). Table 13.1 shows the increase in the number of women in a variety of professional occupations.

Table 13.1   *Increase in the Percentage of Women in Managerial and Professional Jobs*

	1970	1983	1988
Occupation:			
College teacher	29.1%	36.3%	38.5%
Lawyer	4.9%	15.3%	19.3%
Physician	9.7%	15.8%	20.0%
Natural scientist	13.6%	20.5%	24.1%
All professions	44.0%	48.1%	49.8%
Executive/Administrative	18.5%	32.4%	39.3%

Source: U.S. Bureau of Labor Statistics, 1985, 1989.

Although such figures are encouraging, sex segregation in the workplace is still the rule and not the exception. Almost half of all employed women work in occupations that are at least 80% female—librarians, nurses, elementary school teachers, secretaries, and so on (Philipson, 1993; Reskin & Hartmann, 1986). A report by the National Committee on Pay Equity (1992) found that women constitute 99% of all secretaries, 94.5% of all registered nurses, 97% of all child care workers, 89% of all telephone operators, and 74% of all teachers, excluding colleges and universities. On the other hand, women make up only 9.5% of all dentists, 19% of all physicians, 8% of all engineers, 20% of all lawyers and judges, and 14% of all police officers. It's estimated that about two-thirds of American men and women would have to change jobs today in order to achieve equal gender distribution across occupations, a figure that was the same in 1900 (Philipson, 1993).

Most of the changes that *have* taken place in the sex distribution of different occupations have been due to women entering male lines of work. While women have entered traditionally male occupations at a steady clip since the 1970s, men have not noticeably increased their representation in female-dominated occupations. The number of male nurses, kindergarten teachers, librarians, and secretaries has increased only minimally if at all (Reskin & Hartmann, 1986). One recent study found that some men would rather suffer unemployment than accept "women's jobs," even if they are high-paying ones, because of the potential damage to their masculinity (Epstein, 1989).

This kind of "one-way" occupational shift is troubling and may actually lead to the resegregation of the workforce. Historically, when large numbers of women enter a particular occupation previously closed to them, there is an accompanying decrease in the number of men in that occupation. Given the fact that in this society greater value is usually awarded to male pursuits, such occupations become less prestigious as men leave them. In fact, the higher the proportion of female workers in an occupation, the less both male and female workers earn (Reskin & Padavic, 1994).

During the early part of this century, for example, the job of bank teller was a well-respected and exclusively male occupation. Between World War I and World War II, bank telling was reorganized along the lines of *deskilling*, in which complex jobs are broken down into simpler tasks. Within the bank structure, a hierarchy of jobs was created, which meant a hierarchy in salaries. Because of these changes, women entered the field at increasing rates. They were more willing than men to work for lower wages and were viewed by employers as appropriate for the work assignments at the lower end of the hierarchy. By the beginning of World War II, women had come to constitute 37% of bank tellers (Philipson, 1993). This figure increased even more during the war as women were hired to replace men who had entered the military.

The nature of banking was also changing. Prior to World War II, banks primarily served corporations and wealthy individuals. Few people had checking accounts. During the Depression and war years, however, banks began offering services to larger segments of the population in order to provide people with greater access to funds. They introduced economy checking accounts with no minimum balance requirements, made installment loans for consumer purchases, real estate, and small business investments, and began accepting phone and utility payments (Philipson, 1993). Between 1939 and 1952 the number of checking accounts in the United States nearly doubled. Consequently, banks expanded their number of branches and, in turn, the number of bank employees.

With this shift from "class" to "mass" banking, the status of bank telling declined, and with it the wages relative to other occupations. Bank telling ultimately lost its attractiveness to male employees. After the war, men did not reclaim these jobs. By 1950 women filled almost half of all bank telling positions. By 1990, 90% of bank tellers were women (Philipson, 1993; Reskin & Padavic, 1994).

It should also be noted that greater female entry into a traditionally male line of work doesn't necessarily mean gender equality. Segregation *within* occupations is still strong. For instance, although half of all assemblers in the manufacturing industry are women—a fact that suggests occupational integration—upon closer inspection women make up 75% of electrical assemblers but only 17% of motor vehicle assemblers, which is a higher paying job (Reskin & Hartmann, 1986). Women who work as sales clerks in department stores are likely to be in the lower paying departments (e.g., clothing and housewares), whereas men are likely to be in the more lucrative departments (e.g., furniture and large appliances). Female physicians are substantially overrepresented in specialties like pediatrics, obstetrics, and gynecology and underrepresented in more prestigious and lucrative areas like neurosurgery (Patterson & Engelberg, 1978).

Such within-occupation segregation reinforces gender stereotypes. A study of jobs in a McDonald's restaurant found that although there was roughly the same number of male and female workers, most of the women worked at the counter or the drive-up window and most of the men worked at the grill. Many of the workers found this arrangement unremarkable. They simply assumed that women were more interested in working with people and that the job requirements of smiling and showing deference to customers was best suited to a feminine style of interaction (Leidner, 1991).

Finally, at the personal level, many women who do enter traditionally male occupations find they must continuously confront their marginal status and the differential treatment resulting from it. It is common for businesses with few women in upper-level positions to give the outward appearance of equality by placing them in highly visible positions.

Micro-Macro Connection

Tokenism in the Workplace

Sociologist Rosabeth Moss Kanter (1977) observed and interviewed employees at a large industrial supply company she called Industrial Supply Corporation over a period of 5 years. She used the word *tokens* to refer to the relatively few women given prominent positions in a particular occupational setting.

Whether they are women, minorities, people with handicaps, or the elderly, tokens are often treated as symbols or representatives of the marginal social group to which they belong. As a result, the thoughts, beliefs, and actions of the lone woman in a predominantly male company are likely to be taken as typical of all women. Some women at Industrial Supply Corporation were even told that their job performance could affect the prospects of other women in the company. In short, the token is less an individual than a social category.

Tokens must perform their jobs under conditions very different from those facing other workers. Consequently, token status has important social and psychological consequences. The token doesn't have to work hard to be noticed, but she does have to work hard to have her achievements noticed. Kanter found that many of the women she studied told of situations in which their abilities were eclipsed by their physical appearance, creating additional performance pressures.

Token women also experienced the added pressure of trying not to make male co-workers look bad. Tokenism sets up conditions that make women afraid of performing too well on group tasks. Because of her visibility, her actions can never be hidden. The irony is that, while they must work twice as hard just to be seen as competent, they also feel that their successes should be kept to themselves. There is a fine line between doing just well enough and too well (Kanter, 1977). The choice is either to turn their noticeability to their advantage or to try to become socially invisible. To limit visibility is to risk being overlooked; to take advantage of publicity is to risk being labeled a troublemaker.

Kanter also found that tokens are constantly being reminded of their outsider status. Their presence actually increases group solidarity and camaraderie among men. Typical male behavior—telling tales of sexual adventure, sharing off-color jokes, talking about sports—becomes more dramatic and is acted out more fervently in the presence of token women. This reinforces the feeling that she is not part of the "club."

Kanter also discovered that in more formal settings like meetings and conferences, men would often preface their acts with apologies or questions about appropriateness directed toward the token woman, such as, "I probably shouldn't say this in mixed company?" or "Can we still use technical jargon?" This makes the token feel as though she is "interrupting" the usual course of events. Rarely do token women feel comfortable enough to prevent a large number of men from engaging in an activity they consider normal. By saying these things, men make their dominant culture clear to the tokens and effectively state the terms under which they will be allowed to participate as outsiders.

Tokens can never be seen as who they really are. They must always fight stereotypes and tailor their actions to the desires and tastes of others. We can see the self-fulfilling prophecy at work here. Stereotypical assumptions about what tokens "must be like" force them into playing limited and caricatured roles. This serves the interests of those in the dominant group, who can fall back on preexisting expectations and traditional behaviors. The courteous, polite, gentlemanly behavior of men toward women, such as opening doors for them or expressing excessive concern for their safety, implies, on the surface, respect and affection. But this behavior not only subordinates women, it also limits their employment opportunities because it reinforces the notion that women are in need of special protection:

> [Mary's] male counterparts in the company frequently were invited to out-of-town business meetings and social functions from which she was excluded. These occasions were a source for information on business trends and store promotions and were a rich source of potentially important business contacts. When [Mary] asked why she was not invited to these meetings and social gatherings, the response was that her employer thought it was "too dangerous for her to be driving out of town at night by herself . . . "
> (quoted in Benokraitis & Feagin, 1993, p. 335)

Kanter argues that the implications of token status can apply to people of any social category who find themselves few of a kind among a majority of others. This is an important point sociologically because it shows that the treatment of certain social groups is not fixed by inflexible characteristics but can depend on their relative numbers vis-à-vis the majority. Workplace discrimination is a product of the system as much as it is a product of individuals within it.

Nevertheless the actual experience of tokenism can vary between social groups. For instance, men in traditionally female jobs (e.g., male nurses, librarians, elementary school teachers) and women in traditionally male jobs (e.g., physicians, engineers, carpenters) both face prejudice and discrimination. But the nature and consequences of such treatment can be quite different (C. L. Williams, 1992).

The discrimination token women workers face is the kind that first comes to mind when we consider sexism on the job: difficulties getting hired, earning promotions, and getting respect from supervisors and colleagues. These obstacles come from *within* the job itself, either from its basic organizational structure or from the people in it. However, the prejudice men feel from working in nontraditional occupations is more likely to come from *outside* the job. Men often encounter stigmatizing negative stereotypes when they come into contact with clients and people outside of work. Male nurses are assumed to be gay, and male librarians or social workers might be considered feminine. Male elementary school teachers often have to confront suspicions that they are potential child molesters (C. L. Williams, 1992).

The obstacles to integrating predominantly female occupations are more psychological than structural. But while such outside prejudice is enough to prevent large numbers of men from entering traditionally female professions, those that do enter them often find that they receive fair, sometimes even preferential, treatment. For many men, their token status as males in predominantly female professions works to their advantage in hiring and promotions. As opposed to the "glass ceiling" encountered by women in which invisible obstacles prevent them from moving up in a company, many men in female occupations encounter a "glass escalator": invisible pressures to move up in their professions (C. L. Williams, 1992).

In sum, men are able to take their culturally derived gender privilege with them when they enter predominantly female professions. This becomes an advantage despite the fact that they make up only a small percentage of all people in that profession.

The institutional structure of contemporary American labor markets segregates women into relatively low-wage occupations or excludes them entirely. Although the motivation for such discrimination may be primarily economic, the role of sexist ideology and gender stereotypes cannot be overlooked. Employers as well as the public at large still believe there are certain jobs for which women and men are naturally inclined (Reskin & Hartmann, 1986).

Sociologist Richard Levinson (1975) had male and female undergraduate sociology students make job inquiries in response to 256 classified advertisements. The jobs were categorized as "male" (security guard, truck driver, car sales, etc.) or "female" (receptionist, hostess, cosmetic sales, etc.). Working in male-female pairs, one partner made a telephone inquiry about a "sex inappropriate" job, for example a man asking about a receptionist position or a woman asking about a truck driver job. About 30 minutes later, the other partner called about the same job. This time the person was "sex appropriate"—the woman called about the receptionist job or the man called about the truck driver opening. The students were instructed to be polite and use identical words in their inquiries.

Levinson found clear-cut discrimination in 35% of the cases. The sex inappropriate caller might be told that the person doing the hiring was out of town or that the position had already been filled. However, when the sex appropriate caller phoned a half hour later, he or she might be told that the position was still open or was even encouraged to come in for an interview. Ambiguous discrimination was found in another 27% of the cases. This type of discrimination ranged from expressions of surprise to subtle attempts on the part of employers to discourage the sex inappropriate caller from applying for the job. A more recent replication of this study found that these forms of sex discrimination, while not as common as they were in Levinson's study, still exist (Winston, 1988).

Such thinking about the sex-appropriateness of certain jobs also leads employers to make personnel decisions on the basis of characteristics believed to be typical of a group. Consider the different reactions employers commonly have toward their male and female employees getting married. For men, marriage is likely to be seen as a "stabilizing" influence. From the point of view of management, he's settling down and will make a better, more dependable worker. He might even need a raise, since fatherhood is probably looming not far down the road.

But for women, marriage is still likely to be seen as disruptive to their careers. The employer may jump to the conclusion that a newly married woman will soon be seeking maternity leave or quitting altogether. Rather than making her a more dependable worker, marriage actually may make her less dependable in the eyes of management. These beliefs subtly influence hiring and promotion decisions (Reskin & Hartmann, 1986).

We continue to have a dual labor market made up of one set of jobs that employs almost exclusively women and another that employs almost exclusively men. Such segregation has consequences that extend beyond its mere existence (Reskin & Hartmann, 1986). When people are allocated jobs on the basis of sex rather than ability to perform the work, chances for self-fulfillment are limited. Society also loses because neither men nor women are free to do the jobs for which they might best be suited. Sex segregation represents a failure of the economy to use the available labor force most efficiently. However, segregation is most harmful to women primarily because the occupations they predominantly hold tend to be less desirable than those held predominantly by men. In particular, occupational segregation contributes to the lower wages earned by women.

The Wage Gap

> The Lord spoke to Moses and said, "When a man makes a special vow to the Lord which requires your valuation of living persons, a male between twenty and sixty years old shall be valued at fifty silver shekels. If it is a female, she shall be valued at thirty shekels. (Lv. 27:1-4, cited in Corcoran, Duncan, & Hill, 1986)

You don't have to go back to the Bible to find evidence of the practice of setting women's pay at about three-fifths that of men's. In 1991 all men working full-time year-round earned a median salary of $27,719 per year. All women working full-time year-round earned a salary of $19,829 per year (U.S. Bureau of the Census, 1992c). For every dollar a man earned, a woman earned approximately 71 cents. The differences are even more pronounced for African-American and Hispanic women, who earn 65 and 57 cents respectively for every dollar a man earns. While these figures are an improvement over past wage differences—in 1973, for instance, all women earned only 56.6 cents for every dollar a man earned—the discrepancy between men's pay and women's pay has proved remarkably resilient. This wage gap has persisted despite the 1963 Equal Pay Act, which guaranteed equal pay for equal work, and Title VII of the 1964 Civil Rights Act, which banned job discrimination on the basis of sex (as well as race, religion, and national origin).

I should point out that the wage gap is not an exclusively American phenomenon. To varying degrees in every country around the world, men earn more than women. In the developing countries of Latin America, Africa, and Asia, women commonly earn 25% or less of what men earn (Tiano, 1987). In Korea and Japan, women earn barely half of men's income. In some countries however, such as France, Sweden, Australia, and Denmark, the wage gap is actually much narrower than it is here, with women earning 80 to 90% of what men earn (Reskin & Padavic, 1994).

Multinational corporations frequently export our wage gap abroad by paying female factory workers in developing countries as little as half of what they pay men. In many countries, women comprise over three-quarters of unskilled assembly workers. This preference for women is sometimes rationalized by beliefs that they have a high tolerance for monotonous work, an inherent dexterity that suits tasks that involve tiny parts, and a docile nature that allows them to withstand the pressure of closely supervised production (Tiano, 1987).

Why does the wage gap exist? One reason, of course, is occupational segregation and the types of jobs women are most likely to have. Studies suggest that occupational segregation accounts for about 40% of the gender differences in average earnings (Reskin & Hartmann, 1986). For the five "most female" jobs (that is, those more than 96% female)—which are secretary, receptionist, licensed practical nurse, private household worker, and child care worker—the average weekly salary is $219. For the five "most male" jobs (those less than 3% female)—which are airplane pilot, construction worker, truck driver, firefighter, and miner—the average weekly salary is $506 (adapted from Barrett, 1987).

Some economists and policy makers argue that the wage gap is essentially an institutional by-product that exists because men on the whole have more work experience, more training, and higher education than women. The U.S. Bureau of the Census, however, reports that gender differences in education, labor force experience, and seniority—factors that might make discrepancies in salary justifiable—account for less than 15% of the wage gap between men and women (cited in National Committee on Pay Equity, 1992). For instance, according to the U.S. Department of Commerce, the average earnings of full-time female

Table 13.2   *Median Annual Earnings by Sex and Educational Attainment of Full-time, Year-round Workers, 1992*

| | EARNINGS | |
Level of Educational Attainment	Male Workers	Female Workers
8 years of schooling	$18,539	$11,885
High school dropout	19,392	13,411
High school graduate	24,148	16,392
Less than 4 years college	29,871	20,578
College graduate	36,733	26,241
Some graduate school	46,913	31,861

Source: U.S. Bureau of the Census, 1992c.

workers in 1991 were significantly lower than men's with the same level of educational training. In fact, women with a college degree can expect to earn just slightly more than men with only a high school diploma ($26,241 compared to $24,148 a year) (U.S. Bureau of the Census, 1992c). These statistics are shown in Table 13.2.

There are also broader economic reasons for the existing wage gap. Because of the type of occupations women tend to have, their labor force participation is more likely to be determined by the fluctuating needs of the economy. By nature of their position within the occupational structure, women are easily exploited and are used as cheap labor and quickly dispensed when no longer needed (J. Smith, 1981). More than two-thirds of temporary or part-time workers in this country are women (Baca-Zinn & Eitzen, 1993). During hard times these workers are the first ones pushed out of employment not because they're women, but because their jobs are the most expendable.

Overcoming Economic Discrimination: Comparable Worth

You have seen the various ways in which women are economically discriminated against in American society. What can be done about it? How would you reduce the large gap between men's and women's earnings? One controversial policy to achieve pay equity is called comparable worth.

Comparable worth is the principle that different jobs that are of equal value to society and require equal training ought to be paid equally. This principle rejects the premise that women's work is inherently worth less than men's and the related assumption that workers are paid according to their needs and that women need less money than men (Feldberg, 1984). The ultimate goal is to raise the wages of underpaid, female-dominated occupations.

Going beyond the principle of "equal pay for equal work," comparable worth acknowledges that women and men do not do the same work and that sex segregation is the rule, not the exception (Ciancanelli & Berch, 1987). The assumption is that to achieve any equality in a work world already structured around difference, it is necessary to use comparability as a criterion for judging the *relative* worth of certain occupations.

Comparable worth is now used routinely to set pay scales in corporations. A job is broken down into the various skills required of the jobholder: education, special abilities, and experience. The job is also broken down in terms of difficulty: Does it require physical labor, manual dexterity, responsibility for important decisions, supervising others? It then becomes possible to compare how these skills and requirements are valued in dollar amounts across different jobs (P. Simpson, 1983). Panels of experts assign point values to jobs based on their judged "worth." If, for example, nurses are paid less than tree trimmers, can such a difference be justified by the skills and training required for these different jobs? Or is the wage difference simply illustrative of a pattern of discrimination against women?

At present, all but five states have addressed the issue of pay equity (National Committee on Pay Equity, 1992). Almost half of all states have conducted job evaluation studies to determine if their systems for setting the wages of state workers are discriminatory. In Minnesota, a job evaluation study determined that there was a 20% gap between comparable male-dominated and female-dominated jobs. Adjustments are being phased in over a 4-year period.

Critics claim that comparable worth attacks free market capitalism and destroys economic competition (Aaron & Lougy, 1986). They feel employers should be free to pay workers the "going market rate." Women's low-wage position is simply the result of the workings of economic forces dictating that higher wages ought to be paid to workers in the more socially valuable or useful positions. If these forces were truly at work, however, the drive to maximize profits by using cheap labor would create a uniform wage structure in which everyone was paid poorly, not one characterized by huge gender differences. Instead, the low wages women earn must be the result of a socially constructed labor market that incorporates history, customs, prejudices, and belief systems that connect the worth of different jobs with ideas about the inherent worth of the people who perform them (Feldberg, 1984).

Even those who wish to implement comparable worth pay policies acknowledge some practical difficulties. For example, it may actually *dis*courage women from seeking jobs in what are considered to be traditionally male occupations if they can earn the same salary in traditionally female occupations. Comparable worth may end up establishing wage equality but still not end the sex segregation of occupations (Kelly & Bayes, 1988). There is some merit to this argument. Setting salaries according to an occupation's worth will reduce the gender gap in wages *only* if women have access to the jobs that society values (Feldberg, 1984). If men continue to dominate the jobs deemed to be most socially "worthy," then pay equity will never be achieved.

This raises a larger point regarding cultural perceptions. The skills required in many predominantly female occupations are often not socially recognized as skills and therefore are not included in the formal evaluation of the worth of those occupations. For instance, much of the work teachers, nurses, and secretaries do is often geared toward recognizing and responding to subtle cues from others and understanding other people's needs (Feldberg, 1984). These skills are difficult to quantify and may not be perceived as compensable because they are likely to be viewed as an extension of women's unpaid domestic skills (Renzetti & Curran, 1989). When these skills are overlooked, strange rankings may result, as when the job of nursery school teacher was rated lower than dog trainer (Feldberg, 1984).

In sum, comparable worth is a useful tool in reducing wage discrimination. However, because of practical issues of implementation as well as continuing prejudices and cultural stereotypes, full equality is not being reached. It seems that comparable worth, at present, may have more symbolic than practical value. Nevertheless, it is an attempt to overcome sexual inequality at the institutional rather than personal level.

Conclusion

Sexual inequality goes beyond the degrading media and cultural images of women, face-to-face interactions that reinforce the devaluation of women, and the stereotypes of individual people. It is woven into the institutional and cultural fabric of our society. It is as much a part of the American scene as baseball, apple pie, and the Fourth of July. Every woman in the country has felt sexism at some level, whether as personal violence, sexually suggestive leers and comments, fear of going out at night, job discrimination, legal obstacles, or subtle encouragement toward "appropriate" sports, hobbies, and careers.

We have seen in this chapter that men tend to benefit from living in a society where language, identity, intimacy, history, culture, and institutions are built on gender distinctions, *even if the men themselves do not support such inequality.* Most men do not see sexual inequality as their problem; it's a "woman's issue." Like most people whose interests are being served by the system, men are largely unaware of the small and large advantages the social structure provides them (W. J. Goode, 1981). Therefore men are less likely to see inequality as unjust or to see change as necessary.

The first step toward sexual equality is that men will have to come to understand their role in the process, even in the absence of blatant, personal sexism. We are all tacitly involved in the oppression of women each time we automatically giggle at sexist jokes, mistake female doctors for nurses, see women in purely physical terms, expect less from them on the job or in school, or expect more of them at home.

The next step will require a fundamental transformation of institutional patterns and cultural values. Such a solution sounds too massive to be possible. But today we are seeing early steps in that direction: changing conceptions of familial roles, increasing (though not yet equal) labor force participation, growing political power, and greater awareness of sexual exploitation and violence. How far these changes will take us in the future remains to be seen.

CHAPTER HIGHLIGHTS

■ Personal sexism is most apparent during the course of everyday interaction in the form of communication patterns and gestures. It can be particularly dangerous when expressed in the form of sexual harassment and sexual violence.

■ Sexual stratification is perpetuated by a dominant cultural ideology that devalues women by attributing sexual inequality to inherent biological differences between men and women.

■ Institutional sexism exists in the law, in the family (in terms of reproductive choices, fetal rights, and the domestic division of labor), and in economics. Women have entered the paid labor force in unprecedented numbers, but they still tend to occupy jobs that are typically considered "female" and still earn significantly less than men.

■ Not only are social institutions sexist in that women are systematically segregated, exploited, and excluded, they are also "gendered." Institutions themselves are structured along gender lines so that traits associated with success are usually stereotypically male characteristics: tough-mindedness, rationality, assertiveness, competitiveness, and so forth.

YOUR TURN

To understand how beliefs are translated into action, it is important to examine how sexism influences people's activities. One fruitful area of examination is the home. Locate at least one of each of the following types of couples in which both partners work full-time outside the home:

■ newly married without children (married less than one year)
■ married without children (married 10 years or more)
■ married (older or younger) with at least one child living at home
■ cohabiting (heterosexual or homosexual)

Ask *each* person to make a list of *all* the household chores that need to be done during the course of a week. Ask them to be as specific and exhaustive as possible (e.g., "cleaning windows" rather than "cleaning the house"). After the lists are completed, ask each person to indicate which of these tasks he or she is primarily responsible for, which his or her partner is responsible for, and which are shared.

Ask the participants also to estimate the total amount of time spent each week on all these tasks combined. Finally, ask them if they are employed outside the home and, if so, about how many hours they work during a typical week. Note: It is important that partners are not in each other's presence when answering these questions.

In comparing responses, see if there are any differences—in terms of time spent doing housework and the number of tasks for which each one is responsible—between

- partners in the same couple
- men and women
- younger and older couples
- married and cohabiting couples

Do women still bear the primary responsibility for housework? Is this true even for women who work outside the home? Are there certain types of couples for which this is not the case? If partners within the same couple had different ideas about housework responsibilities, to what can you attribute this lack of agreement? Describe the tensions men and women experience when trying to balance work and home responsibilities.

CHAPTER 14

The Architecture of Population

Demographic Trends

In his novel *Generation X: Tales for an Accelerated Culture*, Douglas Coupland (1991) describes the experiences of three friends in their 20s who quit their "low-pay, low-prestige, low-benefit, no-future jobs" and move to Palm Springs, California, in search of new experiences they hope will give meaning to their lives. In one scene Andy, the narrative voice of the book, describes an experience with his friend Dag:

> Just after 2:00 a.m., Dag got off of shift at Larry's Bar where along with me he is a bartender. While the two of us were walking home, he ditched me right in the middle of a conversation we were having and darted across the road, where he then scraped a boulder across the front hood and windshield of a Cutlass Supreme. This is not the first time he has impulsively vandalized like this. The car was the color of butter and bore a bumper sticker saying WE'RE SPENDING OUR CHILDREN'S INHERITANCE, a message that I suppose irked Dag . . .
>
> "I don't know, Andy," he said . . . "whether I feel more that I want to punish some aging crock for frittering away my world, or whether I'm just upset that the world has gotten too big—way beyond our capacity to tell stories about it, and so all we're stuck with are these blips and chunks and snippets on bumpers . . . I feel insulted either way."

The disillusionment and frustration voiced by Dag symbolizes the fears and anxieties of a specific segment of the American population. But this is not a group of people characterized by common skin color, ethnicity, religion, or sex, nor is it a social group brought together by the same occupation or an emotional political issue. These individuals are bonded by one simple and unchangeable fact: They are members of the same **birth cohort**—a set of people who were born during the same time period and who must face similar societal circumstances brought about by their position in the age structure of the population.

In the past several chapters I have examined the various interrelated sources of social stratification: class, race, and gender. We have seen how the distance between the haves and the have-nots continues to grow wider as a result of their different levels of access to important resources. We have seen how race and gender continue to determine access to cultural, economic, and political opportunities. Yet another source of inequality that has enormous local, national, and global significance is the changing size and shape of the human population. Globally, population imbalances between richer and poorer societies underlie most if not all of the other forces for change that are taking place today. In the United States, the domestic population imbalances between various age and ethnic groups will be our defining feature in the decades to come.

This chapter examines the relationship between population trends and everyday life. First I describe how the time in which we were born influences our everyday experiences. Next, I look at three population trends occurring across the globe today: population growth, changing age structures, and migration. I then turn my focus to some of the key population trends occurring in our society. How are the changing age structure of American society and the growing number of legal and illegal immigrants affecting our ability to provide people with the resources they need for a comfortable life? How are our important social institutions functioning as a result of population shifts? Do these institutions now benefit some cohorts at the expense of others?

The Influence of Birth Cohorts

You've no doubt asked yourself questions like: What career will I pursue? Where will I live? Will I be able to afford a house? Will I have a spouse? children? The answers to these questions are influenced by your personal desires, traits, values, ambitions, and abilities as well as your social class, gender, race, religion, and ethnicity. But they are also affected by your place in the population at a given point in time. The sheer number of people living in a society will affect the availability of affordable houses, high-paying jobs, attractive potential mates, and so on. More than that, the shape of your birth cohort or "generation" and its position and size relative to other cohorts will be tremendously influential. Each cohort has distinctive properties, such as initial size, ethnic composition, age-specific birth rates, and average life expectancies, that set it apart from other cohorts.

Cohorts and Everyday Life

Cohorts influence the everyday lives of individuals in two fundamental ways (Riley, 1971). First, there is the life course dimension, or what sociologists call

cohort effects. People born at roughly the same time tend to experience life course events or social rites of passage at the same time, including puberty, marriage, childbearing, graduation, entrance into the workforce, and death. Think of this as the collective experience of aging.

Second, people born at the same time share a common history. A cohort's place in time tells us a lot about the opportunities and constraints placed on its members. Historical events and major social trends, called **period effects,** contribute to the unique shape and outlook of each cohort. Many historians, for instance, believe that a period of drought and famine caused the abandonment of the great cities of the Mayan civilization nearly a thousand years ago. Those who were young when this period began enjoyed comfortable lives, reveled in the high culture of the Mayans, and had tremendous prospects for the future. But for their children, born just a generation later, starvation, death, and social dislocation were basic facts of life (Clausen, 1986).

Cohort and period effects combine to profoundly affect the lives of cohorts because members experience the same major societal or world circumstances at about the same stage in their lives. Consider what people born just prior to 1920 have experienced: They survived World War I and the flu epidemic of 1919-1920 as infants; they lived through the Depression era of the 1930s as young teens; they experienced World War II, perhaps even firsthand, as young adults; and they witnessed the Vietnam War in middle age. They have also seen the advent of airplanes, radio, television, space travel, and computers, not to mention dramatic changes in sexual, political, educational, and religious values (Clausen, 1986).

Notice how it's not only exposure to these events that shaped their cohort histories, it's also how old people were when they occurred that distinguishes them from other cohorts (Soldo & Agree, 1988). For instance, cohorts who experienced the Great Depression during their peak childbearing years have the lowest birth rate of any cohort observed so far in this century. Therefore, people born between 1900 and 1910 have smaller families to rely on in old age and will have similar worries about how they will be cared for in their old age. These experiences contrast sharply with people born only 10 years later or earlier who either were past their prime childbearing years during the Depression or were too young to have children, and therefore tend to have larger families today (Soldo & Agree, 1988).

Your cohort may be as influential in forming your worldview and self concept as your race, class, gender, or family. Think how different your goals and ambitions would be had you experienced childhood during the Depression as opposed to a period of relative affluence. Rights and privileges considered unattainable dreams by one cohort are likely to be taken for granted by a future one. Similarly, the differences in attitudes and values between people who became adults during the Vietnam War and people who became adults during the Persian Gulf War are not only a function of simple age differences but a function of differences in prevailing social and historical conditions. Think how different your perceptions of the world and your ideas about solving international conflicts would be if your most vivid teenage memory was one of angry crowds jeering soldiers going off to fight an unpopular war or adoring crowds cheering soldiers going off to fight a popular one.

Indeed, different cohorts develop and mature in what amounts to fundamentally different societal environments. The very nature of society—its size, age distribution, and racial or ethnic proportions—will vary between cohorts. We start our lives in one historical period with a distinct age pattern of behavior and set of social norms, and we end our lives in another. As we grow older, we develop and change in a society that itself is developing and changing.

Throughout most of the 20th century, for instance, each succeeding generation has received substantially more schooling than the previous one. Early in the century most people went to school for only 6 or 7 years, which yielded an adequate education for the sorts of jobs their parents and older siblings held. Today, most people are in school 12 years or more. As a result, older cohorts on the whole tend to score substantially lower on standardized intelligence tests than younger ones. Because of such a trend, it was long assumed that intelligence declined markedly with age. But we now know that these differences are not the result of aging but of changing societal values regarding education (Clausen, 1986).

Even the way people experience the aging process is affected by the character of the cohort to which they belong and by the social, cultural, and environmental changes to which their cohort is exposed in moving through the life course. People are living longer, and advancements have been made in nutrition, education, sanitation, and other areas. As a result, cohorts experience the physical consequences of aging in different ways (Riley, Foner, & Waring, 1988). For instance, the average age of menarche (a girl's first menstrual period) has gradually lowered from about 14 a century ago to 12.5 today (Darton, 1991). When combined with changing social norms, values, and cultural beliefs, such a change will inevitably speed up the point at which young people become sexually curious and explorative.

In sum, to understand the impact cohorts exert on everyday life, we must place them within their relevant historical and demographic contexts. Birth cohorts are more than just a collection of individuals born within a few years of each other; they are distinctive generations tied together by historical circumstances, population trends, and societal changes. However, we must also realize that when many individuals in the same cohort are affected by social events in similar ways, the changes in their collective lives can *produce* changes in the social structure. Each succeeding cohort leaves its mark on the prevailing culture. Each helps create and is shaped by its own *zeitgeist*, the intellectual, moral, and cultural spirit of the time (Mannheim, 1952). In other words, cohorts are not only affected by social changes, they contribute to them as well (Riley, Foner, & Waring, 1988).

Baby Boomers and Generation X

The birth cohort that has received the most national attention is, without a doubt, the baby boom generation, those 75 million or so people born between 1946 and 1964. They now comprise almost one-third of the entire U.S. population. Preceded and followed by much smaller cohorts, they stand in sharp political, economic, and cultural contrast to those around them:

> They grew up as the first standardized generation, drawn together by the history around them, the intimacy of television, and the crowding that came from the sheer onslaught of other Baby Boomers. They shared the great economic expectations of the 1950's and the fears that came with Sputnik and the dawn of the nuclear era. They shared the hopes of John F. Kennedy's New Frontier and Lyndon Johnson's Great Society, and the disillusionment that came with the assassinations, Viet Nam, Watergate, and the resignations. (P. Light, 1988, p. 10)

The passing of this massive cohort through the life course has been described metaphorically as "a pig in a python." If you've ever seen one of those *National Geographic* films of snakes digesting small animals you can see how apt the metaphor is. As this cohort bulge works its way through the life course, it stretches the parameters of the relevant social institutions at each stage. Baby boomers packed hospital nurseries as infants, school classrooms as children, and college campuses, employment lines, and the housing markets as young adults (P. Light, 1988).

As the baby boomers reach their golden years, those institutions concerned with later life—pension plans, Social Security, medical and social care—will be seriously stressed, leading one gerontologist to call the baby boomers a "generation at risk" (Butler, 1989). By the year 2030, one out of every three Americans will be over 65. At that time, there will be over 50 million retired baby boomers, about twice the number of retirees there are today. Some have even predicted a huge surge in business for the funeral industry by then as this generation reaches the end of its collective life cycle (Schodolski, 1993).

Baby boomers have also left a particularly influential mark on the institution of the family. Their generation was the first to redefine families to include a variety of living arrangements like cohabitation, domestic partnerships, and never-married women with dependent children (Wattenberg, 1986). They were also the first to acknowledge the expectation of paid work as a central feature of women's lives. And they were the first to grow up with effective birth control, making delayed childbearing and our present low birth rate possible.

Hence baby boomers are responsible for the smaller families we have today. Consequently, as they reach old age, they will have fewer children to turn to for the kind of help they gave in earlier years (Butler, 1989). This, along with the trend toward greater mobility and independent living, means that the baby boom elders will be more likely to turn to social service and health care organizations to care for them.

Wade Clark Roof
Religion in the
Nineties

Because of its size and influence, the baby boom generation is often used as a measuring stick against broader cultural trends. Consider the place that religion occupies in the national consciousness. In the United States today, religious faith and spirituality are in question more than ever. Such concern is due primarily to what is perceived to be the abandoning of religion by the baby boomers. After all, it was the boomers who grew suspicious of the faith and morality handed down to them by their elders in the sixties and seventies and who got caught up in their own selfish pursuits in the eighties. Two-thirds of all baby boomers brought up in a religious tradition dropped out of their churches and synagogues during their late teens and early 20s (Roof, 1993a). Hence it is no surprise that mainline religions (Lutherans, Methodists, Episcopalians, Presbyterians, Jews, and so on) have seen their memberships decline steadily over the past several decades (Jacquet and Jones, 1991).

Some observers of American culture suggest that the baby boom generation has almost completely severed its religious loyalties, creating what amounts to a national spiritual crisis (e.g., Bellah et al., 1985). According to sociologist Wade Clark Roof (1993a), however, what has happened is not so much an abandonment of religion but a shift in the way religion is practiced both within and outside existing institutions.

Over a period of 4 years Roof interviewed and surveyed baby boomers in a variety of social settings, including churches, seminaries, folk festivals, airplanes, bars, and ticket lines, about their religious values and goals and their visions for the country. From these data he found that only about a third of the boomers have remained actively involved in organized religion. Another quarter dropped out of organized religion for a while but later returned to some form of institutional involvement. The rest, about 42%, remain "dropouts." Yet even among dropouts there is still a significant amount of religious activity and involvement. Some are what Roof calls "believers, not belongers," people who maintain their religious faith but are not involved in any institutional religion. These individuals are likely to express their religiosity privately. Others are "seekers," individuals who choose either mysticism and New Age spiritualism on the one hand or theologically conservative fundamentalist religion on the other. For instance, at the same time the membership of mainline religions has declined, that of "evangelical" churches (Church of the Nazarene, Seventh Day Adventist, Assemblies of God, Church of God) has increased (Hunter, 1987; Jacquet & Jones, 1991).

American religion in the nineties has become remarkably fluid. People move in and out of organized religion with ease and frequency. According to Roof, about half of all Americans will drop out of active religious participation for a period of at least 2 years. Of those, 80% return at some point, usually to a church or synagogue. Consider the religious biography of this 36-year-old man:

- raised as a Methodist
- dropped out as a teenager, preferring to play Beatles records rather than go to church
- attended a Lutheran church for a while
- dropped out and began attending Buddhist services
- explored the Baha'i faith and attended its meetings
- attended spiritual seminars on Judaism and Hinduism
- currently describes himself as a fundamentalist Christian (Roof, 1993a, p. 175)

Most people don't explore so many religious alternatives, but in general they do feel freer to switch religions than their predecessors did. Some have interpreted this trend to mean that religious loyalties have become superficial and impermanent, with people choosing religion as they would items on a restaurant menu. Roof claims, though, that the people who switch do not do so for frivolous reasons but for moral and religious ones. Boomers want results and see no reason *not* to search for a comfortable environment in which to express themselves religiously or spiritually. Indeed, baby boomers have adopted a uniquely noninstitutional, individualistic approach to religion. They look at religion much the same way they look at lifestyle and consumption choices. Although they still utilize insitutional religion during certain life events—birth, marriage, death— they are finding less traditional ways to forge a link between their individual experiences and their spirituality. The traditional human concerns for sharing, caring, and belonging are as real today as ever before, but they find expression in new and varied ways:

> Women explore their own spirituality in Goddess groups, but also in home churches; many people, both men and women, find support in adult-children-of-alcoholics meetings and in other 12-step groups but also in evangelical prayer groups; there are meaningful group experiences . . . whether among those spending a week working with Habitat for Humanity or among those exploring the meaning of visualization and dream analysis; there is community and celebration on Jesus Day but also on Earth Day. (Roof, 1993b, p. 167)

A major restructuring of American religion is under way. The religious and spiritual concerns of baby boomers run deeper than the simple notion of a "return to religion" would imply (Roof, 1993a). Only a small percentage of the population will "return" to the religion into which they were born. The rest will be involved in various types of religious activities. They may or may not describe themselves as religious, and they may or may not view themselves as related to existing establishments. But there is little doubt that religion, in whatever form it takes, still plays an important role in the lives of baby boomers.

While the baby boomers have dominated the cultural and religious spotlight, American society is just beginning to take notice of its next generation, known in the media as "twentysomethings," "baby busters," or "Generation X." Today there are roughly 48 million people either in or approaching their 20s, a sort of lost cohort tucked between the massive baby boom generation and their offspring. The birth rate during the 1970s, when these individuals were born, was about half as large as it was during the post-World War II years of the baby boomers.

These young people are less likely to get married than other generations and more likely to delay marriage if they do. In 1970, 55% of men and 36% of women between the ages of 20 and 24 had never married. In 1988 the figures were 77 and 61%, respectively (D. M. Gross & Scott, 1990). Furthermore, the high divorce rate over the past several decades has had a direct and lasting impact on this cohort. Roughly 40% of people in their 20s are children of divorce. Even more of them were so-called latchkey children, the first generation of children to experience the wholesale effects of two working parents. For many, childhood was marked by dependence on secondary relationships—teachers, friends, day care.

Like the fictional Dag at the beginning of this chapter, members of this cohort are disillusioned over shrinking opportunities due to poor economic times and angry that they have inherited a variety of gargantuan crises, from the national debt and the savings and loan bailout to the degradation of the natural environment and growing urban decay. Resentful of the wasteful excesses of their elders, they are experiencing unprecedented apprehension about their own futures. Many sense they are destined to become society's sacrificial "clean-up crew."

But rather than evoke sympathy from other cohorts, they have instead become a symbol of a nation in decline. From the perspective of older generations, Generation X has become a metaphor for despair over the state of American culture and fear for our collective future (Howe & Strauss, 1992). This generation is described in dismal terms:

> They have trouble making decisions. . . . They have few heroes, no anthems, no style to call their own. They crave entertainment, but their attention span is as short as one zap of a TV dial. They hate yuppies, hippies and druggies. They postpone marriage because they dread divorce. They sneer at Range Rovers, Rolexes and red suspenders. . . . They possess only a hazy sense of their own identity but a monumental preoccupation with all the problems the preceding generation will leave for them to fix. (D. M. Gross & Scott, 1990, p. 57)

Demographic Dynamics

Many aspects of your personal life are influenced by your birth cohort, but your life is also affected by macro-level population trends. The sociologists who study these trends in population characteristics are called **demographers.** Demographers examine several important and interrelated population processes in order to explain current social problems or project future ones: birth or fertility rates (changes in the number of children people are having), death or mortality rates (changes in people's life expectancy), and patterns of migration (the movement of people in and out of a society). These three processes influence a population's growth, overall age structure, and movement.

Population Growth

The most fundamental population characteristic is size. No other phenomenon has the ability to touch the lives of everyone on the planet as profoundly as the growth of the human population. Changes in population size are a function of birth and death rates. As long as people are dying and being born at similar rates, the size of the population stabilizes (barring large changes due to migration). But when birth rates increase and death rates decrease, the population grows.

It took hundreds of thousands of years, from the beginning of humanity to the early 19th century, for the earth's population to reach 1 billion. However, it only took an additional hundred years to reach 2 billion. Three billion was reached 30 years later; 4 billion, 16 years later; and 5 billion a little over 10 years after that. Today we are fast approaching 6 billion and will exceed 7 billion by 2010. Ten thousand years ago the world's population was 8 million. Today it takes a little over a month for the population to grow by that much (Farley, 1991). Figure 14.1 charts world population growth since 8000 B.C.

The bulk of the growth is occurring in developing countries. The annual rate of growth between 1990 and 1995 will be approximately 1.7%. But that figure masks dramatic differences, from Europe's tiny 0.22% per year to Africa's massive 3.0% per year. In 1950 Africa's population was half that of Europe. By 2025 its population is expected to be three times as large as that of Europe, and about 95% of *all* global population growth will take place in Africa alone. It's estimated that by the year 2025, 83% of the world's population will reside in the developing countries of Africa, Asia, and Latin America (Kennedy, 1993). World population growth by region is tracked in Figure 14.2.

There is no denying that the world's population is growing at unprecedented speed. However, there is some disagreement as to what the consequences of that growth will be. In the past, large numbers of people were seen as a precious resource. The Bible urged humanity to be fruitful and multiply. One 18th-century British scholar, referring to the strategic importance of a large population, called a high birth rate "the never-failing nursery of Fleets and Armies" (quoted in Mann, 1993, p. 49). A larger population creates greater division of

Figure 14.1 *World Population Growth Since 8000 B.C.*

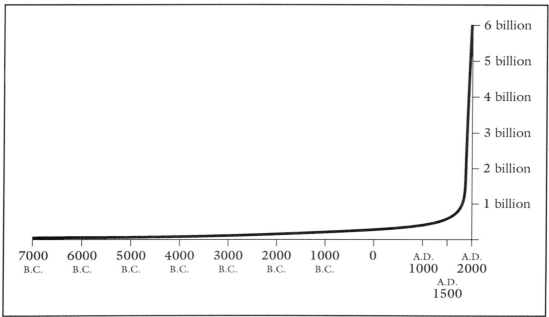

Source: Farley, 1992.

labor and a larger market to support highly specialized services. More people will be available to contribute to production.

Although few people today sing the praises of massive population growth, some argue that it isn't particularly troublesome. A study in the early 1980s concluded that by using modern agricultural technology, developing countries could support an additional 30 *billion* people (cited in Mann, 1993). The Food and Agriculture Organization estimates that there are nearly 80 billion acres of usable farmland lying idle, four times what is now being cultivated (Percival, 1989). Pollution is decreasing, resources are becoming more available, average food consumption levels are improving, and people are living longer (J. Simon, 1983).

Others, however, haven't been so optimistic. Population growth can compound, magnify, or even create a wide variety of important social, economic, and political problems such as food shortages, pollution, housing shortages, high inflation, energy shortages, unemployment, illiteracy, and the loss of individual freedom (Weeks, 1992). Thousands of years ago, philosophers in ancient China worried about the need to shift the masses to underpopulated areas. Plato said that cities with more than 5,040 landholders were too large (Mann, 1993). According to some contemporary demographers, global population growth will destroy the onetime bonanza of environmental resources like fossil fuel, rich soil,

Figure 14.2   *World Population Growth by Region*

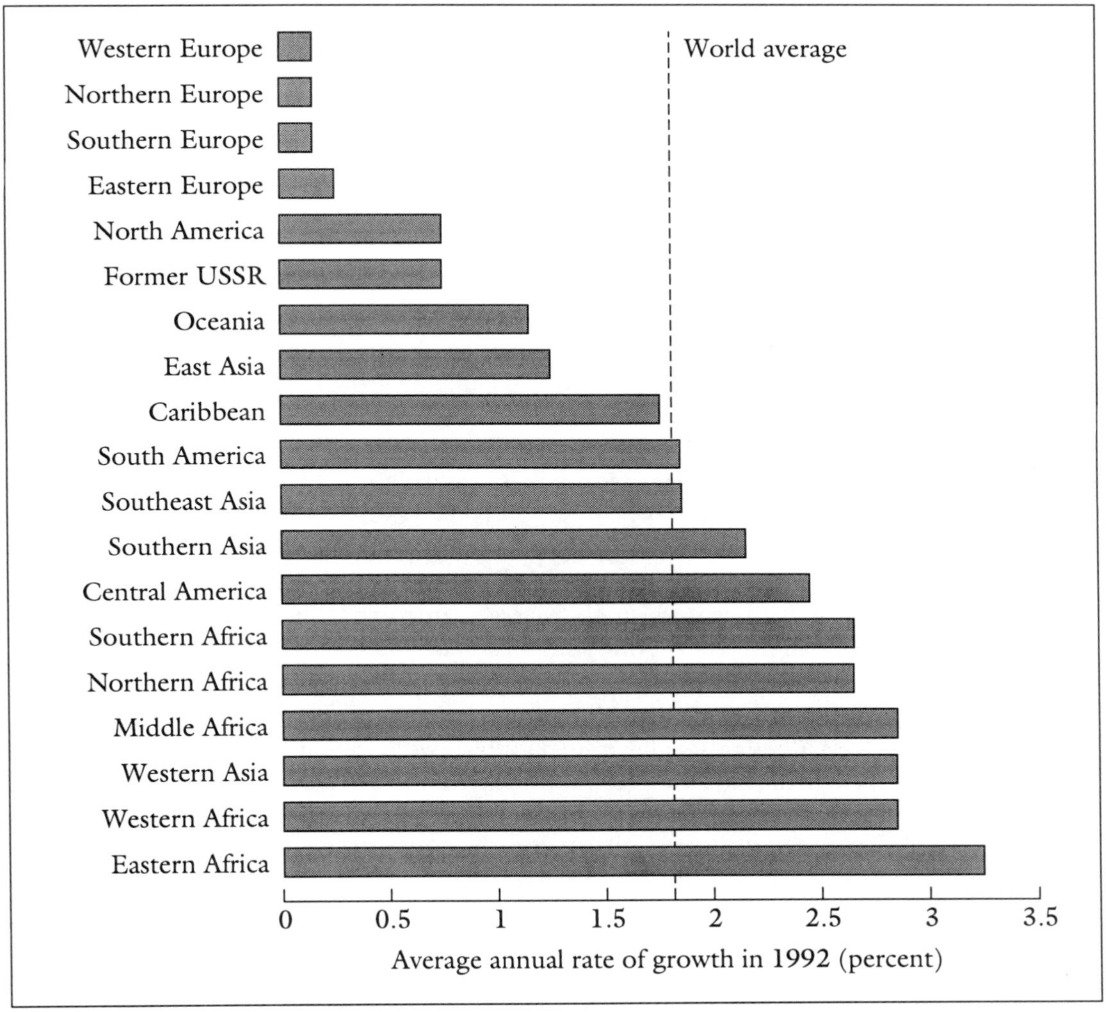

Source: Weeks, 1992.

and certain plant and animal species, widen the gap between rich and poor nations, perpetuate social and economic inequality within nations, give rise to racial and ethnic separatism, as we are seeing in the former Soviet Union and Yugoslavia, and increase already high levels of world hunger and unemployment (Ehrlich & Ehrlich, 1993).

Population growth saps important resources and taxes the entire social system. When a particular population is excessively large, individuals are forced to compete for limited food, space, jobs, and salaries. People's ability to achieve a standard of living they feel they are entitled to will be hampered by the size of the population.

In sum, the problem is not so much that the earth's population is expanding but that different countries are experiencing vastly different rates of growth. Populations in poor, developing countries of the world are rapidly expanding, while those in wealthy, developed countries have either stabilized or are declining. These imbalances influence how people view one another, affect global and domestic policies, and determine the availability of food, energy, and adequate living space (Kennedy, 1993).

The Demographic Transition

In 1972 a group of researchers at the Massachusetts Institute of Technology predicted that because of rapid population growth, the world would run out of gold by 1981, oil by 1992, usable farmland by 2000, and civilization itself would collapse by 2075 (Mann, 1993). If Nigeria were to continue at its present rate of population growth (around 3.4% annually), in 140 years its population would be equal to that of the entire world today (Keyfitz, 1990). Needless to say, none of these things has happened or is going to happen. Sooner or later growth will have to stop. But why?

An 18th-century English clergyman named Thomas Malthus argued that populations always grow faster than food supplies. As the gap widens, starvation will ensue. Famines, combined with wars, plagues, diseases, and the like, eventually act as natural limits to population growth.

Malthus assumed that food supplies were the ultimate population check. But he couldn't have foreseen the ability of trade and technology to solve the food supply problem. Japan's population, for instance, would have started dying off long ago if it had to rely on its own food production instead of imports from other countries. In addition, agricultural progress over the last two decades has enabled societies to produce food more abundantly and more efficiently than was possible during Malthus's time. Global food production actually rose more than 10% between 1968 and 1990 (Mann, 1993). Many of the nations today that are experiencing famines actually have food *surpluses* (Keyfitz, 1990). The starvation is not being caused by a lack of food per se but by maldistribution, which is often made worse by politics and/or civil war (see chapter 11).

A less grim and more popular theory of population growth and contraction is what demographers call the **demographic transition.** Underlying this model is the assumption that all societies go through similar stages of economic and social development. During the first, preindustrial stage of development, both birth and death rates tend to be quite high. People have lots of children, but life expectancy is so low that roughly the same number of people die as are born each year. Hence the size of the population remains fairly stable.

The second stage occurs when societies begin to industrialize and living conditions improve. The first demographic phenomenon to improve is usually the death rate. New technology often means better food supplies and increased knowledge about disease. Societies learn how to keep their water supplies clean and how to dispose of garbage and sewage. But for a considerable period of time after the death rate begins to fall there isn't an accompanying drop in the birth rate. The end result is a dramatic increase in the size of the population. Many demographers feel that most of the world's developing countries are in this second stage of the demographic transition. In these countries women will bear an average of 3.6 children in their lifetimes, and the number reaches an astronomical 8 in Malawi in Africa. In industrialized countries women on average will have a statistical 1.9 children in their lifetimes. (In the United States the number is slightly higher: 2.1.)

You might find it hard to understand why poor parents in developing countries who already face enormous difficulties would continue to produce more mouths to feed. Part of the reason is the lack of access to effective birth control. But it goes beyond that. For a period of time during this stage of the demographic transition, traditional beliefs about the importance of large families still remain. Often established laws, customs, and religious norms continue to exert strong influence on people's reproductive behavior. In developing nations children are likely to be perceived as economic assets. They are the "Social Security" of traditional cultures and a form of savings few people can do without (Mann, 1993).

As countries modernize, they reach the third and final stage, which is marked by a low birth rate and a low death rate. People moving into the city soon begin to realize that large families are an economic liability rather than an asset. They discover that raising large numbers of children in a city is exceedingly difficult. Traditional and religious beliefs become weaker as a result. Therefore, population growth in modern countries like the United States and the countries of Western Europe is quite a bit slower than that in the developing countries of Africa, Latin America, and Asia.

Although the demographic transition model is useful in understanding the unequal rates of population growth, it has its drawbacks. The model is based on processes of urbanization and modernization that characterized 18th-century Europe but may not apply to developing countries today. Death rates fall at a much more accelerated rate in today's developing countries than they did 200 years ago. This is because immunizations, antibiotics, pesticides, and other health advances are likely to be imported from more advanced countries instead of arising from economic and scientific development within that country. As a result, declining mortality is not accompanied by an increase in the standard of living, as it was in the past. Because birth rates tend to fall when standards of living increase, there is currently less pressure in developing countries today to drive down their birth rates. Hence developing countries are stalled in the second stage of the model with no realistic chance of moving on to the final stage.

There are signs, though, that this assessment may be too pessimistic. Results from a study by the Population Crisis Committee found that there has been an increase, worldwide, in overall access to birth control ("World progress in birth control," 1993). Of the 87 developing nations studied, 57 had improved birth control substantially over the last 5 years. Forty percent of the countries surveyed had decreased their average family size by a third, and another 42% exhibited smaller but noticeable differences.

We must keep in mind, however, that while the *rate* of population growth may be declining, annual *absolute* increases in the number of people continue to mount in many countries and will continue to be large for several decades to come (Merrick, 1986). When a country has a large and young population base, it may take several generations for a declining rate of growth to offset the sheer number of people produced by the high rates of the past. Even though individual people might be producing fewer children, so many of them are having kids that the population continues to grow anyway.

Politics, Culture, and Population Growth

You might get the impression from the above discussion that population growth is a "natural" process that works its influence relentlessly and inevitably on unsuspecting populations. Yet there have been times when human intervention—governmental intervention, more specifically—has purposefully altered the size or even the configuration of a population for political or economic reasons.

Take China, for example. Because of this country's massive population of more than 1.2 billion and its limited resources, China's leadership has been struggling for decades to limit family size. One out of every five humans alive today is Chinese, but China has only 7% of the earth's farmland, much of it of poor quality. In response, the government enacted a strict birth policy to stem the population growth. Couples must wait until their mid-20s to marry. Provinces and cities are assigned yearly birth quotas. Neighborhood committees determine which married couples can have a baby and when they can start trying. The committees also oversee contraceptive use and even record women's menstrual cycles (Ignatius, 1988). In some areas, groups of family planners visit each village once or twice a year and take all women who have already had children to a nearby clinic to be sterilized (Kristof, 1993b). Couples who have only one child are rewarded with salary bonuses, educational opportunities, and housing priorities. Penalties are imposed on couples who have more than one child. For instance, a couple may be fined more than a year's salary, lose access to apartments, schools, and free education, or be fired from their jobs (Ignatius, 1988).

The effectiveness of China's birth policy has amazed demographers. Population targets have been reached that weren't expected until 2010. The average number of births per woman has decreased from more than seven in the 1960s to less than two in 1992 (Kennedy, 1993; Kristof, 1993a). In contrast, the average woman in India, a country with similar population problems, still gives birth to four children in her lifetime. Only 9% of all Chinese births in 1992 were third, fourth, or subsequent children, down from over 15% in 1988. Over 80% of all Chinese couples of childbearing age are sterilized.

Ironically, at the same time people are being encouraged to limit the size of their families, cultural tradition continues to express a deep preference for male children, forcing some couples, especially peasants, to illegally have more than one baby if the first one is a girl. Sons are preferred because only they can perpetuate the family line. Sons also represent an economic asset to the family and a source of security for parents when the latter reach old age (Heise, 1989).

Such devaluation of female children in China can lead to extreme acts. A few years ago I was stunned by the following passage in a newspaper article:

> At least 60 million females in Asia are missing and feared dead, victims of nothing more than their sex. Worldwide, research suggests, the number of missing females may top 100 million. (Kristof, 1991)

Reading this, I felt as though 40% of the entire American population were gone and presumed dead. If this many people were missing because of a war, earthquake, tidal wave, or plague, we surely would have heard something about it. How could something as massive and hideous as this happen so quietly?

Before I address this question, let me describe how demographers arrive at such an estimate in the first place. These figures are based on a few fundamental facts about the natural gender configuration of human populations. Worldwide there are 5 or 6% more male babies born than female babies. But under normal circumstances males die at higher rates at every age thereafter. In the United States and Europe, the number of men and women evens out by the time a cohort reaches its 20s or 30s (Kristof, 1991). Later in life, though, there is a higher number of women because women tend to live longer than men. The overall sex ratio in developed countries is approximately 105 women for every 100 men.

However, the figures in many developing countries contrast sharply with these demographic expectations. In India, for instance, the figure is only 92 females for every 100 males. In China, it is 84 females for every 100 males (Kristof, 1993b). Similar deficiencies of women have been found in Pakistan, Bangladesh, Nepal, and Papua New Guinea. Hence the 100 million estimate cited represents the difference between the actual number of females in the world and the number that should be expected under normal demographic circumstances.

The "missing" females may include children of all ages who are aborted, killed at birth, abandoned, neglected, given up for foreign adoption, or hidden (Kristof, 1993b). Some girls die because they are given less food than boys, or because family members view a sick daughter as a nuisance but a sick son as a medical crisis requiring immediate attention. In Punjab, India, parents spend more than twice as much on medical care for boy infants as for girls (Heise, 1989).

While countries like China see their future in reducing the size of their populations, other countries are starting to worry that their populations aren't growing enough. The developed, industrialized countries of the world, which tend to have higher standards of living and superior health care, enjoy low mortality rates. But these countries have also experienced drastically lower fertility rates over the past 30 years. Taiwan has experienced a dramatic drop in its birth rate over the last 30 years from 5.3 births per woman in 1963 to 1.7 today (Weeks, 1992). Because of the high cost of living, childlessness and even singlehood have become more popular, even fashionable lifestyles. The government, fearing a future population with too many old people and not enough young people, is trying to reverse its approach to population growth and adopt a low-key "pro-baby" policy which, among other things, encourages early marriage and procreation and offers inexpensive specialist advice to infertile couples ("Taiwan's little problem," 1993).

In other cases governments have used much more drastic measures in an attempt to *increase* the size of their populations. In 1966, Romanian dictator Nicolae Ceausescu decided that his country's strength lay in its numbers. He called for a plan to increase the country's population from 23 million to 30 million by the year 2000. Ceausescu declared that "the fetus is the property of the entire society. Anyone who avoids having children is a deserter who abandons the laws of national continuity" (quoted in Breslau, 1990).

Within several years Romania's birth rate nearly doubled. However, because the country still provided virtually no prenatal care and was ravaged by poor nutrition, the infant mortality rate soared to 83 deaths per every 1,000 births (to give you an idea of how high that is, the infant mortality rate for most Western European countries is less than 10 deaths per 1,000 births). This population growth plan also contributed to the increased institutionalization of children, the spread of infant AIDS, and large-scale international trafficking in babies and children through adoption.

But Ceausescu pressed on with his plan. He outlawed sex education, classifying books on sexuality and reproduction as state secrets (Breslau, 1990). Women under the age of 45 were rounded up at their places of work every 2 or 3 months and taken to clinics, where they were examined for signs of pregnancy in the presence of government agents. A pregnant woman who had a miscarriage would automatically be suspected of arranging an illegal abortion and could be summoned for questioning. If a child died in a doctor's district, that doctor could lose 10% to 25% of his or her salary.

The world was given its first glimpse of this policy when Ceausescu was overthrown in December of 1989. The consequences of his "program" have been tragic. Not only have thousands, perhaps millions of women suffered through unwanted pregnancies and self-induced illegal abortions, but the country's orphanage system is bulging today with unwanted and unhealthy children.

Age Structure

In addition to affecting the size of the population, birth and death rates also combine to affect that society's **age structure,** the balance of old and young people. For areas in which recent population growth is exceedingly rapid and in which life expectancy remains low, as in Southeast Asia, Latin America, the Indian subcontinent, the Middle East, and Africa, the age structure will be increasingly dominated by young people. In Pakistan, Nigeria, Egypt, Turkey, Mexico, India, and most other developing countries, 40 to 50% of the population is now under the age of 15 (L. R. Brown, 1988; Burdett et al., 1990). On the other hand, those countries that are experiencing low birth rates coupled with increasing life expectancy have a much different age structure: More old people are living, and fewer young people are being born.

The international implications of these different age structures are worth mentioning. When young people become so numerous in a particular country, they are likely to achieve higher visibility and overwhelm social institutions like the economy and the educational system (K. Davis, 1976). The resulting economic stresses generate political conflict as well. A steady decline in living standards will no doubt mean growing unrest, which can have an impact on *our* lives here in America if the unrest takes place in countries we depend on for certain resources, goods, or services. According to one columnist:

> Given what is coming—unemployed youths roaming the streets in countries where half the population often is under 18 years of age, and looking to irregular leaders to lead them in new and as yet unpredictable movements—there is little question that even more political explosions are on the immediate horizon. (quoted in L. R. Brown, 1988, p. 33)

The obvious consequence of today's population trends is that developing nations will have the burden of trying to support millions of people under the age of 15, while developed nations will have the burden of trying to support millions of people over the age of 65. As the prosperous societies of the world struggle with the problem of allocating more resources to the elderly, the rest of the planet must deal with the demands of growing numbers of children and infants (see Figure 14.3).

Figure 14.3   *Age Distribution in Less Developed and Developed Countries*

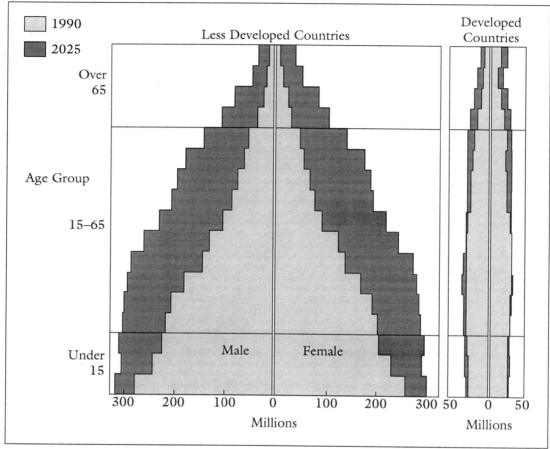

Source: Keyfitz, 1990.

Immigration

In response to these problems, many people will be motivated to move to another place where prospects for a comfortable life are brighter. Therefore, large-scale migration, the third major demographic process, is an important factor to consider in the growth and decline of populations. According to a recent report from the United Nations, more than 100 million people worldwide have left their homes in search of a better life somewhere else. Whereas in the past migration meant moving to uncharted or newly developed areas, today it means pushing into territories already occupied by others.

The pressures that encourage migration are growing and fundamentally arise from disparities in opportunities. Poverty, political instability, famine, high birth

Table 14.1   *Urban Overcrowding Worldwide*

Persons per square mile (cities ranked by population size) 1991:

Tokyo-Yokohama	25,018
Mexico City	40,037
São Paulo	41,466
Seoul	49,101
New York City	11,480
Osaka-Kobe-Kyoto	28,025
Bombay	127,461
Calcutta	56,927
Rio de Janeiro	44,952
Buenos Aires	21,790

Source: U.S. Bureau of the Census, 1993a.

rates, environmental deterioration, high unemployment, and the lure of richer countries continue to drive the world's poorest people to seek safety and a better life in more prosperous nations (Honebrink, 1993). Even developing countries are experiencing widespread growth of already overcrowded cities as people move in from rural areas. Today 1.4 billion people in the world live in the cities of developing countries; by 2025 there will be 4.1 billion. Of the 20 "megacities" with a population of over 11 million that will exist by the end of the century, 17 will be in the developing world, including such places as Mexico City, São Paulo, Calcutta, Bombay, and Shanghai. It is estimated that by the year 2000, 90% of the poorest people in Latin America will live in cities.

This transformation illustrates more than just a shift of living tendencies; it has changed our assumptions about what urban living means worldwide. In the past, cities were meccas of great wealth, cultural activities, fine houses, impressive streets, and so on. Today, however, urban life is associated with poverty and social devastation. The sheer number of people crammed into these large cities makes it impossible for residents to enjoy some of the benefits of urban living. At 11,480 people per square mile, you may think New York City is crowded. But it is a veritable open prairie compared to Bombay, India, where there are 127,461 people per square mile (see Table 14.1).

It would seem that, when people migrate from underdeveloped, over-crowded countries to more developed, technologically advanced countries, everyone would benefit. After all, migration lowers population pressures and unemployment at home while offsetting the problems of negative population growth and an aging workforce in developed countries. As one author puts it:

> Why . . . should North America not allow the influx of millions of families from south of the Rio Grande; or labor-short Japan admit vast numbers of willing workers from Southeast Asia; or the European Community, with its

> graying populations, welcome the millions of unemployed of North Africa?
> Since most of Europe has a negative replacement fertility rate and the
> populations of Algeria, Morocco, and Tunisia are expected to double over
> the next few decades this seems . . . "the perfect match." (Kennedy, 1993,
> pp. 42-43)

From a sociological point of view, however, people in receiving countries
perceive the influx of immigrants and their economic impact in personal rather
than societal terms. Instead of seeing their contribution to the overall economy,
immigrants are seen as an immediate threat. Furthermore, immigrants seek to
satisfy the same needs as everyone else. They require housing, education, and
medical attention, all of which are in short supply. They also bring with them
foreign habits, traditions, norms, and cultural ways of life.

Even though laws in most countries ban discrimination against foreigners,
deep-seated resentment and prejudice is growing. In Great Britain the resentment is directed against Indians and Pakistanis; in France it's Algerians and
Moroccans; in Germany it's the Turks; in Sweden it's Iraqis and Kurds; and in
the United States it's immigrants from Latin America and Asia.

Industrialized countries face an uncontrollable tide of people from poorer
countries, and many are closing their gates. In 1991 there were more than 1,500
attacks in Germany against foreigners. Even though such violence is carried out
by a relatively small number of extremists, up to 40% of the German population
can be characterized as "silent sympathizers," people who express at least some
sympathy for issues of "racial purity" and "foreigners out" raised by extremists.
In France, mounting resentment against Muslim Arab immigrants forced the
government to place tight restrictions on immigration. One survey found that
76% of French citizens believe there are too many Arabs in the country. In Italy,
75% of the population favor closing the borders to all new immigrants (J. Levin,
1993).

These responses show that migration is quickly becoming one of the world's
major social and political issues. To some, the consequences of current migratory
trends are nothing short of apocalyptic:

> The most potent political force shaping the civilization of the future may
> well be one that has no place in any ideology: the sheer movement of
> people from one place to another. It is changing the face of the world,
> rendering old boundaries and policies obsolete, and laying the foundation
> for a "new world order" quite unlike anything foreseen by any political
> leader or theorist—a boundary-less world in which people live where they
> choose. (quoted in Honebrink, 1993, p. 47)

Immigration creates a variety of cultural fears: the fear that there is no control
over national boundaries, the fear that an ethnically homogeneous race will be
altered through intermarriage, the fear of an influx of a "strange" way of life with
religious rituals and cultural habits, and the fear that newcomers will encroach

upon property, clog the educational system, and suck up social benefits owned and largely paid for by natives (Kennedy, 1993). Many people also express concern that immigrants are responsible for outbreaks of diseases like AIDS, measles, and cholera, which strain the health care system and create even more resentment. Above all, there is the fear that immigrants might one day become a statistical majority, rendering the "natives" powerless in their own country.

Population Trends and the Impact on the American Experience

How are these processes affecting the population in our country? It is difficult to talk about common American population trends because different ethnic, religious, and gender groups experience these processes differently. Hispanic Americans, for instance, have a significantly higher birth rate than whites. Catholics and Mormons have higher birth rates than other religions (Weeks, 1992). American women, on average, can expect to live longer than American men.

Nevertheless, two important demographic trends in the United States will exert a profound effect on the entire population in years to come: the growing proportion of nonwhite, non-English-speaking immigrants and their children and the shifting age structure of the population marked by a growing proportion of elderly and shrinking proportion of native-born young people. These two trends together strain America's social fabric as questions about the fair distribution of social resources become more and more insistent.

Immigration and the Changing Face of America

Because we live in a society where the population grows at a manageable rate, it is hard for us to understand how population explosions in other countries can affect us. But as populations burst the seams of national boundaries elsewhere, degrading the environment, reducing the number of available jobs, and creating political turmoil, individuals move, often to those countries that they perceive hold the most promise and opportunities. Many end up here in the United States. Some arrive legally by plane, boat, or train. Others arrive illegally by foot or are smuggled in the backs of trucks or the bottoms of boats.

In the mid-1980s the U.S. Census Bureau predicted that by the year 2050 the United States would have a population of 300 million (there are roughly 250 million Americans today). In the early 1990s, however, the Bureau revised its estimate, projecting instead a population of 383 million by 2050 (Pear, 1992). Part of the reason these projections were adjusted was that immigration has played a more significant role in our population growth over the last several years than had been anticipated. Over one million documented immigrants enter this country each year. In California alone, immigrants represent 37% of the state's population growth during the 1980s (Reinhold, 1993). The Census Bureau predicts that over 90% of the growth in the U.S. population by the year 2050 will be due to immigration that occurred *after* 1991 (cited in Honebrink, 1993).

This isn't the first time our country's population has been radically increased by a flood of immigration. In the first decade of the 20th century, nearly 9 million immigrants entered the country (Weeks, 1992). What makes contemporary immigration different, though, is that relatively few of these newcomers will be white. In the late 19th century, 90% of the immigrants who came to this country were from northern and southern Europe. But by the mid-1980s only 11% were from Europe; 46% were from Asia and 37% from Latin America (Bouvier & Gardner, 1986). Roughly 60% of the 2 million or so *illegal* immigrants who enter the country each year come from Latin America (Robey, 1987).

Not surprisingly, the racial and ethnic composition of the country changed more quickly and dramatically in the past decade than at any previous time in the 20th century. In chapter 12, I described the fact that our population is becoming less white. Experts estimate that by the year 2000 the Hispanic population will increase by 21%, the Asian-American population by 22%, and the African-American population by 12%. In contrast, the white population will increase by about 2% (Baca-Zinn & Eitzen, 1993).

The strains of high immigration levels are likely to continue for some time. Most people who immigrate to this country are pulled by the lure of employment and a better life. Until population and economic pressures ease in other regions of the world, the United States will remain an appealing destination. And as long as U.S. employers are willing to hire illegal immigrants, then it seems unlikely that enhanced efforts to seal the borders against them or to limit their access to education and social programs will be successful (R. L. Clark & Passel, 1993).

As their numbers grow, immigrants find that they are becoming the targets of a variety of social anxieties, from economic tension to outright anger (D. Sontag, 1992). Although immigrants contribute to the economy through their work and the taxes they pay, they are widely perceived to be an economic drag on society, using health, school, and police services while spreading crime, drug trafficking, and disease (Reinhold, 1993). One study estimates that the millions of immigrants, legal and illegal, who will enter the country in the next decade will cost taxpayers approximately $668 billion dollars in welfare, primary and secondary education, and Medicaid (Huddle, 1993).

The problem is particularly acute in California. In a 1992 survey, 76% of Californians felt there were too many immigrants entering their state; 78% said immigrants had become a financial burden on the state; and 80% thought steps should be taken to limit immigration (cited in Miles, 1992).

Violence against immigrants, or "immigrant bashing," is becoming more common throughout the United States. A Salvadoran dishwasher was beaten and robbed; his attackers told him: "You steal our jobs, we steal your money." A Mexican immigrant who sells flowers on a street corner was routinely spat upon and told to return to her country by passersby. A few years ago in Houston, a 15-year-old Vietnamese boy was stomped to death by two skinheads. As he was dying, he reportedly cried out, "God forgive me for coming to this country!" (D. Sontag, 1992). In Detroit, a Chinese American was beaten to death with a baseball bat as his assailants shouted, "It's because of you that we're out of work!" (J. Levin, 1993).

The growing hostility directed toward immigrants has been fueled, to a large degree, by anti-immigrant sentiments voiced by politicians, lobbyists, academics, and writers who have capitalized on the frustration of some Americans over increasing competition for jobs and social services. Pat Buchanan and David Duke, two unsuccessful presidential candidates in 1992, ran their campaigns on a theme that new immigrants would "dilute" the country's European character. A plank in the Republican Party's 1992 platform called for a barrier along the border between the United States and Mexico to keep illegal aliens out (D. Sontag, 1992). The animosity crosses party lines. Some liberal Democratic politicians have also called on the government to seal the nation's border. In 1993 alone, 21 different bills aimed at controlling the flow of immigrants—such as denying illegal immigrants health care, education, driver's licenses, and housing—were introduced in the California State Legislature (Reinhold, 1993).

The changing ethnic configuration of the population will not just heighten tensions between immigrant groups and whites but may also increase animosity between minority groups. As discussed in chapters 11 and 12, we have a two-tiered occupational structure in which jobs on the lower rung tend to belong to members of racial minorities. To the extent that vast waves of immigration mean greater competition for unskilled labor jobs, those most affected by the presence of immigrants may well be other people of color. For instance, janitorial companies serving downtown Los Angeles have almost entirely replaced their unionized black workforce with nonunionized, and therefore less expensive, immigrants from Latin America and Asia. African Americans are also being forced out of jobs as gardeners, busboys, construction workers, and nannies (Miles, 1992).

New immigrants even face animosity from members of their own racial or ethnic groups who arrived earlier. According to the 1992 Latino National Political Survey, over 70% of the respondents, which included people of Cuban, Mexican, and Puerto Rican descent, felt there were too many Hispanic immigrants coming into this country (Suro, 1992). About two-thirds of them felt that special preferences should not be given to Latin American immigrants. The researchers concluded that the strain of economic competition from recent Hispanic immigrants is felt as strongly by Hispanics as it is by whites.

In sum, our country has always had a love-hate relationship with immigrants. In good times they have been inexpensive and welcome contributors to the economy. Their labor helped build our rail system and our roads. They filled unwanted jobs, opened businesses, and improved the lives of many Americans by working cheaply as housekeepers, dishwashers, and gardeners. When times are bad, however, the inclination is to shut the door and blame them for many of the country's economic woes.

The "Graying" of America

At the same time that the United States must deal with the changing ethnic and racial configuration of its population, it also has to address a monumental shift in its age structure. The age structure of a society is one of the key factors determining the extent of an individual's needs. Very young people require physical care and protection. Educational requirements are based, in large part, on the age of an individual. Workers at the beginning and end of their careers are more susceptible to unemployment than those at midcareer. And age is the major determinant of decisions to retire.

The age structure can even influence certain social problems in ways that are not immediately apparent. Take crime, for instance. According to the FBI there were almost 50% more arrests in the United States in 1980 than in 1970. To some this was evidence that society had fallen apart. To others it was proof that the country had turned into a police state. Actually, neither was true. What happened was that the large baby boom cohort had reached its late teens and early 20s, a period in the life course when criminal activity is most common (L. E. Cohen & Land, 1987). The crime rates went up not because crime became a more desirable pursuit or because Americans as a whole became less respectful of the law, but simply because there were more people at the age when criminal activity is statistically more likely to take place.

Perhaps the most important and most problematic demographic trend in this country involves the increasing average age of the population. Two hundred years ago, the median age for Americans was 16. Today it is about 33 and is expected to be about 43 by the middle of the next century as the massive baby boom cohort reaches old age (Taeuber, 1988).

Two developments in the 1960s and 1970s changed the age structure of the United States in dramatic ways (Preston, 1984). The first was a decrease in the number of children being born. From 1960 to 1982, the number of children under 15 fell by 7%. During this period the birth rate dropped from 3.7 births per woman to about 1.8 (Yorburg, 1993). Furthermore, more families than ever chose to have only one child.

The other development was a rapid increase in the number of people surviving to old age. Between 1960 and 1980, the proportion of people over 65 grew by 54%. By 2030 there will be more old people in this country than children. The number of people over 85, an age group for which health care costs are exceptionally high, will grow fastest of all, doubling to 6.5 million by

Table 14.2 *Distribution of the Population by Age: 1990-2050 (in percentages)*

	1990	2000	2010	2030	2050
Total	100.0	100.0	100.0	100.0	100.0
under 5	7.6	6.9	6.6	6.4	6.4
5 to 13	12.8	13.1	11.9	11.7	11.6
14 to 17	5.3	5.7	5.7	5.3	5.2
18 to 24	10.8	9.5	10.1	9.1	9.0
25 to 34	17.3	13.6	12.9	12.4	12.5
35 to 44	15.1	16.3	13.0	12.9	12.2
45 to 64	18.6	22.2	26.5	22.1	22.5
65 & over	12.5	12.7	13.3	20.2	20.6
85 & over	1.2	1.6	1.9	2.4	4.6
100 & over	0.0	0.0	0.1	0.1	0.3

Source: U.S. Bureau of the Census, 1993b.

2020 and soaring to 17.7 million by 2050. There will be more than one million people over the age of 100 by then as well (Pear, 1992) (see Table 14.2). Technological advances in medicine and nutrition have extended the lives of countless numbers of Americans who would have routinely died several decades ago. Life expectancy has risen from 69.6 in 1955 to 73.6 in 1980 and will probably be over 80 by the year 2000 (Monk, 1988).

Why should we be concerned about the "graying" of the American population? The answer is that a society with an aging population will inevitably experience increased demands for pensions, health care, and other social services catering to the needs of the elderly (OECD, 1988). Moreover, aging populations change the assumptions we make about our economy, the family, and the larger culture.

Graying and the Economy

One of the key concerns arising out of this trend is whether society, and in particular the working population, will be able and willing to bear the additional burden of caring for the growing number of elderly people. This concern has led demographers to look at the statistical relationship between the elderly and the rest of the population. To the extent that old people have to be supported by the society to which they have contributed throughout their lives, this relationship tells us a great deal about the social, political, and economic effort society may be asked to make in support of its elderly (Kart, 1990). By 2030 the ratio of elderly people (i.e., those over 65) to people of working age (18 to 64) will be three times greater than it was in 1950. This means that workers, on average, will have to support three times as many older people.

This figure is probably exaggerated. Not all people over 65 are retired, nor are they all in poor health. And not all people between the ages of 18 and 64 are working, nor are they all in good health (Friedland, 1989). Nevertheless, the retirements of older people will be directly or indirectly financed by the working-age population through Social Security and other pension programs. Unless the future's elderly are better able to support themselves financially than today's elderly, the government, through tax dollars, will have to play an even larger role in providing health care and other services.

The growing number of elderly people and shrinking number of young people are challenging employers to restructure the workplace. With the population getting older, many more workers are choosing early retirement, and there are fewer young workers to replace them. As a result, the cost of labor is likely to go up in the future and will garner different responses from employers depending on the type of industry. Some will be forced to focus more attention on employee productivity, perhaps turning to machines to replace workers. On the positive side, however, because of the impending labor shortage, employers will have to pay attention to meeting the needs of their valuable employees and finding better ways to attract and retain them (Friedland, 1989). We may see more employers providing assistance with child and elderly care. Employers may also have to find ways to keep older workers interested in working longer rather than retiring, by offering bonuses for continued employment or by creating prestigious and well-paid part-time positions.

Graying and the Family

The growth of the elderly population will have an enormous impact on the American family as well. The vast majority of deaths today are postponed to old age (Riley, 1983). In other words, most people will live to be old. This will require us to rethink our very view of family relations. In the distant past it was quite rare for a child to know, let alone grow up with, his or her grandparents. It made sense to focus academic, cultural, and political attention on the nuclear family. However, with many families today having four or even five generations alive at the same time, it becomes increasingly difficult to conceptualize the family simply in terms of parents and children. Today over half of all people over 65 have great-grandchildren (Baca-Zinn & Eitzen, 1993).

One important familial consequence of increasing longevity is prolonged marriage. When life expectancy was lower, the average marriage ended as a result of the death of one of the spouses after only 20 or so years of marriage. At the turn of the century, more than half of all marriages were ended by the death of one spouse before the last child had left home (Kart, 1990). Today, the average couple could live 30 years or more after the last child has left home. It's estimated that, apart from divorce, one out of every five married couples will celebrate their 50th anniversary (Glick & Norton, 1977).

While this means that married couples will have more time to compile extensive common experiences and share broad historical changes, it also means that there will be more time for them to get on each other's nerves (Preston, 1976). As a result, divorce among older people—a segment of the population typically assumed to be beyond the reach of national trends in divorce—has more than doubled since 1960 (Uhlenberg & Myers, 1981). Now, in a sense, people are "outliving" their marriages.

Increased longevity also extends the amount of time parents spend with their children. It will not be uncommon, in the near future, for a significant number of parents and children to spend 60 years together, of which only 18 are in the traditional parent-child relationship (Riley, 1983). A government study found that one or both parents are still alive for 44% of people between the ages of 58 and 66 (Kolata, 1993). Certainly this increases the number of important experiences that parents and children can share. It also means, however, that there will be increasing financial and emotional burdens on the children when they reach adulthood, resulting in role conflict. The likelihood that one's parents will live well into their 80s means that, for many people, their role as someone's child and the accompanying responsibilities will long overlap their roles as someone's spouse and parent (see chapter 2).

Graying and Culture

The care of the growing numbers of elderly will be one of the country's most urgent social issues over the next several decades. It is further complicated by the low cultural value traditionally placed on the elderly in this society. For many of us, the elderly represent precisely what we spend a significant portion of our lives trying to deny: our own mortality. They symbolize disease, disability, and death (Butler, 1975). As a result, old people are one of the most excluded age groups in American society today.

Elderly people are likely to experience prejudice, discrimination, and residential segregation simply because they are old. Common stereotypes about the elderly—that they're sick, slow-witted, senile, mean, depressed, and drive too slowly—reinforce the public perception that they are socially worthless (Neugarten, 1980). As with other forms of prejudice, these perceptions are usually translated into action, that is, discrimination. The Age Discrimination Employment Act of 1967 prohibits hiring, firing, wage determination, or other privileges and conditions of employment on the basis of age. It is clear, however, that age discrimination in employment practices still exists today. Mandatory retirement policies in some businesses operate on the assumption that all people experience a decrease in mental and physical capabilities when they reach a certain age. As long as the elderly are perceived to be rigid, unhealthy, unhappy, and unemployable, discriminatory treatment accorded them will continue to be justified and it will be difficult to convince younger people that tax dollars ought to go to supporting them.

Micro-Macro Connection

The Elderly in Japan

Not all cultures express disdain for their elderly. The population of Japan, for instance, is aging faster than any on earth. By 2025, one-quarter of the Japanese population will be 65 or older (Dentzer, 1991). However, unlike Americans, the Japanese have traditionally maintained a relatively high level of respect for elders, integrating them into work and family (Palmore, 1975). The most common word for the aged in Japanese is *otoshiyori*, which literally means "honorable elders." Although the days when elderly people were assumed to be superior simply because they were old have disappeared, rules of etiquette still give elders priority in most social settings such as public seating arrangements and serving order. There is even a national holiday called Respect for Elders Day. In Japan people use the age of 61 as an occasion for celebration, much like the American tradition of celebrating the age of 21. Japan's 1963 National Law for the Welfare of the Elders states: "The elders shall be loved and respected as those who have for many years contributed toward the development of society, and a wholesome and peaceful life shall be guaranteed to them" (quoted in Kart, 1990, p. 203).

Over 60% of Japan's elderly live with their children or extended families, compared with less than 10% in the United States (Dentzer, 1991). The majority of Japanese men over 65 are in the paid labor force. Although most Japanese industries have mandatory retirement, which was raised to age 65 in 1986, almost all provide some kind of employment for older workers even after they retire. This may mean extending the old job, creating a new one not subject to compulsory retirement, or offering a part-time or lower paying job (Kart, 1990). Voluntary organizations called Silver Human Resource Centers assist older workers in finding part-time or temporary work, like supervising parking lots or cleaning parks (L. Martin, 1989). Those who are not employed remain useful in terms of housekeeping, child care, shopping, gardening, and other household tasks (Palmore, 1975).

Why do the Japanese attach such high social value to their aged citizens? Japanese society is "vertically" structured, meaning that most relationships are hierarchical rather than egalitarian. Age is the most important dimension for determining who is above and who is below. In addition, religious principles of *filial piety* dating back to Confucius suggest that respect and duty toward one's parents is one of the most important personal virtues an individual can possess.

But in recent years attitudes toward the elderly in Japan have changed, particularly among the young. There has been a weakening of the belief that children are obligated to care for their aging parents. Traditionally, wives bore the responsibility of taking care of aged parents and in-laws. However, since more women are working outside the home, they are less inclined to take on this duty. A Japanese newspaper survey of wives in their childbearing years shows that the proportion who plan on depending on their children in old age has declined from 55% in 1950 to 18% in 1988. As a result, the proportion of elderly people living with their children has started to fall (L. Martin, 1989). Many people in Japan are worried that the government will soon be expected to provide financial support for the rapidly growing elderly population in the form of health care, social services, and nursing homes.

Cohort Inequality and the Tarnished American Dream

In all societies, different age groups have different rights, duties, and privileges (Riley, Johnson, & Foner, 1972). They are subjected to different societal expectations and accorded different access to social resources. Such age stratification is as influential as class, race, and gender stratification. The changing racial configuration and age structure of America are prompting spirited debate over the distribution of social resources among various cohorts in our society. You might think that a change in America's age structure would help young people and hurt old people because more older people are living longer and fewer people are being born. Fewer young people should mean less competition for resources and greater availability of social services but an increase in old people should strain institutions such as nursing homes, hospitals, and Social Security.

Increasingly, the gap between the rich and poor in this country is becoming a gap between the old and young. The economic well-being of the elderly has actually been steadily improving since the 1960s, while that of the younger cohorts—baby boomers and Generation X alike—has been steadily deteriorating (Preston, 1984). According to the U.S. Census, real income for people over 65 increased 52.6% between 1967 and 1987; the increase for all others was about 7%. During the 1980s the only age group to suffer a drop in real income— 10.8%—were people under 25.

In the early 1970s a typical 30-year-old male made 6% more than a typical 60-year-old male; today he makes 14% *less*. Although most teens today expect to have an annual income over $30,000 by the time they're 30, according to the U.S. Census Bureau in 1990, the number of Americans between ages 25 and 29 who made less than $30,000 outnumbered those who made more by eight to one (Howe & Strauss, 1992).

For people beginning their families and careers in the late 1980s and early 1990s, inflation widened the gulf between their quality of life and that of their parents and grandparents. The average price of a new house went up 294% during the 1980s. Federal income taxes went up 175%, and state taxes increased by 520%. Social Security taxes went up 331%. The cost of having a baby in a hospital increased 233%. Tuition costs at private universities doubled or even tripled (P. Light, 1988). On virtually every available economic indicator, today's young people lag behind previous generations.

Consequently, over the past several decades there have been dramatic changes in the proportion of young people who live in poverty relative to the proportion of elderly. In 1970, 16% of children under age 16 lived in poverty compared to 25% of those older than 65 (Preston, 1984). By 1991 the situation had been completely reversed: 22% of children lived in poverty compared to 12% of the elderly (U.S. Bureau of the Census, 1992a). Sixty-nine percent of the wealthiest 400 people in this country are 65 years of age or older ("The Forbes Four Hundred," 1990). Certainly not all old people are this wealthy, but their economic status as a group does continue to improve.

Not surprisingly, many young people today feel that the American Dream is unattainable, at least for them. They fear they will be the first generation to fail to match their parents' economic success (Shapiro, 1993). In a 1990 poll, two out of three Americans between the ages of 18 and 29 thought it would be much harder for people in their generation to live as comfortably as previous generations. Sixty-nine percent believe they will have more trouble buying a house, 52% feel they will have less leisure time, and 53% are worried about their future (D. M. Gross & Scott, 1990). Today, 75% of Americans between the ages 18 and 24 still live at home—the largest percentage since the Great Depression of the 1930s (D. M. Gross & Scott, 1990). These so-called boomerang kids are finding independent life away from home difficult, if not impossible, to sustain.

Ruth Sidel
"Twentysomething"
Women on Their
Own

To examine the life outlooks of today's young people, sociologist Ruth Sidel interviewed 150 women in their late teens and early 20s. She wanted to know what members of this generation thought about family, work, and women's roles in contemporary society. Sidel found that many young women today have an overwhelming desire for material wealth and feel it is possible to achieve this goal through individual effort. They feel very strongly that they can and should take control over their own lives, planning their own success stories instead of playing supporting roles in someone else's. Few of them indicate any interest in traditionally female occupations like teaching or nursing. In short, they believe very strongly in the basic tenets of the American Dream: that with enough hard work they will "make it." As Sidel put it, "They have bought into the image of a bright future" (1990, p. 18).

Such dreams are quite different from those held by young women only two generations ago. Those women, for the most part, did not perceive themselves as independent individuals with their own futures and their own needs. Their identities were determined by their ability to satisfy the needs of others, usually as wives or mothers. But by the 1970s and 1980s women had come to feel that they were entitled to play roles formerly reserved for men. They saw no reason why they couldn't contribute to fields like medicine, law, or politics. Most agreed that if they were ever to gain the same recognition and respect as men, they would have to enter the male-dominated public sphere, for that is where the *real* money, power, and status lie.

The young women in Sidel's research had a strong commitment to career, material wealth, success, and independence. One of the common desires of all of the women interviewed was to be affluent. In fact, the dreams of these women were remarkably similar across racial and ethnic groups, class lines, and levels of education. Today's young women are the first generation to take for granted that they, like men, deserve their fair share of the American Dream.

But how do these visions for the future compare to the demographic and cultural realities of life in the late 20th century? Sidel found that lurking behind all these dreams and ambitions is an almost overwhelming sense of despair:

> [It is] the despair of those who cannot envision a future beyond tomorrow, of those whose lives have been shaped at a young age by personal circumstances and social and economic forces often beyond their control, of eighteen- and nineteen-year-olds who seem old before their time. (Sidel, 1990, p. 219)

The young women Sidel interviewed consistently expressed the belief that they were, essentially, on their own. They are convinced that if they are to "make it" they will have to do it by themselves. The dreams of success have become symbols of identity in an era of "fragmented family life, insecure, often transient work relationships, and a vanishing sense of community" (Sidel, 1990, p. 223).

On the one hand this focus on individualism signals a growing sense of independence and personal responsibility among young women, a sign that they had acquired the voice of hearty American individualism that had long been suppressed. On the other hand, Sidel speculates that perhaps the women of this generation have been hoodwinked into believing that they can do it all, have it all, and be it all while society itself remains largely unchanged in its neglect of youth. In other words, is the self-sufficiency this generation perceives to be necessary possible within the current structure of American society? Clearly the dilemmas facing young women today are as much a function of their times as their gender. The baby boomers raised women's expectations to unprecedented levels. Yet the increasing economic burdens on today's young women limit their ability to fulfill these expectations. We can see the enormous generational relevance of the subtitle of Sidel's book: *Growing Up in the Shadow of the American Dream*. The dream looms large—casting a broad shadow over all aspects of life—yet it remains a shadow, something that can be seen but not grasped.

Conclusion

The interconnectedness of private experiences and macro-structural forces is clearly felt in the relationship between population trends and everyday life. You have seen in this chapter that our destinies, whether positive or negative, can be profoundly influenced by the size, ethnic makeup, and age structure of the population in our country as well as in other countries. You have also seen how the experiences of your birth cohort are shaped by the processes, events, and social changes that occur in society as you progress through the life course. In sum, the process of growing older is much more complex than simply adding a year to your age each birthday. It involves the private experience of major world events, cultural trends, and shifts in population characteristics.

I must confess that in discussing current and future demographic trends I can't help but think about my own children and their as yet unnamed generation. As I write this book they are 5 and 8. Their generation will be the first to reach the teen years during the 21st century. I wonder what kind of impact being born in the late 1980s and growing up in the 1990s will have on their lives? Will the world's population reach the predicted catastrophic proportions, or will we figure out a way to control population growth and enable all people to live quality lives? Will the growing ethnic diversity of this society continue to create tension and conflict, or will we eventually learn how to be a truly multicultural nation? What will be their cohort's single, most definitive "punctuating" event: a war, an assassination, a severe economic depression, or some other unimaginable catastrophe? Or will it be world peace, an end to hunger and homelessness, or a cure for AIDS?

I also wonder how our important social institutions will serve their generation. What will their experience in higher education be like? Will there be jobs waiting for them when they are ready to enter the labor force? What will be their share of the national debt? How will they perceive family life? Will marriage be an outdated mode of intimacy by the time they reach adulthood? What will be a desirable family size?

As a parent, of course, I'm more than a little curious about how these questions will be answered. I want to know the answers right now! But as a sociologist, I realize that they will emerge only from the experiences and interactions of my kids, and others their age, as they progress through their lives. Herein lies the unique and fundamental message of the sociological perspective. As powerful and relentless as the demographic and generational forces described in this chapter are in determining my children's life chances, the responsibility for shaping and changing this society in the 21st century ultimately rests in the hands of their generation. It is this topic—the ability of individuals to change and reconstruct their society—that will serve as the theme for the next, and final, chapter.

CHAPTER HIGHLIGHTS

- Often overlooked in our quest to identify the structural factors that shape our everyday experiences are the effects of our birth cohort. Birth cohorts are more than just a collection of individuals born within a few years of each other; they are distinctive generations tied together by historical events, national and global population trends, and large-scale societal changes.

- The earth's population is growing at an unprecedented rate. But different countries experience different rates of growth. Poor, developing countries are expanding rapidly, while the populations in wealthy, developed countries have either stabilized or, in some cases, declined.

■ When the population of a country grows rapidly, the age structure will be increasingly dominated by young people. In slow-growth countries with low birth rates and high life expectancy, the population will be much older.

■ As conditions in developing countries grow worse, pressures to migrate increase, creating a variety of cultural, political, and economic fears in countries experiencing high levels of immigration.

■ All societies have a system whereby different age groups are stratified and given different rights, duties, and privileges. The changing age structure of the American population—more older people and fewer younger people—has meant that the gap between rich and poor has increasingly become a gap between old and young.

Y O U R   T U R N

Demographers often use "population pyramids" to graphically display the age and sex distributions of a population. These pictures are often used to draw conclusions about a population's most pressing economic, educational, and social needs. Using information from the most recent U.S. Census (available in the government documents section of your school's library), construct population pyramids for several different types of cities:

■ a college town (e.g., Ann Arbor, Michigan; Iowa City, Iowa)

■ a military town (e.g., Norfolk, Virginia; Annapolis, Maryland)

■ a large urban city (e.g., New York, Chicago, Los Angeles)

■ a small rural town

■ an affluent suburb

■ a city with a large elderly retirement community (e.g., St. Petersburg, Florida; Sun City, Arizona)

The pyramid should utilize the following structure:

```
                    Male              │              Female

Age:
75+
65-74
55-64
45-54
35-44
25-34
15-24
5-14
0-4
        20 18 16 14 12 10 8 6 4 2   2 4 6 8 10 12 14 16 18 20
              (percent of the population in each age group)
```

Describe how the age and sex profiles of these cities differ. What other characteristics of these cities would be different as a result of the shape of their populations? Consider the following:

- the nature of the educational system
- the types of businesses that would succeed and fail
- the sorts of recreational opportunities available
- important political issues and the degree of citizen involvement in political activity
- important health care issues
- crime rates
- divorce rates
- suicide rates

From these differences draw some general conclusions about how people's lives are influenced by the age and sex distribution of the population in their cities.

Profiles of Contemporary Immigration

PHOTOGRAPHS AND CONCEPT BY STEVE GOLD

One of the most powerful population processes at work in the world today is international migration—the movement of people to countries other than those into which they were born. Immigrants must face the difficult task of adapting and integrating into the dominant culture. Sometimes people move because they seek better economic opportunities elsewhere; other times they are "refugees," who are forced to flee their country of origin in order to survive.

Immigration authorities differentiate between "immigrants"(those who have come voluntarily) and "refugees"(those who have fled persecution). Not all refugees receive refugee status, but those that do have several advantages over immigrants upon entering the United States: they are eligible for resettlement services, training programs, cash assistance, and are offered permanent resident status. Their disadvantages stem from the reasons they left their countries in the first place: they usually have little time to plan for their move, learn English, or collect capital. Furthermore they may be less willing to adapt to an alien culture than immigrants who have chosen to move here.

Sociologist Steve Gold compared two refugee groups in the United States, Soviet Jews and the Vietnamese, from 1982 to 1990. These groups share several common elements, including an emphasis on educational attainment, high levels of skill and urban experience, a common place of arrival (large fractions of both populations settled in urban areas of California), and origins in communist nations. Yet he also discovered that there is a great deal of diversity and complexity *within* both the Jewish and Vietnamese refugee communities. As you look at these photographs, notice the different ways refugees are able to maintain separate ethnic communities while still adapting to the dominant culture.

*S*oviet Jews have been emigrating to the United States since the 1970s when Soviet immigration policies were loosened. Because of widespread anti-Semitism in the former USSR, access to jobs, higher education, and housing were restricted.

Soviet Jews usually emigrate to this country in intact family units. Extended families of several generations are used to living together in close quarters because of the shortage of housing in the former Soviet Union. Unlike American youth, who are socialized by their peers, Soviet Jewish youth are more involved with their families, maintaining strong ties to relatives throughout their lives.

Unlike other refugee and immigrant populations, Soviet Jewish families typically contain many elderly persons, especially women, such as these shown here working on their English in a Los Angeles park. Over 50 percent of Soviet Jews are over the age of 45. The average is 40.5 (Gold, 1992).

Soviet Jews typically achieve a high level of education. Most women are accustomed to working outside the home; Svetlana Siegel (left) is a cardiologist in Los Angeles.

Immigrant and refugee business owners often hire Mexican, Chicano/a, and Central American workers. Entrepreneurs associate several advantages with these employees: they feel they are physically strong and hard-working, are easy to control, don't demand favors based on common ethnicity, and, as cultural outsiders who don't speak the owner's language, are unlikely to open a competing business. The woman here runs a clothing store and, with the help of her Chicana seamstress, repairs damaged Levi's for resale.

Although you'd expect this religiously defined refugee group to have strong spiritual ties, Soviet Jews are fractured in their religious orientations. Elderly émigrés tend to be religiously involved upon resettlement, having been exposed to traditional Eastern European Judaism before the restrictions of the 1930s. The younger generations, who grew up in largely secular, communist countries are much less religiously involved.

*V*ietnamese refugees have come to the United States in three waves: the expatriate elite in 1975, the "boat people" since 1978, and most recently the ethnic Chinese Vietnamese, a minority group within Vietnam. The first group, who left their country quickly after the fall of Saigon, were highly educated and competent in English. They adjusted quickly to their new lives in this country. The second group came largely from rural areas. Their trips were arduous and many were forced to spend months in refugee camps before entering the United States Due to these dangers there were many more men than women, children, and elderly. Their lack of marketable skills and knowledge of English made it difficult for them to find work. The third group also experienced difficult passage to the U.S. Their situation is made worse by the fact that they are often treated harshly by the Vietnamese population already here.

Family is an important part of Vietnamese culture. In an effort to provide themselves with social support, many young male refugees who have no blood relatives in this country form "pseudofamilies" that are based on the traditional Vietnamese family model. Although the members of this "pseudofamily" are of very different class, regional, and ethnic origins, they share accommodations, money, and advice in Oakland, California.

Although the Vietnamese family is patriarchal, the culture has a strong tradition of female autonomy and independence. The propensity of Vietnamese women to open small businesses in California is in part due to the Vietnamese village women's practice of running small enterprises as an extension of their domestic duties. Here a food distributor gives orders to one of her employees.

Faced with economic difficulties, many Vietnamese refugees turn to their ethnic communities for support, information, and diversion. Above, Vietnamese Catholics participate in a religious parade to celebrate the Feast of the Immaculate Conception.

Although Vietnamese history has involved conflicts between China and Vietnam, at the same time, the Vietnamese have been largely influenced by their northern neighbor. This tradition is reflected in the photo above, where a Vietnamese family celebrates a wedding at an Oakland Chinese Vietnamese restaurant.

CHAPTER 15

Architects of Change

Reconstructing Society

The 1992 film *Lorenzo's Oil* dramatized the true story of a couple, Augusto and Michaela Odone, who discover their son, Lorenzo, is suffering from a rare disease known as adrenoleukodystrophy (ALD). ALD destroys the protective coating around nerve fibers, progressively impairing victims' ability to talk, walk, and care for themselves. Death is slow, painful, and certain. When the Odones sought medical assistance for their son through ordinary channels, they came face-to-face with a health care system that was apparently too large and bureaucratic for its own good and was more concerned with disease processes than with diseased people. Frustrated by the doctors' overwhelming pessimism and resignation, and having no scientific training whatsoever, the Odones launched a two-person crusade to find a treatment for their son's disease. They read obscure medical journals and managed to find a few medical and chemical experts who were willing to help them. Through hard work and perseverance, they eventually discovered that a combination of two natural oils stopped the physical decline brought about by ALD. The film ends with a visual testimony to the many other children who used the Odones' oily concoction and were spared the debilitating effects of the disease.

As with all films derived from real-life events, there is some debate as to whether the facts of Lorenzo's life and the actions of his parents are different from what were portrayed in the film. Nevertheless, the message is sociologically compelling: Two individuals were able to overcome the institutional indifference of the medical establishment to find their own solution to a seemingly insoluble problem.

The Odones succeeded in helping their son precisely because the medical establishment could not. From an institutional perspective, there is little profit for pharmaceutical companies that invest in so-called *orphan diseases* that affect only a small percentage of the total population. Furthermore, new drugs must be tested meticulously to determine their effectiveness and to identify all potentially dangerous side effects. There must be a sharp line drawn between the need to satisfy the principles of sound scientific method and the desire to help individual people (D. J. Rothman & Edgar, 1992). As we have seen throughout this book, institutions must operate in a highly structured, standardized, and impersonal way, at a level above the interests and personalities of the individual people they are created to serve. Imagine the chaos that would ensue if all parents with sick children went around challenging medical science and creating their own treatments. The entire system would quickly collapse.

But such institutional needs are often little comfort to the individuals whose lives operate under the influence of that institution. Lorenzo's story, while illustrating the inherent tension between individuals and institutions, also shows that individuals can overcome bureaucratic lethargy and actually change a part of their social structure. As a result of the Odones's actions, the standard medical approach to ALD will probably never be the same again.

The Odones aren't the only individuals who have succeeded in "altering the system." AIDS activists, frustrated by mounting deaths and a government drug approval process that often takes years to get drugs into the hands of the people who need them, have succeeded in changing the way drugs are developed and regulated for AIDS so that potentially helpful treatments can be produced more quickly (Arno & Feiden, 1992).

This theme, the power of individuals to influence the structural elements of their society, guides us through this final chapter of the book. I have spent the previous 14 chapters discussing how our society and everything in it is socially constructed and how these social constructions, in turn, impact the lives of individuals. At times the message has been pessimistic, even downright gloomy. It's hard not to feel a little helpless when discussing the control that culture, bureaucracies, institutions, and systems of social stratification have over our lives. And it's hard to be upbeat when discussing things like poverty, racism, sexism, and the global population explosion. It's only fitting, then, to end on a positive note with a discussion of social change and how individuals can reconstruct their society.

The Elements of Social Change

Whether it occurs in our personal relationships, in our cultural norms and values, in our systems of stratification, or in our institutions, change is the preeminent characteristic of modern human societies. During the 1992 presidential election, Bill Clinton based his entire campaign on the concept of change. We heard terms like *a new age, revolutionary, a time of great excitement,* and *a new world order.* Granted, these phrases may simply have been hollow campaign rhetoric. But beyond politics they do seem to characterize all corners of human life as we approach the 21st century.

As you read this book, there is no doubt that the world in which you are living right now is, in many ways, different from the one I experienced when I wrote it. I've had to revise several examples in this book at the last minute because some things have changed so abruptly. Modern electronic telecommunications technology can link people around the world in milliseconds, creating what amounts to a massive global information community (Zukin, 1991). Through vast computer networks and bulletin boards, individuals with similar interests can anonymously form long-lasting relationships and establish complex electronic communities without ever coming into actual contact with one another. Cyberspace has become the singles bar, support group, and social club of the nineties. And it won't be long before we will be able to shop, bank, trade stocks, design our own personalized newscasts, and access any movie we want through our interactive televisions.

International developments once considered impossible, like peace in the Middle East and black majority rule in South Africa, are becoming realities, changing the shape of world politics and economics. At the same time, however, ancient tribal hatreds and nationalistic desires have reemerged, creating a growing number of new, hostile, and ethnically homogeneous subnations. And map makers are one of many who have to keep up with shifting national boundaries around the world.

It seems that everywhere you look—your relationships, your school, your job, your home, your entertainment equipment, your diet, your clothes, and your government—institutional and cultural change is the rule, not the exception. Consider family life in America over the past 30 or 40 years. Divorce rates skyrocketed, then stabilized. Women have entered the workforce in unprecedented numbers. People are waiting longer to get married, and once they do, they are having fewer children. Cultural concerns over gender equality have altered the way men and women relate to one another inside and outside the home. Social and sexual rules that once seemed permanent have disintegrated: Unmarried couples can live openly together, unmarried women can have and keep their babies, remaining single and remaining childless have become acceptable lifestyle options (Skolnick & Skolnick, 1992). In short, today's American family bears little resemblance to the cultural ideal of the 1950s.

These changes have, in turn, affected other institutions. Because so many families are headed by dual-earner couples, children spend less time with their parents than they did in the past, forcing them to depend on secondary relationships: paid caregivers, friends, teachers. Schools are being called on to address many of society's social problems by providing students with training in moral values and technological "literacy," the provision of adequate nutrition, and practical instruction to help them avoid drug and alcohol abuse, teen pregnancy, and AIDS. It's no surprise that the very nature of childhood is also changing.

Social critics have argued that childhood has all but disappeared. Children today are exposed to events, devices, and ideas that would have been inconceivable to their baby boom parents. The cultural "secrets" of adulthood—death, illness, violence, and sexuality—are revealed to them in their homes, in their schools, in their neighborhoods, and on television.

We read about sixth graders who have to pass metal detectors in order to enter their schools; 7-year-olds being tried for such crimes as murder, rape, and drug smuggling; and 12-year-olds becoming pregnant. One in six children between the ages of 10 and 17 has seen someone shot or knows someone who has been shot. The number of violent crimes committed by children in this age group has more than tripled since 1965. A study by the Centers for Disease Control found that 1 in 12 high school students has attempted suicide and that 1 in 4 has seriously considered it. Kids today worry about everything from contracting AIDS to not being able to find a good job (Kantrowitz, 1993; Adler, 1994). Psychologists estimate that children today are about 2 to 3 years ahead of children their age 25 years ago:

> The idea of childhood as a sheltered time, free from adult anxieties, is becoming a nostalgic luxury in a world where young people die of AIDS and TV newscasts are filled with stories of child-pornography rings, kidnappings and the sorrowful faces of abused children. (Darton, 1991, p. 62)

The fundamental nature of work in American society has changed, too. If you were to have taken this course 30 years ago, the only tools your instructor would have needed to teach it were a well-stocked collection of books, a manual typewriter, some pencils, a stack of carbon paper, and a love of the discipline. While good instructors today still need a love of the discipline (I hope), it's becoming increasingly difficult to teach interestingly, effectively, and efficiently without taking advantage of state-of-the-art technology: a high-speed desktop computer, electronic mail, on-line databases, computerized test banks, colorful overhead projections, a video library, and access to photocopy and fax machines.

In the 1950s no one doubted that technology would dramatically improve their work lives. The automated future was going to be efficient, clean, and beautiful. Machines would take the drudgery out of virtually every task. However, no one foresaw the impact of automation. Sophisticated machines and computers have reduced or, in some cases, completely displaced the need for human labor in many areas of manufacturing and business.

As a result, we have become what some sociologists call a **postindustrial society,** one in which knowledge and the control of information are more important than manufacturing and production (Bell, 1976). An economic way of life that once centered around factories and the production of material goods now revolves around information and service industries, including public relations, tourism, advertising, insurance, banking and finance, and computer systems.

Sources of Social Change

Where do all these technological, cultural, and institutional changes come from? Sociologists tell us that social change can come from a variety of sources.

- *Environmental and population pressures:* The increasing degradation of the land, sea, and air due to pollution not only has fostered changes in individual and community behavior, such as recycling and conservation, but has also served as the motivation behind innovations in environmentally safe products and services. Likewise, natural disasters like earthquakes and tornadoes often inspire improvements in home safety products and architectural design.

  Consider also how the shifting size and shape of our population creates change in society. In the previous chapter I discussed how the movement of the baby boom cohort through the life course has and will continue to force all relevant social institutions to change along the way.

- *Cultural innovation:* Sometimes change is spurred by scientific discoveries and technological inventions within a society. The discovery of fire, electricity, and disease processes changed the nature of human lives and cultures for all time. The invention of the internal combustion engine, television, the microchip, and effective birth control have been instrumental in determining the course of history in the 20th century.

  Social institutions can sometimes be slow to adjust to scientific and technological innovation. Artificial insemination, in vitro fertilization, surrogate motherhood, and other medical advances in the area of infertility have increased the number of people who can now have children. Yet these technological developments were changing the face of parenthood well before society began to recognize and address the ethical, moral, and legal issues raised by them.

  Similar problems are created by the growth of computer technology. Computers have become an indispensable tool in postindustrial society and have had a lasting effect on the culture (Hollinger & Lanza-Kaduce, 1988). They now keep track of vast quantities of crucial information in practically every area of society, including banks, schools, hospitals, credit companies, the military, and the government. Certainly our day-to-day lives have become more efficient as a result. But it wasn't long before clever computer operators began to figure out how they could use their own personal computers for nefarious purposes, breaking into larger systems to alter important and highly confidential information like bank accounts and credit ratings. When these acts, known as computer hacking, were first recognized as a potentially dangerous problem, there were no laws against them. The legal system had not yet adjusted to this new activity. It took several years for a new body of criminal law to evolve that specifically focused on computer crimes (Hollinger & Lanza-Kaduce, 1988).

■ *Diffusion of technological or cultural practices.* Another source of social change is diffusion: the process by which beliefs, technology, customs, and other cultural items are spread from one group or society to another. Most of the taken-for-granted aspects of our lives originally came from somewhere else. For instance, pajamas, clocks, toilets, glass, coins, newspapers, soap, even our alphabet and language were once imported from other cultures (Linton, 1937). Japanese innovations in microelectronics have dramatically altered the patterns of communication, transportation, and personal entertainment in American society. At the same time, American culture, as expressed in fashion, art, music, and food, is being incorporated into the lives of many young Japanese.

The diffusion process is not always so friendly. When one society's territory is taken over by another society, people may be required to adapt to new customs and beliefs. When the Spanish conquered the New World, Native American people were forced to abandon their cultural ways of life and become more "civilized." Hundreds of thousands of Indians died in the process, not only from ensuing warfare but also from new diseases inadvertently brought over by their conquerers.

The Speed of Social Change

Whatever the source, it is clear that a universal feature of all societies is change. But change is not always immediately apparent to individuals within a society. In the distant past change tended to be slow, almost imperceptible, during the course of one's lifetime. Family and community traditions typically spanned many generations:

> From the time of the great pyramids in Egypt, built 4,700 years ago, to the time of Cleopatra, a bit over 2,000 years ago, the pace of change was so slow that few people in Egypt were aware of it. During that time there were significant advances in metallurgy, agriculture, ship building, astronomy, mathematics, statecraft, historiography and much more. But most Egyptian peasants in the Nile valley and delta were largely ignorant of these changes; for them life continued much as it was hundreds, even thousands of years before. (Chirot, 1994, p. 14)

Throughout the centuries, change has become more accelerated. You can see evidence of this in how we characterize separate periods of history. We frame distant eras—periods with their own distinct cultures and social structures—in chunks of time hundreds of years long: the Middle Ages, the Dark Ages, the 19th century, and so forth. More recent eras, however, are packaged in terms of decades (the Roaring Twenties, the turbulent sixties). In fact, today it may take

as little as half a decade for the culture to adopt a new set of characteɪ.
a new identity: the early 1980s versus the late 1980s. A recent newspaper ⸌
described an "'80s revival" complete with 1980s theme parties and radio shoⱳ
As the columnist put it, "We've sped up to the point where we're looking back
to three years ago. Everything is happening faster in popular culture" (quoted
in Silver, 1992, p. B4).

Because we live in a world that is in a constant state of flux, it's tempting to
see concern with rapid social change as an exclusively contemporary issue. Keep
in mind, however, that sociologists and other scholars have always expressed
deep concern over the effects these changes have on people. Victorian social
observers, for example, linked accelerated social change with England's high
incidence of insanity:

> I doubt if ever the history of the world, or the experience of past ages, could
> show a larger amount of insanity than that of the present day. It seems, in-
> deed, as if the world was moving at an advanced rate of speed proportion-
> ate to its approaching end; as though, in this rapid pace of time, increasing
> with each revolving century, a higher pressure is engendered on the minds
> of men and with this, there appears a tendency among all classes constantly
> to demand higher standards of intellectual attainment, a faster speed of in-
> tellectual travelling, greater fancies, greater forces, larger means than are
> commensurate with health. (quoted in Showalter, 1985, p. 25)

The 19th-century sociologist Émile Durkheim argued that rapid social change
created a normative vacuum—what he called **anomie**—in which the old cultural
rules that governed people's lives no longer applied. When things change
quickly, through sudden economic shifts, wars, natural disasters, population
explosions, or rapid transitions from a traditional to a modern society, people
become disoriented and experience anomie as they search for new guidelines and
rules.

Widespread anomie affects the larger society as well. When norms are
disrupted by rapid social change, our naturally greedy impulses are unleashed.
Without moral norms to constrain our unlimited aspirations and with too few
resources to satisfy our unlimited desires, we are in a sense doomed to a
frustrating life of striving for unattainable goals (Durkheim, 1897/1951). The
result, Durkheim felt, is higher rates of suicide and criminal activity as well as
weakened ties to family, neighborhood, and friends.

What Durkheim considered rapid social change, though, would appear
sluggish by contemporary standards. The velocity of change today has affected
the way sociologists go about their work. When American society was understood to be relatively stable, sociological study was fairly straightforward. Most
social researchers in the 1950s believed that one could start a 5- or 10-year study
of some social institution, like the family or work, and assume that that
institution would still be much the same when the study ended (A. Wolfe, 1991).

Today, such assumptions about the staying power of society are dubious at best. There is no such thing as a permanent social institution.

Collective Action and Change

One of the dangers of talking about the structural sources of social change or its cultural, environmental, and institutional consequences is that it is easy to see change as a purely macro-structural phenomenon that *happens* to us rather than something we *create*. But social change is not some huge, invisible hand that descends from the heavens to arbitrarily disrupt our routine way of life. It is, in the end, a phenomenon driven by human action. In chapter 10 I discussed the fact that some segments of the population have greater access to important social and financial resources and therefore have greater power than other segments of the population. This might imply that only powerful people have the where-withal to change society. We also saw that people without access to such resources are rarely completely powerless. By acting collectively, individual people can sometimes create sweeping, historic changes in our culture and in the structure of our major social institutions.

Collective action is group behavior that is not derived from, and may even be opposed to, the institutional norms of society (J. Lofland, 1981). The term encompasses spontaneous as well as organized group behavior.

Collective actions vary in terms of their goals, shape, and duration (Michener, DeLamater, & Schwartz, 1986). The goal of collective action may be *expressive* (to publicly display emotions such as joy or hostility) or *instrumental* (to achieve some concrete goal like the redistribution of power in society). Collective actions also range from unorganized, such as street riots, to highly organized, such as social movements with formal leadership, bureaucratic organization, and a planned program of action. Finally, collective actions vary in terms of duration. Some activities, such as victory celebrations, last a few hours; others, like riots, last for days; still others, like the civil rights movement, may last for years.

Whether expressive or instrumental, organized or diffuse, short or long, all types of collective action require a redefinition of a situation from routine to problematic. This shared redefinition of right and wrong prompts a relatively large number of people to begin to feel that events in a community or in society as a whole are not proceeding as they should. The norms that emerge rationalize activity that would not be acceptable under ordinary conditions. One of the key features of collective action is that citizens acting in groups do things they would not usually do. They may panic, riot, loot from stores, march, demonstrate, engage in civil disobedience, or launch terrorist campaigns because they find immediate social support for the view that what they are doing is the right thing given present circumstances (Turner & Killian, 1987).

There is always the possibility, of course, that incorrect redefinitions will predominate. Take, for instance, the mass hysteria that resulted from the discovery of the AIDS virus in the mid-1980s. Panic and anxiety over the deadly disease spread quickly. Misinformation about how it is transmitted was disseminated nationwide and took on the appearance of fact. People began to believe that it could be passed on merely by being near or touching someone with the disease. Homosexuals, the subset of the population most closely identified with the disease, were fired or denied housing and, at worse, became the objects of violent attacks. Children diagnosed as having the AIDS virus were forced out of school by their classmates' parents and school officials. Some doctors, dentists, and hospital workers refused to treat not only AIDS patients but all homosexuals; undertakers refused to embalm AIDS patients; police officers wore rubber gloves and masks when arresting anyone they thought was homosexual (Conrad, 1992; A. G. Johnson, 1992). A legitimate and tragic medical emergency had been made even worse by widespread hysterical fears created by the spread of false definitions.

Social Movements

Collective action directed toward an issue of concern to large numbers of people can be continuous and organized and extend beyond the immediate confines of groups or mobs. These actions are called **social movements** (Zurcher & Snow, 1981). Underlying all social movements is change: the desire to enact it, stop it, or reverse it. Social movements tend to involve a variety of activities, from signing petitions, participating in demonstrations, donating money, protesting in the streets, and campaigning during elections to more violent means like riots and government coups d'etat.

Types of Social Movements

On the basis of their size and the magnitude of their goals, social movements can be categorized as either reform or revolutionary movements. A **reform movement** attempts to change limited aspects of a society but does not seek to alter or replace major social institutions. Take the civil rights movement of the 1960s. It did not call for an overhaul of our economic system (capitalism) or our political system (two-party democracy). Instead, it advocated a more limited change: opening up existing institutions to full and equal participation by members of minority groups (DeFronzo, 1991). Similarly, the anti-Vietnam War movement sought to change government policy rather than change the form of government itself. Other recent examples of reform movements include the women's movement, the nuclear freeze movement, the union movement, and the environmental movement.

Because reform movements seek to alter some aspect of existing social arrangements, there will always be people and groups opposed to such changes. Reform movements typically spawn organized **countermovements** designed to prevent or reverse the changes sought or accomplished by an earlier movement. Countermovements are most likely to emerge when the reform movements against which they are reacting become large and effective in pursuing their goals and therefore come to be seen as threats to personal and social interests (Chafetz & Dworkin, 1987; Mottl, 1980).

The emergence of the conservative and religious New Right in the mid-1970s and 1980s was provoked by a growing perception of enormous social upheaval, breakdown of traditional roles and values, and challenge to existing institutions like education, religion, and the family brought about by the civil rights, anti-war, student, and women's movements of the 1960s and 1970s (Klatch, 1991). The women's movement in particular is perceived by the New Right as having launched an ideological attack on the family. Indeed, the leaders of the New Right were the first to articulate that women's equality was responsible for women's unhappiness and the weakening of the American family (Faludi, 1991). The rising divorce rate and the increased number of working mothers are seen as eroding the moral bases of family life (Klatch, 1991). One New Right minister said, "We're not here to get into politics. We're here to turn the clock back to 1954 in this country" (quoted in Faludi, 1991, p. 230).

Through organizations such as the Moral Majority, the Heritage Foundation, and the Eagle Forum, and many smaller religious groups around the United States, the New Right has sought to restore the faith, morality, and decency they feel America has lost in recent years. Over the past two decades the New Right has been somewhat successful in shifting the political and social mood of the country. It gained legitimacy in 1980 when Ronald Reagan and several senate candidates it supported won election. Its most notable triumphs, however, have been at the state and local levels, where it has succeeded in influencing public school curricula as well as antiabortion and anti-gay rights legislation.

Both reform movements and countermovements operate *within* the existing social system. **Revolutionary movements** are attempts to overthrow the entire system itself, whether it be the government or the existing class structure, in an effort to replace it with another (Skocpol, 1979). Although revolutionary change in basic social institutions can be brought about through nonviolent means (peaceful labor strikes, democratic elections, civil disobedience, etc.), most successful revolutions have involved some level of violence on the part of both movement participants and groups opposing revolution (DeFronzo, 1991).

The Development of a Social Movement

Whether reform or revolutionary, social movements occur when unsatisfied people see their condition as resulting from society's inability to meet their needs. Many movements develop when certain segments of the population conclude that society's resources—access to political power, higher education, legal justice, medical care, a clean and healthy environment, and so on—are distributed unequally and unfairly (R. Brown, 1986). People come to believe that they have a moral right to the satisfaction of their unmet expectations and that this cannot or will not occur without some effort on their part. This perception is often based on the experience of past failures of working within the system.

As individuals and groups who share this sense of frustration and unfairness interact with one another, the existing system begins to lose its perceived legitimacy (Piven & Cloward, 1977). In large numbers, individuals who ordinarily might have considered themselves helpless come to believe they have the capacity to change things and significantly alter their lives and the lives of others.

The Role of Ideology

A social movement must also have an **ideology,** a coherent system of beliefs, values, and ideas that justifies its existence (Turner & Killian, 1987; Zurcher & Snow, 1981). Consider the antiabortion movement. Its ideology rests on several assumptions about the nature of childhood and motherhood (Luker, 1984). For instance, each conception is an act of God, therefore abortion violates God's will; life begins at conception; the fetus is an individual who has a constitutional right to life; and every human life should be valued (Michener, DeLamater, & Schwartz, 1986). Believing that every child is wanted, the antiabortion movement subscribes to the belief that everyone can "make room for one more," reinforcing the view that abortion is both evil and self-indulgent (Luker, 1984). Anyone who favors continued legal abortion is automatically defined as immoral.

An ideology fulfills several functions. It defines the group's interests and helps to identify people as either supporters or enemies, creating an identifiable group of "good guys" and "villains." An ideology also provides participants with a collective sense of what the goals of the movement are or should be. Misdirected or ill-conceived ideologies can sometimes break a social movement: It has been argued that organized opposition to the 1991 Persian Gulf War was ineffective primarily on ideological grounds. Instead of focusing on support for continuing nonviolent sanctions against Iraq, antiwar activists were committed to an ideological script that was used successfully in the movement against the war in Vietnam 20 years earlier: portray the United States as the hostile aggressor (Goertzel, 1993). Their effectiveness in garnering widespread public support was limited.

Given the reports of Iraqi atrocities and the unsavory actions of Saddam Hussein, it was difficult to convince the public that the American military response was wrong. Indeed, 90% of Americans supported President Bush's handling of the crisis. There was no "innocent victim" the United States was attempting to destroy, as had been the case in Vietnam. This antiwar movement was caught between two conflicting ideological positions: opposing Iraqi aggression on the one hand, but wanting to paint the United States as the bad guy on the other hand. By acting against only American military action, those involved in the movement became, for all intents and purposes, allies of Hussein. In a speech broadcasted on CNN on January 28, 1991, Hussein stated:

> All the people of Iraq are grateful to all the noble souls amongst the United States people who are coming out into the street demonstrating against this war. We follow with keenness this sublime level of humanity, which comes out to counter the policies of aggression. (quoted in Goertzel, 1993, p. 143)

The leadership of the U.S. Army was, in fact, quite reluctant to go to war, and there was considerable public reluctance as well. In addition, the congressional vote authorizing the use of force passed only by a narrow margin. If the movement had focused its support on legislators who favored stronger economic sanctions against Iraq rather than military intervention, it might have been more effective. But this approach would have required the movement to abandon its "America as the hostile aggressor" stance. The movement failed to make a clear ideological distinction between opposition to war and selective opposition to only those wars conducted by the United States (Goertzel, 1993).

I should point out that while the content of the ideology might be what attracts people to a movement, it must be spread through social networks of friends, family, co-workers, and so on (Zurcher & Snow, 1981). For some people, the ideology of the movement is secondary to other social considerations. Potential participants in a social movement usually are unlikely to join without being informed about it and introduced to it by someone they know. While the ideological leaders of a social movement might want to believe that participants are there because of "the cause," chances are they have a friend or acquaintance who convinced them to be there (Stark & Bainbridge, 1980; Gerlach & Hine, 1970).

Ironically, social movements sometimes require involvement on the part of individuals from *outside* the group of people whose interests the movement represents. Those individuals who are the most deprived and most in need of massive changes in social arrangements are not necessarily those who are most likely to subscribe to the ideology that sustains the movement. People who are already disadvantaged often lack the money, time, skills, and connections that successful movements require. The ideological supporters of the environmental movement, for example, are more likely to be affluent suburbanites (whose environments are relatively unpolluted) than residents of urban areas (who live closest to polluting factories and dirty highways). Many of the people who would benefit the most from an improved environment are actually highly skeptical of "environmentalists" who they feel are taking away their jobs rather than protecting their interests.

Sometimes the activities required to promote or sustain a particular movement run counter to the ideological goals of the movement itself. The leaders of successful political revolutions, for example, soon realize that in order to run the country they now control they must create highly structured bureaucracies not unlike the ones they have overthrown.

Individuals in reform movements may also be forced to engage in behaviors that conflict with the ideological tenets of the movement. The New Right movement was organized, in part, as a backlash against the women's movement. Its profamily, promotherhood, and anti-equal rights for women positions are clearly designed to turn back the feminist agenda. However, early in the movement it became clear that in order to be successful it would have to enlist high-profile women to campaign against feminist policies. New Right women had to abandon their families, travel the country to make speeches, and display independent strength—characteristics that were anything but the ideal models of passive womanhood they were publicly promoting. Phyllis Schlafly, a woman who has vehemently argued that a woman's natural place is to be a wife and mother in a house supported by her husband, is a Harvard-educated lawyer, author of nine books, and a two-time congressional candidate (Faludi, 1991).

The Role of Rising Expectations

You might think that major social movements, particularly revolutionary ones, would be most likely to occur when people's lives are at their lowest and most desperate point. Certainly huge numbers of disadvantaged people, who think there is little chance that things will improve and who perceive the government as unwilling or unable to meet their needs, are necessary for any massive movements for change (Tilly, 1978).

But some sociologists argue that such movements are actually more likely to arise when things are getting *better* (C. Brinton, 1965; Davies, 1962). Constant deprivation does not necessarily make people want to revolt. Instead, they are more likely to be preoccupied with daily survival than with demonstrations and street protests. Improvements in living conditions, however, show those who are deprived that their society is capable of being different, raising their expectations and sparking a desire for large-scale change. When these expectations aren't met, these people become angry. The gap between what they expect and what they have now seems intolerable. Although they may actually be better off than they had been in the past, their situation *relative to their expectations* now appears much worse (Davies, 1962). Such frustration makes participation in protest or revolutionary activity more likely.

Consider the short-lived pro-democracy movement in China in 1989. During the early 1980s the Chinese government began to introduce economic reforms that would open up markets and create faster growth and political reforms to provide citizens with more freedom. These reforms inspired a popular demand for even greater freedom and democracy, a movement that was violently squashed in Tiananmen Square.

Resource Mobilization and Movement Organization

At any point in time there are numerous potential problems in a society that need fixing. And yet at that same point in time there are relatively few major social movements. If widespread dissatisfaction and frustration were all that is needed to sustain a social movement, "the masses would always be in revolt" (Trotsky, 1959). What allows a social movement to get started, gain support, and achieve its goals?

According to *resource mobilization theory*, effective organization keeps a movement going and enables it to be successful. How far a movement goes in attaining its goals depends on its ability to expand its ranks, acquire large-scale public support, and transform those who join into committed participants (Zurcher & Snow, 1981). Thus, no social movement can exist unless there is an organized system for acquiring the necessary resources for operation like money, labor, recruitment of participants, legal aid, access to the media, and so on (McCarthy & Zald, 1977).

Douglas Murray
The Abolition of the Short-Handled Hoe

Some social movements become successful only when they secure organizational support. Sociologist Douglas Murray examined the process by which a simple farm tool, the short-handled hoe, came to symbolize the exploitation of California farm workers and served as a focal point for a successful social movement. During the early 20th century, the short-handled hoe became the principal tool used by farm laborers for thinning and weeding crops. Growers claimed that it was more accurate and efficient than the long-handled hoe. However, farm laborers saw another motive: the increased supervision and control of the workers. With the long-handled hoe, supervisors sometimes couldn't tell when a worker was working or just leaning on the hoe. With the short-handled hoe it became easier to see when they were working because they had to stand up to rest.

Use of the short-handled hoe came to be called "squat labor" or "stoop labor" because of the bent-over position one had to be in to use the tool correctly. Numerous physicians and medical experts pointed out that use of this tool over long periods of time caused a degeneration of the spine, leading to permanent disabilities. According to one farm worker:

> When I used the short-handled hoe my head would ache and my eyes hurt because of the pressure of bending down so long. My back would hurt whenever I stood up or bent over. I moved down the rows as fast as I could so I could get to the end and rest my back for a moment. (quoted in Murray, 1982, p. 29)

As early as the 1920s farm workers engaged in isolated protests and work stoppages over the use of the short-handled hoe. During the Depression, though, poor people from Oklahoma, Arkansas, and elsewhere flocked to

California willing to do any work, including using the short-handled hoe, for lower wages. Hence the protests of the 1920s were rendered ineffective.

It wasn't until the early 1970s, when the civil rights movement was in full swing and the United Farm Workers union had been organized, that the issue of the short-handled hoe was resolved:

> Late one afternoon in the spring of 1973, farm workers leaving the fields of the fertile Salinas Valley in Central California gathered beside the buses which would take them to the nearby labor camps for the night. They moved nervously about a large pile of short-handled hoes which they had been using that day to thin and weed long rows of lettuce. One farm worker quickly doused the hoes with gasoline; another tossed a match, setting them ablaze. Cries of protest swept through the crowd as the farm workers served their bosses with a defiant notice: no longer would they work with "el cortito," the short-handled hoe. (Murray, 1982, p. 26)

The protesters were finally able to mobilize state and legal organizations to bring the growers to court. Because of heightened access to the media, farm worker strikes drew national attention. With the help of national labor unions, government agencies such as the Office of Economic Opportunity, and legal assistance agencies for the disadvantaged, the short-handled hoe was eventually declared to be in violation of federal worker health and safety protections.

Since the short-handled hoe was banned, farm worker conditions have improved. Growers report fewer worker compensation claims due to back injuries. The success of the case, along with the powerful organizational structure representing farm workers, encouraged labor protests over other conditions such as exposure to dangerous pesticides. In sum, the protest over this little tool, made more effective by the use of government and legal organizations, spawned the farm workers movement that exists to this day.

Most large, long-term social movements involve a national, even international coalition of groups. Such widespread organization makes the movement more powerful by making the mobilization of resources, in the form of people and fund-raising, more efficient.

The ongoing environmental movement relies on high-level organization. Many individuals today are emotionally and fervently committed to environmental quality. Environmental degradation is perceived by many young people to be the most urgent national and global issue. Yet most of the movement's successes are accomplished not by highly visible parades, protests, and concerts, but by the quieter activities of several large bureaucratic organizations, including the Sierra Club, the Audubon Society, the National Wildlife Federation, the National Parks and Conservation Association, and Greenpeace.

In addition, highly organized social movements must have established networks of communication (McCarthy & Zald, 1977). The ability to mobilize people for, say, a march on the nation's capital, in a very short time depends on extensive communications networks: phone systems, direct mailing systems, or computers. Movements need both an effective system of mass communication for recruiting and fundraising and a way for information to get to all participants when ongoing face-to-face interaction is impossible.

In sum, the movements that succeed in enacting substantial social change are not necessarily those with the most compelling ideological positions or the highest emotional appeal. Instead, they are the ones with the necessary high-level organization and communication networks to mobilize supporters, and the necessary media access to neutralize the opposition and transform the public into sympathizers. Those movements that historically have been the most long-lasting—the women's movement, the civil rights movement, and the environmental movement—are those that are supported by large organizations such as the National Organization for Women, the National Association for the Advancement of Colored People (NAACP), and the Sierra Club. These organizations also have full-time lobbyists or political action committees that connect them to the national political system. Few movements can succeed without such connections because achieving social change often requires changing laws or convincing courts to interpret laws in particular ways.

The Bureaucratization of Social Movements

It makes sense that the most successful social movements are the ones that are best organized. However, high-level organization is not necessarily a guarantee for success. The formal structuring of a social movement can sometimes prove unwieldy when constituent organizations differ in their philosophies and tactics. There may be tremendous in-fighting and bickering among groups ostensibly working toward the same goal. For instance, the civil rights movement during the 1950s and 1960s included many diverse, seemingly incompatible organizations. The NAACP was large, racially integrated, legalistic, and bureaucratic in form. The Student Non-Violent Coordinating Committee was younger, more militant in its tactics, and after a while excluded whites from participation. The Southern Christian Leadership Conference was highly structured, utilized a religious ideology, and was dominated by male clergy. Finally, the Black Muslims and the Black Panthers advocated extreme, sometimes violent methods to achieve civil rights.

In sum, no matter what their shape, size, or motive, social movements require sustained activity over a long period of time (Turner & Killian, 1987). Unlike riots, which are of limited duration, social movements may become *permanent* fixtures in the political and social environment of society. It is ironic that a social phenomenon whose goal is a large-scale alteration of some aspect of society can become part of the establishment. People who devote their lives to the movement come to depend on it for their own livelihood. Hence social movements organized for the purposes of enacting social change actually provide structure and order for the lives of their members, acting as sources of opportunities, careers, and rewards (Hewitt, 1988).

Reconstructing Society: The Sociological Imagination Revisited

In the summer of 1981 I had the good fortune to visit Florence, Italy. While there I made it a point to go to the Galleria dell' Accademia, the museum where one of my favorite works of art, Michelangelo's statue of David, resides. The statue stands in a bright rotunda at the end of a long hallway. To my eye it is truly a masterpiece in sculpture, nearly flawless in its detail.

I stood there admiring this amazing work of art for close to 2 hours. Afterward, as I contentedly made my way back down the hallway, I noticed a series of sculptures that had escaped my attention when I first entered the museum. I found out that they, too, were created by Michelangelo. What made them particularly interesting was that they were all unfinished. Some were obviously near completion, but others looked to me like shapeless blocks of granite.

There was something astounding in these pieces. As I looked closer it wasn't difficult to see the actual chisel marks that the great sculptor had made. I could imagine the plan Michelangelo had in his head as he worked. I could envision him toiling to bring form to the heavy stone. These imperfect slabs of rock showed evidence of *human creation* in a way that the perfect finished statue of David never could. At that moment I realized that Michelangelo was a real person who fashioned beauty from formlessness. I began to admire the genius of the creator and not just the creation. I went back to look at David again with a newfound appreciation.

Society isn't nearly as perfect as Michelangelo's artwork, yet it is easy to see social structure as a product that exists on its own and not as something that people collectively created. We sometimes forget that many of the realities of our lives that we take for granted were the result, at some point in history, of the handiwork of individuals. One generation's radical changes become another's common features of everyday life. The fact that you can't be forced to work 70 or 80 hours a week, can't be exposed to dangerous working conditions without your knowledge, and are entitled to a certain number of paid holidays a year are a result of the actions of real people in early labor union movements.

Because we take many of our freedoms, rights, and desires for granted, we may not only overlook the struggles of those who came before us, but also downplay the extent to which inequities and injustices existed in the past. For instance, many young women today have never even considered that they might have to struggle against closed educational opportunities, the secondary importance of their careers, and the expectation that they would be the sole caregivers for their children. Like most beneficiaries of past movements, they simply take their freedoms and opportunities for granted, sometimes even expressing contempt for the movement responsible for the rights they so casually enjoy (Stacey, 1991). The irony of social movements, then, is that the more profound and far-reaching their accomplishments, the more likely it is that the efforts of the individuals who produced them will eventually be forgotten. Like Michelangelo's sculpture, these achievements ultimately become objectified and begin to exist independently of the individuals and groups who created them. While full incorporation of changes into mainstream society is the ultimate goal of any social movement, there is a cultural and historical price to pay as the efforts and sacrifices made by real individuals to re-create our society fade into collective oblivion.

Fundamentally, not only the nature of social movements, but the nature of human society itself—whether stable or rapidly changing—must be understood by examining what people do and think. We must remember that societies remain stable because enough individuals define existing conditions as satisfactory, and that societies change because enough individuals define situations that were once tolerable as problems that must be acknowledged and solved. As one author wrote regarding the antiwar movement during the 1960s and 1970s:

> Ten years and 12 days after the first busloads of demonstrators rolled into Washington to protest U.S. involvement in Indochina, the last planeloads of Americans left Saigon. . . . The standard American histories of the Vietnam War, when they are culled from the memoirs of the generals and politicians . . . are unlikely to record this coincidence. But the decisions about the pursuit of those generals' and politicians' objectives in Indochina were not made only in their carpeted offices. They were also made in the barracks, in the schools, in the streets, by the millions of Americans—Blacks and whites, students, workers, nuns and priests, draftees and draft resisters— who made up the Anti-War Movement. (Cluster, 1979, p. 131)

Some influential acts of individuals may at first blush appear rather insignificant. Early in 1960, four black students at North Carolina Agricultural & Technical State University in Greensboro engaged in a series of discussions in their dormitory rooms about the state of the civil rights movement. They came to the conclusion that things weren't progressing quickly enough in the still segregated South and that it was time for action. They decided to go to the lunch counter at the local Woolworth's department store and order coffee and doughnuts. In the 1960s South it was forbidden by law to serve blacks at public eating facilities that weren't for blacks only.

After purchasing some school supplies in another part of the store, they sat down at the lunch counter and placed their orders. As anticipated, the reply was "I'm sorry, we don't serve you here" (McCain, 1991, p. 115). They remained seated for 45 minutes, citing the fact that they had been served in another part of the store without any difficulty. They returned the next week with more demonstrators. Word of their actions spread quickly. Within 2 months sit-ins had spread to 9 states and 54 cities in the South as well as to areas in the North, where sympathetic pickets of department stores took place. This eventually proved to be one of the most effective tactics of the civil rights movement, a movement that had itself been set into motion 5 years earlier by the refusal of one woman, Rosa Parks, to give up her seat on a Montgomery, Alabama, city bus to a white man.

Some social observers even argue that many of the political movements for change that burst onto the scene in the 1960s—including the women's movement, the antiwar movement, and the student free speech movement—could trace their philosophical and tactical roots to this small act (Cluster, 1979). That's not to say that those movements wouldn't have developed had these four men been served that coffee and those doughnuts. The point is, the actions of these seemingly insignificant individuals had an enormous impact on the massive changes that occurred in our country during that decade.

We re-create society not only through acts of defiance and organized social movements, but also through our daily interactions. The driving theme throughout this book has been that society and its constituent elements is simultaneously a human creation and a phenomenon that exists independently of us, influencing and controlling our private experiences at every turn.

Organizations and institutions exist and thrive because they implicitly or explicitly discourage individuals from challenging the rules and patterns of behavior that characterize them. Imagine what would happen to the system of higher education if you and others like you challenged the authority of the university. You could establish a new order in which students would dictate the content of courses, take control of the classroom, abolish grading or any other evaluative mechanism used for assessing student performance, do away with tuition, and so on. But because you have an education and a career to gain from the institutional structure as it stands, it's not very likely you'd do something to jeopardize it.

Are we then to believe that we are all helpless leaves in the wind, buffeted here and there by the powerful and permanent forces of a structure that dwarfs us? To some extent the answer is yes. I subscribe to the sociological imagination and strongly believe that to fully understand our lives we must acknowledge that processes larger than us determine some of our private experiences. Along the way, though, we sometimes lose sight of our important role as shapers of society:

> We know when to tear down a building that has ceased to serve any useful function and may even be a source of danger. However, we sometimes rattle around in dusty old social institutions that are cracked and crumbling simply because we fail to realize that it is within our power to step beyond the confines of this structure and build others. . . . What may have served as a useful basis for achieving some particular end becomes an ideology and an

end in itself. When this occurs our social constructions may cease to serve any useful function but we may persist in maintaining them simply because they have become permanent, hardened features of our social landscape. (Kollock & O'Brien, 1993, p. 503)

Although society presents itself as largely unchangeable, our culture is based at least in part on the value of the American "can do" attitude. I recall, as a child, sitting in a darkened living room with my parents on a warm July evening in 1969. The only light in the room came from the gray-blue glow of the television. I watched with great amazement the fuzzy, almost imperceptible image of astronaut Neil Armstrong taking the first tentative steps on the moon and stating: "That's one small step for man, one giant leap for mankind." I didn't realize then how the power of that statement stretched beyond the space program. People *can* influence the world in which they live.

In this chapter you've seen that we *do* have some influence over shaping and changing our dusty old institutions. Individuals, bound together by only the thin strand of an idea that things ought not to be the way they are, can change the course of social history. We are active participants in the construction of our realities. Yes, we are affected by social forces. Yes, our lives are influenced, maybe even determined, by social institutions. But we have the ability and the obligation to be aware of that influence, to analyze it, and to act on it. And, as the efforts of Rosa Parks, the four young men in Greensboro, and the California farm laborers proved, one small act can change society.

Conclusion and Farewell

Sociology is not one of those disciplines that draws from a long-standing body of scientific facts and laws. We do have some good explanations of why certain important social phenomena happen, and we can make reasonable predictions about future developments, but sociology is not inherently a discipline of answers. It's a discipline of questions, one that provides a unique and useful method for solving the puzzles of your life and your society.

This discipline scrutinizes, analyzes, and dissects institutional order and its effects on our thinking. It exposes the vulnerable underbelly of both objective and official reality and, by doing so, prods us into taking a closer look at ourselves and our private worlds, not an easy thing to do. Sociology makes everyday life an unsafe place. I don't mean that it makes people violent or dangerous, I mean that it makes perceptions of social stability unstable or at least fair game for analysis. We don't want to admit that our reality may be a figment of our collective minds and just one of many possible realities. We live under a belief system that tells us our unchallenged assumptions are simply the way things are.

Sociology is a "liberating" perspective (Liazos, 1985). It forces us to look at the social processes that influence our thoughts, perceptions, and actions, and helps us see how social change occurs and the impact we can have on others. In doing so, sociology also points out the very limits of liberation. We are aware of the chains that restrict our "movements," but we also have the tools to break those chains. The sociological imagination goes beyond a description of powerful social forces to a questioning of them and ultimately a push toward social action. Sociology gives us a glimpse of the world both as it is and as it could be. To be a sociologically astute observer of the world as it is, you must be able to strip away fallacies and illusions and see the interconnected system underneath. Only then can you take full advantage of your role as a cocreator of society.

I leave you with one final thought: If you now look at your life and the lives of those around you differently, if you now question things heretofore unquestionable, if you now see where you fit in the bigger societal picture, if you now see orderly patterns in areas you previously thought were chaotic, or chaos in areas you previously thought were orderly, then you are well on your way to understanding the meaning—and the promise—of sociology.

CHAPTER HIGHLIGHTS

- Whether at the personal, cultural, or institutional level, change is the preeminent feature of modern societies.

- Social change has a variety of sources: adaptation to environmental pressures, the importation of cultural practices from other countries, internal population changes, and technological discoveries and innovations.

- Social change is not some massive, impersonal force that arbitrarily disrupts our routine way of life; it is a human creation.

- Social movements are long-term collective actions that address an issue of concern to large numbers of people.

- The nature of society, from its large institutions to its tiny, unspoken rules of everyday life, can be understood only by examining what people do and think. Societies remain stable because enough people define existing conditions as satisfactory, and they change because enough people define once accepted conditions as problems that must be solved.

YOUR TURN

It's one thing to read about people taking an active role in reconstructing a part of their personal lives or of their society, but it's quite another to see such people in action. Most communities contain people who were at one time active in a major movement for social change: the labor movement, the antiwar movement, the women's movement, the civil rights movement, and so forth. Find a few people who were involved in one such movement. Ask them to describe their experiences. What was their motive for joining the movement? What sorts of activities did they participate in? What were the goals they wanted to accomplish? Looking back, do they feel the movement accomplished those goals? If not, why not? What else needs to be done? What did they feel they, as individuals, accomplished?

For purposes of historical comparison, see if you can identify a movement that is currently under way in your community. It might be a drive to promote environmental or AIDS awareness, an antiabortion movement, or a group organized to address an issue of local interest such as a neighborhood improvement drive or an attempt to stop the construction of a factory or business.

Try to attend a gathering in which the movement is involved. It might be an organizational meeting, a town council meeting, a protest march, or a demonstration. What happened at the gathering? What seemed to be the overall atmosphere? Was it festive? solemn? angry? businesslike? Was any opposition present?

Interview some of the participants. Ask them the same questions you asked the participants who were in past movements. Do people get involved in social movements for the same reasons they did in the past?

Relate your observations and the information from the interviews to the discussion of social movements in this chapter. What are the most effective tactics and strategies? How are resources mobilized? Why do some movements succeed and others fail?

REFERENCES

Aaron, H. J., & Lougy, C. M. 1986. *The comparable worth controversy*. Washington, DC: Brookings Institution.

Acitelli, L. 1988. "When spouses talk to each other about their relationship." *Journal of Social and Personal Relationships, 5,* 185-199.

Acker, J. 1978. "Issues in the sociological study of women's work." In A. H. Stromberg & S. Harkees (Eds.), *Women working.* Palo Alto, CA: Mayfield.

———. 1988. "Class, gender and the relations of distribution." *Signs, 13,* 473-497.

———. 1992. "From sex roles to gendered institutions." *Contemporary Sociology, 21,* 565-569.

Adamec, C., & Pierce, W. L. 1991. *The encyclopedia of adoption.* New York: Facts on File.

Aday, D. P. 1990. *Social control at the margins.* Belmont, CA: Wadsworth.

Adler, J. 1994. "Kids growing up scared." *Newsweek,* January 10.

Ahrons, C. R., & Rodgers, R. H. 1987. *Divorced families: A multidisciplinary developmental view.* New York: Norton.

Ainlay, S. C., Becker, G., & Coleman, L. M. 1986. *The dilemma of difference.* New York: Plenum.

Aldous, J., & Dumon, W. 1990. "Family policy in the 1980's: Controversy and consensus." *Journal of Marriage and the Family, 52,* 1136-1151.

Allon, N. 1982. "The stigma of overweight in everyday life." In B. B. Wolman (Ed.), *Psychological aspects of obesity.* New York: Van Nostrand Reinhold.

Allport, G. 1954. *The nature of prejudice.* Reading, MA: Addison-Wesley.

Altman I., & Taylor, D. A. 1973. *Social penetration: The development of interpersonal relationships.* New York: Holt, Rinehart & Winston.

American Psychiatric Association. 1987. *Diagnostic and statistical manual of mental disorders* (3rd ed.). Washington, DC: Author.

"America's poor showing." 1993. *Newsweek,* October 18.

Amir, M. 1971. *Patterns of forcible rape.* Chicago: University of Chicago Press.

Anderson, M. L., & Collins, P. H. 1992. *Race, class and gender: An anthology.* Belmont, CA: Wadsworth.

Andrews, E. L. 1992. "Broadcasters, to satisfy law, define cartoons as education." *New York Times,* September 30.

Angier, N. 1993. "Drug works, but questions remain." *New York Times,* December 13.

Archer, D. 1985. "Social deviance." In G. Lindzey & E. Aronson (Eds.), *Handbook of social psychology* (3rd ed., Vol. 2). New York: Random House.

Arendell, T. 1984. "Divorce: A woman's issue." *Feminist Issues, 4,* 41-61.

Arendt, H. 1963. *Eichmann in Jerusalem: A report on the banality of evil.* New York: Viking Press.

Aries, P. 1962. *Centuries of childhood: A social history of family life.* New York: Vintage Books.

Armstrong, P. J., Goodman, J. F. B., & Hyman, J. D. 1981. *Ideology and shop-floor industrial relations.* London: Croom Helm.

Arno, P. S., & Feiden, K. L. 1992. *Against the odds: The story of AIDS drug development, politics and profits.* New York: HarperCollins.

Asch, S. 1958. "Effects of group pressure on the modification and distortion." In E. E. Maccoby, T. M. Newcomb, & E. L. Hartley (Eds.), *Readings in Social Psychology.* New York: Holt, Rinehart, & Winston.

Auletta, K. 1982. *The underclass.* New York: Random House.

Babbie, E. 1986. *Observing ourselves: Essays in social research.* Belmont, CA: Wadsworth.

———. 1988. *The sociological spirit.* Belmont, CA: Wadsworth.

————. 1992. *The practice of social research.* Belmont, CA: Wadsworth.

Baca-Zinn, M., & Eitzen, D.S. 1993. *Diversity in families.* New York: HarperCollins.

Bagdikian, B. H. 1991. "Missing from the news." In J. H. Skolnick & E. Currie (Eds.), *Crisis in American institutions.* New York: HarperCollins.

Bailey, B. L. 1988. *From front porch to back seat: Courtship in 20th century America.* Baltimore: Johns Hopkins University Press.

Bailey, C. A. 1993. "Equality with difference: On androcentrism and menstruation." *Teaching Sociology, 21,* 121-129.

Ballard, C. 1987. "A humanist sociology approach to teaching social research." *Teaching Sociology, 15,* 7-14.

Bandura, A., & Walters, R. H. 1963. *Social learning and personality development.* New York: Holt, Rinehart & Winston.

Banfield, E. 1970. *The unheavenly city.* New York: Little, Brown.

Barber, B. 1992. "Jihad vs. McWorld." *Atlantic Monthly,* March, pp. 53-65.

Barcus, F. E. 1978. *Commercial children's television on weekends and weekday afternoons.* Newtonville, MA: Action for Children's Television.

Barnett, N. J., & Feild, H. S. 1977. "Sex differences in university students' attitudes toward rape." *Journal of College Student Personnel,* 93-96.

Baron, A. 1987. "Feminist legal strategies: The powers of difference." In B. Hess & M. M. Ferree (Eds.), *Analyzing gender: A handbook of social science research.* Newbury Park, CA: Sage.

Barrett, N. 1987. "Women and the economy." In S. E. Rix (Ed.), *The American woman, 1987-88.* New York: Norton.

Barringer, F. 1992. "Whether it's hunger or 'misnourishment,' it's a national problem." *New York Times,* December 27.

————. 1993a. "Anger in the post office: Killings raise questions." *New York Times,* May 8.

————. 1993b. "Immigration in the '80's made English a foreign language for millions." *New York Times,* April 28.

Basch, C. E., & Kersch, T. B. 1986. "Adolescent perceptions of stressful life events." *Health Education,* June/July, 4-7.

Beaman, A. L., Klentz, B., Diener, E., & Svanum, S. 1979. "Objective self awareness and transgression in children: A field study." *Journal of Personality and Social Psychology, 37,* 1835-1846.

Beck, M. 1990. "Be nice to your kids." *Newsweek,* March 12.

Becker, H. 1952. "Social class variations in the teacher-pupil relationship." *Journal of Educational Sociology, 25,* 451-466.

————. 1963. *The outsiders.* New York: Free Press.

Becker, H. S., & Geer, B. 1958. "The fate of idealism in medical school." *American Sociological Review, 23,* 50-56.

Bedard, M. 1991. "Captive clientele of the welfare supersystem: Breaking the cage wide open." *Humanity and Society, 15,* 23-48.

Beeghley, L. 1984. "Illusion and reality in the measurement of poverty." *Social Problems, 31,* 322-333.

Belkin, L. 1990. "Airport anti-drug nets snare many people fitting 'profiles.'" *New York Times,* March 20.

Bell, D. 1976. *The coming of post-industrial society.* New York: Harper & Row.

Bell, D. J., & Bell, S. L. 1991. "The victim-offender relationship as a determinant factor in police dispositions of family violence incidents: A replication study." *Policing and Society, 1,* 225-234.

Bellah, R., Madsen, R., Sullivan, W. M., Swidler, A., & Tipton, S. M. 1985. *Habits of the heart.* New York: Harper & Row.

Belsky, J. 1988. "The effects of infant day care reconsidered." *Early Childhood Research Quarterly, 3,* 235-272.

Bennett, N. G., Bloom, D. E., & Craig, P. H. 1986. *Black and white marriage patterns: Why so different?* (Discussion Paper No. 500). New Haven, CT: Economic Growth Center, Yale University.

Benokraitis, N. V., & Feagin, J. R. 1993. "Sex discrimination: Subtle and covert." In J. Henslin (Ed.), *Down to earth sociology.* New York: Free Press.

Ben-Yehuda, N. 1990. *The politics and morality of deviance.* Albany: State University of New York Press.

Berg, B. 1992. "The guilt that drives working mothers crazy." In J. Henslin (Ed.), *Marriage and family in a changing society.* New York: Free Press.

Berg J. H., & McQuinn, R. D. 1986. "Attraction and exchange in continuing and noncontinuing dating relationships." *Journal of Personality and Social Psychology*, 50, 942-952.

Berger, P. L. 1963. *Invitation to sociology*. Garden City, NY: Anchor.

Berger, P. L., & Kellner, H. 1964. "Marriage and the construction of reality: An exercise in the microsociology of knowledge." *Diogenes*, 46, 1-23.

Berger, P. L., & Luckmann, T. 1966. *The social construction of reality*. Garden City, NY: Anchor.

Bernard, J. 1972. *The future of marriage*. New York: Bantam.

————. 1981. "The good provider role: Its rise and fall." *American Psychologist*, 36, 1-12.

Berndt, T. J., & Heller, K. A. 1986. "Gender stereotypes and social inferences: A developmental study." *Journal of Personality and Social Psychology*, 50, 889-898.

Bernstein, S. 1990. "Getting it done: Notes on student fritters." In J. W. Heeren & M. Mason (Eds.), *Sociology: Windows on society*. Los Angeles: Roxbury.

Berscheid, E., and Walster, E. 1974. "Physical attractiveness." In L. Berkowitz (Ed.), *Advances in experimental social psychology*. New York: Academic Press.

Bertenthal, B. I., & Fischer, K. W. 1978. "Development of self-recognition in the infant." *Developmental Psychology*, 14, 44-50.

Best, J. 1990. *Threatened children: Rhetoric and concern about child-victims*. Chicago: University of Chicago Press.

Best, R. 1983. *We've all got scars: What boys and girls learn in elementary school*. Bloomington: Indiana University Press.

Birchler, G. R., Weiss, R. L., & Vincent, J. P. 1975. "Multimethod analysis of social reinforcement exchange between maritally distressed and non-distressed spouse and stranger dyads." *Journal of Personality and Social Psychology*, 31, 349-360.

Birenbaum, A., & Sagarin, E. 1976. *Norms and human behavior*. New York: Praeger.

Bishop, K. 1991. "Ads on Holocaust 'hoax' inspire campus debates." *New York Times*, December 23.

Blackwell, J. E. 1990. "Current issues affecting blacks and Hispanics in the educational pipeline." In G. E. Thomas (Ed.), *U.S. race relations in the 1980's and 1990's*. New York: Hemisphere.

Blau, P. M. 1964. *Exchange and power in social life*. New York: Wiley.

Blau, P. M., & Duncan, O.D. 1967. *The American occupational structure*. New York: Wiley.

Blau, P. M., & Meyer, M. W. 1987. "The concept of bureaucracy." In R. T. Schaeffer & R. P. Lamm (Eds.), *Introducing sociology*. New York: McGraw-Hill.

Blauner, R. 1964. *Alienation and freedom*. Chicago: University of Chicago Press.

————. 1972. *Racial oppression in America*. New York: Harper & Row.

————. 1992. "The ambiguities of racial change." In M. L. Anderson & P. H. Collins (Eds.), *Race, class and gender: An anthology*. Belmont, CA: Wadsworth.

Block, J. H. 1983. "Differential premises arising from differential socialization of the sexes: Some conjectures." *Child Development*, 54, 1335-1354.

Blood, P., Tuttle, A., & Lakey, G. 1992. "Understanding and fighting sexism: A call to men." In M. L. Anderson & P. H. Collins (Eds.), *Race, class and gender: An anthology*. Belmont, CA: Wadsworth.

Blumstein, P. 1975. "Identity bargaining and self-conception." *Social Forces*, 53, 476-485.

Blumstein, P., & Kollock, P. 1988. "Personal relationships." *Annual Review of Sociology*, 14, 467-490.

Blumstein, P., & Schwartz, P. 1983. *American couples*. New York: Morrow.

Bohlen, C. 1989. "Holtzman may appeal probation for immigrant in wife's slaying." *New York Times*, April 5.

Bonnie, R. J., & Whitebread, C. H. 1974. *The marijuana conviction*. Charlottesville: University of Virginia Press.

Boshier, R., & Johnson, D. 1974. "Does conviction affect employment opportunities?" *British Journal of Criminology*, 14, 264-268.

Bouvier, L. F., & Gardner, R. W. 1986. "Immigration in the U.S.: The unfinished story." *Population Bulletin*, 41, 1-50.

Bowles, S., & Gintis, H. 1976. *Schooling in capitalist America: Educational reform and the contradictions of economic reform*. New York: Basic Books.

Bradley, G. W. 1978. "Self-serving biases in the attribution process: A reexamination of the fact or fiction question." *Journal of Personality and Social Psychology*, 36, 56-71.

Bradsher, K. 1993. "Mark Twain would understand the water crisis that's corrupting Iowans." *New York Times*, July 22.

Brand, D. 1987. "The new whiz kids." *Time*, August 31.

Braun, D. 1991. *The rich get richer: The rise of income inequality in the United States and the world.* Chicago: Nelson-Hall.

Brehm, S. 1992. *Intimate relationships.* New York: McGraw-Hill.

Breslau, K. 1990. "Overplanned parenthood." *Newsweek*, January 22.

Bridges, J. S. 1988. "Sex differences in occupational performance expectations." *Psychology of Women Quarterly, 12,* 75-90.

Brim, O. 1968. "Adult socialization." In J. A. Clausen (Ed.), *Socialization and society.* Boston: Little, Brown.

Brinton, C. 1965. *The anatomy of revolution.* New York: Vintage.

Brinton, M. 1988. "The social-institutional bases of gender stratification." *American Journal of Sociology, 94,* 300-334.

Brooke, J. 1985. "The unexplained lost years of Gladys Burr." *New York Times*, July 11.

Broverman, I., Vogel, S., Broverman, D., Clarkson, F., & Rosenkrantz, P. 1972. "Sex role stereotypes: A current appraisal." *Journal of Social Issues, 28,* 59-78.

Brown, J. L. 1987. "Hunger in the U.S." *Scientific American, 256,* 37-41.

Brown, J. L., & Pizer, H. F. 1987. *Living hungry in America.* New York: Mentor.

Brown, L. R. 1988. "Analyzing the demographic trap." *Current*, March/April.

Brown, R. 1986. *Social psychology.* New York: Free Press.

Brownmiller, S. 1975. *Against our will: Men, women and rape.* New York: Simon & Schuster.

———. 1984. *Femininity.* New York: Fawcett.

Bryjak, G. J., & Soroka, M. P. 1992. *Sociology: Cultural diversity in a changing world.* Boston: Allyn & Bacon.

"Buchanan talks tough about the homeless, visits a soup kitchen." 1991. *Washington Post*, December 25.

Buikhuisen, W., & Dijksterhuis, P. H. 1971. "Delinquency and stigmatization." *British Journal of Criminology, 11,* 186.

Bumpass, L., Sweet, J., & Castro Martin, T. 1990. "Changing patterns of remarriage." *Journal of Marriage and the Family, 52,* 747-756.

Burdett, H., Fornos, W., Kinkade, S., & Meyer, D. 1990. "A continent in crisis: Building a future for Africa in the 21st century." In K. Finsterbusch & G. McKenna (Eds.), *Taking sides: Clashing views on controversial social issues.* Guilford, CT: Dushkin.

Butler, R. 1975. *Why survive? Being old in America.* New York: Harper & Row.

———. 1989. "A generation at risk: When the baby boomers reach Golden Pond." In W. Feigelman (Ed.), *Sociology Full Circle.* New York: Holt, Rinehart & Winston.

Cameron, M. 1964. *The booster and the snitch: Department store shoplifting.* New York: Free Press.

Campbell, A. 1987. "Self-definition by rejection: The case of gang girls." *Social Problems, 34,* 451-466.

Campbell, A., Converse, P. E., & Rodgers, W. L. 1976. *The quality of American life.* New York: Russell Sage Foundation.

Cancian, F. 1987. *Love in America: Gender and self-development.* New York: Cambridge University Press.

Cantor, M. G. 1987. "Popular culture and the portrayal of women: Content and control." In B. B. Hess & M. M. Ferree (Eds.), *Analyzing gender: A handbook of social science research.* Newbury Park, CA: Sage.

Carr, J. 1988. *Crisis in intimacy.* Pacific Grove, CA: Brooks/Cole.

Carter, H., & Glick, P. C. 1976. *Marriage and divorce: A social and economic study.* Cambridge: Harvard University Press.

Celis, W. 1993. "Study finds rising concentration of black and Hispanic students." *New York Times*, December 14.

Cetron, M. J., Rocha, W., & Luckins, R. 1991. "Into the 21st century: Long term trends affecting the United States." In L. Cargan & J. H. Ballantine (Eds.), *Sociological footprints.* Belmont, CA: Wadsworth.

Chafetz, J. S. 1978. *A primer on the construction and testing of theories in sociology.* Itasca, IL: Peacock.

Chafetz, J. S., & Dworkin, A. G. 1987. "In the face of threat: Organized anti-feminism in comparative perspective." *Gender and Society, 1,* 33-60.

Chambliss, W. 1964. "A sociological analysis of the law of vagrancy." *Social Problems, 12,* 66-77.

————. 1974. "The state, the law and the definition of behavior as criminal or delinquent." In D. Glaser (Ed.), *The handbook of criminology*. Chicago: Rand McNally.

Chambliss, W., & Nagasawa, R. H. 1969. "On the validity of official statistics: A comparative study of white, black and Japanese high-school boys." *Journal of Research in Crime and Delinquency, 6*, 71-77.

Charon, J. 1989. *Symbolic interactionism: An introduction, an interpretation, an integration*. Englewood Cliffs, NJ: Prentice Hall.

————. 1992, *Ten questions: A sociological perspective*. Belmont, CA: Wadsworth.

Cherlin, A. 1978. "Remarriage as an incomplete institution." *American Journal of Sociology, 84*, 634-650.

————. 1992. *Marriage, divorce, remarriage*. Cambridge: Harvard University Press.

Chernin, K. 1981. *The obsession: Reflections on the tyranny of slenderness*. New York: Harper & Row.

Cherry, R. 1989. *Discrimination: Its economic impact on blacks, women and Jews*. Lexington, MA: Lexington Books.

Chirot, D. 1994. *How societies change*. Newbury Park, CA: Pine Forge Press.

Ciancanelli, P., & Berch, B. 1987. "Gender and the GNP." In B. B. Hess & M. M. Ferree (Eds.), *Analyzing gender: A handbook of social science research*. Newbury Park, CA: Sage.

Cicirelli, V. G. 1983. "Adult children and their elderly parents." In T. H. Brubaker (Ed.), *Family relationships in later life*. Beverly Hills, CA: Sage.

Cirino, R. 1973. "Bias through selection and omission: Automobile safety, smoking." In S. Cohen & J. Young (Eds.), *The manufacture of news*. Beverly Hills, CA: Sage.

Clark, B. 1960. "The 'cooling out' function in higher education." *American Journal of Sociology, 65*, 569-576.

Clark, R. D., III, & Word, L. E. 1972. "Why don't bystanders help? Because of ambiguity." *Journal of Personality and Social Psychology, 24*, 392-400.

Clark, R. L., & Passel, J. S. 1993. "Studies are deceptive." *New York Times*, September 3.

Clausen, J. A. 1986. *The life course: A sociological perspective*. Englewood Cliffs, NJ: Prentice-Hall.

Clifford, M. M. & Walster, E. 1973. "The effect of physical attractiveness on teacher expectations." *Sociology of Education, 46*, 248-258.

Clinard, M. B., & Meier, R. F. 1979. *Sociology of deviant behavior*. New York: Holt, Rinehart & Winston.

Cloward, R., & Piven, F. F. 1993. "The fraud of workfare." *The Nation*, May 24, 693-696.

Cluster, D. 1979. *They should have served that cup of coffee*. Boston: South End Press.

Cobb, N. J., Stevens-Long, J., & Goldstein, S. 1982. "The influence of televised models on toy preference in children." *Sex Roles, 8*, 1075-1080.

Cockerham, W. C. 1992. *Sociology of mental disorder*. Englewood Cliffs, NJ: Prentice Hall.

Coe, R. M. 1978. *Sociology of medicine*. New York: McGraw-Hill.

Cohen, A. K. 1955. *Delinquent boys: The culture of the gang*. New York: Free Press.

————. 1966. *Deviance and control*. Englewood Cliffs, NJ: Prentice Hall.

Cohen, A. M., & Brawer, F. 1982. *The American community college*. San Francisco: Jossey-Bass.

Cohen, B. 1991. "Taking time off: Leave provision in the European community for parents of school age children." *Women's Studies International Forum, 14*, 585-598.

Cohen, F. G. 1986. *Treaties on trial: The continuing controversy over Northwest Indian fishing rights*. Seattle: University of Washington Press.

Cohen, L. E., & Land, K. C. 1987. "Age structure and crime: Symmetry vs. asymmetry and the projection of crime rates through the 1990's." *American Sociological Review, 52*, 170-183.

Colburn, D. 1992. "A vicious cycle of risk." *Washington Post Health Magazine*, July 28.

Collins, R. 1971. "Functional and conflict theories of educational stratification." *American Sociological Review, 36*, 1002-1019.

————. 1981. "On the microfoundations of macrosociology." *American Journal of Sociology, 86*, 984-1014.

————. 1992. *Sociological insight: An introduction to non-obvious sociology*. New York: Oxford.

Collins, R., & Coltrane, S. 1991. *Sociology of marriage and the family: Gender, love and property*. Chicago: Nelson-Hall.

Collins, R., & Makowsky, M. 1984. *The discovery of society*. New York: Random House.

Conrad, P. 1975. "The discovery of hyperkinesis: Notes on the medicalization of deviant behavior." *Social Problems, 23,* 12-21.

————. 1992. "The social meaning of AIDS." In J. W. Heeren & M. Mason (Eds.), *Sociology: Windows on Society*. Los Angeles: Roxbury.

Conrad, P., & Schneider, J. W. 1980. *Deviance and medicalization: From badness to sickness*. St. Louis: C. V. Mosby.

Cookson, P., & Persell, C. 1985. *Preparing for power*. New York: Basic Books.

Cooley, C. H. 1902. *Human nature and social order*. New York: Charles Scribner's Sons.

Coontz, S. 1992. *The way we never were*. New York: Basic Books.

Corcoran, M., Duncan, G. J., & Hill, M. S. 1986. "The economic fortunes of women and children: Lessons from the panel study of income dynamics." In B. C. Gelpi, et al. (Eds.), *Women and poverty*. Chicago: University of Chicago Press.

Cose, E. 1993. *The rage of the privileged class*. New York: HarperCollins.

Coser, L., & Coser, R. 1963. "Time perspective and social structure." In A. W. Gouldner & H. P. Gouldner (Eds.), *Modern sociology*. Orlando, FL: Harcourt Brace Jovanovich.

————. 1993. "Jonestown as a perverse Utopia." In K. Finsterbusch & J. S. Schwartz (Eds.), *Sources: Notable selections in sociology*. Guilford, CT: Dushkin.

Coulson, M. A., & Riddell, C. 1980. *Approaching sociology*. London: Routledge & Kegan Paul.

Coupland, D. 1991. *Generation X: Tales for an accelerated culture*. New York: St. Martin's Press.

"Court rules city may oust unwed couple." 1986. *Seattle Times,* 19:6, November 8.

Cowan, R. 1991. "More work for Mother: The postwar years." In L. Kramer (Ed.), *The sociology of gender*. New York: St. Martin's Press.

Crittenden, K. S. 1991. "Asian self-effacement or feminine modesty? Attributional patterns of women university students in Taiwan." *Gender and Society, 5,* 98-117.

Crittenden, K. S., & Wiley, M. G. 1985. "When egotism is normative: Self-presentational norms

guiding attributions." *Social Psychology Quarterly, 48,* 360-365.

Cross, J., & Guyer M. 1980. *Social traps*. Ann Arbor: University of Michigan Press.

Cummings, S., & Taebel, D. 1978. "The economic socialization of children: A neo-Marxist analysis." *Social Problems, 26,* 198-210.

Cunningham, J. A., Strassberg, D. S., & Haan, B. 1986. "Effects of intimacy and sex-role congruency on self-disclosure." *Journal of Social and Clinical Psychology, 4,* 393-401.

Curran, D. J., & Renzetti, C. M. 1990. *Social problems*. Boston: Allyn & Bacon.

Cushman, J. H. 1993. "U.S. to weigh Blacks' complaints about pollution." *New York Times,* November 19.

Dabbs, J. M. 1992. "Testosterone and occupational achievement." *Social Forces, 70,* 813-824.

Dahl, R. 1961. *Who governs? Democracy and power in an American city*. New Haven, CT: Yale University Press.

Dahrendorf, R. 1959. *Class and class conflict in industrial society*. Stanford, CA: Stanford University Press.

Darton, N. 1991. "The end of innocence." *Newsweek* [special summer issue].

Davies, J. C. 1962. "Toward a theory of revolution." *American Sociological Review, 27,* 5-19.

Davis, A. J. 1984. "Sex-differentiated behaviors in non-sexist picture books." *Sex Roles, 11,* 1-16.

Davis, F. J. 1991. *Who is Black?* University Park: Pennsylvania State University Press.

Davis, J. A., & Smith, T. 1986. *General social survey cumulative file 1972-1982*. Ann Arbor, MI: Inter-University Consortium for Political and Social Research.

Davis, K. 1937. "The sociology of prostitution." *American Sociological Review, 2,* 744-755.

————. 1976. "The world's population crisis." In R. K. Merton & R. Nisbett (Eds.), *Contemporary social problems*. New York: Harcourt Brace Jovanovich.

Davis, K., & Moore, W. 1945. "Some principles of stratification." *American Sociological Review, 10,* 242-247.

DeFronzo, J. 1991. *Revolutions and revolutionary movements*. Boulder, CO: Westview.

Della Fave, L. R. 1980. "The meek shall not inherit the Earth: Self evaluation and the legitimacy of stratification." *American Sociological Review*, 45, 955-971.

"Denny's Restaurant hit with discrimination suit," 1993. *Jet Magazine*, April 12.

Dentzer, S. 1991. "The graying of Japan." *U.S. News and World Report*, September 30.

Denzin, N. 1969. "Symbolic interaction and ethnomethodology: A proposed synthesis." *American Sociological Review*, 34, 922-934.

———. 1977. *Childhood socialization: Studies in the development of language, social behavior, and identity*. San Fransisco: Jossey-Bass.

———. 1989. *The research act: A theoretical introduction to sociological methods*. Englewood Cliffs, NJ: Prentice Hall.

DeParle, J. 1990. "In debate over who is poor, fairness becomes the issue." *New York Times*, September 3.

Derber, C. 1979. *The pursuit of attention*. New York: Oxford University Press.

Derlega, V. J., Harris, M. S., & Chaikin, A. L. 1973. "Self-disclosure reciprocity, liking and the deviant." *Journal of Experimental Social Psychology*, 9, 277-284.

DiMaggio, P. J., & Powell, W. W. 1983. "The iron cage revisited: Institutional isomorphism and collective rationality in organizational fields." *American Sociological Review*, 48, 147-160.

Dion, K. K. 1972. "Physical attractiveness and evaluations of children's transgressions." *Journal of Personality and Social Psychology*, 24, 207-213.

Dion, K., Berscheid, E., & Walster, E. 1972. "What is beautiful is good." *Journal of Personality and Social Psychology*, 24, 285-290.

Dobash, R. E., & Dobash, R. P. 1979. *Violence against wives: A case against the patriarchy*. New York: Free Press.

"Does doctor know best?" *Newsweek*, 1990. September 24.

Domhoff, G. W. 1983. *Who rules America now? A view from the eighties*. Englewood Cliffs, NJ: Prentice Hall.

Dugger, C. W. 1992. "U.S. study says Asian-Americans face widespread discrimination." *New York Times*, February 29.

Duncan, G. J. 1984. *Years of poverty, years of plenty*. Ann Arbor: University of Michigan Press.

Durkheim, E. 1951. *Suicide*. New York: Free Press. (Original work published 1897)

———. 1954. *The elementary forms of religious life* (J. Swain, Trans.). New York: Free Press. (Original work published 1915)

———. 1958. *The rules of sociological method* (G. E. G. Catlin, Ed.; S. A. Solovay & J. H. Mueller, Trans.). Glencoe, IL: Free Press.

Eagly, A. H., Wood, W., & Fishbaugh, L. 1981. "Sex differences in conformity: Surveillance by the group as a determinant of male nonconformity." *Journal of Personality and Social Psychology*, 40, 384-394.

Ebaugh, H.R.F 1988, *Becoming an ex*, Chicago: University of Chicago Press.

Edelman, M. W. 1988. "Growing up black in America." In J. Skolnick & E. Currie (Eds.), *Crisis in American institutions*. Glenview, IL: Scott, Foresman.

Edney, J. 1979. "Free riders en route to disaster." *Psychology Today*, August, pp. 80-102.

Edney, J. J., & Harper, C. S. 1978. "The commons dilemma: A review of contributions from psychology." *Environmental Management*, 2, 491-507.

Egan, T. 1993. "A cultural gap may swallow a child." *New York Times*, October 12.

Ehrenreich, B. 1989. *Fear of falling: The inner life of the middle class*. New York: Harper.

———. 1990. "Is the middle class doomed?" In B. Ehrenreich (Ed.), *The worst years of our lives*. New York: Harper.

Ehrenreich, B. & English, D. 1979. *For her own good: 150 years of the experts' advice to women*. Garden City, NY: Anchor.

Ehrlich, P. R., & Ehrlich, A. H. 1993. "World population crisis." In K. Finsterbusch & J. S. Schwartz (Eds.), *Sources: Notable selections in sociology*. Guilford, CT: Dushkin.

Eitzen, D. S., & Baca-Zinn, M. 1989. *Social problems*. Boston: Allyn & Bacon.

———. 1991. *In conflict and order: Understanding society*. Boston: Allyn & Bacon.

Eitzen, D. S., Jung, M. A., & Purdy, D. A. 1982. "Organizational linkages among the inner group of the capitalist class." *Sociological Focus*, 15, 179-189.

Ekman, P., & Friesen, W. V. 1969. "Nonverbal leakage and clues to deception." *Psychiatry*, 32, 88-106.

Elder, G. H., & Liker, J. K. 1982. "Hard times in women's lives: Historical influences across 40 years." *American Journal of Sociology*, 88, 241-269.

Emerson, R. 1962. "Power-dependence relations." *American Sociological Review*, 27, 31-41.

English, C. 1991. "Food is my best friend: Self-justifications and weight loss efforts." *Research in the Sociology of Health Care*, 9, 335-345.

Epstein, C. F. 1989. "Workplace boundaries: Conceptions and creations." *Social Research*, 56, 571-590.

Erickson, P. G., & Goodstadt, M. S. 1979. "Legal stigma for marijuana possession." *Criminology*, 17, 208-216.

Erikson, K. 1966. *Wayward puritans*. New York: Wiley.

Ervin-Tripp, S. 1964. "Interaction of language, topic and listener." *American Anthropologist*, 66, 86-102.

Escobar, G. 1991. "A death near White House again underscores peril for homeless." *Washington Post*, December 12.

Eskenazi, G. 1992. "The plan no one wants to use." *New York Times*, May 22.

Evans, S. M. 1987. "Women in twentieth century America." In S. E. Rix (Ed.), *The American Woman, 1987-88*. New York: Norton.

Evans-Pritchard, E. E. 1937. *Witchcraft, oracles and magic among the Azande*. Oxford: Oxford University Press.

Evered, R. 1983. "The language of organizations: The case of the Navy." In L. R. Pondy, P. J. Frost, G. Morgan, & T. C. Dandridge (Eds.), *Organizational symbolism*. Greenwich, CT: JAI Press.

Ewen, S., & Ewen, E. 1982. *Channels of desire: Mass images and the shaping of the American consciousness*. New York: McGraw-Hill.

Ewing, W. 1992. "The civic advocacy of violence." In M. S. Kimmel & M. A. Messner (Eds.), *Men's Lives*. New York: Macmillan.

Fairchild, H. H. 1985. "Black, negro or Afro-American? The difference is crucial!" *Journal of Black Studies*, 16, 47-55.

Faludi, S. 1991. *Backlash: The undeclared war against women*. New York: Crown.

Farb, P. 1983. *Word play: What happens when people talk*. New York: Bantam.

Farhi, P. 1992. "Number of U.S. millionaires soars." *Washington Post*, July 11.

Farley, J. 1982. *Majority-minority relations*. Englewood Cliffs, NJ: Prentice Hall.

————. 1991. *Sociology*. Englewood Cliffs, NJ: Prentice Hall.

Fausto-Sterling, A. 1985. *Myths of gender: Biological theories about women and men*. New York: Basic Books.

————. 1993. "How many sexes are there?" *New York Times*, March 12.

Feagin, J. R. 1975. *Subordinating the poor*. Englewood Cliffs, NJ: Prentice Hall.

————. 1991. "The continuing significance of race: Anti-black discrimination in public places." *American Sociological Review*, 56, 101-116.

Federal Bureau of Investigation. 1991. *Uniform crime reports for the United States*. Washington, DC: U.S. Government Printing Office.

Fee, E., & Fox, D. M. 1992. *AIDS: The making of a chronic disease*. Berkeley: University of California Press.

Feigelman, W., & Silverman, A. B. 1984. "The long-term effects of transracial adoption." *Social Service Review*, 58, 588-602.

Feldberg, R. L. 1984. "Comparable worth: Toward theory and practice in the United States." *Signs*, 10, 311-328.

Felmlee, D., Sprecher, S., & Bassin, E. 1990. "The dissolution of intimate relationships: A hazard model." *Social Psychology Quarterly*, 53, 13-30.

Ferraro, K. J., & Johnson, J. M. 1983. "How women experience battering: The process of victimization." *Social Problems*, 30, 325-339.

Festinger, L., Riecken, H., & Schacter, S. 1956. *When Prophecy Fails*. New York: Harper & Row.

Fincham, F., & Bradbury, T. N. 1987. "The impact of attributions in marriage: A longitudinal analysis." *Journal of Personality and Social Psychology*, 53, 510-517.

Fine, G. A. 1990. *Talking sociology*. Boston: Allyn & Bacon.

Fineman, H. 1991. "The new politics of race." *Newsweek*, May 6.

Finlay, B. 1985. "Right to life vs. right to die: Some correlates of euthanasia attitudes." *Sociology and Social Research*, 69, 548-560.

Fitchen, J. M. 1992a. "Homelessness in rural places: Perspectives from upstate New York." *Urban Anthropology*, 20, 177-210.

————. 1992b. "On the edge of homelessness: Rural poverty and housing insecurity." *Rural Sociology*, *57*, 173-193.

"The Forbes four hundred." *Forbes Magazine*, 1990. *147*, 318-327.

Foucault, M. 1965. *Madness and civilization*. New York: Vintage.

Fox, J., & Levin, J. 1993. "Postal violence: Cycle of despair turns tragic." *USA Today*, May 12 [and personal correspondence].

Frank, M., Ziebarth, M., & Field, C. 1982. *The life and times of Rosie the Riveter*. Emeryville, CA: Clarity Educational Productions.

Franklin, B. A. 1987. "Agency imposes $111,470 in penalties for mine fire that killed 27 in 1984." *New York Times*, May 12.

Franklin, C. W., II, 1988. *Men and society*. Chicago: Nelson-Hall.

Freedman, R. 1986. *Beauty bound*. Lexington, MA: Lexington Books.

Freiberg, P. 1991. "Self-esteem gender gap widens in adolescence." *APA Monitor*, *22*, 29.

Friedland, R. 1989. "Questions raised by the changing age distribution of the U.S. population." *Generations*, *13*, 11-13.

Friedson, E. 1970. *Profession of medicine*. New York: Dodd, Mead.

Frieze, I. H., Parsons, J. E., Johnson, P. B., Ruble, D. N., & Zellman, G. L. 1978. *Women and sex roles: A social psychological perspective*. New York: Norton.

Furstenberg, F. F. 1981. "Conjugal succession: Re-entering marriage after divorce." In P. B. Baltes & O. Brim (Eds.), *Life span development and behavior*. New York: Academic Press.

Gaertner, S., & Dovidio, J. 1990. "The aversive form of racism." In A. G. Halberstadt & S. L. Ellyson (Eds.), *Social psychology readings: A century of research*. New York: McGraw-Hill.

Gailey, C. W. 1987. "Evolutionary perspectives on gender hierarchy." In B. B. Hess & M. M. Ferree (Eds.), *Analyzing gender: A handbook of social science research*. Newbury Park: Sage.

Galambos, N. L., & Maggs, J. L. 1991. "Children in self-care: Figures, facts and fictions." In J. V. Lerner & N. L. Galambos (Eds.), *Employed mothers and their children*. New York: Garland.

Gans, H. 1971. "The uses of poverty: The poor pay for all." *Social Policy*, Summer, 20-24.

Garfinkel, H. 1967. "Common sense knowledge of social structures: The documentary method of interpretation in lay and professional fact finding." In H. Garfinkel (Ed.), *Studies in ethnomethodology*. Englewood Cliffs, NJ: Prentice Hall.

Gargan, E. A. 1993. "For many brides in India, a dowry buys death." *New York Times*, December 30.

Garner, D. M., Garfinkel, P. E., Schwartz, D., & Thompson, M. 1980. "Cultural expectations of thinness in women." *Psychological Reports*, *47*, 483-491.

Garson, B. 1988. *The electronic sweatshop*. New York: Penguin.

Gates, H. L. 1992. "TV's black world turns—but stays unreal." In M. L. Anderson & P. H. Collins (Eds.), *Race, class and gender: An anthology*. Belmont, CA: Wadsworth.

Geerken, M., & Gove, W. R. 1983. *At home and at work: The family's allocation of labor*. Newbury Park, CA: Sage.

Gelles, R. J., & Cornell, C. P. 1990. *Intimate violence in families*. Newbury Park, CA: Sage.

Gelles, R. J. & Straus, M. A. 1988. *Intimate Violence*. New York: Simon & Schuster.

Gergen, D. 1991. "Not in my backyard." *U.S. News and World Report*, July 22.

Gergen, K. J. 1991. *The saturated self*. New York: Basic Books.

Gerlach, P., & Hine, V. H. 1970. *People, power, change: Movements of social transformation*. Indianapolis: Bobbs-Merrill.

Gerson, K. 1985. *Hard choices: How women decide about work, career, and motherhood*. Berkeley: University of California Press.

Gertsel, N. 1987. "Divorce and stigma." *Social Problems*, *34*, 172-186.

Gibbons, D. C. 1992. *Society, crime and criminal behavior*. Englewood Cliffs, NJ: Prentice Hall.

Gibbons, F. X. 1986. "Stigma and interpersonal relations." In S. C. Ainlay, G. Becker, & L. M. Coleman (Eds.), *The dilemma of difference*. New York: Plenum.

Giddens, A. 1991. *Introduction to sociology*. New York: Norton.

Gillen, B. 1981. "Physical attractiveness: A determinant of two types of goodness." *Personality and Social Psychology Bulletin, 7,* 277-281.

Gillespie, C. K. 1989. *Justifiable homicide.* Columbus: Ohio State University Press.

Gilligan, C. 1990. "Teaching Shakespeare's sister: Notes from the underground of female adolescence." In C. Gilligan, N. P. Lyons, & T. J. Hanmer (Eds.), *Making connections.* Cambridge: Harvard University Press.

Gitlin, T. 1979. "Prime time ideology: The hegemonic process in television entertainment." *Social Problems, 26,* 251-266.

Gleason, H. A. 1961. *An introduction to descriptive linguistics.* New York: Holt, Rinehart & Winston.

Glenn, N. 1982. "Interreligious marriage in the United States: Patterns and recent trends." *Journal of Marriage and the Family, 44,* 555-566.

Glick, P. C., & Norton, A. J. 1977. "Marrying, divorcing, and living together in the U.S. today." *Population Bulletin, 32.* Washington, DC: Population Reference Bureau.

Goertzel, T. G. 1993. "Some observations on psychological processes among organized American opponents to the Gulf War." *Political Psychology, 14,* 139-146.

Goetting, A. 1982. "The six stations of remarriage: Developmental tasks of remarriage after divorce." *Family Relations,* April, 213-222.

Goffman, E. 1952. "On cooling the mark out: Some aspects of adaptation to failure." *Psychiatry, 15,* 451-463.

———. 1959a. *The presentation of self in everyday life.* Garden City, NY: Doubleday.

———. 1959b. "The moral career of the mental patient." *Psychiatry, 22,* 125-131.

———. 1961. *Asylums.* Garden City, NY: Anchor.

———. 1963. *Stigma: Notes on the management of spoiled identity.* Englewood Cliffs, NJ: Prentice Hall.

———. 1967. *Interaction ritual.* Chicago: Aldine.

Gold, S. 1992. *Refugee Communities: A Comparative Field Study.* Thousand Oaks, CA: Sage.

Goldberg, S. 1974. *The inevitability of patriarchy.* New York: Willam Morrow.

Goldberg, S., & Lewis, M. 1969. "Play behavior in the year-old infant: Early sex differences." *Child Development, 40,* 21-31.

Goleman, D. 1984. "Rethinking IQ tests and their value." *New York Times,* July 22.

———. 1986. "Perception of time emerges as a key psychological factor." *New York Times,* December 30.

———. 1989. "Sensing silent cues emerges as key skill." *New York Times,* October 10.

———. 1990. "The group and the self: New focus on a cultural rift." *New York Times,* December 25.

———. 1991a. "When ugliness is only in the patient's eye, body image can reflect a mental disorder." *New York Times,* October 2.

———. 1991b. "Parents' warmth is found to be key to adult happiness." *New York Times,* April 18.

———. 1993. "Therapists find some patients are just hateful." *New York Times,* May 4.

Goodchilds, J., Zellman, G., Johnson, P., & Giarusso, R. 1988. "Adolescents and the perceptions of sexual interaction outcomes." In A. W. Burgess (Ed.), *Sexual assault.* New York: Garland.

Goode, E. 1984. *Deviant behavior.* Englewood Cliffs, NJ: Prentice Hall.

———. 1989. *Drugs in American society.* New York: McGraw-Hill.

Goode, W. J. 1971. "World revolution and family patterns." *Journal of Marriage and the Family, 33,* 624-635.

———. 1981. "Why men resist." in B. Thorne & M. Yalom (Eds.), *Rethinking the family: Some feminist questions.* New York: Longman.

Gordon, D. M., Edwards, R., & Reich, M. 1982. *Segmented work, divided workers: The historical transformation of labor in the United States.* Cambridge: Cambridge University Press.

Gordon, M. M. 1964. *Assimilation in American life.* New York: Oxford University Press.

Gottfredson, M., & Hirschi, T. 1989. "Why we're losing the war on crime." *Washington Post Magazine,* September 10.

Gottfried, A. E. 1991. "Maternal employment in the family setting: Developmental and environmental issues." In J. V. Lerner & N. L. Galambos (Eds.), *Employed mothers and their children.* New York: Garland.

Gough, K. 1971. "The origin of the family." *Journal of Marriage and the Family, 33,* 760-770.

Gould, S. J. 1981. *The mismeasure of man.* New York: Norton.

Gove, W. 1982. *Deviance and mental illness*. Beverly Hills, CA: Sage.

Gove, W., Hughes, M., & Geerkin, M. R. 1980. "Playing dumb: A form of impression management with undesirable effects." *Social Psychology Quarterly*, 43, 89-102.

Gracey, H. L. 1991, "Learning the student role: Kindergarten as academic boot camp." In J. Henslin (Ed.), *Down to earth sociology*. New York: Free Press.

Granovetter, M., & Tilly, C. 1988. "Inequality and labor processes." In N. J. Smelser (Ed.), *Handbook of sociology*. Newbury Park, CA: Sage.

Grant, L. 1984. "Black females' 'place' in desegregated classrooms." *Sociology of Education*, 57, 98-111.

Green, M. 1984. "When money talks, is it democracy?" *The Nation*, September 15, pp. 200-204.

Greencastle Banner Graphic. 1992. Letter to the editor. March 7.

Greenhouse, L. 1986. "The rise and rise of McDonald's." *New York Times*, June 8.

————. 1990. "Use of illegal drugs as part of religion can be prosecuted, high court says." *New York Times*, April 18.

Griffin, J. L. 1993. "Domestic partners getting benefits." *Indianapolis Star*, November 28.

Griffin, S. 1986. *Rape: The power of consciousness*. New York: Harper & Row.

————. 1989. "Rape: The all American crime." In L. Richardson & V. Taylor (Eds.), *Feminist frontiers II*. New York: Random House.

Gross, D. M., & Scott, S. 1990. "Proceeding with caution." *Time*, July 16.

Gross, E. 1984. "Embarrassment in public life." *Society*, 21, 48-53.

Gross, E., & Etzioni, A. 1985. *Organizations and society*. Englewood Cliffs, NJ: Prentice Hall.

Gross, E., & Stone, G. P. 1964. "Embarrassment and the analysis of role requirements." *American Journal of Sociology*, 70, 1-15.

"A growing percentage of the homeless are families, a reports says." 1993. *New York Times*, December 22.

Gruber, K. J., & White, J. W. 1986. "Gender differences in the perceptions of self's and others' use of power strategies." *Sex Roles*, 15, 109-118.

Gruson, L. 1985. "Groups play matchmaker to preserve Judaism." *New York Times*, April 1.

Gusfield, J. R. 1963. *Symbolic crusade: Status politics and the American temperance movement*. Urbana: University of Illinois Press.

Hacker, A. 1992. *Two nations: Black and white, separate, hostile, unequal*. New York: Charles Scribner's Sons.

Hafferty, F. W. 1991. *Into the valley: Death and socialization of medical students*. New Haven, CT: Yale University Press.

Hagan, J. 1985. *Modern criminology: Crime, criminal behavior and its control*. New York: McGraw-Hill.

Hall, E. T. 1969. *The hidden dimension*. Garden City, NY: Doubleday.

————. 1983. *The dance of life*. Garden City, NY: Anchor.

Hall, P. 1990. "The presidency and impression management." In J. W. Heeren & M. Mason (Eds.), *Sociology: Windows on society*. Los Angeles: Roxbury.

Hall, R. M., & Sandler, B. R. 1985. "A chilly climate in the classroom." In A. G. Sargent (Ed.), *Beyond sex roles*. New York: West.

Hall, W. 1986. "Social class and survival on the S.S. Titanic." *Social Science and Medicine*, 22, 687-690.

Halle, D. 1984. *America's working man: Work, home, and politics among blue collar property owners*. Chicago: University of Chicago Press.

Hallin, D. C. 1986. "We keep America on top of the world." In T. Gitlin (Ed.), *Watching television*. New York: Pantheon.

Hamilton, D. L. 1981. *Cognitive processes in stereotyping and intergroup behavior*. Hillsdale, NJ: Erlbaum.

Hammer, J. 1992. "Must Blacks be buffoons?" *Newsweek*, October 26.

Hane, M. 1982. *Peasants, rebels and outcastes: The underside of modern Japan*. New York: Pantheon

Hardin, G., & Baden, J. 1977. *Managing the commons*. New York: W. H. Freeman.

Hareven, T. K. 1978. *Transitions: The family and the life course in historical perspective*. New York: Academic Press.

————. 1992. "American families in transition: Historical perspectives on change." In A. S. Skolnick

& J. H. Skolnick (Eds.), *Family in transition.* New York: HarperCollins.

"Harper's Index." 1986. *Harper's Magazine,* December, p. 13.

Harris, M. 1964. *Patterns of race in the Americas.* New York: Norton.

Harrison, B., & Bluestone, B. 1988. *The great U-turn: Corporate restructuring and the polarizing of America.* New York: Basic Books.

Hartmann, H., Kraut, R. E., & Tilly, L. A. 1989. "Job content: Job fragmentation and the deskilling debate." in D. S. Eitzen & M. Baca-Zinn (Eds.), *The reshaping of America.* Englewood Cliffs, NJ: Prentice Hall.

Hatfield, E., Traupmann, J., Sprecher, S., Utne, M., & Hay, J. 1985. "Equity and intimate relations: Recent research." In W. Ickes (Ed.), *Compatible and incompatible relationships.* New York: Springer-Verlag.

Hatfield, E., Walster, G. W., & Traupmann, J. 1978. "Equity and premarital sex." *Journal of Personality and Social Psychology, 37,* 82-92.

Heise, L. 1989. "The global war against women." *Washington Post Magazine,* April 9.

Helmreich, W. B. 1992. "The things they say behind your back: Stereotypes and the myths behind them." In H. F. Lena, W. B. Helmreich, & W. McCord (Eds.), *Contemporary issues in sociology.* New York: McGraw-Hill.

Hendrick, S. S. 1981. "Self-disclosure and marital satisfaction." *Journal of Personality and Social Psychology, 40,* 1150-1159.

Henley, N. 1977. *Body politics.* Englewood Cliffs, NJ: Prentice Hall.

Henslin, J. 1991. *Down to earth sociology.* New York: Free Press.

Henslin, J., & Biggs, M. A. 1978. "Dramaturgical desexualization: The sociology of the vaginal examination." In J. Henslin & E. Sagarin (Eds.), *The sociology of sex: An introductory reader.* New York: Schocken.

Herbert, B. 1993. "The real jobless rate." *New York Times,* August 4.

Herman, E. S., & Chomsky, N. 1988. *Manufacturing consent: The political economy of the mass media.* New York: Pantheon.

Hertz, R. 1986. *More equal than others: Women and men in dual-career marriages.* Berkeley: University of California Press.

Hewitt, J. P. 1988. *Self and society: A symbolic interactionist social psychology.* Boston: Allyn & Bacon.

Hewitt, J. P., & Hewitt, M. L. 1986. *Introducing sociology: A symbolic interactionist perspective.* Englewood Cliffs, NJ: Prentice Hall.

Hewitt, J. P., & Stokes, R. 1975. "Disclaimers." *American Sociological Review, 40,* 1-11.

Hiller, D. V., & Philliber, W. W. 1986. "The division of labor in comtemporary marriage: Expectations, perceptions and performance." *Social Problems, 33,* 191-201.

Hiller, E. T. 1933. *Principles of sociology.* New York: Harper & Row.

Hills, S. 1980. *Demystifying social deviance.* New York: McGraw-Hill.

Hirschi, T. 1969. *Causes of delinquency.* Berkeley: University of California Press.

Hochschild, A. 1983. *The managed heart.* Berkeley: University of California Press.

Hofferth, S. 1983. "Updating children's life course." Bethesda, MD: Center for Population Research, National Institute for Child Health and Human Development.

Hollinger, R. C., & Lanza-Kaduce, L. 1988. "The process of criminalization: The case of computer crime laws." *Criminology, 26,* 101-126.

Holmes, S. A. 1991. "Homelessness rises, but not as an issue." *New York Times,* December 25.

Holstrom, N. 1982. "Do women have a distinct nature?" *The Philosophical Forum, 14,* 25-42.

Holtzworth-Munroe, A., & Jacobson, N. S. 1985. "Causal attributions of married couples: When do they search for causes? What do they conclude when they do?" *Journal of Personality and Social Psychology, 48,* 1398-1412.

Homans, G. 1961. *Social behavior: Its elementary forms.* New York: Harcourt Brace Jovanovich.

Honebrink, A. 1993. "Migrants create a new world order with their feet." *Utne Reader,* May/June, pp. 46-49.

Hossfeld, K. J. 1990. " 'Their logic against them': Contradictions in sex, race and class in Silicon Valley." In K. Ward (Ed.), *Women workers and global restructuring.* Ithaca, NY: ILR Press.

House, J. 1981. "Social structure and personality." In M. Rosenberg & R. H. Turner (Eds.), *Social psychology: Sociological perspectives.* New York: Basic Books.

Howard, J. A., Blumstein, P., & Schwartz, P. 1986. "Sex, power and influence tactics in intimate relationships." *Journal of Personality and Social Psychology, 51*, 102-109.

Howe, N., & Strauss, W. 1992. "The new generation gap." *Atlantic Monthly*, December.

Huber, B. 1994. Internal memorandum of the American Sociological Association, February 10.

Huber, J., & Form, W. H. 1973. *Income and ideology.* New York: Free Press.

Huddle, D. L. 1993. "Immigrants: A cost or a benefit?" *New York Times*, September 3.

Hughes, L. 1958. *The Langston Hughes reader.* New York: George Braziller.

Humphry, D. 1991. *Final exit: The practicalities of self-deliverance and assisted suicide for the dying.* Eugene, OR: Hemlock Society.

Hunt, J. 1985. "Police accounts of normal force." *Urban Life, 12*, 315-341.

Hunt, J. G., & Hunt, L. L. 1990. "The dualities of careers and families: New integrations or new polarizations?" In C. Carlson (Ed.), *Perspectives on the family: History, class and feminism.* Belmont, CA: Wadsworth.

Hunter, J. D. 1987. *Evangelicalism: The coming generation.* Chicago: University of Chicago Press.

————. 1991. *Culture wars: The struggle to define America.* New York: Basic Books.

Hurst, C. 1979. *The anatomy of social inequality.* St. Louis: C. V. Mosby.

Huston, T. L. 1983. "Power." In H. Kelley et al. (Eds.), *Close relationships.* New York: W. H. Freeman.

Ignatius, A. 1988. "China's birthrate is out of control again as one-child policy fails in rural areas." *Wall Street Journal*, July 14.

Inciardi, J. A. 1992. *The war on drugs II.* Mountain View, CA: Mayfield.

Institute on Hunger and Development. 1992. *Hunger 1992: The 2nd annual report on the state of world hunger*, Washington, DC: Author.

Instone, D., Major, B., & Bunker, B. B. 1983. "Gender, self-confidence, and social influence strategies: An organizational simulation." *Journal of Personality and Social Psychology, 44*, 322-333.

"Is there a Santa Claus?" 1897, *New York Sun*, September, 21.

Jackall, R. 1988. *Moral mazes: The world of corporate managers.* New York: Oxford University Press.

Jackman, M. R., & Jackman, R. W. 1983. *Class awareness in the United States.* Berkeley: University of California Press.

Jackson, J. 1954. "The adjustment of the family to the crisis of alcoholism." *Quarterly Journal of Studies on Alcohol, 15*, 564-586.

Jacobs, P. 1988. "Keeping the poor, poor." In J. H. Skolnick & E. Currie (Eds.), *Crisis in American institutions.* Glenview, IL: Scott, Foresman.

Jacquet, C. H., & Jones, A. M. 1991. *Yearbook of American and Canadian churches.* Nashville: Abingdon.

James, W. 1890. *Principles of psychology.* New York: Holt.

Janis, I. 1991. "Groupthink." In L. Cargan & J. H. Ballantine (Eds.), *Sociological footprints.* Belmont, CA: Wadsworth.

Janoff-Bulman, R. 1979. "Characterological versus behavioral self-blame: Inquiries into depression and rape." *Journal of Personality and Social Psychology, 37*, 1798-1809.

Jaynes, G. 1982. "Suit on race recalls lines drawn under slavery." *New York Times*, September 30.

Jencks, C., Bartlett, S., Corcoran, M., Crouse, J., Eaglesfield, D., Jackson, G., McClelland, K., Mueser, P. Olneck, M., Schwartz,, J., Ward, S., and Williams, J. 1979. *Who gets ahead?* New York: Basic Books.

Jhally, S., & Lewis, J. 1992. *Enlightened racism: The Cosby Show, audiences, and the myth of the American Dream.* Boulder, CO: Westview.

Johnson, A. B. 1990. *Out of bedlam: The truth about deinstitutionalization.* New York: HarperCollins.

Johnson, A. G. 1992. *Human arrangements.* Fort Worth, TX: Harcourt Brace Jovanovich.

Johnson, D. 1991. "Polygamists emerge from secrecy, seeking not just peace but respect." *New York Times*, April 9.

Johnson, P. 1976. "Women and power: Toward a theory of effectiveness." *Journal of Social Issues, 32*, 99-110.

Johnson, R. 1987. *Hard time: Understanding and reforming the prison.* Monterey, CA: Brooks/Cole.

Johnston, D. 1992. "Survey shows number of rapes far higher than official figures." *New York Times*, April 24.

Jones, E. E., Farina, A., Hastorf, A. H., Markus, H., Miller, D. T., & Scott, R. A. 1984. *Social stigma: The psychology of marked relationships.* New York: W. H. Freeman.

Jones, E. E., & Pittman, T. S. 1982. "Toward a general theory of strategic self-presentation." In J. Suls (Ed.), *Psychological perspectives on the self* (Vol. 1). Hillsdale, NJ: Lawrence Erlbaum.

Jones, J. M. 1986. "The concept of racism and its changing reality." In B. P. Bowser & R. G. Hunt (Eds.), *Impacts of racism on white Americans.* Beverly Hills, CA: Sage.

Jones, S. M. 1978. "Divorce and remarriage: A new beginning, a new set of problems." *Journal of Divorce, 2,* 217-227.

Kagan, J. 1976. *Raising children in modern America: Problems and prospective solutions.* Boston: Little, Brown.

Kagay, M. R., & Elder, J. 1992. "Numbers are no problem for pollsters. Words are." *New York Times,* August 9.

Kain, E. 1990. *The myth of family decline.* Lexington, MA: Lexington Books.

Kamerman, S. B. 1985. "Time out for babies." *Working Mother, 4,* 80-82.

Kamm, H. 1993. "In new Eastern Europe, an old anti-Gypsy bias." *New York Times,* November 17.

Kanter, R. M. 1975. "Women and the structure of organizations: Explorations in theory and behavior." In R. M. Kanter & M. Millman (Eds.), *Another voice.* New York: Doubleday.

————. 1977. *Men and women of the corporation.* New York: Basic Books.

Kanter, R. M., & Stein, B. A. 1979. *Life in organizations: Workplaces as people experience them.* New York: Basic Books.

Kantrowitz, B. 1993. "Wild in the streets." *Newsweek,* August 2.

Karabel, J. 1972. "Community colleges and social stratification." *Harvard Educational Review, 42,* 521-559.

Kariya, T., & Rosenbaum, J. E. 1987. "Self selection in Japanese junior high schools: A longitudinal study of students' educational plans." *Sociology of Education, 60,* 168-180.

Karp, D. A., & Yoels, W. C. 1976. "The college classroom: Some observations on the meanings of student participation." *Sociology and Social Research, 60,* 421-439.

————. 1985. *Sociology and everyday life.* Itasca, IL: Peacock.

Kart, C. S. 1990. *The realities of aging.* Boston: Allyn & Bacon.

Kasarda, J. D. 1985. "Urban change and minority opportunities." In P. E. Peterson (Ed.), *The new urban reality.* Washington, DC: Brookings Institution.

————. 1989. "Urban industrial transition and the underclass." In W. J. Wilson (Ed.), *The ghetto underclass: Social science perspectives.* Newbury Park, CA: Sage.

Katz, J. 1975. "Essences as moral identities: Verifiability and responsibility in imputations of deviance and charisma." *American Journal of Sociology, 80,* 1369-1390.

Katz, P. A. 1986. "Modification of children's gender-stereotyped behavior: General issues and research considerations." *Sex Roles, 14,* 591-602.

Kaufman, M. 1987. *Beyond patriarchy: Essays by men on pleasure, power, and change.* Toronto: Oxford.

Kearl, M. C. 1989. *Endings: A sociology of death and dying.* New York: Oxford University Press.

Kearl, M. C., & Gordon, C. 1992. *Social psychology.* Boston: Allyn & Bacon.

Kelley, H., Berscheid, E., Christensen, A., Harvey, J. H., Huston, T. L., Levinger, G., McClintock, E., Peplau, L. A., & Peterson, D. R. 1983. *Close relationships.* New York: W. H. Freeman.

Kelly, R. M., & Bayes, J. 1988. *Comparable worth, pay equity and public policy.* Westport, CT: Greenwood Press.

Kennedy, P. 1993. *Preparing for the 21st century.* New York: Random House.

Kerbo, H. R. 1991. *Social stratification and inequality.* New York: McGraw-Hill.

Kessler, R. C., et al. 1994. "Lifetime and 12-month prevalence of DSM-III-R psychiatric disorders in the United States." *Archives of General Psychiatry, 51,* 8-19.

Kessler, S. J., & McKenna, W. 1978. *Gender: An ethnomethodological approach.* Chicago: University of Chicago Press.

Keyfitz, N. 1990. "The growing human population." In *Readings from Scientific American: Managing Planet Earth.* New York: Freeman.

Kilborn, P. T. 1993a. "Inside post offices, the mail is only part of the pressure." *New York Times,* May 17.

————. 1993b. "New jobs lack the old security in time of 'disposable workers.' " *New York Times*, March 15.

Kilbourne, J. 1992. "Beauty and the beast of advertising." In P. S. Rothenberg (Ed.), *Race, class & gender in the United States*. New York: St. Martin's Press.

King, M. L. 1991. "Letter from Birmingham City Jail." In C. Carson, D. J. Garrow, G. Gill, V. Harding, & D. Clark Hine (Eds.), *Eyes on the Prize civil rights reader*. New York: Penguin.

Kirk, S. A., & Kutchins, H. 1992. *The selling of DSM: The rhetoric of science in psychiatry*. Hawthorne, NY: Aldine deGruyter.

Klatch, R. 1991. "Complexities of conservatism: How conservatives understand the world." In A. Wolfe (Ed.), *America at century's end*. Berkeley: University of California Press.

Kleck, R. 1968. "Physical stigma and nonverbal cues emitted in face to face interaction." *Human Relations, 21*, 19-28.

Kleck, R., Ono, H., & Hastorf, A. 1966. "The effects of physical deviance and face to face interaction." *Human Relations, 19*, 425-436.

Kleck, R., & Strenta, A. 1980. "Perceptions of the impact of negatively valued physical characteristics on social interaction." *Journal of Personality and Social Psychology, 39*, 861-873.

Kligman, G. 1992. "Abortion and international adoption in post-Ceausescu Romania." *Feminist Studies, 18*, 405-419.

Kluegel, J. R., & Smith, E. R. 1986. *Beliefs about inequality: Americans' views of what is and what ought to be*. New York: Aldine deGruyter.

Kobrin, F. E. 1976. "The fall in household size and the rise of the primary individual in the United States." *Demography, 31*, 127-138.

Kohlberg, L. A. 1966. "A cognitive-developmental analysis of children's sex-role concepts and attitudes." In E. Maccoby (Ed.), *The development of sex differences*. Stanford, CA: Stanford University Press.

Kohn, M. L. 1979. "The effects of social class on parental values and practices." In D. Reiss & H. A. Hoffman (Eds.), *The American family: Dying or developing*. New York: Plenum.

Kokopeli, B., & Lakey, G. 1992. "More power than we want: Masculine sexuality and violence." In M. L. Anderson & P. H. Collins (Eds.), *Race, class and gender: An anthology*. Belmont, CA: Wadsworth.

Kolata, G. 1993. "Strong family aid to elderly is found." *New York Times*, May 3.

Kollock, P., Blumstein, P., & Schwartz, P. 1985. "Sex and power in interaction: Conversational privileges and duties." *American Sociological Review, 50*, 34-46.

Kollock P., & O'Brien, J. 1993. *The production of reality*. Newbury Park, CA: Pine Forge Press.

Kovel, J. 1980. "The American mental health industry." In David Ingleby (Ed.), *Critical psychiatry*. New York: Pantheon.

Kozol, J. 1988. *Rachel and her children: Homeless families in America*. New York: Crown.

————. 1991. *Savage inequalities: Children in America's schools*. New York: Harper & Row.

Kristof, N. D. 1991. "Stark data on women: 100 million are missing." *New York Times*, November 5.

————. 1993a. "China's crackdown on births: A stunning and harsh success." *New York Times*, April 25.

————. 1993b. "Peasants of China discover new way to weed out girls." *New York Times*, July 21.

Ladner, J. 1978. *Mixed families: Adopting across racial boundaries*. Garden City, NY: Anchor Press.

Lakoff, R. 1973. "Language and woman's place." *Language and Society, 2*, 45-80.

————. 1975. *Language and woman's place*. New York: Harper & Row.

Lamanna, M. A., & Reidmann, A. 1994. *Marriages and families: Making choices and facing change*. Belmont, CA: Wadsworth.

Lander, L. 1988. *Images of bleeding: Menstruation as ideology*. New York: Orlando.

Langston, D. 1992. "Tired of playing monopoly?" In M. L. Anderson & P. H. Collins (Eds.), *Race, class and gender: An anthology*. Belmont, CA: Wadsworth.

Lasch, C. 1977. *Haven in a Heartless World*. New York: Basic Books.

Laslett, B., & Warren, C. A. B. 1987. "Losing weight." In E. Rubington & M. S. Weinberg (Eds.), *Deviance: The interactionist perspective*. New York: Macmillan.

Latané, B., & Darley, J. 1970. *The unresponsive bystander: Why doesn't he help?* New York: Appleton-Century-Crofts.

Latané, B., & Rodin, J. 1969. "A lady in distress: Inhibiting effects of friends and strangers on bystander intervention." *Journal of Experimental Social Psychology, 5*, 189-202.

Lauderdale, P. 1980. *A political analysis of deviance.* Minneapolis: University of Minnesota Press.

Lauer, R., & Handel, W. 1977. *Social psychology: The theory and application of symbolic interactionism.* Boston: Houghton Mifflin.

Lawson, C. 1992. "Who believes in make-believe? Not these new toys." *New York Times,* February 6.

————, 1993. "Stereotypes unravel, but not too quickly, in new toys for 1993." *New York Times,* February 11.

Leidner, R. 1991. "Serving hamburgers and selling insurance: Gender work and identity in interactive service jobs." *Gender and Society,* 5, 154-177.

Leinberger, P., & Tucker, B. 1991. *The new individualists: The generation after the organization man.* New York: HarperCollins.

Lekachman, R. 1991. "The specter of full employment." In J. H. Skolnick & E. Currie (Eds.), *Crisis in American institutions.* New York: HarperCollins.

Lemert, E. 1972. *Human deviance, social problems, and social control.* Englewood Cliffs, NJ: Prentice Hall.

Lerner, M. 1970. "The desire for justice and reactions to victims." In J. Macauley & L. Berkowitz (Eds.), *Altruism and helping behavior.* New York: Academic Press.

Leslie, C. 1991. "Classrooms of Babel." *Newsweek,* February 11.

Levant, R. F., Slatter, S. C., & Loiselle, J. E. 1987. "Fathers' involvement in housework and child care with school age daughters." *Family Relations,* 36, 152-157.

Levin, D. P. 1991. "Latest slayings at post office spur a review of all workers." *New York Times,* November 16.

Levin, J. 1993. *Sociological snapshots.* Newbury Park, CA: Pine Forge Press.

Levine, R., & Wolff, E. 1988. "Social time: The heartbeat of culture." In E. Angeloni (Ed.), *Annual editions in anthropology 88/89.* Guilford, CT: Dushkin.

LeVine, R. A., & White, M. 1992. "The social transformation of childhood." In A. S. Skolnick & J. H. Skolnick (Eds.), *Family in Transition.* New York: HarperCollins.

Levinson, M. 1991. "Living on the edge." *Newsweek,* November 4.

Levinson, R. M. 1975. "Sex discrimination and employment practices: An experiment with unconventional job inquiries." *Social Problems,* 22, 533-543.

Lewin, T. 1989. "Aging parents: Women's burden grows." *New York Times,* November 14.

————. 1990. "Suit over death benefits asks, what is a family?" *New York Times,* September 21.

————. 1991. "Jobless pay for mother." *New York Times,* March 13.

Lewis, M. 1978. *The culture of inequality.* New York: New American Library.

Lewis, M. M. 1948. *Language in society.* New York: Social Science Research Council.

Lewis, N. A. 1988. "For New York City, the lessons are hard and the gold stars are few." *New York Times,* September 4.

Lewis, O. 1968. "The culture of poverty." In D. P. Moynihan (Ed.), *On understanding poverty: Perspectives from the social sciences.* New York: Basic Books.

Liazos, A. 1985. *Sociology: A liberating perspective.* Boston: Allyn & Bacon.

Light, P. 1988. *Baby boomers.* New York: Norton.

Light, D., & Keller, S. 1985. *Sociology.* New York: Knopf.

Lindesmith, A. R., Strauss, A. L., & Denzin, N. K. 1991. *Social psychology.* Englewood Cliffs, NJ: Prentice Hall.

Link, B. G., Cullen, F. T., Frank, J., & Wozniak, J. F. 1987. "The social rejection of former mental patients: Understanding why labels matter." *American Journal of Sociology,* 92, 1461-1500.

Link, B. G., Mirotznik, J., & Cullen, F. T. 1991. "The effectiveness of stigma coping orientations: Can negative consequences of mental illness labeling be avoided?" *Journal of Health and Social Behavior,* 32, 302-320.

Linton, R. 1937. "One hundred percent American." *The American Mercury,* 40, 427-429.

Lippmann, L. W. 1922. *Public opinion.* New York: Harcourt Brace Jovanovich.

Lips, H. M. 1993. *Sex and gender: An introduction.* Mountain View, CA: Mayfield.

Lizotte, A. J. 1978. "Testing the conflict model of criminal justice." *Social Problems,* 25, 564-580.

Lofland, J. 1981. "Collective behavior: The elementary forms." In M. Rosenberg & R. H. Turner

(Eds.), *Social psychology: Sociological perspectives.* New York: Basic Books.

Lofland, L. H. 1971. "Self-management in public settings, Part I." *Urban Life and Culture, 1,* 93-117.

————. 1973. *A world of strangers: Order and action in urban public space.* New York: Basic Books.

Lopez, G. A. 1991. "The Gulf War: Not so clean." *Bulletin of the Atomic Scientists, 47,* 30-35.

Lorber, J. 1989. "Dismantling Noah's Ark." In B. J. Risman & P. Schwartz (Eds.), *Gender in intimate relationships: A microstructural approach.* Belmont, CA: Wadsworth.

Lord, W. 1956. *A night to remember.* New York: Bantam.

Lott, B. 1987. *Women's lives: Themes and variations in gender learning.* Monterey, CA: Brooks/Cole.

Loury, G. C. 1985. "Beyond civil rights." *The New Republic,* October.

Lubeck, S., & Garrett, P. 1990. "Child care 2000: Policy options for the future." In C. Carlson (Ed.), *Perspectives on the family.* Belmont, CA: Wadsworth.

Luker, K. 1984. *Abortion and the politics of motherhood.* Berkeley: University of California Press.

Lyman, S. M., & Douglass, W. A. 1973. "Ethnicity: Strategies of collective and individual impression management." *Social Research, 40,* 344-365.

Lynch, M. 1983. "Accommodation practices: Vernacular treatments of madness." *Social Problems, 31,* 152-164.

Lytton, H., & Romney, D. M. 1991. "Parents' differential socialization of boys and girls: A meta-analysis." *Psychology Bulletin, 109,* 267-296.

MacAndrew, C., & Edgerton, R. B. 1969. *Drunken comportment: A social explanation.* Chicago: Aldine.

MacDonald, K., & Parke, R. D. 1986. "Parent-child physical play: The effects of sex and age on children and parents." *Sex Roles, 15,* 367-378.

Makinson, L. 1993. *Open secrets: The encyclopedia of congressional money and politics.* Washington, DC: Congressional Quarterly Inc.

Mann, C. C. 1993. "How many is too many?" *Atlantic Monthly,* February.

Mannheim, K. 1952. "The problem of generations." In P. Kecskemeti (Ed. and Trans.), *Essays on the sociology of knowledge,* London: Routledge & Kegan Paul.

Mannon, J. 1990. *American gridmark.* Tucson, AZ: Harbinger House.

Margolick, D. 1990. "Death and faith, law and Christian Science." *New York Times,* August 6.

Martin, L. 1989. "The graying of Japan." *Population Bulletin, 44,* 1-43.

Martin, M. K., & Voorhies, B. 1975. *Female of the species.* New York: Columbia University Press.

Martin, T. C., & Bumpass, L. L. 1989. "Recent trends in marital disruption." *Demography, 26,* 37-51.

Marx, K., & Engels, F. 1982. *The Communist manifesto.* New York: International Publishers. (Original work published 1848)

Massey, D. 1990. "American apartheid: Segregation and the making of the underclass." *American Journal of Sociology, 96,* 329-357.

Matthews, J. 1989. "Rescue plan for Africa." *World Monitor,* May, pp. 28-36.

Mayo, J. M. 1990. "Propaganda with design: Environmental dramaturgy in the political rally." In D. Brissett & C. Edgley (Eds.), *Life as theater: A dramaturgical sourcebook.* New York: Aldine de-Gruyter.

McCain, F. 1991. "Interview with Franklin McCain." In C. Carson et al. (Eds.), *The Eyes on the Prize civil rights reader.* New York: Penguin.

McCall, G. J. 1982. "Becoming unrelated: The management of bond dissolution." In S. Duck (Ed.), *Personal relationships 4: Dissolving personal relationships.* London: Academic Press.

McCall, G. J., & Simmons, J. L. 1978. *Identities and interactions.* New York: Free Press.

McCarthy, J. D., & Zald, M. N. 1977. "Resource mobilization and social movements: A partial theory." *American Journal of Sociology, 82,* 1212-1241.

McClelland, K. E., & Auster, C. J. 1990. "Public platitudes and hidden tensions: Racial climates at predominantly white liberal arts colleges." *Journal of Higher Education, 61,* 607-642.

McClendon, M. J. 1985. "Racism, rational choice and white opposition to racial change: A case study of busing." *Public Opinion Quarterly, 49,* 214-233.

McFadden, R. D. 1983. "Comments by Meese on hunger produce a storm of controversy." *New York Times,* December 10.

McGrath, J., & Kelly, J. 1986. *Time and human interaction: Toward a social psychology of time.* New York: Guilford Press.

McHugh, P. 1968. *Defining the situation.* Indianapolis: Bobbs-Merrill.

McPhee, J. 1971. *Encounters with the archdruid.* New York: Noonday.

McRoy, R. G., & Zurcher, L. A. 1983. *Transracial and inracial adoptees: The adolescent years.* Springfield, IL: Charles Thomas.

Mead, G. H. 1934. *Mind, self and society.* Chicago: University of Chicago Press.

Mead, M. 1963. *Sex and temperment in three primitive societies.* New York: William Morrow.

Medvedev, Z. A., & Medvedev, R. A. 1971. *A question of madness.* New York: Norton.

Mehan, H., & Wood, H. 1975. *The reality of ethnomethodology.* New York: Wiley.

Merrick, T. W. 1986. "World population in transition." *Population Bulletin, 41,* 2.

Merton, R. 1948. "The self fulfilling prophecy." *Antioch Review, 8,* 193-210.

———. 1957. *Social theory and social structure.* New York: Free Press.

Messick, D. M., & Brewer, M. B. 1983. "Solving social dilemmas: A review." In L. Wheeler & P. Shaver (Eds.), *Review of personality and social psychology.* Beverly Hills, CA: Sage.

Meyer, J. W., & Rowan, B. 1977. "Institutionalized organizations: Formal structure as myth and ceremony." *American Journal of Sociology, 83,* 340-363.

Miall, C. E. 1989. "The stigma of involuntary childlessness." In A. S. Skolnick & J. H. Skolnick (Eds.), *Family in transition.* Boston: Little, Brown.

Michener, H. A., DeLamater, J. D., & Schwartz, S. H. 1986. *Social psychology.* San Diego, CA: Harcourt Brace Jovanovich.

Miles, J. 1992. "Blacks vs. browns." *Atlantic Monthly,* October.

Milgram, S. 1974. *Obedience to authority.* New York: Harper & Row.

Miller, C. L. 1987. "Qualitative differences among gender-stereotyped toys: Implications for cognitive and social development." *Sex Roles, 16,* 473-488.

Miller, J. 1984. "Culture and the development of everyday explanation." *Journal of Personality and Social Psychology, 46,* 961-978.

Miller, T. M., Coffman, J. G., & Linke, R. A. 1980. "Survey on body-image, weight and diet of college students." *Journal of the American Dietetic Association, 77,* 561-566.

Millman, M. 1980. *Such a pretty face.* New York: Norton.

Mills, C. W. 1940. "Situated actions and vocabularies of motive." *American Sociological Review, 5,* 904-913.

———. 1956. *The power elite.* New York: Oxford University Press.

———. 1959. *The sociological imagination.* New York: Oxford University Press.

Mills, J. L. 1985. "Body language speaks louder than words." *Horizons,* February.

Minzesheimer, B. 1989. "PACs play both sides of fence." *USA Today,* May 9.

Mitford, J. 1963. *The American way of death.* Greenwich, CT: Fawcett Crest.

Moffatt, M. 1989. *Coming of age in New Jersey.* New Brunswick, NJ: Rutgers University Press.

Mokhiber, R. 1989. "Crime in the suites." *Greenpeace, 14,* 14-17.

Molotch, H., & Lester, M. 1974. "News as purposive behavior: On the strategic use of routine events, accidents, and scandals." *American Sociological Review, 39,* 101-112.

———. 1975. "Accidental news: The great oil spill as local occurrence and national event." *American Journal of Sociology, 81,* 235-260.

Monk, A. 1988. "Aging, generational continuity and filial support." *The World and I, 3,* 549-561.

Moore, R. B. 1992. "Racist stereotyping in the English language." In M. L. Anderson & P. H. Collins (Eds.), *Race, class and gender: An anthology.* Belmont, CA: Wadsworth.

Moorhead, G., Ference, R., & Neck, C. 1991. "Group decision fiascoes continue: Space shuttle *Challenger* and a revised groupthink framework." *Human Relations, 44,* 539-550.

"More children taking hyperactivity drugs." 1988. *Hartford Courant,* October 21.

Morgan, G. 1986. *Images of organizations.* Newbury Park, CA: Sage.

Morgan, J. N. 1978. "A potpourri of new data gathered from interviews with husbands and wives." In G. J. Duncan & J. N. Morgan (Eds.), *Five thou-*

sand American families: Patterns of economic progress* (Vol. 6). Ann Arbor: University of Michigan, Institute for Social Research.

Morgan, M. 1982. "Television and adolescents' sex role stereotypes: A longitudinal study." *Journal of Personality and Social Psychology, 48,* 1173-1190.

———. 1987. "Television sex role attitudes and sex role behavior." *Journal of Early Adolescence, 7,* 269-282.

Morgan, P., Wallack, L., & Buchanan, D. 1988. "Waging drug wars: Prevention strategy or politics as usual?" *Drugs and Society, 3,* 99-124.

Morganthau, T. 1992. "Losing ground." *Newsweek,* April 6.

Morris, M., & Williamson, J. B. 1987. "Workfare: The poverty/dependence tradeoff." *Social Policy,* Summer, *13-16,* 49-50.

Morton, T. U. 1978. "Intimacy and reciprocity in exchange: A comparison of spouses and strangers." *Journal of Personality and Social Psychology, 36,* 72-81.

Mottl, T. L. 1980. "The analysis of countermovements." *Social Problems, 27,* 620-635.

Murdock, G. 1957. "World ethnography sample." *American Anthropologist, 59,* 664-687.

Murray, D. L. 1982. "The abolition of el cortito, the short-handled hoe: A case study in social conflict and state policy in California agriculture." *Social Problems, 30,* 26-39.

Myrdal, G. 1944. *An American dilemma.* New York: Harper & Row.

Nanda, S. 1994. *Cultural anthropology.* Belmont, CA: Wadsworth.

Nasar, S. 1992. "The 1980's: A very good time for the very rich." *New York Times,* March 5.

National Center for Education Statistics. 1989. *1989 education indicators.* Washington, DC: U.S. Government Printing Office.

National Committee on Pay Equity. 1992. "The wage gap: Myths and facts." In P. S. Rothenberg (Ed.), *Race, class and gender in the United States.* New York: St. Martin's Press.

National Institute on Drug Abuse. 1992. *Smoking, drinking and illicit drug use among American secondary school students, college students, and young adults, 1975-1991.* Washington, DC: U.S. Government Printing Office.

Neary, I. J. 1986. "Socialist and communist party attitudes towards discrimination against Japan's Burakumin." *Political Studies, 34,* 556-574.

Neubeck, K. 1986. *Social problems: A critical approach.* New York: Random House.

Neugarten, B. L. 1980. "Grow old along with me! The best is yet to be." In B. Hess (Ed.), *Growing old in America.* New Brunswick, NJ: Transaction Books.

Newman, K. 1988. *Falling from grace: The experience of downward mobility in the American middle class.* New York: Free Press.

Njeri, I. 1990. *Every good-bye ain't gone.* New York: Random House.

Nolan, J. D., Galst, J. P., & White, M. A. 1977. "Sex bias on children's television programs." *Journal of Psychology, 96,* 197-204.

Norton, A. J. 1987. "Families and children in the year 2000." *Children Today,* July/August, 6-9.

Novac, V. 1988. "Formula for profit: How private corporations grow fat from a program designed to feed the poor." *Seeds,* August, 22-25.

Oakes, J. 1985. *Keeping track: How high schools structure inequality,* New Haven: Yale University Press.

OECD (Organization for Economic Co-operation and Development). 1988. *Aging populations: The social policy implications.* Washington, DC.

Olsen, M. 1965. *The logic of collective action.* Cambridge: Harvard University Press.

Omi, M., & Winant, H. 1992. "Racial formations." In P. S. Rothenberg (Ed.), *Race, class and gender in the United States.* New York: St. Martin's Press.

O'Neill, M. 1992. "As the rich get leaner, the poor get french fries." *New York Times,* March 18.

Oreskes, M., & Toner, R. 1989. "The homeless at the heart of poverty and policy." *New York Times,* January 29.

Ostrander, S. 1980. "Upper class women: Class consciousness as conduct and meaning." In G. W. Domhoff (Ed.), *Power structure research.* Beverly Hills, CA: Sage.

O'Sullivan See, K. & Wilson, W. J. 1988. "Race and ethnicity." In N. Smelser (Ed.), *Handbook of sociology.* Newbury Park, CA: Sage.

O'Toole, R., & Dubin, R. 1968. "Baby feeding and body sway: An experiment in George Herbert Mead's 'Taking the Role of the Other.'" *Journal of Personality and Social Psychology, 10,* 59-65.

Palmore, E. 1975. *The honorable elders: A cross cultural analysis of aging in Japan.* Durham, NC: Duke University Press.

Parenti, M. 1986. *Inventing reality.* New York: St. Martin's Press.

————. 1988. *Democracy for the few.* New York: St. Martin's Press.

Parlee, M. B. 1989. "Conversational politics." In L. Richardson & V. Taylor (Eds.), *Feminist frontiers II.* New York: Random House.

Parsons, T. 1951. *The social system.* New York: Free Press.

————. 1971. "Kinship and the associational aspect of social structure." In F. L. K. Hsu (Ed.), *Kinship and culture.* Chicago: Aldine.

Parsons, T., & Bales, R. F. 1955. *Family, socialization and interaction process.* Glencoe, IL: Free Press.

Parsons, T., & Smelser, N. 1956. *Economy and society.* New York: Free Press.

Passell, P. 1993. "Like a new drug, social programs are put to the test." *New York Times,* March 9.

Patterson, M., & Engelberg, L. 1978. "Women in male-dominated professions." In A. H. Stromberg & S. Harkess (Eds.), *Women working.* Palo Alto, CA: Mayfield.

Payer, L. 1988. *Medicine and culture.* New York: Penguin.

Pear, R. 1983. "Study says affirmative action rule expands hiring of minorities." *New York Times,* June 19.

————. 1992. "New look at the U.S. in 2050: Bigger, older and less white." *New York Times,* December 4.

————. 1993a. "Wide health gap, linked to income, is reported in the U.S." *New York Times,* July 8.

————. 1993b. "Poverty in U.S. grew faster than population last year." *New York Times,* October 5.

Pearce, D. 1979. "Gatekeepers and homeseekers: Institutional patterns in racial steering." *Social Problems, 26,* 325-342.

Percival, R. 1989. "Malthus and his ghost." *National Review,* August 18.

Perlez, J. 1991. "Madagascar, where the dead return, bringing joy." *New York Times,* August 31.

Perlman, D., & Fehr, B. 1987. "The development of intimate relationships." In D. Perlman & S. Duck (Eds.), *Intimate relationships: Development, dynamics and deterioration.* Newbury Park, CA: Sage.

Perrow, C. 1986. *Complex organizations: A critical essay.* New York: Random House.

Perrow, C., & Guillen, M. 1990. *The AIDS disaster: The failure of organizations in New York and the nation.* New Haven, CT: Yale University Press.

Persell, C. H. 1991. "Schools under pressure." In A. Wolfe (Ed.), *America at century's end.* Berkeley: University of California Press.

Pescosolido, B. A. 1986. "Migration, medical care and the lay referral system: A network theory of role assimilation." *American Sociological Review, 51,* 523-540.

Pescosolido, B. A., & Georgianna, S. 1989. "Durkheim, suicide, and religion: Toward a network theory of suicide." *American Sociological Review, 54,* 33-48.

Petersilia, J. 1985. *Probation and felony offenders.* Washington, DC: U.S. Department of Justice.

Peterson, J., & Kim, P. 1991. *The day America told the truth.* New York: Prentice Hall.

Peterson, P. 1991. "The urban underclass and the poverty paradox." In C. Jencks & P. Peterson (Eds.), *The urban underclass.* Washington, DC: Brookings Institution.

Peterson, S. B., & Lach, M. A. 1990. "Gender stereotypes in children's books: Their prevalence and influence in cognitive and affective development." *Gender and Education, 2,* 185-197.

Petrunik, M., & Shearing, C. D. 1983. "Fragile facades: Stuttering and the strategic manipulation of awareness." *Social Problems, 31,* 125-138.

Pettigrew, T. F., & Martin, J. 1987. "Shaping the organizational context for black American inclusion." *Journal of Social Issues, 43,* 41-78.

Pfohl, S. J. 1977. "The discovery of child abuse." *Social Problems, 24,* 310-323.

————. 1985. *Images of deviance and social control.* New York: McGraw-Hill.

Philipson, I. J. 1993. *On the shoulders of women: The feminization of psychotherapy.* New York: Guilford.

Piaget, J. 1954. *The construction of reality in the child.* New York: Basic Books.

Piliavin, I., & Briar, S. 1964. "Police encounters with juveniles." *American Journal of Sociology, 70,* 206-214.

Piven, F. F., & Cloward, R. A. 1977. *Poor people's movements: Why they succeed, how they fail.* New York: Vintage.

Pollitt, K. 1991. "Fetal rights: A new assault on feminism." In J. H. Skolnick & E. Currie (Eds.), *Crisis in American institutions*. New York: HarperCollins.

Postman, N. 1982. *The disappearance of childhood*. New York: Delacorte Press.

Powell, W. W. 1991. "Expanding the scope of institutional analysis." In W. W. Powell & P. J. DiMaggio (Eds.), *The new institutionalism in organizational analysis*. Chicago: University of Chicago Press.

Pratkanis, A., & Aronson, E. 1991. *Age of propaganda*. New York: W. H. Freeman.

Preston, S. H. 1976. *Mortality patterns in national population: With special references to recorded causes of death*. New York: Academic Press.

————. 1984. "Children and the elderly in the U.S." *Scientific American*, December, 44-49.

Pryor, J. B., & Ostrom, T. M. 1981. "The organization of social information: A converging-operations approach." *Journal of Personality and Social Psychology*, *41*, 628-641.

Pugliesi, K. 1987. "Deviation in emotion and the labeling of mental illness." *Deviant Behavior*, *8*, 79-102.

Quinney, R. 1970. *The social reality of crime*. Boston: Little, Brown.

Ramirez, A. 1988. "Racism toward Hispanics: The culturally monolithic society." In P. A. Katz & D. A. Taylor (Eds.), *Eliminating racism*. New York: Plenum.

Ramos, R. 1990. "Movidas: Mexican-American interactional strategies." In J. W. Heeren & M. Mason (Eds.), *Sociology: Windows on society*. Los Angeles: Roxbury.

Reiman, J. 1990. *The rich get richer and the poor get prison*. New York: Macmillan.

Reinharz, S. 1992. *Feminist methods in social research*. New York: Oxford University Press.

Reinhold, R. 1993. "A welcome for immigrants turns to resentment." *New York Times*, August 25.

Reiss, I. L. 1960. "Toward a sociology of the heterosexual love relationship." *Marriage and Family Living*, *22*, 139-145.

Reiss, I. L., & Lee, G. R. 1988. *Family systems in America*. New York: Holt, Rinehart & Winston.

Renwick, T. J., & Bergmann, B. R. 1993. "A budget-based definition of poverty." *Journal of Human Resources*, *28*, 1-24.

Renzetti, C. M., & Curran, D. J. 1989. *Women, men and society: The sociology of gender*. Boston: Allyn & Bacon.

Reskin, B., & Hartmann, H. 1986. *Women's work, men's work: Sex segregation on the job*. Washington, DC: National Academy Press.

Reskin, B., & Padavic, I. 1994. *Women, men and work*. Newbury Park, CA: Pine Forge Press.

Reynolds, J. M. 1973. "The medical institution." In L. T. Reynolds & J. M. Henslin (Eds.), *American society: A critical analysis*. New York: David McKay.

Richardson, L. 1987. "Gender stereotyping in the English language." In L. Richardson & V. Taylor (Eds.), *Feminist frontiers II*. New York: Random House.

Riesman, D. 1950. *The lonely crowd*. New Haven, CT: Yale University Press.

Riley, M. W. 1971. "Social gerontology and the age stratification of society." *The Gerontologist*, *11*, 79-87.

————. 1983. "The family in an aging society: A matrix of latent relationships." *Journal of Family Issues*, *4*, 439-454.

Riley, M. W., Foner, A., & Waring, J. 1988. "Sociology of age." In N. J. Smelser (Ed.), *Handbook of sociology*. Newbury Park, CA: Sage.

Riley, M. W., Johnson, M., & Foner, A. 1972. *Aging and society III: A sociology of age stratification*. New York: Russell Sage Foundation.

Ritzer, G. 1993. *The McDonaldization of society*. Newbury Park, CA: Pine Forge Press.

Robey, B. 1987. "Locking up haven's door." *American Demographics*, *9*, 24-29.

Robins, L. N., & Regier, D. A. 1991. *Psychiatric disorders in America: The epidemiologic catchment area studies*. New York: Free Press.

Robinson, R. V., & Bell, W. 1978. "Equality, success and social justice in England and the United States." *American Sociological Review*, *43*, 125-143.

Robinson, R. V., & Kelley, J. 1979. "Class as conceived by Marx and Dahrendorf: Effects on income inequality and politics in the United States and Great Britain." *American Sociological Review*, *44*, 38-58.

Rodin, J. 1985. "The application of social psychology." In G. Lindzay & E. Aronson (Eds.), *The handbook of social psychology*. New York: Random House.

Rodman, H., Pratto, D. J., & Nelson, R. S. 1985. "Child care arrangements and children's functioning: A comparison of self care and adult care children." *Developmental Psychology, 21,* 413-418.

Roethlisberger, F. J., & Dickson, W. J. 1939. *Management and the worker.* Cambridge: Harvard University Press.

Rohter, L. 1993. "Miami meals tax to aid homeless." *New York Times,* August 3.

Roof, W. C. 1993a. *A generation of seekers: The spiritual journeys of the baby boom generation.* San Francisco: Harper.

———. 1993b. "Toward the year 2000: Reconstructions of religious space." *The Annals of the American Academy of Political and Social Science, 527,* 155-170.

Rosenhan, D. 1973. "On being sane in insane places." *Science, 179,* 250-258.

Rosenthal, R., & Jacobson, L. 1968. *Pygmalion in the classroom.* New York: Holt, Rinehart & Winston.

Ross, C. E., Mirowsky, J., & Goldstein, K. 1990. "The impact of family on health: The decade in review." *Journal of Marriage and the Family, 52,* 1059-1078.

Rossi, A. 1968. "Transition to parenthood." *Journal of Marriage and the Family, 30,* 26-39.

Rossi, P. 1988. *Down and out in America: The origins of homelessness.* Chicago: University of Chicago Press.

Rothenberg, P. S. 1992. *Race, class and gender in the United States.* New York: St. Martin's Press.

Rothman, B. K. 1987. "Reproduction." In B. B. Hess & M. M. Ferree (Eds.), *Analyzing gender: A handbook of social science research.* Newbury Park, CA: Sage.

Rothman, D. J., & Edgar, H. 1992. "Scientific rigor and medical realities: Placebo trials in cancer and AIDS research." In E. Fee & D. M. Fox (Eds.), *AIDS: The making of a chronic disease.* Berkeley: University of California Press.

Rothschild, N. 1990. *New York City neighborhoods.* New York: Academic Press.

Rowland, R. 1990. "Technology and motherhood: Reproductive choice reconsidered." In C. Carlson (Ed.), *Perspectives on the family: History, class and feminism.* Belmont, CA: Wadsworth.

Roy, D. 1959. "Banana time: Job satisfaction and informal interaction." *Human Organization, 18,* 158-168.

Rubin, J. Z., Provenzano, F. J., & Luria, Z. 1974. "The eye of the beholder: Parents' views on sex of newborns." *American Journal of Orthopsychiatry, 44,* 512-519.

Rubin, L. 1976. *Worlds of pain.* New York: Basic Books.

Rubin, Z. 1973. *Liking and loving.* New York: Holt, Rinehart & Winston.

Rubin, Z., Hill, C. T., Peplau, L. A., & Dunkel-Schetter, C. 1980. "Self-disclosure in dating couples: Sex roles and the ethic of openness." *Journal of Marriage and the Family, 42,* 305-317.

Ruether, R. 1980. "Politics and the family: Recapturing a lost issue." *Christianity and Crisis, 40,* 261-267.

Ruggles, P. 1990. "The poverty line—too low for the 90's." *New York Times,* April 26.

Rusbult, C. E. 1983. "A longitudinal test of the investment model: The development (and deterioration) of satisfaction and commitment in heterosexual involvement." *Journal of Personality and Social Psychology, 45,* 101-117.

Rusbult, C. E., Zembrodt, I. M., & Iwaniszek, J. 1986. "The impact of gender and sex-role orientation on responses to dissatisfaction in close relationships." *Sex Roles, 15,* 1-20.

Ryan, W. 1976. *Blaming the victim.* New York: Vintage Books.

Sadker, M., & Sadker, D. 1985. "Striving for equity in classroom teaching." In A. G. Sargent (Ed.), *Beyond sex roles.* New York: West.

Salholz, E. 1986. "Too late for Prince Charming?" *Newsweek,* June 2.

Sapir, E. 1929. "The status of linguistics as a science." *Language, 5,* 207-214.

———. 1949. *Selected writings* (D. G. Mandelbaum, Ed.). Berkeley: University of California Press.

Satchell, M. 1991. "Poisoning the border." *U.S. News and World Report,* May 6.

Saul, L. 1972. "Personal and social psychopathology and the primary prevention of violence." *American Journal of Psychiatry, 128,* 1578-1581.

Schacter, S. 1951. "Deviation, rejection, and communication." *Journal of Abnormal and Social Psychology, 46,* 190-207.

Scheff, T. 1966. *Being mentally ill: A sociological theory.* New York: Aldine.

Schlesinger, A. 1992. *The disuniting of America*. New York: Norton.

Schodolski, V. J. 1993. "Funeral industry, pitching videos, 2-for-1 specials to baby boomers." *Indianapolis Star*, December 26.

Schofield, J. 1982. *Black and white in school*. New York: Praeger.

Schor, J. B. 1991. "Global equity and environmental crisis: An argument for reducing working hours in the north." *World Development, 19*, 73-84.

Schuman, H., Steeh, C., & Bobo, L. 1988. *Racial attitudes in America: Trends and interpretations*. Cambridge: Harvard University Press.

Schur, E. M. 1984. *Labeling women deviant: Gender, stigma and social control*. New York: Random House.

Schwartz, B. 1973. "Waiting, exchange and power: The distribution of time in social systems." *American Journal of Sociology, 79*, 841-870.

Schwartz, C. G. 1970. "Strategies and tactics of mothers of mentally retarded children for dealing with the medical care system." In N. R. Bernstein (Ed.), *Diminished people: Problems and care of the mentally retarded*. Boston: Little, Brown.

Schwartz, R. D., & Skolnick, J. H. 1962. "Two studies of legal stigma." *Social Problems, 10*, 133-138.

Schwarz, J. E., & Volgy, T. J. 1993. "Above the poverty line—but poor." *The Nation*, February 15.

Scott, M., & Lyman, S. 1968. "Accounts." *American Sociological Review, 33*, 46-62.

Scott, R. 1967. "The selection of clients by social welfare agencies: The case of the blind." *Social Problems, 14*, 248-257.

Scull, A., & Favreau, D. 1986. "A chance to cut is a chance to cure: Sexual surgery for psychosis in three nineteenth century societies." In S. Spitzer & A. T. Scull (Eds.), *Research in law, deviance and social control* (Vol. 8). Greenwich, CT: JAI Press.

Scully, D., & Marolla, J. 1984. "Convicted rapists' vocabulary of motive: Excuses and justifications." *Social Problems, 31*, 530-544.

Seedman, A. A., & Hellman, P. 1975. *Chief*. New York: Avon.

Segall, A. 1987. "Sociocultural variation in sick role behavioral expectations." In H. D. Schwartz (Ed.), *Dominant issues in medical sociology*. New York: Random House.

Senior, J. 1994. "Sign language reflects changing sensibilities." *New York Times*, January 3.

Sennett, R. 1984. *Families against the city: Middle class homes in industrial Chicago*. Cambridge: Harvard University Press.

Sennett, R., & Cobb, J. 1972. *The hidden injuries of class*. New York: Vintage Books.

Shakin, M., Shakin, D., & Sternglanz, S. H. 1985. "Infant clothing: Sex labeling for strangers." *Sex Roles, 12*, 955-964.

Shanker, A. 1990. "The Family Medical Leave Act." *New York Times*, June 24.

Shapiro, J. P. 1993. "Just fix it." *U.S. News and World Report*, February 22.

Shaw, C. R., Forgaugh, F. M., McKay, H. D., & Cottrel, L. S. 1929. *Delinquency areas*. Chicago: University of Chicago Press.

Sheffield, C. J. 1987. "Sexual terrorism: The social control of women." In B. B. Hess & M. M. Ferree (Eds.), *Analyzing gender: A handbook of social science research*. Newbury Park, CA: Sage.

Sherman, S. R., Ward, R. A., & LaGory, M. 1988. "Women as caregivers of the elderly: Instrumental and expressive support." *Social Work*, March-April, 164-167.

Sherraden, M. 1988. "Rethinking social welfare: Toward assets." *Social Policy*, Winter, 37-43.

Shibutani, T. 1961. *Society and personality: An interactionist approach to social psychology*. Englewood Cliffs, NJ: Prentice Hall.

Shilts, R. M. 1987. *And the band played on: Politics, people and the AIDS epidemic*. New York: St. Martin's Press.

Shireman, J. F., & Johnson, P. R. 1986. "A longitudinal study of black adoptions: Single parent, transracial and traditional." *Social Work, 31*, 172-176.

Shon, S. P., & Ja, D. Y. 1992. "Asian families." In A. S. Skolnick & J. H. Skolnick (Eds.), *Family in transition*. New York: HarperCollins.

Shotland, R. L., & Straw, M. K. 1976. "Bystander response to an assault: When a man attacks a woman," *Journal of Personality and Social Psychology, 34*, 990-999.

Showalter, E. 1985. *The female malady*. New York: Penguin.

Sidel, R. 1986. *Women and children last*. New York: Penguin.

———. 1990. *On her own: Growing up in the shadow of the American Dream*. New York: Penguin.

Signorielli, N. 1990. "Children, television and gender roles." *Journal of Adolescent Health Care, 11*, 50-58.

Silver, V. 1992. "Barely gone, the 80's are ripe for a revival." *New York Times*, December 15.

Silverman, D. 1982. *Secondary analysis in social research: A guide to data sources and methods with examples*. Boston: Allen & Unwin.

Simon, J. 1983. "Life on earth is getting better." *The Futurist*, August.

Simon, R., & Alstein, H. 1981. *Transracial adoption: A follow up*. Lexington, MA: D. C. Heath & Co.

Simons, M. 1993. "Dutch parliament approves law permitting euthanasia." *New York Times*, February 10.

Simpson, I. H. 1979. *From student to nurse: A longitudinal study of socialization*. Cambridge: Cambridge University Press.

Simpson, P. 1983. "The fight for pay equity." *Working Woman*, April.

Singleton, R., Straits, B. C., & Straits, M. M. 1993. *Approaches to social research*. New York: Oxford University Press.

Siwek, J. 1992. "Plight of the homeless shows flaws in the system." *Washington Post Health Magazine*, July 28.

Skocpol, T. 1979. *States and social revolutions: A comparative analysis of France, Russia and China*. New York: Cambridge University Press.

Skolnick, A. S. 1981. "Married lives: Longitudinal perspectives on marriage." In D. H. Eichorn, J. A. Clausen, N. Haan, M. P. Honzik, & P. H. Mussen (Eds.), *Present and past in middle life*. New York: Academic Press.

———. 1987. *The intimate environment: Exploring marriage and the family*. Boston: Little, Brown.

———. 1991. *Embattled paradise*. New York: Basic Books.

Skolnick, A. S., & Skolnick, J. H. 1992. *Family in transition*. New York: HarperCollins.

Smeeding, T., Torrey, B. B., & Rein, M. 1988. "Patterns of income and poverty: The economic status of children and the elderly in eight countries." In T. Smeeding, J. L. Palmer, & B. B. Torrey (Eds.), *The Vulnerable*. Washington, DC: Urban Institute Press.

Smith, D. A. 1993. "Technology and the modern world system: Some reflections." *Science, Technology and Human Values, 18*, 186-195.

Smith, J. 1981. *Social issues and the social order: The contradictions of capitalism*. Cambridge, MA: Winthrop.

Smolowe, J. 1993. "Giving the cold shoulder." *Time*, December 6.

Sniderman, P. M., & Tetlock, P. E. 1986. "Symbolic racism: Problems of motive attribution in political analysis." *Social Forces, 42*, 129-150.

Snipp, C. M. 1986. "American Indians and natural resource development." *American Journal of Economics and Sociology, 45*, 457-474.

Snow, D. A., Baker, S. G., Anderson, L., & Martin, M. 1986. "The myth of pervasive mental illness among the homeless." *Social Problems, 33*, 407-423.

Snow, D. A., Robinson, C., & McCall, P. 1991. " 'Cooling out' men in singles' bars and nightclubs." *Journal of Contemporary Ethnography, 19*, 423-449.

Soldo, B. J., & Agree, E. M. 1988. "America's elderly." *Population Bulletin, 43*, 1-45.

Solomon, J. 1988. *The signs of our times: The secret meanings of everyday life*. New York: Harper & Row.

Sontag, D. 1992. "Across the U.S., immigrants find the land of resentment." *New York Times*, December 11.

Sontag, S. 1979. *Illness as metaphor*. New York: Random House.

Sowell, T. 1977. "New light on black IQ." *New York Times Magazine*, March 27.

Spanier, G. B. 1989. "Cohabitation in the 1980's: Recent changes in the United States." In A. S. Skolnick & J. H. Skolnick (Eds.), *Family in Transition*. Boston: Little, Brown.

Spence, J. T., Deaux, K., & Helmreich, R. L. 1985. "Sex roles in contemporary American society." In G. Lindzey & E. Aronson (Eds.), *The handbook of social psychology*. New York: Random House.

Spickard, P. R. 1989. *Mixed blood*. Madison: University of Wisconsin Press.

Spitze, G. 1988. "Women's employment and family relations: A review." *Journal of Marriage and the Family, 50*, 595-618.

Spretnak, C. 1982. "The Christian Right's 'holy war' against feminism." In *The politics of women's spirituality*. New York: Anchor.

Squires, G. D. 1980. "Runaway factories are also a civil rights issue." *In These Times*, May, 14-20.

Srole, L., Langner, T. S., Michael, S. T., Opler, M. K., & Rennie, T. A. C. 1962. *Mental health in the metropolis: The midtown Manhattan study.* New York: McGraw-Hill.

Stacey, J. 1991. "Backward toward the postmodern family." In A. Wolfe (Ed.), *America at century's end.* Berkeley: University of California Press.

Stacey, J., & Thorne, B. 1985. "The missing feminist revolution in sociology." *Social Problems, 32,* 301-316.

Staples, R. 1992. "African American families." In J. M. Henslin (Ed.), *Marriage and family in a changing society.* New York: Free Press.

Staples, R., & Mirande, A. 1980. "Racial and cultural variations among American families: A decennial review of the literature on minority families." *Journal of Marriage and the Family, 42,* 157-173.

Stark, R., & Bainbridge, W. S. 1980. "Networks of faith: Interpersonal bonds and recruitment in cults and sects." *American Journal of Sociology, 85,* 1376-1395.

Starr, P. 1982. *The social transformation of American medicine.* New York: Basic Books.

Steele, S. 1990. *The content of our character: A new vision of race in America.* New York: HarperCollins.

Stein, L. I. 1967. "The doctor-nurse game." *Archives of General Psychiatry, 16,* 699-703.

Steinfels, P. 1992. "Apathy is seen toward agony of the homeless." *New York Times,* January 20.

Steinmetz, S. K., Clavan, R., & Stein, K. F. 1990. *Marriage and family realities: Historical and contemporary perspectives.* New York: Harper & Row.

Stephens, W. N. 1963. *The family in cross cultural perspective.* New York: University Press of America.

Stevenson, R. W. 1992. "Maker is accused of faulty tests on parts for missiles and aircraft." *New York Times,* April 23.

Stewart, J. E. 1980. "Defendant's attractiveness as a factor in the outcome of criminal trials: An observational study." *Journal of Applied Social Psychology, 10,* 348-361.

Stockard, J., & Johnson, M. M. 1992. *Sex and gender in society.* Englewood Cliffs, NJ: Prentice Hall.

Stokes, R., & Hewitt, J. P. 1976. "Aligning actions." *American Sociological Review, 41,* 837-849.

Stone, G. P. 1981. "Appearance and the self: A slightly revised version." In G. P. Stone & H. A. Farberman (Eds.), *Social psychology through symbolic interaction.* New York: Wiley.

Stone, L. 1979. *The family, sex and marriage in England 1500-1800.* New York: Harper Torchbooks.

Straus, M. A. 1977. "A sociological perspective on the prevention and treatment of wife beating." In M. Roy (Ed.), *Battered women.* New York: Van Nostrand.

Straus, M. A., & Gelles, R. J. 1986. "Societal change in family violence from 1975 to 1985 as revealed by two national surveys." *Journal of Marriage and the Family, 48,* 465-479.

Straus, M. A., Gelles, R. J., & Steinmetz, S. K. 1980. *Behind closed doors.* New York: Bantam.

Strong, B., & DeVault, C. 1992. *The marriage and family experience.* St. Paul, MN: West.

Strube, M. J., & Barbour, L. S. 1983. "The decision to leave an abusive relationship: Economic dependence and psychological commitment." *Journal of Marriage and the Family, 45,* 785-793.

Stryker, S. 1980. *Symbolic interactionism.* Menlo Park, CA: Benjamin/Cummings.

Sudnow, D. 1965. "Normal crimes: Sociological features of the penal code in a public defenders' office." *Social Problems, 12,* 255-264.

Sullivan, M. A., Queen, S., & Patrick, R. 1958. "Participant observation as employed in the study of a military training program." *American Sociological Review, 23,* 660-667.

Sunstein, C. 1991. "Why markets don't stop discrimination." In E. F. Paul, F. D. Miller, & J. Paul (Eds.), *Reassessing civil rights.* Cambridge, MA: Blackwell.

Suro, R. 1992. "Poll finds hispanics desire to assimilate." *New York Times,* December 15.

Sutherland, E., & Cressey, D. 1955. *Criminology.* Philadelphia: Lippincott.

Swanson, G. 1992. "Doing things together: On some basic forms of agency and structuring in collective action and on some explanations for them." *Social Psychology Quarterly, 55,* 94-117.

Sykes, G., & Matza, D. 1957. "Techniques of neutralization: A theory of delinquency." *American Sociological Review, 22,* 664-670.

Szasz, T. 1984. *The therapeutic state.* Buffalo, NY: Prometheus Books.

———. 1990. *Insanity: The idea and its consequences.* New York: Wiley.

Taeuber, C. M. 1988. "Demographic perspectives in an aging society." *The World and I, 3,* 591-603.

"Taiwan's little problem." 1993. *The Economist,* June 5.

Takagi, D. Y. 1990. "From discrimination to affirmative action: Facts in the Asian-American admissions controversy." *Social Problems, 37,* 578-592.

Tannen, D. 1990. *You just don't understand: women and men in conversation.* New York: Ballantine.

Tannenbaum, F. 1938. *Crime and community.* New York: Ginn.

Tavris, C. 1992. *The mismeasure of woman.* New York: Touchstone.

Tavris, C., & Offir, C. 1984. *The longest war: Sex differences in perspective.* New York: Harcourt Brace Jovanovich.

Tauber, M. A. 1979. "Parental socialization techniques and sex differences in children's play." *Child Development, 50,* 225-234.

Taylor, R. J., Chatters, L. M., Tucker, M. B., & Lewis, E. 1990. "Developments in research on black families: A decade review." *Journal of Marriage and the Family, 52,* 993-1014.

Taylor, S. J., & Bogdan, R. 1980. "Defending illusions: The institution's struggle for survival." *Human Organization, 39,* 209-218.

Thibaut J., & Kelley, H. 1959. *The social psychology of groups.* New York: Wiley.

Thoits, P. 1985. "Self labeling process in mental illness: The role of emotional deviance." *American Journal of Sociology, 91,* 221-249.

Thomas, D. L., Franks, D. D., & Calonico, J. M. 1972. "Role taking and power in social psychology." *American Sociological Review, 37,* 605-614.

Thompson, P. 1989. *The nature of work.* London: Macmillan.

Thompson, R. A. 1991. "Infant day care: Concerns, controversies, choices." In J. V. Lerner & N. L. Galambos (Eds.), *Employed mothers and their children.* New York: Garland.

Thorne, B., & Luria, Z. 1986. "Sexuality and gender in children's daily worlds." *Social Problems, 33,* 176-190.

Thorne, B., & Yalom, M. 1982. *Rethinking the family: Some feminist questions.* New York: Longman.

Tiano, S. 1987. "Gender, work and world capitalism: Third world women's role in development." In B. B. Hess & M. M. Ferree (Eds.), *Analyzing gender: A handbook of social science research.* Newbury Park, CA: Sage.

Tilly, C. 1978. *From mobilization to revolution.* Reading, MA: Addison-Wesley.

Timms, E., & McGonigle, S. 1992. "Psychological Warfare." *Indianapolis Star,* April 5.

Tobin, J. J., Wu, D. Y. H., & Davidson, D. H. 1989. *Preschool in three cultures: Japan, China and the United States.* New Haven, CT: Yale University Press.

Tocqueville, A. de. 1969. *Democracy in America.* New York: Doubleday. (Original work published 1835)

Toennies, F. 1963. *Community and society.* New York: HarperCollins. (Original work published 1887)

Torrey, E. F. 1988. *Surviving schizophrenia.* New York: Harper & Row.

Trepanier, M. L., & Romatowski, J. A. 1985. "Attributes and roles assigned to characters in children's writing: Sex differences and sex role perceptions." *Sex Roles, 13,* 263-272.

Triandis, H. C., McCusker, C., & Hui, C. H. 1990. "Multimethod probes of individualism and collectivism." *Journal of Personality and Social Psychology, 59,* 1006-1020.

Trice, H. M., & Roman, P. M. 1970. "Delabeling, relabeling and alcoholics anonymous." *Social Problems, 17,* 538-546.

Trotsky, L. 1959. *The history of the Russian Revolution* (F. W. Dupee, Ed.). Garden City, NY: Doubleday.

Trudgill, P. 1972. "Sex, covert prestige and linguistic change in the urban British English of Norwich." In B. Thorne & N. Henley (Eds.), *Language and society.* Cambridge: Cambridge University Press.

Tumin, M. 1953. "Some principles of stratification: A critical analysis." *American Sociological Review, 18,* 387-393.

Turner, R., & Edgley, C. 1976. "Death as theater: A dramaturgical analysis of the American funeral." *Sociology and Social Research, 60,* 377-392.

———. 1983. "From witchcraft to drugcraft: Biochemistry as mythology." *Social Science Journal, 20,* 1-12.

Turner, R. W., & Killian, L. M. 1987. *Collective behavior.* Englewood Cliffs, NJ: Prentice Hall.

Uchitelle, L. 1993. "Use of temporary workers is on rise in manufacturing." *New York Times*, July 6.

Uhlenberg, P., & Myers, M. A. 1981. "Divorce and the elderly." *The Gerontologist, 21,* 276-282.

"Uninsured hospital patients found far more likely to die." 1991. *New York Times*, January 16.

United States Bureau of Justice Statistics. 1983. *Report to the nation on crime and justice: The data.* Washington, DC: U.S. Government Printing Office.

————. 1993. *Sourcebook of criminal justice statistics—1992.* Washington, DC: U.S. Government Printing Office.

United States Bureau of Labor Statistics. 1985. *Handbook of labor statistics.* Washington, DC: U.S. Government Printing Office.

————. 1989. *Handbook of labor statistics.* Washington, DC: U.S. Government Printing Office.

United States Bureau of the Census. 1988. *Statistical abstract of the United States.* Washington, DC: U.S. Government Printing Office.

————. 1990a. "Marital status and living arrangements." *Current population reports.* Washington, DC: U.S. Government Printing Office.

————. 1990b. "Poverty in the United States: 1990." *Current population reports.* Washington, DC: U.S. Government Printing Office.

————. 1991a. *Statistical abstract of the United States.* Washington, DC: U.S. Government Printing Office.

————. 1991b. *Census and you, 26,* September, p. 3.

————. 1991c. "Money income and poverty status of persons and families in the U.S." *Current population reports.* Washington, DC: U.S. Government Printing Office.

————. 1992a. *Statistical abstract of the United States.* Washington, DC: U.S. Government Printing Office.

————. 1992b. *Census and you, 27,* November, p. 7.

————. 1992c. "Educational attainment in the United States: March 1991 and March 1990." *Current population reports.* Washington, DC: U.S. Government Printing Office.

————. 1992d. *Population projections of the United States by age, sex, race and Hispanic origin: 1992 to 2050.* Washington, DC: U.S. Government Printing Office.

————. 1993a. *Census and you, 28,* April, p. 14.

————. 1993b. *Census and you, 28,* January, p. 1.

United States Commission on Civil Rights. 1986. *The economic progress of black men in America.* Washington, DC: Clearinghouse Publication.

United States Commission on Human Rights. 1992. "Indian tribes: A continuing quest for survival." In P. S. Rothenberg (Ed.), *Race, class and gender in the United States.* New York: St. Martin's Press.

United States Department of Health and Human Services. 1988. "The health consequences of smoking." *Nicotine addiction: A report of the Surgeon General.* Washington, DC: U.S. Government Printing Office.

————. 1990. *Report of the United States Advisory Board on Child Abuse and Neglect.* Washington, DC: U.S. Government Printing Office.

United States Department of Health, Education and Welfare. 1973. *Work in America: Report of a special task force to the Secretary of Health, Education and Welfare.* Cambridge: MIT Press.

United States Department of Justice. 1983. *Report to the nation on crime and justice.* Washington, DC: U.S. Government Printing Office.

United States Senate Committee on Governmental Affairs. 1978. *Interlocking directorates among the major U.S. corporations.* Washington, DC: U.S. Government Printing Office.

Useem, M. 1978. "The inner group of the American capitalist class." *Social Problems, 25,* 225-240.

Utne, M. K., Hatfield, E., Traupmann, J., & Greenberger, D. 1984. "Equity, marital satisfaction, and stability." *Journal of Social and Personal Relationships, 1,* 323-332.

Valdivieso, R., & Davis, C. 1991. "U.S. Hispanics: Challenging issues for the 1990's." In J. Skolnick & E. Currie (Eds.), *Crisis in American institutions.* New York: HarperCollins.

Vanek, J. 1980. "Work, leisure and family roles: Farm households in the United States: 1920-1955." *Journal of Family History, 5,* 422-431.

Van Willigen, J., & Channa, V. C. 1991. "Law, custom and crimes against women: The problem of dowry death in India." *Human Organization, 50,* 369-377.

Vaughan, D. 1986. *Uncoupling.* New York: Vintage.

Veblen, T. 1953. *The theory of the leisure class: An economic study of institutions.* New York: Mentor. (Original work published 1899)

Vega, W. A. 1990. "Hispanic families in the 1980's: A decade of research." *Journal of Marriage and the Family, 52,* 1015-1024.

Vergara, C. J. 1994. "Our fortified ghettos." *The Nation,* 31 January.

Viets, E. 1992. "Give a whistle, he'll love it." *Indianapolis Star,* November 29.

Vincent, J. P., Weiss, R. L., & Birchler, G. R. 1975. "Dyadic problem solving behavior as a function of marital distress and spousal vs. stranger interactions." *Behavior Therapy, 6,* 475-487.

von Baeyer, C. L., Sherk, D. L., & Zanna, M. P. 1981. "Impression management in the job interview: When the female applicant meets the male (chauvinist) interviewer." *Personality and Social Psychology Bulletin, 7,* 45-51.

Voyandoff, P. 1990. "Economic distress and family relations: A review of the eighties." *Journal of Marriage and the Family, 52,* 1099-1115.

Wagner, D. G., Ford, R. S., & Ford, T. W. 1986. "Can gender inequalities be reduced?" *American Sociological Review, 51,* 47-61.

Wallerstedt, J. F. 1984. "Returning to prison." *Bureau of Justice Statistics special report.* Washington, DC: U.S. Government Printing Office.

Wallerstein, I. 1974. *The modern world system.* New York: Academic Press.

Walsh, E. J., & Warland, R. H. 1983. "Social movement involvement in the wake of a nuclear accident: Activists and free riders in the TMI area." *American Sociological Review, 48,* 764-780.

Walton, J. 1990. *Sociology and critical inquiry.* Belmont, CA: Wadsworth.

Warshaw, R. 1988. *I never called it rape.* New York: Harper & Row.

Wattenberg, E. 1986. "The fate of baby boomers and their children." *Social Work, 31,* 20-28.

Watzlawick, P. 1976. *How real is real?* Garden City, NY: Doubleday.

———. 1984. "Self fulfilling prophecies." In P. Watzlawick (Ed.), *The invented reality: How do we know what we believe we know? Contributions to constructivism.* New York: Norton.

Weber, M. 1946. "Bureaucracy." In H. H. Gerth & C. W. Mills (Eds.), *From Max Weber: Essays in sociology* (pp. 196-244). New York: Oxford University Press.

———. 1947. *The theory of social and economic organization.* New York: Free Press.

———. 1968. *Economy and society* (G. Roth and C. Wittich, Eds.). New York: Bedminster Press.

———. 1970. *From Max Weber: Essays in sociology* (H. H. Gerth & C. W. Mills, Eds.). New York: Oxford University Press.

———. 1977. *The Protestant ethic and the spirit of capitalism.* New York: Macmillan. (Original work published 1904)

Weeks, J. 1992. *Population: An introduction to concepts and issues.* Belmont, CA: Wadsworth.

Weinstein, E. A., & Deutschberger, P. 1963. "Some dimensions of altercasting." *Sociometry, 26,* 454-466.

Weitzman, L. 1985. *The divorce revolution: The unexpected consequences for women and children in America.* New York: Free Press.

Weitzman, L., Eifler, D., Hodada, E., & Ross, C. 1972. "Sex-role socialization in picture books for preschool children." *American Journal of Sociology, 77,* 1125-1150.

Welsh, J. F. 1984. "The presentation of self in capitalist society: Bureaucratic visibility as a social source of impression management." *Humanity and Society, 8,* 253-271.

Weston, K. 1991. *Families we choose: Lesbians, gays, kinship.* New York: Columbia University Press.

Whalen, C. K., & Henker, B. 1977. "The pitfalls of politicization: A response to Conrad's 'The discovery of hyperkinesis: Notes on the medicalization of deviance.'" *Social Problems, 24,* 590-595.

White, L., & Brinkerhoff, D. 1981. "The sexual division of labor: Evidence from childhood." *Social Forces, 60,* 170-181.

"Whites retain negative view of minorities." 1991. *New York Times,* January 10.

Whorf, B. 1956. *Language, thought and reality.* Cambridge: MIT Press.

Whyte, M. K. 1990. *Dating, mating and marriage.* New York: Aldine deGruyter.

Whyte, W. H. 1956. *The organization man.* Garden City, NY: Doubleday.

Wiesel, E. 1986. *Night.* New York: Bantam Books.

Wilkerson, I. 1991a. "As interracial marriage rises, acceptance lags." *New York Times,* December 12.

————. 1991b. "Shift in feelings on the homeless: Empathy turns to frustration." *New York Times*, September 2.

Wilkinson, L. C., & Marrett, C. B. 1985. *Gender influences in classroom interaction.* Orlando, FL: Academic Press.

Will, J., Self, P., & Datan, N. 1976. "Maternal behavior and perceived sex of infant." *American Journal of Orthopsychiatry, 46*, 135-139.

Williams, C. L. 1992. "The glass escalator: Hidden advantages for men in the 'female' professions." *Social Problems, 39*, 253-267.

Williams, L. 1991a. "In a 90's quest for black identity, intense doubts and disagreements." *New York Times*, November 30.

————. 1991b. "When blacks shop bias often accompanies sale." *New York Times*, April 30.

————. 1992a. "Girls' self-image is mother of the woman." *New York Times*, February 6.

————. 1992b. "Scrambling to manage a diverse workforce." *New York Times*, December 12.

Wilson, W. J. 1980. *The declining significance of race.* Chicago: University of Chicago Press.

————. 1987. *The truly disadvantaged.* Chicago: University of Chicago Press.

Winick, C. 1982. "The image of mental illness in the mass media." In W. Gove (Ed.), *Deviance and mental illness.* Beverly Hills, CA: Sage.

Winston, N. A. 1988. "Sex-bias response to telephoned job inquiries, Tampa, 1987." *Sociology and Social Research, 72*, 121-124.

Wolfe, A. 1991. *America at century's end.* Berkeley: University of California Press.

Wolfe, S. M. 1991. *Women's health alert.* Reading, MA: Addison-Wesley.

Woliver, L. R. 1989. "The deflective power of reproductive technologies: The impact on women." *Women and Politics, 9*, 17-47.

Wood, P. L. 1975. "The victim in a forcible rape case: A feminist view." In L. G. Schultz (Ed.), *Rape victimology.* Springfield, IL: Charles Thomas.

Wooton, A. 1975. *Dilemmas of discourse.* London: Allen & Unwin.

Word, C. O., Zanna, M. P., & Cooper, J. 1974. "The nonverbal mediation of self-fulfilling prophecies in interracial interaction." *Journal of Experimental Social Psychology, 10*, 109-120.

"World progress in birth control." *The Futurist*, 1993. August.

Wright, E. O. 1976. "Class boundaries in advanced capitalist societies." *New Left Review, 98*, 3-41.

Wright, E. O., Costello, C., Hachen, D., & Sprague, J. 1982. "The American class structure." *American Sociological Review, 47*, 709-726.

Wright, E. O., & Perrone, L. 1977. "Marxist class categories and income inequality." *American Sociological Review, 42*, 32-55.

Wrong, D. 1988. *Power: Its forms, bases, and uses.* Chicago: University of Chicago Press.

Yarrow, M. R., Schwartz, C. G., Murphy, H. S., & Deasy, L. C. 1955. "The psychological meaning of mental illness in the family." *Journal of Social Issues, 11*, 12-24.

Yorburg, B. 1993. *Family relationships.* New York: St. Martin's Press.

Young, T. R. 1993. "Dress, drama and self: The tee shirt as text." In P. Kollock & J. O'Brien (Eds.), *The production of reality.* Thousand Oaks, CA: Pine Forge Press.

Zastrow, C. 1977. *Outcome of black children–white parents transracial adoptions.* San Francisco: R & E Research Associates.

Zborowski, M. 1952. "Cultural components in responses to pain." *Journal of Social Issues, 8*, 16-30.

Zelizer, V. 1985. *Pricing the priceless child.* New York: Basic Books.

Zerubavel, E. 1985. *The seven day circle: The history and meaning of the week.* New York: Free Press.

Zimbardo, P. 1971. "The pathology of imprisonment." *Society, 9*, 4-8.

Zola, I. 1986. "Medicine as an institution of social control." In P. Conrad & R. Kern (Eds.), *The sociology of health and illness.* New York: St. Martin's Press.

Zucker, L. G. 1991. "The role of institutionalization in cultural persistence." In W. Powell & P. DiMaggio (Eds.), *The new institutionalism in organizational analysis.* Chicago: University of Chicago Press.

Zukin, S. 1991. *Landscapes of power: From Detroit to Disney World.* Berkeley: University of California Press.

Zurcher, L. A., & Snow, D. A. 1981. "Collective behavior: Social movements." In M. Rosenberg & R. H. Turner (Eds.), *Social psychology: Sociological perspectives.* New York: Basic Books.

A

Abortion, 82, 227, 413, 415, 484, 485. *See also* Fetal rights

Absolute poverty the inability to afford the minimal requirements necessary to sustain a reasonably healthy existence, 340

Absolutism an approach to defining deviance that rests on the assumption that all human behavior can be considered either inherently good or bad (compare to *relativism*), 179-181, 183, 184

Abuse. *See* Violence

Account a verbal statement designed to explain unanticipated, embarrassing, or unacceptable behavior after the behavior has occurred, 159-161

Accuracy, of social research, 69-72

Acquaintance rape, 404, 406

Actions, influence of others on, 23-25

Adoption, 89-91, 95

Adornment, impression management and, 144-145. *See also* Clothing

Affirmative action a program designed to seek out members of minority groups for positions from which they had previously been excluded, thereby attempting to overcome institutional racism, 380, 392-395

African Americans
adoption by white parents, 89-91
arrest of, 180, 181
Asian Americans vs., 455
"blacks" designation, 382

color divisiveness among, 112
discrimination against, 377-379, 380-381
drug courier profiles and, 202-203
education of, 363, 390-392
as executives, 277
family structure of, 231
income of, 311, 371, 393, 426
institutional racism and, 385-395
Jim Crow laws, 369, 371
Latins Americans vs., 455
middle-class, 309, 367-368, 378-379
occupations of, 387, 389
one-drop rule, 110-112
oppression of, 368, 371, 373
population size of, 373, 454
poverty of, 342, 360, 368
racist language and, 382, 383
residential segregation and, 386-387
social class distribution of, 309
socialization of, 113
stereotypes of, 375, 376, 379
success of, 367-368, 371
television portrayal of, 376-377, 389-390
unemployment and, 388
upper-class, 309, 367-368, 378-379
victimization and, 394
whites' beliefs about, 109-110
See also Affirmative action; Civil rights movement; Slavery

Age Discrimination Employment Act of 1967, 459

Age structure a population's balance of old and young people, 449-450, 456-461. *See also* Elderly

Aging process, birth cohorts and, 436. *See also* Elderly

AIDS, 287-291, 476, 478, 482-483

Aid to Families With Dependent Children, 354, 360. *See also* Welfare system

Alcohol consumption
family violence and, 248
as legal drug use, 202
Prohibition and, 58
situation and, 183
social behavior and, 36-37

Alcoholics Anonymous, 187

Alcoholism
causes of, 8, 186
a century ago, 46, 222
homelessness and, 346
medicalization of, 46, 204, 205
social vs. personal forces and, 8
stereotypes of, 188

Aleuts, 373

Aligning action action taken to restore an identity that has been damaged by an unwelcome event, 158-161

Aloneness, 20, 21-22

Altercasting the use of verbal strategies to impose on others an identity we want them to have, 147-148

Alyha, 122

Americanization, 373

Ancestor worship, in Madagascar, 75, 76, 81

Anglo-American conformity, 373

Anomie a condition in which rapid change disrupts society's ability to adequately regulate and control its members; the old rules that governed people's lives no longer seem to apply, 48

Antiabortion movement. *See* Abortion

Anticipatory socialization the process through which people acquire the values and